Research Methods in Psychology 3rd edition

Research Methods
in Psychology 3rd edition

Edited by
Glynis M. Breakwell,
Sean Hammond,
Chris Fife-Schaw and
Jonathan A. Smith

Los Angeles | London | New Delhi
Singapore | Washington DC

First edition published 1995, reprinted three times
Second edition published 2000, reprinted 2001, 2002, 2004

This edition published 2006
Reprinted 2009, 2010

SAGE Publications Ltd
1 Oliver's Yard
55 City Road
London EC1Y 1SP

SAGE Publications Inc.
2455 Teller Road
Thousand Oaks, California 91320

SAGE Publications India Pvt Ltd
B 1/I 1 Mohan Cooperative Industrial Area
Mathura Road
New Delhi 110 044

SAGE Publications Asia-Pacific Pte Ltd
33 Pekin Street 02-01
Far East Square
Singapore 048763

British Library Cataloguing in Publication data

A catalogue record for this book is available from the British Library

ISBN 978-1-4129-1127-6
ISBN 978-1-4129-1128-3 (pbk)

Library of Congress Control Number: 2005935774

Typeset by C&M Digitals (P) Ltd, Chennai, India
Printed in Great Britain by Ashford Colour Press Ltd, Gosport, Hants.
Printed on paper from sustainable resources

Summary of Contents

Contents   vii
List of Contributors   xiv
Preface   xviii
How to use this Textbook and Companion Website   xxii

Part 1   The Bases of Research   **1**

1 **Theory, Method and Research Design**   2
   Glynis M. Breakwell and David Rose
2 **Practical and Ethical Issues in Planning Research**   24
   Martyn Barrett
3 **Levels of Measurement**   50
   Chris Fife-Schaw
4 **The Experimental Method in Psychology**   64
   Alyson Davis and Gavin Bremner
5 **Quasi-experimental Designs**   88
   Chris Fife-Schaw
6 **Surveys and Sampling**   104
   Patrick Sturgis

Part 2   Data Gathering   **123**

7 **Observational Methods**   124
   Rudi Dallos
8 **Psychophysiological Methods**   146
   Paul Sowden and Paul Barrett
9 **Psychophysical Methods**   160
   David Rose

10 **Using Psychometric Tests** 182
Sean Hammond

11 **Questionnaire Design** 210
Chris Fife-Schaw

12 **Interviewing Methods** 232
Glynis M. Breakwell

13 **Using Self-recording: Diary and Narrative Methods** 254
Glynis M. Breakwell

14 **Focus Groups** 274
Lynne J. Millward

15 **Ethnographic and Action Research** 300
David Uzzell and Julie Barnett

Part 3 Data Treatment 321

16 **Interpretative Phenomenological Analysis** 322
Jonathan A. Smith and Virginia Eatough

17 **Grounded Theory** 342
Karen Henwood and Nick Pidgeon

18 **Discourse Analysis** 366
Adrian Coyle

19 **Principles of Statistical Inference Tests** 388
Chris Fife-Schaw

20 **Introduction to Multivariate Data Analysis** 414
Sean Hammond

21 **Introduction to Structural Equation Modelling** 444
Chris Fife-Schaw

22 **Meta-analysis** 466
David O'Sullivan

References 482
Index 510

Contents

LIST OF CONTRIBUTORS   xiv
PREFACE   xviii
HOW TO USE THIS TEXTBOOK AND COMPANION WEBSITE   xxii

PART 1   THE BASES OF RESEARCH   1

1   THEORY, METHOD AND RESEARCH DESIGN   2
Glynis M. Breakwell and David Rose
   1.1   THEORY BUILDING AND THEORY TESTING   4
   1.2   MATCHING METHODOLOGIES TO THEORY   17
   1.3   INTEGRATING FINDINGS FROM DIFFERENT METHODOLOGIES   22
   1.4   FURTHER READING   23

2   PRACTICAL AND ETHICAL ISSUES IN PLANNING RESEARCH   24
Martyn Barrett
   2.1   INTRODUCTION   26
   2.2   FORMULATING RESEARCH QUESTIONS   26
   2.3   ASSESSING THE PRACTICAL FEASIBILITY OF THE RESEARCH   33
   2.4   ASSESSING THE ETHICAL FEASIBILITY OF THE RESEARCH   38
   2.5   CONSIDERING THE POSSIBLE OUTCOMES OF THE RESEARCH IN ADVANCE   43
   2.6   APPLYING FOR RESEARCH FUNDING   43
   2.7   CONCLUSION   47
   2.8   BPS AND APA ADDRESSES AND WEBSITES   48
   2.9   FURTHER READING   48

3   LEVELS OF MEASUREMENT   50
Chris Fife-Schaw
   3.1   INTRODUCTION   52
   3.2   CLASSIFYING MEASUREMENTS   53
   3.3   DISCRETE VERSUS CONTINUOUS VARIABLES   58

3.4 MEASUREMENT ERRORS 59

3.5 CHOICES OVER LEVELS OF MEASUREMENT 60

3.6 THE RELATIONSHIP BETWEEN LEVEL OF
MEASUREMENT AND STATISTICS 61

3.7 CONCLUSION 63

3.8 FURTHER READING 63

4 THE EXPERIMENTAL METHOD IN PSYCHOLOGY 64
Alyson Davis and Gavin Bremner

4.1 INTRODUCTION 66

4.2 EXPERIMENTATION AND THE SCIENTIFIC METHOD 66

4.3 WHAT IS AN EXPERIMENT? 67

4.4 CAUSALITY AND EXPERIMENTATION 69

4.5 VARIABLES 69

4.6 RELIABILITY AND VALIDITY 73

4.7 EXPERIMENTAL MANIPULATION AND CONTROL 74

4.8 BASIC EXPERIMENTAL DESIGNS 74

4.9 EVALUATING THE EXPERIMENTAL METHOD 85

4.10 CONCLUSION 86

4.11 FURTHER READING 87

5 QUASI-EXPERIMENTAL DESIGNS 88
Chris Fife-Schaw

5.1 INTRODUCTION 90

5.2 PRE-EXPERIMENTS 90

5.3 QUASI-EXPERIMENTS 92

5.4 NON-EQUIVALENT CONTROL GROUP DESIGNS 93

5.5 TIME SERIES DESIGNS 96

5.6 TIME SERIES WITH NON-EQUIVALENT
CONTROL GROUP DESIGNS 98

5.7 MODIFICATIONS TO THE BASIC DESIGNS 102

5.8 CONCLUSION 103

5.9 FURTHER READING 103

6 SURVEYS AND SAMPLING 104
Patrick Sturgis

6.1 INTRODUCTION 106

6.2 STATISTICAL INFERENCE: FROM SAMPLE TO POPULATION 106

6.3 NONRESPONSE 111

6.4 SAMPLING STRATEGIES 113

6.5 SURVEY MODE 118

6.6 SMALL-SAMPLE ISSUES 119

6.7 CONCLUSION 121

6.8 FURTHER READING 121

PART 2   DATA GATHERING   123

7   **OBSERVATIONAL METHODS**   124
    Rudi Dallos
        7.1   INTRODUCTION   126
        7.2   WHAT IS OBSERVATIONAL RESEARCH?   126
        7.3   LEVELS OF OBSERVATION: BEHAVIOUR AND TALK   132
        7.4   OBSERVATION AND THEORETICAL LENSES   133
        7.5   DECIDING WHAT TO OBSERVE – CODING SCHEMES   134
        7.6   INTERPRETATIVE ORIENTATION TO OBSERVATION   138
        7.7   PARTICIPANT OBSERVATION RESEARCH   139
        7.8   VALIDITY   144
        7.9   CONCLUSION   145
        7.10 FURTHER READING   145

8   **PSYCHOPHYSIOLOGICAL METHODS**   146
    Paul Sowden and Paul Barrett
        8.1   INTRODUCTION   148
        8.2   THE PRINCIPAL AREAS OF PHYSIOLOGICAL
              DATA ACQUISITION   149
        8.3   QUANTIFYING BIOSIGNAL DATA   156
        8.4   CONCLUSION   159
        8.5   FURTHER READING   159

9   **PSYCHOPHYSICAL METHODS**   160
    David Rose
        9.1   INTRODUCTION   162
        9.2   PRINCIPLES OF ABSOLUTE THRESHOLDS   162
        9.3   FORCED-CHOICE TECHNIQUES   167
        9.4   METHODS FOR MEASURING ABSOLUTE THRESHOLDS   168
        9.5   DIFFERENCE THRESHOLDS   174
        9.6   SENSATIONAL MEASUREMENTS   175
        9.7   SOME GENERAL TIPS ON RUNNING EXPERIMENTS   178
        9.8   CONCLUSION   181
        9.9   FURTHER READING   181

10 **USING PSYCHOMETRIC TESTS**   182
    Sean Hammond
        10.1 INTRODUCTION   184
        10.2 TYPES OF PSYCHOMETRIC TEST   185
        10.3 CLASSICAL TEST THEORY   189
        10.4 THE PROBLEM OF VALIDITY   199
        10.5 ITEM RESPONSE THEORY   203
        10.6 CONCLUSION   208
        10.7 FURTHER READING   209

11 QUESTIONNAIRE DESIGN 210

Chris Fife-Schaw

11.1	INTRODUCTION	212
11.2	WHAT INFORMATION DO YOU WANT?	212
11.3	OPEN VERSUS CLOSED RESPONSE FORMATS	214
11.4	COMMON RESPONSE FORMATS	215
11.5	COMMON WORDING PROBLEMS	218
11.6	TYPES OF INFORMATION GLEANED FROM QUESTIONNAIRES	223
11.7	EXISTING SCALES AND MEASURES	228
11.8	QUESTIONNAIRE LAYOUT	228
11.9	CONCLUSION	231
11.10	FURTHER READING	231

12 INTERVIEWING METHODS 232

Glynis M. Breakwell

12.1	INTRODUCTION	234
12.2	THE INTERVIEW STRUCTURE	235
12.3	PILOTING THE INTERVIEW	240
12.4	CONDUCTING THE INTERVIEW	241
12.5	MEDIUM OF THE INTERVIEW	243
12.6	INTERVIEWING CHILDREN	244
12.7	VALIDITY AND RELIABILITY OF INTERVIEW DATA	247
12.8	ANALYSING INTERVIEW DATA	250
12.9	REPORTING INTERVIEW RESEARCH	252
12.10	CONCLUSION	253
12.11	FURTHER READING	253

13 USING SELF-RECORDING: DIARY AND NARRATIVE METHODS 254

Glynis M. Breakwell

13.1	INTRODUCTION	256
13.2	WHAT ARE DIARY TECHNIQUES?	256
13.3	WHAT SORTS OF DATA ARE SUITABLE FOR DIARIES?	258
13.4	THE PROS AND CONS OF THE DIARY APPROACH	259
13.5	GETTING THE BEST OUT OF DIARY TECHNIQUES	263
13.6	WHAT ARE NARRATIVE TECHNIQUES?	266
13.7	ELICITING THE NARRATIVE	267
13.8	ANALYSING DIARY AND NARRATIVE RECORDS	269
13.9	CONCLUSION	271
13.10	FURTHER READING	272

14 FOCUS GROUPS 274

Lynne J. Millward

14.1	INTRODUCTION	276
14.2	THE APPROPRIATENESS OF THE FOCUS GROUP METHOD	277

14.3	WHAT TYPE OF EVIDENCE DO FOCUS GROUPS YIELD?	278
14.4	THE FOCAL STIMULI	281
14.5	FOCUS GROUP DESIGN AND PLANNING	283
14.6	FOCUS GROUP IMPLEMENTATION	286
14.7	RECORDING THE DATA	291
14.8	TRANSCRIPTION	291
14.9	ANALYSIS OF FOCUS GROUP DATA	291
14.10	FEEDBACK OF RESULTS/FINDINGS	296
14.11	FUTURE DEVELOPMENTS IN FOCUS GROUP RESEARCH	296
14.12	CONCLUSION	297
14.13	FURTHER READING	298

15   ETHNOGRAPHIC AND ACTION RESEARCH   300
David Uzzell and Julie Barnett

15.1	INTRODUCTION	302
15.2	WHAT IS ETHNOGRAPHY?	302
15.3	PROBLEMS IN ETHNOGRAPHY	305
15.4	MEASURING QUALITY IN ETHNOGRAPHIC RESEARCH	309
15.5	ACTION RESEARCH	311
15.6	DISTINGUISHING CRITERIA OF ACTION RESEARCH	315
15.7	CONCLUSIONS	319
15.8	FURTHER READING	320

PART 3   DATA TREATMENT   321

16   INTERPRETATIVE PHENOMENOLOGICAL ANALYSIS   322
Jonathan A. Smith and Virginia Eatough

16.1	INTRODUCTION	324
16.2	IPA AND PSYCHOLOGY	325
16.3	SUITABLE RESEARCH QUESTIONS FOR IPA	326
16.4	HOW MANY PARTICIPANTS?	327
16.5	DATA COLLECTION METHODS	329
16.6	STAGES OF ANALYSIS	332
16.7	WRITING UP AN IPA STUDY	338
16.8	CONCLUSION	340
16.9	FURTHER READING	340

17   GROUNDED THEORY   342
Karen Henwood and Nick Pidgeon

17.1	INTRODUCTION	344
17.2	EMERGENT DESIGN, FLEXIBILITY AND ITERATION	346
17.3	THE ORIGIN POINT AND USE OF THE PRIOR LITERATURE	348
17.4	THEORETICAL SAMPLING	350
17.5	STORAGE: THE RESEARCH RECORD	352
17.6	OPEN CODING AND CONSTANT COMPARISON	353

	17.7	THEORETICAL MEMOS	357
	17.8	CORE ANALYSIS I: REFINING AND SATURATING CATEGORIES	358
	17.9	CORE ANALYSIS II: BUILDING THEORY AND MODELS	359
	17.10	WRITING AND EVALUATING GROUNDED THEORY STUDIES	361
	17.11	CONCLUSION	363
	17.12	FURTHER READING	364

18 DISCOURSE ANALYSIS   **366**
Adrian Coyle

	18.1	INTRODUCTION	368
	18.2	DISCOURSE ANALYSIS: ASSUMPTIONS, APPROACHES AND APPLICATIONS	368
	18.3	SAMPLING DISCOURSE	374
	18.4	TECHNIQUES OF DISCOURSE ANALYSIS	375
	18.5	WORKING WITH DATA	377
	18.6	EVALUATING DISCOURSE ANALYTIC WORK	382
	18.7	PROBLEMS IN DISCOURSE ANALYTIC WORK	384
	18.8	CONCLUSION	386
	18.9	FURTHER READING	387

19 PRINCIPLES OF STATISTICAL INFERENCE TESTS   **388**
Chris Fife-Schaw

	19.1	INTRODUCTION	390
	19.2	SOME BASIC DEFINITIONS	390
	19.3	WHAT ARE BIVARIATE STATISTICAL ANALYSES?	393
	19.4	CLASSICAL BIVARIATE DESIGNS	393
	19.5	THEORIES AND HYPOTHESES	396
	19.6	TYPE I AND TYPE II ERRORS	397
	19.7	PROBABILITY	398
	19.8	PARAMETRIC VERSUS NON-PARAMETRIC TESTS	406
	19.9	CHOOSING A STATISTICAL TEST	407
	19.10	CONCLUSION	413
	19.11	FURTHER READING	413

20 INTRODUCTION TO MULTIVARIATE DATA ANALYSIS   **414**
Sean Hammond

	20.1	INTRODUCTION	416
	20.2	EXAMINING DIFFERENCES BETWEEN GROUPS	416
	20.3	MAKING PREDICTIONS	424
	20.4	EXPLORING UNDERLYING STRUCTURE	430
	20.5	THE SPECIAL CASE OF CATEGORICAL DATA	440
	20.6	CONCLUSION	441
	20.7	FURTHER READING	442

21 INTRODUCTION TO STRUCTURAL EQUATION MODELLING   **444**

Chris Fife-Schaw

21.1   INTRODUCTION   446
21.2   THE IDEA OF MODEL FITTING AND MODEL COMPARISON   447
21.3   MEASUREMENT MODELS AND CONFIRMATORY
       FACTOR ANALYSIS   450
21.4   STRUCTURAL MODELS   458
21.5   ANALYSIS STRATEGY   460
21.6   OTHER THINGS THAT CAN BE DONE WITH SEM   461
21.7   CAUTIONARY NOTES   463
21.8   CONCLUSION   464
21.9   FURTHER READING   464

22 META-ANALYSIS   **466**

David O'Sullivan

22.1   INTRODUCTION   468
22.2   QUANTIFYING THE REVIEW PROCESS   469
22.3   STEPS IN CONDUCTING A META-ANALYSIS   473
22.4   CONCLUSION   480
22.5   FURTHER READING   481

REFERENCES   **482**
INDEX   **510**

List of Contributors

*Julie Barnett is a Senior Research Fellow at the University of Surrey. Much of her research focuses on risk issues. She is also interested in how experts think about and engage with publics and in the contribution that different methods can make to addressing particular research questions.

*Martyn Barrett is Professor of Psychology in the Department of Psychology at the University of Surrey. He has worked extensively on the development of language in children and on the development of children's drawings. More recently he has been working on processes of national and ethnic enculturation in childhood and adolescence, the development of prejudice and stereotyping in children and adolescents, and acculturation processes in ethnic minority individuals. He is Editor of the British *Journal of Developmental Psychology*, Academic Director of the multidisciplinary Centre for Research on Nationalism, Ethnicity and Multiculturalism at the University of Surrey and an Academician of the Learned Societies for the Social Sciences.

*Paul Barrett is an adjunct professor of psychometrics and performance measurement at the University of Auckland, and an adjunct associate professor of psychology at the University of Canterbury, New Zealand. His primary research interests are in the areas of psychological measurement, predictive modelling of behavioural outcomes, and the development of innovative methods of psychological assessment. His applied work is largely in the fields of organizational and forensic psychology, concerned mainly with issues of measurement, meaning, and prediction of relevant outcomes (e.g. job performance, recidivist risk).

*Glynis M. Breakwell is Vice-Chancellor of the University of Bath. She is a chartered health psychologist and an academician of the Academy of Social Sciences. She researches identity processes, the psychology of risk, and leadership in complex organizations, including the military and universities.

*Gavin Bremner is Professor of Developmental Psychology at Lancaster University. He is an experimental developmental psychologist with research interests in perception and cognition in infancy and early childhood. In addition to his core interest in perception and cognition in infancy, he has done research on spatial cognition and spatial aspects of graphical skill in children. In addition to his publications in journals, he is author of the text *Infancy*, and has edited numerous books at various levels.

*Adrian Coyle is a Senior Lecturer in the Department of Psychology at the University of Surrey, where he is currently part of the team which runs the University of Surrey's Practitioner Doctorate Programme in Psychotherapeutic and Counselling Psychology. His research interests include lesbian and gay psychology, the psychology of religion/spirituality and the development of qualitative research methods.

*Rudi Dallos is Professor and Programme Director on the Doctorate in Clinical Psychology training programme at the University of Plymouth where he is involved in teaching researching methods and supervising clinical research projects. He is also a consultant psychologist who specializes in systemic family therapy. His clinical work and research involves live and recorded observation of family dynamics. He also has a current interest in attachment theory and family dynamics.

*Alyson Davis is a Reader in Psychology at the University of Surrey. She has research interests in children's representations (drawing, writing and number) and in the development of pretence and imagination.

*Virginia Eatough is a lecturer in psychology at Birkbeck University of London, where she teaches qualitative research methods at postgraduate level. Her main research interests are emotions, in particular the role of feelings in emotional experience. Currently she is undertaking a project on adult crying which is looking at the subjective experience and structure of crying episodes, and the functional and situational aspects of crying.

*Chris Fife-Schaw is a Senior Lecturer and former Head of Psychology at the University of Surrey. His research has included studies of perceptions of food-related hazards, young people's responses to AIDS/HIV, public responses to genetic technologies and risk perception and communication of water-borne hazards. He lectures in social psychology, research methods and structural equation modelling and his research interests are in risk perception, models of behavioural regulation, and developing alternative measures of attitudes that do not involve questionnaires.

*Sean Hammond is a Statutory Lecturer and former Head of Applied Psychology at University College Cork, Ireland. He is currently the Director of the Postgraduate Forensic Psychology Programme. His primary interests are in forensic and health psychology and he has particular expertise in psychometrics and multivariate statistics. Current work involves risk assessment of mentally disordered offenders and the development of procedures for assessing sex offenders. He is currently the Research Director for the RAMAS Foundation, an organization set up to promote best practice in psychiatric risk management and assessment.

*Karen Henwood is a Senior Lecturer in Social Science in the Cardiff School of Social Sciences. She has substantive research interests in the role of culture, difference and life history in the formation of identity and subjectivity. Currently she is involved in a research project with Nick Pidgeon investigating a narrative approach to values, identity and risk, as part of ESRC's 'Risk and Social Context Network'. She has a long-standing interest in the role of qualitative methods in psychology and the social sciences.

*Lynne Millward is Senior Lecturer and leads the Master's programme in Occupational and Organizational Psychology. Her recent textbook called 'Understanding Occupational and Organizational Psychology' published by Sage in 2005 consolidates and reflects over 15 years of teaching, research and practice in this area. From both a research and practise point of view, her primary interest is in application of social psychological thinking to address issues or problems arising in vocational, occupational and organizational contexts with view to intervention.

*David O'Sullivan is a lecturer in the Department of Applied Psychology, University College Cork. He obtained his DPhil in 2000 at the University of York in educational aspects of human–computer interaction. His current research interests are in the areas of applied cognition and forensic psychology.

Nick Pidgeon is Professor of Applied Psychology at Cardiff University. He has research interests in people's perception of risk and its communication with particular applications to public policy decision-making, environmental issues (such as biotechnology, nuclear power and climate change) and industrial safety. He has authored (jointly with Karen Henwood) a number of methodological papers on grounded theory for psychologists.

*David Rose is a Reader in Psychology at the University of Surrey. He is interested in wide areas of brain research, visual perception, cognition, philosophy of mind and philosophy of science. His research has centred mainly on visual psychophysics, but he also has experience in broad areas of neuroscience and is currently extending his investigations to theories of consciousness. He has edited two books, *Models of the Visual Cortex* and *The Artful Eye*, and authored a third, *Consciousness: Philosophical, Psychological and Neural Theories*, published in 2006.

*Jonathan A. Smith is Reader in Psychology, Birkbeck University of London, where he teaches social psychology and qualitative research methods on the undergraduate as well as a number of postgraduate programmes. He has been developing and applying interpretative phenomenological analysis over the last ten years. Much of his recent research has been in psychosocial aspects of the new genetics.

*Paul Sowden** is a Senior Lecturer in Psychology at the University of Surrey. His research aims to understand the basis of improvements in sensory and perceptual processing as a result of learning and experience, and to understand how they contribute to perceptual expertise at complex visual tasks such as medical image inspection.

*Patrick Sturgis** is a lecturer in the Department of Sociology at the University of Surrey. His research interests focus on the social psychology of political behaviour, with a particular focus on how political knowledge and information influence decision making and belief system structure. He has done extensive work in the area of survey methodology, particularly focusing on survey nonresponse and the design and analysis of Time Use surveys. More recently, he has conducted research in the area of Public Understanding of Science, examining the interacting effects of different domains of knowledge on public perceptions of and attitudes toward science.

*David Uzzell** is Professor of Environmental Psychology at the University of Surrey. He specializes in research on sustainability and sustainable development, crime and the environment, architectural appraisal and social exclusion. He is also Visiting Professor at the UFR de Sciences Psychologiques et de Sciences de l'Education, Université de Paris X – Nanterre and the Department of Architecture, University of Strathclyde.

Preface Introducing Research Methods in Psychology

Glynis M. Breakwell, Scan Hammond,
Chris Fife-Schaw and Jonathan A. Smith

This is the third edition of *Research Methods in Psychology*. In deciding to produce a third edition, we felt it was necessary to significantly revise and restructure the book. In the five years since the second edition was published there have been important developments in techniques of data gathering and data treatment available to psychology researchers. There has been some change in the arena of the statistical modelling of data, and this is represented. However, the most significant changes have occurred in the qualitative methods that are used, and this edition of the book has been designed to reflect these developments. The editorial team has been enhanced with the addition of Jonathan Smith who has been at the forefront of the articulation of the new qualitative approaches. The result, we believe, is a book that truly reflects the rich diversity of methods used currently by the leading researchers in psychology, encompassing qualitative and quantitative traditions.

The purpose of this book is to offer students at the undergraduate and postgraduate levels a clear and reasonably comprehensive introduction to the research methods which can be used in the exploration of psychological processes. Psychology is concerned with identifying how processes operate. A process here is defined as a series of changes. The task of the psychological researcher is to plot and examine patterns of changes in variables and in relationships between variables. Theories essentially specify the principles or rules which describe these relationships. A variable is used here to refer to a construct or a property of an individual or social system that is an object for description and/or explanation. The variables which interest theorists in psychology lie at intra-individual, interpersonal and societal levels of analysis. They range from the biochemical and genetic, through the physiological, to the cognitive and affective, and beyond to interpersonal networks and communication, and further still to social power hierarchies and ideologies. In so far as the psychological processes they study are influenced by the material context or physical environment, many psychologists see these also as a target of their analysis. Such diversity of subject matter requires a diversity of research methods. Students of psychology are therefore usually offered research methods training which is simultaneously both broader and more intensive than in virtually any other discipline.

This book is designed to provide the basic information a student might need about each of the common research strategies used to examine psychological processes. In presenting these approaches, we have tried to be value-neutral: we do not play favourites; there are no methodological heroes or design villains in this text. Each approach is presented as robustly and fairly as possible by an expert in the field. While the individual contributors unequivocally present the value of the method they describe, there is no attempt within this book as a whole to proselytize for any one approach in particular. In fact, the assumption underlying this collection of approaches is that the usefulness of any method can only be judged against the nature of the research question that you wish to answer and the theoretical predilections that you espouse. More importantly, it is assumed that all methods have weaknesses and limitations. Therefore, it is argued that researchers will want to have recourse to a variety of methods that they will need to implement in an integrated fashion. Most especially, new students of psychology need to be aware of the full range of methods that they can deploy.

Any book on methods in psychology is inevitably grounded in the epistemological debates that underpin the discipline. There is the ever-present schism between the realist essentialists and the constructionists. Questions abound about the relationship of explanation and prediction, the viability of any general theory, the feasibility of hypothesis testing, the value of experimentation, the limitations of measurement, the ethics of manipulation, the role of reactance in the research process, the status of data interpretation, the objectivity of data, the implications of sampling, and so on. These debates, and others, are partly what make psychology a fascinating area. Students of psychology need to understand these arguments. In this book, these issues are embedded in the consideration of each of the methods and addressed in a way designed to illustrate their meaning and relevance.

In this third edition of the book we have decided to divide chapters into three parts. These, three parts essentially mirror the three major ingredients in conducting research: the specification of the research question and design of the research activity; the choice of data gathering method; and the selection of data treatment regime.

Part 1, 'The Bases of Research', provides an introduction to the relationship between theory method and research design. It offers practical advice on planning, executing and disseminating research, including ethical issues. It outlines the variety of levels of measurement possible within psychological research. It explains the role and structure of experimental, quasi-experimental, and survey research designs.

Part 2, 'Data Gathering', presents nine important methods of collecting data: observation; psychophysiological; psychophysical; psychometric; questionnaire;

interviewing; free-form self-recording; focus groups; and ethnography and action research. Taken together, this represents a comprehensive examination of the data collection techniques current in psychology.

Part 3, 'Data Treatment', summarizes seven approaches to the analysis of data: interpretative phenomenological analysis; grounded theory; discourse analysis; bivariate statistical analysis; multivariate statistical analysis; structural equation modelling; and meta-analysis. The first three might be said to represent the qualitative developments in psychological research, whereas the last four fall into the quantitative tradition. The purpose of these last four chapters is not to provide detailed explanations of specific statistical tests. The object is to explain the logic which should dictate which statistical test you should choose to use and what this sort of test is capable of telling you about your data. A basic understanding of statistical assumptions is often slow to mature and can be delayed by dealing too soon with the mathematical details of specific tests. Here, you are introduced to these fundamental statistical assumptions in a way which shows how they are linked to types of research design and levels of measurement and, perhaps, this makes them more comprehensible. Readers needing detailed information on specific statistical tests are directed to appropriate alternative texts.

The distinction between data gathering and data treatment is highlighted for the purpose of structuring this book, but the dividing line is never so clear in practice. It is evident even in the chapters here that ways of collecting data are frequently intimately linked to the ways researchers assume that they will be analysed. Nevertheless, it is worth maintaining this distinction between how the data are gathered and how they are treated or analysed. Data collected using a single method, for instance interviewing, can be analysed in many different ways. Similarly, it is worth noting that the same data gathering method can be used in many different types of research design.

Data gathering itself falls into two recognizably different activities: data elicitation and data recording. Elicitation is about accessing the information, opening it up for examination. Recording is about codifying the revealed information in such a manner that it allows the research question to be addressed. Data elicitation typically involves three major forms: direct observation *in situ* (and this can include technologically assisted monitoring, e.g. of heartbeat); self-report (where information is provided by the participants); and archival (where information is derived from records or artefacts not originally produced for purposes of the research). Observation, self-report and archival methods of data elicitation dominate in psychology. Others are largely just variants of these. The information these three provide can be recorded in many ways. All three can generate either qualitative or quantitative data records. In the most basic sense, the form of data elicitation does not dictate the form of data record – specifically, it does not predetermine whether the record is qualitative or quantitative. The distinction between qualitative and quantitative methods is not a division inevitably determined by the nature of data elicitation used but in the way data are recorded and then subsequently treated. Data recording really matters. The way data are recorded fundamentally determines how they can be analysed later (and analysis is used here in the widest sense, not merely to encompass statistical analysis). The chapters is this book are explicit in the way they describe the data elicitation and recording methods they introduce in the hope that students will focus upon the real flexibility that is inherent in the way these approaches can be used individually and in concert.

Each chapter attempts to present a practical guide to the research approach it covers. The object is to demythologize where necessary, to systematize and summarize succinctly relevant information, and to offer advice which will be useful when you try to use the approach yourself. Each chapter should provide you with enough information so that you can judge whether that approach will be of any use to you in addressing a particular research problem. Typically, the chapters are structured so as to introduce the approach, illustrate its potential and the details of using it, identify its weaknesses (where possible showing how they can be overcome), and suggest further literature which can be used to acquire a better understanding of it.

Contributors to this edition have been asked to ensure that where appropriate they explain the underlying role of certain basic principles of data structuring in the method they describe – making communalities across methods more evident. They have been asked to ensure that factors affecting the selection of participants in research using their method are outlined – making implicit limitations in generalizability more manifest. They have been instructed to show how the participants' characteristics (e.g. cultural background or physical or cognitive abilities) might impact upon the validity or reliability of the method – making the inevitable importance of cross-cultural or subcultural comparability more focal. They examine the full spectrum of factors that influence the method's appropriate use, relevance, reliability and validity – making explicit the variety of criteria that can be used in evaluation. They use boxes in the text to highlight key information or to illustrate important arguments – making some quite complex material easily accessible.

Given the variety of approaches covered in this book, we expect that it will be useful throughout the course of an individual's research training. Chapters which are not used at an undergraduate level may well be central to a postgraduate course or be valuable later when considering further research activity. Effectively the book can be used in modules, and progress towards a thorough understanding and skilled use of these various approaches can be achieved in easy stages. As a reference text for more experienced researchers, the book has been written as far as possible so as to incorporate current and recent developments. This is done in the hope that this book can be used as a resource in the process of continuing professional development.

How to use this Textbook and Companion Website

This third edition of *Research Methods in Psychology* purposely doesn't take a 'bells and whistles' approach to pedagogical support unlike many other textbooks on the market. Our focus in all three editions to date has been to provide broad methodological coverage written by people who we believe to be experts in using a particular approach, and we've received some wonderful feedback over the years that the book is very accessible to students.

However, in the current climate of higher education – and particularly in response to feedback from our Publisher – we recognize the value that certain heuristic devices (both inside the textbook and online) can add to the experience of using any textbook from either a lecturer or student perspective. Accordingly, we have now decided to incorporate a range of features to make the third edition even more user-friendly. Much of this development has arisen from direct feedback from 'end users' of the second edition so we trust that these features will strike a chord with readers and users of this book.

TEXTBOOK

Key features inside the textbook – in every chapter – include the following:

1   A range of text boxes. These have multiple functions, and some of these include:

   ➢   summaries of similarities/differences in contrasting approaches to doing psychological research;
   ➢   a checklist of all ethical issues in conducting research systematically;
   ➢   outlines of key psychological studies;

> ➤ overviews of new advances, methods or technologies used in conducting research (e.g. imaging technologies);
> ➤ summaries of concepts, statistical formulae and methodological debates in an interesting manner for the student.

2 Opening chapter introductions and reflective chapter summaries.
3 Emboldened key terms, also listed at the end of every chapter.
4 Suggested further readings at the end of every chapter.

COMPANION WEBSITE

A companion website is also available to accompany this textbook and can be accessed by visiting **www.sagepub.co.uk/breakwell**. The features on this website are all designed to help lecturers use the textbook in a variety of teaching and assessment situations with confidence (only available to those who adopt the textbook via a password), and for students to self-test their knowledge from the book. The features of this website are as follows:

Lecturer Resources

1 A set of PowerPoint slides, arranged by chapter, containing images from the book.
2 A full suite of Blackboard/WebCT compatible multiple choice questions, again arranged by chapter (**NB**: this may not apply to some qualitative methods chapters). In total there are 220–250 questions in this testbank.

Student Resources

1 Interactive multiple choice questions (ten per chapter) for self-testing, arranged by chapter.
2 A flashcard glossary related to the key terms in bold throughout the textbook so that students can test their understanding of key methodological concepts.

We hope that these features will make the experience of using *Research Methods in Psychology*, third edition even easier and more enjoyable.

PART 1
THE BASES OF RESEARCH

1

Theory, Method and Research Design

Glynis M. Breakwell and David Rose

1.1   Theory building and theory testing
    1.1.1   The importance of theories
    1.1.2   The basic construction of a theory
    1.1.3   The nature of explanation: process and functional
    1.1.4   Building more complex theories: induction and deduction
    1.1.5   Theory testing
    1.1.6   Advanced theory structures
    1.1.7   Testing a theory structure
    1.1.8   The meaning of theories
1.2   Matching methodologies to theory
    1.2.1   Type of data elicited
    1.2.2   Technique of data elicitation
    1.2.3   Type of design for monitoring change
    1.2.4   Amount of manipulation
    1.2.5   Treatment of data as qualitative or quantitative
1.3   Integrating findings from different methodologies
1.4   Further reading

AIMS

The purpose of this chapter is to introduce the importance of theory building and the difficulties associated with theory testing. In order to do this, the scientific method and its limitations are described. The relevant, and often debated, distinctions between positivist and constructionist approaches to theory and research are summarized. Different types of data elicitation are outlined and their relationship to data analysis considered. The varieties of research designs that can be used for monitoring change are examined and the role of manipulation in research designs is explained. The chapter concludes by discussing the significance of integrating findings from different types of methods.

Key terms

anomalies	Occam's razor
cross-sectional design	paradigm shift
deduction	positivist
Duhem–Quine thesis	process explanation
falsify	relational rules
functional explanation	revolution
hypotheses	sequential design
induction	stipulative statement
longitudinal design	theory
manipulation checks	qualitative treatment
normal science	quantitative treatment

1.1 THEORY BUILDING AND THEORY TESTING

1.1.1 The importance of theories

We do psychological research to make sense of the thinking, feeling and actions of people. We do it to try to understand what is happening. To be more precise, we do research to find out what has happened, how it happened, and, if possible, why it happened. We use 'happened' rather than 'happening' because by the time we have recorded something it is inevitably in the past. But there is more: once we have some idea of the kinds of things that may happen and their relationship –

theory   in other words, when we have a **theory** – we can use that theory to predict what will happen in the future. If we also understand why things happen the way they do, we may even be able to improve the future by intervening in the world. Knowledge is said to be power, and knowledge is stored elegantly and systematically in the form of theory. Consequently, good theory is both powerful and of practical relevance.

Research is not inevitably tied to formal theory building or theory testing. Some researchers self-consciously eschew the construction of theory for philosophical reasons. They use their research to describe in detail specific happenings without any attempt to use these as instances to illustrate or test some general underlying explanatory framework. Other researchers ignore theory because they do their research for purely practical reasons. They think they only need to know what has happened in order to decide what they (or their clients) should do next.

Yet it could be argued that even those researchers who have no time for formal theories are in fact working with implicit theories. Any set of ideas about the relationships between variables (or what are sometimes referred to as constructs or concepts) has the attributes of a theory. Implicitly, we build theories all the time. In fact, George Kelly (1955), when he developed the theory of personal constructs to explain personality and cognitive processes, based his argument on the metaphor of 'man the scientist'. Kelly suggested that we all behave as scientists in so far as we are inveterate constructors of theories. They help us to navigate in the world by letting us explain to ourselves what we think is happening and why it is happening. Informal theories of this type are particularly valuable because we invariably use them as the basis for predicting what will happen next.

So, for instance, you might observe events which lead you to conclude that men in their late teens or early twenties are more likely than other people to drive their cars aggressively and erratically, with their windows open, with heavy bass music blaring, on sunny days. From this you might generate an informal theory that attributes their driving behaviour to their age or possibly some interaction of their age with the music and the sunshine. As a naïve scientist, you are not obliged to test your theory. You can go ahead to predict from it that young men playing audible music on sunny days are more likely to be a danger to you and adjust your own behaviour accordingly. Theory building of this sort has survival value – though when it goes wrong it also has the capacity seriously to endanger you. Such theories can mislead you, directing you to cues in the situation which are irrelevant. Your sunny day, music-loving bad driver theory is only really valuable if it turns out that in the rain young men are at least as good as any other driver. However, Kelly pointed out that the erroneous theory is usually just a staging post to a better version. As naïve scientists, we are mostly willing to refine our theories on the basis of new information which proves the earlier versions wrong. This is a characteristic of the scientific approach properly pursued.

The implicit theories which inform some research have the same sort of power to both aid and hinder survival. Even while they remain unmentioned, these implicit theories direct the attention of the researcher to focus on some things rather than others, to use certain research approaches rather than others, and to try this rather than that form of analysis. In most cases, it would be better if the researcher did articulate these implicit theories. By doing so, it is possible to analyse their logical weaknesses (e.g. inconsistencies) and their substantive weaknesses (e.g. omission of important variables). Some researchers resist making their implicit theories explicit because they do not see their task as theory building. Yet this is actually a poor excuse. It does not really preclude the need to specify what theoretical assumptions underlie your work. Since these assumptions will inevitably affect what you do, they should be described so that other researchers can judge how far your research activities and findings are influenced by them (e.g. Dobson & Rose, 1985). Researchers who do try to lay bare these underlying assumptions often find that the discipline needed to articulate them has the effect of leading them to a new understanding of their research problem. Essentially, whether you see yourself as a theory builder or not, it is always useful to examine the implicit theories which affect your research. Indeed, many approaches in psychology (e.g. those in Chapters 13, 15, 16, 17 and 18) now require the researcher to be explicit about their own position in relation to their research question and data, tasking them to be self-reflexive and to lay bare their own preconceptions and expectations. Thus even where researchers might be rejecting the application of a priori theoretical frameworks, they are seeking to expose their preconceptions. This is undoubtedly important in order to allow others to interpret the nature of data and explanations ultimately presented.

The basic steps in the scientific method might be summarized as:

1 Formulate the research problem clearly, simply and completely. It might be: what is the relationship between variable X and variable Y?
2 Develop an idea of what might be the form of the relationship between X and Y and outline it in general terms. It might be: X results in Y.
3 Specify an exact hypothesis about the relationship between X and Y. It might be: the occurrence of X always precedes the occurrence of Y and X never occurs without Y following it.
4 Set up a controlled test of the hypothesis, specifically attempting to engender conditions where the hypothesis can be shown to be wrong. It might entail describing all naturally occurring incidences of X and Y to determine whether they always co-occur. It might entail inducing the occurrence of X under a variety of constrained conditions and establishing whether Y will always occur.
5 If the test shows the hypothesis to be wrong, it should be abandoned or, more likely, amended.
6 If the test fails to disprove the hypothesis it may be accepted conditionally before designing further tests and refining the range of its applicability. The object is always to define the limits of the predictive power of the theoretical model.

Some of the limitations of this basic scientific approach to theory construction are given in Sections 1.1.4–1.1.6. Of particular importance is the critique of this approach from those researchers who would not accept that hypothesis testing is an appropriate approach.

Of course, the assertion that everyday thought parallels scientific thought is based on a set of assumptions about what constitutes the scientific approach. Box 1.1 outlines some basic elements of the traditional scientific method. There has been endless debate in psychology about whether it can consider itself a science. There is no final answer to this question: not all psychological research deploys the scientific method; not all psychologists would aspire to do so. The fundamental problem that faces psychology in the pursuit of scientific status is that the majority of the constructs that it finds interesting (e.g. intelligence, motivation, identity) lie at a level of analysis that means that they can only be defined after many levels of extrapolation from any objectively measurable events.

1.1.2 The basic construction of a theory

The process of formal theory building was traditionally supposed by philosophers of science to proceed in an orderly manner from description, to taxonomy, and thence to testable causal **hypotheses**. This would mean that the first task of the hypotheses theorist is to describe the phenomena of interest thoroughly and systematically. The next task is to categorize phenomena, showing how specific instances are characterized by common attributes which make them capable of being treated in some sense as equivalent to each other. Such categorization is one way of ordering the plethora of data which are generated whenever descriptions are not prestructured. The categorization scheme can be labelled as a theoretical construct. Learning theory has categorized phenomena to generate two very salient constructs: stimuli and responses. To the behaviourist, all phenomena at any one moment can be categorized as either a stimulus or a response. By this act of definition, suddenly the multitudinous world is dichotomized, order is imposed and it is our task to explain the relationship between stimulus and response.

Once the taxonomy is complete, the theorist's next task entails stating how one category of phenomena is related to another. The description of a single set of relationships between phenomena does not become a theory unless general principles about the relationships of similar phenomena are formulated. The observation 'The woman kicked the dog after he bit her and he was never found to bite her again' is a description of a pattern of events: it is not a theory. But if one were to say, 'The woman punished the dog for biting and he never did it again', there remains only one further step towards generalization before a theory comes into being: 'Punishment of a behaviour leads to the diminution of that behaviour'. The result is a recognizable basic tenet of learning theory (to be much qualified later by statements about the frequency of punishment, the temporal relationship of the punishment to the behaviour, and the availability of alternative rewards for the behaviour, etc.). Basic theories are sets of what might be called **relational rules**. The relational rule specifies how variation in one theoretical relational rules construct is related to variation in one or more others.

1.1.3 The nature of explanation: process and functional

An explanation can be of two sorts: the mechanistic or process variety or the functional variety. The **process explanation** accounts for a phenomenon in terms process explanation of phenomena which are its precursors. It is usually in the form: if A and B occur, then C will follow. In contrast, the **functional explanation** accounts for a phenomenon in terms of the consequences it has. It is usually in the form: A occurs in functional explanation order that B will follow. The functional explanation assumes that the phenomenon to be explained is purposive, intentional or teleological (i.e. it occurs to achieve some goal).

Another way of talking about the distinction between the process and functional types of explanation is to say that the former is concerned with causes and the latter with reasons: with how as opposed to why. Traditional theories, for example in physics, tend to deal only with the first of these. However, psychological theories use both types of explanation. Some theorists use both explanatory forms to account for a single psychological phenomenon. For instance, in studying altruism (helping or pro-social behaviour) researchers have found that people are less likely to offer someone help if they perceive that person to be in need because he or she has made too little effort, not used his or her own ability and not chosen to get out of the difficulty when it was possible to do so. One explanation of helping suggests that people see the need for assistance, then assess whether the individual is responsible for his or her own predicament; if he or she is responsible this leads to anger and no helping, but if he or she is deemed not to be responsible this leads to sympathy and helping. This is clearly a process explanation. Another explanation of helping suggests that people are unwilling to help an unfortunate whom they see to be the origin of his or her own fate because they wish to punish the miscreant for failures of effort or judgement. In this explanation the punishment (i.e. failure to help) serves the function in some way of exacting restitution and may warn others that such slack behaviour is unacceptable and not rewarded with help. It should be noted that these two explanations of the same phenomenon are not mutually exclusive. The functional explanation may serve to account for the anger, so central to the process explanation, which is aroused when the needy are shown not to have tried to shift for themselves.

1.1.4 Building more complex theories: induction and deduction

This mixing of mechanistic and functional explanations is common in psychological theories. It may emanate, in part, from the way psychological processes and thus psychological theories often traverse many levels of analysis. It is argued here (see also Breakwell, 1994; Rose & Dobson, 1985) that psychologists should be building theories which encompass processes at the intrapsychic (i.e. physiological, cognitive, affective and oretic) level, the interpersonal level and the societal level of analysis. These theories should be integrative, linking the hypotheses and models that explain specific psychological processes. But we are currently a long way away from the grand theory in psychology. We have low- or middle-range theories designed to explain relatively narrow bands of phenomena. Thus, for instance, we have theories of aggression distinct and separate from theories of altruism when common sense might think them to be in some way connected. While these low-level theories may offer a detailed process explanation of their target phenomena, they tend to rely upon what Israel (1972)

stipulative statements   called **stipulative statements** that concern assumptions about the nature of the individual, the nature of society and the nature of the relationship between the individual and society. These stipulative statements are often functionalist (e.g. a variety of social Darwinism as illustrated in the theory of altruism described above). This results in a strange mixture of explanatory types being moulded together in many psychological theories – made more strange by the fact that some significant element of the explanation remains unsaid. Those elements which lie at a different level of analysis from that of the main theory will reside at the margin, unexamined and untested.

Just as process and functional explanations are not so simple to keep apart, the distinction between theories built from **induction** and theories developed through **deduction** is not easy to maintain in practice. Induction entails inferring a general law from particular instances (such as the theory about young men drivers given above). Deduction entails drawing from the general an inference to the particular. In practice, theory building is a messy, iterative process. Relational rules that seem to be valid are usually crafted by successive approximation. This process of approximation will involve both deductive and inductive reasoning (Oldroyd, 1986). You may well, for instance, in developing a theory of how identity processes which concern self-esteem affect memory capacity, set off by cataloguing the range of examples of instances where memory capacity has been shown to be greater for self-relevant information and where it has been proven to be more accurate for information which is positive about the self. From this you might induce a generalization: the memory for self-evaluative information will be greater and more accurate if that information is positive than if it is negative. From this generalization, you might go on to deduce that memory for exam results will be better if they are the individual's own results and especially if they were good results.

In summary, the process of induction allows us to produce theoretical generalizations which are based on evidence about a range of specific instances; one reason for doing research is to collect this evidence. The process of deduction allows us to derive specific predictions from those generalizations, and another reason for doing research is to test these predictions.

induction
deduction

1.1.5 Theory testing

For a long time, it was thought that theory testing involves showing that a theory gives rise to accurate predictions about what will happen under a particular set of circumstances. However, this method is not really convincing, since it can never prove that the theory will always be right under every possible set of circumstances, no matter how many times it is tested. Instead, it has been suggested that what we should do in testing a theory is to try to prove it wrong (Popper, 1959). By showing where a theory is wrong, we show which bits need to be removed and in most cases we also show what needs to be substituted in their place. Research designed to test a theory will be organized so as to show whether a prediction deduced from that theory is wrong. This would **falsify** the theory. If we fail to disprove the prediction, the theory survives to face another test. Research can never prove a theory, it can merely accumulate examples of where the theory has not been disproved. The reason why a theory cannot be proven in absolute terms is that it must entail generalization and the empirical research can

falsify

only ever sample specific instances of that generality. A good theory is one which survives intact through many sincere and severe attempts at falsification.

One problem with this approach is that theories may survive because they are not strictly falsifiable. Some theories are unfalsifiable because they rest upon a tautology. For instance, some critics of learning theory would argue that one of its fundamental assertions cannot be falsified because the concept of a reinforcer is defined in a tautological way. Thus a reinforcer is defined as anything which acts to increase the frequency of a response. The theory then goes on to state that responses which are reinforced increase in frequency. The circularity in the argument is clear when the theory is reduced to its fundamentals in this way. Such a tautology means that the theory cannot be tested because a key concept cannot be operationally defined independently of other concepts within the theory.

Another problem is the Freudian theory of ego-defence mechanisms, which cannot be falsified for a different reason. In this case, the theory attempts to explain how the conscious mind protects itself from material which must remain in the unconscious or preconscious mind. Freud explained that such material is handled by a series of ego-defence mechanisms (sublimation, displacement, regression, fixation, etc.). What makes this aspect of psychoanalytic theory untestable is the fact Freud offers such an array of defence mechanisms that it is impossible to formulate a test of the operation of one which would not be potentially abrogated by the operation of another. For instance, one might set out to test the notion of sublimation which would say that an unacceptable unconscious impulse driven by the id should be translated into one which is socially acceptable before it could gain access to the conscious mind. The first problem the empiricist would have is in knowing that the impulse existed at all. The second would be that the impulse need not be dealt with by sublimation: it could be treated through reaction formation. This would mean that even if you established when the impulse was occurring and monitored no evidence of sublimation, you would not have falsified the theory because the impulse had been dealt with by another equally valid defence mechanism. Freud basically produced what could be called an overdetermined model: a theory which allows multiple determiners of outcomes in such a way that no single determiner can be empirically proven to be irrelevant.

1.1.6 Advanced theory structures

Other problems with falsifiability appear when we consider theories in advanced areas of research. Although induction can give us our initial ideas when we first begin to investigate a fresh research field, delving further into an already established area of research requires new skills entirely. Deductive skills will serve for testing simple theories, but in advanced areas of research the theories have been built into complex structures, with many levels and enormous ranges of applicability.

Some philosophers have divided the components of such theories into two types: the fundamental 'hard core' of assumptions and presuppositions that are basic to the whole enterprise, and a collection of auxiliary hypotheses that derive from the hard core and make predictions about what will happen in particular situations (Lakatos, 1970). The whole complex is known as a research programme. Everyday research concerns tests of the auxiliary hypotheses, and the more the programme generates new hypotheses, and the more these find empirical support, the more 'progressive' the research programme is said to be.

A single experiment is, however, not sufficient to falsify a complex theory: instead, only a series of negative results (failed predictions), together with a paucity of new ideas stemming from within the programme, can suggest that the programme is 'degenerative'. Only after a period of such degeneration may the situation be considered so bad that it is necessary to revise or even reject the whole theory.

Of course, in practice it is difficult to judge when this latter course of action is necessary. This is because one of the characteristics of a complex theory structure is that it can be so easily modified by adding or subtracting new components. In fact a fundamental problem with these structures is that just about any negative or unexpected empirical result can be accommodated by adding *ad hoc* hypotheses to the theory. This is known as the **Duhem–Quine thesis**.

Duhem–Quine thesis

For example, the presupposition that children learn by copying others might lead to the hypothesis that children who view violent cartoons on television will subsequently show similar antisocial behaviour. Suppose then that observations of a group of ten-year-olds who regularly watch 'Tom and Jerry' cartoons reveal no difference in some measure of violent social behaviour, when compared with ten-year-olds who do not watch 'Tom and Jerry'. The theorist can then say: ah, well, the antisocial behaviour will only be revealed later, when the child enters adolescence and encounters more testing situations such as gang fights. Or the cartoons do have the predicted effect but only on children of a particular age, for example below ten years old, because by age ten the children have learned the difference between cartoons and reality. Or only cartoons involving violence between humans will lead to antisocial behaviour. And so on. In each of these cases, the theorist has added an additional hypothesis after the facts of the experiment have become known. These hypotheses act to save the core tenets of the theory from falsification (disproof), by making the theory a little more complicated. Although in principle we should not allow such *post hoc* theorizing, it is inevitable, given that life is complicated, that a correct theory will therefore also need to be complex if it is to specify in exact detail what will happen when and under what circumstances. However, the indefinitely large number of these possible *post hoc* hypotheses does make it very difficult to disprove a theory conclusively.

1.1.7 Testing a theory structure

Although psychology as a whole does not yet have a single grand unifying theory, many of the theories you encounter will nevertheless be so complex as to render simple interpretation and methods inadequate. This fact has several consequences for research methodology in those situations.

Firstly, the choice of which observations it is worthwhile to make is informed by the background knowledge that has already been built up in that field. This requires you to know not only what observations have already been accrued, but also which theories and hypotheses are still under development and are worthy of further investigation.

Secondly, the meaning of any new observations you make depends on the background theory: you have to interpret your empirical findings in the light of the theory. For example, criminal behaviour can appear very different, depending whether your underlying theory of behaviour is genetic or behaviourist or whatever: are violent criminals just basically evil, or victims of their hormones, or morally corrupted by a corrupt society around them, or copying the example set by their violent parents, or suffering from brain damage?

You also have to know what the implications of the observation are for the whole structure of the theory: for example, is an unexpected observation inconsistent only with the particular hypothesis you are testing, or does it count against the underlying assumptions of the whole theory? In other words, does the failure of prediction arise because the fundamental tenets of the whole approach are wrong, or merely one of the auxiliary hypotheses – and if so which one? How can you tell? Falsifiability becomes problematic when there are so many interacting hypotheses, data bases and collateral assumptions that any one of them might be in error, so throwing your prediction out.

Take, for example, Bandura's (1997) theory of self-efficacy, which states that people vary in the extent to which they believe that they can achieve whatever they set out to do (i.e. they vary in self-efficacy). People who have high self-efficacy expectancies are healthier, more effective and generally more successful than those with low self-efficacy expectancies. From this theory we may derive a hypothesis that a person who is high in self-efficacy and who becomes ill will be more likely to take medication to cure the condition. However, this behaviour will only take place if the person has a belief that the medication will be efficacious. A method of testing this hypothesis is to monitor whether people with high self-efficacy who become ill are actually more likely to take medicine when advised to do so. Suppose, however, we find they do not. Is this because Bandura's theory is wrong, because our hypothesis is wrong, because the variables of self-efficacy and belief in the medication have been indexed inappropriately, or because our method of measuring behaviour was inadequate or inappropriate?

All predictions also have a *ceteris paribus* clause attached: they assume that no extraneous variables or factors will interfere with the observations or invalidate them in any way. It is a frequent occurrence for data not to be as expected, and perhaps the commonest way of explaining the anomaly is to postulate an extra variable that is affecting the outcome. In the above example, for instance, people might not take medicine voluntarily because they have an additional belief, such as that medication in general does not work, or is immoral on religious grounds, or would cause too many side-effects. Controlled experiments that are designed to reveal any such extraneous variable are accordingly often performed on an *ad hoc* basis after the main body of observations has been made.

Thirdly, the empirical methods used are themselves theory relative. It is not possible to divide science into theory and observation, as was claimed by **posi-** **tivist** philosophers earlier in the last century. Although empirical science worships the idol of the 'neutral' observer who is an unbiased recorder of nature, in practice this standard is an unattainable ideal. Thus we all have some idea of what we might find when we make an observation, and in many cases we know what we want to find. The techniques of 'blind' experimentation have been developed to help cope with exactly this problem.

positivist

Additionally, the very measuring instruments we use have been developed under particular theoretical backgrounds; their construction depends upon a whole network of theoretical assumptions about the nature of the materials used and the way these interact with the subjects of the experiment. For example, psychoanalytic theory developed the Rorschach inkblot test as an instrument to facilitate behaviour sampling. Responses to this test have been used to make inferences about a person's 'personality' type. However, the results do not make sense under modern personality theory, which instead uses complex statistical analyses of responses to a much wider variety of simpler but more strictly defined tests (e.g. questionnaires). The kinds of personality categories recognized under psychoanalytic theory are not commensurate with those of alternative theories. Another example would be trying to assess memory ability by presenting nonsense syllable pairs on a memory drum to see how many associations can be remembered. This makes sense under behaviourism; but under Gestalt theory, or modern cognitive theory, the number of associations is just not interesting: instead it is the emergent, holistic and semantic organizational properties of memory that are relevant, and the kinds of tests that are considered appropriate are very different (e.g. structuring in free recall). Moreover, under some theories there is no such thing as a 'nonsense syllable': all stimuli are taken to have meaning.

The idea that the interpretation of the data generated always depends upon a network of background theory does not just apply to the 'apparatus' by which we interact with the subject; it is no less true of the quantitative numerical techniques we use to analyse the data (Lamiell, 1995). For example, the basic methods of statistics were developed under positivist principles, which are now considered obsolete. They assume that theory-neutral observations can be made by unprejudiced objective impartial observers. The process of using statistics thus creates a delusion of certainty that makes it all too easy for us to fall into the trap of letting the empirical results and the significance levels of the associated analyses tell us what to believe. You should not allow yourself to be dominated by the probability level in deciding what conclusions to draw. Quantitative results have to be interpreted in the light of a whole lot of background knowledge, theory and opinion.

Finally, an established theory will have accreted to itself the results of numerous empirical tests, some of which support the theory and some of which do not. If the supporting evidence comes from many different sources and is of many different types, the convergence on to the same conclusion from all these sources is regarded as making the theory stronger or more valid than if the evidence comes from repeated observations all of the same type because the latter might be caused by some artefact or error in the method. Predicting new observations is also generally regarded as carrying more weight than fitting retrospectively an old body of obser-

anomalies

vations. False predictions of the theory are categorized as **anomalies**, and most advanced theories bear a number of these – although not all the supporters of the theory will necessarily admit their existence. This is because evidence is not always accepted at face value, if only because experiments are complicated and not per-fectly reliable. It is only with years of hindsight that empirical outcomes can be classified as valid or invalid, in the light of which a theory has turned out to be the correct one (Lakatos, 1970). In the interim, it is conventional to live with the ano-malies, provided they are not too many in number or too crucial and convincing.

normal science

Periods in which scientists beaver away collecting data under a generally accepted theory have been described as **normal science** (Kuhn, 1962). Complete rejection of such generally accepted theories does not usually occur unless there exists an alternative or competing theory (as well as many anomalies in the old theory). Until such arrives, researchers have no real alternative but to carry on using the old theory, despite all its faults. When another theory exists, it predicts a pattern of results that differs from the pattern predicted by the old theory. If the new pattern fits the actual data better, the new theory is likely to be adopted (allow-ing also for the other criteria for theory acceptance outlined below). Once such a

revolution
paradigm shift

revolution or **paradigm shift** occurs, the meaning of all the empirical results is reinterpreted: what previously appeared to be peculiar if not downright bizarre data may now be seen to be understandable, given the new theory. So previous anomalies are now consonant with expectation, in that they can be deductively related to the covering laws (relational rules) in the new theory. Any observa-tions that remain unexplained become anomalies under the new theory; adop-tion of the new theory is intended to reduce the number of anomalies as much as possible. Positivist philosophers suggested one could simply count up the number of successful empirical predictions of a theory, subtract the number of anomalies, and pick the theory with the highest score. However, this assumed all observations carry equal weight and each is an isolated nugget of fact. Instead, observations fit together to form a pattern, and the links between them should form a logically coherent structure.

The psychological process of reinterpreting and reorganizing the whole set of empirical data has been likened to the Gestalt-like change in perception and under-standing that can occur in individual knowledge following an act of 'insight' (Kuhn, 1962). A novel synthesis of the data into a new pattern is usually presented in the form of a review article and brings great credit to its originators. While you will almost always undertake a 'literature review' as part of any research project, in which you summarize the extant findings in the field, if you perceive a novel pattern by which more of the data can be accounted for by some new theory than by any existing theory, your contribution will be highly valued.

We have discussed theory testing as involving primarily empirical testing and observation, but given the existence of complex theory structures and the Duhem–Quine thesis, reliance on simple observational evidence is clearly not enough. The alternative is to use rationalist principles alongside empiricist ones: theories can be evaluated according to several non-empirical criteria, such as their parsimony, ease of communication, flexibility, fruitfulness, insightfulness, internal consistency, simplicity, elegance, breadth, and so on. Such principles are used implicitly by all scientists and are actually a central reason for the success of science. No one criterion alone is sufficient: a judicious and balanced combination of arguments should guide one's choice.

Consider simplicity, for example. A corollary of the Duhem–Quine thesis is that any given set of data can in principle be explained by an infinite number of theories. The thesis states that theories can be elaborated to any degree of complexity we wish. It is therefore possible to take almost any theory and by adding sufficient auxiliary hypotheses modify that theory so it can explain a particular set of data. In such cases, our choice of which theory to adopt is 'underdetermined' by the data, since the data do not point unequivocally to one theory and one theory only. The normal response to this problem is to choose the simplest theory, applying what is called **Occam's razor** (sometimes spelt **Ockham's** razor), which states that we should not multiply hypotheses needlessly. A problem with simplicity is that it assumes that the complexity of a theory can be measured in some objective way so that different theories can be compared. However, advanced theory structures differ so much qualitatively as well as in their quantitative 'complexity' that comparison by any single common yardstick may in practice be impossible. Thus theories are often incommensurable because their underlying purposes and assumptions are different; they have different criteria for their own success, since their aims and intended context of application are very different. Theory comparison and selection may then appear a matter of subjective judgement.

Occam's razor
Ockham's

1.1.8 The meaning of theories

The notion that a theory can be successful for a period of time, and can then be replaced by a totally different and incommensurable theory that is even more successful, leads to the question of why the first theory should have been successful at all, given that it was wrong. Research into scientific practice itself has shown that science is not so different from other spheres of life: it is a social activity, and the choice of which theory to believe, which data to accept as correct, which professor or department to rely on, is as much a matter of attitude and opinion formation as is any other psychological belief. Personal and social factors cannot be excluded from science. At its most extreme, this school of opinion (known as the strong programme in the sociology of knowledge) denies that any theory describes an objective reality: it is just a matter of socially reached consensus among the scientific community as to what to believe (relativism).

Other researchers treat theories as useful ways of predicting what will happen under given circumstances, but without making any claim one way or the other as to whether the theories describe an actual 'reality' (this attitude is variously called pragmatism, operationalism or instrumentalism). This issue is still the subject of intense debate in the philosophy of science. Moderating voices accept the (empirically observed) fact that social factors do operate in science, but that objective empirical data about the world play their part too: the social factors are not the sole determinants of theory acceptance or rejection. Thus although interpersonal disputes play a crucial part at the cutting edge of research, where the truth is still uncertain, in the long run scientists are kept on the right path by some kind of objective reality operating via the empirical observations (e.g. Oldroyd, 1986; Hull, 1988; Kitcher, 1993; Klee, 1997).

Box 1.2 summarizes in bald terms the distinction between the approach of positivist-realists and the constructionist-relativist traditions.

The Duhem–Quine thesis and the strong programme in the sociology of knowledge have led some people to conclude that relativism is the norm. Thus

Box 1.2 Comparison of positivist and constructionist* approaches to research	
POSITIVIST	**CONSTRUCTIONIST**
Facts can have an objective reality	Facts are subjective constructs
Data validity and reliability are sought	Reliability and validity are irrelevant concepts since the data are not judged in terms of any external notion of truth
Hypotheses should be explicit and pre-date data collection	Understanding is emergent and explanation can emerge after data are collected
Prediction is an objective Falsification of hypotheses is an objective	Description is an objective Usefulness of interpretation is an objective
*There are many labels used to describe these broad traditions and there are many subsets within each, all having somewhat different philosophies. The comparison here is in bald terms and at the most generic level.	

although everybody starts out believing that there is an absolute truth about how the world is, and there is a single correct answer to every problem, which it is science's job to find, we soon realize that life is more complicated, that people in positions of authority can hold differing opinions (often diametrically opposed) and that no one can be 100% sure about anything. Most research students reach a point when they realize that observations are not pure nuggets of truth, and that they all depend upon a network of assumptions (about the nature of the measuring instrument, the theoretical and observational presuppositions from which the hypotheses were derived, and so on, as explained above). At this point it is important not to despair; life goes on and science does work. You have to realize that all beliefs have pros and cons, that whatever theory you adopt will have some evidence and arguments in favour of it and some against. You have to decide which theory to believe in, otherwise you cannot act. You will select what is in your opinion the best theory, given the currently available theories and evidence. However, your choice of theory should not be adhered to as a dogma that cannot be contradicted. You must adopt a flexible attitude: you must realize that your choice is provisional, and you must always be ready to change your belief in the light of new evidence and arguments.

Nowadays, there is increasing appreciation of the complexity of psychological systems and processes. Psychologists and biologists look for particular causal mechanisms, rather than for universal covering laws (e.g. Bechtel & Richardson, 1993). This avoids the problems of the grand theory structures outlined above. The idea is still to explain the phenomena that are observed, but to give understanding of how and why they arise, in terms of what causes them, not which universal law of nature they are deductively in accordance with. The idea of simple universal laws arose within seventeenth-century physics; more recently, however, we have come to realize that biological systems are too complex to analyse using the same methods, and entirely different principles are called for. Functional and process or mechanistic explanations (Section 1.1.3) must be given together. People and animals evolved and survived within a chaotically changing range of environments that have shaped and altered us over the aeons in ways that no simple law will describe. Our aims as psychologists therefore have to be to explain the particulars of mental life and behaviour we encounter in terms of the individual people we are observing, their constitutions and their immediate and past circumstances. To do so we have to use multiple methods, both rationalist and empiricist in nature. It is to this end that many of the methods described in the following chapters of this book are directed.

1.2 MATCHING METHODOLOGIES TO THEORY

Different types of theory have to be tested using different types of research method. The nature of the theory limits the range of research methods which can be meaningfully used to test it. For example, a theory explaining variation in visual acuity is likely to need to measure acuity using some psychophysical technique (see Chapter 9). However, the extent of these limitations should not be overestimated. Most psychological theories can be tested using more than one method. In fact, it is advisable to try to test a theory using a variety of methods in order to prove that it is no artefact of the method which results in the theory being supported.

A piece of research can differ along a series of five independent dimensions:

1 type of data elicited;
2 technique of data elicitation;
3 type of design for monitoring change;
4 amount of manipulation used;
5 treatment of data as qualitative or quantitative.

1.2.1 Type of data elicited

In psychological research the data can vary in origin: they can be intrapersonal (e.g. genotypic information, cognitions, emotions), interindividual (e.g. friendship networks, communication patterns), or societal (e.g. institutional hierarchies, ideological systems).

1.2.2 Technique of data elicitation

Data can be elicited directly or indirectly from a target. Direct elicitation methods would include any stimulus to self-report (e.g. interviewing, self-completion questionnaires) or self-revelation through behaviour (e.g. role play, performance on tasks). Indirect elicitation methods would include techniques that rely upon the researcher observing behaviour (e.g. participant observation) or using informants about the target's behaviour, thought or feelings (e.g. archival records, witnesses).

Data elicitation can vary in terms of the amount of control exerted by the researcher upon a target. This control can be manifest in restrictions imposed upon the freedom of the target to give information (e.g. forced-choice options rather than open-ended responses to questions). It can be evident in the extent to which the target is manipulated (e.g. in experiments through the creation of artificial contexts or in surveys through the use of cover stories designed to mislead the target about the purpose of the study).

1.2.3 Type of design for monitoring change

A central task for psychological theories is to explain change. Researchers whose objective is to identify and explain change have a choice of three main classes of design for data collection: longitudinal, cross-sectional or sequential.

A **longitudinal design** involves data being collected from the same sample of individuals on at least two occasions. The interval between data collections and the number of data collections vary greatly: the research can be contained in a few days or spread over several decades. A longitudinal design allows researchers to establish changes in individuals over time as the sample ages or experiences some identifiable alteration in experience. In experimental parlance, a longitudinal design might be called a repeated measures or within-subject design (see Chapter 4).

longitudinal design

A **cross-sectional design** involves eliciting information at a single time from people in a number of different conditions that are expected to be significant to the change. Often this means studying people in different age cohorts because, particularly in theories of developmental psychology, age is deemed to be a major determinant of change. The term 'age cohort' refers to the total population of individuals born at approximately the same time, which is usually taken to mean in the same calendar year. The cross-sectional design permits age-related changes to be gauged.

cross-sectional design

A **sequential design** will choose samples from a particular condition (e.g. a specific age cohort) but will study them at different times. The periodicity in sequential data gathering varies across studies. A simple sequential design might involve sampling the 21-year-old cohort of 1989, the 21-year-old cohort of 1979, and the 21-year-old cohort of 1969. This type of design would be targeted at revealing whether changes in a particular age group are affected by factors which are associated with their specific sociohistorical era.

sequential design

When studying patterns of change that are age-related there are always three factors which could possibly explain observed relationships: development tied to the ageing of the individual; characteristics associated with the particular age cohorts studied; and impact of the specific time of measurement. Time of measurement is the term suggested by Schaie (1965) to refer to the set of pressures upon the individual generated by the socio-environmental context at the point data are collected. The difficulty facing researchers interested in explaining age-related changes lies in establishing which of these three factors is the source of the change. The strategy adopted by most researchers is to keep one of the factors constant. For instance, the longitudinal design keeps the cohort constant. The cross-sectional design keeps the time of measurement constant. The sequential design keeps the chronological age constant. Of course, this means that explanation of any observed age-related trend remains problematic since these designs always leave two of the three explanatory factors free to vary simultaneously. Irrespective of which of these three designs is adopted, two explanatory factors will be confounded. This represents the major methodological drawback in using such relatively simple designs.

There is a secondary problem. By holding one factor constant, the design obviously rules out the possibility of exploring the effects of that factor in interaction with the others. Yet, in virtually all complex systems of change, one would expect interaction effects between developmental, cohort and time of measurement factors. The solution to this fundamental methodological problem has been to integrate the three design types in what is known as a longitudinal cohort sequential design. This combines the longitudinal follow-up of a series of cohorts first sampled simultaneously as in a cross-sectional study with the sequential addition of new cohorts of the same ages to the study at each subsequent data collection point.

Even if a researcher believes the psychological construct under investigation is not influenced by the chronological maturation of the individual and not affected by the sociohistorical context of the data collection, the burden of proof rests upon that researcher to show that they are not important. It used to be thought that only a developmental psychologist really needed to consider whether to use a longitudinal cohort sequential design. Now, particularly as lifespan development becomes an accepted stipulative adjunct to most theories of psychological functioning, all researchers need to understand the implications of these different types of design.

1.2.4 Amount of manipulation

Research designs differ in the extent to which they rely upon the researcher manipulating the experience of participants in order to induce reactions. The fundamental differences between experimental, quasi-experimental, and other non-intrusive (or, more accurately, less intrusive) approaches are described in subsequent chapters in this book. For current purposes, it may be enough to highlight that researchers must make decisions about the nature of the interventions and control they will deploy in order to create the context in which they can study their target variables. Some research traditions eschew all manipulation and seek only to record naturally occurring phenomena. Others engage in highly elaborate environmental and social manipulation to create artificial but closely controlled conditions under which data are collected. Understanding where you are in any particular research design on this continuum of manipulation is important. It is important for two reasons. First, the greater the level of manipulation, the greater the degree of artificiality in the data and the greater the need to check whether the results can be generalized beyond the research context. Second, one of the most frequent reasons why research fails is that the manipulations used are inadequate. They can be inadequate in a number of ways:

- they can fail to reflect the construct or variable the impact of which the researcher wishes to study (for instance, the researcher wants to threaten the participant's sense of self-esteem and seeks to do this by providing false feedback of failure on an IQ test but the feedback represents what the participant would have expected to achieve);

- they can introduce unanticipated changes in ancillary variables that the researcher does not wish to study (for instance, the researcher wants the participant to focus on their family history and presents a family photograph but the photo includes in the background a fair and the participant focuses upon the fairground not the family element in the stimulus);
- they can fail to mean the same thing to the participant as they mean to the researcher (for instance, the researcher wishes to frighten someone and uses a manipulation involving the sudden presentation of a large spider, but the participant finds spiders not frightening but comic).

Ironically, the problem with manipulation is that it is difficult to control. Care in choosing manipulations pays dividends. **Manipulation checks** are now the norm in good research. These are designed to test whether the manipulation you think you introduced worked in the way you thought it would. In evaluating the research of others it is always a good idea to assess the effectiveness of the manipulations used.

manipulation checks

1.2.5 Treatment of data as qualitative or quantitative

Research methods can be differentiated according to whether data are submitted to a qualitative or quantitative treatment. A **qualitative treatment** describes what processes are occurring and details differences in the character of these processes over time. A **quantitative treatment** states what the processes are, how often they occur, and what differences in their magnitude can be measured over time. Subsequent chapters in this book deal in detail with data treatment techniques and this is not the place to go into them in detail.

qualitative treatment

quantitative treatment

It is important to reiterate that these five dimensions on which a piece of research can be described are independent of each other. Data type, elicitation technique, the design for monitoring change, amount of manipulation and the qualitative or quantitative treatment of the data can be put together in many varieties. For instance, it is possible to use a qualitative treatment of data acquired as part of an experiment conducted in a longitudinal study.

A researcher, in structuring a study along these five dimensions, will have to make hard decisions. The decisions will in part be determined by whether theory building is at an inductive or deductive phase. A broader range of data types, elicitation techniques with lower control, cross-sectional designs, and qualitative treatment of data may be most appropriate in the early inductive phase. The deductive phase leading to testable predictions is likely to be linked to the narrowing of data types, direct and controlled data elicitation, a mixture of change-monitoring designs, and the quantitative treatment of data. Sadly the decision is also too often influenced by preconceptions, prejudices and fears. Researchers get trapped into one methodological approach (i.e. a package of one type of data, one elicitation technique, one design, and one data treatment). Once a routine sets in this can be easier than getting to know (or even remembering) how to do the other things. Also, of course, often researchers acquire their reputation on the basis of using a specific sort of methodology. To relinquish it is tantamount to abandoning their claim to fame. The solution may lie in practising eclecticism of methodology from an early stage in a research career.

Such eclecticism is fostered by forcing yourself, when faced with the task of constructing any study to test a hypothesis deduced from your theory, to provide at least two realistic alternative methodologies. Then weigh the pros and cons of each. Work out the differences between what they will tell you. In most cases, even minor variations of methodology will substantially affect what you can conclude. Ultimately, researchers have to choose between alternative feasible methodologies in the full knowledge of what they might lose by passing over those which they reject. The chapters in this book make an attempt to help you to see what are the strengths and weaknesses of various techniques, designs and data treatments.

1.3 INTEGRATING FINDINGS FROM DIFFERENT METHODOLOGIES

If you understand different methodologies and use them in concert, there comes a point when you must ask yourself: how do I put the findings from one methodology together with those from another? The easy answer focuses upon the theory. Assuming that each methodology is used to test one or more hypotheses derived from the theory, as long as the various methodologies yield conclusions which are compatible with the theory there is no problem. They are merely vehicles for theory testing; they may travel by different routes but they get to the same destination ultimately.

The problems arise when different methodologies produce contradictory or inconsistent conclusions about the hypothesis tested. In the baldest terms, one may support the hypothesis, whereas another may generate evidence which indicates that it is incorrect. The first step in this situation is to check that the methodologies were both executed properly. If they were, you should, if possible, collect further data using the same methodologies. If the inconsistent result is repeated, it is necessary to examine whether there is some identifiable attribute differentiating between the methodologies which could explain their inconsistent results. If such an attribute can be identified, it should be incorporated into another study in a controlled way so that its effect can be studied systematically. This may support the introduction of some caveat into the original hypothesis. If no such attribute can be identified, the hypothesis should be retested using a series of completely different methodologies. If these yield contradictory evidence, it is reasonably certain that the hypothesis will need to be reformulated. The combination of evidence from the various methodologies should show where its limitations lie and point to an appropriate revision.

Obviously, all this procedure of iterative data collection takes time and resources. The researcher will have to decide whether this aspect of the theory is sufficiently important to merit such effort. If the procedure is not followed, it is essential that the original finding which refuted the hypothesis is treated seriously. The temptation to dismiss the finding in such a situation must be resisted. There are many siren voices which will offer ways of discounting the finding in terms of the relative merits of the methodologies. Unless you clearly stated on an a priori basis that one methodology would be given priority in the event of inconsistencies in the findings, the methodologies must be treated retrospectively as having equivalent standing.

When there are inconsistent results, an integrated approach to the use of several methodologies may be inconvenient but it also has great advantages. Every methodology has its limitations. The nature of these limitations differs. Using a series of methodologies allows you to compensate for the weaknesses of one methodology in a domain by supplementing or complementing it with another methodology which is stronger in that domain. The development of a coherent strategy for integrating methodologies, designed to test clearly defined hypotheses comprehensively, is the basic foundation for researching psychological processes.

1.4 FURTHER READING

There are some excellent handbooks that offer comprehensive coverage of the central issues. Denzin and Lincoln's (2005) text provides a clear and concise introduction to the major methods of qualitative research, with details of how data can be interpreted. Scott and Xie (2006) provide a fundamental introduction to the key quantitative methods in the social sciences beyond the discipline of psychology, assuming no prior knowledge of the statistical methods necessary to analyse quantitative data. Scott (2006) presents the variety of ways in which documentary evidence is interpreted, and is valuable particularly because it shows how texts are used by scholars outside social science, for instance in literature or history. Finally, M. Smith's (2005) text is useful for those who would unearth some of the greater complexities of the philosophical arguments that underlie the choice of a method of data collection or analysis.

2

Practical and Ethical Issues in Planning Research

Martyn Barrett

2.1   Introduction
2.2   Formulating research questions
    2.2.1   Selecting a topic to study
    2.2.2   The need to formulate specific research questions
    2.2.3   Strategies to adopt when formulating specific research questions
    2.2.4   Choice of possible research methods
    2.2.5   The literature review
    2.2.6   Accessing the relevant literature
2.3   Assessing the practical feasibility of the research
    2.3.1   Participants required for the research
    2.3.2   Equipment and materials required for the research
    2.3.3   Consumable items required for the research
    2.3.4   Other costs which may be incurred by the research
    2.3.5   Pilot work
    2.3.6   Identifying the statistical analyses needed and rechecking the sample size
    2.3.7   Formulating a timetable
    2.3.8   Conclusions
2.4   Assessing the ethical feasibility of the research
    2.4.1   The protection and welfare of participants
    2.4.2   The principle of informed consent
    2.4.3   The use of deception
    2.4.4   The debriefing of participants
    2.4.5   Participants' right to withdraw from an investigation
    2.4.6   The invasion of privacy in observational research
    2.4.7   Confidentiality and the anonymity of data
    2.4.8   Conclusions
2.5   Considering the possible outcomes of the research in advance
2.6   Applying for research funding
2.7   Conclusion
2.8   BPS and APA addresses and websites
2.9   Further reading

This chapter aims to introduce the reader to many of the practical and ethical issues which need to be considered when planning psychological research. The chapter discusses how to formulate suitable research questions, how to access the relevant background research literature, and how to assess the practical and ethical feasibility of a research study. We look at issues concerning the role of pilot work, participant availability and recruitment, the availability of equipment and materials, the assessment of the financial costs which are associated with conducting research, and how to apply for research funding. We also examine how ethical principles should always form an integral part of the planning process and, in particular, how the welfare of participants should always be protected through confidentiality, anonymity and the principle of informed consent. The chapter concludes with a checklist of all of the key issues which should be considered during the course of planning a psychological research study.

Key terms

anonymity
confidentiality
debriefing
deception
ethical principles
gatekeeper
invasion of privacy
informed consent
literature review
operational definitions
participant attrition

participant availability
participant non-compliance
pilot work
research costs
research dissemination
research funding
research questions
right to withdraw
timetable
welfare of participants

2.1 INTRODUCTION

This chapter is concerned with the practical and ethical issues which need to be considered when planning psychological research systematically. There are many different issues which need to be taken into account if a piece of psychological research is to achieve its intended goal, and each of these issues requires careful decisions to be made during the course of the planning process. Of necessity, this chapter will have to discuss these issues and decisions in a particular sequence. However, it is important to bear in mind that these decisions are not independent of one another, and that making one decision can have important implications for other decisions (e.g. choosing to use a particular statistical procedure will have implications for the minimum size of sample which ought to be

invasion of privacy

used, or an ethical decision concerning the **invasion of privacy** might lead one to choose interviewing rather than naturalistic observation for collecting data). This complex interdependence means that the process of planning psychological research does not consist of a simple linear sequence of decisions. Instead, as we seek operational definitions of the theoretical concepts that are contained in the hypotheses which we wish to test by means of our research, we are of necessity having to think simultaneously about possible ways of measuring these concepts in particular types of settings with various types of participants; this means that we also have to think, at the same time, about whether we have access to those participants, and whether it is feasible to collect the data on an appropriate timescale with the resources which are available to us in such a way that those data can then be analysed by the types of statistics which are pertinent to testing the hypotheses from which we started out. This complex interdependence of the various decisions which together comprise the planning process should be borne in mind throughout this chapter.

To a certain extent, many of the issues which will be discussed in this chapter might appear to be a matter of simple common sense. However, if this is the case, it is surprising how often such common sense fails researchers, particularly those early in their careers. There are all sorts of pitfalls which can bedevil psychological research and can prevent that research from achieving its intended goals. The hope is that this chapter will at least help to sensitize the beginning researcher to some of the major pitfalls.

2.2 FORMULATING RESEARCH QUESTIONS

2.2.1 Selecting a topic to study

When planning a piece of psychological research, there is of course one particular step which needs to be taken first, and that is to identify and select a topic to study. There are all sorts of reasons why psychologists choose to study particular topics. They might do so because of a personal interest in the topic or because they make a value judgement about the importance of that topic. Or they may choose a topic for a theoretical reason, perhaps because they have spotted an assumption or a prediction made by a particular theory which has never been tested empirically. Alternatively, they may have a concern with a particular social problem and want to contribute towards the resolution of that problem, or wish to help improve the quality of life for a particular group of individuals. All of these reasons are equally valid. Essentially, they all boil down to an assessment that the topic which has been chosen is either interesting, important or useful.

However, from a practical point of view, it is crucial also to take into account a further criterion when selecting a particular topic to investigate: is it realistic and feasible to conduct research into this topic, given the practical and ethical restrictions on what the researcher is able to do? In order to derive an answer to this question, it is essential to move on from the general topic to the formulation of the specific questions concerning that topic which will be addressed by means of the research, so that the researcher can work out precisely what is required in practice in order to answer those questions, and can then work out whether or not these requirements can be met.

2.2.2 The need to formulate specific research questions

To take an example, the researcher might believe that aggression in children is an important topic to study. However, selecting this general topic for research is not sufficient to enable us to say whether the intended research is or is not feasible. Firstly, it is necessary to state exactly what it is that the researcher wants to find out about this topic. For example, does the researcher want to discover how aggressive behaviour in children varies as a function of age, or the factors which cause children to be aggressive to others, or the responses which children's aggressive behaviour elicits from other people, or what? Notice that in all cases, if the researcher's goal is to discover something about the topic which has been selected, then it is always possible to state that research goal in the form of a question. How does children's aggressive behaviour vary as a function of age? What are the factors which cause children to be aggressive to others? What are the responses which children's aggressive behaviour elicits from other people? If the intended goal of the research cannot be formulated as an explicit question, or as a series of such questions, then that research does not have a coherent goal.

Let us pursue our hypothetical example a little further. Let us assume that the researcher decides that the question to be addressed by means of the research is the relatively mundane one of: how does children's aggressive behaviour vary as a function of age? Notice that it is clearly impossible for any researcher to study children's aggressive behaviour in all contexts at all ages. Consequently, in order to assess the feasibility of the research, the researcher now needs to qualify the research question further by stipulating the appropriate contexts which are of interest. For example: how does children's aggressive behaviour in the school playground, in the home, in the streets (say) vary as a function of age? The feasibility of the study can now begin to be assessed against the criterion of whether the researcher can obtain access to children in the contexts which are of interest. The researcher also needs to specify the ages of the children who would be studied. Would the study cover children of all ages (is this feasible?) or just children of particular ages? (If so, of what ages, and does the researcher have access to children of those ages?) In addition, notice that the term 'aggressive behaviour' must also be defined in order to assess the feasibility of the research. For example, does 'aggressive behaviour' include inflicting psychological injury on others, as well as physical injury? If so, is it feasible to assess whether or not psychological injury has been inflicted? Also, must aggressive acts be intentional? If so, is it feasible to assess intentionality in children of the ages which would be studied?

Ethical considerations must also play a role in assessing the feasibility of studying this topic. For example, most people today would consider it unethical for a psychologist to deliberately elicit aggressive behaviour from children so that the characteristics of that behaviour can be studied. This would not be feasible on ethical rather than practical grounds. However, in the past, different ethical standards have applied. For example, Albert Bandura's classic studies into aggressive behaviour in children (Bandura, Ross & Ross, 1961, 1963; Bandura & Walters, 1963), which were conducted in the late 1950s and early 1960s, entailed the provision of role models of aggressive behaviour for children to imitate (see Box 2.1). In other words, the ethical considerations which are used to evaluate the feasibility of a piece of research change over time, and past practices should not be used as an automatic guide to what is ethically acceptable today. It should be clear from the example given here that, in order to decide whether or not a particular topic which has been selected for investigation passes the criterion of feasibility, it is essential to formulate not just research questions, but highly specific research questions.

Box 2.1   The study by Bandura _et al._ (1961)

This study was designed to investigate whether aggressive behaviour can be transmitted to children by exposing them to a display of aggressive behaviour by an adult. A total of 72 children, aged between 3 years 1 month and 5 years 9 months, who were enrolled in a nursery school, were divided into three groups containing 24 children each. The children in one of the groups were exposed to an

(_Continued_)

Box 2.1   (Continued)

adult who behaved aggressively towards a 5-foot inflated Bobo doll; the adult punched the doll, sat on it and punched it repeatedly on the nose, hit it with a mallet, threw it up in the air, kicked it around the room, and uttered aggressive remarks such as 'Sock him on the nose', 'Kick him', 'Pow', as well as non-aggressive remarks such as 'He keeps coming back for more' and 'He sure is a tough fellow'. At the time of their exposure to these behaviours, each child was occupied on a diverting task sitting in the same room, and was not given any explicit instructions to either observe or learn the behaviours in question. The exposure session lasted for ten minutes. The children who were in a second experimental group were exposed to the adult for the same length of time, but here the adult simply sat at a second table in the same room as the child assembling some toys in a quiet subdued manner and totally ignoring the Bobo doll. The children in the third control group had no exposure to the adult. For half of the children in the first two groups, the adult was male, while for the other half the adult was female.

The children were then taken to another room which contained a variety of toys, including a 3-foot Bobo doll, a mallet, dart guns, and various other more neutral toys such as a tea set, bears, and crayons and colouring paper. Each child was observed for 20 minutes through a one-way mirror. The frequency with which the child produced physically aggressive behaviours, verbally aggressive remarks, and non-aggressive verbal remarks was recorded. It was found that the children in the aggression condition produced high levels of physically and verbally aggressive behaviour, and of non-aggressive remarks, which were very similar to the behaviours and remarks of the adult model to which they had been exposed. By contrast, the children in the other two groups displayed very low levels of aggression. Interestingly, the children's imitation of the adult model in the exposure condition varied according to gender. Boys displayed more aggression than girls when they had been exposed to the male model, whereas girls exposed to the female model produced more verbal aggression and more non-imitative aggression (e.g. using the dart guns) than boys.

The research paper does not report details of how the children were recruited to the study, nor any details about the treatment or **debriefing** of the children (or their parents) after the study had taken place. Do you think that this study is ethically acceptable? What are the reasons for your judgement?

debriefing

However, there is an additional reason why it is necessary to formulate specific research questions at the outset of the planning process. This is so that the researcher can ensure, during the course of planning, that the data which are collected will actually address the research questions which are of interest. There is very little point in jumping directly from the identification of a general topic to the collection of data, and then trying to articulate specific questions about that general topic afterwards. Such a procedure is extremely unlikely to result in any of the data which are collected being appropriate for addressing the particular questions which the researcher will really want to ask about that topic. Instead, in order to ensure that the data which are collected are relevant to answering the specific questions which are of interest to the researcher, it is vital to use the specific research questions themselves to inform the design of the research from the outset, so that the researcher can be certain that the data which are collected will actually answer those questions.

2.2.3 Strategies to adopt when formulating specific research questions

When thinking about specific research questions, several strategies may be used to ensure that the questions which are formulated are suitable for the further planning purposes for which they are required. First of all, it is always helpful to formally articulate research questions in words. If you cannot articulate these questions in words, they are unlikely to lead to any productive research. Secondly, the articulated questions should contain specifications of the particular situations or conditions in which the phenomena of interest would be studied, as well as specifications of the precise type of participants who would be used in the research.

Thirdly, it is important to articulate these questions in such a way that they can be addressed by means of a specified type of empirical evidence. This is **operational definitions** achieved by providing **operational definitions** of the concepts which are included in the research question. An operational definition of a concept is a statement of the activities or operations which are needed to measure that concept in practice (or, in the case of an independent variable, a statement of the activities or operations which are needed to manipulate that variable in practice). For example, if the research question is 'How does children's aggressive behaviour vary as a function of age?', we need an operational definition of the concept of 'aggressive behaviour', that is, a statement of how it would be measured in practice. For example, it might be defined operationally as 'any behaviour which two or more independent adult observers classify as having aggressive intent' or as 'any behaviour which, when a video recording of it is played back to the child and the child is questioned about it, the child admits was intended to hurt another person'. Similarly, if a research question contains references to participants' personalities or intelligence, the concepts of 'personality' and 'intelligence' could be operationally defined as the measures which are obtained by using a particular personality test (such as the EPQ) or intelligence test (such as the WISC-R), respectively.

A fourth point to bear in mind when formulating specific research questions is that all such questions must be empirically testable. For example, 'Do different people have the same subjective experience of the colour red?' and 'If a child believes in God, is that a true or a false belief?' are both empirically untestable questions. This is because at least one of the concepts which each question contains cannot be given a satisfactory operational definition (i.e. the concepts of 'subjective experience' and 'God', respectively). Thus, the testability of research questions is very closely linked to whether or not it is possible to provide adequate operational definitions of their constituent concepts.

2.2.4 Choice of possible research methods

Having identified the specific research questions, and having established adequate operational definitions of the concepts, the researcher is then in a position to be able to select possible research designs and methods of data collection which could be used to obtain the data to address these questions. For example, let us suppose that our hypothetical researcher has decided to investigate aggression in children by trying to answer the specific research question 'Do seven-year-old children produce more aggressive acts than five-year-old children in the school playground?', and has operationally defined 'aggressive act' as 'any act which two or more independent adult observers classify as having aggressive intent'. In that case, the researcher is now in a position to choose either a cross-sectional or a longitudinal research design for studying the children at the two different ages, and is able to choose naturalistic observation as an appropriate method for collecting the data.

The specific considerations which should motivate the choice of any particular research design and any particular method of data collection at this point in the planning process are beyond the scope of the present chapter. The reader is therefore referred to the contents of the other chapters in this book in order to find out how particular research questions and particular operational definitions should feed into the decision to use or not to use any particular research design or method.

For present purposes, however, let us assume that the bridge has now been made from the specific research question to the possible research designs and possible methods of data collection.

2.2.5 The literature review

So far in this chapter, no mention has been made of the role which the literature review ought to play in planning a piece of psychological research. Obviously, though, a thorough review of the literature is an essential component of planning research into any topic. The literature contains accounts of all the existing psychological theories and concepts which can be used to generate or to structure research ideas; of the findings which have been obtained by previous researchers and which can therefore be either assumed and built upon, or questioned, when planning further research into that topic; of the arguments and lines of thinking which have proved profitable to previous researchers and which may therefore prove profitable to pursue further; and of the blind alleys down which previous researchers have gone and which therefore ought to be avoided.

Furthermore, the existing literature is an enormously rich repository which contains a massive amount of information about the topics which have been investigated in the past, about the specific research questions which have been asked by previous researchers, about the operational definitions which have been adopted in previous studies, and about the research designs and methods which have been used by previous researchers. Thus, the existing literature can be used as an invaluable source from which to mine all sorts of research topics, research questions, operational definitions, research designs and methods, all of which can be used to inform the process of planning research.

2.2.6 Accessing the relevant literature

There are two principal ways in which to access the literature relevant to any given topic. The first is to use a standard abstracting source. The most useful such source for the research psychologist is the PsycINFO database. This is an online database which contains the abstracts of psychology journal articles and of psychology books and book chapters, which can be searched systematically by typing into the computer the key words which define the topic in which you are interested. PsycINFO then displays the abstracts of the articles, books and chapters which have been located, and by reading these abstracts, it is usually possible to work out whether or not any given item is of sufficient relevance to merit reading in full (if your own library does not subscribe to the journal in which an article appeared, it may be possible for them to obtain it for you through their inter-library loans system).

An alternative way of searching the literature is to begin from the reference lists of the central textbooks that have been written on the topic in which you are interested. It is often useful to begin by picking out from these reference lists the most recent major review articles which have been written on the topic in which you are interested, as well as any recent empirical articles which seem to be particularly important. The reference lists of both types of articles can then be used to locate other relevant empirical articles, and the reference lists of these empirical articles can be used to locate further empirical articles. If you use this method of accessing the literature, however, you should bear in mind that there is usually, at the very least, a two-year lag between the publication of a journal article, chapter or book and these publications being picked up by and referred to in textbooks. Consequently, this method of searching the literature must always be accompanied by a systematic search through the most recent issues of all the major journals which publish articles on the topic in which you are interested, to ensure that you do pick up on any article which has not yet penetrated the textbooks.

Whichever method is used to locate the relevant literature, that literature should then be used to inform the entire planning process, from the selection of an appropriate topic, through the formulation of specific research questions and operational definitions, to the identification of the possible research designs and methods which could be used to address those research questions.

2.3 ASSESSING THE PRACTICAL FEASIBILITY OF THE RESEARCH

Having reached this point, the research is now sufficiently well articulated to enable the researcher to assess the practical feasibility of conducting the research. This assessment may well lead the researcher to reject some possible designs or methods, or even to revise some of the operational definitions or research questions, if these now prove not to be feasible on purely practical grounds. It is therefore essential that, at this point, the researcher systematically thinks through all of the following issues.

2.3.1 Participants required for the research

First of all, the researcher must think through the issue of **participant availability**. What type of participants, with what particular characteristics, will the research require? Will these participants need to be in any particular location, situation or context for the research to take place? How many participants are needed? In answering this last question, account should be taken of the power of the statistical methods which are to be used to analyse the data, and power tables, which are sometimes included in statistics textbooks, should be consulted in order to help determine an appropriate sample size (see Chapter 19). Finally, are such participants in this number available to the researcher?

If the answers to all of these initial questions are satisfactory, further questions then need to be asked. Are the participants themselves willing to participate in the research? If payment is required in order to entice the participants into taking part in the research, is the necessary budget available?

In thinking about this issue of participant availability, there are many factors which need to be borne in mind. For example, there are the problems of uncontrolled **participant attrition** (i.e. participants dropping out of the study while it is in progress) and **participant non-compliance** (i.e. participants not complying with the research procedure). Participant attrition and non-compliance are not always a consequence of participants being bloody-minded. In large-scale longitudinal studies, for example, which take place over a period of many years, it is perhaps inevitable that at least some participants in the study will move home, fall ill, or even die during the course of the study. Of course, if there are high levels of participant attrition or non-compliance, this leads to the sample of participants

participant availability

participant attrition
participant non-compliance

becoming systematically biased, either for lack of mobility, or for staying power, or for willingness to co-operate with the research procedure. Furthermore, it is always possible that such characteristics are related in a systematic manner to the psychological phenomena which are being studied. The problem of non-compliance can be particularly serious in research which involves questionnaires about a sensitive topic being mailed to participants for completion and return. Such questionnaires may only have a return rate somewhere in the region of 10–40%. This rate of self-selection from a sample which was originally constructed on systematic principles represents a very serious biasing of the sample which will inevitably affect the generalizability of the findings which are obtained.

There are, however, some general precautions which can be taken by the researcher concerning participant attrition and non-compliance. Firstly, the sample which is planned should always be large enough to allow for possible attrition and non-compliance. Secondly, when recruiting participants, the researcher should always try to make participation in the study sound as interesting as possible; it is important to emphasize any parts of the study that might be especially interesting to participants themselves. Avoid saying that participating in the study is a way of 'doing your bit for science'; this is not a formula which wins over hesitant participants. Thirdly, you should always assure potential partici-

confidentiality, anonymity pants of complete **confidentiality** and **anonymity** of their results. Fourthly, you can offer to inform the participants of the eventual outcome of the research; this may be done by producing a simple written summary of the research findings at the end of the study in jargon-free language, which can be sent to the participants who took part in the research.

In some cases, the recruitment of participants for the study can depend upon

gatekeepers certain key individuals, or '**gatekeepers**', who have to give their permission and co-operation in order for the participants who are the target of the research to be used. Perhaps the two most common types of gatekeepers are the head teachers of schools, who control access to the children in their schools, and doctors, who can provide access to patients. Obviously, the feasibility of the research will then depend upon winning over the co-operation of these gatekeepers. Gatekeepers can have both disadvantages and advantages. For example, it may be difficult to win a head teacher over to the idea of a study of playground aggression if that head teacher maintains that no aggressive behaviour occurs in the playground of his or her school. However, once a head teacher has been won over, the researcher will then have open access to the very large numbers of children who attend that school.

Because the feasibility of such studies depends crucially upon the co-operation of the gatekeeper, it is always extremely important to ensure that gatekeepers are treated with courtesy. It is important that gatekeepers are only approached after the researcher has fully thought through all the precise details of what needs to be done in the study, so that the researcher is able to answer any questions concerning the study which may arise when discussing the research with the gatekeeper. This presents a professional image which helps to inspire the gatekeeper's confidence in the researcher. Again, during such discussions, the purpose of the study should be made to sound interesting, and the researcher can offer to send the gatekeeper a written summary of the findings of the research when the study has been completed.

One problem which can be unintentionally caused by gatekeepers is that they take it upon themselves to select which particular participants are used in the research. For example, if the research requires schoolchildren to be tested individually outside their classroom, teachers may select only their brightest children to send to the researcher, hoping to impress the researcher with their abilities. However, such a process obviously results in a biased sample being used for the research. Thus, it is always sensible for the researcher to plan a systematic method for selecting which particular participants should participate in the research (e.g. picking every other child from the class register irrespective of their ability), and to agree this plan with the gatekeeper at the outset.

2.3.2 Equipment and materials required for the research

In assessing the practical feasibility of the research, the researcher must also consider very carefully all the equipment and materials which are needed for the study to take place. If any special materials or equipment are needed, does the researcher already have them or not? If not, and if they have to be specially purchased or constructed, are the necessary funds available for these purposes? If the funds are not available, could the materials or equipment be borrowed from or used at another institution or department of psychology? If materials have to be specially designed, or if equipment has to be specially constructed, can this be done on an appropriate timescale? Can such purpose-built equipment be properly tested to eliminate any possible teething and technical problems which it might have so that it will be fully functional by the time that it is needed?

Finally, under this heading, the researcher should consider whether he or she needs time to learn how to use the relevant materials and/or equipment. For example, it can take a lot of time for a novice to learn how to customize computer software (e.g. for presenting visual stimuli to participants, or for recording participants' reaction times) or to learn how to administer and score a standardized psychometric test. If time is required for mastering the materials or the equipment, it is important that the timetable for the research is drawn up in such a way that it allows an adequate amount of time for these purposes.

2.3.3 Consumable items required for the research

The researcher also needs to think through, at the planning stage, all the consumable items which will be needed for the research (i.e. items which will be completely used up during the course of conducting the research). It is important that all consumables are properly costed to ensure that the funds which are required in order to conduct the research do not exceed the total budget available for the research. For example, any photocopying (of, for example, interview schedules or questionnaires), postage (for mailing out postal questionnaires), video or audio recording tapes, computer disks, computer printing, etc. should all be properly costed out in order to ascertain whether the budget is sufficient for conducting the research.

2.3.4 Other costs which may be incurred by the research

Finally, there may be other costs involved in conducting the research. For example, will the researcher be able to conduct all the work on his or her own? If it is necessary for the researcher to have assistance from others in conducting the research, and if the people who provide this assistance need to be paid for their time, are the funds available to pay these people at the appropriate rate? For example, if the researcher needs help to collect the data (e.g. to help interview participants, to make independent observations of participants, or to act as stooges in an experiment), or if assistance is needed in coding the data (e.g. for running checks on the reliability of the coding), it may be necessary to pay the people who provide this help. If so, the total number of hours of assistance which will be needed must be properly costed in advance, in order to see whether the research can be conducted within the budget which is available.

Also, if the researcher and/or any person assisting them needs to travel from their normal place of work to another location in order to test participants (e.g. to a school or to a hospital), this will require funds to cover the costs of the travel and of any subsistence which might be needed by the researchers (such as food or overnight accommodation). Once again, the costs involved need to be worked out in advance, taking into account the location of the participants, the size of the sample, and the length of time that it will take to collect the data from each participant. Once again, the research will only be feasible if the total budget available to the researcher is able to cover these costs.

2.3.5 Pilot work

Let us assume that the researcher has run through all the preceding checks on participant availability and access, the availability of materials and equipment, and the availability of the funds which are needed to cover consumable costs, research assistance costs, and travel and subsistence costs. If all of these considerations indicate that the research is feasible, it is often extremely useful to then conduct pilot work, in order to try out the methods, materials, equipment, etc. in advance of running the full-scale study itself.

Such pilot work should be conducted using a smaller group of participants who have similar characteristics to those of the participants who will be used in the main study itself. Pilot work can be used to test out the various operational definitions and research methods which are still under active consideration, and to see if some of these methods and definitions are more useful or are simpler to administer than others. Pilot work can also be used to establish whether participants understand instructions, to ascertain how much time it takes to test each participant, to obtain practice in administering all the tasks and in making all the necessary measurements (ideally, the researcher should be trained to saturation before the main study commences, so that any training effects do not contaminate the main study itself), to find out whether tasks are sufficiently sensitive to discriminate amongst participants, to examine whether the measures which are being made have stable measurement properties (i.e. are reliable), etc.

It is often the case that, if a variety of different possible research methods and operational definitions have still been under active consideration up to this point in the planning process, the pilot work helps to sort out the more useful and reliable methods and definitions, thereby facilitating the final selection by the researcher of those particular methods and definitions which will be used in the main study itself.

2.3.6 Identifying the statistical analyses needed and rechecking the sample size

Once the research design, operational definitions, and methods of data collection have been selected for use in the study, it is then essential for the researcher to identify in advance the types of data which will be collected, and the types of statistical analyses which will be performed on those data in order to answer appropriately the research questions which have been posed. The choice of statistical analyses will be determined by the research design, by the type of data which will be collected, and by the research questions which are being asked (see Chapters 19 and 20). Having selected appropriate methods of analysing the data, it is then necessary, at the planning stage, to check back to the sample size which is being planned, and to the availability of the participants who are required for the study. It is vital to do this, in order to ensure that sufficient data will be collected from a large enough sample to enable the proposed statistical analyses to detect the relationships and effects which are being sought, assuming they are present in the data.

2.3.7 Formulating a timetable

Another important aspect of planning research systematically is the formulation of an explicit timetable for the research. This timetable needs to contain all the intermediate staging posts, and their deadlines, which will punctuate the research (e.g. when the data collection will begin and end, when data coding will begin and end, when the statistical analyses will be conducted, when the research will be written up, etc.). In producing this timetable, it is essential to adopt a realistic stance, and to allow sufficient time for all the component activities which are involved, including any final piloting that may be required, the time that may be required for training additional researchers, the time needed for recruiting participants and the time needed for testing all participants or for collecting all data. (Does this involve testing all participants simultaneously, or in sequence? Will you have to wait for participants to make their returns of a mailed questionnaire through the post? Is it necessary to build in time for the replacement of participants who fail to attend for testing or fail to reply? etc.) Also, the time which is needed for debriefing participants, transcribing any data from audio or video recordings, coding the data, running reliability checks upon the data coding, entering the data into the computer, analysing the data, interpreting the results of the analyses, and writing the report.

Having produced an explicit timetable with a realistic estimate of the amounts of time needed for all the component activities, it is then necessary to go back yet again and recheck the availability of participants, equipment and all other resources which will be used for the research. In particular, it is essential to check that participants, equipment and resources will be available at the times which are required according to the timetable that has been worked out. After all, if the participants, for example, are not available for testing when the timetable stipulates (e.g. if schoolchildren are required for testing during a school's summer vacation), then, quite simply, it will not be feasible to conduct the research on that timetable. If there are any problems concerning participant, equipment or resource availability, then it is necessary for the researcher to revise either the timetable or the content or structure of the study itself so that it fits into a feasible timetable.

2.3.8 Conclusions

Assessing the practical feasibility of a piece of research is clearly a complex activity. Not only are there many different aspects of the research that need very careful checking in order to ensure that the research is feasible in practice but also, if the research proves unfeasible on just one count, it may be necessary to revise the entire study. Nevertheless, having planned a piece of research through to this level of detail, if it turns out not to be feasible to run the study as planned, it is always worth considering the possible modifications which could be made to it before abandoning it entirely and starting from scratch once again (e.g. other possible sources of participants could be tried, extravagant but unnecessary costs could be cut back, or the timetable for the study could be extended).

2.4 ASSESSING THE ETHICAL FEASIBILITY OF THE RESEARCH

In the preceding section, we considered issues concerning the practical feasibility of a piece of research. The present section considers issues which are to do with the ethical feasibility of a piece of research. It is quite possible that a research study is feasible on practical grounds, but is unfeasible because it would be judged to be unethical to conduct that study. The criteria which ought to be used by psychologists in order to assess whether a particular study is or is not ethically acceptable have been formalized in statements issued by the British Psychological Society (BPS, 2004) and by the American Psychological Association (APA, 1992) – see Section 2.8. Any person who is intending to conduct psychological research should obtain a copy of, and should study in full, one or other of these two statements (or an equivalent statement which has been issued by a corresponding professional body). The postal addresses and websites from which the BPS and the APA statements may be obtained are given at the end of this chapter. The following account draws heavily upon the principal criteria which are contained in the current BPS statement.

2.4.1 The protection and welfare of participants

A fundamental principle which underpins all ethical codes relating to psychological research is that psychologists must always consider the welfare of the participants who take part in their research, and must protect them from being either physically or mentally harmed by the research process. In practice, this means that the risk of harm to someone who participates in a psychological study should normally never be greater than the risks which that person would encounter during the course of their normal lifestyle. If there are any aspects of the study which might result in any harm or undesirable consequences for the participants, the researcher has a responsibility to identify and remove or correct these consequences. If this is not possible, and if there is a risk that the participants in the research will suffer in any way, either physically or psychologically, as a result of the research, then that research would normally be considered to be ethically unacceptable.

Of course, there are certain types of psychological research where the risk of harm, unusual discomfort, or other negative consequences for the participant's future life might occur or might be greater than in everyday life (e.g. in certain types of psychopharmacological studies, there may be unanticipated side-effects of the drugs which are administered to participants). In such cases, the researcher must always obtain the disinterested approval of independent advisers before the research takes place (usually this advice is obtained from an independent ethics committee, either of the university or of the hospital in which the research is based). In addition, in such cases, the participants must be fully informed of the possible risks to them, and real informed consent must be given by each participant individually.

2.4.2 The principle of informed consent

More broadly, the BPS **ethical principles** stipulate that, wherever it is possible, researchers should inform participants in psychological research of all aspects of

ethical principles

that research which might reasonably be expected to influence their willingness to participate in that research; in addition, researchers should usually explain any aspect of the research about which a participant enquires. Thus, when a participant agrees to participate in a study, that person's consent should normally be informed by knowledge about the research. This is the principle of informed consent.

In some cases, of course, participants may be unable to give informed consent. This is the case whenever the research involves either young children or adults with impairments in understanding or communication. In all such cases, informed consent should instead be given either by parents or by those *in loco parentis*. In addition, it may be necessary in such cases (depending upon the potential risks to the participants) also to obtain advice and approval from an independent ethics committee. If such permission or approval cannot be obtained, then the study would be considered to be ethically unacceptable and ought to be either revised or abandoned.

It is important to bear in mind, when considering the application of the principle of informed consent, that a researcher is often in a position of authority or influence over the participants. This position should never be used to pressurize the participants to take part in, or to remain in, an investigation. Similarly, the payment which may be offered to participants should not be used to induce them to accept risks which they would not normally accept in their everyday life without payment.

2.4.3 The use of deception

In the case of some psychological studies, however, it is simply not possible to tell the participants everything which they could be told about the study because, if they had knowledge about the actual purpose of the investigation, they might alter those critical aspects of their behaviour which are of interest to the investigator, thereby undermining the purpose of the study. Alternatively, it is sometimes simply impossible to study a particular psychological process without deliberately misleading the participants. According to section 4, paragraph 1 of the BPS ethical principles (BPS, 2004), the basic guidelines which should be followed in all such situations are the following:

> The withholding of information or the misleading of participants is unacceptable if the participants are typically likely to object or show unease once debriefed. Where this is in any doubt, appropriate consultation must precede the investigation. Consultation is best carried out with individuals who share the social and cultural background of the participants in the research, but the advice of ethics committees or experienced and disinterested colleagues may be sufficient.

deception   However, the BPS principles also add that the intentional **deception** of participants ought to be avoided wherever this is possible. Consequently, the researcher should always first consider whether there are alternative procedures available which do not require deception. If no such alternatives are available, and if it is judged that the intended deception is an ethically permissible procedure, then the participants should be debriefed at the earliest opportunity.

2.4.4 The debriefing of participants

In all studies where participants are aware that they have taken part in an investigation, after the data have been collected, the participants should be given any information which they might need or request concerning the nature of the study. The researcher should also discuss with the participants their experience of the research process, so that if there are any unintended or unanticipated effects of the research, these can be monitored. Researchers also have a responsibility to ensure that, if any active intervention is required to negate the effects of an investigation upon a participant, such intervention is provided before the participants leave the research setting. Consequently, when drawing up the timetable for the research for the purposes of assessing whether or not the research will be feasible on practical grounds, sufficient time must be built into that timetable to allow for the debriefing of participants after testing, wherever this may be necessary.

2.4.5 Participants' right to withdraw from an investigation

Researchers should also make it clear to participants at the outset of the study that they have a right to withdraw from the research at any time, irrespective of whether or not payment or any other inducement has been offered. In the case of children, their avoidance of the testing situation ought to be taken as evidence of a failure to consent to the research procedure, and should be acknowledged.

Furthermore, the BPS ethical principles state that participants should always have the right to withdraw any consent which they may have given previously to participate in the study, either in the light of their experience of the investigation, or as a result of their debriefing. In such cases, participants also have a right to require that any data pertaining to themselves, including any recordings, be destroyed. Obviously, if a large proportion of the participants exercise this right in any individual study, a sampling bias will be introduced to the study which could limit the generalizability of the results. However, this is a limitation which the researcher must accept, as the retention and use of the data which were provided by a participant who has subsequently withdrawn his or her consent is an ethically unacceptable practice.

2.4.6 The invasion of privacy in observational research

Research which is based upon the naturalistic observation of participants in their everyday settings raises particular ethical concerns, because in such studies informed consent may not be given by the participants. Such studies must, therefore, respect the privacy and psychological well-being of the participants who are studied. Furthermore, if consent is not obtained in advance, observational research is only acceptable in places and situations where those observed would expect to be observed by strangers. Particular account should always be taken of local cultural values, and of the possibility that the participants might consider it to be an invasion of their privacy to be observed whilst believing themselves to be unobserved, even though they are in a normally public place.

2.4.7 Confidentiality and the anonymity of data

The BPS ethical principles stipulate that all information which is obtained about a participant during an investigation must be confidential unless it has been agreed otherwise in advance. All participants in psychological research have a right to expect that the information which they provide will be treated confidentially and, if published, will not be identifiable as theirs. If such confidentiality or anonymity cannot be guaranteed, then the participant must be warned of this before he or she agrees to participate in the study.

In addition, it should be noted that, in the UK, when data about an individual person are stored on a computer in such a form that the individual is personally identifiable, then the researcher storing those data must comply with the provisions of the Data Protection Act 1998. This Act is designed to ensure that those who use computerized information (and some paper records) about identifiable individuals are always open and honest about their use of that information and follow sound and proper practices. This involves notifying key details about their use of the information to the Information Commissioner, who makes these details publicly available in a register. For researchers who work within an institution, such as a university, there is usually an institutional administrator who handles these matters.

2.4.8 Conclusions

From the preceding account, it should be clear that there are not only many practical considerations which need to be borne in mind while planning psychological research; there are also many different ethical considerations which have to be accommodated if the planned research is to be ethically feasible. If the research which is being planned requires any of the preceding ethical principles to be violated in an unacceptable manner, then that research must be assessed as being ethically unfeasible. However, should a study be judged to be unacceptable on ethical grounds, having reached this point in the planning process, it is always worth reconsidering those specific aspects of the study which have been found to be problematic in order to see whether there are any alternative procedures which may be adopted which would be ethically acceptable. But if no such alternative procedures are available (and remember that any such alternative procedures would also have to be assessed as being feasible on practical as well as ethical grounds), then the researcher is obliged to abandon the research which has been planned.

Having read the contents of this section on how to assess the ethical feasibility of a piece of research, go back to Box 2.1, in which the study by Bandura *et al.* (1961) was described. As a practical exercise, try to apply all of the ethical principles which have been described in this section to the study, and evaluate the ethical status of the study once again from the perspective of our current codes of research ethics.

2.5 CONSIDERING THE POSSIBLE OUTCOMES OF THE RESEARCH IN ADVANCE

Finally, it can help to focus the mind while planning a piece of research to consider the possible outcomes of the research in advance. To this end, it is useful to break down possible outcomes into those things which will be delivered immediately upon the completion of the research, and the longer-term outcomes which might emerge eventually from the work.

Things which are immediately deliverable upon completion of the research would include: the answers to the specific research questions which the research was designed to provide; and the immediate research report (whether this is in the form of a final-year undergraduate research project report, an MSc thesis, or an end-of-project report for a funding agency).

Longer-term products of the research could include: any further studies which might be required to clarify or to extend the results which will be obtained (focusing upon further studies which might be required for clarification purposes can be an extremely useful process for thinking through the limitations of the planned study); any applied policy recommendations which might be able to be made on the basis of the research to relevant authorities; and the publication of the findings of the research. Publication should, under normal circumstances, always be regarded as the proper endpoint of research. This is because it is only when research is published that it enters the public domain, becomes available to the scientific community, and can be properly regarded as contributing to the general scientific understanding of the issues which it has been designed to study.

2.6 APPLYING FOR RESEARCH FUNDING

As noted earlier, an important part of the process of planning research is working out the costs which will be incurred in carrying out the planned research (e.g. the costs of your equipment and materials, of your consumable items, of any research assistance, and of your travel expenses). If you do not have sufficient funds yourself in order to be able to cover all of these costs, you will need to apply for the money from a research funding source in order to be able to carry out the research. In some departments of psychology, students are able to apply for funds from a specific budget to cover the costs of conducting their research; alternatively, you may be thinking about applying for funding to an external organization such as a research council or a charity in order to obtain a more substantial sum of money than an internal source will allow. Or, if you are a student who wishes to conduct the planned research for your PhD, you may need to apply to a research council or some other body to cover not only your research costs but also your university registration fees and your maintenance.

If you are intending to apply for funding, there are a few useful rules which you should always try to follow. Firstly, you should always read very carefully the detailed notes which accompany any application form, in order to see whether the terms of reference of the funding body or funding scheme apply to the particular piece of research which you wish to conduct. Sometimes, funding bodies specify that they will only fund research on certain specific topics; sometimes they specify that, while they are willing in principle to fund research in any number of areas, priority will nevertheless be given to projects on particular topics. Obviously, if you wish to maximize your chances of being awarded the funding, you should always make sure that your project or area of research closely matches the topics or priority areas specified by the funding body to which you are applying. The reality is that applying for external research funding is a fiercely competitive process these days, and if you ignore the funding priorities of the bodies to which you are applying, your application is very unlikely to be successful.

Secondly, when reading the guidance notes which accompany the application form, look to see if there are any particular features of proposals which are encouraged by or are of special interest to the funding body (e.g. involving a partner from another discipline). Here, if it is at all possible to build these favourable features into your own proposal (but without compromising the scientific and methodological integrity of your research, of course!), you should always try to do so. Such a strategy can only enhance the prospects of a successful outcome.

Thirdly, if you have planned your research properly, you should be able to give very precise details in the application about exactly what it is you are going to be doing. Under most circumstances, these details should minimally include: an indication of the existing body of research which you have drawn upon in developing the proposed research; the specific research questions which the research will address, and why these are interesting or important; the research methods which are going to be used and the motivation for using these particular methods; exact details of the sample characteristics and sample size (and if there are any possible questions about your access to the sample, copies of letters of support from potential gatekeepers might usefully be included); the type of equipment and materials which will be used; the role and content of any pilot work in the research; the methods of statistical analysis that will be used to analyse the data; any ethical issues that may be involved in conducting the research and how you will ensure that your research complies with an established set of ethical guidelines (and if there are any major ethical issues entailed by your research, a copy of a letter from an ethical committee granting you permission to conduct the research might also be usefully included); the timetable on which the various phases of the research will be conducted; the outputs and deliverables of the research, including your plans for disseminating the findings of the research through conference presentations and publications; and how your research will be useful, and to whom (e.g. whether your research will be useful to other researchers; to particular groups of people such as social workers, teachers, or clinical psychologists; or to organizations such as a particular government department or a local authority).

Fourthly, in writing the proposal, be open about any obvious problems which the research might encounter, and explain how you will tackle these problems if they do occur. Your application and proposal will almost certainly be read by someone who has a good understanding of the realities of the research process, and they will know only too well that research does not always proceed as planned. So they will be looking to see if you are being realistic in your plans, and whether you give any evidence in your application that you will be able to respond appropriately to problems if these do occur.

Fifthly, always make sure that you fill in the application form exactly as required and to the letter. If you cannot even follow the simple instructions for filling in an application form, the funding body will have very little confidence in your ability to execute a piece of original research, and they may even reject your application without considering it properly if you fail to provide information which they regard as crucial for evaluating the application.

Sixthly, always type or word-process your application: it is a nightmare for an evaluator to try to read and assess a handwritten proposal. The presentation and appearance of an application are extremely important, and poor presentation is highly likely to affect the judgement which an evaluator forms of your proposal. Correct spelling and use of grammar are important too.

Finally, if you are posting your application close to a specified deadline, it is always sensible to obtain proof of posting, just in case there are any unexpected postal delays which might lead to your application arriving after the specified deadline. It should go without saying that the application should arrive before the stated deadline. Many bodies will simply ignore applications that arrive late.

Box 2.2 contains a checklist of all the things which research funding agencies usually look for in a research proposal when making a decision about whether or not to make the funding available for a proposed study. A funding agency is only likely to agree to fund the proposed research if the answers to most, if not all, of these questions are affirmative. This checklist also provides a useful summary of the various practical and ethical issues which have been discussed in the course of this chapter.

Box 2.2   A checklist of all the practical and ethical matters which should be taken into account when planning a piece of research systematically

- Is the research based upon an adequate review of the existing literature?
- Is the research based upon coherent research questions?
- Have the various concepts which are included in the research questions been given suitable operational definitions?
- Are the proposed research design and methods appropriate for answering the research questions?
- Are the proposed research design and methods clearly defined and feasible?
- Are the intended participants for the research likely to be available to the researcher?
- Has sufficient attention been paid to the potential problems of participant attrition and participant non-compliance, and are suitable procedures in place to deal with these problems?
- Does the researcher have access to all of the equipment and materials which are required for the research, if the costs for these are not being requested from a funding agency?
- Has appropriate pilot work been conducted in order to test the feasibility of the research methods which are going to be used?
- Are appropriate methods of analysing the data being proposed?
- Is the sample large enough for all of the statistical analyses which are being proposed?
- Is the proposed timetable for all the different stages of the research appropriate, feasible and realistic, and will the participants, equipment and other resources be available to the researcher at the time when they are required according to this timetable?
- Have the welfare and the protection of the participants, and any foreseeable risks to either the participants or the researcher, been considered in an appropriate manner?
- Will the principle of informed consent be implemented in an appropriate manner?
- Has the potential deception of the participants been kept to a minimum, given the goals of the research?

(Continued)

Box 2.2 (Continued)

- Will the participants be debriefed after the research in an appropriate manner?
- Will the participants be given the right to withdraw from the study?
- Will the data from the study be treated confidentially and anonymously?
- Will the research take due notice of locally existing legal requirements (such as the Data Protection Act in the UK)?
- Have the possible deliverables and outcomes of the research been considered in an appropriate manner?

In the case of research proposals which are submitted to external funding bodies, the following additional questions also come into play.

- Is the research likely to make a significant, original and distinctive contribution to our knowledge of the topic, or to advance research methods or theory in a significant way?
- Does the proposal show that the applicant is aware of the full range of previous research which has been conducted on the topic?
- Are the costs which are being requested from a funding agency necessary and appropriate, and does the research represent good value for money?
- Have appropriate plans been made for the dissemination of the findings of the research?
- Have appropriate plans been made to engage potential users of the research findings (e.g. government departments, social policy makers, commercial users) in the design and the dissemination of the research?

2.7 CONCLUSION

This chapter has discussed the numerous practical and ethical issues which always have to be considered when planning a piece of psychological research. As was noted in the introduction, although this chapter has necessarily had to discuss these various issues in a particular sequential order, the decisions that have to be made about them are invariably interdependent, and a decision made about one issue (such as an ethical one) may well have important implications for how a decision about another issue (such as the choice of research method) is made. This complex interdependence of decisions always has to be borne in mind throughout the planning process.

As any experienced researcher will be able to tell you, the research process often does not run smoothly. However, the problems that may occur in the course of conducting a piece of psychological research can usually be minimised by trying to think through every single aspect of the research in minute detail in advance. While such double-checking and triple-checking of details may not always ensure a trouble-free journey, it can certainly help researchers to arrive at their research destinations with only a minimum of complications.

2.8 BPS AND APA ADDRESSES AND WEBSITES

A copy of the British Psychological Society's *Ethical Principles for Conducting Research with Human Participants* may be obtained from: The British Psychological Society, St Andrews House, 48 Princess Road East, Leicester LE1 7DR, UK. It can also be downloaded over the web as part of a larger document entitled 'Code of Conduct, Ethical Principles and Guidelines' from: http://www.bps.org.uk/the-society/ethics-rules-charter-code-of-conduct/ethics-rules-charter-code-of-conduct_home.cfm. At the time of writing (2005), the British Psychological Society is in the process of developing a new *Code of Ethics and Conduct*, which it is anticipated the Society will adopt in 2006. Interested readers should monitor the BPS website (http://www.bps.org.uk) for future developments.

A copy of the American Psychological Association's *Ethical Principles of Psychologists and Code of Conduct* may be obtained from: Ethics Office, American Psychological Association, 750 First Street, NE, Washington DC 20002-4242, USA. It can also be downloaded over the web from http://www.apa.org/ethics/code2002.html

2.9 FURTHER READING

Detailed discussions of the various issues which are involved in selecting research topics, formulating specific research questions, and formulating operational definitions of concepts, are contained in Kerlinger and Lee's (2000) text. In addition, Shaughnessy, Zechmeister and Zechmeister's (2006) text contains excellent discussions of ethical issues in the conduct of psychological research, and of many of the practical issues which are involved in assessing the feasibility of such research.

3

Levels of Measurement

Chris Fife-Schaw

3.1   Introduction
3.2   Classifying measurements
   3.2.1   Categorical measures
   3.2.2   Ordinal level measures
   3.2.3   Interval level measures
   3.2.4   Ratio scale measures
3.3   Discrete versus continuous variables
3.4   Measurement errors
3.5   Choices over levels of measurement
3.6   The relationship between level of measurement and statistics
3.7   Conclusion
3.8   Further reading

This chapter introduces the reader to the common categories of measurement used in psychological science. This traditional categorization system is fundamental to under-standing how to conduct good research but is also key to making decisions about how to analyse the data generated by a study. The chapter also briefly describes some chal-lenges to this orthodox view.

Key terms

approximate value	interval measurement
categorical measurement	mutual exclusivity
conjoint measurement theory	non-parametric tests
continuous variables	ordinal measurement
discrete variables	parametric tests
exhaustiveness	ratio scale measurement
	real limits

3.1 INTRODUCTION

While there are many aspects of the research process that do not involve measurement and, indeed, some fields of research where explicit measurement is avoided altogether, the great majority of research studies will involve it in some form. Whether a research hypothesis stands or falls may depend on how well the key concepts have been measured, independently of whether or not it is a worthy hypothesis. What follows in this chapter is a discussion of measurement issues that have been central to the pursuit of 'positivist' psychological science. Key amongst the assumptions (see Cattell, 1981) is that before we can construct grand psychological theories and laws, we must first be able to measure and describe things with reasonable accuracy.

For the purposes of this chapter, measurement is defined as the assigning of numbers to objects, events or observations according to some set of rules. Sometimes these numbers will be used merely to indicate that an observation belongs to a certain category; at other times these numbers will indicate that the observation has more of some property than an observation that is assigned a lower number.

In much of psychology we have to measure psychological properties indirectly because we have no direct access to the mental constructs we want to measure. It is a straightforward matter to measure length and we can do this fairly directly by offering up our measuring instrument (ruler or tape measure) to the object we want to measure. In the case of IQ, however, we can only infer levels of intelligence from tests that ask people to solve problems of varying difficulty. We assume that people who get more of the more difficult items correct are more intelligent, but we cannot yet observe intelligence in any more direct way than this. In many respects the existence of something called intelligence is itself a hypothesis and the debate about what IQ tests *actually* measure has often been a heated one in the past. While few people would argue about what a ruler measures, the quantities measured by many psychological measurement instruments are more open to debate and much more obviously depend on the theoretical perspective of the researcher than is the case in the physical sciences.

This is not to say that psychological measurements are of little value. A great deal of effort has been expended in establishing the reliability and validity of psychological measures over the last century. There are now libraries of well-validated tests for all sorts of psychological phenomena which can be used very effectively as long as the manuals are used appropriately. Chapter 10 outlines the principles involved in test construction and development commonly used in psychology.

While many established tests exist, researchers are often confronted by the need to create their own measures to deal with the specific problems they have. This may be because nobody has yet fully developed a test for the particular kinds of observations you are interested in. It may be that you are measuring something which has not been measured before or, perhaps, that the existing tests are too cumbersome for your purposes. Here, you will have to pay particular attention to the precise meaning and nature of your new measures.

It should go without saying that the goal is always to measure things as well as possible. There are often trade-offs that have to be made, however. Measures that demand lots of time and effort from participants may induce fatigue and boredom that may simply introduce unwanted 'noise' into your measurements. On the other hand, measures that are very simple and quick for the respondents to complete are frequently crude and inaccurate. Ultimately you will have to make the judgement as to whether your measures are 'good enough' for your purposes.

3.2 CLASSIFYING MEASUREMENTS

Whether you use a ready-made measure or create your own, you always need to know what class of measurement you have made. How you classify a measurement will have an impact on the kinds of numerical analyses you can perform on the data later on. Stevens (1946) proposed that all measurements can be classified as being of one of four types. This system has become dominant within psychology and no methods textbook would be complete without describing it. There are, however, other important alternative conceptualizations of measurement, such as those of Luce, Krantz, Suppes and Tversky (1990) and Adams (1966), and objections to the way psychologists think (or rather, do not think) about their measures (see Box 3.1). Stevens's classification remains the best-known but it is only one way of thinking about measurement.

3.2.1 Categorical measures

Categorical measurements (variables), also called nominal measurements, reflect qualitative differences rather than quantitative ones. Common examples include categories such as yes/no, pass/fail, male/female or Conservative/Liberal/ Labour. When setting up a **categorical measurement** system the only requirements are those of mutual exclusivity and exhaustiveness. **Mutual exclusivity** means that each observation (person, case, score) cannot fall into more than one category; one cannot, for example, both pass and fail a test at the same time. **Exhaustiveness** simply means that your category system should have enough categories for all the observations. For biological sex there should be no observations (in this case people) who are neither male nor female.

A key feature of categorical measurements is that there is no *necessary* sense in which one category has more or less of a particular quality: they are simply

categorical measurement
mutual exclusivity

exhaustiveness

different. Males are different from females (at least at some biological level) and northerners come from the north and southerners do not. Sometimes, however, this will seem like an odd assumption. Surely 'passing', for example, is better than 'failing'? Well, yes, in certain cases this would be so, but this would depend on what your a priori theory about the measure was. If you believed that 'passing' was more valuable and reflected more positively on somebody (e.g. that they were more intelligent, or paid more attention) then that is a matter for you as a researcher; the use of a pass/fail category system does not inherently contain any notion of greater or lesser value.

For the purposes of using computers to help with our analyses, we commonly assign numbers to observations in each category. For instance we might assign (code) a value of 1 for males and 2 for females. The important point is that although females have a numerically larger number there is no suggestion that being female is somehow better or more worthy. Again, this can cause confusion, especially as your computer deals only with numbers and not their meanings. You could, for instance, ask it to calculate the mean sex of the respondents and it might come up with a figure like 1.54; clearly this is pretty uninformative other than that it tells you that there are more females than males.

Although the categories of a categorical variable do not necessarily have any value associated with them, this does not mean that they cannot reflect some underlying dimension in some instances. As an example, you might classify people you are observing in the street as 'young' or 'old' because you are unable to approach them to ask their ages directly. While this is likely to be an extremely crude and inaccurate classification, this system implies an underlying continuous dimension of age even though we place people in only two categories.

The criteria for categorical measurement do not preclude the possibility of having a category of 'uncategorizable'. If you were to have such a category you would satisfy both the mutual exclusivity and exhaustiveness criteria, but if there were a lot of 'uncategorizable' observations then the value of your categorization system might be brought into question. How useful is it to have a variable on which the majority of observations are 'uncategorizable'? This can only truly be answered with reference to your research question.

3.2.2 Ordinal level measures

ordinal measurement **Ordinal measurement** is the next level of measurement in terms of complexity. As before, the assumptions of mutual exclusivity and exhaustiveness apply and cases are still assigned to categories. The big difference is that now the categories themselves can be rank-ordered with reference to some external criterion such that being in one category can be regarded as having more or less of some underlying quality than being in another category. A lecturer might be asked to rank-order their students in terms of general ability at statistics. They could put each student into one of five categories: excellent, good, average, poor, appallingly bad. Clare might fall into the 'excellent' category and Jane into the 'good' category. Clare is better at statistics than Jane, but what we do not know is just how much better Clare is than Jane. The rankings reflect more or less of something but not *how much* more or less.

Most psychological test scores should strictly be regarded as ordinal measures. For instance, one of the subscales of the well-known Eysenck Personality Questionnaire (Eysenck & Eysenck, 1975) is designed to measure extroversion. As this measure, and many like it, infer levels of extroversion from responses to items about behavioural propensities, it does not measure extroversion in any direct sense. Years of validation studies have shown how high scorers will tend to behave in a more extroverted manner in the future, but all the test can do is rank-order people in terms of extroversion. If two people differ by three points on the scale we cannot say *how much* more extroverted the higher-scoring person is, just that he or she is more extroverted. Here the scale intervals do not map directly on to some psychological reality in the same way that the length of a stick can be measured in centimetres using a ruler. The fundamental unit of measurement is not known.

Since many mental constructs within psychology cannot be observed directly, most measures tend to be ordinal. Attitudes, intentions, opinions, personality characteristics, psychological well-being, depression, etc. are all constructs which are thought to vary in degree between individuals but tend only to allow indirect ordinal measurements.

This conclusion is a point of contention for many researchers since one of the implications of assuming these measures to be ordinal is that some parametric statistical tests should not be used with them. Indeed, even the humble mean is not used appropriately with ordinal measures (the median is a more appropriate measure of central tendency). This sits uneasily with what you will see when you read academic journal articles, where you will regularly find means and parametric statistics used with ordinal measures. We will deal with this issue later in this chapter (see also Chapter 19).

3.2.3 Interval level measures

Like an ordinal scale, the numbers associated with **interval measurement** reflect more or less of some underlying dimension. The key distinction is that with interval level measures, numerically equal distances on the scale reflect equal differences in the underlying dimension. For example, the 2°C difference in temperature between 38°C and 40°C is the same as the 2°C difference between 5°C and 7°C.

As we will see later, many behavioural researchers are prepared to assume that scores on psychological tests can be treated as interval level measures so that

interval measurement

they can carry out more sophisticated analyses on their data. A well-known example of this practice is the use of IQ test scores. In order to treat scores as interval level measures, the assumption is made that the 5-point difference in IQ between someone who scores 75 and someone who gets 80 means the same difference in intelligence as the difference between someone who score 155 and someone who scores 160.

3.2.4 Ratio scale measures

ratio scale measurement

Ratio scale measurement differs from interval measurement only in that it implies the existence of a potential absolute zero value. Good examples of ratio scales are length, time and number of correct answers on a test. It is possible to have zero (no) length, for something to take no time, or for someone to get no answers correct on a test. An important corollary of having an absolute zero is that, for example, someone who gets four questions right has got twice as many questions right as someone who got only two right. The ratio of scores to one another now carries some sensible meaning which was not the case for the interval scale.

The difference between interval and ratio scales is best explained with an example. Suppose we measure reaction times to dangers in a driving simulator. This could be measured in seconds and would be a ratio scale measurement, as 0 seconds is a possible (if a little unlikely) score and someone who takes 2 seconds is taking twice as long to react as someone who takes 1 second.

If, on average, people take 800 milliseconds (0.8 seconds) to react we could just look at the *difference* between the observed reaction time and this average level of performance. In this case the level of measurement is only on an interval scale. Our first person scores 1200 ms (i.e. takes 2 seconds, 1200 ms longer than the average of 800 ms) and the second person scores 200 ms (i.e. takes 1 second, 200 ms more than the average). However, the first person did not take 6 times as long (1200 ms divided by 200 ms) as the second. They did take 1000 ms longer, so the *interval* remains meaningful but the ratio element does not.

True psychological ratio scale measures are quite rare, though there is often confusion about this when it comes to taking scores from scales made up of individual problem items in tests. We might, for instance, measure the number of simple arithmetic problems that people can get right. We test people on 50 items and simply count the number correct. The number correct is a ratio scale measure since four right is twice as many as two right, and it is possible to get none right at all (absolute zero). As long as we consider our measure to be *only* an indication of the number correct there is no problem and we can treat them as ratio scale measures.

If, however, we were to treat the scores as reflecting ability at arithmetic then the measure would become an ordinal one. A score of zero might not reflect absolutely no ability at all as the problems may have been sufficiently difficult so that only those with a moderate degree of ability would be able to get any correct. It would also be a mistake to assume that all the items were equally difficult. Twenty of the questions might be easy and these might be answered correctly by most people. Getting one of these correct and adding one point to your score would be fairly easy. The remaining items may be much more difficult and earning another point by getting one of these correct might require much more ability. In other words, the assumption that equal intervals between scores reflect equal differences in ability is not met and we should strictly treat the scores as an ordinal measure of ability. Even when doing this we are assuming that ability is a quantitative entity though we will not have established this directly (see Box 3.1).

Box 3.1 Are we deluding ourselves about our measures? A word of caution

Recent years have seen a challenge to the orthodoxy on measurement presented in this book, most notably by Joel Michell (e.g. Michell, 2000). Michell's arguments are highly detailed philosophical ones and it is difficult to represent them fairly in a short space; however, a key idea in his work is that, in the rush to appear to be 'hard' scientists like physicists, psychologists, and psychometricians in particular, have failed to consider some fundamental questions about what they are assuming when they attempt to measure psychological attributes. When coming up with a quantitative measure of some attribute, psychologists are assuming that the attribute concerned has a quantitative structure, yet this is rarely, if ever, tested – even though, Michell argues, that this is in principle an empirical question open to investigation. If trying to measure job satisfaction, say, psychometricians rarely stop and ask the question 'is job satisfaction really a quantitative attribute?' – it is already assumed to be quantitative and indeed it is necessary to assume this if the quantitative test scores are to have any sensible meaning. The focus usually moves directly to how satisfaction test scores are quantitatively related to other variables, even though the quantitative nature of satisfaction was never established. Satisfaction could be a categorical state for instance, and it is far from proven that dissatisfaction is the dimensional opposite of satisfaction.

The existence of a test that produces numbers does not establish that the attribute being 'measured' is really quantitative and a lot of bogus 'science' may be built on flawed measurement assumptions. Although Michell speculates about why psychologists and psychometricians have not bothered with establishing that given attributes are quantitative, doing so is not a simple matter. **Conjoint measurement theory** (e.g. Luce & Tukey, 1964) offers one of the few ways to address this at the moment, and Michell (2000) gives a nice illustrative example. Other methods have proven elusive, yet the need for them is clear – we should not be attempting to present psychology as a rigorous science that measures quantitative things if we cannot establish that the things we want to measure are actually quantitative in the first place.

conjoint
measurement theory

As hopefully it will have become clear, there is a hierarchical distinction between the types of measurement described in this section. Nominal measures give information on whether two objects are the same or different, ordinal measures add information concerning more or less of a quantity, interval measures add information on the distance between objects, and ratio scale measures add the absolute zero standard.

3.3 DISCRETE VERSUS CONTINUOUS VARIABLES

Many types of measurement result in indices that consist of indivisible categories. If someone scores 13 on our 50-item arithmetic test, they might have scored 14 on a better day but they could never have scored 13½. The score 13½ was not possible as the individual questions can be marked only correct or incor-

discrete variables rect. Measures like this are called **discrete variables** since they can have only discrete, whole number values.

continuous variables Some variables such as height and time are referred to as **continuous variables** since they could be divided into ever smaller units of measure. We could measure height in metres, then centimetres, then millimetres, then micrometres, then nanometres and so on until we got to the point where our measuring instrument could not make any finer discrimination. There are an infinite number of possible values that fall between any two observed values. Continuous variables can be divided up into an infinite number of fractional parts. Ultimately it is the accuracy of our measuring instrument that puts limits on the measurement of continuous variables. If our ruler can measure accurately only to the nearest millimetre we must settle for that degree of precision.

When measuring a continuous variable you end up recording a single figure, but this really represents an interval on the measurement scale rather than a

approximate value single value. It is therefore always an **approximate value**. If we time someone doing a task to the nearest second, and it takes them 20 seconds, we are really saying that the time taken lies somewhere in the interval between 19.5 s and 20.5 s. Had it actually taken them 19.4 s we would have rounded the time to 19 s, not 20 s (note: to avoid rounding bias when rounding a number that ends exactly with a numeral 5, round to the nearest even number). Similarly, an elapsed time of 20.6 s would have been rounded to 21 s. This is shown in the diagram.

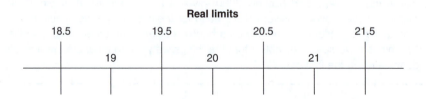

In this example we are deliberately recording times only to the nearest second but, in principle, the choice of any measurement tool carries with it a limit to the degree of accuracy that can be achieved and thus the rounding process will have to happen even if we are unaware of it. We will still be reporting a time that corresponds to an interval and not a discrete value. If our stopwatch could record times to the nearest hundredth of a second, say, and we recorded a time of 20.12 s, this would still mean we were saying that the time taken lay somewhere in the interval between 20.115 and 20.125 s. These boundary values are referred to as **real limits**.   real limits

It is always appropriate to use the most accurate measure practicable. Any calculations you do using approximate values necessarily include that approximation in the final result. Use two or more approximate values in a calculation and the scope for misleading results increases dramatically. Hence it is always preferable to use approximate measures associated with the smallest intervals possible so as to minimize this problem. You should also note that, although our variables might be theoretically continuous, such as time and length, the act of measurement always reduces the measure to a discrete one.

3.4 MEASUREMENT ERRORS

The goal of all researchers should be to minimize measurement errors. Put formally, these are the discrepancies between the observed value of your measurement and the 'true' value. There is a simple formula to illustrate this:

Observed score = True score + Error.

The 'error' term may be positive or negative. Obviously it would be nice to have the error term as small as possible. If you were measuring people's heights with a ruler marked off in inches then you could probably only measure accurately to within half an inch. Having a ruler marked off in millimetres would give rise to much more accurate measurement, and finer distinctions between individuals could be made (see the previous section). In a similar way, psychological measures should strive to make as fine a set of distinctions between people as possible. Assuming your measure is valid, it makes sense to have more points on your measurement scale rather than fewer.

This holds true only so long as you believe the individual points on the scale carry the same meaning for all participants. When it comes to ratio scale and interval level measures, this is not a problem. You could measure time to the nearest millionth of a second, though you might find the necessary timing equipment a little expensive! For most psychological research, timing to the nearest millisecond is probably accurate enough. Things get much more difficult when you have ordinal measures, however. Problems arise when you try to label individual responses on your ordinal scale. Take the following as an example.

Let us assume you have an attitude statement about a political issue and you would like people to tell you how much they agree or disagree with it. You could provide a five-point scale as follows:

1	2	3	4	5
Strongly agree	Agree	Neither agree nor disagree	Disagree	Strongly disagree

Most respondents would know what they were required to do with such a response scale. While you could not be certain that all those who 'agreed' had agreed to the same extent, you would probably feel reasonably happy that they did not intend to tell you they had very strong views on the topic. Similarly, it is probably safe to assume that they are not entirely equivocal about the issue either.

If you gave this question to several hundred people in a survey, however, you might find that so many people had the same score on the item that it did not discriminate very much between people. In this situation you might want to increase the number of response options available. A seven-point scale could be used and it would be reasonably easy to label the response options. You might even think a nine-point scale was appropriate, though labelling all the points might prove more of a challenge. Indeed, you could simply label the end- and mid-points, leaving the rest unlabelled.

Why not opt for a 29-point scale instead? This would give even greater discrimination, surely? The answer is, regrettably, no. Respondents would now have trouble working out where they should indicate their response on the scale. Should it be the 18th or the 19th point or even the 20th? Such a response format increases the scope for confusion on the part of the respondent and thus will introduce, rather than reduce, measurement error. There is also the problem that we still do not know that all people responding at point 19 agree to the same extent. Such multi-point ordinal scales introduce an unfortunate illusion of precision.

3.5 CHOICES OVER LEVELS OF MEASUREMENT

In the previous and very traditional section you will have noticed that I have implicitly suggested that ratio and interval level measurement is to be preferred over ordinal or categorical measures. The reason for this is that in most cases a good ratio scale measure will contain more information about the thing being measured than a good ordinal measure. You would probably rather have temperature reported in degrees Celsius than on a scale of very cold, cool, neither warm nor cold, warm, very hot. You should always strive for greater accuracy of measurement where possible.

Naturally some kinds of variable are always going to be categorical (e.g. sex) and some are always going to be ordinal (e.g. most scaled measures; but see Section 3.6). In such cases you should not regard your measures as somehow inferior. Whilst it would be nice to think that ultimately we will have access to more direct measures of attitudes and personalities, for example, these are not likely for the foreseeable future.

There are, however, some common practices which should be discouraged. The most notorious of these is the collapsing of ordinal measures into categorical ones. It is quite common to see researchers take an attitude item with a seven-point agree/disagree response format and collapse the data into a simple three-point scale of agree/uncertain/disagree. This practice degrades the measurement by removing the extremity information.

There are three kinds of motive for collapsing data in this way. One is the desire to use simpler statistical procedures; a second is to make graphs and tables clearer; and the third is that you might not believe that your seven-point measure is very accurate or valid. With the ready availability of comprehensive statistics books and computer programs the first problem is easily overcome. While clarifying graphs and tables is an admirable aim, it would be desirable to collapse the scores only for this purpose and conduct statistical analyses on the uncollapsed data. The third justification is also a justification for not using the measure. If you doubt the validity or accuracy of a measure then you should think twice about using it at all.

3.6 THE RELATIONSHIP BETWEEN LEVEL OF MEASUREMENT AND STATISTICS

Most good statistics texts present 'decision trees' which help you select the correct statistical test to use providing you know the answers to a number of simple questions about your data and research design. These are very useful, and simple versions are provided in Chapter 19 on bivariate analyses.

These decision trees ask about the level of measurement for your data as well as the nature of the distribution of scores on the measure that you expect in the population from which your sample scores were drawn. The topic of distributions of scores is dealt with in Chapter 19 but the level of measurement issue is pertinent here, particularly at the boundary between ordinal and interval level measures.

The attraction of **parametric tests**, ones that assume something about the distribution of scores in the population (e.g. *t*-test, ANOVA), is that there are many more of them than **non-parametric tests**. They often allow you to ask interesting questions about your data that are not easily answered without using such parametric procedures. To say that your measure is only ordinal, rather than interval level, usually rules out these useful procedures. Chapter 20 outlines some of the many possibilities. Two views have developed over the appropriateness of treating ordinal measures as interval ones. Those interested in reading more on this debate should see Henkel (1975), Labovitz (1975), Davison and

parametric tests

non-parametric tests

Sharma (1990), Townsend and Ashby (1984) and Stine (1989), among many others.

One view states that, most of the time, providing you have a good-quality ordinal measure, you will arrive at the same conclusions as you would have using more appropriate tests. It is sometimes argued (see Minium, King & Bear 1993) that while most psychological measures are technically ordinal measures, some of the better measures lie in a region somewhere between ordinal and interval level measurement.

Take a simple example of a seven-point response scale for an attitude item. At one level this allows you to rank-order people relative to their agreement with the statement. It is also likely that a two-point difference in scores for two individuals reflects more of a difference than if they had only differed by one point. The possibility that you might be able to rank-order the magnitude of *differences*, while not implying interval level measurement, suggests that the measure contains more than merely information on how to rank-order respondents. The argument then runs that it would be rash to throw away this additional useful information and unnecessarily limit the possibility of revealing greater theoretical insights via more elaborate statistical procedures.

The more traditional and strict view (e.g. Henkel, 1975; Stine, 1989) says that using sophisticated techniques designed for one level of measurement on data of a less sophisticated level simply results in nonsense. Computer outputs will provide you with sensible-looking figures but these will still be nonsense and should not be used to draw inferences about anything. This line of argument also rejects the claim that using parametric tests with ordinal data will lead to the same conclusion *most of the time* on the grounds that you will not know when you have stumbled across an exception to this 'rule'.

The debate on this issue continues. The safest solution, advocated by Blalock (1988), is to conduct analyses on ordinal measures using both parametric and non-parametric techniques where possible. Where both procedures lead you to the same substantive conclusion then, when reporting parametric test results, you will at least know that you are not misleading anyone. You should be guided more by the non-parametric procedures if the conclusions are contradictory.

What is unacceptable is to select the statistical procedure that leads to results that support your hypothesis. You should attempt consistency in reporting findings so that you decide either that your data meet the assumptions for parametric procedures or that they do not.

Ultimately, whether this issue matters will depend on the seriousness of making a mistake and who your audience is likely to be. Research on a drug or an intervention that may change people's lives demands the strictest and most conservative approach to your analysis. On the other hand, if your research topic is more esoteric and your audience is researchers in a field that has regularly used (abused?) parametric techniques on ordinal data, then you may find it difficult to get a hearing if you do not report findings in the accepted way.

3.7 CONCLUSION

This chapter has attempted to alert you to the main issues surrounding levels of measurement. As time marches on, the research community may come to an alternative system of classifications (cf. the debate discussed above). However, the Stevens system described here remains the dominant one in psychology for the time being. Chapter 19 takes this a step further by looking at the principles of statistical inference in more detail. Be sure that you have understood this chapter before you read Chapter 19.

3.8 FURTHER READING

All good statistics textbooks explain Stevens's classification system and the relationship levels of measurement and statistics, though few books will go much beyond what has been presented here and in Chapter 19. Minium *et al.* (1993) have the virtue of spelling out many of the debates in a clear and accessible way. Many of the key papers on the debate about measurement and statistics have appeared in the *Psychological Bulletin* and are likely to continue to appear in that journal.

4

The Experimental Method in Psychology

Alyson Davis and Gavin Bremner

4.1   Introduction
4.2   Experimentation and the scientific method
4.3   What is an experiment?
4.4   Causality and experimentation
4.5   Variables
   4.5.1   Independent variables
   4.5.2   Dependent variables
4.6   Reliability and validity
4.7   Experimental manipulation and control
4.8   Basic experimental designs
   4.8.1   Between-subjects designs
   4.8.2   Randomization
   4.8.3   Matching
   4.8.4   Within-subject designs
4.9   Evaluating the experimental method
4.10 Conclusion
4.11 Further reading

AIMS

This chapter attempts to explain the ideas underlying commonly used experimental designs in psychology. We attempt to justify the widespread use of experiments within psychology and, in doing so, we will concentrate on the reasons why the principles of the experimental method should be adhered to (most but not all of the time), for the sake of psychological theory and not just in the interests of 'good science'.

Key terms

between-subjects designs	incomplete counterbalancing
carry-over effects	independent groups designs
ceiling effects	independent variable
confounding	Latin square designs
counterbalancing	method of difference
dependent variable	operational definition
differential treatment	order effects
ecological validity	participant bias
experimental treatment	related groups designs
external validity	reliability
floor effects	validity
hypotheses	within-subject designs

4.1 INTRODUCTION

Psychological research has two major goals. The first is to provide a description of human behaviour and its underlying psychological processes, and the second is to provide an explanation for that behaviour. The task of generating sufficient evidence to enable the descriptive task of research is well met by many different systematic research methods, including experiments. However, the uniqueness and power of the experimental method is that it allows us to address the problem of explanation. It goes beyond the descriptive problem towards providing answers as to how and why that behaviour comes about. In other words, by using experiments it is possible to answer questions about the causes of behaviour. For this reason both undergraduate and postgraduate students receive substantial training in the principles of experimental design and carrying out experiments for themselves. Is this time well spent? The purpose of this chapter is to convince you that the answer is 'yes'. We shall outline the basic tenets of the experimental method and principles of designing experimental research in an attempt to justify the widespread use of experiments within psychology. In doing so, we will concentrate on the reasons why the principles should be adhered to (most but not all of the time), for the sake of psychological theory and not just in the interests of 'good science'.

4.2 EXPERIMENTATION AND THE SCIENTIFIC METHOD

Historically, the widespread use of experiments in psychological research began in nineteenth-century German psychophysics, in particular with Helmholtz's empirical studies of visual perception during the 1860s (see Helmholtz, 1962) and Wundt's founding of the first experimental psychology laboratory in 1879. The methodology of experimental design then developed with the rise of statistics and behaviourism early in the twentieth century (e.g. Fisher, 1935; Skinner, 1953). Since then the use of experiments in psychological research has become synonymous with psychology's acceptance as a scientific discipline. This said, these early influences have also led to experimental methodology being associated with a mechanistic approach to human thinking and behaviour. While there is a relationship between method and theory, most psychologists who adopt experimental methodology are testing theories far removed from behaviourist learning theory and are interested in precisely those unobservable mental processes which the behaviourists found so abhorrent. Nevertheless, there are some basic assumptions underlying experimentation in terms of its relationship with the scientific method which must be accepted by the researcher in adopting experimental methodology. The method by which experiments seek out the causes of human behaviour assumes acceptance of a deterministic and atomistic framework, whereby behaviour and its causes are seen as being objectively specifiable and divisible into discrete units. Moreover, the complexity of real-life stimuli and responses can be simplified, controlled and quantified without losing the meaningfulness of the results. On these grounds alone some psychologists reject the experimental method as an unacceptable and inappropriate research methodology and propose instead alternative methodologies. Therefore, from the outset it must be appreciated that in using experiments in research you are adopting a methodology which, like any other, carries with it acceptance of certain ruling principles.

4.3 WHAT IS AN EXPERIMENT?

In the British television series *The Good Life* popular in the 1970s and 1980s one of the leading characters, Tom, is seen in the kitchen contemplating a row of three seed boxes. He declares to his wife his intention of carrying out an experiment into the effects of talking to his plants. All the boxes contain the same seeds. The seeds in box A, he announces, are to be spoken to for ten minutes every morning in a calm, gentle manner, the seeds in box B are to be shouted at for the same length of time, while those in box C are to be ignored and not spoken to at all. Not perhaps, you may say, cutting-edge science, but it serves a purpose very well as providing an example against which to test the formal definition of an experiment. Is Tom carrying out an experiment? At the minimal level he is, not a perfect one, but one which meets the basic criteria. As mentioned briefly above, an experiment is a test of cause–effect relationships by collecting evidence to demonstrate the effect of one variable on another. In its simplest form, two groups of people are treated in exactly the same way with one exception (the **experimental treatment**, also called the **differential treatment**) and any observed difference between the groups is then attributed to the different treatment. Tom has these basic ingredients in his three seed boxes. He is testing the effect of speech (a variable) on another variable (growth rate of the seeds). He treats his groups of participants (seed boxes) in exactly the same way with one exception (whether they are spoken to kindly or shouted at). In fact, he goes one step further by introducing a different level of his variable by including a baseline or control condition whereby one box is not spoken to at all. There are, of course, many questions which would have to be answered in order to evaluate the appropriateness of Tom's experimental design – such as whether all the seeds are of equivalent gestation, and whether they would all be kept under the same conditions of lighting – but the essential ingredients for an experiment are present. In later sections we shall unpack in some detail what these ingredients are, but first we need to take a step back and ask how experiments come about. Experiments do not design themselves simply by following a set of rules. They are designed

experimental treatment
differential treatment

as a means of answering questions, of testing hypotheses and predictions about the psychological world. All of us carry theories about why people behave and think the way they do, and the following is a series of hypotheses or predictions which serve as illustrations:

Watching aggressive television programmes makes people more aggressive.

Men believe they are better car drivers than women.

Children who are sensitive to rhyme in early childhood make better progress in learning to read than those who do not.

Mothers who concentrate their babies' attentions on objects are more likely to have children whose early vocabulary contains a large number of object names than mothers who do not.

Remembering a list of items is easier if the list is read twice rather than once.

At one level these are all hypotheses, in that they predict some relationship between the different variables (type of television and aggressive behaviour, sex and driving ability beliefs, reading ability and academic progress etc.). **hypotheses** **Hypotheses** are formal statements of predictions derived from evidence from earlier research and theory, or simply the result of a hunch. All these examples lie in the realm of psychological inquiry and yet not all lend themselves particularly well to the experimental method. Why? The crux of making decisions about appropriate methodology is the appropriateness of a particular method for addressing a particular type of research question. For example, in the case of men's belief about sex differences and driving skills, the example is formulated as a hypothesis but not one in which an experimental design would be most appropriate since the question is about belief rather than behaviour. This kind of attitudinal claim lends itself to questionnaire and survey methodology rather than experimentation.

Similarly, the example about children's early vocabulary illustrates another way in which experimental methodology is not necessarily the most appropriate. By definition, natural language is not easily manipulated, and yet the hypothesis as stated is empirically testable, by means of systematic observation alone without experimental intervention. The final example is the most obvious case for experimental testing under classic experimental design since it would be relatively simple to compare groups of people who were given differential levels of repetition of an initial list to remember and compare their performance. However, the relevance of the experimental method to these and any other hypotheses is that whereas other methods would establish the existence of the relationship being claimed, one cannot address the question of causality without appeal to experimentation. For this reason we now turn to a more detailed look at causal relationships and how they can be established using experiments.

4.4 CAUSALITY AND EXPERIMENTATION

Psychology students are reminded repeatedly of the dangers of inferring causality from a correlation. It is a lesson well worth learning since the pitfalls are not always obvious. The correlation may be spurious or caused by a third variable that affects both the first two (a 'common cause'). An example should help illustrate this point. In 1993 the truancy figures in UK secondary schools increased and during the same period school examination scores likewise increased. While it seems counter-intuitive that non-attendance at school causes improved exam performance, we might have been tempted to accept it had the correlation been a negative one. In addition, what right have we to interpret the correlation as suggesting truancy causes good exam scores: why not good exam scores causing truancy? There is no principled way of inferring the direction of causality from the correlation alone; other factors must be considered. We can extend this example even further. During the same period there was increased global warming, increased crime in Moscow, and increased ageing in pet hamsters. Truancy levels can correlate with many other phenomena, and we cannot just choose one at random and then draw conclusions. The principle remains the same: causality needs to be established over and above the description of an existing relationship between two variables.

How can this be achieved? The experimental method does this by manipulating one factor and looking for evidence that this produces a change in another factor. If there is such an effect, we know that there is a causal relationship between the factor manipulated and the factor affected. This is the most commonly used technique in psychological experiments and is based on the canon put forward by the philosopher J.S. Mill in 1874 – the **method of difference** (see Mill, 1950). Using this method one applies a test twice (say, to the same people twice each, or to two groups of people: see below). These test applications are identical except in one respect and any observed differences in the participants' performance can then be attributed to the difference in treatment. Careful use of this method should indicate whether or not the particular treatment that is being varied can have a causal influence on behaviour (other factors might of course intervene in more complex situations; see Lipton, 1991). But in principle the aim of establishing causality is to provide an explanation that is the only explanation for the observed phenomenon.

method of difference

4.5 VARIABLES

Variables and the control and manipulation of variables are central both to defining what constitutes an experiment and to distinguishing a good experiment from a weak one. A variable is any characteristic that can vary across people or situations and that can be of different levels or type. Thus in the list of examples given above, aggressive behaviour, type of television, sex, driving ability, age, and reading ability are all types of variable. There are two basic kinds – independent variables and dependent variables. This distinction is central to experimental design and so we shall take each in turn.

4.5.1 Independent variables

independent variable

The **independent variable** is that which the experimenter manipulates or controls and as such is the variable in whose effect the researcher is interested. It is the one that differs between the treatments in Mill's method of differences, described above. The experimental hypothesis proposes that the independent variable will actually cause the change in the behaviour being measured (dependent variable). For example, from our selection of illustrations the hypotheses suppose that the type of television viewed will determine the levels of aggression, and likewise that phonological skill will determine reading ability. Note that, in principle, variables may be independent or dependent depending on the formulation of the research hypothesis: they can be causes or effects. In practice, however, some variables such as sex, age, and type of life experience are fixed – that is, they cannot be manipulated within the experiment. However, the experimenter can select groups that differ in terms of these variables.

One way of classifying independent variables is in terms of those which can be quantified in some way in that the experimenter can determine the amount or levels presented in the study, such as amount of drug administered or time allowed to perform a task. Such variables are termed quantitative. In contrast, other independent variables differ in kind and are termed categorical. Examples of qualitative, categorical independent variables include the race and sex of people chosen, type of drug administered and type of experimental instructions given. The conditions of an experiment refer to the levels of independent variable received by the participants, or the levels of treatment. True experiments require at least two conditions in order that variable manipulation can occur but in principle there is no limit to the maximum number of conditions (see Chapter 3 for further discussion on levels of measurement).

4.5.2 Dependent variables

dependent variable

Essentially, the **dependent variable** (sometimes called the 'response variable') is the behavioural measure made by the experimenter; it is the outcome which may or may not, depending on the hypothesis, be predicted to depend on the independent variable. Thus in our earlier examples, aggressive behaviour, reading ability, early vocabulary and driving ability are all examples of dependent variables. Just as independent variables must be carefully selected so that they can be easily and systematically controlled within the experiment, so must the dependent variable be selected so that it can be sensibly and meaningfully measured. The dependent variable must not only be measurable with enough sensitivity to detect some effect that stands up to statistical testing but also be potentially sensitive to alterations in the level of the independent variable. Thus, in the example of our aggressive television experiment we have within our theoretical stance an assumption that the amount of aggressive programme exposure will impact on the amount of aggressive behaviour exhibited by viewers. To test this we would need to plan very carefully how aggressive behaviour was to be measured in our experiment to pick up our predicted experimental effects.

The fundamental problem of deciding on an appropriate dependent variable stems from the very nature of psychological inquiry. Most psychological research is interested in outcome measures that are only indirectly related to the psychological process in which we are interested. Much present-day research is dealing with questions about mental processes which are not directly observable but where some behavioural measure is taken as being symptomatic of some underlying process. It is this inferential nature of psychological research which makes it so difficult. Learning, problem solving, developmental change and so on cannot be directly observed and so even the most clearly specifiable of problems needs great care in the selection of our outcome measure. One way of addressing this issue is by the use of an **operational definition** of the dependent variable, **operational definition** where one makes an explicit statement about the precise way in which observed behaviour is going to be scored or categorized as the dependent variable. In the case of our aggressive behaviour following violent television we would need to specify what constitutes aggression – whether it be acts of physical violence against others or against objects or includes verbal aggression.

The difficulties of precision in designing experiments cannot really be appreciated by reading textbooks or even scientific journal articles: direct personal experience, however, is very effective! Developmental psychologists are interested in the development of babies' ability to retrieve hidden objects since there are theoretical reasons for supposing that this provides some measure of the baby's general level of cognitive development (Piaget, 1952a). As such there is a relatively large literature reported in the scientific journals on the infant's reaction to hidden objects. Such experiments involve a dependent variable which measures whether or not the infant retrieves or searches for an object when it is hidden in various locations and through various means of concealment. It sounds simple enough; the reality, however, is far from simple. For example, what constitutes an effective attempt at search? The nine-month-old infant will move his or her hands around and in doing so displace the cover: is this searching behaviour? Likewise he or she may wait some time, cry, giggle, look around and then move towards an object, pick it up, drop it and even replace it. How can such behaviour be classified?

It is tempting to suppose that these difficulties arise out of attempting experiments with types of people who are implicitly difficult to work with. The problem, we suspect, is much more fundamental to all forms of experimental research. Working with infants and young children simply makes explicit those problems of defining psychological measurement in general. For example, adult participants often adopt particular stances with regard to the experiment, which depend on what they think of you, of psychology, or of science in general. This is known as **participant bias**. Disgruntled, depressed or downright antisocial people (i.e. anyone who doesn't like you) may deliberately fail to conform to the experimental instructions, often in subtle and undetectable ways. Conversely, most people are happy to comply, but go to the opposite extreme. They wish to do what they are supposed to, and to do it well – but they form assumptions about exactly what it is they are supposed to do. The instructions given to participants usually deliberately leave out the real reason for doing the experiment, because if the participants know, they will adapt their performance in ways they think appropriate to your aims, rather than just behaving as they would normally (see Chapter 3 for discussion of the ethical issues that arise here). In the absence of reasons, people often make up their own; they try to guess what you want from the experiment, and they then behave according to their false presumption about the real situation. For example, a common test of 'creativity' is to ask someone to write down as many uses for a brick as they can think of in one minute. Suppose the participant does not know this is a straightforward quantitative test of creativity, but guesses it to be a personality test, and so guesses it is the content of the ideas that will be analysed, not simply their number. Any unpleasant ideas that occur, such as 'hit an old lady over the head with the brick and steal her purse', will thus be suppressed on the assumption they will create a negative opinion of the thinker. This might be true, but from the experimenter's point of view the test will be covertly flawed, in that it no longer gives a true measure of the individual's creativity.

    A further issue related to the selection and measurement of the dependent variable is that of floor and ceiling effects. A **floor effect** occurs where a null result emerges because the majority of the participants score at the very bottom end of the scale. Whatever condition they perform in, a floor effect may well emerge simply because the task is too difficult for the participants and the experiment is thus insensitive to changes in the independent variable. An obvious example is a psychophysical task where the stimulus is too weak to be detected. If the purpose of the experiment is to compare people's sensitivity to lights of different colours, but all the colours are below threshold, no meaningful data will be obtained. **Ceiling effects** are the converse of floor effects and are found when people score too close to the top of the scale. Continuing with the example, if all the coloured lights are so bright as to be clearly visible, the task would be too easy and therefore result in a ceiling effect. Floor and ceiling effects can, we emphasize, be obtained with any task in which dependent variable cannot track the full range of the independent variable. Unfortunately, preventing floor and ceiling effects involves more than common sense

participant bias

floor effect

ceiling effects

and a good grasp of the relevant scientific literature. It is almost always necessary to carry out pilot studies to check the appropriateness of your subject pool and variables before carrying out the experiment proper. In addition, Chapter 9 describes techniques for adjusting the difficulty of a task continually during the experiment to keep the subject's responses near the middle of the available response scale, so that floor and ceiling effects never occur.

4.6 RELIABILITY AND VALIDITY

In experiments, as in all systematic research, the stakes are very high. Claiming psychological causality on the basis of poorly designed studies renders experiments worthless at best and potentially damaging at worst. These difficulties can be formalized by using the concepts of reliability and validity.

Reliability refers to the consistency or stability of any experimental effect. The most common technique for establishing reliability is by replication. If the same experimental design leads to the same results on subsequent occasions and using different samples then the experiment is said to be reliable. Typically, however, experimenters do not replicate their own experiments on more than one occasion for pragmatic reasons and so reliability is commonly established by other researchers replicating a particular experimental paradigm within their own research.

Unfortunately, evidence suggesting that an experiment is reliable is no guarantee of its validity. **Validity** refers to whether or not an experiment explains what it claims to explain: in other words, the truth of the causality which is being inferred. Validity can be dealt with to some extent by providing adequate operational definitions, although these can sometimes be reduced to rather unhelpful truisms such as the frequently cited claim that 'intelligence is what intelligence tests measure'. The importance of validity in psychological experimentation cannot be overstressed, not only because of its status as a basic tenet of experimental method but also because of the very real human consequences which potentially arise when claims of causality arise from an invalid dependent measure.

An example comes from the work of Milgram (1974) where, in a series of famous experiments on obedience, he asked people to administer electric shocks to other people when they failed to get simple learning problems correct (the 'victims' were confederates of the experimenter who were just acting and were, in fact, not shocked). Usually over half of the participants would end up administering apparently dangerous levels of electric shock to the 'victims' when told to do so. Milgram concluded that these studies had demonstrated high levels of obedience to authority in many apparently ordinary people. The validity problem here is that it is unclear that obedience, and obedience alone, was the cause of the people's behaviour. Some may have 'seen through' the experiment and some may have felt that no serious academic could actually allow people to

reliability

validity

be hurt in an experiment. Milgram has also been criticized for creating an extremely stressing and distressing novel experimental environment that does not mirror 'real-world' situations at all. The debate about the value and validity of Milgram's work continues even to this day.

4.7 EXPERIMENTAL MANIPULATION AND CONTROL

The power of the experimental technique rests on its ability to ensure that only the independent variable is permitted to vary systematically across the conditions of the experiment. Where one or more other variables unintentionally vary along-

confounding side the manipulated variable, this results in **confounding**. Confounding of variables can render an experiment useless since it makes the results uninterpretable.

An example should make this clear. Suppose you were investigating the effects of different techniques of teaching reading to children. To do this three teachers are trained in three different techniques and the children's reading ability is assessed before and after receiving one of the three methods. Any observed differences are then attributed to differences in teaching method. However, there are real difficulties in making such claims because the variable 'teacher' is confounded with the manipulated variable 'method'. In other words, one cannot distinguish whether any effects arise out of teacher differences or differences in teaching method.

Even where it seems intuitively unlikely that a confounding matters, the danger is a very real one. In the above example the confounding would be serious since there is, in fact, good evidence to suggest that individual teachers can have differential effects on children's performance (Tizard, Blatchford, Burke, Farquar & Lewis, 1988). Some confoundings are obvious while others are far more subtle yet equally damaging to the strength of the experiment. Even in laboratory settings confoundings can easily occur, such as testing people at different times of the day where the dependent variable is very sensitive to fatigue effects. As these examples demonstrate, the more closely related the confounded variable is to the independent variable the more serious the consequences. Recognizing confoundings after data have been collected is too late – the experiment is already ruined. Therefore checking for possible confoundings before running the experiment is essential.

4.8 BASIC EXPERIMENTAL DESIGNS

There are two fundamental experimental designs, which form the basis of all the

between-subjects designs more complex designs and which differ according to the way in which they deal with the control of subject variation. These are **between-subjects designs** and

within-subject designs **within-subject designs**. (Between-subjects designs are sometimes called independent or separate groups designs, while within-subject designs are sometimes called related or repeated groups designs or repeated measures designs.) If two or more totally separate groups each receive different levels of the independent variable then this constitutes a between-subjects design. In contrast, if the same group of people receive all the various conditions or levels of the independent variable then this is an instance of within-subject design. Both these methods carry advantages and disadvantages (see Box 4.1), and the selection of basic design must rest on the nature of the research hypothesis as well as pragmatic concerns.

Box 4.1 Advantages and disadvantages of experimental designs

The advantages and disadvantages of the two main experimental designs in an experiment with two conditions are given below (A and B). In the between-subjects design participants are allocated to *either* condition A *or* condition B. In the within-subject design participants are allocated to *both* conditions.

	Advantages	Disadvantages	Possible ways to overcome disadvantages	Situations where you have no choice
Between-subjects design	• Participants in each condition are naïve as to purpose of the study • No order effects	• Larger number of participants needed • Differences between conditions may be due to group differences	• Increase sample size • Random assignment to groups	• If independent variable makes it impossible for participants to be in both conditions (e.g. sex/age)
Within-subject design	• Fewer participants needed • Equivalent sample in each condition	• Aim of study may become obvious in later conditions • Order effects	• Counter-balance or randomize order of conditions	• If trials are very short (e.g. reaction time) • Participants are difficult to recruit (e.g. brain surgeons, serial murderers)

You should note that while it is no longer considered appropriate to refer to participants in experiments as 'subjects', the terms for types of experimental design have yet to change. We will continue to refer to between-subjects designs and within-subject designs here for the sake of consistency with other texts.

4.8.1 Between-subjects designs

Allocating people to different conditions within an experiment rather than presenting people with all the experimental conditions consecutively is the most common experimental paradigm used in experimental psychology. Immediately, this method poses a threat to the power of the experiment because by definition there are different people in each group and these groups may share different characteristics at the outset of the experiment which will influence their performance. Let us take the example of the children in our earlier hypothetical experiment who are in three different classes each receiving a different method of being taught to read. In the discussion of confounding variables it was pointed out that there is a risk of teacher differences interfering with teaching method effects. In addition to this possibility there is a chance that the three groups of children differed before the introduction of the different teaching problems. Perhaps the groups differ by chance, one class being significantly more able than the others, or they may differ by some predetermined factor such as the type of teaching method they received in an earlier class. So, how can this type of problem be overcome? The answer is by adhering to a fundamental principle of experimental design known as randomization.

4.8.2 Randomization

Randomization is a technique to ensure that as few differences as possible exist between different subject groups by giving every subject an equal chance of being allocated to each of the experimental conditions. Procedurally, randomization is relatively straightforward to achieve. One assigns arbitrary numbers to each subject and literally pulls out these numbers from a hat. In a two-group design with ten people in each group, the people corresponding to the first ten numbers selected would constitute one group and the second ten the other group. The mechanics of this procedure are simplified by the use of random number tables found in most statistics textbooks or generated on a computer. Other methods of attaining random allocation to groups can be used such as tossing a coin or, in the case of our classes of schoolchildren, alphabetical lists of children's names might be used. The precise method is irrelevant as long as the procedure ensures that each individual has an equal chance of appearing in each of the experimental groups. It is important to note that this procedure does not eliminate or even reduce individual differences: it simply distributes those differences randomly between the groups. So, continuing our example, those children whose previous reading experience might facilitate their performance in the experiment appear in all the groups in roughly equal numbers. The ideal being aimed at is of totally equal distribution, but because allocation is done on a random probabilistic basis this can never be guaranteed. However, because the chance of a very biased distribution is very small indeed, randomization of participants is an important step in setting up even the smallest of experiments. If we did not do this, we could end up with a more able group in one condition, and any difference between conditions might be due to a systematic effect of individual differences rather than to differences in experimental treatment between the groups. By randomizing, we very much reduce the possibility of a systematic bias of this sort.

As the number of people in an experiment increases, so does the likelihood of attaining an equal distribution of those subject variables which might interfere with the causal relationship being tested for. For this reason, psychologists generally regard an experiment as more reliable if there are large numbers of people involved (see Chapter 19 for additional statistical justifications for large samples). Consider the extreme opposite case. If there were only one subject in each group, different outcomes might be due to individual differences in reaction to the independent variable, rather than reflecting any general reaction, principle or law that applies to all people and that can thus be used in the future to make predictions or decisions. Despite the strength of randomization as a technique and its relative ease of implementation, it is surprising how many experiments remain uninterpretable because of the researcher's failure to ensure random distribution of people across groups. See also Chapter 5 for a discussion of quasi-experimental designs.

4.8.3 Matching

The sensitivity of an experiment refers to its ability to pick up any effect of the independent variable. Sometimes experimental effects may be very small and yet of great psychological significance. A classic example of such a situation is in sex differences. On most measures males and females do not respond differentially: the similarities far outweigh the differences. However, those psychological areas in which one sex outperforms the other are of great psychological interest even though the actual size of the effects can be very slight indeed. Therefore, researchers interested in this area must make sure that the experiment is designed to be maximally sensitive. Randomization of participants to experimental groups will guard against certain error but will not increase sensitivity. All is not lost, however, since there are steps which will achieve this, namely various means of matching participants.

If we take our example of a group of schoolchildren embarking on their different programmes of being taught to read, there are many instances of existing differences between those children which might interfere with our ability to assess the effectiveness of the different programmes. Prior reading training is one we have already mentioned, but other factors such as intelligence and age are also potentially significant. When running experiments with children, age is a difficult variable to deal with because development is so rapid in early childhood that even a six-month age difference between two children might exert a significant effect on their performance. Therefore, we would want to be sure that the children in each condition were of a similar age. Randomization of our class of children would help ensure that the average age of our groups was similar, but we may need to do more than that. Where there is reason to believe that some variable which is not manipulated by the experiment may exert an effect then it is necessary to take the additional step of actually matching children. In the case of age, we would make sure that for each subject in group A there was a child of exactly the same chronological age (in years and months) in each of groups B and C. Furthermore, if intelligence were a concern to us then we might take a further step of assessing IQ on some standardized test and then match children across groups according to IQ. When these kinds of precautions are taken the probability of revealing a true causal relationship between our independent variable of teaching method and our dependent variable of reading performance is dramatically increased. A numerical example may make this clear. Suppose we have two groups, each of three people, who participate in an experiment that gives a numerical score outcome reflecting their level of performance. We obtain scores from the first group of 1, 26 and 39, and from the second group 2, 27 and 40. The mean scores of the two groups are 22 and 23 respectively – a difference, but one so small compared to the variability between people within each group that we would probably not credit that it tells us anything meaningful or reliable about whether there is a real difference between the two groups. Consider, however, what would have happened had the participants been matched, and if one pair of participants had scored 1 and 2, the second pair 26 and 27, and the third pair 39 and 40. In each case there is a consistent difference such that people in the second group scored higher. The difference in scores is only 1, but it is so consistent that we would be much more likely to believe there is an actual difference between the two groups. The experiment with the matched pair design is much more sensitive.

The importance of matching becomes more salient when the experiment comprises very different participant groups. Suppose the experiment is comparing some kind of treatment intervention on groups of people with some disability such as autism, schizophrenia, dyslexia or Down's syndrome. How can these people be matched? The answer to this lies very much in the realm of the experimental hypothesis. We shall use the example of dyslexia to highlight some of the traditional matching techniques and point out how these have recently been improved. Some people, who have average or significantly above average IQs, have pronounced difficulties with reading and writing. The term 'dyslexia' is often applied to these people to describe this paradoxical gap between their intelligence and their literacy skills. The theoretical debate around the causes of dyslexia has assumed a specific cognitive or neuropsychological deficit and, not surprisingly, has been the focus of many research studies and experiments. The typical experimental paradigm has been to take a group of people with reading difficulties and compare them with people of the same age and intelligence. Thus the groups were matched for mental age and the experiments then went on to probe the nature of the reading difficulty of the dyslexic group.

However, research by Bryant and colleagues has criticized this approach on both methodological and theoretical grounds (Bryant & Bradley, 1985). The traditional approach assumes that reading difficulties are caused by some deficit, but the methodology used does not allow us to distinguish cause and effect. As Bryant points out, reading difficulties not only have causes but also exert effects: a person with reading difficulties will be less able to deal with other aspects of the world because print is so endemic to everyday life. While experimental methods employing the mental age matched design allow us to look at causal relationships, they do not allow us to decide which is the cause and which is the effect (see also Box 4.2). A beautifully simple way around this problem is to introduce an additional matched group of people – those who are matched with the people with dyslexia according to reading age – which is precisely what Bryant did in his series of experiments. This way, differences between people at the same level of reading ability might truly reveal something about the nature of the 'deficit'. For example, the dyslexic group might make different types of errors from the ability matched group.

Box 4.2   The difficulty of pinning down developmental causality: the case of locomotion onset and visual cliff avoidance

In a classic study, Gibson and Walk (1960) tested infants on what they called a visual cliff. Infants were placed on a central platform with a shallow drop to one side and a deep drop to the other, both covered by strong glass. They found that infants willingly traversed the shallow side but few ventured onto the deep side. It

(Continued)

Box 4.2 (Continued)

is generally accepted that this 'deep side avoidance' indicates both perception of the deep drop and wariness of it. However, given that these infants had to be able to crawl to be tested, it was unclear whether this ability was innate or had developed in the months prior to crawling onset at between seven and nine months. However, it has proved possible to adapt the task to allow testing of prelocomotor infants. Schwartz, Campos and Baisel (1973) measured infants' heart rate as they were lowered on to the deep and shallow sides of a visual cliff. Taking heart rate on the shallow side as baseline, they found that prelocomotor five-month-olds showed a deceleration in heart rate on the deep side relative to the shallow side, whereas nine-month-olds showed an increase. Since a heart rate reduction is generally taken as an indicator of attention and an increase is taken as an indicator of stress or unease, Schwartz *et al.* (1973) concluded that the younger infants perceived the difference between deep and shallow sides but that only the older ones showed wariness of the drop. This led to the suggestion that wariness of vertical drops followed from early locomotor experience.

Although the proposal that the onset of crawling leads to developments in spatial awareness is quite straightforward, investigating a direct causal link of this sort is far from simple. In the above study there is a major confounding between age and mobility status. The mobile group was older than the immobile so would be likely to be more advanced cognitively as well as motorically. Svejda and Schmid (1979) attempted to surmount this problem by gathering two groups of infants who differed in whether or not they could crawl but whose average ages were the same. They found that even with age held constant, those infants with crawling experience showed evidence of wariness on the visual cliff, whereas those who were still immobile did not. Even in this study, however, there is an interpretative problem. As Campos, Svejda, Campos and Bertenthal (1982) point out, infants who crawl early may do so because they are generally more advanced, cognitively as well as motorically. This means that simply holding test age constant is no guarantee that all variables other than mobility will be controlled.

This problem can be counteracted by matching the two groups on a range of general ability tests, but of course it is still possible that some infants crawl early because they are more advanced in specific spatial skills. Although the tendency is to assume that locomotor experience may lead to cognitive development, the reverse is also possible. Prior to acquisition of locomotion, infants spend quite some time attempting to crawl but either failing to move or actually moving backwards. It is quite possible that these continuing attempts come at this point not just because of motor maturation but because some new knowledge motivates their attempts. For instance, they may begin their attempts on realization that the space out of reach is navigable territory.

Two pieces of evidence suggest, however, that this model is inappropriate. Campos, Hiatt, Ramsay, Henderson and Svejda (1978) tested newly crawling infants on the locomotor version of the visual cliff task, and found that it took

(Continued)

Box 4.2   (Continued)

some time before they began to avoid the deep side of the cliff. Nearly half of infants with 11 days' crawling experience crossed the deep side, whereas less than a quarter did after 41 days' experience. A close temporal lag of this sort looks like reasonable evidence that the direction of causality is from mobility to cognition rather than the reverse. Stronger evidence of such a link comes from a study by Campos, Svejda, Bertenthal, Benson and Schmid (1981), who selected two groups of infants according to whether their parents had provided baby-walkers for them during their fifth month. These two groups were matched for age and general cognitive ability, and subsequently their responses on the visual cliff were compared. Those given early locomotor experience were more likely than control infants to show wariness on the deep side of the cliff. However, neither of these findings is completely conclusive. The second looks most convincing, but becomes less so when we start to ask questions about what determines whether or not parents decide to give their infant a baby-walker. Possibly those who do so wish to promote exploration and spatial awareness in their infant, and if so it is likely that they will do this in many other ways in addition to providing them with early mobility.

This example points up the difficulty in demonstrating this sort of real-life developmental causality. None of these studies manipulates a variable in a controlled fashion. Instead, difference in the independent variable is arrived at by group selection. And no matter how hard one tries to control other variables by matching, there are some that are outside the investigator's control. For this reason, such investigations are often called pseudo-experiments. However, they are often the only way of gaining evidence about developmental change. Returning to the example of locomotion and visual cliff avoidance, Campos, Anderson, Barbu-Ruth, Hubbard, Hestenstein & Witherington (2000) argue cogently that the relationships here are multifaceted, involving locomotor, perceptual, emotional, and social factors in a complex interplay. Faced with the complexity of reality, and clear ethical objections to intervening to manipulate infants' long-term experience for non-therapeutic purposes, the solution left to us is to build the most plausible picture emerging from different approaches to the same issue.

One reason why we particularly like this example is that it shows that changes in methodology are not introduced purely in the interests of better scientific method such as enhancing the sensitivity of the test. They have real and sometimes very dramatic theoretical consequences. It also illustrates how generations of scientists accept particular methods without noticing the flaws in current procedure.

4.8.4 Within-subject designs

Some types of experiment solve the problem of differences between people and the need for matching by using the same people in each of the experimental conditions. Within-subject designs, as they are called, have one very obvious advantage since each individual is tested under both or all conditions of the study. In experiments containing a control or baseline group, each individual acts as his or her own control. When the same person performs quite differently under each of the treatments then the effect of the independent variable is very clear indeed, because the difference cannot be caused or diluted by individual differences. But this method carries with it some disadvantages which in some cases make the method inappropriate but in others can be dealt with by following certain precautions.

The first problem which within-subject designs pose is that which arises because by definition the different levels or tasks in the experiment must be completed serially, one after another. The serial nature of testing can easily give rise to **order effects**, where doing one task first and another second influences the person's performance. A clear example might be a task involving high levels of concentration, such as an auditory discrimination task in which two words are simultaneously presented in each ear and the participant has to identify one on the basis of some given criterion which differs in each experimental condition. In such a situation, the participant is quite likely to show an incremental improvement from one condition to the next as they gain experience with the nature of the task, such that performance in the first condition would always be inferior to performance in later conditions. Any experiment in which familiarity with the experimental set-up and procedure can grow is at risk of showing order effects which will distort the interpretation of the results. Similarly, fatigue and boredom can also increase over time and affect the outcome. Moreover, these types of order effect will arise regardless of the precise sequencing of conditions since they arise simply out of the fact that one condition must be first, second, third and so on.

A more specific kind of difficulty arising out of order of presentation is the potential for **carry-over effects**. These come into play when performance on one condition is dependent in part on the conditions which precede it; this runs the risk of lowering the experiment's validity. Carry-over effects can be characterized in a number of ways. The first is where the participant gains experiment-relevant skills in one task which spill over into the next task presented. So in an experiment with two conditions (A and B) let us suppose that while undertaking A the subject picks up skills which will enhance performance on B. The participant's score on B will be artificially inflated compared with the same experiment run as a between-subjects design. An obvious example is learning set material under different environmental conditions. Obviously, once the material has been learned, it does not have to be learned again (or at least there will be considerable retention). And so the effect of this is likely to outweigh any effect of different environmental conditions.

order effects

carry-over effects

Another common carry-over situation is when two tasks differ in difficulty. Suppose task A is easy and task B difficult, and you intend to assess people's abilities on each task, such as how quickly they finish or how many problems they solve correctly. An individual who does task A first will get the impression the experiment is easy, and will therefore approach task B with that in mind: this individual will work quickly and therefore make many mistakes. Conversely, the individual who does task B first will come to think the experiment difficult, and will therefore perform slowly and carefully when it is time to do task A. The participants may thus score differently on task A, depending on whether it was attempted first or second, and the same may be true for task B. So which is the appropriate score on each task? From the theoretical point of view, it is also interesting to ask what 'skills' the participants acquired or developed during the first task that they then use to do the second task. In other words, participants' performance on the task they do first is the 'clean measure' of ability under that condition, but equally we may be interested in the effect experience of one task has on another. So we may want to compare the 'clean measure' when the task is done first, with the 'experience-altered measure' when the same task follows the other.

A further scenario is where experience of one task actually creates a situation where the participant reinterprets the meaning of the experiment and the experimenter's intentions (either rightly or wrongly) and therefore changes their behaviour on all subsequent tasks. Examples of this latter type are particularly common when testing young children's cognitive understanding and indeed have been exploited in developmental psychology for their theoretical interest. One familiar example is in testing young children's understanding of number. Piaget (1952b) showed how children under the age of five or six often report that the number of objects in a row actually changes simply because an adult (acting as experimenter) spreads the row of objects out so that the row appears longer. This phenomenon is said to arise because the young child does not understand number invariance or number conservation. It is a very powerful and convincing effect to witness. It is even more striking if one then retests the child and, instead of the adult spreading out the row, the adult picks up a teddy bear and the teddy is seen as spreading out the row of objects. Experiment after experiment has shown how children who fail to conserve when the transformation is undertaken by an adult, change to give conserving responses when a cuddly toy performs the action. Furthermore, these studies show significant carry-over effects. If children are tested in the teddy bear condition first then they are more likely to give correct conserving responses on the adult condition than children who are given the reverse order of presentation. Note the difference between order effect and carry-over effect here; it is not that children show an improvement from first to second task but that they show improvement only with a particular sequence of conditions.

So, we have been trying to suggest that carry-over effects can be of theoretical interest rather than simply viewing them as experimental pitfalls to be avoided at all costs. This said, they can only provide valuable insight if the experiment is designed so that they can be recognized. In the number conservation examples above, the relevant experimental manoeuvre employed was that of **counterbalancing**: half the children were given the Piagetian version of the task first followed by the modified task involving the toy, and the other half were given the toy condition followed by the standard Piagetian condition. In a two-treatment design, this AB, BA counterbalancing is effective, efficient and easy to implement. Both order and carry-over effects can be readily recognized. Note, however, that this procedure does not eliminate such effects, it just makes them separable from the effect of the independent variable. But what of more complex designs involving many levels of the independent variable? True counterbalancing becomes very unwieldy as the number of conditions increases: 3 conditions give 6 different orders, and 5 generate 120. Consequently, researchers using more than three or four treatments will settle for **incomplete counterbalancing** as in **Latin square design**. A Latin square ensures that each level or condition appears equally in each position (Fisher, 1935). An example with four levels of treatment (A, B, C and D) is shown in Table 4.1. Such an experiment would require at least four participants or multiples of four so that they are evenly divided among the four possible orders of treatment. It is worth noting that in a design as complex as this, any carry-over effects are being controlled for by being randomly distributed across the experiment and are not likely to be as clearly apparent as in a two-condition design (AB, BA) unless very large numbers of people were being tested, such that a good number perform under each order.

counterbalancing

incomplete counterbalancing
Latin
square design

Table 4.1 Counterbalancing by Latin squares

Subject 1	A	B	C	D
Subject 2	B	C	D	A
Subject 3	C	D	A	B
Subject 4	D	A	B	C
Subject 5	A	B	C	D
Subject 6	B	C	D	A
Subject 7	C	D	A	B
Subject 8	D	A	B	C
Subject 9	A	B	C	D
⋮	⋮	⋮	⋮	⋮
Subject n	D	A	B	C

We have organized this section along the dichotomy of between-subjects versus within-subject design. Like many of the other concepts that have been considered this is an oversimplification and to some extent a fairly arbitrary distinction made in the interests of ease of presentation and learning. In practice many experiments involve the use of both within-subject and between-subjects measures. These mixed designs are increasingly common as access to complex statistical analysis becomes more available on personal computers. This said, it is not the case that complex design is on the increase simply for pragmatic reasons: there are good theoretical grounds for this change. Psychological processing is a multivariate activity: there is probably not one single phenomenon in psychology which can be described by appeal to a single variable.

4.9 EVALUATING THE EXPERIMENTAL METHOD

Throughout this chapter we have avoided having a section on advantages and disadvantages of the experimental method; however, the discussion which follows might well have fallen under such a heading. Although the whole enterprise of experimental design rests on quantification, we would argue that the decision about what type of methodology to employ is not easily quantifiable. The decision rests on the nature of the research question, one's own experience and expertise and a host of other essentially qualitative factors. Some questions do literally cry out for experimental investigation and it would be plain silly in some instances to use other methodologies. But our own personal view of progression in psychology is not one where experimental methodology continues to be more and more sophisticated, thus squeezing out alternatives. There are two issues at stake: one is whether or not the experimental method has a significant role to play in psychological research, and the second is the subtlety of our ability to combine different methodologies. In the pursuit of causal explanations, experimental methods are identified as the only way of achieving such goals, but there is a certain arrogance attached to this claim because it tends to blur the unavoidable fact that there is little point in searching for causality unless we can be sure that a meaningful relationship exists which warrants our efforts to determine cause and effect in the first place. It is quite possible to follow the rules of experimental methodology to answer a ridiculous question in just the same way as a computer will calculate the average gender of people. The suggestion we are making is that the experimental method is dependent for its success on living alongside other methodologies for one very simple reason. The weaknesses of the key alternative to experimentation, namely correlational techniques, can be complemented by the strengths of the experimental method and vice versa (see Bryant, 1990, for a full discussion of this point). Experiments are frequently criticized (and rightly so) for the fact that they lack **ecological validity**. Findings generated in laboratory conditions where behaviour must be tightly controlled may not tell us anything interesting about life outside the laboratory. In other words they lack **external validity**. However, they are a good way, in fact the only way, of definitively answering causal questions. Correlational studies, on the other hand, tell us very little about the causes of relationships between events, but they can be carried out in natural 'real-life' settings and so tell us a good deal about people's normal behaviour. There are a few, but very powerful, instances where researchers have capitalized on the dovetailing characteristics of combined methodologies to great effect (see Bryant & Bradley, 1985).

ecological validity

external validity

4.10 CONCLUSION

We hope that in the course of this chapter we have not only highlighted the issues one needs to be aware of when designing effective psychological research but also gone some way in explaining why the experimental method has a real contribution to offer. Yet there is a sense in which one feels 'but life is not like that' when trying to define the ideal control condition or a readily measurable dependent variable. One of the overriding difficulties of the experimental method is that the ideal often is humanly impossible, as in the case where it would be too time-consuming or where certain groups, conditions or variables literally do not exist. Sometimes it is not possible to meet the criteria formally demanded by experimental designs discussed here and we have to resort to quasi-experimental methods or adopt alternative methodologies entirely. Furthermore, because scientific research is a human endeavour, researchers themselves as much as their participants get involved in chains of unavoidable events which mean that the most clearly defined of objective plans get waylaid. Even Skinner, as a disciple of objective methodology, laid down some less than scientific principles of the pragmatics of carrying out research, in a talk about his own experiences (for a discussion of these, see Christensen, 1988). Does the fact that our research will fall short of logical purity negate the whole exercise of striving for systematic objective study? The answer must be a definite 'no'. There is such a thing as good evidence and experimental methodology is currently one of the best research tools we have at our disposal to uncover it.

4.11 FURTHER READING

There is no shortage of good textbooks on experimental design issues, but the following are very helpful and clear. Christensen's (1988) is a good detailed guide to the principles of experimental design. Keppel and Saufley (1980) outline the main types of experimental design alongside appropriate techniques for analysis. A more recent text is Field and Hole's (2003) which also deals with appropriate ways to report experimental work.

5

Quasi-experimental Designs

Chris Fife-Schaw

5.1   Introduction
5.2   Pre-experiments
5.3   Quasi-experiments
5.4   Non-equivalent control group designs
  5.4.1   Problems with NECG designs
5.5   Time series designs
  5.5.1   Problems with time series designs
5.6   Time series with non-equivalent control group designs
  5.6.1   Problems with TSNECG designs
5.7   Modifications to the basic designs
5.8   Conclusion
5.9   Further reading

This chapter deals with experiments where, for whatever reason, the researcher does not have full control over allocation of participants to experimental conditions. It describes three common quasi-experimental designs: the non-equivalent control group design, the time series design and the time series with non-equivalent control group design. Single case studies are also considered.

K ey terms

compensatory rivalry
external validity
Hawthorne effect
history effects
instrumentation effects
internal validity
maturation effects
non-equivalent control group
   design
participant mortality
pre-experiments

quasi-experiments
sample selection
selection biases
selection–maturation
   interaction
statistical regression
   towards the mean
testing effects
time series designs
time series with non-equivalent
   control group designs

5.1 INTRODUCTION

In Chapter 4 the basics of classical experimental designs were discussed. Most psychology degree courses stress the value of doing experiments since they offer the most clear-cut route to testing hypotheses about causes and effects. The experimenter has control over the relevant independent variables and allocates participants to conditions at random in an attempt to make sure that they know exactly what is responsible for the changes observed.

This is to be contrasted with observational and correlational approaches, where we can observe that two variables appear related to one another but it is difficult to determine whether there is a causal relationship between the variables (where one 'causes' the other) or some third variable is responsible for the observed relationship (see Chapter 19). Although this state of affairs may seem less than satisfactory – after all, we usually want to be able to say what caused what – correlational studies are often the best we can hope for in many real-world situations. Practical considerations limit the amount of control we can expect to have in such situations, so we have to be careful whenever we try to interpret relationships between variables.

pre-experiment
quasi-experiment
In between correlational and experimental approaches lie two other kinds of study: the **pre-experiment** and the **quasi-experiment**. Pre-experiments are discussed in the next section, and quasi-experiments in Section 5.3.

5.2 PRE-EXPERIMENTS

Pre-experiments are best thought of as studies that are done simply to get an initial feel for what is going on in a particular situation prior to conducting a more rigorous investigation; this is probably best illustrated by an example.

I once attended a course on rapid reading in an attempt to increase the speed with which I could get through paperwork. The university was pleased to supply such training as it would help the staff perform better and this should, in turn, help the university to be more efficient. A consultant was hired to do the training. With the current political concern to evaluate everything, the consultant felt obliged to conduct an experiment to see if the training had actually worked. Before the training started we were given a report to read and we were asked to time our reading of it and answer some factual questions about the report's content. Having done this, the training went ahead and at the end of the day we were tested on our reading again. So that the times and test scores would be readily comparable we read the same text and answered the same questions. Needless to say reading speed had increased dramatically (four times quicker in my case) and accuracy remained high. The consultant, with obvious satisfaction, declared the day a success. Of course the problem here is that we do not really know if the training had any effect on reading speed at all. Whether we have been able to accurately detect the effect of the training is referred to as the **internal validity** of the experiment.

There are several problems with this procedure which challenge its internal validity even though at first sight it looks like a reasonable thing to have done. First, the test materials were the same on both occasions and since we had seen them only about seven hours previously there is a strong possibility that we would remember the content. Thus the improvements may be reflecting memory for the material rather than any increased reading speed. One does not need to be a psychologist to know that it is easier to read something quickly if you already know what it is about. The same applies to the 'test' questions. Such threats to the experiment's internal validity are called **testing effects**. In all sorts of studies, repeatedly exposing participants to the test materials is likely to make them familiar with them and less anxious about what they have to do. Such effects tend to inflate post-test scores.

In fairness, were the consultant to have used a different report and different test questions, it would have been even more difficult to know what any differences in reading speed could be attributed to. The second text might be naturally easier to read or, possibly, more difficult.

A second problem concerns what are called **maturation effects**. Merely having the time to concentrate on reading speed even without experiencing the training may have led to improvements. As none of those tested had been allowed to spend the day thinking about rapid reading without also being exposed to the training, we do not really know whether the training *per se* had an effect.

Another problem concerns **sample selection**. All those present felt that they had a reading speed problem and, at least at the start of the day, were motivated to improve. You had to volunteer for the course and there was no external pressure on people to attend. Having put a day aside to improve performance, not trying hard to improve would have been somewhat perverse. This factor, in conjunction with the potential maturation effects noted above, may have served to increase scores on the retest. Again, we cannot really say how effective the training was, and even if it was effective here, it might be somewhat less useful when people are not so keen to be trained. This latter point refers to the **external validity** of the study: just how generalizable are the findings? If training works, does it only work for very committed people?

It should be noted that all of these problems are concerned with the experiment (as a pre-experiment) and do not say anything about the virtues of the course. It may have worked very well or it may not. Whichever is the case, this study shed very little light on the issue. This is obviously not an ideal way to demonstrate that the training package increased reading speed.

Other common forms of pre-experiment are frequently found in news stories where some sort of intervention has to be evaluated. A crude example would be to see if peer teaching improved computing skills by comparing children's exam performances in schools that had adopted peer teaching with ones that had maintained traditional teacher-led methods. At one level this looks like a legitimate comparison between treatment groups – one that gets peer teaching and one that does not. Clearly a true controlled experiment is not possible as it would be ethically and politically unacceptable to randomly allocate children to schools and thus to the 'treatment' conditions.

Numerous problems follow in interpreting any differences that are observed between the groups. First, there is the question of whether the schools are comparable. Perhaps the schools that adopt peer teaching simply have more able or more socially advantaged children in them. Those children from higher socio-economic backgrounds may be expected to have home computers and thus be more computer literate, for instance. There is also a possibility that some event, such as a cutback in funds for computer maintenance, may occur in one school and not another. **history effects** Sudden changes of this kind in one of the groups are known as **history effects** and may lead to a difference between the groups which is not attributable to the treatment (here peer teaching) but is due to something else. While pre-experiments as I have presented them here may seem so flawed as to be pointless they do serve a purpose of highlighting problems that need to be addressed when the resources become available to do something more impressive and rigorous.

5.3 QUASI-EXPERIMENTS

Many of the problems discussed in relation to pre-experiments reduce the degree of certainty you can have that the 'treatment' actually caused the observed differences in the dependent variable of interest (i.e. the study's internal validity). Because of this, it is rare to see pre-experiments in high-status academic journals. However, many of the research questions that we would like to answer simply cannot be answered by resorting to true experiments. This is usually because either we cannot randomly allocate participants to treatment conditions for practical reasons or it would be unethical to do so (e.g. if it would mean withholding treatment from someone who needs it). In the computer skills example above, for instance, we could not randomly allocate children to schools.

Quasi-experiments should not be seen, however, as always inferior to true experiments. Sometimes quasi-experiments are the next logical step in a long research process where laboratory-based experimental findings need to be tested in practical situations to see if the findings are really useful. Laboratory-based experiments often reveal intriguing insights yet the practical importance, or substantive significance, of these can only be assessed quasi-experimentally. Laboratory studies may have shown that, under certain highly controlled conditions, peer teaching improves computer test scores, but the 'real' issue is whether peer teaching is good for children in their schools. This is a question about the **external validity** of the laboratory-based studies.

external validity

Three classical quasi-experimental designs exist which attempt to overcome these threats to internal validity discussed above. What is presented below is a summary of the three prototypical designs; many variations of these are possible (see Cook & Campbell, 1979).

5.4 NON-EQUIVALENT CONTROL GROUP DESIGNS

As we saw in the computer skills example, the two groups (as defined by which school they attended) may not have been comparable. The intervention of peer teaching (the treatment) may have had an effect on test scores but we cannot be sure that the peer teaching group was not already better at computing, prior to the inception of the new programme. The **non-equivalent control group design** (NECG) overcomes this by requiring a pre-test of computing skill as well as a post-test. The pre-test allows us to have some idea of how similar the control and treatment groups were before the intervention.

non-equivalent control group design

Figure 5.1 shows a range of possible outcomes from a simple NECG design. In graph A the control group starts off scoring less than the treatment group, reflecting the non-equivalence of the two groups; finding a control group with exactly equivalent scores in a quasi-experimental design is difficult. Both groups improve after the intervention, but the treatment group has clearly improved more than the control group. This is quite a realistic picture to find in studies of educational interventions like the computer skills study discussed earlier. We would expect the control group to improve a bit as, after all, they are still being taught and are maturing. If the treatment had an effect, then scores should have improved more than might have been expected if the intervention had not taken place. Graph B shows what might have happened if the treatment had no effect. Scores in both groups changed about the same amount.

The graphs in Figure 5.1 are prototypical and reflect improvements over time. It is, of course, possible for all sorts of patterns to be found. Non-equivalent controls may outscore the treatment group at the pre-test; they may even be equal. Perhaps a treatment serves to allow the treatment group to 'catch up' with the controls. The treatment might *decrease* scores. There are many possibilities. In all cases you are looking for an interaction between treatment condition (treatment v control) and time of measurement (pre-test v post-test). You would obviously test for such an interaction statistically (see Chapter 20), but by plotting graphs like these you should observe lines of differing gradients; parallel lines usually indicate no treatment effect (but see below).

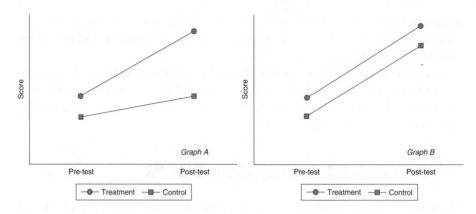

Figure 5.1 Non-equivalent group designs

5.4.1 **Problems with NECG designs**

selection biases

Almost by definition, NECG designs suffer from potential sample **selection biases**. In studies of 'alternative' therapeutic interventions in particular, there is often a problem that those who get a new treatment had actually sought it out, perhaps because traditional treatments had not worked for them. Such people may be highly motivated to see the new treatment succeed and might have ideological objections to existing treatments. There is also the possibility that those offering the therapy may select people they believe would benefit from it or who they think will comply with the regimen. Those who are thought likely to be 'difficult' cases, or for whom the disease may have progressed too far, might not be selected and may even end up appearing in the control group.

Clearly it would be unethical to refuse a new treatment to those who want it or to force those content with existing treatments to receive a new and presumably still untested treatment. However, where possible, you should attempt to have control over, or at least full knowledge of, how the samples are selected. Be aware that those whose efforts are being evaluated may have a vested interest in the outcome of your study.

Even though we have pre-test measures on which we can compare samples, this does not guarantee that the two groups were truly equivalent before the treatment started. If one group was more able or brighter, maturation may proceed at a faster rate in that group than the other. We might expect, for instance, that children's computer skills improve with age (maturation) and that more able kids learn these skills more quickly and easily. Were the treatment group to contain proportionately more high-ability children, group differences may arise out of

selection–maturation interaction

these differential rates of maturation rather than exposure to the peer teaching method. This is referred to as a **selection–maturation interaction**. As the pre-test is usually only used to compare groups on the dependent variable, such a problem may remain undetected. One obvious solution would be to measure variables that might conceivably lead to differential maturation rates at the pre-test (e.g. IQ) though this also increases demands on participants.

Statistical regression towards the mean is another phenomenon which may influence interpretation of the data. Regression towards the mean is reflected in very high pre-test scorers scoring lower at post-test and very low pre-test scorers scoring higher at post-test. If we are studying people who score at the extremes on the dependent variable we may mistake changes at post-test for this regression to the mean. Why this happens is a little difficult to grasp at first but depends on the fact that our test measures will inevitably contain some errors (see Chapter 10). Cook and Campbell (1979) use an everyday example which is fairly easy to understand; the following is an embellished version of their example.

statistical regression
towards the mean

If we have an ability test, say an exam, we might do worse than our 'true' ability would merit because we were distracted by other students, we were extremely badly hung over (worse than usual) and we had revised the topics which did not come up in the paper. We know that if we took an exam for the same subject again we might expect to do better next time, more accurately reflecting our ability. This is because we would expect these sources of error (failures to record our true ability) to be less likely to *all* co-occur next time around. Similarly, if we were very lucky, the exam might only contain questions on the topics we had revised and we might be fortunate enough to sit the exam on the only day of the year when we were not hung over and everybody behaved themselves in the exam hall. This time we might get a mark that somewhat overstated our true ability in the subject. However, we probably would not expect to be so lucky if we took a similar exam again without further revision.

Across a sample of people, those with mid-range scores are likely to be about equally influenced by these errors (inflating and reducing scores) so they would cancel out on average, leading to no systematic bias in our experiment. People at the extremes, however, are *less likely* to score more extremely on being retested as some of those who had extreme scores at pre-test will have done so because their scores had already been inflated (or reduced) by large errors. Since extremely large errors are relatively less likely than moderate size errors, two consecutive large errors in the same direction are very unlikely. This means that post-test scores will tend towards the population's mean score.

For quasi-experiments, this is a particular problem when the treatment group has been selected because of the participants' low scores on the dependent variable (e.g. selecting people with poor computing skills for the peer teaching method). The simplest way to guard against this (though easier said than done) is to ensure that your control group is also drawn from the pool of extreme scorers. The ethics of denying an intervention to children who are particularly bad at computing are clearly an issue here. The problem is also more likely to influence results if your dependent measure has low test–retest reliability. The less reliable the measure (i.e. the more error-prone it is) the more there is likely to be regression to the mean.

Finally, for now, history effects can affect the validity of NECG studies. If some event, in addition to the treatment intervention, occurs between pre-test and post-test in one group only, then it is not clear what any group differences at post-test should be attributed to. For example, an evaluation of a persuasive campaign to promote commuting to work by urban railways in different cities may be invalidated if the 'treatment' city suffers from road travel chaos caused by unanticipated roadworks on the main commuter routes during the period of the study. People may flock to the trains but only because driving to work (their preferred method) was nearly impossible.

You should be aware that history, selection and maturation effects can work both to enhance group differences *and* to obscure them.

5.5 TIME SERIES DESIGNS

time series design   A **time series design** involves having only one sample but taking measurements of the dependent variable on three or more occasions. Such designs are sometimes referred to as 'interrupted time series' designs as the treatment intervention 'interrupts' an otherwise seamless time series of observations. Figure 5.2 gives an illustration of some hypothetical time series data.

As you can see, the main feature that you are looking for when collecting time series data is that the only substantial change in scores coincides with the intervention. The virtue of such a design is that it is relatively less likely that short-term historical events (i.e. history effects) will (a) co-occur with the treatment and/or (b) have a lasting effect over time. It is also unlikely that small differences pre- and post-intervention will be maintained if the treatment really has no effect. Any maturation effects should be reflected in gradual trends in time series data and not radical changes occurring at the same time as the intervention.

For time series studies to work well, multiple data collection/observation points are required. It is difficult to detect trends of any kind with just three observation points so, where possible, opt for as many observation points as is realistic but pay due regard to participant fatigue, boredom and irritation.

5.5.1 Problems with time series designs

Time series studies potentially suffer from the threat of testing effects to their validity. As these studies, by definition, require repeated administration of the same dependent measures, there is a tendency for people gradually to do better

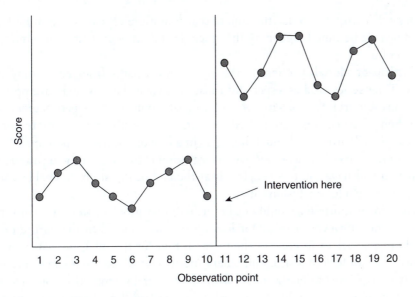

Figure 5.2 Example time series data

as time goes on. This is a separate phenomenon from maturation effects, as testing effects arise out of familiarity with the measurement procedures. When presented with a novel test, for instance, we usually do not know what is required and may be anxious about our performance. Repeated exposure to the test material should reduce these anxieties and allow us to perform better. It is also possible that respondents might come to know what they are being asked about and develop more efficient answering strategies, allowing them to respond more quickly. This is especially a problem where measurements are timed.

The net impact of testing effects is that, if the *magnitude* of the treatment effect itself is small, it may get swamped by the testing effects. If the size of the treatment effect is relatively large there will be little problem in determining that the treatment actually had an effect.

Another potential problem concerns **instrumentation effects**. These refer to changes in the accuracy of measurements over time. One good example would be the reporting of crimes. Over time the likelihood of reporting (and of the police recording) crimes changes as a function not only of their frequency but also of the social representation of the crimes. What may have been regarded as common assault in the past may come to be seen as a racially motivated attack in more enlightened times. Similarly, women are now encouraged to report sexual attacks and the social opprobrium that used to follow a claim of rape is now somewhat reduced, though still present. What this is really about is a change in the way the measures are taken and their relative accuracy. Studies that involve measures taken by observers are particularly at risk from instrumentation effects as

instrumentation effects

observers learn how to use the coding schedule more efficiently or, more likely (and worse), become fatigued by the schedule and attempt their own reinterpretation of it.

participant mortality

Participant mortality refers to the loss of participants from your study over time. Time series studies, especially those that cover long periods, are prone to participant mortality problems which are usually outside the experimenter's control. Some participants may indeed die during the study, but it is more normal that some will drop out through boredom or a lack of interest, or perhaps because they move house. If you do not have a large sample to start with you run the risk that you will have too few people left at the end of the study to enable you to draw any reliable conclusions at all.

Participant mortality would not be such a great problem were it a truly random event. However, reasons for leaving that are related to the nature of the study (e.g. a lack of interest in the research topic or the intrusive nature of the measures) can lead to a situation where the surviving sample becomes progressively more biased in favour of showing that the treatment works. Suppose you were trying to evaluate the effect of a local waste recycling advertising campaign and had started regular assessments of how much waste people recycled. Even if you started with a fairly representative sample of the population, you might well find that by the time you had started the adverts and were collecting post-intervention observations, only environmentally committed people were still ready and willing to help you with the project. In all likelihood, your estimates of average post-intervention waste recycling behaviour would be considerably higher than the pre-intervention average, but this would be mainly due to sample mortality rather than the effect of the adverts.

Careful mapping of sample survivors' pre- and post-intervention behaviour would overcome this problem, but this is naturally a rather unsatisfactory solution since such a campaign was presumably intended to change the behaviour of the less environmentally committed people who were lost to the study. Needless to say, strenuous efforts have to be made to maintain the sample.

5.6 TIME SERIES WITH NON-EQUIVALENT CONTROL GROUP DESIGNS

time series with non-equivalent control group

Many of the problems associated with time series and NECG designs are neatly overcome by the combination of the two approaches in the **time series with non-equivalent control group** (TSNECG) design, sometimes also called the 'multiple time series design'. An extended series of data collection points are used with both the treatment group and the non-equivalent control. The key advantage of the TSNECG design is that you should be able to tell both whether a treatment

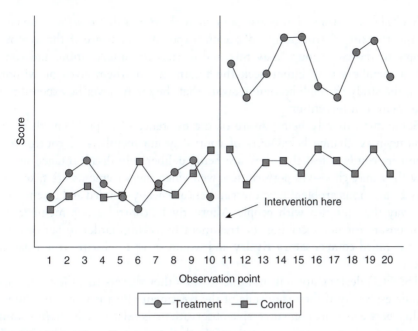

Figure 5.3   Time series with non-equivalent control group

has an effect compared with a control group and that the effect only occurs at a point after the introduction of the treatment. It helps to rule out many of the individual threats to validity outlined above.

Figure 5.3 illustrates what we would hope to find if there really was a strong treatment effect. While it is clear from Figure 5.3 that there is variability in scores over time and that there appears to be a gradual improvement in scores in the control group, potentially via testing, instrumentation or maturation effects, the post-intervention scores for the treatment group are considerably higher than for the controls.

5.6.1 Problems with TSNECG designs

The price to be paid for minimizing so many threats to validity is all-round increased cost and the need to study many more people. This is not a problem when conducting research on existing archival data, but may be a serious problem if you intend to collect fresh data.

Differential sample mortality in the two groups can be a problem. If people who are somewhat apathetic to the study are differentially more likely to be lost from one group than the other, then group differences may be artificially enhanced or constrained. It is also possible with studies that last for some period of time that the control group will become exposed to, or aware of, the treatment. People in the two groups may mix and discuss the intervention, and control group members may either seek the treatment for themselves or withdraw from the study through becoming aware that they may never be exposed to the treatment or intervention.

Sometimes, merely being aware of the existence of a 'problem' that needs treating may change behaviours of control group members. If control group members come to feel that they are being deliberately disadvantaged in some way they may choose to perform less well when measurements are taken. This may be a serious problem when researchers are heavy-handed and insensitive in the way they interact with people. Alternatively, control group members may compensate for not receiving the treatment by trying harder to perform well.
compensatory rivalry This is called **compensatory rivalry** and would serve to obscure true treatment effects.

TSNECG designs are not immune to the other threats to validity discussed earlier, especially if the magnitude of the treatment effect is weak and the variability between scores on successive observations is relatively high. In common with the single-case designs (see Box 5.1), detecting a treatment effect is easiest when it is possible to establish a fairly clear-cut stable baseline in both the control group and the treatment group prior to the intervention. As with true experiments, it may be necessary to increase sample sizes substantially in order to provide the necessary statistical power to detect these weak effects.

Box 5.1   Single-case designs

Although elsewhere in this book researchers are encouraged to seek out large samples in order to increase their confidence in the conclusions they draw from a study, it is perfectly possible to conduct meaningful experiments on single cases. The most basic single-case design is the ABA design which shares many of the characteristics of the time series design discussed in this chapter.

The ABA design is the best-known single-case experimental design in which the target behaviour or response is clearly specified and measurements are carried out continuously throughout three phases of the experiment, A, B and A again. The first occurrence of phase A is the baseline phase during which the natural occurrence of the target behaviour or response is monitored; in phase B the treatment variable is introduced. To increase our confidence that the treatment in phase B is responsible for any changes we see, the treatment is then removed and responses monitored in what amounts to another baseline phase A. A hypothetical example of an ABA design is shown in Figure 5.4.

Box 5.1   (Continued)

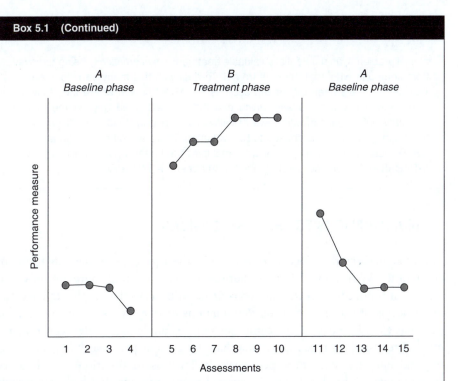

Figure 5.4 Example of an ABA design

There is, however, an important reservation concerning the clinical application of the ABA design; this is that it may not be possible to tell whether any behaviour change that occurs following onset of the treatment results from the treatment *per se* or from changes that are part of the recovery process that would have happened even without the treatment. This issue is particularly problematic when there is only weak evidence of an experimental effect, that is, only a slight improvement is seen. One way of overcoming this problem is to use a control variable. A control variable is another aspect of behaviour which would be as susceptible to the effects of recovery as the experimental variable, but is not thought to be something that will be influenced by the treatment. If the effects found following treatment were due to naturally occurring, non-treatment-related recovery then the curves for the treatment and control variables should be parallel.

ABA designs are most commonly used in clinical settings where clinicians are interested in finding out whether a treatment intervention will work for a particular patient, usually with a relatively unique combination of problems (treatments for comparatively common conditions are usually tested using true experiments in the form of randomized control trials). The ABA design presents some fairly obvious

(Continued)

Box 5.1 (Continued)

ethical problems, as a potentially valuable treatment is systematically being removed from someone who might benefit from it. To deal with this many variations on the ABA design have been suggested such as the ABAB design where the study finishes with a treatment phase which can then be extended beyond the end of the study, but a phase of withdrawal still allows the opportunity for the efficacy of the treatment given in the B phases to be evaluated. There are other variations on the ABAB design, for example having multiple treatment and baseline phases (ABABABABAB) or incorporating another treatment (ABACABAC).

5.7 MODIFICATIONS TO THE BASIC DESIGNS

The basic designs described here are really the tip of the iceberg in terms of possibilities. With NECG designs there is no necessity that there are only two treatment conditions (treatment and control). It is perfectly possible to have different levels of the treatment or combinations of treatments in one design. For example, we might extend the computer skills example to include a control (traditional teaching) group, a group that had two periods per a week of peer teaching and one that had three per week. In fairness to traditional methods of teaching, we might also divide the control group into one that had two periods per week and one that had three periods of traditional teaching. Clearly, this new design is much more useful to curriculum developers since it tells us not only whether peer teaching is better than traditional methods but also whether spending more time on computing yields worthwhile increases in skill level. Assuming we had enough schools prepared to help, we could even add a group that gets both traditional and peer teaching for a total of three periods.

Sometimes concerns about testing effects may lead us to believe that post-test measures will be unduly influenced by people having completed the pre-test. An example might be of a knowledge test with a short period between pre- and post-test. In such a situation we might expect people to remember the items, thus inflating the apparent power of any intervention. It is also often the case that merely asking people about some aspect of their lives changes their behaviour in that domain. For instance, merely asking about your waste recycling activities might make you think that you ought to recycle more waste. Somebody show-Hawthorne effect ing interest in your behaviour may change it. This is called the **Hawthorne effect** after the electricity plant in Illinois where the phenomenon was first formally described in studies on attempts to enhance worker performance (Roethlisberger & Dickson, 1939). It is possible to get over both sorts of problem by using separate pre- and post-test samples so that different individuals take the pre- and post-tests. This approach is only sensible if you have a large pool of people from which to draw your samples and you can draw them by some fairly random procedure.

For time series designs and TSNECG designs it is possible to adopt treatment withdrawal designs. These involve intervening with the treatment and then, at a later point, withdrawing it and observing a subsequent fall in scores on the dependent measure. This approach works best when the treatment is not expected to have a lasting effect on the dependent variable and has to be 'maintained' in some sense for the effect to be shown. An example might be to evaluate the effectiveness of camera-based speed checks on stretches of road. Speeds could be monitored surreptitiously for some period before erecting the camera systems; then, after a period with the cameras in place, they could be removed to see if speeds gradually increased in their absence. The cameras could be re-erected later to see if speeds fell again.

5.8 CONCLUSION

Having read through this chapter and followed all the potential problems associated with each quasi-experimental design, you might be forgiven for concluding that such approaches are too fraught with difficulties to make them worthwhile. The difficulties, however, are inevitable whenever you forgo experimental control in order to do research outside the laboratory. What I hope to have shown you is that there are some rigorous methods available and, while they will not necessarily lead you to unambiguous answers to your research questions, they do at least highlight the likely threats to validity. If you know where potential interpretative problems lie then you can address them and make some estimate of the likely impact these could have had on the results of your study. Quasi-experiments, providing they are conducted with due care, can be the most powerful available means by which to test important hypotheses.

5.9 FURTHER READING

The classic text in this area is Campbell and Stanley's (1966). This is a very short book of only 70 pages which had first appeared as a chapter in Gage's (1963) text. It is the place where quasi-experimental designs were first comprehensively explained. The more detailed text by Shadish, Cook and Campbell (2001) contains discussions of the major designs and a few more, as well as information about the appropriate statistical models to be used with each design. For single-case studies Todman and Dugard (2001) expand on the examples given here.

6

Surveys and Sampling

Patrick Sturgis

6.1   Introduction
6.2   Statistical inference: from sample to population
   6.2.1   Sampling distributions
   6.2.2   The normal distribution
   6.2.3   Confidence levels and confidence intervals
   6.2.4   Factors affecting the precision of estimates
6.3   Nonresponse
6.4   Sampling strategies
   6.4.1   Simple random sampling
   6.4.2   Complex sample designs
   6.4.3   Complex designs and variance estimation
   6.4.5   Quota sampling
6.5   Survey mode
6.6   Small-sample issues
6.7   Conclusion
6.8   Further reading

This chapter introduces the notion of inference from sample to population by way of random sampling. Key concepts from statistical theory are discussed and some of the main practical sampling strategies reviewed. We then move on to consider some of the factors affecting the precision of survey estimates and the importance of interview mode in determining response rates and data quality.

Key terms

census	sampling frame
central limit theorem	sampling without replacement
clustering	seed number
complex sample designs	simple random sample
confidence intervals	standard error
confidence levels	stratification
epsem designs	survey mode
population	systematic random sampling
probability distribution	unbiased estimator
sample	weighting
sampling distribution	

6.1 INTRODUCTION

This chapter will focus on the use of random sampling for making inferences from samples to populations. Random sampling is dealt with in some depth in sociology and political science and, though psychologists regularly conduct surveys, it is fair to say that psychologists' surveys might benefit from the methodological sophistication found elsewhere in the social sciences. In particular, the chapter focuses on the concept of sampling distributions and how they can be used to draw inferences from samples to populations. We also consider the threat to the validity of inference in the presence of nonresponse and review some of the primary practical strategies for drawing samples and obtaining data from sampled units.

Conceptually, surveys and sampling techniques are not tied to any particular philosophical viewpoint. Those adopting a hypothetico-deductive approach will be concerned to sample appropriately, as will those taking a more constructivist perspective. Whenever the goal is to make statements about a group of people then, unless you approach all the members of that group, how you draw your sample from that group will determine how much confidence you can have in the generality of your findings.

Similarly, surveys are not tied to any particular data gathering technique. Whilst structured questionnaires are by far the most common form of data collection in surveys, it is perfectly possible to collect qualitative data, or to count, weigh and observe population units within a sample survey. Even experimental investigations can be done using survey techniques, with respondents randomly allocated to treatment and control groups, usually differing in question wording or information provided in the questionnaire. Physiological and other, more invasive, measures can also be collected in surveys. The Health Survey for England (see: http://www.dh.gov.uk), for instance, collects height, weight, blood pressure and lung function measurements as part of the interview.

6.2 STATISTICAL INFERENCE: FROM SAMPLE TO POPULATION

population

The underlying motivation of sampling is to make statistical inferences from samples to populations. That is, we wish to use known facts (responses from the sample) to understand unknown facts (responses of the population) (King, Keohane & Verba, 1994). A **population** is the universe of objects in the 'real world' in which we are interested. These objects may be individuals, households, organizations, countries or practically anything we can define as belonging to a single taxonomic class. Because populations are often extremely large, or even infinite, it is usually impossible – for cost and practical reasons – to take measurements on every element in the population. For this reason, more often than not, we draw a **sample** and generalize from the properties of the sample to the broader population. In addition to the cost savings this entails, we are usually able to make more – and more detailed – observations on each sample element. When we do make observations on every element in the population, we are conducting a population **census** and the issue of inference is not applicable as we will know from our data the true score of the population on the variable of interest, measurement error notwithstanding.

sample

census

Making valid and reliable inferences from a sample to a population is a cornerstone of science and there are many pitfalls that may crop up along the way in our efforts to do this. Because of such difficulties, we often hear researchers attempting to limit the claims they are making for their analyses by saying their results 'apply only to the sample at hand and should be generalized to the broader population with caution'. Such claims should be viewed with scepticism, for we are hardly ever interested in the idiosyncratic characteristics of a particular sample. Furthermore, even when this sort of statement is made, generalization to a population is usually implicit in the conclusion being drawn.

Fortunately, however, if a sample is collected properly, it is possible to make valid and reliable generalizations to the broader population within quantifiable bounds of error. To appreciate how this is done, it is first necessary to understand the concept of sampling distributions, as this is the key that allows us to link our specific sample with the broader population.

6.2.1 Sampling distributions

When we talk about distributions, we usually understand this as referring to the distribution of values on a particular variable in our sample or in the broader population. Such a distribution is known as a **probability distribution**, as it describes the probability of observing each of the different possible values a variable can take in the sample or population. Probability distributions have different shapes and are named according to the shape they assume. For example, the normal distribution – or bell curve – describes how human samples and populations vary on characteristics such as height or intelligence (see Figure 6.1 for an example of a normal distribution).

probability distribution

The logic of probability distributions, however, can also be applied to statistics. A statistic is just a mathematical transformation or formula applied to a set of numerical data. The distribution of possible values of a statistic in a population is referred to as the **sampling distribution** of that statistic. The difference between the distribution of a variable (a probability distribution) and the distribution of a statistic (a sampling distribution) can be somewhat confusing. However, it is important to understand this distinction if the rationale of inferential statistics using random sampling is to be properly understood.

sampling distribution

When we draw a random sample from a population, it is just one of many samples that might have been drawn using the same design and, therefore, observations made on any one sample are likely to be different from each other and from the 'true value' in the population (although some will be the same). Imagine we were to draw 10,000 (or some other very large number) random samples of individuals from a population. On each sample we calculate a statistic, say, the mean age in years and we then plot the mean age obtained from each sample on a histogram (a histogram is chart using bars to represent the number of times a particular value occurred). This histogram would represent the **sampling distribution** of the arithmetic mean of age in this population. Do not worry about the practicalities of actually drawing all these samples, as we are only talking about a *hypothetical* set of possible samples that could, in theory, be drawn.

Sampling distributions are useful because they allow us to make statements about how likely it is that the true population value will fall within the margin of error of the estimate we make from the sample we have drawn. This is because the sampling distribution tells us the frequency with which the statistic in our particular sample would be found in the population of all possible samples. But how do we know the sampling distribution of our statistic without drawing a huge number of samples each time we wish to make use of it? Fortunately, we do not need to actually draw all the samples that would be necessary to physically plot sampling distributions because of known mathematical links between the parameters of a random sample and the sampling distribution from which it is taken.

If we draw a sufficiently large random sample, all the information necessary for drawing inferences about the population from which the sample was drawn is contained within the sample data. To understand how this is so, it is important to understand a number of additional, interrelated ideas. The first, and possibly the most important, of these is the concept and properties of the normal distribution.

6.2.2 The normal distribution

The exact shape of the normal distribution is defined by a function which has only two parameters: mean and standard deviation. The standard deviation is a measure of dispersion and can be thought of as a measure of how much, on average, people differ from the sample mean.

A characteristic property of the normal distribution is that 68% of all of its observations fall within a range of ±1 standard deviations from the mean, a range of ±1.96 standard deviations covers 95% of the scores, and ±2.58 standard deviations covers 99% of all the observed scores. This has the useful consequence that, when a variable is normally distributed, we are able to tell what proportion of a sample falls within a range of values around the sample mean.

For example, Figure 6.1 shows an example of a normally distributed variable. Let us imagine that this is the distribution of the variable 'age in years' from a randomly drawn sample. We know, then, that the mean age in our sample is

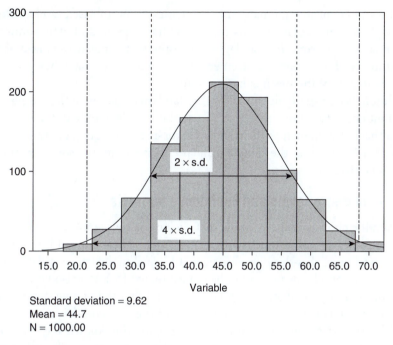

Figure 6.1   Normal probability distribution

45 and the standard deviation is 10. Because the data are normally distributed, we know that 95% of sample cases will be within the range of 45 plus or minus $1.96 \times 10 = 19.60$, which is the range of 25.4 to 64.6. (Note that, had we wanted to talk about a more precisely defined group, say 99% of cases, we would have multiplied the standard deviation by 2.58 rather than 1.96. The consequence of this would have been a widening of the range of values to 25.8–70.8.) Another way of putting this is that the probability of a given case being over 64.6 or under 25.4 is .05 (or 5%).

So, the normal distribution is useful in that it enables us to make statements about the probability of observing particular values. But so far, this only refers to the characteristics of our particular sample. How can we use the sample data to make statements about the whole population? This is possible because of the following links between the properties of sample statistics and their corresponding sampling distribution.

1   When the distribution of a variable is normal in the population, the sampling distribution of the mean (and many other statistics) is also normal.
2   Even when the distribution of the variable in the population is not normal, **central limit theorem** tells us that, as sample size increases, the sampling distribution of the mean (and many other statistics) becomes normal.

central limit theorem

unbiased estimator 3 The sample mean (and many other statistics) is an **unbiased estimator** of the population mean. This means that if we draw repeated random samples (of the same size) from the population and estimate the mean, the mean of these estimates of the mean will itself equal the population mean when the sample of estimates of the mean is large enough.

4 Although we usually do not know the standard deviation of the sampling distribution, it turns out that we can use the sample standard deviation as an estimate of it, known as the **standard error** of the sampling distribution. This is done by dividing the sample standard deviation by the square root of the sample size.

6.2.3 Confidence levels and confidence intervals

So, from the above points, we know that, so long as the sample is random and of sufficient size, we can assume it provides an unbiased estimate of the true population mean (note that this does not mean it is equal to the true population mean, just that the sample mean is an unbiased estimate of it). We also know that the shape of the sampling distribution is normal and that the sample standard deviation provides us with a very good estimate of the standard deviation (standard error) of this sampling distribution. Armed with this knowledge, we can use exactly the same logic as we did on individual cases in our sample earlier in discussing the properties of normal distributions, but this time referring to the target population.

Rather than merely saying that 95% of observations in our sample fall within ±1.96 standard deviations of the mean, we can say that if we were to draw 100 samples of the same size, we would expect only 5 of them to have means that fall outside our estimate of the mean ±1.96 standard errors. Another (more common) way of saying the same thing is that we are 95% confident that the true population mean falls within the range of the sample mean ±1.96 standard errors.

To illustrate, if we drew a random sample of 1000 individuals (assuming no nonresponse or measurement error) and calculated the mean age to be 45 and the standard deviation (s.d.) to be 10, we could say that we are 95% confident that the true population mean age is 45 years plus or minus $1.96 \times 10/\sqrt{1000} = 0.62$ years.

confidence levels
confidence intervals This introduces the linked ideas of **confidence levels** and **confidence intervals** – for a given level of confidence, say 95%, we specify the interval within which the true population value is likely to fall. Although this discussion has been concerned with the arithmetic mean, the same logic applies to many other inferential statistics, such as proportions, differences between means and regression coefficients.

It is important to note that this 'magical process' linking sample to population parameters can break down at various points in the research process, predominantly during the sampling and measurement stages. However, if we are confident that our sample has been properly drawn (i.e. randomly and without nonresponse bias), the sample size is large enough (greater than about 100) and the characteristic of interest has been validly measured (i.e. without bias or random error), the logic of inference is unassailable and can be proven mathematically. It is this logic that enables us to make very definite statements about the characteristics of populations such as 'people in Britain' (which at the last count approached 60 million) based on samples of only around 1000 individuals.

6.2.4 Factors affecting the precision of estimates

The width of the confidence interval determines the precision of the estimate we are making. The wider the confidence interval, the less precise the estimate and vice versa. From the discussion above, we can tell that the two factors affecting the precision of our estimates are the population variance and sample size. The more variable the thing we are measuring is in the population, the less precise our estimates will be – holding sample size constant.

The larger the size of our sample, the more precise our estimates will be – holding population variance constant. However, as the standard error decreases as a function of the square root of the sample size, there are steadily diminishing returns for increasing sample size. Thus increasing sample size from 500 to 1000 reduces the standard error by 29%, while increasing it from 1000 to 1500 reduces the standard error by only 18%. This is why many opinion poll samples have a sample size of around 1000.

Another factor affecting the precision of estimates is the way in which a random sample is drawn. As we shall see in Sections 6.4 and 6.5, there are a number of different ways of drawing random samples and which one we chose influences the reliability of the estimates we make from the obtained sample data.

6.3 NONRESPONSE

The logic of statistical inference using random sampling derives its strength from its mathematical underpinning. If all relevant theoretical assumptions are met, we can have great confidence in the inferences made from sample to population. In the real world of survey research, however, human populations rarely conform to the assumptions of neat mathematical laws!

One of the primary areas in which the mathematical assumptions underpinning random sampling are rarely met in practice is that of response rate. The response rate is calculated by dividing the number of achieved interviews by the total sample size. Although this sounds straightforward, what goes into the numerator and what goes into the denominator of this equation can vary in practice and have a substantial influence on the overall response rate (see Lynn,

Beerten, Laiho & Martin, 2001). So, if we drew a sample of 1000 households and were able to conduct interviews with only 650 of these, the response rate would be 650/1000 = 65%. Conversely, the nonresponse rate for this survey would be 35% (one minus the response rate). Nonresponse occurs for many different reasons but the commonest are 'non-contact', when no contact is made with the selected unit (usually a person) for the duration of fieldwork, and 'refusals', when contact is made but the selected unit declines to participate. This type of nonresponse is referred to as unit nonresponse, as no information is obtained at all on the nonresponding sample unit. A second type of nonresponse is when a respondent provides an interview but does not complete all the items in the questionnaire. This item nonresponse might be deliberate, in the case of sensitive questions such as those relating to income or drug use. Alternatively, respondents may omit items inadvertently through haste or as a result of poor questionnaire design.

The basic sampling theory outlined in Section 6.2 assumes that responses are obtained to all items from all sampled population units. However, if for various reasons, some sample members fail to provide measurements, there is the real risk that survey estimates will be biased. That is to say, the survey estimate will be systematically different from the true value in the population. Because the precision of estimates is a function of sample size, nonresponse also results in less reliable estimates. The latter problem is not particularly serious, however, because we can build an anticipated level of nonresponse into our survey design and still achieve our required sample size by drawing a larger initial sample than would be necessary with 100% response.

While a low response rate may indicate the existence of nonresponse bias, it is important to note that a low response rate does not automatically mean a sample estimate will be biased. Bias only arises if nonresponse is correlated with the variable in question. So, for instance, if a survey measures people's annual income and richer individuals are less likely to respond to the survey than poorer individuals, the sample estimate of mean income would be biased (we would underestimate mean income in the population). However, if nonresponse is completely uncorrelated with income, our estimate would be unbiased, no matter what the response rate is.

Similarly, bias should be thought of as relating to estimates, not samples. One estimate from a sample with non-zero nonresponse might be biased while another estimate from the same survey may have no bias at all – what determines whether an estimate is biased or not is the correlation between tendency to respond and the variable on which the estimate is being made. Survey researchers are currently very concerned about nonresponse bias as studies show that response rates around the world have been in steady decline for the past 20 to 30 years (de Leuw & Hox, 2001).

Fortunately, high and rising rates of nonresponse can be mitigated by improving interviewer training, the timing of calls at addresses and the general design of surveys. Nonresponse **weighting**, a process whereby underrepresented groups in the sample can be weighted up to match their composition in the population, can also be used during analysis to remove or reduce bias arising as a result of nonresponse.

weighting

6.4 SAMPLING STRATEGIES

Thus far we have focused on the conceptual foundations of survey sampling. In practical terms, though, how do you go about selecting a sample from a population? This decision will depend on the type of measurements you want to make, the nature of the population being studied, the complexity of your survey design and the resources available.

The first stage in any survey is to define the population from which you want to draw your sample. For example, you might be interested in the effects of youth unemployment on psychological well-being and thus need to study samples from the population of employed and unemployed youth. Or you might have a developmental hypothesis that some cognitive abilities change around the seventh or eighth year, so you might sample from the population of children aged 5, 7, 9 and 11. Determining the exact population from which you wish to sample is important as you must be clear about the population to which inferences are being made.

Having an explicit and detailed description of your population is also important because for most sampling strategies you will need a **sampling frame,** which is a list of all members of the population. This might sound easy at first, but practical restrictions often curb your initial ambitions. For large-scale surveys of the general population of adults in the UK, the *electoral register* and the *postcode address file* (PAF) are the most commonly used sampling frames. The electoral register is available in libraries and main post offices and lists people eligible to vote. It is used only rarely these days because it does not have anywhere near complete coverage (many people are not listed). Recent legislation also allows people who are registered to vote to be removed from the publicly available register. The PAF lists all UK addresses to which mail can be sent and is available in computerized form. It has very high coverage of UK addresses (approaching 100%) and is regularly updated. As the PAF is not a list of individuals but of addresses, contact must first be made with the household and a randomly selected household member interviewed (if the survey is of individuals, rather than households). The PAF contains approximately 13% non-domestic addresses, so many of the sampled addresses are considered ineligible for the survey. This

sampling frame

proportion of addresses being ineligible needs to be factored into estimates of sample size requirements. Several companies now exist which will draw samples from PAF and other population frames at a commercial rate.

We now turn to a consideration of the different ways in which samples can be drawn from the sampling frame, once the population has been defined and the list obtained.

6.4.1 Simple random sampling

simple random sample

Although it is rarely used in practice, the **simple random sample** (SRS) is the yardstick by which other sampling strategies are judged. An SRS gives every unit in the population an equal probability of selection. For this reason, simple random samples are referred to as **epsem designs** (for Equal Probability of SElection Method). To draw an SRS, every population unit must be assigned a unique identification number from 1 to N (where N is the total population size). Random numbers between 1 and N are then drawn (using a random number table or other random number generating device) until the required sample size is achieved. If the same number is drawn more than once, it is not selected into the sample multiple times, we simply draw another number until we select one that has not already been selected. This is called **sampling without replacement** and is the normal practice in survey sampling.

epsem designs

sampling without replacement

In practice simple random sampling can be cumbersome and time-consuming. An alternative approach – **systematic random sampling** – is simpler and more convenient. To draw a systematic random sample, begin by assigning every population unit a unique number in ascending order. Next, calculate the sampling interval, i, which is the ratio of the required sample size to the population total, $i = N/n$. A random number between 1 and i is then generated, called the **seed number**, representing the unique identifier of the first population unit to be included in the sample. Next the sampling interval, i, is summed with the random number between 1 and i and this is taken as the second unit in the sample. The process is continued until the end of the sampling frame has been reached and the desired sample size achieved.

systematic random sampling

seed number

To illustrate, let us assume that you have a sampling frame containing 1600 names and you want a random sample of 200 to receive your questionnaire. The sampling interval here would be 1600/200 = 8. The next step is to use random number tables to select a number between 1 and 8 to give the seed number to start with. Say you get a 5. You would select the 5th person on the list, then the 13th (5 + 8), then the 21st (13 + 8) and so on. Strictly speaking, this procedure is not an epsem design, since once the 5th person has been selected the 4th and 6th cases cannot be selected as the order of the list determines who is now selected. However, for most practical purposes, systematic random sampling can be considered as equivalent to simple random sampling.

6.4.2 Complex sample designs

Simple random sampling techniques are impractical when you wish to sample from large and geographically diffuse populations, such as 'adults in the UK'. Interviewers would need to be sent to all corners of the country, at great practical inconvenience and expense. For this reason, SRS designs are rarely used in practice. Where sample designs divert from epsem methods, they are referred to as **complex sample designs**.

complex sample designs

The two main ways in which sample designs divert from epsem methods is in the use of **clustering** and **stratification**. Clustering – or multi-stage selection of sample units – is almost always used on national, face-to-face interview surveys, as non-clustered designs are both impractical from the perspective of data collection agencies and prohibitively expensive for funders of research. The basic idea of a clustered design is to select the sample in stages so that individual sample units are kept in relative geographical proximity. Consider conducting a survey of secondary school pupils. We might begin by drawing a sample of schools and then randomly selecting pupils within each school. This would make the interviewers' job much easier than if an SRS had been used as they would need to visit only one or two schools to conduct all their interviews.

clustering stratification

For a fixed cost, clustering produces more precise population estimates than an SRS design would achieve. However, for a fixed sample size, clustered designs are subject to larger standard errors. This is because there tend to be greater similarities, on many attributes, between members of the same geographical subunit than between independently selected members of the total population. For instance, size of garden, number of bedrooms and household income are all variables that are intuitively likely to be more similar within than between postcode sectors. Clustering, therefore, underestimates true population variance and this is reflected in standard errors that are larger, if correctly estimated, than those that would have been obtained from an SRS of the same size.

National probability surveys also routinely employ stratification in the selection of sample units. Stratification divides the sample up into separate subgroups and then selects random samples from within each group. These subsamples are then combined to form the complete issued sample. Strata are created through the cross-classification of variables contained on the sampling frame, which are known or believed to correlate with key survey variables. So long as the latter assumption holds true, stratification will reduce sampling error, relative to an unstratified sample design of the same size.

Sampling within strata can be either proportionate or disproportionate to population totals. In addition to obtaining increases in statistical efficiency, disproportionate stratification is often used to ensure that robust estimates can be made within substantively important strata. For instance, surveys of the population of Great Britain might disproportionately sample within strata formed by the three constituent countries. 'Oversampling' within the Wales stratum would enable separate estimates to be produced for people living in Wales, where sample size might be too small under a proportionate stratification. To produce estimates representative of the GB population from such a disproportionate allocation, however, sample units from Wales would need to be downweighted to their correct population proportion.

A third complex design factor employed by most national probability samples is the use of post-survey weighting. Weighting is generally applied to correct for unequal selection probabilities and nonresponse bias. The main purpose of this weighting is to reduce bias in population estimates by upweighting population subgroups that are underrepresented and downweighting those that are overrepresented in the sample. A less desirable by-product of weighting, however, is that it can, when the variance of the weights is large, result in a loss of precision; that is, standard errors that are larger than they would be for unweighted estimates.

6.4.3 Complex designs and variance estimation

The net effect of clustering, stratification and weighting, therefore, is that the standard errors of these 'complex' sample designs tend to be different (smaller or larger, but usually larger) than those of an SRS. The difference in the precision of the estimates produced by a complex design relative to an SRS is known as the *design effect*. The design effect is the ratio of the actual variance, under the sampling method used, to the variance calculated under the assumption of simple random sampling. This number will obviously vary for different variables in the survey – some may be heavily influenced by design effects and others less so.

For cluster samples, the main components of the design effect are the *intraclass correlation* and the number of units within each cluster. The intraclass correlation is a statistical estimate of within-cluster homogeneity. It represents the probability that two units drawn randomly from the same cluster will have the same value on the variable in question, relative to two units drawn at random from the population as a whole. Thus, an intraclass correlation of 0.10 indicates that two units randomly selected from within the same cluster are 10% more likely to have the same value than are two randomly selected units in the population as a whole. Estimation of intraclass correlation is beyond the scope of this chapter, but it can be easily obtained from commercially available statistical software. The design effect is calculated as follows:

$$deff = 1 + rho\ (n - 1),$$

where *deff* is the design effect, *rho* is the intraclass correlation for the variable in question, and *n* is the size of the cluster (an average is taken when clusters differ in size). From this formula, we can see that the design effect increases as the cluster size (in most instances the number of addresses sampled within a postcode sector) increases, and as the intraclass correlation increases.

A somewhat more readily interpretable derivation of the design effect is the *design factor*, which is simply the square root of the design effect. The design factor effectively gives us an inflation factor for the standard errors obtained using a complex survey design. For example, a design factor of 2 indicates that the standard errors are twice as large as they would have been had the design been an SRS. The design factor can also be used to obtain the *effective sample size* which, as the name suggests, gives, for a complex survey design, the sample size that would have been required to obtain the same level of precision in an SRS.

In order to correctly estimate variance when analysing survey data with a complex design, two main statistical approaches are available: Taylor series approximation and balanced repeated replication (BRR). An alternative to BRR, based on the jackknife, can also be used to take account of these complex design factors (see Skinner *et al.*, 1989). An extended discussion of the properties of these estimators is beyond the scope of this chapter, but see Groves *et al.* (2004) for a detailed treatment. For the substantive analyst, however, the important thing to note is that many popular statistical software packages (such as SPSS and SAS) do not implement these procedures as standard. This means that, for a great many statistics routinely used by researchers, these packages produce standard error estimates as if they were taken from an SRS, ignoring any complex design factors. If there is significant within-cluster homogeneity on particular survey variables, if stratification has been used, or if any form of weighting has been applied during estimation, standard errors will, therefore, be biased.

6.4.4 Quota sampling

Quota sampling attempts to create a representative sample by specifying quotas, or targets, of particular types of people who need to be included to represent the population. As an example, let us assume we know that 50% of the population in a particular age group are female and that 16% of males and 14% of females are left-handed pen users. We want a sample that is representative of both sex and handedness: we decide on a sample size, say 100, and then set quotas. We need 50 males and 50 females. We also need to balance the handedness of respondents appropriately within the sexes, so we set four quotas as follows: 8 left-handed males (16% of 50), 42 right-handed males, 7 left-handed females (14% of 50) and 43 right-handed females.

Once the sample is defined, the researcher approaches people in the relevant age group, confirms their sex and asks them about handedness when using a pen. People become sample members as long as the quotas have not been filled. Once we have our seven left-handed females we reject any subsequent left-handed females who come along.

The great advantage of quota sampling is that a sample that looks something like the population in terms of key characteristics can be obtained very quickly and cheaply. No population listing is required; only information about the population characteristics with which to define quotas is needed. However, all sorts of selection biases may serve to render the sample unrepresentative of the target population. People who are not physically or temporally near the sampling point could never enter the sample. The researcher might only approach people who look as if they would be polite and co-operative. People who are not easily classified as male or female just by observation may be excluded by not being approached. If you have multiple levels of controls on the quotas (e.g. male left-handers over 60 with ginger hair) filling some quotas may prove very difficult.

6.5 SURVEY MODE

survey mode

An important decision which must be made before a sample can be drawn is the mode in which the survey is to be conducted. The **survey mode** relates to the way in which the questionnaire (or other survey instrument) is completed and the degree of interviewer involvement. The primary distinction in terms of mode is between whether the questionnaire is administered by an interviewer or is completed by the respondents themselves. Whether a survey is interviewer-administered or self-completion has a strong bearing on the response rate, the quality and quantity of data obtained and the overall cost of the survey.

Most interviewer-administered surveys now use personal computers to enter, store and transmit questionnaire data, which makes fieldwork more efficient and reduces keying and other data entry errors. The 'gold standard' in terms of survey mode is computer-assisted personal interview (CAPI) which achieves the highest response rates, obtains the highest-quality data but comes at the greatest monetary cost, as it requires an expensive human resource – interviewers. Computer-assisted telephone interviewing (CATI) is increasingly common in the UK. It achieves reasonably high response rates, though generally lower than in CAPI surveys, and the interview length is shorter than can be achieved in personal interview surveys. Because all interviews are conducted from a central location, costs are considerably lower than for face-to-face interview surveys. However, the speed with which data can be obtained is significantly faster for CATI than for other survey modes. On the downside, the introduction of call screening technology, the increase in multiple phone lines in residential properties and the widespread use of mobile phones (and increasing replacement of landlines) has made the job of the telephone researcher increasingly difficult.

Using a self-administration mode significantly reduces costs. However, response rates and the quality of data obtained are generally considerably lower when no interviewer is used. Until recently, postal surveys were practically the sole exemplar of self-administered surveys, but the past ten years has witnessed a rapid expansion of Internet-based survey research, offering a vast pool of potential respondents at lightning turnaround times and at vastly reduced cost, relative to other survey modes.

In addition, of course, the Internet is able to harness all the information technology and multimedia functions that are largely absent from phone and face-to-face interactions. There is the realistic possibility, for instance, that 'virtual interviewers' could administer questionnaires to respondents, tailored to each respondent's background and personal preferences, matching 'interviewer' and respondent in terms of race and sex, for example.

Yet, with all the potential benefits of the Web for survey research come many potential pitfalls. The relatively low penetration of Internet use within society as a whole means that representative samples are difficult, if not impossible, to achieve at present. Even with full population penetration, the lack of sampling frames or other ways of generating probability samples of Internet populations means that genuine statistical inference from Web surveys is still a long way off. Likewise the benefits of multimedia applications within online questionnaires are limited by the fact that many potential respondents will be viewing the instrument with low-end browsers and small-bandwidth modems.

6.6 SMALL-SAMPLE ISSUES

In common with lots of textbooks on sampling and survey design, I have stressed the desirability of getting a large sample. Generalizations about the population are likely to be more convincing to others when there is a well-drawn large sample. Large samples produce parameter estimates with small standard errors and increase the statistical power of your hypothesis tests (see Chapter 19). Studies done with small samples can yield ambiguous, non-significant results as you cannot usually tell whether the result was because the null hypothesis was true or because your sample was too small. You cannot turn this around and conclude that because your sample was small any effect you observe must therefore be 'significant', however tempting this might seem!

The realities of doing psychological research on many topics are such that getting large samples is simply not possible. Much clinical research on patients with specific complaints or disorders cannot obtain large samples as, thankfully, such groups are not large. Research on offenders with particular criminal histories (e.g. child murderers) is usually done on small samples as, again, mercifully, there are not lots of such offenders to study. Given this and the desirability of large samples, is such research therefore a waste of time?

Obviously the answer is 'no'. Insights gained from researching such topics can be very valuable and will often have important practical implications. Indeed, studies on single cases can be particularly useful (see Chapter 5), especially when the single individual is studied intensively. What is needed is a recognition that 'research' does not just mean experiments, big samples and lots of statistics. Some useful illustrative examples of important small-sample clinical research can be found in Powell and Adams (1993).

The use of inferential statistics such as t-tests and correlations (see Chapter 19) implies that hypotheses are being tested and that studies have been designed as 'fair' tests of these hypotheses. One of these criteria for 'fairness' is that you have a big enough sample to give you sufficient statistical power to make the results of such tests unambiguous. If you know in advance that your sample will be small then you should not place too much emphasis on statistical tests. It might be better to regard your study as exploratory or as contributing to a data-base that later researchers using meta-analysis (see Chapter 22) might merge together with similar studies. This increases the effective sample size, thereby allowing more powerful statistical testing. You should also remember that the magnitude of any differences or correlations you find (the effect sizes) are of importance separately from their statistical significance.

Studies with small samples may give indications of fruitful avenues for future research. If a phenomenon looks interesting in a small-scale project, funding agencies may be more inclined to put in the resources to allow the collection of data from a larger sample, perhaps by increasing the size of the catchment area or period of time available for data collection. A clinical study, for instance, may have had to be based on clients presenting themselves at a small number of clinics in a relatively short period. Extra resources, made available because of the promise of your initial study, may allow you to go to more clinics over a much longer period, thereby permitting the sampling of much more of the population of interest. Essentially this is to view small-sample work as a kind of pilot study.

Statistical inference and population parameter estimation are not everything, of course. Research using qualitative approaches such as focus groups and ethnographic methods are usually impractical on large samples and it is much more desirable to engage in theoretical sampling where the aim is to approach people who ought, on a priori grounds, to be the most informative. Here you want to get a large amount of information from people in the hope that it will be substantively more informative than what you might have obtained from a large survey.

What is crucial is to distinguish between samples that will be small because the population is hard to access, and samples that are small because not enough effort has been put into the study. Small-sample research, like any other kind, is only meaningful if it is carried out as rigorously as is reasonably possible.

6.7 CONCLUSION

This brief overview of survey sampling should give you some idea of the theory underlying statistical inference from sample to population, the main issues involved in drawing a random sample and some of the main pitfalls of the various kinds of design. The last decade has seen a growth in the number of psychologists involved in large-scale survey investigations, and this trend looks likely to continue. Surveys offer the potential to answer a range of research questions that have until now remained in the realm of speculation. Surveys are now more cost-effective than ever before and funding agencies are progressively more willing to invest in big surveys than at any time in the past. However, the value of such surveys will continue to depend crucially on good design and attention to the kinds of issues discussed here.

6.8 FURTHER READING

Most texts on survey and sampling issues tend to be orientated towards sociologists and other social scientists rather than specifically to psychologists. This should not prevent you reading them since the issues related to sociological data apply equally to psychological data. Moser and Kalton's (1971) text is widely admired as one of the most detailed yet accessible works on survey design and sampling. The more recent book by Groves *et al.* (2004) provides an accessible account of the fundamentals of survey sampling and survey methodology more generally.

PART 2
DATA GATHERING

7

Observational Methods

Rudi Dallos

7.1   Introduction
7.2   What is observational research?
7.3   Levels of observation: behaviour and talk
7.4   Observation and theoretical lenses
7.5   Deciding on what to observe – coding schemes
    7.5.1   *Coding sequences of behaviour*
7.6   Interpretative orientation to observation
7.7   Participant observation research
    7.7.1   *Collecting data*
    7.7.2   *Recording*
7.8   Validity
7.9   Conclusion
7.10   Further reading

AIMS

This chapter attempts to offer an overview of observational methods. It starts with an overview of four core features of observational research and considers these within related theoretical frameworks. It then goes on to outline, with examples from a variety of psychological research, some details of how different types of observation are conducted. The intention is to enable readers to understand and have insight into some techniques of doing observation and ways of coding different types of observational data. The chapter aims to show that observation inevitably involves an interpretative process. Therefore a guiding thread running through the chapter is the suggestion that the choice of focus of the observation, the observational methods employed, and the nature of the subsequent analysis are guided by the researcher's theoretical and personal lenses. Participant observational research is discussed as exemplifying aspects of an interpretative approach to observation. The chapter concludes with a consideration of issues of validity and reliability.

K ey terms

analytic induction	observer as participant
audit trail	paralinguistic
coding schemes	participant as observer
complete observer	participant observer
complete participant	self-reflection
going native	time event analysis
inter-rater reliability	time sampling
investigative journalism	video recording

7.1 INTRODUCTION

Why might we choose to engage in observational research? Salmon (2003) argues that we should select research methods based on the questions that we want to answer and adapt, combine or modify methods to give us the best possible ways of answering these. Our choice of research questions is in turn shaped by our research, personal and professional interests. My own work as a clinical psychologist involves the use of live observation and analysis of videos of family–therapist interactions as an integral part of the process of clinical formulation and intervention (Dallos & Draper, 2005). Arguably all clinicians and applied psychologists employ observation as part of their daily practice to guide day-to-day practice but also to contribute to a larger body of evidence and theory (Rustin, 2002). In addition, practitioners may engage in more formal observational studies to develop understanding or to test particular concepts. Observational research is in a sense ubiquitous and it may be helpful to recognize its importance in generating initial research ideas as well as its contribution to more formal research endeavours.

More broadly, observation is an essential human activity that helps us ensure our safety and survival and to select friends and intimate partners. The continuing popular interest in texts on non-verbal behaviour (Argyle, 1972; Morris, 2002; Beattie, 2003) and reality TV programmes also suggests that observations are of great fascination for many people and indicates that observational skills are fundamental to human activity and not just the province of psychologists. This also suggests that we need to adopt an approach to observational research which recognizes that psychological observation, unlike observation in the physical sciences, involves us making inferences about persons who are similarly engaged in making observations themselves, about the aims, intentions and interest of the researcher.

7.2 WHAT IS OBSERVATIONAL RESEARCH?

Observational research is a research method in its own right as well as being integrated into other kinds of research methods. A variety of research methods, such as interview studies, focus groups, experimental studies and clinical case studies, may include observational data. For example, observation may indicate participants' emotional states or how their actions are connected to aspects and changes in the social setting. Observation may reveal what people do, how they do it and how this is influenced by and in turn influences the social setting within which their actions take place.

Observational studies can broadly be conceptualized in terms of four core dimensions. Each of these dimensions can be seen as involving interpretative processes on behalf of the observer and those observed. Though the extent of this interpretation may vary, nevertheless we are invariably assigning meaning to what we observe, for example in what phenomenon we choose to observe and to which aspects of the phenomenon we choose to direct our attention (Box 7.1).

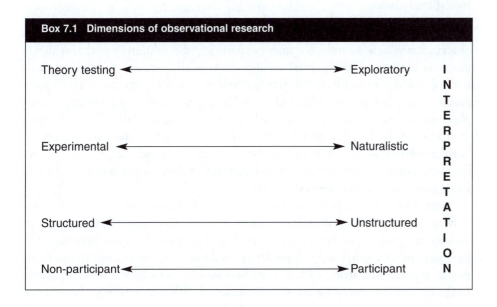

Box 7.1 Dimensions of observational research

Theory testing–exploratory. Firstly, observational studies can be conceptualized in terms of the extent to which the intention is to test existing theory by examining what people do in various situations and circumstances. For example, early social psychological studies explored the broad theoretical proposition that people display conformity in situations when instructed to do so by apparent figures of authority. Observation of participants' behaviour in the famous Milgram (1983) studies more than confirmed this proposition in that they also discovered that people could be persuaded to apply apparently lethal dosages of electric shock to experimental 'subjects' when requested to do so and reassured by a 'scientist' authority figure. Importantly, studies such as these revealed not only what people would do in certain situations but also observational indications of how people were feeling in terms of their hesitations, non-verbal behaviour and what features of the situation were influential, such as the experimenter's white coat as a 'badge of authority'.

In contrast, observation can be employed in a more descriptive way to explore different situations. This can be as a form of 'reconnaissance' – exploratory observation to generate ideas which can be researched more formally when some potential key features have been identified. As with other forms of exploratory research, such as interpretative interview studies, the aims may be to develop understanding in an inductive process (Strauss & Corbin, 1998; see Chapter 17, this volume). A good example of such research was conducted by Marsh, Rosser and Harré (1978) in their exploratory observations of the behaviour of fans at football matches.

Experimental–naturalistic. This dimension connects with a contrast between observation which is conducted under experimental conditions and that which is more naturalistic. Experimental conditions typically impose various types of control in order to facilitate the development of causal explanations. This might involve observing people subjected to similar experiences. An interesting example is the Strange Situation (Ainsworth, Blehar, Waters & Wall, 1978) employed in studies of mother–infant attachment. This consists of a standardized procedure involving several separations between mothers and their infants, and specific aspects of their behaviour, such as signs of distress and patterns of comforting on reunion, are the key measures.

Observation has also been widely used to describe behaviours in 'natural' situations which are contrasted with situations, such as laboratory studies, which are seen as 'artificial' or not belonging to 'real life'. Naturalistic studies have varied in the extent to which they employ predetermined categories, or attempt to test theories as opposed to starting with a more non-specific, 'let's have a look' approach. Examples include observing the play activities of children in school playgrounds (Robson, 2002), psychiatric institutions (Goffman, 1961) and the functioning of families in their own home setting (Vetere & Gale, 1987). The latter study involved the researchers 'living in' with families over a period of several months to observe their actions, for example in various subgroupings – as individuals, couples, parents and children. Naturalistic observation covers a wide range of methods, from a relatively 'outside' perspective where the observer does not engage with the people being observed to a more participant position where the observation involves

going native becoming involved – **going native** to understand the situation from the inside.

There is a wide variety of types of observational research, and the distinction between experimental/artificial and naturalistic is not a straightforward one. For example, it has been argued that even in experimental situations long-term relationships, such as in couples, families and work groups, will settle into and display their well-established patterns. In effect, the 'naturalness' of the relationship can extend into whatever situation they are in. However, this is an important research question, for example whether a group, such as a family, does change its dynamics according to different contexts – at home, shopping, in the therapy unit, at a parents' evening at school, and so on. It can also be possible to gain various forms of natural control of variables in naturalistic situations, for example observing tasks which have a repetitive structure, such as committee meetings, or where certain events occur, for example, greetings and leave taking at airports or railway stations. Advocates of naturalistic research argue that behaviour is context-specific and observation must involve close attention to the parameters of different situations, including cultural definitions. For example, there are important cultural variations in what are regarded as appropriate as opposed to inappropriate ways of behaving in situations such as shops, weddings, parties and with family members. Simply observing behaviour without an understanding of these contextual meanings might only offer a very partial understanding of the phenomenon we wish to explore.

A significant development in observational research has come about through the widespread availability of **video recording** facilities. These are now so widely available that it is possible to incorporate self-recording by participants. For example, we can employ video diaries of people in the home situation or leave video cameras in the situation we wish to observe for extended periods, allowing participants to acclimatize to their presence.

Structured–unstructured. Structured observational studies sometimes employ coding of particular types of behaviour. These may be larger meaningful units (such as an interactional episode) or types of actions (such as showing solidarity or hostility), or more minute aspects of behaviour (such as expressions or movements). A widely used form of structured observation comes from studies of group decision-making processes which employ a taxonomy of different types of communications (Bales, 1950; Ellis, 1993). Observers are trained in the use of these systems and code how different members of a group contribute to the group decision-making process, for example in terms of *task* as opposed to *socio-emotional*-orientated actions, or how the pattern of such communications alters as the group dynamics develop over time.

It is also possible to approach observational research without clearly developed structures for observing events. At the extreme this has included ethnographic studies where the coding schemes are developed as the research progresses (Hammersley & Atkinson, 1995; Gomm, Hammersley, & Foster, 2000). Related to this is the idea that the researcher, though starting with an unstructured approach, can, in collaboration with participants, decide what are the important features, events, actions or sequences that should be recorded.

Non-participant–participant. Observational research varies in terms of the role adopted by the researcher in the situation being observed. Junker (1972) described the social roles of the **participant observer** along a continuum with the complete participant and the complete observer at either extreme, and the participant as observer and observer as participant in intermediate positions (see Box 7.2). At one extreme the researcher actively takes part in the setting and at the other extreme tries to remain detached and objective. The participant

video recording

participant observer

observer working in naturalistic settings may find herself moving in and out of these roles, along the continuum of relative involvement, even though she might emphasize one of these roles (see Vetere & Gale, 1987).

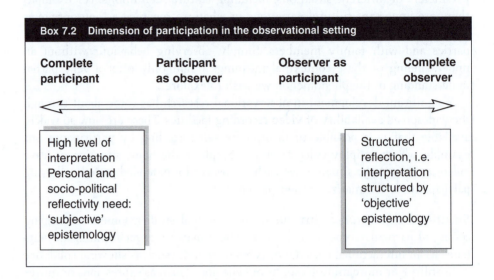

Box 7.2   Dimension of participation in the observational setting

Complete participant	Participant as observer	Observer as participant	Complete observer

High level of interpretation Personal and socio-political reflectivity need: 'subjective' epistemology

Structured reflection, i.e. interpretation structured by 'objective' epistemology

complete participant

The **complete participant** is totally involved with the group of persons under study, and conceals her observational activity from the group. This allows the observer to act as a member of an 'in-group', perhaps sharing private information that would not have been disclosed to an identifiable observer. The advantage is that the observer develops an intimate acquaintance with a particular social role, and has more access to the thoughts, feelings and intentions of the participants. However, there are disadvantages – for example, ethically, our codes of conduct disallow observation without the consent of the participants, and we could be open to accusations of spying. Alongside this is the problem for the observer of subsuming her own identity in order to join the group. Managing relationships in the group, such as alliances, can draw the researcher into being deceptive about how she is feeling and thinking. In turn, opportunities for observation outside the 'in-group' may be limited. Such studies have considerable overlaps with investigative journalism and there have been powerful investigations, for example exploring racist attitudes in the police force. A classic piece of research is the study by Rosenhan (1973) consisting of researchers 'faking' mental illness in order to be admitted to a psychiatric institution and subsequently observing the behaviour of staff in the unit and reflecting on their own experiences. A more recent replication has also been conducted (Slater, 2004).

participant as observer

The **participant as observer** already has or takes on a meaningful social role within the group under study. The role is characterized by relative involvement with the group, for example, Jane Gilgun observed her clinical multi-disciplinary team colleagues' decision-making processes, whilst acting as a member of the team herself (Gilgun, Daly & Handel, 1992). Observational activity is not wholly concealed, but observers often find the group members evaluate them on the basis of their group participation, rather than on their status as an observer.

The advantages include familiarity with a particular role within the group, with increased understanding of group processes from this more subjective and sympathetic position. There is relative freedom to observe within the group, although observational activity may be constrained by the demands of the particular role adopted within the group. Disadvantages include limited access to some private information, with more time and energy spent participating than observing! Another example can be found in the classic work of Whyte (1943) which looked at life on the streets in Italian slums in the USA.

The **observer as participant** joins the group with the expressed intention to observe. Her role as observer is characterized by relative detachment from the group under study, with her objective and empathic positioning emphasized. Advantages include access to a wide range of material, even private information if it becomes known that the observer can maintain anonymity for the group members. The observer is in many ways freer to ask questions in this role, unrestrained by the role demands of participation. The observer as participant is less active than the participant as observer. The latter carries responsibility to participate within the group and initiates activity, whereas the former tends to be more reactive to the initiatives of the group members. Disadvantages of this role can include constraints on confidentiality when reporting, and a sense of marginality since the observer is only partly a part of the world of the group members. The observer needs to be mindful of the need to maintain a degree of even-handedness or neutrality relative to internal alliances and factions within the group. This can be an emotionally demanding task, particularly if the observational study separates the observer from their own social group and sources of social support and affirmation of personal identity. An example of this role can be found in the work of Vetere, in her ecological studies of family life (Vetere & Gale, 1987).

observer as participant

The **complete observer** role is characterized by detachment from the group under study, with no direct contact with group members during the observational work. This is approximated in some clinical work, as well as when activity is viewed from behind a one-way screen, in observations of mother–infant interactions, and in non-declared observation, such as Michael Argyle's (1972) work observing rituals of greeting and leave taking at major international airports. It is possible to use pre-prepared coding schemes, and to subject them to intra-coder and inter-coder reliability studies. Another example can be found in viewing videotapes of clinical work. There are no risks of observational reactivity, but the observer is never *in* the situation, with no opportunity to share in the experiential world of the participants.

complete observer

7.3 LEVELS OF OBSERVATION: BEHAVIOUR AND TALK

Researchers contemplating observational research frequently start with questions of behaviour, what people do, their actions, movements, expressions and gestures. But, apart from young infants and those with a severe learning disability or speech impairment, people's actions are usually accompanied by talk. In most situations, then, we will have a choice to make about whether we in some way separate out the talk from the behaviour or attempt a form of analysis which combines the two. The question applies the other way around as well: much current qualitative research is concerned with analysis of interview material or various forms of text from talk. But talk is accompanied by behaviour and shows many important **para-**

paralinguistic   **linguistic** features, such as the rate of talk, tone, hesitations, pitch, voice tremor, laughter and tears. Hence observational research can be an important accompaniment to interview and other forms of language-based research. It can also be argued (Dallos & Vetere, 2005) that in clinical research and practice such combination of verbal and observational research is essential. Box 7.3 summarizes the potential types of data involved in observational research. We can distinguish between observation of individual pieces of behaviour and actions on the one hand, and sequences of joint behaviours on the other. As we move from relatively objective pieces of behaviour to more complex patterns the level of interpretation in assigning behaviour to particular categories becomes greater. However, the analysis of behaviours, even small relatively uncontested pieces of behaviour, remains a complex interpretative activity. For example, a fleeting look or gesture may be extremely meaningful in an interaction.

Box 7.3   Levels of observation

- Games, roles and scripts

- Interactional episodes/circularities

- Individual behavioural actions

- Micro-processes – segments of actions, e.g. gestures, non-verbal movements

INCREASING LEVEL OF INFERENCE INVOLVED IN CODING

Observational research has been employed in areas where we have to rely on observation because language is absent. For example, with young infants we cannot use methods such as interviews to ask them about what they are doing and their intentions. There is a wide range of fascinating studies, for example Brazelton and Cramer's (1991) observational studies of mother–infant interactions which revealed that attunement of actions and mutual gaze at objects and patterns of smiling develop early in infancy. There have also been studies of children's interactions in school settings, for example play indicating patterns of friendship and gender differences (Robson, 2002).

7.4 OBSERVATION AND THEORETICAL LENSES

All observation can be seen to take place through theoretical lenses. In psychodynamic theory all behaviours and actions that can be seen are regarded as manifestations of dynamic inner processes. For example, they represent attempts to meet basic needs and reveal fundamental internal conflicts, particularly relating to needs to satisfy sexual urges, express hostility and ensure safety. Importantly, when a psychologist from a psychodynamic standpoint undertakes observational research he or she is looking for evidence, such as behavioural indications of such internal struggles. We direct our attention to particular behaviours as opposed to others and some behaviours, for example laughing or blushing, may be seen as particularly significant in revealing sexual desires. Observation from a behavioural perspective, in contrast, involves an emphasis on behaviour in terms of frequency, intensity and the context in terms of stimuli, that may have evoked the behaviour, and contingencies, such as rewards or punishments, that appear to increase or decrease the likelihood of the behaviour occurring again. So, added to the behaviour itself is its location in time and its association in relation to other events. This includes looking for patterns over time. Developmental psychologists have looked for and observed differences in how much infants look at different combinations of visual materials, suggesting that infants have a predisposition for patterns or schemas that look like faces. In this way observation of behaviour is employed to provide evidence about potential mental states, such as interest and attention. Systemic approaches (Dallos & Draper, 2005; Watzlawick, Beavin & Jackson, 1967; Watzlawick, 1964) look for patterns of interconnected actions in families in terms of behaviour but also in terms of patterns of communication such as who talks most, interruptions and manner of talking. Early research also inspired exploration of the links between communication patterns, such as incongruities and development of different types of psychological problems (Bateson, 1972; Dallos & Draper, 2005).

The theoretical perspectives underpinning the observational research guides what we choose to look for, what we attend to rather than ignore, and also what meaning we assign to what we have observed. Observation, like any form of psychological research, has to be at least partly reductionist. We cannot observe absolutely everything because reality is too complex. The point of psychological theory is to make the observation and analysis manageable, but at the same time a core issue is that we do not want to ignore what may be potentially important. As psychology has developed there have been different positions on what is important to observe, and the recent inclusion of social constructionism in psychology emphasizes the need to include a recognition that people, the objects of our observations, are themselves involved in observing and interpreting their own and others' actions.

In Box 7.1, it is suggested that all varieties of observation involve an interpretative component. This is in contrast to a more widely accepted view that exploratory, naturalistic, participant and unstructured approaches to observation fall into a broadly qualitative, and therefore interpretative, approach, and theory-testing, experimental, non-participant and structured approaches fall into a quantitative, and therefore more objective and less interpretative, approach. Though this can be a convenient way of organizing a discussion of observational methods it can be argued that all of the methods can be viewed within an interpretative framework since what we choose to observe and what sense or meaning we give to our observations involves interpretation. In observation which is non-participant, experimental and employs quantitative measures, it is still the case that interpretation is involved in where the researcher directs her gaze, what behaviours are not regarded as important, and what interpretations are given to the data that are gathered.

7.5 DECIDING ON WHAT TO OBSERVE – CODING SCHEMES

A starting point for any observational study is a consideration of what we will be observing. As discussed earlier, this choice will fall on a continuum between being driven explicitly by attempts to test theory and a more open exploratory, 'let's have a look', approach. The schemes that observational researchers employ are called **coding schemes**

coding schemes. These may vary from the use of broad and flexible categories to being highly structured and involving quantification. Even with the use of the latter the underlying research questions can be broader and exploratory. For example, the research question might be about whether there is any observational evidence of discernible differences in how co-operatively as opposed to competitively boys and girls interact in a school playground.

An example of such a study, referred to earlier, was that of Ainsworth *et al.* (1978) which explored attachment patterns exhibited by infants towards their parents. This employed a structured experimental paradigm – the Strange Situation, which is a standardized situation in which infants are subjected to periods of brief separation from their mothers and also to brief interactions with a stranger. These sequences are videotaped and subsequently analysed, with different observers trained in the coding scheme (trained to be 'reliable') independently analysing the interactions and subsequently arriving at agreed codings in terms of patterns defined as secure, avoidant, anxious/ambivalent or extreme/disorganized. Initially these studies employed live observation and note-taking, but this has been developed and elaborated with the availability of sophisticated video-recording facilities. The fine-grained analysis made available by video recording has resulted in increasing differentiation of the attachment behaviours and in the patterns becoming elaborated into a wider range of classifications (Crittenden, 1998).

More generally, Robson (2002) suggests a broad set of guidelines for developing coding schemes.

1　Non-verbal behaviours – bodily movements not associated with language, such as gestures, expressions and rate of movement.
2　Spatial behaviours, for example, proximity and the extent to which individuals move towards or away from one another.
3　Extra-linguistic behaviours, including. speaking rate, loudness and interruptions.
4　Linguistic behaviours, such as the content of talk as well as features such as detail and coherence.

Here we can see that, for example the question of co-operative behaviour can be coded initially in terms of actions which are predominantly behaviours, through to more complex aspects such as the form and content of speech. The different levels can be seen as complementing each other, and differences and incongruities between them as offering points for further consideration. For example, it may be interesting that boys and girls differ in the level of insight and awareness they have about their own and each other's behaviour in this situation or in what aspects they chose to talk about.

The coding scheme that is employed will depend on the research questions guiding it. In some cases there may already be a coding scheme available. If the research is specifically driven by a particular theoretical approach, such as attachment theory, then it may be felt necessary to employ the existing observational system in order that findings are compatible with and comparable to the existing research literature. However, there will be many occasions when either there is no existing system or, where one does exist, modifications need to be made to it for the specific purposes of the research. Broadly, coding systems can be seen to contain a range of issues that need to be taken into account.

Objective–subjective.　The extent to which it is possible to think about the data as objective (e.g. counting specific instances of a behaviour), as opposed to necessarily requiring some subjective interpretation from the observer (e.g. that an action indicates 'criticism' or 'hostility').

Focused–unfocused.	A consideration of the extent to which the observation will have clear parameters about what we look for and what to exclude from the observation. For example, in some observational studies of group decision-making the individual actions of the participants were the focus but other possibilities, such as patterns of interactions between the participants or the impact of the setting, were not included.
Explicit–implicit.	Coding systems may vary in terms of how clearly they define what behaviours and actions are to be included in a category.
Context dependence.	The definition of the category may shift with different contexts. For example, in research on communication in couples the meaning of any specific communication may be defined by the context of the previous one – previous communication could indicate that a given utterance was a neutral statement or a sarcastic negative jibe (see Box 7.4).
Exhaustive–specific.	This is the extent to which coding attempts cover all events as opposed to being more specific in its aims. In some cases attempts to be exhaustive may involve a large residual category (e.g. in attachment research this came to be the 'disorganized' category).

7.5.1 Coding sequences of behaviour

Frequently in observational studies the interest is in exploring sequences of behaviour and how they shift and change over time. Observations may include various counting schemes to record how frequently and when an event has occurred. For example, in a behavioural analysis we may want to code examples of smiling by a member of staff towards residents in a unit. The event coding will count each instance of smiling and then also count the behaviours that follow, to see whether there is a change in the frequency of the behaviours following the smiling to suggest that these are functioning as a rewards. Another form of analysis over time might be concerned with changes in states, for example in emotions from happy to sad, angry and so on.

Time is a key element in such recording and may be employed as a marker or map to check when the events occur. An example of a coding system that is informed by theory and also an open coding system is the work of Gottman (1982) on relationships in couples. This also employs standardized observational scenarios, in this case asking couples to engage in certain types of interactions, such as a discussion of areas of conflict. Gottman combines his observations with direct physiological measures to assess levels of stress and arousal. The research attempted to explore whether couples who are dissatisfied with their relationship display more patterns of reciprocal emotional negative reactions. His analysis includes observing sequences of verbal and non-verbal behaviours and the identification of episodes of reciprocal negative reactions (see Boxes 7.4 and 7.5).

Box 7.4   Observing talk and actions in relationships

H: You'll never guess who I saw today. Frank Dugan.
W: So, *big deal,* you saw Frank Dugan.
H: Don't you remember I had that argument with him last week?
W: I forgot.
H: Yeah.
W: So, I'm sorry I forgot, all right?
H: So it is a big deal to see him.
W: So, what do you want me to do, jump up and down?
H: Well, how was *your* day, honey?
W: Oh brother, here we go again.
H: (pause) You don't have to look at me that way.
W: So what d'ya want me to, do, put a paper bag over my head?

Source: Gottman (1982: 114)

Box. 7.5   Time event analysis

Husband	P		P		N		N		N
Wife		N		X		N		N	
Time (secs)	0	5	10	15	20	25	30	35	40

P   Positive emotional action
N   Negative emotional action
X   Neutral

In this brief example, the coding system in Box 7.5 is mapping the emotional valence of the conversational turns in Box 7.4. We can then examine how the relationship unfolds over time. It is possible to see that the husband's first positive (P) greeting appears to be met with a negative (N) from his wife. This is followed by another (P) response from the husband, in turn responded to by a neutral (X) response from his wife – 'I forgot' (we might need to observe the non-verbal tone of this communication, though, to be able to judge whether it was neutral or, if said in a sarcastic tone, negative). From this point on they appear to move towards a mutually escalating negative pattern.

time event analysis   In the above example of **time event analysis** the events are coded within time scales of five seconds. An alternative is to record the exact time that events occur. For longer periods of observation one method is to employ time sampling so that, for example, an observation of five minutes is carried out every hour. It is important to clarify whether such sampling distorts the observation. For example, some important events may occur very infrequently and be completely missed or occur regularly in the periods between the time samples.

Of course, the data from such sequence analysis can be compared, for example, with the observer's impressions of events from a more narrative observation and the participants' own insights.

7.6 INTERPRETATIVE ORIENTATION TO OBSERVATION

In the rest of this chapter we can look further at approaches where the focus of observational research is a concern to gain a picture of the underlying meanings that actions hold for the participants. This orientation can be seen to be based on a constructivist and social constructionist approach to research (Smith, 2003; Kelly, 1955; Strauss & Corbin, 1998). The point of observation then becomes to observe what people are doing and, importantly, to try to understand why they are behaving as they are. Central to this process is an acknowledgement that this involves a reflexive, interpretative process. It has been argued that observational research in psychology has been guided by notions of science drawn from the physical sciences, especially Newtonian ideas of certainty and predictability. However, even in the inanimate world of physics these have been questioned by theories of 'relativity' which argue that we must take into account the position of the observer and the principle of uncertainty according to which the very process of observation transforms what we are observing:

> Using Einstein's own homespun example of playing table tennis on a moving train, the answer to the question 'How fast was the ball travelling after you hit it?' Has a multitude of answers between which one cannot choose until the question 'Relative to what?' is answered. By analogy, abundant empirical evidence exists to show that the same is true for psychological measurement. (Davies, 2004: 692)

Such relativistic questions become infinitely more complex when we enter into the field of observation of human action.

- Observation as active vs. passive process
- Construction vs. representation of reality
- Theory held in parentheses
- Relativity of observing position acknowledged
- Role of language in interpretation and focus

Observation can be seen as an active process in that what we look for is actively guided by the theoretical lens that we bring to the research. This fits with the second theme in Box 7.6 regarding observational research as construction as opposed to representation. We create or impose meanings on what we observe, in that there is bound to be an element of selection, firstly, in what we look for and, secondly, in how we then analyse our data. The observation can also try to explicitly test theory or alternatively to hold theory in 'parentheses' – to keep it in the background so that theory develops from the data rather being imposed on it. Related to this is the important issue that the observer is invariably bringing his or her assumptions to the process of observation. Even if we attempt to keep our formal theory in the background it is very difficult to remove all our personal assumptions and experiences in order to eliminate 'bias'. Instead, we can recognize and utilize our own assumptions and make these visible in the analysis by revealing our critical reflections on our interpretative processes. Finally, we need to acknowledge the powerful influence of language, and the cultural assumptions that language contains, and which are liable to colour our observations. Our observational data will usually be transformed into language and this process, as well as our interpretations, will in turn be influenced by culturally shared discourses. In addition, these discourses shape the beliefs and actions of the people we are observing, and in order to understand their behaviour we need to take this into account.

7.7 PARTICIPANT OBSERVATION RESEARCH

Earlier the distinction was drawn between participant and non-participant research. Participant research can consist of the researcher as a 'complete participant' who is completely immersed and part of the situation being observed, or a less extreme form of immersion, the 'participant as observer'. Such participant observational methods exemplify many features of an interpretative approach to observation. They recognize that the observation involves a subjective process on the part of the observer in that she utilizes her own experience, thoughts, feelings and actions in the situation as important sources of data. The approach also emphasizes that interpretation is a vital component of the gathering of the data and subsequent analysis. Furthermore, often the research adopts an exploratory approach in which, although there will be some guiding questions or propositions, these are seen to evolve during the process of the research study.

Robson (2002) helpfully suggests that the process of conducting participant observation can be seen as involving an orientation to gathering data which **analytic induction** involves a form of **analytic induction.** He argues that the researcher can helpfully adopt an active approach in which, rather than becoming bogged down in a sea of details, she can proceed more on the basis of 'progressive hypothesizing'. This can be seen to consist of a number of steps.

1 Putting forward a rough definition of the phenomenon of interest. This is supported in turn by developing an initial hypothetical explanation of the phenomenon.
2 Studying a situation in the light of the hypothesis, to determine whether or not the hypothesis fits.
3 Checking whether the hypothesis fits the evidence, if it does not then either the hypothesis must be reformulated, or the phenomenon to be explained must be redefined so that the phenomenon is excluded.
4 This is repeated with a second situation. Confidence in your hypothesis increases with the number of situations fitting the evidence. Each negative one requires either a redefinition or reformulation.

This ensures an active and recursive loop between formulation of the phenomenon being observed and the process of gathering data.

Some preliminary reconnaissance can be helpful, for example to assist the researcher in finding ways of joining the social setting that is the focus of the study. This can help the researcher avoid making errors, such as appearing to differ from other people's opinions or routines, or requiring so much guidance and information as to become a burden on the members. Usually we gain access by making contact and forming a relationship with one or more members of a group, and it can be an important issue who these members are, whether they are representative of the group, their relationships with the other members, and so on. Often a way in is to have a pre-existing relationship with one or more members of a group or setting. The process of immersion can also be complex – for example, initially we might become closer to some members of a setting and sometimes, without being aware of doing so, communicate some level of approval or disapproval for what we observe to be going on. For the complete participant this is difficult since to fully participate does mean to become actively and emotionally engaged, otherwise we might be seen as 'uptight', 'snooty', 'distant' or 'uncaring' about what happens. Where more emphasis is placed on the observer part of the role, this can become easier but at the cost perhaps of losing some of the experiential data about what it feels like to be engaged in their processes.

The observer needs to invest energy in maintaining the observational roles, possibly at some personal cost, and to negotiate a planned withdrawal from the group under study. If the observer has spent significant time with the group under observation, she may have developed a sense of commitment to the group and may wish to keep in touch subsequently. Research supervision is helpful in identifying responsibilities to the group under study and the less helpful breaches of roles and overstepping of responsibilities within the group.

7.7.1 Collecting data

The process of gathering information in participant observation research can be seen as analogous to good **investigative journalism**. An important difference with research is that we will go beyond the description to develop a set of explanatory concepts and connections to psychological theory. For participant observation research this involves a recursive movement between gathering objective and subjective information. As well as collecting details of who is doing what, where and with whom, we need to gather data about what they might be feeling and thinking, judged by what they say and their behaviours. Alongside this we need to gather information about our own reflections, how we feel and think about what we are seeing going on around us.

investigative journalism

We can identify a variety of types of data that we may use in our observation (see Box 7.7). Initially the emphasis is on description, how things are done rather than why events occur. In practice it is very difficult to separate these, and the observer has to work hard to keep a wide focus and not rush to causal formulations. Especially in participant observation, the researcher is also likely to become involved in conversations in which participants may offer their ideas about the reasons behind people's actions and what they think is going on. Moving down this list, it is possible to see that the level of inference required from the observer increases, especially in terms of ideas about what the goals and feelings of the participants might be.

Box 7.7	Basic elements of descriptive observation
Space	layout of the physical setting: rooms, outdoor spaces, etc.
Actors	the names and relevant details of the people involved
Activities	the various activities of the actors
Objects	physical elements, furniture, etc.
Acts	specific individual actions
Events	particular occasions, e.g. meetings
Time	the sequence of events
Goals	what actors are attempting to accomplish
Feelings	emotions in particular contexts

It is also important to recognize the variety of processes that may shape the data that we gather.

Selective attention – invariably we will focus more on some aspects of the situation we are observing than others. Our attention is guided by our interests and our preconceptions but also due to the basic fact that our capacity is limited and we cannot attend to and take in everything. However, we need to strike a balance in participant observation between focusing our attention and staying open to potentially important information. To take a simple example, we need to be in a position where we can see people's faces and pay attention to what the non-speaking participants may be doing.

Selective memory and forgetting – events fade in memory rapidly and we are likely to remember events in terms of our well-established interests and beliefs which may distort events. It helps, therefore, if we write up observational notes quickly and use cues and memory prompts: sometimes these can be a shorthand for particular episodes or visual cues. These can serve as associative prompts to help us recall and fill out details when we write up full notes following the observation.

Selective encoding – related to selective attention and memory, we may engage in selectively recording events. Often this can also involve a tendency, often implicit, to form interpretations from our initial observations. Though, as argued earlier, this is an inevitable psychological process, it is important to stay open to multiple interpretations so that we do not exclude data or narrow our gaze prematurely. To take a common example, we are likely to note unusual or different events, such as confrontations, but ignore periods of agreement or co-operative action and, importantly, how this is achieved.

7.7.2 Recording

Sometimes researchers take audio or video recordings of their participant observation sessions. In some situations this is relatively straightforward – for example, in the practice of family therapy the sessions are routinely recorded. Hence, it is a simple matter subsequently to analyse videotapes at leisure and even for the researcher, who may have been part of the session, to reflect on her feelings and actions during the process. It is also possible to engage in a collaborative analysis and recording by watching the tape together with members of the family – see Elliott (1986) on the subject of structured process recall.

However, there will be many situations where video or audio recording is not feasible, and the recording of information may be more complex. For example, where the researcher is fully a participant, there may be pressure to engage in some form of deception so that the process of recording is hidden. An option here is to regularly remove oneself from the situation and engage in some note-taking – for example, by retreating to the toilet or leaving the room for a drink. However, even short durations place huge demands on the researcher's memory.

Important details are quickly forgotten and selective processes may mean that some important features are overlooked. If possible, note-taking on the spot is preferable, but this is more feasible if the researcher's role as observer is recognized by the group. The question arises, though, that the group processes may have been altered by the participants' awareness of the presence of the researcher.

Another variation on data gathering is **time sampling**, where recording is conducted at particular intervals. This can also be conducted with video recording so that the camera is timed to go off at certain periods during the day. The sampling may be driven by theoretical considerations, such as wanting to observe events at particular parts of the day, such as when people meet in the morning, in committee meetings, break times and endings. Or it may be intended to gain a picture of how events and activities vary over the day to offer an overall profile of activities.

time sampling

Box 7.8   Types of data recording

1   Video recording
2   Intermittent recording – breaks from the observation to write up what was observed
3   Continuous – partly hidden or open note-taking
4   Time sampling – notes taken at regular periods
5   Self-reflection following or during the observation
6   Talking with participants
7   Gathering observations from participants following the observation

---

Box 7.8 illustrates the range of different recording methods for participant observation. Points 5–7 in particular relate to attempts to gather levels of meaning in the observation. **Self-reflection** can provide important information about how it felt to be in the situation, including the emotional atmosphere and communication patterns. However, if this recording occurs too long after the observation, the observer's immediate responses may become smoothed out or interpreted within her framework so that important features experienced at the time become minimized or forgotten. Talking with participants is similarly important in order to gain understandings of their intentions and feelings. However, it can also help focus on events, or some important details that the observer may have missed. Again the timing is important since retrospective accounts may be filtered by the participant's beliefs and defences so that important actions may be ignored, forgotten or their significance minimized.

self-reflection

7.8 VALIDITY

inter-rater reliability

There are broadly two approaches to the issue of validity. Researchers adopting the more structured, theory-testing experimental paradigm employ traditional measures of validity and reliability. For such researchers, therefore, coding schemes must be reliable. This typically involves questions of **inter-rater reliability** based on agreement between different observers using the system to independently code a situation. Frequently this involves a period of training in the use of the system to build observational skills with the method. Reliability can also be offered by observations over time – for example, repetitions of an attachment observation to check if the same classification is derived. The observation scheme can in some circumstances be divided up to offer intra-coding reliability by comparing one part of the coding scheme against another. Various measures exist for calculating reliability effects – for example, inter-rater agreement can be calculated as a percentage agreement in assignation to categories. This can be further analysed statistically employing statistical measures of agreement such as Cohen's kappa (Cohen, 1988; Robson, 2002). There are various 'threats to validity' such as reactivity effects in how the observer's presence may influence the results. In addition, there can be an 'observer drift' in that the observers may come to use certain categories more than others; this may be due to their coming to see what they expect or, alternatively, there may be a shift through a learning effect, so that there is a greater differentiation between observations later in the research.

audit trail

In interpretative orientations to observation there are different questions regarding validity and reliability. These resemble the general questions for qualitative research in adopting an interpretative perspective in which it is recognized that the data are derived through an interpretative lens. One way to increase validity is to offer an **audit trail** – a clear and visible account of the process of the observational research. This will include personal reflections of the impact of the situation on the observer, and details of the analysis of the data. Included in this may be prior knowledge and experience that the observer brings to the study. Interpretative orientations to observational studies can also incorporate inter-observer analysis. It is possible to have several participant observers in a setting or, with the use of videotapes, to conduct independent analyses which can then be compared. The research also needs to make clear and visible how it moves from data collection to the subsequent analysis. Like textual analyses (see Smith, 2003) this can include material to support the analysis, such as segments of field notes, sections of videotape, descriptions of sequences of action, pieces of visual material showing the positions and movements of participants, and so on. The observation may also be supported by accounts from the participants – member validation. Where videotapes are available, this can be done directly with a collaborative analysis of sequences. Finally, as with other forms of research, validity can be enhanced by employing other sources of data or methods of research (triangulation). Observations can be complemented by an interview study, case notes or questionnaires.

7.9 CONCLUSION

Observational research has a long history in psychological research. It has been suggested that it is possible to see observational research as a ubiquitous activity that is a necessary component of other forms of research. It can be extremely useful in generating ideas for psychological research, but is important in its own right for exploring a wide range of important phenomena. It raises a fundamental question for psychology in relation to the need to explore what people do as opposed to what they may say they do, as in interview studies. Importantly, it has been suggested that all forms of observational research involve an interpretative component. This features in what we choose to look for, what categories we decide to employ and how we make sense of our data. It has been argued in this chapter that whether our ways of collecting data employ relatively objective structured observational methods, or use of self in participant observation, at the end of the day an interpretative component is involved. Hence, this chapter argues for a position regarding observation which embraces an interpretative stance and thus encourages a more flexible approach which can help to integrate theory-driven and exploratory approaches to observation.

7.10 FURTHER READING

Barker, Pistrang and Elliott's (2002) text is an excellent general introduction to research methods in clinical situations, with good, accessible overviews of observational methods. Sapsford and Jupp's (1996) is a useful textbook prepared for Open University undergraduate and postgraduate courses (see especially the chapter by Foster, pp. 57–93). Willig's (2001) work is a sophisticated but engaging overview of qualitative methodology, with excellent examples of applications. For a highly readable general text which weaves together both qualitative and quantitative approaches in the context of conducting flexible and applicable research, see Robson's (2002); this has a useful overview of observational approaches. Finally, Smith's (2003) text provides a comprehensive overview of qualitative research methods, which is especially clear in outlining interpretative approaches to research.

8

Psychophysiological Methods

Paul Sowden and Paul Barrett

8.1   Introduction
8.2   The principal areas of physiological data acquisition
   8.2.1   Muscle activity
   8.2.2   Sweat gland activity
   8.2.3   Eye movements – pupillary response
   8.2.4   Cardiac response, blood pressure and blood volume
   8.2.5   Respiration
   8.2.6   Electrical potentials of the brain
8.3   Quantifying biosignal data
   8.3.1   Level of measurement
   8.3.2   Hardware, signal processing and data volume
   8.3.3   Designing the experiment and choosing parameters to measure
8.4   Conclusion
8.5   Further reading

AIMS

This chapter aims to provide the reader with an understanding of the breadth of possibilities in psychophysiological work. The tone of this chapter is less discursive and more didactic than many of the other chapters in this book. It is intended to whet the appetite of those readers who may wish to pursue this kind of research.

Key terms

electrocardiography	photoplethysmograph
electrodermal activity	PQRST complex
electroencephalography	pupillary response
electromyography	skin potentials
electro-oculography	skin resistance
evoked potential electroen-	sphygmomanometer
cephalography	systole
diastole	transducers
galvanic skin response	

8.1 INTRODUCTION

Specifically, the field of psychophysiology is concerned with the manipulation of psychological variables and their corresponding observed effects on physiological processes. Thus, psychophysiology is concerned with observing the interactions between physiological and psychological phenomena. More generally, psychophysiology can be said to encompass both the study of behavioural consequences of physiological properties of the body at a biochemical and anatomical level, and the effects of behaviour on these same physiological properties.

Much of psychophysiological investigation is concerned with examining the concepts of emotion, behavioural states, stress, cognitive task performance, personality and intelligence. In each case, the relationships between psychological factors, stimulus perception and recognition, situational indices and physiological response are used in an attempt to shed light on the initiation, execution, maintenance and termination of behavioural events. Ultimately, the field can be partitioned into six major areas of endeavour as follows.

Social psychophysiology Social psychophysiology is the study of the interactions between physiology and behaviours when those behaviours are involved in social processes. For example, interpersonal phenomena and group dynamics may be investigated by observing the interplay between various behaviours and each individual's dynamic physiological changes such as pupil size, muscle tone and skin electrical resistance (e.g. Birnbaumer & Ohman, 1993; Blascovich & Kelsey, 1990; Diamond, 2001; Wagner & Manstead, 1989).

Developmental psychophysiology This is the study of the ageing process, looking specifically at how changing properties of physiological systems and anatomical structures affect behaviour (e.g. Van der Molen & Molenaar, 1994). In addition, the nature of the interaction between the psychological and physiological factors during development is examined. For example, research may use measures of brain activity (e.g. event-related potentials) to examine ongoing brain function during early development (Ridderinkhof & van der Stelt, 2000; Steinschneider, Kurtzberg & Vaughan, 1992).

Cognitive psychophysiology This concerns the relationship between information processing and physiology (see Jennings & Coles, 1991). That is, it examines the relationships between cognitive task performance and physiological events. For example, it looks at how perception, movement, attention, language and memory may be associated with particular features of brain electrical and magnetic activity (see Kutas & Dale, 1997; Zani & Proverbio, 2002).

Clinical psychophysiology This is the study of psychological disorders and their relationship with physiological functioning and malfunctioning (e.g. Halliday, Butler & Paul, 1987; Magina, 1997). In addition, this area is concerned with the examination of the effectiveness of treatment regimes and drug effects on the psychological behaviour and affect of the individual. For example, in looking at chronic depression, it is sometimes useful to look at the benefits of any treatment applied in terms of both the behavioural outcomes and the changed nature of physiological parameters such as brain activity, sympathetic nervous system responsivity and biochemical substance assays (Carlson, 2004).

Applied psychophysiology This area is involved with the application of psychophysiological techniques and findings to occupational, recreational, clinical and other areas of interest. For example, the monitoring of certain physiological activity within an individual, and providing instant and appropriate feedback of this activity, is known as biofeedback. This technique is used as an aid for relaxation therapy, stuttering, respiration control and a variety of other practical problems whose treatment may be amenable to self-control therapeutic techniques (Schwartz & Andrasik, 2003).

Individual differences This area looks specifically at the relation of physiological processes and anatomical structures to measures of personality and intelligence (generally defined by psychometric measures, e.g. Cooper, 2002; Gale & Eysenck, 1993). These measures may be of typically dynamic psychophysiological form, such as the relationship between the overall amplitude of brain-evoked potentials to varying levels of stimulation, and introversion–extroversion (the augmenting–reducing phenomenon), or may quantify aspects of anatomical physiology and relate these to the psychometric or psychological indices. For example, from histological surveys of human cadavers, the number of dendrites and their length correlate positively with the level of education attainment within individuals.

8.2 THE PRINCIPAL AREAS OF PHYSIOLOGICAL DATA ACQUISITION

This section is a brief summary of important facts and information surrounding the quantification of parameters describing the function of particular physiological structures and systems. It is not intended to be a comprehensive overview but rather is a snapshot of the diversity and richness of the measurement process in psychophysiology.

8.2.1 Muscle activity

Assessing muscle activity is carried out by a technique known as **electromyography** in which the electrical potentials that are associated with contractions of muscle fibres are measured. These potentials are brief impulses lasting between 1 and 5 milliseconds (ms), detected using devices known as **transducers**. These vary from invasive needle electrodes inserted into muscle tissue and recording individual fibre potentials, to non-invasive surface electrodes that are fixed to the skin above the particular muscle of interest, recording the mass action of muscle fibre groups.

electromyography

transducers

The amplitude of recorded signals can vary between about 1 and 1000 microvolts (μV), although recordings of less than 20 μV are difficult to obtain. The frequency of the electrical impulses can be anywhere between 20 and 1000 hertz (Hz). The quantitative measures available will vary depending upon the focus of investigation. For example, when one is looking at the behaviour of a single nerve fibre or a homogeneous group of fibres, the single or compound (many fibres) action potential may be measured in response to a precise, targeted stimulus such as a small electric shock. Measures extracted from this potential include those of impulse amplitude and nerve conduction velocity. Alternatively, when looking at the long-term activity of muscle fibres, the integrated amplitude, frequency of nerve firing (impulses) and gradients of frequency responses may be examined.

One interesting example of electromyograph recordings was reported by Surakka and Hietanen (1998) who assessed muscular activity on the face in response to other peoples' facial expressions of emotion. Their research has revealed that people show different muscular reactions to real (Duchenne) as opposed to deliberate (false) smiles. Also, Winkielman and Cacioppo (2001) showed that electromyographic activity is associated with real smiles when conducting easier mental tasks.

8.2.2 Sweat gland activity

Assessing the activity of the sweat glands relies upon measuring electrical activity on the surface of the skin, a procedure known variously as **electrodermal activity** or **galvanic skin response**. What is actually measured are the electrical properties of the skin that are associated with eccrine sweat gland activity. This activity is responsive to changes in emotionality and cognitive activity in general, and is often used as a general measure of arousal.

Measuring electrodermal activity requires the placement of two non-invasive, metallic, surface electrodes either on the palm or the fingers of one hand. Two types of measure can be recorded: **skin potentials** and **skin resistance**. Skin potentials are recorded by measuring the voltage potential between an electrode over an 'active' site and a reference electrode on an inert site. Alternatively, skin resistance is measured by imposing a constant voltage between the electrodes, across the surface of the skin. The current between these electrodes can be measured, and this provides information about the conductivity of the skin between the two electrodes. In short, sweaty palms are better conductors of current than dry ones and the equipment is designed to register any changes in sweat production. An alternative strategy sometimes used is to maintain a constant current between the two electrodes by constantly adjusting the voltage: this voltage adjustment measures skin resistivity. Both momentary fluctuations (phasic) and relatively stable measures (tonic) can be recorded.

If measuring skin potentials, the voltage amplitude between the two electrodes is recorded, and this normally ranges between about 1 and 6 millivolts (mV). If

electrodermal activity
galvanic skin response

skin potentials
skin resistance

measuring skin resistance, then variation of electrical resistance around a baseline is recorded. Given a relatively stable level of resistance of, say, 100 kilohms (kΩ), to the passage of electric current through the surface of the skin, variability of resistance around this baseline value can reach up to 50 (kΩ) or more in magnitude.

Skin conductance is generally measured in microsiemens (µS), where 1 seimens equals $1\,\Omega^{-1}$. Given a baseline level of conductivity of $10\,\mu S$, conductivity can be seen to vary generally between about $8\,\mu S$ and $20\,\mu S$. A typical response duration would be between about 1 and 3 seconds. Of course, these example values will be heavily dependent on the type of experimental conditions used to elicit changes in potential, resistivity and conductivity.

The quantitative measures derived from electrodermal activity are generally measures of response waveform amplitude and latency, rise/fall times, and frequency of responses. In addition, gradients over time of these measures can be analysed, as in the case of habituation of response amplitude to repetitive stimuli.

Measures of electrodermal activity have been widely used to indicate level of arousal from almost any conceivable stimulus. For instance, Blair, Jones, Clark and Smith (1997) found that psychopathic individuals show a lower electrodermal response to distress cues in others than a group of matched controls (see also Lorber, 2004).

8.2.3 Eye movements – pupillary response

Pupillary response describes the dilation of the pupil of the eye, while **electro-oculography** describes the measurement of eye movement. In addition, eye-blink rate and duration can be measured.

pupillary response

electro-oculography

To measure pupillary response, an individual's eyes are illuminated by low-level infrared light and a low-light-level video camera is used to record pupil size, with digital signal processing of the video images to provide a continuous measurement of pupil diameter. Pupil diameter changes can be measured over a 0.5 mm to 10 mm range. Spontaneous, continuous pupil size changes vary around 1 mm or so. Typically, pupillary response measures encompass pupil diameter and rate of change in diameter in response to either a specific stimulus or a longer-term emotional state.

Electro-oculography is concerned with assessing muscular activity around the eye, and evaluating the change in voltage potential between the positively charged cornea and negatively charged retinal segment of the eye. It uses non-invasive pairs of electrodes placed around the eye. Electrodes placed at the side of the eye record horizontal movement, those placed above and below the eye record vertical movement. Electro-oculographic amplitude varies between about 0.4 and 1 mV. Currently, electro-oculographic signals can record movement up to 70° from a central position, with a resolution of 1°. Eye-blink duration is generally seen to fall between 100 and 400 ms, with rates heavily dependent upon specific situational factors. Electro-oculographic measures encompass eye movement speed, direction, type (smooth pursuit as in tracking tasks, or fast saccades as in reading or examining a static stimulus).

Pupillary dilation is considered to be indicative of heightened interest and arousal, while electro-oculograms are regularly used in sleep research, for instance, as one indicator of entry to the phase of sleep known as REM (rapid eye movement) sleep, which is characterized by the eyes making rapid darting movements (see Carlson, 2004).

8.2.4 Cardiac response, blood pressure and blood volume

electrocardiography

Electrocardiography refers to the recording of the electrical potentials generated by the heart muscles over the period of one heartbeat. The electrical waveform produced by the sequence of contractile responses in a heartbeat is referred to as the

PQRST complex

PQRST complex. The P wave is the small change in potential caused by the initial excitation of the atrial (upper heart chambers) muscles just prior to their contraction. The QRS complex represents the contraction of the left and right ventricular (lower chambers of the heart) muscles that pump blood from the ventricular chambers to the lungs and rest of the body. The R wave is the point of maximum ventricular excitation. The T wave indicates repolarization of ventricular muscle.

systole
diastole

The term **systole** is used to describe the atrial and ventricular contraction phases (P–S) and **diastole** to describe the relaxation phase (T–P) of the passive filling of the atria and ventricles. Blood pressure measurement is based upon the measurement of the systolic and diastolic phase wavefronts in the blood moving through the arteries. Blood volume measurement (plethysmography) assesses the amounts of blood that are present in various areas of the body during particular activities.

To make an electrocardiograph measurement, surface electrodes can be placed on the wrist, ankle, neck or chest. For the measurement of blood pressure, a

sphygmomanometer

sphygmomanometer (pressure cuff) and stethoscope are used to detect the systolic and diastolic pressures. For blood volume measurements, conventionally a

photoplethysmograph

photoplethysmograph is used to detect the amount of blood passing in tissue directly below the sensor (using the principle of light absorption characteristics of blood). This device is normally placed on a fingertip or an earlobe.

The most popular quantitative measures in electrocardiography are of heart rate (counting the number of R waves over a minute) and heart period (the duration between R waves). The average heart rate is around 75 beats per minute, which is equivalent to a cardiac cycle of 800 ms, during which the heart is in ventricular systole for 200–250 ms and in diastole for 550–600 ms. However, with a multi-component waveform as in the PQRST complex, and the physiological processes that underlie the waveform, meaningful measures can be generated from many combinations of latencies or amplitudes between and within the PQRST complex. The measurement of blood pressure yields simple pressure indices; however, the ratio between the systolic and diastolic pressure values is of significance, as is the absolute value of each pressure parameter. Normal systolic blood pressure (measured in millimetres of mercury displacement (mmHg)) ranges from 95 to 140 mmHg, with about 120 mmHg as the average pressure.

Normal diastolic blood pressure ranges from 60 to 90 mmHg, with about 80 mmHg as the average pressure. Blood volume measures are always relative to some baseline within an individual. The signal is generally an amplified analogue voltage that indexes light absorption by the photoelectric sensor.

Measures such as heart rate variability have been widely used to indicate the mental workload (a concept that reflects information processing demands and complexity) imposed by a variety of tasks, such as those involved in flying aircraft (e.g. Backs, 1998; Sammer, 1998).

8.2.5 Respiration

To assess respiration, measures of the breathing and gas-exchange process are made. More specifically, oximetry examines the arterial blood oxygen (O_2) levels and infrared capnometry examines the lung carbon dioxide (CO_2) levels. Abdominal and thoracic respiration rate and depth may also be measured.

Oximetry measures are made using a specially calibrated photoplethysmograph, with output calibrated as percentage of saturated haemoglobin. For capnometry, a nasal catheter is inserted about 6 mm into a nostril and held in place with some tape on the upper lip. CO_2 expiration pressure (PCO_2) and end-tidal CO_2 ($PETCO_2$: the concentration of CO_2 in expired air) can be measured. For abdominal and thoracic breathing measurement, pneumography and strain gauges are most often used.

The different methods of respiration assessment produce analogue voltages, digital values or direct pressure manometer readings that index the gases or strains being measured. There are up to 50 measures that can be extracted from an examination of the output from oximetry, capnography and pneumography. These vary from measures of volume displacement, frequency and pressure, to proportionate fractionation of gases in expired air and oxygenation of the blood. The analysis of respiration has inexplicably been neglected in psychophysiology. However, the book by Fried and Grimaldi (1993) is a remarkable testament to the richness of relationships between respiration and psychological factors, and to the theoretical importance of respiration to conventional models of arousal and physiological functioning.

An interesting finding from the analysis of respiration has been that individuals suffering from panic disorder have greater irregularity and complexity in their breathing patterns, which may make them more vulnerable to panic attacks (e.g. Caldirola, Bellodi, Caumo, Migliarese & Perna, 2004).

8.2.6 Electrical potentials of the brain

The electrical activity generated by the mass action of neurons within the cortex and midbrain structures is measured using a technique known as **electroencephalography**. In addition, since electrical currents generate magnetic fields, these can be measured by magnetoencephalography. Electroencephalograph (EEG) recordings can be made using either invasive needle electrodes, placed directly into the exposed cortex or deeper structures, or non-invasive electrodes placed upon the surface of the scalp

electroencephalography

(up to more than 300 with high-density EEG recording). These electrodes are used to record voltage differences between one or more cortical sites and a relatively electrically inactive area (such as an earlobe). For magnetoencephalograph recording, superconducting quantum interfering devices (SQUIDs) are used to detect the minute dynamically fluctuating magnetic fields within the brain. Unlike EEG electrodes, SQUIDs do not have to be in contact with the scalp or cortical tissue as there is no reliance on electrical conductivity of electrons through body tissues.

The electrical signals emanating from the brain are very small (of the order of microvolts). Spontaneous electroencephalography is the term used to describe the continuous stream of activity that is always present within the brain. This activity can be characterized as patterns of oscillatory waveforms that have conventionally been subdivided in terms of their frequency into four main bands: delta (low frequency, 0.5–4 Hz; amplitude 20–200 μV), theta (low frequency, 4–7 Hz; amplitude 20–100 μV), alpha (dominant frequency, 8–13 Hz; amplitude 20–60 μV) and beta (high frequency, 13–40 Hz; amplitude 2–20 μV). Electroencephalography has frequently been used to study levels of arousal from deep sleep, where delta activity predominates, through to alert attentiveness, where beta activity predominates.

If, instead of recording the spontaneous activity of the brain, a brain response is evoked by a quantifiable stimulus, then it is possible to examine the change in electrical activity in direct response to a known stimulus. This technique is known as **evoked potential electroencephalography**. Some of these evoked potentials can last less than 10 ms (such as the brain-stem auditory evoked potential generated by subcortical brain tissues) or up to a second or longer as in the case of the *Bereitschaftspotential* or readiness potential (a slow shift in voltage that is observed preceding voluntary or spontaneous movement within an individual). Generally, because of the low level of brain response over and above the normal background electroencephalographic activity, many evoked responses are collected and then summed to produce an average evoked response (AER), also known as an average evoked potential (AEP). The basis for this summation is that activity in the waveform that is not generated in response to the stimulus will be almost random and hence sum to near zero over occasions, while activity that is related to the stimulus will be enhanced by adding these stimulus-generated signals together.

For spontaneous EEG data, the most popular method of analysis is based around a mathematical technique known as Fourier analysis. This decomposes the complex EEG waveform into simple separate oscillating components each having a particular frequency of oscillation and magnitude. Following this, the amount of electrical energy accounted for by each particular frequency that could possibly make up the complex waveform provides direct, quantitative measures that index signal power at certain frequencies. More recent methods of analysis have re-expressed multi-electrode output as a spatial contour map – the topographical EEG map. This is a method of interpolating activity between electrodes in order to produce a set of smoothed gradients that can be 'mapped' over the surface of the

evoked potential electroencephalography

scalp, encompassing all electrode positions and the intervening spaces between electrodes. In addition, chaos theory (non-linear dynamic analysis or fractal dimensionality analysis) has very recently been applied to the background EEG as a method for determining the 'complexity' of the EEG. For AEP research, measures invariably focus on peaks and troughs in the waveform, characterizing these components by their amplitude and latency from the point of stimulation. Some work has also focused on the spectral composition of the AEP. Particularly promising has been analysis that uses the wavelet transform, which allows a multi-resolution analysis of time-varying signals and which is especially suited to locating the time interval within which a high-frequency signal, such as the brain-stem auditory evoked potential, occurs (see Samar, Swartz & Raghuveer, 1995).

Contemporary EEG work frequently uses high-density recording (see Oostenveld & Praamstra, 2001) where many electrodes are placed on the scalp, yielding a relatively high-resolution topographical map. Using this type of recording, Huber, Ghilardi, Massimini and Tononi (2004) have been able to show that slow wave sleep may be crucial to learning new tasks. Specifically, they found that learning a new task may trigger an increase in slow wave sleep activity in the relevant brain area, which in turn may enhance task performance.

However, despite advances in the topographic mapping of EEG data its spatial resolution is still relatively poor. Fortunately, complementary techniques for measuring brain activity, such as functional magnetic resonance imaging (see Box 8.1), have relatively good spatial resolution. When used together, these techniques make a particularly powerful combination, effectively measuring the brain activity associated with psychological processes.

Box 8.1   Functional magnetic resonance imaging

Functional magnetic resonance imaging (fMRI) is currently the fastest-growing method for relating brain activity to psychological processes and behaviour. Whilst the hardware and facilities required are extremely expensive, they are becoming increasingly available to researchers working in psychology departments, with a number of departments having their own fMRI facilities.

Functional magnetic resonance imaging works by detecting the radio frequency energy emitted by the nuclei of atoms as they align with a strong magnetic field. Participants in fMRI studies are placed inside a scanner, which fundamentally comprises a large, high-strength magnet, various coils that make local adjustments to the static magnetic field generated by the large magnet, and radio frequency transmitting and receiving coils. The participants are stimulated in some way, for instance, by presentation of visual stimuli, whilst their brain activity is measured as described next.

Essentially, a radiofrequency pulse is used to flip the nuclei out of alignment with the magnetic field and then, as they move back into alignment, they emit radio frequency energy – the magnetic resonance signal – that is measured by a receiver

(Continued)

Box 8.1 (Continued)

coil. Because increased neural processing requires increased oxygen consumption, and because the magnetic resonance signal from deoxygenated blood is reduced relative to oxygenated blood, changes in the blood oxygen level dependent (BOLD) response are related to changes in underlying neural activity in a given brain area. Statistical analysis of fMRI BOLD data attempts to relate changes in stimulation applied by the experimenter to changes in the BOLD response in different brain areas. From this type of analysis various types of deduction can be made including those about the functional role of different brain areas, about the interactions between brain areas, about the mechanisms of learning in the brain and about the modulation of brain activity by factors such as task.

In recent years there has been an explosion of fMRI-based research. To take one example, by using fMRI, researchers have been able to identify brain areas that seem to be associated with psychological cravings (Myrick *et al.*, 2004).

8.3 QUANTIFYING BIOSIGNAL DATA

8.3.1 Level of measurement

As can be seen from the information presented in Section 8.2, the measurements made from psychophysiological data are almost always at true ratio level – that is, they behave like interval level measurements and possess a true zero (see Chapter 3). However, despite the high level of precision of psychophysiological measurements, the psychologist using these measures faces a significant problem. She must determine the psychological meaningfulness of any change in the biosignal. For instance, returning to the earlier example of using heart rate variability as a measure of mental workload, a statistically significant change in heart rate variability may not necessarily signify a psychologically meaningful change in mental workload. Thus, the interpretation of psychophysiological data is often more qualitative than the precision of the measures might seem to imply.

8.3.2 Hardware, signal processing and data volume

Having established that the scale of measurement is superior to that of nearly all psychological data, it is apparent that many issues in the quantification of parameters that bedevil psychology fade into insignificance in this area. However, the price of this philosophical simplicity is computational and methodological complexity. The measures made are invariably electrically based, exact to a predetermined level of accuracy defined by the properties of the sensors and any amplification used, and prone to levels of noise that can utterly distort any parameter or signal. So, in order to attempt to measure any physiological parameter from any part of the human body, fairly detailed knowledge is required of the underlying physiology to be assessed, the physical properties of the sensors or transducers to be applied, the properties of the signals thus generated (electrical engineering and digital signal processing techniques) and the plethora of possible methods of analysis (both bivariate and multivariate methods of waveform analysis, periodicity analysis, event detection, pattern recognition and clustering techniques).

A simple measure such as heart rate (counted in beats per minute) seems a trivial parameter to acquire, until you ask yourself how you are going to measure the heart rate. Having found out that two electrodes placed, say, on each wrist will enable the acquisition of the information, your next problem is to work out how you are going to extract the heart rate parameter itself: that is, how you record the electrical signals. Assume next that you are provided with a computer-based recording system set up to output a number every 10 seconds or so which indicates beats per minute. Looking at the number, you see the heart rate is alternating between 50 and 70 beats per minute. Is this acceptable? The individual being assessed is sitting quietly. Your local expert happens by and notices that the 50 Hz hardware notch filter is off. In addition, checking the earth electrode shows that very poor electrical contact is being made between this and the individual. By improving this contact and switching the notch filter in-line, the heart rate stabilizes around 70 beats per minute. To understand what has happened requires knowledge of the expected heart rate, the properties of metallic electrodes, earthing problems, the operation of a notch filter, and the appreciation of how a heart rate monitor works. This is all *before* you begin to manipulate a single psychological variable. Note also that here you were dealing with a relatively large biological signal. Imagine attempting to measure high-frequency EEG of maybe 5 μV in amplitude with amplifiers that have background, self-generated electronic noise of about 1 μV, and where mains noise can be as large as 10–20 μV. The knowledge required to ensure that the signal you are seeing is actually biologically generated and not some property of the hardware in use, or of bad measurement technique, is quite considerable.

Unlike much purely psychological research, it is possible to generate quantitative physiological data that are literally pure error. This is a problem in some topographic EEG systems that provide maps of brain electrical activity computed from many electrodes placed upon the scalp. Most systems have automated filtering such that only frequencies between 0 and 40 Hz are displayed. However, if an electrode becomes detached from the scalp or its connecting wire breaks (inside the insulating plastic), this electrode will pick up large amounts of background mains noise (and any other stray frequencies present in the environment). Depending upon the efficiency of the filters, this electrode position will be seen as producing either very low-amplitude signals across the signal spectrum or high-frequency beta of moderate amplitude (where beta activity was defined as being from 20 Hz upwards). In this latter case, the filter does not remove *all* 50 Hz activity and, owing to spectral smearing (given a low sampling speed and short segment of EEG), this gets mapped as high-frequency activity in your EEG records. Experienced EEG technicians and researchers can invariably detect this. For a novice researcher, however, it poses a serious problem. Once again, only knowledge of the measurement process and the characteristics of the hardware can guard against this incorrect interpretative process.

8.3.3 Designing the experiment and choosing parameters to measure

If you set up an experiment protocol, and have acquired some psychophysiological data, your next problem is deciding what parameters to extract from these data. This stage of the measurement process *must* be decided on the basis of a priori measurement and psychological hypotheses. Data dredging (extracting every conceivable parameter and attempting to relate them to the psychological parameters) in the hope of finding something is virtually impossible to implement in this area. So many parameters can be computed that attempting to sift through your data in this manner is a recipe for disaster. You will run out of time, computing facilities and energy! Modern laboratories routinely keep all physiological data on some form of archive medium (e.g. magnetic, CD-ROM or DVD). However, only certain hypothesis-specific parameters are extracted from this archive for use in the examination of psychological relationships. Should other hypotheses evolve over time, the archive data can then be reanalysed (where relevant) in order to permit the extraction of the new parameters.

One major problem you may face is that the system you are using to acquire psychophysiological data may permit only certain forms of analysis or, more rarely, provide no parameters at all. That is, you may have access to a computer-based skin conductance recording system, which will acquire and store the continuous conductance levels. However, if you do not have a program that analyses this output in terms of response latency and amplitude, then the data are practically useless. Your only options are to write all the incoming data to a chart recorder and carry out all such measures by hand, or (more usually) obtain or write a computer program yourself that implements the procedures necessary to extract these parameters. This highlights another global feature of psychophysiological data acquisition: the collection of data can take a few minutes, but the volume of data generated can tax the computer system whilst the analysis of one participant's data by hand can take days! This is particularly true for methods that measure brain activity such as electroencephalography, magnetoencephalography and fMRI where several gigabytes of data may be simultaneously recorded from a large number of locations in just a few hours. Even the latest analysis packages running on high-specification computers can take hours to complete each stage of the necessary analysis.

Of course, returning to the heart rate example above, it may be that only five such measures are made throughout an experiment, where (say) the only focus of interest is the effect of difficulty of task problem on heart rate. The drawback to such simple experiments is that the explanatory power of any results is limited by the paucity of variables analysed! As Fried and Grimaldi (1993) also point out in their discussion of pulmonary (respiration) research, using observable movements of the chest or abdomen (pneumography) alone as indicators of respiration activity is not to be recommended, as PETCO$_2$ activity demonstrates that such movement can be quite unrelated to actual airflow in to and out of the lungs. Thus, to use respiration rate or depth as an indicator of increasing or decreasing airflow is liable to be prone to error. In the same way, the use of heart rate alone is not of much practical use except as a simple descriptor of one particular feature of cardiac activity.

8.4 CONCLUSION

Psychophysiological methods offer insights into a wide range of human behaviours and experiences. In this chapter we have attempted to convey the breadth of techniques available to the psychophysiological researcher. In a chapter like this it is not possible to go into much depth, but it is hoped that we have whetted the appetite of students and researchers to look further into this area of investigation. The following short section on further reading should provide the requisite detail for helping a researcher embark on effective psychophysiogical research.

8.5 FURTHER READING

Andreassi's (2000) is an excellent introductory text. It is probably the best general textbook for students who are completely new to the area. Cacioppo *et al.*'s (2000) text should be read straight after Andreassi's. This is a comprehensive book that is intended both as a reference source for the specialist and yet to be accessible to undergraduates.

Dempster's (2001) is a good introductory text on the recording and analysis of psychophysiological data using modern computer-based data acquisition systems. Since electroencephalography is one of the largest research areas in psychophysiology, it is useful to take a look at Fisch's (1999) text. This is written at an introductory level suitable for students who have no prior knowledge of psychophysiology but is also of value to experienced EEG users. For students who wish to undertake projects involving electroencephalography, it is an essential handbook that provides much practical as well as some theoretical information. For those who wish to learn about functional magnetic resonance imaging, Jezzard, Matthews and Smith's (2001) book provides an excellent starting point. Aimed at postgraduate level, it covers the underlying principles of fMRI and the design and analysis of fMRI experiments. Finally, there is Fried and Grimaldi (1993) is an absolutely brilliant book. It contains an excellent introductory section on psychophysiological measurement and provides a masterful description of respiratory functions and processes. In addition, the provocative and challenging hypotheses in the book make this probably one of the best 'specialist' books in this area.

9

Psychophysical Methods

David Rose

<table>
<tr><td>9.1</td><td>Introduction</td></tr>
<tr><td>9.2</td><td>Principles of absolute thresholds</td></tr>
<tr><td>9.3</td><td>Forced-choice techniques</td></tr>
<tr><td>9.4</td><td>Methods for measuring absolute thresholds</td></tr>
<tr><td>9.5</td><td>Difference thresholds</td></tr>
<tr><td>9.6</td><td>Sensational measurements</td></tr>
<tr><td>9.7</td><td>Some general tips on running experiments</td></tr>
<tr><td>9.8</td><td>Conclusion</td></tr>
<tr><td>9.9</td><td>Further Reading</td></tr>
</table>

AIMS

This chapter serves as an introduction to psychophysical methods. First, we summarize theoretical understanding of what limits sensory detection, and then review the techniques available to investigate those limits. Later, procedures for measuring the strengths of percepts above threshold are considered. Finally, some general issues of experimental practicality are discussed.

K ey terms

absolute threshold	method of limits
adaptive techniques	method of single stimuli
bias	method of a thousand staircases
bisection	nulling
criterion	point of subjective equality
cross-modal matching	psychometric function
detection threshold	reaction time
difference threshold	receiver operating characteristic
forced choice	signal-plus-noise
fractionation	staircase methods
interval	standard stimulus
intra-modal matching	steps
iso-intensity contour	stimulus intensity
just noticeable difference	test stimulus
magnitude estimation	trials
matching	two-alternative forced choice
method of adjustment	Weber fraction
method of constant stimuli	Weber's law

9.1 INTRODUCTION

Psychophysical methods are among the oldest and most rigorously developed in psychology and they underpin a vast range of modern applied and academic research in the discipline. They are primarily techniques for measuring the functioning of the sensory and perceptual systems, and of mental information processing in general. However, the techniques have also found application in a wide variety of other applied and theoretical problems, including the assessment of anxiety, stress, memory, criminal behaviour, face recognition, social attitudes, advertising effectiveness, and so on. They are used in ophthalmology and acoustics, and for measuring the taste, touch and smell of commercial products from foodstuffs to soap powder. Additionally, the tests are increasingly used in personnel selection, for jobs where fine sensory aptitudes are predictive of success (e.g. flying, military target recognition, and detecting tumours in X-ray clinics).

detection threshold
absolute threshold
stimulus intensity

Perhaps the commonest use of these methods is for finding the minimum intensity of a stimulus that can be detected, i.e. the **detection threshold** or **absolute threshold**. Hence, for most of this chapter the independent variable under discussion is **stimulus intensity**. However, the principles can be applied to many other types of variable, including sensory (e.g. size, colour), affective (the pleasantness of a perfume, facial attractiveness) and cognitive (word frequency, memory familiarity).

9.2 PRINCIPLES OF ABSOLUTE THRESHOLDS

I have often been amused by the reactions of novice students to near-threshold stimuli. For example, in a practical in which they were required to read words presented very briefly on a screen some students complained that the apparatus was not working properly, because sometimes they could read a word clearly but on other occasions, repeating exactly the same presentation, the word was unrecognizable.

Of course, the apparatus was functioning perfectly; it was the students who were varying from trial to trial. People are not robots (especially not students); they do not function 'like clockwork'. Their reactions to a stimulus are not exactly the same on every occasion. Instead, they fluctuate in their sensitivity. In the terminology of information theory, people are full of noise: random, apparently spontaneous factors, internal to the subject, affect human performance. Biologically based theorists ascribe this noise to the spontaneous firing of action potentials that occurs along sensory nerves; but noise can also be regarded more generally as informational garbage (or information loss) at any level in the system. Some stimuli are so weak they are drowned out by this noise, and hence are not detected at all. Stronger stimuli may be detected, but appear more or less intense, depending on the amount of noise around at the instant when the stimulus occurred.

So consider first a subject's reaction to a simple stimulus presented briefly, say a spot of light shone briefly on to a screen, or an auditory tone, a touch to the skin, or whatever. The magnitude of the sensation felt by the subject will not be constant every time we repeat the stimulus. Sometimes it will be larger, sometimes smaller. If the stimulus is extremely weak, then on some presentations the subject may not notice it at all. Stimulus detection then becomes a probabilistic affair. The weaker the stimulus, the lower the probability of it being detected.

The probability of detecting any given stimulus can be measured by presenting that stimulus repeatedly and counting the number of times the subject perceives it. We then convert that number to a percentage of the number of stimulus presentations or **trials**.

trials

By choosing a series of stimuli that differ in strength, we can in fact estimate the amount of noise in the sensory system. Plotting the probabilities for each stimulus strength gives us a graph called the **psychometric function**. A typical example is shown in Figure 9.1. Probability of detection varies from practically zero for very weak stimuli, to 100% for strong stimuli.

psychometric function

The notion of absolute threshold as an all-or-none detection level is thus somewhat obsolete. Basically, it assumed that weak stimuli are not detected because they do not activate the sensory system sufficiently; only sensory events that exceed a minimum threshold amount are able to pass on to higher levels of perception and action. The word 'threshold' is nevertheless still often used as a shorthand for the dividing line between correct and incorrect performance. In Figure 9.1, the stimulus intensity that would give us 50% detection is conventionally defined as the absolute threshold.

The slope of the psychometric function is proportional to the amount of noise in the system. Steep slopes indicate low noise (a robot with no noise would give a steep function, changing sharply from no response below threshold to 100% responses above threshold), while shallow slopes reveal the presence of much noise, i.e. subject variability over time (Treisman & Watts, 1966).

A problem with the above experiment is that, if the subject knows a stimulus is actually presented on every trial, the subject will maximize the number of trials he or she gets correct by saying 'yes, I detected it' every time (or at least, 'yes, a stimulus was there'). Subjects are notoriously obstreperous in this fashion: they will regard the experiment as a test, and try to score as highly as possible, regardless of what you want them to do. So the only thing to do is to introduce some blank, 'catch' trials, on which you present a stimulus of zero intensity, and make it clear that responding 'yes' to a blank trial will incur horrific penalties, or at least a withering glare.

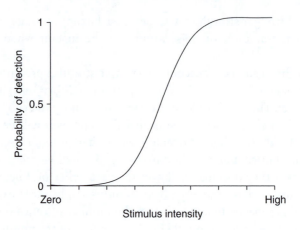

Figure 9.1   The psychometric function

Nevertheless, subjects still do sometimes respond positively to blank trials, even when they are not trying to outguess you but are genuinely trying to respond appropriately. Why does this happen? It is because the noise in their sensory system has momentarily risen to such a large extent it is mistaken for the level of activity normally evoked only by a real (but weak) stimulus.

The situation that pertains in a sensory system during such experiments is illustrated in Figure 9.2. The noise in the system fluctuates from moment to moment, so the probability of there being a given level of activity at any instant in time is described by the distribution labelled 'noise'. A Gaussian curve is usually an accurate description of the noise distribution (Green & Swets, 1966). The sensory system normally lives with this noise within it, and learns to ignore it. When, however, a stimulus occurs, the level of activity within the system is elevated by an amount proportional to the stimulus's strength. Over many, repeated instances of the same stimulus, the probability distribution is shifted to **signal-plus-noise** the right. This is now called the **signal-plus-noise** distribution. It has the same shape as the noise distribution if (as often, but not always, occurs) the stimulus simply adds a constant amount to the level of activity in the system.

If the stimulus is strong, the signal-plus-noise distribution is easily distinguished from the noise-alone distribution, because it constitutes much higher levels of activity. When the stimulus is weak, however, there may be considerable overlap between the two distributions. What can the sensory system do to maximize its performance? If it ignores all levels of activity that are normally present between trials due to the internal noise, it will miss many stimuli, i.e. the ones that occur when there is so little noise that the signal-plus-noise activity is still less than sometimes occurs due to noise alone. If, however, it wants to detect every stimulus, it must accept lower levels of activity as indicative of stimulus

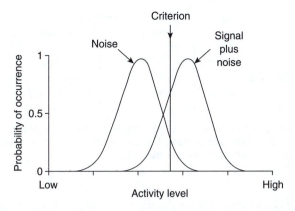

Figure 9.2 The activity levels in the nervous system with and without the presence of a stimulus, expressed as probabilities

occurrence; but then it will mistakenly respond on some catch trials, i.e. those when the level of internal noise is high. According to signal detection theory, the sensory system accepts all levels of activity above a certain **criterion** as indicat- ing that a stimulus has occurred, while all levels below the criterion are rejected as due to internal noise. The criterion is normally set to an intermediate, com- promise level, above the point at which all stimuli are detected, and below the point at which mistakes are made on catch trials (Green & Swets, 1966).

criterion

Four outcomes from each trial are thus possible (Figure 9.3). On catch trials, the subject may deny the occurrence of the stimulus: this is known as a 'correct rejection'. If the subject mistakenly says a stimulus did occur, this is a 'false alarm'. On trials with a stimulus present, denial of the occurrence of the stimu- lus is known as a 'miss', while a claim to have detected the stimulus is called a 'hit'. The probabilities of each of these four possibilities are equal to the areas under the probability distributions in Figure 9.2, above and below the criterion.

The stronger the stimulus, the greater the distance between the means of the two distributions in Figure 9.2. The symbol used to represent this distance is d', while the criterion level of activity is known as β. As stimulus strength increases, the proportion of hits will increase, while the number of false alarms will be unaffected, if β stays the same. However, one of the important postulates of sig- nal detection theory is that β can vary, depending on the circumstances of the experiment (see further, below). So when stimulus strength increases, it is pos- sible for β to increase proportionately, such that the probability of scoring a hit remains constant despite the now higher intensity of the stimulus. In that case, however, the proportion of false alarms will be seen to decrease. So it is always possible to disentangle the effects of the stimulus, in creating a higher mean level of activity in the system, and the effects of changes in criterion. The two

		Response	
		Present	Absent
Stimulus	Present	Hit	Miss
	Absent	False alarm	Correct rejection

Figure 9.3 The four possible logical outcomes of experimental trials in which there either may or may not be a stimulus presented, and in which the subject must either respond that a stimulus was detected or that one was not

variables d' and β, can vary independently, but they are related to the proportions of hits and false alarms.

The values of d' and β can be calculated from the proportions of hits and false alarms, either by looking them up in published tables (e.g. Freeman, 1973), or by computing the integrals under the probability distributions in Figure 9.2 directly (Rose, 1988). (These assume the noise and signal-plus-noise distributions have equal variance.)

receiver operating characteristic

A common way of plotting the results of such experiments is in the form of a **receiver operating characteristic** (ROC) curve (Figure 9.4). This shows the proportions of hits and false alarms in the experiment. Changes in d' or β alter the ratio between the two variables, but in a manner predictable from the theory depicted in Figure 9.2.

Changes in d' and β can be deliberately induced by the experimenter to plot a series of ROC curves. Manipulating stimulus intensity will affect d'. Changes in payoff are the commonest way of altering β; if the reward for scoring a hit is high and the punishment for giving a false alarm is low, subjects will lower their criterion, which has the effect of increasing the proportions of both hits and false alarms, at the expense of correct rejections and misses. Severely punishing any false alarms has the opposite effect. (In practical terms, if you are a radar operator watching for incoming nuclear missiles, you need to set a low criterion to avoid missing any, even though this may mean frequent false alarms. On the other hand, if you are out in a hunting party you need a high criterion for target identification, to be sure you don't shoot your companions by mistake.) β can also be altered by making the probability of stimulus occurrence (i.e. the percentage of catch trials) higher or lower. A neat way of generating an ROC curve is to get your subject to rate the confidence with which his or her judgement is made (Green & Swets, 1966). This is equivalent to asking the subject to generate and maintain several different criterion levels simultaneously. For example, scores might be given on an integer scale from 0 to 5, with 5 indicating complete confidence that the signal was present. Each rating score is treated as reflecting achievement of a separate criterion level, and the analysis then proceeds as usual,

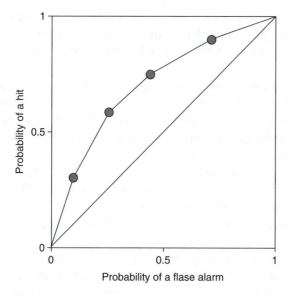

Figure 9.4 A receiver operating characteristic for a constant stimulus intensity. The four points were obtained by varying β. If stimulus intensity were zero, the points would fall on the diagonal; higher intensities, and hence higher *d'* values, cause the points to move towards the top left corner of the graph

by plotting a series of hit and false alarm probability pairs, each of which shows the probabilities cumulated up to one of the rating levels.

9.3 FORCED-CHOICE TECHNIQUES

On every trial there has to be a method by which the subject can tell when the stimulus may occur; on a catch trial, for example, you cannot leave your subject sitting there indefinitely waiting for something to happen. So the trial has to be demarcated in time, with the stimulus presented (if at all) during that time. One way is to allow your subject to 'self-pace', i.e. to start each trial by pressing a button, and the stimulus then occurs immediately or very soon after. (Self-pacing has the advantage of enabling subjects to rest, scratch themselves, sneeze, or whatever, whenever they like.) More common, however, is to signal the trial **interval** with another stimulus. For example, in vision experiments it is usual to sound a (clearly audible) tone when the stimulus might appear. For auditory experiments the signal might be a light coming on. The subject thus knows when to attend and when to make a response.

    A common variation on these techniques is to present two such demarcation indicators. These may follow one another in time, or may be located at different positions in space. The stimulus to be detected is presented on every trial,

interval

together with one of the indicators, and the other indicator accompanies a blank or catch stimulus. The subject knows that every trial contains a stimulus, but has to say with which demarcation indicator it is associated. This is known as a **forced choice**.

forced choice

So in temporal forced-choice experiments there are two indicators, separated by a pause, and the subject has to say whether the stimulus occurred in the first or the second interval. In spatial forced choice, the indicators might be placed, say, to the left and right of each other, and the subject has to say in which location the stimulus was presented.

two-alternative forced choice

In fact, the number of demarcation indicators need not be only two (**two-alternative forced choice** or 2AFC); there can be several, but there is always only one stimulus and hence one correct answer.

The psychometric functions derived from forced-choice tasks are similar to that in Figure 9.1, except that the 'floor' is no longer 0% detection. In a 2AFC task there is a 50% chance of guessing correctly even when the stimulus is very weak, so the function increases from 50% to 100% performance as stimulus intensity rises, and the curve is compressed to fit between those limits.

9.4 METHODS FOR MEASURING ABSOLUTE THRESHOLDS

method of constant stimuli

The experimental technique described above and illustrated in Figure 9.1 is known as the **method of constant stimuli**. It is the most comprehensive way of monitoring a subject's reactions to a stimulus, giving data on both threshold and noise (the slope of the psychometric function). Its main disadvantage is that many trials are required (plus some pilot trials to find which stimulus intensities to use). In most experiments, for example, at least 50 trials are given at each of 4 or more different stimulus intensities. (Recent non-parametric methods, however, suggest that using fewer trials but at least 10 different intensities works better: Ulrich & Miller, 2004.) Note also that the intensities should exclude any for which the subject happens to score 0% or 100%, since (i) it is then impossible to know where the function intersects with the floor or ceiling, and (ii) the data are usually fitted with a cumulative Gaussian curve, and this goes to infinity at 0% and 100%. In total, 300 trials are usually regarded as an absolute minimum for reliable estimates of threshold (and even more trials for estimates of noise). At (typically) 5 seconds per trial, this means 25 minutes of intense concentration by the subject. Even with frequent rests, subjects are unable to maintain a constant state of alertness for such long periods: fatigue, boredom and other extraneous variables will alter their operating characteristics during the experiment. In many practical circumstances, these factors are exacerbated: testing young children, busy executives, or patients in hospital, for example. For this reason, other techniques abound that measure threshold more quickly. They do so by using more efficient methods, and of these the simplest is to abandon any attempt to estimate noise accurately, concentrating instead on collecting data near threshold.

First consider how one should collect data to give the quickest, most efficient estimation of threshold. In Figure 9.1, the threshold or 50% performance level is the point where the slope (of a cumulative Gaussian) is maximal. In general, it makes sense to collect data near the point of maximal slope, because at that point small changes in the stimulus give the biggest changes in the subject's behaviour. Stimuli that the subject gets 98% or 99% right do not tell us so much about the threshold as stimuli the subject gets 49% or 51% right.

So, many techniques attempt to present the stimuli only at those medium intensities. The subject's responses during the experiment are often used to help the experimenter adjust, from trial to trial, the intensities chosen for presentation. These are generally known as **adaptive techniques**. Sometimes, these are used in preliminary investigations to pilot the choice of stimuli to be presented later in a full-blown method of constant stimuli experiment, but nowadays they are used very often in their own right.

At one extreme, the subject may be given absolute control over stimulus intensity, and the experimenter does nothing. Thus in the **method of adjustment**, the subject alters the stimulus by turning a knob at will, or pressing two buttons that respectively increase or decrease intensity. The instructions are to adjust the stimulus to the point of detectability (or loss of detectability). This adjustment may be repeated many times, beginning alternately from above or below threshold, and the results averaged. Alternatively, the subject may be asked to track the threshold, perhaps oscillating the setting continuously by a small amount around the threshold. This can be a useful technique in situations where the threshold may be changing, for example in the period immediately after exposure to an intense stimulus. The method of adjustment is quick and easy to do. However, one can never be certain what criterion the subject is using. Some particularly naïve subjects will refuse to admit they detect the stimulus unless it is clearly present, and will adjust intensity accordingly. Other subjects may move the setting to the point just below the level where the stimulus has disappeared. There is no way of finding out from the data alone what kind of strategy the subject is using. Also, the setting from an individual can be quite variable, perhaps due to the subject changing criterion during the experiment.

In the **method of limits**, the experimenter adjusts the stimulus in a more formal simulation of the method of adjustment. The stimulus is initially set well above threshold and is reduced in **steps** from trial to trial until the subject

adaptive techniques

method of adjustment

method of limits

steps

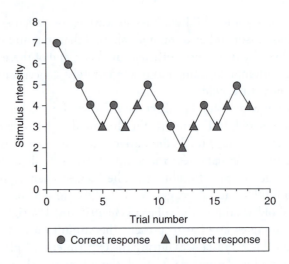

Figure 9.5 Changes in stimulus level during a staircase experiment

fails to detect it; the stimulus level at that point is recorded. The stimulus is then set well below threshold and its intensity is increased from trial to trial until the subject succeeds in detecting it. The point at which the subject's response changes is recorded. These descending and ascending series are repeated until enough data have been collected, and the endpoints of all the series are averaged. It is normal to find some overshoot in this system, i.e. the ascending series give higher estimates of threshold than the descending series. Also, subjects can anticipate what kind of response is expected in the next trial, since it is easy for them to work out the rules that determine stimulus intensity from trial to trial.

staircase methods Another disadvantage of the method of limits is that many trials present stimuli clearly above or below threshold, and thus elicit largely predictable responses from the subject. In **staircase methods**, however, the stimuli are focused more closely around the threshold level. As before, the stimulus is initially presented above threshold and then lowered in steps until the subject fails to detect it. The next step is then an increase in intensity, but starting from the point of failure, not from well below threshold as in the method of limits. The stimulus level continues to be raised from trial to trial until a successful detection is made, and then the stimulus is stepped progressively down until the subject fails to detect it again. This sequence of ascending and descending runs continues, with the stimulus level thus oscillating closely around the threshold (Cornsweet, 1962). Figure 9.5 shows the typical course of an experiment. A block of trials may continue until, say, 10 reversals of the direction of stimulus change have occurred, which would take typically 40–70 trials (depending how large the step size is, relative to the subject's noise level). The reversal points are noted, and are averaged at the end of the experiment to give an estimate of threshold.

Staircase techniques are very common, and there are many variations. The first is designed to cope with the possibility that the subject may anticipate the next stimulus; knowing that clear detections will lead to a reduction in stimulus contrast on the next trial, and that failures to detect will lead to an increase, the subject may realize what kind of response would be expected on the next trial, and respond appropriately. This problem is removed by interleaving two or more staircases (Cornsweet, 1962). In its simplest form, the first trial begins staircase one, the second begins staircase two, the third trial is the second on staircase one, the fourth trial is the second on staircase two, and so on. The subject soon loses track of which staircase is which. Better still is to pick the staircase randomly on each trial, rather than presenting them in strict alternation. With more than two staircases interleaved, the situation is even better. Moreover, these staircases need not be identical in terms of the stimulus tested. For example if you wish to know whether red, green or blue lights are seen equally well you can present three staircases, randomly interleaved, one staircase for each colour. (Although the subject may know from the colour which staircase has just been tested, as long as he or she cannot anticipate which colour will be tested on the next trial, the results will be valid.) What is also beneficial is that the three thresholds will be assessed simultaneously, thus avoiding the possibility of subject practice, fatigue or boredom biasing the result, as they might if you tested each colour sequentially.

A popular variation is to alter the rules, so the stimulus intensity is not lowered every time the subject gets one right, but only after two (or three, or more) correct responses from the subject. (The subject still has to get only one wrong, however, to cause an increase in stimulus intensity on the next trial.) The effect of this is to converge the staircase on to a higher point on the psychometric function: for example, 71% for the two-down/one-up rule, instead of 50% for the normal one-down/one-up rule (Wetherill & Levitt, 1965). This makes the staircase slightly longer to run, but gives it a number of advantages as follows.

Firstly, subjects are in general much happier if they know the stimulus they are looking out for. Presenting the occasional clearly detectable stimulus helps, since it literally reminds the subject of the target. If the staircase presents stimuli that on average are detected 71% of the time, this problem is reduced, relative to those with near 50% detectability levels.

Secondly, some workers collect all the data from a staircase experiment and, instead of simply averaging the reversal points and ignoring the trials in between each reversal, they use all the data to build a psychometric function (e.g. Figure 9.1; Hall, 1981). Thus many stimulus levels may be presented during a staircase, most of them several times over. This enables the probability of response to be calculated for each stimulus level. A collection of these probabilities can be used to form a psychometric function. By presenting several staircases with different rules, perhaps interleaved, for example staircases that converge on the 50% level, the 71%, and so on, the data can be deliberately spread out to give a good coverage of the full range of the psychometric function. (Using the method of constant stimuli, you need to find out before the experiment what that range is; with staircases, the stimulus levels adjust themselves automatically to fill the range.) From psychometric functions, it will be remembered, an estimate of the noise can be obtained as well as the threshold level.

bias

Thirdly, with forced-choice staircases, the threshold measure obtained is often an underestimate of the true threshold (Rose, Teller & Rendleman, 1970). This is called **bias**, and occurs because of the nature of guessing when the stimulus level is low. Consider a very weak stimulus that evokes activity below β. The subject is then forced to guess which demarcation indicator is correct, and will do so approximately 50% of the time on a 2AFC task. A correct guess has the effect of lowering the stimulus on the next trial, so the subject will likely have to guess again. The net effect is that the stimulus level drifts down well below threshold. (It is a fact that random guesses may carry on being right in an unbroken sequence more often than most people think; it takes longer than you would expect to even out right and wrong guesses.) So in the end some of the reversal points in the staircase will be much too low. The converse problem does not occur: correct guesses elevate stimulus intensity, so the subject soon detects the stimulus correctly without guessing. The problem of bias can be reduced by keeping the stimulus level up, for example near 71% detection level rather than 50%. (However, there is an even better way of avoiding this problem, which is to increase the number of alternatives in the forced-choice task to three or four, so the subject does not guess correctly so often.)

Further variations on the staircase technique are designed to converge progressively to the threshold, by starting with fairly large step changes in the stimulus between one trial and the next, and reducing the step size as the experiment progresses. The reduction is usually made at reversal points. Thus the early trials direct the stimulus quickly to the approximate region of threshold, and subsequent trials fine-tune the stimulus closer and closer to the threshold level (Taylor & Creelman, 1967; Pentland, 1980; Tyrrell & Owens, 1988).

method of a thousand staircases

Staircases can, like the method of adjustment, be used to track a changing threshold, provided the rate of change is slow. If the changes are rapid, the only alternative is the **method of a thousand staircases**. For example, adaptation to an intense stimulus experienced for a minute or two usually leads to an after-effect that lasts at most a few minutes. Tracking these changes cannot be done with a conventional staircase: instead, the experiment has to be repeated many times, with sufficient time between experiments for complete recovery. In each experiment a number of trials (notionally 1000) are presented, each at strictly the same time relative to the period of adaptation (e.g. the first trial might be five seconds after adaptation, the next ten seconds, and so on). The outcome of the first trial in the first experiment is used to determine the stimulus level that will be presented in the first trial of the second experiment. The response to the first trial in the second experiment determines the stimulus in the first trial of the third experiment. Meanwhile, the second trial in the first experiment determines the second trial in the second experiment. And so on. Each staircase consists of a series of trials, one trial in each experiment. The length of the staircase equals the total number of experiments done. Each staircase converges on the threshold at the particular instant in time its trials were all presented, relative to the time of exposure to the adapting stimulus (Cornsweet & Teller, 1965).

The most modern adaptive techniques use far more complicated calculations between each trial to decide which stimulus level to present next. They use information not just from the previous trial but from all the preceding trials in the block. They also incorporate theoretical assumptions about how to quantify efficiency and about the shape of the underlying psychometric function. The computer programs are however not necessarily long; for example, the best known, Quest, contains only about 40 commands in Basic (Watson & Pelli, 1983). The number of trials needed to obtain a measure of threshold can be as few as 20–40, depending how accurate you want your answer to be: the more trials, the more precise your estimate will be. I cannot go into numerical detail about the methods here, but merely mention that they generally concentrate upon placing the next stimulus at a level that will give most information about the location of the threshold (e.g. Harvey, 1986; King-Smith, Grigsby, Vingrys, Benes & Supowit, 1994; Treutwein, 1995; Alcalá-Quintana & García-Pérez, 2004). This level is not always where the threshold is currently believed to be, because (i) the point of maximum slope of the psychometric function is not always at the threshold (the underlying curve is not always a symmetrical cumulative Gaussian), and (ii) binomial sampling error is maximal at 50% response levels, which makes response probabilities near 50% less reliable than those at higher or lower values. The errors become progressively smaller above and below the 50% level. In 2AFC experiments, a 50% response level is expected for very weak stimuli, and in this case the optimal stimulus to present is somewhat above the threshold intensity. The optimal level in any given experiment thus depends on the number of forced-choice alternatives, and on the slope of the psychometric function.

Further, recent techniques enable the slope (i.e. the subject's internal noise) to be estimated adaptively during the experiment as well as the threshold

(King-Smith & Rose, 1997; Kontsevich & Tyler, 1999; Treutwein & Strasburger, 1999). This is done by searching through the bivariate space of values for threshold and slope, and by placing stimuli nearer the locations optimal for slope estimation than for threshold.

9.5 DIFFERENCE THRESHOLDS

The field of psychophysics is not, thankfully, limited to studying absolute thresholds. We can also investigate what happens when clearly detectable stimuli are presented. The first question we can ask is, however, still one about thresholds: namely, what is the minimum detectable difference between two stimuli that can be noticed? This is known as the **difference threshold** or **just noticeable difference** (JND). The basic methods available to us include all those listed above: constant stimuli, adjustment, limits and staircases, with or without forced choice. For example, the subject might be shown two spots of light and asked to adjust the intensity of one until it is just noticeably brighter than the other. The variable stimulus may be called the **test stimulus** (or probe stimulus) while the other, kept constant, is the **standard stimulus** (or comparison stimulus).

The first parameter we can vary in experiments on difference thresholds is the intensity of the standard stimulus. In other words, we can test whether a weak but clearly detectable stimulus has to be incremented by a lesser or greater amount than a strong stimulus must be incremented, to enable a subject to detect the difference. This is the basic paradigm that led to **Weber's law**, which states that the increment threshold is a constant fraction of the standard stimulus. So if a dim spot of light has to be increased in intensity by 2% before the subject can see the difference, an intense spot must also be incremented by 2% of its luminance before the subject will notice. Weber's law applies to a large number of sensory situations, although the value of the **Weber fraction** varies enormously (e.g. 2% for light intensity, 3.3% for weight, 33% for sound intensity, 0.3% for sound frequency, 20% for taste intensity). The Weber fraction rises above its normal value at very low intensities, where noise becomes significant (so a standard of zero intensity has a difference threshold not of zero, but of the absolute threshold). The fraction also tends to deviate for very intense stimuli.

A second issue in difference threshold experiments is whether the standard stimulus is presented with the same time-course as the test stimulus. There are two common paradigms here. Firstly, the standard may consist of a continuously presented background, while the test is a brief probe presentation superimposed on the background. Secondly, the background may be set to zero intensity, while

difference threshold
just noticeable difference

test stimulus

standard stimulus

Weber's law

Weber fraction

the standard and test are both (equally) brief; the subject has to discriminate between the two types of brief stimulus. (A third situation is possible but rarer: stimuli may be given for the same long period and the subject has as long as desired to inspect the stimuli before responding.) The first paradigm bears on many real-world tasks, but has some disadvantages: (i) for stable performance, the subject first has to adapt to the background, and this often takes longer than is generally thought (this problem applies to the second paradigm too); (ii) brief, 'transient' test stimuli might be detected by different mechanisms from those that detect continuously presented 'sustained' background stimuli. The second paradigm can also resemble some real-world tasks, but may run into problems about what the subject is actually doing. Thus it is possible for the subject to build up in memory, over the course of many trials, a representation of an 'average' stimulus. The subject may then judge which of the two brief stimulus presentations was most clearly the greater relative to that memory trace rather than to each other. In fact, some experimenters deliberately leave out the standard stimulus and merely ask the subjects to judge whether the test stimuli are above or below average: this is the **method of single stimuli**. This can give quite good results, showing that memory for the stimulus can act as a stable reference (Woodworth & Schlosberg, 1954).

method of single stimuli

The third point to note is that difference thresholds can be measured for decrements as well as increments away from the standard. These two thresholds are not always identical. For example, luminance decrements are easier to detect than increments of equal physical magnitude.

An alternative approach is to present a series of test stimuli that range both above and below the standard in the same experiment. The subject is forced to choose whether the test appears greater or less than the standard. A single curve (usually a cumulative Gaussian) is fitted to all the data. The stimulus level where both responses are equally (50%) probable is identified and is labelled the **point of subjective equality** (PSE). The standard deviation of the Gaussian is taken as a measure of the difference threshold. This method is, however, used principally where the PSE is the main parameter of interest. The use of a single cumulative Gaussian rather than two such ogives, one for the increment threshold and one for the decrement threshold, shows that the theoretical underpinnings of the PSE approach are somewhat different from those used for assessing JNDs directly.

point of subjective equality

9.6 SENSATIONAL MEASUREMENTS

A major concern of the early psychophysicists was to measure the strength of sensation. The commonest technique for doing this is **magnitude estimation**.

magnitude estimation

Individuals are first shown a standard stimulus and asked to associate that stimulus with a particular number, for example 100. They are then shown a test stimulus and asked to rate the strength of that stimulus relative to the standard. So if, for example, they thought the test stimulus to be half the strength of the standard, they would give the test a rating of 50. If they thought it twice as strong, the rating would be 200. A series of test stimuli of various strengths can be used to build a picture of how apparent magnitude ψ varies with physical magnitude ϕ. Generally, it is found that the relationship is a power function, $\psi = \phi^i$ where $i = 0.67$ for sound intensity, 0.3 for brightness, 3.5 for electric shock, and other sensory dimensions have other values. Magnitude estimation is a simple technique which requires little training of the subject and yet elicits reliable data from an individual. However, there can be wide variability between subjects, so many have to be studied if normative statistics are required.

matching

A variation on the response technique is **matching**. People are asked to adjust the strength of a comparison stimulus to 'match' the intensity of a test stimulus that differs in some way. The setting can be made by the method of adjustment, or by any other technique. In **cross-modal matching** the stimuli are in completely different sense modalities, for example a spot of light might be adjusted to match the perceived intensity of a touch to the skin. However, it is also common to see **intra-modal matching**, for example adjusting the intensity of a red light to match the intensity of a white light.

cross-modal matching

intra-modal matching

There are in fact two ways this procedure can be used. Firstly, a range of different test stimuli can be adjusted to match the intensity of a standard. For example, different coloured lights can be matched in apparent intensity to a standard white light. Plotting the data as a function of the wavelength of the test stimulus then gives an **iso-intensity contour**. A family of such contours can be plotted for standard stimuli of different intensities. For example, if the white light is just at absolute threshold, then lights of all the other colours will be adjusted to their respective thresholds. The lowest possible contour in the family will thus be the threshold for light detection as a function of wavelength. For a comparison (e.g. white light) stimulus above threshold, lights on its iso-intensity curve will all appear equally strong. In many cases (e.g. sound intensity, black–white contrast), these curves tend to flatten out at high intensities, so perceived intensity becomes independent of the physical parameter under consideration.

iso-intensity contour

Alternatively, the adjustable stimulus may remain the same, in all but intensity, throughout (in our example, it remains a white light), while the test stimuli are of different qualities (e.g. colours) but constant physical intensity. This gives measures of the apparent intensities of the test stimuli that are more akin to those obtained by magnitude estimation; in effect, the subject is adjusting the intensity of the (white) light to match the apparent intensity of the test stimulus.

Another technique for scaling the apparent intensity dimension is **fractionation**, in which subjects are presented with two stimuli that are identical in all but intensity, e.g. white lights. They are asked to adjust one of the stimuli so it appears half the intensity of the other. Subjects can be asked to quarter, or to double, the apparent intensity, but it is easier to stick to halving and build up a scale of apparent intensity by varying the intensity of the comparison stimulus. For some stimulus dimensions, **bisection** can be used. A stimulus has to be adjusted so it lies exactly half-way between two other stimuli. (This is more common for dimensions other than intensity, an obvious example being spatial distance judgements.) In effect, the subject has to decide whether the two intervals between the three stimuli are identical.

Magnitude and scaling techniques do not depend upon there being a linear relationship between perception and response. Any monotonic relationship will do. Another response that can be used under some circumstances is **reaction time** (RT). In general, reaction times decrease as stimulus intensity rises. This effect is clearest at low intensities; RT tends to stabilize at higher intensities. Measures of RT are therefore sometimes used to assess stimulus strength. The procedure is relatively simple: subjects merely have to press a button as quickly as they can when the stimulus occurs. A warning signal is usually given first, and there is then a waiting period of random duration before the stimulus is presented (to prevent the subject anticipating when it might occur). A lot of trials are needed for each RT measurement (of the order of 100 repetitions at minimum), and a lot of practice trials have to be given before performance stabilizes. Moreover, it is problematic how to average the data, since the RT distribution is almost always positively skewed (i.e. there are more very long RTs than there are very short). Some workers transform the data non-linearly, averaging the logarithm or arcsine of the RT; others use the median, or average only the central 90% or 95% of the distribution. Finally, the procedure requires stimuli with sudden onset, so sensory mechanisms detecting sustained stimuli cannot be assessed in this fashion.

In some cases, perceptual effects can be monitored by **nulling** them with another stimulus. This method can be used in situations where the perceptual effect is illusory, or a distortion of the real stimulus. Such distortions include those induced by surrounding stimuli (simultaneous contrast; e.g. when a small stationary visual stimulus is viewed against a moving background, the stimulus appears to drift in the opposite direction). Alternatively, the distortions might be after-effects of adapting to an intense stimulus (successive contrast; e.g. the motion after-effect: Mather, Verstraten & Anstis, 1998). There must be a clear null point along the stimulus dimension, for example stationariness in the case of movement, white in the case of apparent colour, or constant intensity in the case of stimuli that appear to be increasing or decreasing in intensity. The idea is

fractionation

bisection

reaction time

nulling

that the illusory or distorted percept will be cancelled by the perceptual effect of the real, ongoing input, yielding a percept that is at the neutral or null point. So apparent movement, for example, may be nulled by moving the test stimulus in the opposite direction and asking the subject to judge whether the stimulus appears stationary (Blake & Hiris, 1993). The dependent variable is the amount of real movement that exactly cancels the apparent movement. This technique is quite sensitive and is relatively easy for the subject to do. However, issues of interpretation arise, in that the test stimulus is not neutral, but is entering the sensory system and affecting it during the test period. There may be quite complex or unknown interactions between the system's response to the test stimulus and the processes within the system that are generating the effect you are trying to measure.

9.7 SOME GENERAL TIPS ON RUNNING EXPERIMENTS

Performance on novel tasks is not necessarily stationary over time. Practice makes subjects better, while fatigue and boredom may have the opposite effect. The number of practice trials that should be given before the data collection proper starts is an empirical matter: one should always check that performance has levelled off (or at least is minimal compared with the variability intrinsic to performance). The usual procedures of randomization or counterbalancing of conditions should be followed to reduce the effects of residual non-stationariness on the interpretation of the results. Most psychophysical tasks are in fact extremely boring to do, involving intense concentration on a stimulus array that hardly ever varies. Motivation is therefore very important, as are frequent recreational breaks from the laboratory. Uninterrupted sequences of trials (blocks) should not exceed about 100 trials in length, or last more than 10 minutes. Successive trials may follow one another closely in time to speed things up, but subjects will be happier, and less likely to make errors, if they can pause at any time during a block for a rest. In many experiments data will need to be combined from different blocks; this involves theoretical assumptions about stationariness, but is usually unavoidable.

Other refinements allow for human fallibility. Subjects can make errors not just because of sensory limitations but also for mechanical or for other extraneous reasons. Firstly, their fingers may slip or become misaligned when pressing the response keys, so they activate the wrong one by accident. Secondly, their attention may wander during a trial, or they may sneeze or be distracted. So in vision experiments they may blink, or allow their eyes to deviate from the fixation point; in auditory experiments the telephone in the next room may ring or their stomachs may gurgle; in olfactory experiments they may fart (well, the experimenter never does); and so on. There are two ways of coping with this. One is to allow for it in the data analysis, for example by assuming that the psychometric function (Figure 9.1) will never reach 100% even for very strong stimuli, because of these errors (Hall, 1981). The curve can then be compressed so it asymptotes at, say, 99% instead of 100% (i.e. assuming 1 error in 100 trials; other figures are of course possible if your subject is more or less reliable – it is a matter of judgement). The second method is to give your subject a 'cancel-the-previous-trial' key, so if a problem arises that the subject is aware of, he or she can press the emergency button and the computer will reset the values of all its variables as though that trial had never occurred. The latter method can, of course, be used only if the stimulus presentation order contains some random-ness, so the subject cannot cheat by simply pressing the button over and over to obtain multiple presentations of the same stimulus before making a decision.

In detection tasks, an important consideration, as mentioned previously, is the subject's knowledge or memory of the target. Knowing what the stimulus appears like aids performance and lowers threshold; uncertainty has the opposite effect. There are two ways uncertainty can arise. One is memory loss. This can be reduced by allowing the subject to see the stimulus consciously and clearly, either (i) occasionally during the experiment (e.g. by presenting a range of stim-ulus intensities that includes some well above detection threshold) or (ii) delib-erately at the beginning of each block of trials. Some workers present a supra-threshold stimulus before every trial in the experiment; however, this is dangerous, because that stimulus could easily mask the near-threshold test stim-ulus that follows it, or it may cause adaptation, or it may have unknown effects on memory. (Is it a sensory buffer, working memory or long-term memory that needs to be activated? Will it cause retinal after-images in visual experiments?)

The second common source of uncertainty is the random mixing of different stimuli within the same block of trials. Thresholds are higher when the subject knows that the stimulus on any given trial may take one of two (or more) forms, such as different colours of lights, rather than all the stimuli being the same (apart, of course, from intensity). In fact the more uncertain the subject, the worse performance gets for each stimulus individually.

Knowledge of results, or feedback, is also important. Subjects perform better and more stably when they receive feedback. This is usually given in the form of a brief indicator as to whether they were right or wrong on the previous trial. For example, in an experiment on vision, a tone may sound only after correct trials (a tone that is clearly different from the tone that demarcated the observation inter-val), or there may be two different tones, for correct and incorrect trials.

Whatever your chosen technique, with recent advances in computer technology the number of software and hardware tools available to set up your experiment and analyse the data is now very large (see Box 9.1). This makes it much easier to get started, setting up new tasks has become convenient and flexible, and collect-ing lots of valuable data a pleasure!

Box 9.1 **Tools and tips on the Web**

It would appear from the text that to carry out an experiment in psychophysics takes more than just persistence and patience; you also have to perform complex sums in your head in between every trial! Naturally, this is a delusion. Just as the presentation of stimuli has to be exact and is thus typically carried out by hardware, so the calculation of which stimulus to present next is performed by software. Indeed, the two tasks are normally combined into a single program which selects or modifies the stimulus, presents it to the subject, registers the subject's response, and computes which stimulus should be given on the next trial. It also stores the data, checks whether the block of trials has finished, analyses the results, and perhaps even performs some statistical test that may be of immediate use to the experimenter (e.g. to guide a decision about what to do in the next block of trials).

How does one obtain such marvellous software? Of course, you can write your own, and most psychophysicists learn to do just that. (They then go on to get well-paid jobs in computer programming rather than continue their careers in psychology; but that is another story.) However, there is an increasing number of such heroes who have made their programs freely available to the research community. Their software can in most cases be downloaded via the Internet and run on common desktop computers. The programs can be very easy to use, but in many cases the user does require some under-the-bonnet knowledge of how they work – not just in theory (as given in the text of this chapter) but also as to the practicalities of how the software controls the particular hardware you have for creating or handling the stimuli. Such factors may well be laboratory-specific, and having an experienced practitioner and/or a technician on hand to guide you will be a help. Nevertheless such technical skills are not difficult to acquire and tips and guides are also available on the Web about how to set up experiments, perform calibrations and standardize conditions so replication can take place between laboratories.

For example, a useful review of software packages can be found on http://vision.nyu.edu/Tips/FaithsSoftwareReview.html, and a comprehensive overview is given on:
http://www.visionscience.com/documents/strasburger.html
For further links go to the VisionScience website at:
http://www.visionscience.com and under the Resources menu click on Software, Products and Guides&FAQs. The last two include also tips on hardware; see particularly http://vision.nyu.edu/Tips

If you like programming yourself, an easy basic tool is NIH Image, which enables you to generate your own images and run experiments using macros. It is available free from:
http://rsbweb.nih.gov/nih-image/index.html

Although these resources seem mainly orientated towards vision research, remember that for many studies in both general and experimental psychology the stimulus materials are presented on a screen. These software packages therefore have general applicability; for example, you can copy and paste digital photographs, words or other material into many of these packages directly. For some general psychology packages, see:
http://www.visionscience.com/documents/strasburger.html#Psychol_Exp

9.8 CONCLUSION

Psychophysics attempts to grapple quantitatively with phenomenology and not just behaviour. A century's research on imporving the methods has now given us a range of fast, efficient and flexible techniques for measuring both minimal and noticeable subjective experience, as well as perhaps subliminal reactions. Sensitivity can be distinguished from motivational bias or prejudice and both assessed separately. The procedures can be implemented easily on modern computers, not just in the laboratory but also in field settings.

9.9 FURTHER READING

Excellent introductory textbooks with chapters on psychophysical methods include Levine's (2000) Blake and Sekuler's (2005) text. Pelli and Farell's (1995) and Farell and Pelli's (1998) texts also provide useful material, as do Chapters 2 and 3 of Pashler and Wixted's (2002) book. Book-length explanations of psychophysical theory and practice that are both clear and detailed include Gescheider's (1997) and Macmillan and Creelman's (2005) texts. Finally, a series of methodologically orientated research papers on psychophysics can be found in a special issue of the journal *Perception & Psychophysics* edited by Klein and Macmillan (2001), among which the review by Klein (2001) is particularly useful.

10

Using Psychometric Tests

Sean Hammond

10.1   Introduction
10.2   Types of psychometric test
   10.2.1   Projective tests
   10.2.2   Self-report questionnaires
   10.2.3   Objective tests
   10.2.4   Normative or criterion reference
   10.2.5   Idiographic measurement
10.3   Classical test theory
   10.3.1   Defining reliability
      10.3.1.1   Consistency between parallel tests
      10.3.1.2   Internal consistency
      10.3.1.3   Consistency across time (test–retest reliability)
      10.3.1.4   Inter-rater consistency
   10.3.2   General considerations with regard to reliability
10.4   The problem of validity
   10.4.1   Content validation
   10.4.2   Criterion validation
   10.4.3   Construct validation
   10.4.4   General issues of validation
10.5   Item response theory
10.6   Conclusion
10.7   Further reading

This chapter introduces the reader to the major issues in the use of psychometric tests. It will concentrate on the most widely used approach in testing commonly known as classical test theory, but will finish by briefly introducing a more recent approach known as item response theory. The chapter attempts to provide the reader with the basic knowledge required to make considered decisions in developing a research study using psychometric tests as its means of measurement.

Key terms

ceiling effect	postdictive validation
Cohen's kappa	power tests
concurrent validation	projective tests
construct validation	Rasch models
content validation	reliability coefficient
criterion referenced	repertory grid
criterion validation	response set
Cronbach's alpha	self-report
face validity	speed tests
faking good	split-half
floor effect	stability
guessing parameter	standard error of
idiographic	measurement
item parameter	systematic error
item response theory	test–retest
normative	tests of knowledge
norm referenced	tests of performance
norms	true score model
person parameter	unidimensional scale
predictive validity	unsystematic error

10.1 INTRODUCTION

One of the most widely used methods of data collection in psychological research is psychometric testing. However, it must be said that there is a plethora of suboptimal studies in the psychological research literature whose major failing is the ill-advised use of psychometric methodology. In this chapter I intend to address some of the main issues in psychometric testing in the hope that the reader will be able to make informed decisions when selecting a test for use in a research project.

There appear to be two main reasons for the popularity of psychometric tests in psychological research. Firstly, psychometric tests have been developed to measure an extremely broad range of mental characteristics, including aptitudes, competencies, personality traits, mood states, psychopathology, psychosomatic symptomatology, attitudes, motives and self-concept. These developments have provided the researcher with a wide variety of measurement tools that make a large number of psychological variables accessible for research. A second reason for the popularity of psychometric methods is the relative ease with which it is possible to collect large amounts of data. A great many psychometric tests, though by no means all, allow the researcher to gather data at one sitting from large numbers of respondents.

However, one reason why so many studies based on psychometric test data remain unconvincing is that the interest in using psychometric tests is not attended by an equal interest in the technicalities and sophistication of the psychometric principles that underlie their proper use. This lack of interest in psychometrics itself, coupled with an uninformed use of psychometric methods, has burdened the psychological research literature with poorly operationalized studies with little or no potential for replication.

Psychometrics means literally 'measurement of the mind', and psychometric tests are designed to measure the intrinsic mental characteristics of a person. One of the main problems confronting the researcher in psychology is how this measurement can be effected. Almost by definition, the variables under consideration will be those characteristics of the individual that do not lend themselves to simple physical measurement. For example, the degree of extroversion that an individual has or their level of numerical reasoning ability are characteristics that are not accessible to such measuring devices as rulers or weighing scales. Nevertheless, accurate measurement is a necessary prerequisite for any scientific endeavour.

Owing to the lack of direct access to the mental characteristics under scrutiny, the discipline of psychometrics has developed a detailed set of procedures and models for statistical estimation. Essentially, these procedures rely on the presence of a large number of indicators allowing us to 'focus in' on or triangulate the characteristic being measured. In most psychometric tests these indicators may be viewed as the individual items or questions of which they are composed.

10.2 TYPES OF PSYCHOMETRIC TEST

There are many different types of psychometric test, each using a different strategy for data elicitation. The type of test is dictated by the theoretical orientation of the researcher as well as the kinds of questions being asked. For our purposes we will broadly describe the various types under four headings: projective tests, self-report inventories, objective tests and idiographic measures. Each of these types of test has a place in psychological measurement, although each has its own area of application, advantages and limitations. It is always depressing to read an account by a researcher who believes that his or her preferred technique should be used in preference to all others. The choice of test must depend entirely on the nature of the research and the theoretical framework being applied. However, the underlying psychometric issues are similar irrespective of the test form. These are that the test should be reliable, valid and appropriate for the particular study it is being used for.

10.2.1 Projective tests

Projective tests are designed to be indirect measures of an individual's mental state. The common element in all these tests is that the testee is asked to proffer an unstructured response to some form of stimulus or task. Projective tests are typically used to identify personality characteristics related to abnormal psychological functioning. One primary use of such tests is to examine aspects of the person that are considered to be unconscious. The basic idea is that issues a person would not normally be able to articulate directly may be accessed by the process of projective testing.

projective tests

The most widely known projective test is the Rorschach inkblot test in which the respondent is presented with a series of ambiguous stimuli in the form of inkblots and is required to say what each brings to mind (Rorschach, 1921; Erdberg & Exner, 1984). The tester then interprets the responses according to a scoring protocol derived from some a priori theory (often psychoanalytic). She or he is then able to derive a score for the respondent, often leading to placing the respondent within a diagnostic category.

A wide variety of projective tests is available (Klopfer & Taulbee, 1976; Ziller, 1973). One popular form involves presenting respondents with pictures and asking them to compose a story around the image. Themes within these stories are then identified by the tester, again using an a priori theoretical framework, which enables a categorical judgement to be made of the respondent's mental state. Examples of these tests are the Blackie Test (psychoanalytic framework) (Blum, 1949) and the Thematic Apperception Tests (Murray's Needs framework) (Atkinson, 1958).

One of the weaknesses of projective tests is that they typically operate at the nominal level of measurement, that is, simply provide a categorical description of the respondent. Procedures for more elaborate quantification of an individual's responses do exist for some of the most well-used projective tests, although they are nearly always complicated to learn (Exner, 1986; Atkinson, 1958). This is because of the almost infinite variety of possible responses that need to be coded and categorized.

Projective tests are frequently criticized on the grounds that they appear to lack objectivity. The tester's interpretation of open-ended information is often said to be subjective and arbitrary. While this is certainly a major issue in projective testing, it is one that can be addressed with care and the rigorous application of objective scoring criteria. Of course, the basis of these criteria resides in the a priori theoretical model upon which the test is built. This means that projective tests are not normally appropriate in an eclectic research context, and for this reason they are not widely used in research and tend to occur in therapeutic contexts.

10.2.2 Self-report questionnaires

self-report The use of **self-report** questionnaires as a means of measuring psychological characteristics grows out of the simple assumption that the best way of finding out about an individual is to ask them direct questions. A huge number of well-used self-report questionnaires exist, and most of them are designed to measure personality traits or attitudes. The reason for this abundance is their comparative ease in administration and the almost limitless range of psychological characteristics that can be addressed.

One of the first self-report questionnaires to be developed was the Woodworth Personal Profile used during World War I as a means of screening army conscripts; examples of some of the questions asked are as follows.

- Do you daydream frequently?
- Do you usually feel well and strong?
- Do you think you have hurt yourself by going too much with women?

Woodworth's questionnaire is bizarre by today's standards but it is a useful reminder of how test items will reflect the attitudes and values that prevailed at the time they were developed.

It is important that the questions or items in a self-report questionnaire are relevant to the characteristic being examined. Clearly the accuracy of the measurement depends to a great extent upon this relevance. Thus, if we were developing a questionnaire to measure extroversion we might include questions on social activities and impulsivity, whereas a question on a person's fondness for bicycles would have no bearing on the domain in question. This is an issue of content validity, and we return to it later.

Questionnaires are often criticized as research tools owing to the problem of response bias. This describes the situation in which a respondent systematically fails to answer the questions accurately. There may be many reasons for response bias. It may be due to a deliberate attempt on the part of the respondent to present an image of him or herself that is not true, a situation known as **faking good**. In addition, respondents may possess an in-built tendency to answer 'yes' or 'no' to our questions, producing a response bias termed a **response set**. Alternatively, the respondents may simply not know the answer to the question either through lack of self-knowledge or because the question is posed in an ambiguous manner, and so the response may be a random guess. Thus, an important assumption in using self-report questionnaires is the accuracy of individuals' responses.

faking good

response set

10.2.3 Objective tests

The development of the discipline of psychometrics grew out of early attempts to measure human abilities. The social Darwinist approach of Sir Francis Galton, based on his desire to estimate intellectual potential from physical characteristics, soon gave way to the more pragmatic approach of Alfred Binet. Binet devised a series of tasks, performance on which served to indicate the intellectual level of young children. Some examples of Binet's tasks are as follows.

- Point to various parts of face (age level 3).
- Repeat five digits (age level 7).
- Recite days of the week (age level 9).
- Repeat seven digits (age level 12).

Nearly all ability tests developed since have been based on Binet's basic strategy. Thus, tests of numerical reasoning present the respondent with a series of numerical tasks (addition, division, etc.) while tests of verbal reasoning present the respondent with verbal tasks (synonyms, comprehension).

A distinction is often drawn between **tests of knowledge** and **tests of performance**. The former type of test simply prompts the respondent to provide information, as in a history test with the item 'What year was the Battle of Hastings?' Alternatively, the test may ask the respondent to carry out a task, as in the numerical reasoning test with the item 'What is 16 multiplied by 7?'

tests of knowledge
tests of performance

A further distinction may be made between **power tests** and **speed tests**. A power test asks the respondent to respond to each item in their own time, placing no time constraints upon them, while a speed test asks the respondent to respond to as many items as they can within a specific time frame. Obviously, the speed test is more practical to administer, but it does carry the assumption that speed is associated with ability.

power tests
speed tests

For the test to be useful it must be able to discriminate between respondents. Therefore, it is important that the tests are appropriate for the particular group of respondents on whom they are used. If the test is too easy a large number of the respondents may get every answer correct, and this will mean that the resulting measurement will not enable the tester to discriminate between respondents. In other words, our research would be compromised by the existence of a **ceiling effect** or **floor effect**.

ceiling effect or floor effect

10.2.4 Normative or criterion reference

When we have obtained a test score, the problem remains of how to interpret it. Simply having a neuroticism score of 12 tells us nothing about the respondent unless we can refer the score to some kind of standard. Most psychometric tests in use today are **normative** or **norm referenced**, which means that data exist which tell us what range of scores is expected from the population under consideration. This requires that the means and standard deviations of a large representative sample are available to the tester so that she or he can interpret the meaning of an individual's score. These descriptive statistics are termed the **norms**.

normative or norm referenced

norms

For example, most intelligence tests will be constructed so as to produce scores with a mean of 100 and a standard deviation of 15. A respondent with an IQ score of 130, therefore, is deemed to have a high IQ, while a respondent with a score of 100 is deemed to be of 'average' intelligence. This means that the interpretation of the test score requires that there exists some normative information in the form of means and standard deviations relevant to the population from which a particular respondent is drawn. A vast majority of psychometric tests are developed as normative tests in which the test norms serve as a standard against which individuals are measured.

Of course, this assumes that the test score occupies a point along a continuum and that the population scores will conform to a normal distribution. Without a normal distribution the mean is not a useful measure of central tendency and so the standard deviation is meaningless as an index of variation. All norm referenced psychometric tests make this assumption of normality by definition.

It is possible to use criteria other than test norms for interpreting test scores, as long as they are clearly specified in advance. This strategy is employed by a class of tests known as **criterion referenced** (Glaser, 1963). In this case an external performance criterion becomes the standard against which a respondent is judged. Typically, criterion-referenced tests are used in the assessment of competencies particularly in an educational assessment context (Nitko, 1988).

criterion referenced

For example, a set of reading problems may be given to a child. The criterion for entering a particular class is that the child will correctly solve each problem. If the child does not answer each question correctly they fail to reach the criterion and are not accepted into the class. The main point in criterion-referenced tests is that the respondent either reaches a prespecified criterion or does not. Obviously, this means that the criteria have to be established very accurately and precisely justified before the test is made available for use. Criterion-referenced tests may also be interpreted normatively since the resulting score is usually a continuous, number correct, value. The test norms may be used for interpretation as well as the criterion pass mark as long as normative information exists.

10.2.5 Idiographic measurement

The tests described so far rely for their interpretation upon a comparison, either with normative or with external a priori criteria, so that an individual respondent can be placed in position relative to either a 'norm' or a specific criterion. However, there are situations in psychological research where focus is upon the individual respondent and placing them on a relative scale is irrelevant. An example of such a study might be one where a researcher wishes to follow a single patient over a course of psychotherapy and attempt to measure the change in their psychological state. In this case, the respondent may be asked to respond to a test designed specifically for them on a number of occasions. The focus of interest is on the change manifest in the individual's responding on each occasion.

This approach is known as **idiographic** since it focuses on the individual respondent in isolation. This means that the questions that are asked of the respondent may be unique to them, and indeed one of the most popular strategies for idiographic measurement is the use of a **repertory grid** in which the respondent generates the constructs that are of most relevance to them. This means that the assessment device is idiosyncratic and there is no commonality between respondents in the constructs being measured.

idiographic

repertory grid

The idiographic approach has the drawback that comparisons between respondents are difficult if not impossible, and the aggregation of idiographic data is meaningless. However, the approach may be of great value when the focus of interest is upon the dynamic processes within individuals. This is often the case in therapeutic evaluation research or audit.

10.3 CLASSICAL TEST THEORY

As we have seen above, psychometric measurement depends upon estimation rather than direct measurement. As a result psychologists cannot expect perfectly accurate measurement. The role of the test developer is to produce tests which have the greatest accuracy possible and to provide the test user with details of the degree of accuracy they can expect when using the test in question.

The earliest psychometric measurement theory stems from the work of Charles Spearman and is variously called classical test theory, true score theory or reliability theory; it remains today the most widely applied basis for psychometric measurement. A number of other psychometric models have grown out of this classical approach, notably generalizability theory (Cronbach, Gleser, Nanda & Rajaratnam,

1972; Shavelson & Webb, 1991) and item response theory (Hambleton, Swaminathan & Rogers, 1991; Suen, 1990; Lord & Novick, 1968; Mislevy, 1993).

true score model   The **true score model** serves as the basis for classical test theory. In this model it is assumed that the test score is influenced by two factors: firstly, and most obviously, the true extent of the characteristic being measured; and, secondly, random error. This may be represented formally as:

$$\text{Observed score} = \text{True score} + \text{Error}.$$

Thus the test score, or observed score, is a function of the 'true' variance and the error variance. The variance due to error may be positive or negative, so that when we obtain a score from a test it may be an overestimate of the true score or an underestimate. It is the job of the test developer to produce reliable psychometric tests in which the error variance is minimized. A reliable test is one where the 'true' score is close to the 'observed' score.

The error associated with a test score may be systematic or unsystematic.

systematic error   **Systematic error** refers to aspects of error that are built into the test itself and biases the resulting score consistently in one direction. Such error may be due to the use of ambiguous items or the situation where the test is influenced by

unsystematic error   another variable which is not being assessed. **Unsystematic error** refers to error that is external to the test itself and is assumed to be random such that it might equally result in an overestimate or an underestimate. Classical test theory is built upon the assumption that the test has been constructed with sufficient care such that systematic error is negligible and only unsystematic error exists.

Classical test theory also makes a number of assumptions about the nature of this error.

1 Error variation is random.
2 Error variation is normally distributed with a mean of zero.
3 Error variance is completely independent of people's 'true' scores.
4 The error variance of different tests is not correlated.

The implications of these assumptions are that, if we test an individual on a large number of tests for a single characteristic, the mean of these 'observed' scores will equal the 'true' score for that individual. This is because the error variance is partialled out by the operation of adding all the test scores together. This is shown in Table 10.1.

10.3.1 Defining reliability

The reliability of a test is an indication of whether it measures anything at all. As we have already said, the reliability of a test is an indication of the similarity

Table 10.1 Simple example of the basic premise of classical test theory

	Observed score	True score	Error
Test 1	22	21	1
Test 2	24	21	3
Test 3	18	21	-3
Test 4	19	21	-2
Test 5	22	21	1
Mean	21	21	0

between the 'true' and 'observed' scores. One way of conceiving reliability, therefore, is to think of the correlation between the 'true' score and the 'observed' score. Similarly, it may be possible to conceive of reliability (r_{tt}) as the ratio of 'true' variance to the total test variance:

$$r_{tt} = \frac{\sigma^2_{true}}{\sigma^2_{observed}}$$

In this way reliability can also be seen as the proportion of variance in test scores that is due to the variability of true scores. This is equivalent to the squared correlation between 'true' and 'observed' scores. The simple correlation between true and observed is known as the reliability index, while the squared correlation between true and observed is termed the **reliability coefficient**.

reliability coefficient

The greater the reliability a test has, the less the error; and the less the error, the greater the accuracy. Therefore, reliability is associated with the accuracy of the test. If we are looking at the score of one person on a test of known reliability, it is possible to estimate the accuracy of that person's score by calculating what is called the **standard error of measurement** (SEM):

standard error of measurement

$$SEM = \sigma_{observed} \sqrt{(1 - r_{tt})}$$

The SEM allows us to generate confidence intervals for a single respondent's score, and it is a vital piece of information if we are examining a respondent's score change across time (see Box 10. 2). Nunnally and Bernstein (1994, Chapter 6) give a readable account of the main issues surrounding the SEM.

So far we have talked about reliability theoretically and have shown that it may be conceptualized as the correlation between true and observed scores. However, in practice we do not know the value of true scores and so the estimation of reliability is not quite as simple as this account might suggest. In order to estimate the reliability of a test, psychologists have adopted the notion of consistency. The idea is that randomness is inconsistent: therefore, if we can identify consistency in our test we have the confidence of knowing that it is not simply a function of random error. There are a number of kinds of consistency that we can explore in our test but there are essentially four that are traditionally used.

10.3.1.1 *Consistency between parallel tests*

As we have seen, the idea of large numbers of parallel tests forms the basis of the development of classical test theory. The argument follows that if a perfectly parallel pair of tests exists then differences in scores must be due to measurement error, since the true score will be the same for both tests. Where no error exists, the scores between the two tests will be perfectly consistent with each other. If enough parallel tests are used the average score of all the tests will equal the true score, given that the error variance is random. Of course, we must assume, as with classical test theory, that the tests have equal variance and the error variances of the tests are uncorrelated. Having made this assumption we can then estimate our correlation coefficient in the case of two parallel tests by calculating the correlation between them. The correlation between the two parallel forms is equivalent to the squared correlation between the 'observed' and 'true' scores. Box 10.1 demonstrates how this is, in fact the case, and in so doing provides the basic formulae that underlie classical test theory.

Box 10.1   The basic formulae of classical test theory

How can a simple correlation between parallel tests become the reliability coefficient (a squared correlation between the observed score and the true score)? In this box we will attempt to show you how the assumptions of classical test theory make this possible. The population correlation between two parallel tests X and Y is given by:

$$\rho_{xy} = \frac{\sigma_{xy}}{\sigma_x \sigma_y}$$

(Continued)

Box 10.1   (Continued)

Now, assuming that $X = T_x + e_x$ and $Y = T_y + e_y$, this may be written as:

$$\frac{\sigma_{(T_x+e_x)(T_y+e_y)}}{\sigma_x \sigma_y}$$

and, assuming X and Y are parallel forms:

$$\frac{\sigma_{(T_x+e_x)(T_y+e_y)}}{\sigma_x^2}$$

This is also the term for the population regression coefficient for predicting Y from X and may be rewritten as:

$$\frac{\sigma_{T_x T_y} + \sigma_{e_x T_y} + \sigma_{T_x e_y} + \sigma_{e_x e_y}}{\sigma_x^2}$$

Assuming complete independence of the error terms, this may then be reduced to:

$$\frac{\sigma_{T_x}^2}{\sigma_x^2} \quad \text{or} \quad \frac{\sigma_{T_y}^2}{\sigma_y^2}$$

Reliability is defined as the ratio of true score variance to observed score variance:

$$\frac{\sigma_T^2}{\sigma_x^2}$$

Thus the reliability coefficient, conceived as the squared correlation between the true and observed scores, is identical to the population correlation between two parallel test scores.

   For greater detail the reader should consult Suen (1990) or Allen and Yen (1979).

Despite the fact that consistency between parallel forms is theoretically directly linked to the concept of reliability (Gulliksen, 1950) there are a number of glaring practical problems with this approach to reliability estimation. Most obviously, the procedure requires that we develop not one but two tests for the characteristic in question. Having done this, we then have to ensure equivalence between the two forms. As we will see, test development is not a trivial procedure and requires a great deal of investment of time and resources. In addition, the time required for test administration is doubled because both tests must be taken by the respondents.

10.3.1.2 *Internal consistency*

A more practical method for estimating the reliability of a test that builds upon the theory of parallel tests is to examine its internal consistency. This is based on the principle that each part of the test should be consistent with all other parts (i.e. should represent parallel forms of the same test). An early approach based on this principle was suggested by Spearman (1907) and came to be called the **split-half** **split-half** approach. In this procedure, as its name suggests, the test is administered to a large sample and is then divided in half. This may be done by taking even-numbered items as one half and odd-numbered items as the other half. A score is obtained for each half of the test and a correlation r between the two halves is calculated. The split-half reliability coefficient is then estimated by the formula:

$$r_{tt} = \frac{2r}{1 + r}$$

However, although the principle of split-half reliability is reasonably straightforward, there is one fundamental drawback, which is that different ways of splitting the test can produce quite different reliability coefficients. What is needed is a procedure that gives the average of all the possible combinations of split halves. This was precisely what Kuder and Richardson (1937) provided in a formula that came to be called the KR20 (Kuder and Richardson's 20th formula):

$$KR20 = \left(\frac{N}{N - 1} \right) \left(\frac{\sigma^2_{observed} - \sum pq}{\sigma^2_{observed}} \right)$$

The KR20 was developed for use with dichotomous items but it is very simply generalized for use with items measured on continua or rating scales. This generalization was described by Cronbach (1951) and came to be called

Cronbach's alpha. The alpha coefficient can be calculated in a number of ways but two methods are as follows:

$$\alpha = \left(\frac{N}{N-1}\right)\left(\frac{\sigma_x^2 - \sum \sigma_i^2}{\sigma_x^2}\right)$$

and

$$\alpha = \left(\frac{N}{N-1}\right)\left(1 - \frac{N}{N + 2\sum r_{ij}}\right)$$

where N is the number of items, σ_x^2 is the variance of the total test score, σ_i^2 is the variance of item i, and $\sum r_{ij}$ is the sum of the off-diagonal entries of the $N{\times}N$ inter-item correlation matrix.

The second formula (sometimes known as standardized alpha) shows the relationship that alpha has to the inter-item correlations. As we would expect with a procedure designed to estimate internal consistency, alpha is related to the average of all the inter-item correlations. The higher the correlations between the items, the greater the internal consistency. This makes sense if we assume that all the items are indicators of a common underlying characteristic. Thus each item must have variance in common with all the other variables. In other words, the reliability of a test is related to the homogeneity of the items with each other.

10.3.1.3 *Consistency across time (test–retest reliability)*

Another approach to reliability estimation involves assessing the consistency of a test over time. To assess reliability, a test is given to a sample of respondents at time 1 and then is administered to the same respondents later at time 2. The interval between the two administrations may vary from a few days to a few years. The consistency of the scores between the two administrations of the test is a measure of the reliability. In this case reliability is viewed as an index of **stability** in which the test is thought of as parallel with itself. **stability** The assumption is that any differences across time will be due to measurement errors. The same basic assumptions can be made as with parallel tests. Therefore, the correlation of the two administrations is an estimate of the reliability coefficient.

test–retest   One of the problems with estimating reliability by **test–retest** is deciding on the appropriate interval between administrations. If the interval is too short respondents may remember their responses to the first administration, and this may distort their responses at time 2. Usually, test–retest reliability estimation requires an interval of a month or more. A second problem is that this type of reliability assessment assumes that the characteristic being measured is stable over time. It would make little sense to assess test–retest reliability for a test of mood state, since we would fully expect changes in the characteristic to occur over time. Certain personality traits such as extroversion are generally held to be stable over time, as is intelligence. However, the test user should be clear that this form of reliability estimation makes assumptions not only about measurement error, but also about the stability of the characteristic being measured.

Often, the focus of a research study is upon the assessment of change in which psychometric scores are compared over time. This can only be done meaningfully if the psychometric test in question has good test–retest reliability. Box 10.2 describes how the researcher can make use of the psychometric details of a test to evaluate the meaningfulness of test-score change.

Box 10.2   Measuring individual change

A simple paradigm for the measurement of change is to give an individual a test at time 1 and then, usually following some form of intervention, give them the same test at time 2. The difference between the two administrations of the test, often known as the gain score, is then taken as a measure of change. There is still much debate about the use of these simple gain scores (Mcllenbergh, 1999; Linn & Slinde, 1977) but for the researcher simply looking for a measure of change in their respondents the primary thing to consider is measurement error.

As we have seen, a test score is an estimate of a person's position along a continuum and the accuracy of the estimate is indicated by the standard error of measurement. Thus, if someone obtains a score of 5 at time 1 and 7 at time 2 we need to be sure that this 'change' is not simply due to a random fluctuation in an unreliable test. To assess the meaningfulness of this change we need to know the standard error of measurement of the test. It is vital that the SEM is calculated using the test–retest reliability coefficient rather than an internal consistency coefficient, since the stability of the test is the central concern here. The formula for arriving at a measure of change is then:

(Continued)

Box 10.2 (Continued)

$$Z = \frac{x_2 - x_1}{SEM\sqrt{2}}$$

This formula is found in Lord and Novick (1968) but is now widely referred to as the **reliable change index** (RCI) after Jacobson *et al.* (1984). It is a normally distributed index with a mean of 0 and a standard deviation of 1. This means that, if its absolute value exceeds 1.96, the observed change has a probability of 0.05 or less.

reliable change index

Let us consider the example above where a respondent obtains a score of 5 and time 1 and 7 at time 2. Let us assume the standard deviation of the test score for a representative sample has been found to be 1.50. Below are two calculations, the first assuming a reliability of 0.90 and the second assuming a reliability of 0.70. As you can see, the higher the reliability, the more meaningful the gain score.

Test score		Gain	Standard deviation	Test–retest reliability	SEM	RCI
Time 1	Time 2					
5	7	2	1.50	0.90	0.47	3.01
5	7	2	1.50	0.70	0.82	1.72

10.3.1.4 *Inter-rater consistency*

So far we have assumed that the test score is measured on a continuum, and this is usually the case. However, we mentioned in Section 10.2.1 that some psychometric tests produce measurement at the nominal level. Clearly, the procedures for estimating reliability detailed above, relying as they do on the correlation coefficient, are not appropriate for such data. In this case it is usual to estimate reliability by examining inter-rater consistency. For this procedure, at least two test scorers are used to generate the categorical score for a number of respondents. A contingency table is then drawn up to tabulate the degree of agreement between the raters. The percentage agreement gives a rough estimate of reliability, although a better estimate is obtained by calculating an index of agreement. This **Cohen's kappa** is usually **Cohen's kappa**, which ranges between 0 and 1 and represents the proportion of agreement corrected for chance (Cohen, 1960):

$$\kappa = \frac{p_a - p_c}{1 - p_c},$$

where p_a is the proportion of times the raters agree and p_c is the proportion of agreement we would expect by chance. This formula holds for the case of two raters, but it is possible to extend kappa to take into account more than one test scorer and so achieve an even more accurate estimate of reliability. We will not provide the formulae here, but the interested reader is referred to the basic papers of Fleiss (1971) and Light (1971).

10.3.2 General considerations with regard to reliability

Unlike the kinds of statistical coefficients psychologists commonly deal with such as t, F and r, reliability coefficients are population parameter estimates and not sample statistics. This means that strictly speaking we should not generalize from one sample to another. However, for the sake of simplicity they are usually treated as sample statistics and this does mean that they should be estimated on very representative samples. If the test reliability was estimated on a sample that differs from the sample upon which the test is to be used, there is no guarantee that it will have a similar reliability on the new sample. For example, giving an IQ test developed for the general population to a sample of university students may produce reliability coefficients markedly lower than expected because the students would produce smaller test score variance. For this reason care must be taken when choosing a ready-made psychometric test for a research project.

It is also worth noting that the estimates of reliability described above are lower bound estimates. Thus, Cronbach's alpha coefficient gives us a low estimate of the reliability. The actual reliability may be slightly higher. While the type of test dictates the type of reliability estimate that is appropriate, it is generally assumed that KR20 and Cronbach's alpha are about the most accurate estimates of reliability available within the classical test approach.

We should now turn to the tricky question of what is a 'good' reliability coefficient. Received wisdom (Nunnally, 1978) suggests that reliability coefficients should be greater than 0.7 before we can assume sufficient reliability for a research tool. However, if a psychometric test is being used as a diagnostic for job selection purposes, it should have a reliability of at least 0.9.

The basic principle in deciding whether a test is reliable is to remember that the reliability coefficient is a measure of the proportion of overlapping of 'true' and 'observed' variance. Thus, a test with a reliability of 0.7 means that 30% of its variance is residual and irrelevant; a reliability of 0.6 suggests a test in which 40% of its variance is made up of error. You must ask yourself how much error you are prepared to tolerate in your measurement.

The reliability of a test is dependent on the number of items in the test. Providing the items are of sufficient quality, the more items there are, the greater the reliability. This is entirely to be expected given that items are indicators of an underlying characteristic. Obviously, the greater the number of indicators, the more accurate our estimate of the 'true' score. This has often been used as an argument to excuse poor tests. A test with, for example, five items may be found to have a reliability of 0.5; test developers have been known to argue that the reason for the low reliability is that the test has only five items and that it is a good test nevertheless. In fact, the test is not a good test on two counts: firstly, it is inadequate because it does not have enough items to describe the underlying characteristic; and, secondly, it is highly unreliable. A small number of items does not excuse poor reliability estimates.

10.4 THE PROBLEM OF VALIDITY

In estimating the reliability of a test, we are examining its viability as a measurement device. If we find that the reliability is low, we have to assume that the test does not measure anything with any degree of credibility. The reliability of a test is not specific to the characteristic being measured. In other words, we may have a highly reliable test but discover that it does not measure the thing we think it does. This leads us to the problem of validity, which may be posed as the question: how well does the test measure what it purports to measure?

As reliability asks whether a test measures anything at all, it should be apparent that reliability logically precedes validity. We may have a reliable test that is not valid, but we cannot have a valid test that is not reliable. Without reliability we cannot have validity. In other words, reliability is a necessary but not sufficient property for a valid test.

An example of how we may have a reliable test without validity came to the author's attention a few years ago while conducting an undergraduate research methods class. The task was to construct a personality measure of a Freudian construct, and the topic chosen was penis envy. The students dutifully set to work to write a set of questions that tapped this particular domain. Eventually a 50-item questionnaire was constructed which was then distributed to about 200 young women (the theory suggests that males do not manifest penis envy). Upon analysing the responses, we were pleased to note that our internal consistency coefficient exceeded 0.8, suggesting that we had constructed a reasonable measurement device. However, a small but enterprising group of students had also collected data on a group of males, the expectation being that since the domain was not relevant to this population the responses to the questions would be random and produce very low reliability. As it happened the reliability was higher for males and, disconcertingly, males appeared to manifest higher scores on penis envy than did females. The problem was one of validity. We had constructed a reliable test, but it was not a test of penis envy as was supposed. In fact it was probably better described as a test of salaciousness.

Assessing the validity of a test, therefore, requires a precise knowledge of the psychological domain under consideration, together with a clear operational definition of each characteristic being measured. There are essentially three approaches to test validation. These are termed **content validation, criterion validation** and **construct validation**. Cronbach (1971) sees them as three different methods of inquiry.

content validation
criterion validation
construct validation

10.4.1 Content validation

face validity

Content validation simply asks whether the content of the test is relevant to the characteristic being measured. We may check the **face validity** of a test, which is simply the subjective evaluation of the relevance of the test items. This particular form of validity check does have a place, although it is often not given much credence because it lacks objectivity. Let us suppose that we have a particular characteristic we wish to measure (e.g. degree of psychosis). We would first search through the literature until we came across a number of tests that purported to measure psychoticism. We would then need to examine the content of the test items to assure ourselves that the test did coincide with our own operational definition of the construct to be measured. In other words, is our operational definition the same as that of the test which is manifested in the content of its items? Thus, Eysenck and Eysenck's (1976) test of psychoticism measures what most people might term 'psychopathy', while the Minnesota Multiphasic Personality Inventory (MMPI) scale for 'schizophrenia' is more closely associated with the traditional use of the term 'psychotic'.

Having a test with clear face validity may also be useful in obtaining compliance from respondents since, if the items appear irrelevant, testees may become irritated. Nevertheless, in some cases face validity may be a liability since the respondent may identify the purpose of the questions and then proceed to answer them in a biased manner. Clearly, it is up to the researcher to determine whether a high degree of face validity is important for their own study.

Content validation procedures are important when developing a test as it is necessary to construct items that sample the psychological domain in question. One strategy is to ask 'expert' judges to evaluate the relevance of the items to the characteristic being measured. If the judges agree that an item is not measuring the characteristic or they disagree on its relevance, the item may be considered equivocal and its content validity is questionable.

In content validation, an important consideration is the complexity of the test item. A highly complex item may diffuse the focus of the question and result in contamination from some other characteristic that is not being measured. For example, the following two questions require the respondent to perform a simple arithmetic operation:

(a) $2 + 6 + 4 - 6 = ?$
(b) Bill has two apples; Jane gives him six bananas. Sam, who is trying to impress Jane with his generosity, gives Bill four more apples. Maggie then steals six apples from Bill. How many pieces of fruit does Bill have left?

However, (b) is far more complex than (a) and requires that the respondent has a reasonable reading ability. As a result, if item (b) was found in a test of children's arithmetic reasoning, we would have to question its content validity, since it is contaminated by the irrelevant variable 'reading ability'.

Content validation, then, is largely a qualitative process and depends upon the tester having a clearly defined idea of what it is she or he wishes to measure.

10.4.2 Criterion validation

Criterion validation involves testing the hypothesized relationship of the test with external criteria. This is a more quantitative process than content validation but it requires that the tester is able to generate a reasonable set of hypotheses as to how the test should relate to the criteria variables. Criterion validation may be carried out under a number of headings, including predictive validation, concurrent validation, convergent validation and divergent validation.

Predictive validity is concerned with whether the test predicts later behaviour. For example, a child's IQ score may be expected to predict scholastic success; a person's score from a test of the type A behaviour pattern should predict the later development of heart disease.

predictive validity

Predictive validation is vital when developing tests for aptitude or job selection since these tests are designed specifically to measure the potential of a person. It is necessary that a test being used to assess a respondent's potential should have a convincing body of empirical evidence demonstrating its relevance to the characteristics under consideration. Certainly, 'off-the-shelf' tests of personality appear to be poor predictors of job performance (Blinkhorn & Johnson, 1990).

Obviously predictive validity is a very important feature of psychometric tests since our choice of a psychometric test in research is commonly informed by assumptions of its predictive quality. However, when constructing a psychometric test the practicality of predictive validation is quite difficult owing to the time involved. Many test constructors will adopt the shorter-term strategy of **post-dictive validation,** in which test scores of individuals who already own the characteristic being predicted are compared with those without it. Thus, if our test purports to predict performance in a particular job, high-fliers in the job will be

postdictive validation

compared with those who are less adept. This is not strictly predictive validation, because we cannot be sure that the variables being measured by the test have not been modified by an interaction between the person and the job. If high-fliers and inept employees had been screened before they started work we may have found no difference in test scores, but the experience of the job may have differentially modified the characteristics being tested.

concurrent validation

Concurrent validation involves observing the relationship between the test and other criteria that are measured at the same time. More often than not, this involves a correlation between the test in question and one or more other measures for which a hypothesized relationship is posited. Thus, for example, scores on a self-report test of extroversion may be correlated with peer ratings of sociability. Usually multiple criteria are used and the pattern of correlations between the test in question and its validating criteria is examined to assess the concurrent validity of the test. It is always a good idea to include, among the validating variables, a number of variables which are not expected to correlate with the test. In this way we can also check the specificity of the test.

10.4.3 Construct validation

It is important for multiple-item tests that the internal structure of the test is examined. This often involves fitting the observed responses to some kind of measurement model. We have already seen that one way of assessing reliability is to examine internal consistency of the test items. The resulting coefficient (usually Cronbach's alpha) is based upon the homogeneity of the items, a high alpha occurring when the items correlate well together. Thus reliability evaluation may be viewed as a kind of construct validation. In this case the internal structure of the items is assumed to reveal inter-item homogeneity.

unidimensional scale

Another commonly hypothesized structure is that the items form a **unidimensional scale.** In this case the items are expected to have a particular pattern of correlations which reflects their order along a single latent trait. Some authors have confused unidimensionality with internal consistency, and it is important to realize that alpha coefficients may tell us something about the average size of the inter-item correlations but tell us nothing about their pattern. The way to assess the unidimensionality of a scale is to use multivariate data analytic methods which allow you to examine the underlying structure of the test items (see Chapter 20).

It is also common for the test developer to suggest that there may be multiple dimensions underlying the test items. In this case, a number of distinct scales are expected to be found within the item pool. A good example of this is the 90-item Eysenck Personality Questionnaire which measures four traits: extroversion, neuroticism, psychoticism and response bias. The structure of the inter-item correlations is such that all the items designed to measure extroversion correlate well together but correlate less well with items from the other scales. This is expected to be true for each of the remaining traits. The procedure that is commonly used when assessing this multidimensional measurement model is known as factor analysis (see Chapter 20).

Construct validation, then, involves testing hypotheses about the structure of the test. This often involves the use of quite sophisticated data analytic methods.

10.4.4 General issues of validation

Up to this point the reader would be excused for thinking that validity is an intrinsic feature of the test in question. In fact, one of the most widespread problems of validity in the use of psychometric tests in research relates not so much to invalid tests as to the invalid *use* of tests. When scholars are casting around for a standard test to use in their research they need to be particularly careful that the test they choose is appropriate for their use.

For example, British researchers often make use of tests developed on American samples. It is important that the test user justifies the use of such tests on British samples. Equally, a great many tests in common use are very old, and there is no particular guarantee that items constructed even ten years ago have the same meaning as they do today. The onus is on the researcher to provide a full and informed justification of his or her choice of psychometric test.

There are essentially four points about validity that should be borne in mind.

1 There are numerous methods of validation which may be seen as different modes of enquiry (Cronbach, 1971). Their relative importance depends upon the test in question, its proposed usage and the conceptualization of the construct it purports to measure.
2 Validity cannot be estimated by a single coefficient, but is inferred from an accumulation of empirical and conceptual evidence.
3 Validation is cumulative. The validation of a test is an ongoing process which should last for as long as the test is used.
4 Validity is as much a function of the appropriate use of a test as of the test itself.

10.5 ITEM RESPONSE THEORY

In this chapter we have concentrated exclusively upon the classical test model. However, it is not possible to conclude a chapter on psychometric tests without mentioning **item response theory** (IRT). We can give only the briefest of introductions to this important and rapidly growing area of psychometrics here, and the interested reader is referred to Embretson and Reise (2000) for an excellent introductory account. IRT integrates early work on scaling (Guttman, 1941) and the statistical modelling of human responses (Rasch, 1960; Birnbaum, 1968) and

item response theory

Table 10.2 Three item profiles producing equivalent scores

	Items					Score
	A	**B**	**C**	**D**	**E**	
Respondent 1	1	1	0	1	0	3
Respondent 2	0	0	1	1	1	3
Respondent 3	1	1	1	0	0	3

is exemplified in the seminal works of Frederick Lord (Lord & Novick, 1968; Lord, 1980). This approach represents a radical departure from classical test theory in which the test score is the fundamental unit of interest, because it concentrates instead upon the probability of a particular item response. This is the probability that an individual with a certain ability or trait strength will respond in a given way to a particular item within a test.

In Table 10.2 the responses of three individuals to a five-item numerical reasoning test are presented. A value of 1 means that the respondent provided a correct answer and 0 indicates an incorrect answer. As we can see, the respondents have the same number of correct responses. In classical test theory terms, this means that they share the same score and thus have the same ability.

However, we can also see that each of the three respondents presents a qualitatively distinct profile of item responses which indicates that they are not equivalent in their numerical reasoning. Item response theory addresses this anomaly by explicitly modelling the response profile expected from a person with a given ability. The ability of an individual is estimated statistically using information from a large data set. In IRT terminology the ability of a person is a **person parameter**. In addition, the difficulty of each item and its ability to discriminate between high- and low-ability respondents are estimated, and these are known as **item parameters**. It is even possible to estimate a third parameter which describes the degree to which the answer to an item is correctly guessed (a **guessing parameter**). A large number of item response models exist, but most can be described under three main headings based on the number of item parameters that are free to vary as follows.

person parameter

item parameters

guessing parameter

Rasch models

One-parameter or **Rasch models** treat the item discrimination and guessing parameters as fixed (usually the guessing parameters are fixed at zero). This is a relatively strict model in which the only item parameter free to vary is the difficulty. This is the model most favoured among European psychometricians, perhaps because of the seminal influence of the Danish statistician Georg Rasch (1960) who developed the basic model. It may be viewed as a probabilistic extension of Guttman's (1941) scalogram approach.

Two-parameter models allow the difficulty and discrimination parameters to vary. These models appear to be favoured among American psychometricians and are slightly more relaxed in terms of model constraints than the Rasch models. However, in allowing the item discrimination to vary, this model loses the advantage of fitting data to a cumulative scale.

Three-parameter models allow difficulty, discrimination and guessing parameters to vary. These are the most relaxed of the available models, but they are extraordinarily complex because of the numbers of unknown parameters that need to be estimated (Birnbaum, 1968; Lord, 1980). It is also necessary to have very large sample sizes before consistent estimates can be made, and this makes these models impractical except in the case where many thousands of respondents are available. A brief demonstration of the manner in which these models compare is presented in Box 10.3.

Of all the models available the Rasch model has particular advantages that cannot be detailed here. In brief, the main advantage of the Rasch model is that

---

Box 10.3   Item characteristic curves

IRT is built around the notion of an item characteristic curve (ICC). This is a plot of the probability that a respondent will answer an item in a particular way. Using the simple example of a knowledge test, as the general knowledge of a person increases so the probability of them answering the item correctly increases. In most IRT models this probability plot describes a logistic curve.

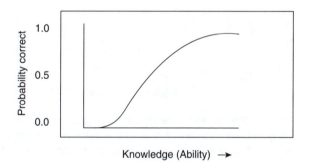

If two items are plotted on the same graph we can compare how they function within the test. Using a Rasch model where the only item parameter free to vary is item difficulty, we can see that any two items are always parallel with each other although they vary according to difficulty. Note that they cannot intersect, this is a requirement of a cumulative scale and means that people with identical scores are assumed to have a similar profile of item responses.

(Continued)

Box 10.2 (Continued)

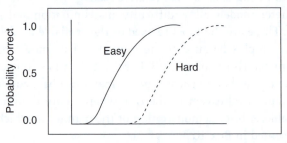

If, however, we apply a two-parameter model, we allow the items to differ on difficulty and discrimination. Discrimination is represented by the steepness of the curve. Because the steepness of any two ICCs can vary, this model does not imply a cumulative scale. In practice, what this means is that the total score is not a very meaningful way of defining a person's position on the latent trait in question, since it can represent very different item profiles. Typically, tests designed by the two-parameter model require a complicated statistical method of scoring a person's position.

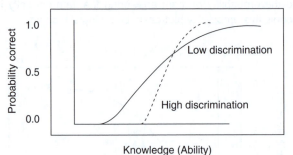

The three-parameter model allows for the possibility of guessing so that nobody has zero probability of getting an item correct. This means that the curve begins at a probability higher than zero. Different items can vary according to how guessable they are.

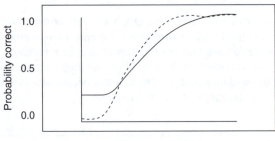

Box 10.2   (Continued)

The Rasch model is the most rigorous of the three models described here and it is also the simplest to use. As more parameters are included, it becomes easier to fit data to the model although the mathematical jiggery-pokery becomes a great deal more complex. Data fit is a holy grail to statisticians, but psychometricians are more concerned with whether a measurement model makes sense to their application. For proponents of the Rasch model data–model fit is important, but it is more the need for robust cumulative scales to justify our measurements that is the key issue. For this reason many Rasch modellers are a little wary of thinking of the Rasch model as being one in a hierarchy of IRT models, preferring to consider it qualitatively distinct from the two- and three-parameter approaches.

it describes a cumulative scale. In so doing it provides the basis for extremely robust and defensible measurement. There are even some who would argue, with considerable justification, that Rasch modelling is the only truly defensible way of developing psychological measurements. Therefore, students wishing to explore issues of psychometric measurement should acquaint themselves with Rasch modelling and are encouraged to consult Andrich (1988) and Bond and Fox (2001) or to take a look at the website www.rasch.org

We are painfully aware that the above descriptions of IRT models are too brief to provide a full understanding of IRT and all we can hope, given the space allotted to the subject, is that the reader is made aware of these alternative, statistically sophisticated approaches to psychological measurement. Item response theory is fast becoming the chosen approach among psychometricians, although it is only slowly being adopted in mainstream psychology as an alternative to classical measurement procedures.

The main reason for its rise among psychometricians is that it answers a number of problems in classical test theory. For example, it provides SEM estimates for each person rather than relying on general test-based estimates. Its slow acceptance in mainstream psychology probably reflects the general lack of interest in measurement and a resistance among many psychologists to statistically sophisticated procedures. It is perhaps necessary to alert the reader to the work of Joel Michell (1997) at this point, in which the scientific pretensions of psychology are cast into doubt. Michell argues convincingly that the naïveté exhibited by psychologists towards measurement militates against our discipline ever achieving a realistic scientific status. Although Michell's concerns are not all answered by IRT, Rasch models come close to doing so.

10.6 CONCLUSION

In this chapter we have discussed the two main issues in the use of psychometric tests: reliability and validity. The development of a psychometric test is a long and detailed process and a full account is beyond the scope of this chapter. However, the issues that we have raised while discussing the problems of reliability estimation and validation are central to test construction. Nevertheless, the psychological literature is peppered with poorly constructed tests where even these basic principles have not been adhered to. The continuing use of such weak tests does nothing for the science of psychology and simply serves to generate more random numbers to distract us from our true purpose as researchers, the identification of replicable and stable laws that govern behaviour. It is the role of researchers who wish to use psychometric tests to maintain high standards in the selection of the tests they use. This requires that researchers using psychometric tests should be aware of the major issues in psychometric methodology. This chapter has attempted to provide a basis for this awareness, but its necessary brevity means that it cannot hope to provide a full account. It is hoped that researchers planning on using psychometric tests will consult further texts such as Nunnally and Bernstein (1994) or Suen (1990).

10.7 FURTHER READING

There are many excellent modern texts on psychometric testing available, and in this section I list a few of my favourites. You will see that I am not necessarily advocating the most recent texts: some of the best early texts have not been bettered and should be available in most libraries. A very comprehensive book is that by Nunnally and Bernstein (1994). This is an update on Nunnally's seminal editions of the 1960s and 1970s. These books became the bible for generations of psychometrics students, and some say that the earlier editions are even better than the update. In a slightly more accessible vein, Paul Kline has written a number of introductory books in the area of psychometrics: Kline's (1993) text is still hard to beat as a good comprehensive introduction that should be accessible to both undergraduate and postgraduate students. For the complete beginner, Rust and Golombok's (1999) book offers a very accessible introduction.

Any researcher who is seriously considering psychometric research should consult a text on measurement theory. De Gruijter and van der Kamp's (2005) is a truly excellent book, which is freely available on the Web. A shorter text, old but still very accessible and informative, is Suen's (1990). Finally, all psychologists, whether they are interested in psychometrics or not should be expected to read Michell's (1999) challenging account of psychological measurement.

For the reader interested in IRT another free text is Baker's (2001). This not only is very readable but also has the extra benefit of coming complete with a simple computer program. Suen's text mentioned above certainly bears study, as does Hulin, Drasgow and Parsons's (1983), which is an early and straightforward treatment. A very useful concise and accessible account is to be found in Hambleton *et al.'s* (1991) book, but for more detail consult Van der Linden and Hambleton's (1997). For a readable and applied account, see Embretson and Reise's (2000) text.

For those interested in finding out more about the Rasch model, a classic and very approachable treatment can be found in Andrich's (1988) book. For a good applied treatment, Bond and Fox's (2001) text is excellent, although for more statistical detail consult Fischer and Molenaar's (1995). Finally, just about everything Ben Wright wrote on the Rasch model is pithy and to the point, and a lot of his material can be found at www.rasch.org

11

Questionnaire Design

Chris Fife-Schaw

11.1   Introduction

11.2   What information do you want?

   11.2.1   Hypothesis generating

   11.2.2   Test development and validation

   11.2.3   Population parameter estimation

   11.2.4   Hypothesis and model testing

11.3   Open versus closed response formats

11.4   Common response formats

11.5   Common wording problems

11.6   Types of information gleaned from questionnaires

   11.6.1   Background and demographic data

   11.6.2   Behavioural reports

   11.6.3   Attitudes and opinions

   11.6.4   Knowledge

   11.6.5   Intentions, expectations and aspirations

11.7   Existing scales and measures

11.8   Questionnaire layout

11.9   Conclusion

11.10   Further reading

AIMS

This chapter will introduce the reader to the uses of, and common problems associated with, questionnaires. It deals with the types of research question that can be addressed with questionnaires, common wording and response formats, as well as outlining common problems.

K ey terms

acquiescence bias
back-translation
bogus pipeline
categorical responses
closed-ended formats
coding errors
filter questions

multiple-response items
non-attitude problem
open-ended formats
ranking scales
rating scales
satisficing

11.1 INTRODUCTION

The humble questionnaire is probably the single most common research tool in the social sciences. The principal advantages of the questionnaire are its apparent simplicity, its versatility and its low cost as a method of data gathering. For many research topics, questionnaires provide data which are of a good enough quality both to test hypotheses and to make real-world policy suggestions. Where people wish to make population parameter estimates (i.e. make estimates of numerical characteristics of a population such as the average number of visits to church per week), the cost advantage of questionnaires over interviews means that many more people can be sampled for a given budget than might otherwise be possible. Questionnaires are a relatively well-understood technology and there are numerous guides to designing good questionnaires (e.g. Sudman & Bradburn, 1982; Oppenheim, 1992).

Designing the perfect questionnaire is probably impossible, however. Experience shows that you can rarely design one that all your respondents, let alone your academic peers, are happy with. Similarly, it is unlikely that you will complete a questionnaire study without asking yourself the 'Why didn't I ask about that?' question. This should not be seen as a failing of questionnaire methods themselves so much as an inevitable part of the research process. This is not to say that careful questionnaire design can be ignored. There have been too many questionnaires produced over the years that contain simple errors that have seriously undermined the value of the data collected. You should always strive to minimize the number of these errors, and hopefully what follows will alert you to the more obvious problems.

The focus of this chapter is on self-completion questionnaires, though the section on item wording contains some ideas that apply equally to interview schedules. You should read this chapter in conjunction with Chapter 6 on surveys and sampling.

11.2 WHAT INFORMATION DO YOU WANT?

The very versatility of the questionnaire as a data gathering technique means that it is difficult to generalize about its appropriate uses. It is, however, useful to try to classify common aims since the temptation is often to milk questionnaire data to meet a number of these aims simultaneously while fulfilling none of the aims particularly well. An awareness of these general purposes should help focus the questionnaire design process.

11.2.1 Hypothesis generating

In this mode, questionnaires are useful for asking a large number of people 'what if', exploratory types of question. The intention is to get a feel for how people respond to certain issues. When attempting to elicit interesting insights in this way, it is often desirable to allow people to make open-ended responses, unconstrained by your prior expectations of what classes of response are useful to you. While this kind of information can also be obtained by unstructured interviews and group discussions, a questionnaire study can give you a feel for the range of likely responses and a rough idea of how common certain responses are.

Sometimes the goal is to see if there is any underlying dimension, or putative cause, that influences responses to a set of items. In such cases, exploratory data analytic procedures, such as exploratory factor analysis and cluster analysis, are commonly used (see Chapter 20). As there is often no established theory generating hypotheses about the items, only your hunches and intuitions, such analytic procedures are best thought of as generating hypotheses about the nature of certain items for future studies.

11.2.2 Test development and validation

A common application of questionnaires is in the realm of test development. This can take many forms. A set of items (questions on the form) may be being tested as a potential scale to measure a psychological construct such as, say, depression or agreeableness. The aim is to collect responses to the items so that various psychometric procedures can be used to test reliability and/or validity. A set of items supposedly measuring some psychological construct may be administered to groups with known characteristics so as to attempt to assess the validity of the measure. Chapter 10 outlines many of the standard procedures associated with this use of the questionnaire.

11.2.3 Population parameter estimation

Once a range of measures exists, either as published tests or as the result of procedures outlined in Section 11.2.2, questionnaires can be used to estimate population scores on such tests. For instance, you might be interested in estimating the levels of psychological well-being among police officers. After appropriate sampling, you could administer a questionnaire containing the General Health Questionnaire (Goldberg, 1972) and treat the resulting scores as an estimate of the 'true' level of psychological well-being among police officers. These estimates can then be compared with norms, the responses of other groups who have taken the General Health Questionnaire in the past. Parameter estimates can be made for almost any type of question you could ask.

11.2.4 Hypothesis and model testing

If measures of key constructs already exist then questionnaires can be useful for hypothesis-testing purposes. Common examples would include testing causal models (e.g. the theory of planned behaviour) or confirming the factor structure underlying responses to a set of pre-existing items. Hypothesized differences between identifiable groups on specified measures are another common application, as is the evaluation of an intervention (e.g. a teaching programme).

Ideally, you should keep the above aims separate and conduct different studies to deal with each aim in turn. In reality, however, limited resources are likely to mean that you will combine some of these aims within one questionnaire study. For instance, it is common practice to specify a new measure (e.g. a set of scaled items) and then attempt hypothesis testing within the same data set. This practice tends to mean that the validity of the measure is not established and, while inter-item reliability can be assessed, the interpretation of the data necessarily requires greater caution than would be the case had established measures been used.

There is an important distinction to be made here between dishing out lots of questionnaires and fishing through the data to find statistically significant relationships and a more theoretically driven exercise. With the advent of easy-to-use computer programs such as SPSS, there is a growing temptation to confuse exploratory, hypothesis-generating uses of questionnaires with hypothesis testing. This should be avoided where possible.

11.3 OPEN VERSUS CLOSED RESPONSE FORMATS

Before looking at individual types of question, it is worth saying something about possible response formats.

A major distinction lies between open-ended and closed-ended response formats. With **open-ended formats**, respondents are asked to write down their response to a question in any terms that they see fit. When asking about occupations it would be prohibitive to list all possible occupations, so you would normally allow respondents to make an open-ended response and simply write down their occupation. As another example, you might ask people to give their reasons for recycling glass bottles and allow them to list as many reasons as they felt they had for recycling. **Closed-ended formats** require the researcher to have a reasonable idea of the likely responses to the items. In the recycling example, they would need to provide a list of likely reasons for recycling and ask respondents to indicate which of the reasons applied to them.

The advantages of closed-ended formats are that they clarify the response alternatives for the respondent and they reduce the number of ambiguous answers that might be given. Open-ended questions often prompt people into providing multiple responses even if these responses are substantively the same. Also, from a clerical point of view, they reduce the number of **coding errors** in the data set. Coding errors occur when the researcher misinterprets an open-ended response at the stage of turning verbal responses into numbers that can be used for computer analysis. Respondents can answer closed-format items

open-ended formats

closed-ended formats

coding errors

quickly, making responding to you at all more attractive if they are under time pressure.

The disadvantages of closed-ended formats are of many kinds, but perhaps the most important is that they can create artificial forced choices and rule out unexpected responses. Your list of reasons for recycling may not include one that is very important for some people. Making up the response categories is often difficult as they must cover the full range of likely responses.

Another problem concerns the shared meanings attached to the words used in the questionnaires. For instance, the term 'tea' is used differently by people from different social strata and different geographical locations. Most people would recognize 'tea' as a drink, but for some people it is also a light snack in the afternoon and for others a larger meal in the early evening. This is rather a quaint example, but closed-ended response formats assume that people share the same understanding of the items and response categories as does the researcher. There are many other biasing effects that occur when using closed-ended formats; these will be discussed in more detail later in this chapter.

While it might seem that the problems with closed-ended response formats are legion, the main reason for their continued popularity lies in the difficulties of analysing open-ended responses. Open-ended responses simply do not lend themselves to easy numerical analysis in the same way that closed response formats do. It is possible to turn such responses into numbers and, of course, it is possible to analyse data without recourse to numbers and statistics, but most questionnaire designers tend towards maximizing the number of closed-ended items wherever possible.

To get over the problems with closed-ended items, it is essential that the items you choose to use and the response options you give are ones that potential respondents would use and understand. This means that you must go out and talk to likely respondents to find out what they think the key questions are and what their responses would be. Running a series of focus groups (see Chapter 14) is often very useful for this purpose. Taped interviews or focus groups, once transcribed, give useful insights that ought to be drawn upon when designing your questionnaire. Having done this, it is still important that careful pilot work is done to see if respondents understand your questions and respond appropriately.

11.4 COMMON RESPONSE FORMATS

Categorical. Examples may include those in Figure 11.1. Note that with **categorical responses** it is possible to have items where respondents can circle more than one response, as is the case with question 4 in the figure. Such items are referred to as **multiple-response items**. Care is needed when coding the responses to such items into a computer since, for example, question 4 contains effectively three

categorical responses

multiple-response items

1	Have you ever attended school in the UK? *(please circle one answer)*	YES	NO
2	Are you male or female *(please circle one answer)*	MALE	FEMALE
3	If there were a General Election tommorrow, which political party would you vote for? *(please circle one answer)*	CONSERVATIVE LIBERAL LABOUR OTHER PARTY WOULD NOT VOTE DO NOT KNOW	
4	Which of the following items have you purchased in the past week? *(you may circle more than one item)*	APPLES PEARS ORANGES	

Figure 11.1 Examples of categorical response formats

Please say how much you agree or disagree with the following statement *(please circle one response only)*:

Government policy on public transport will be good for the environment in the long term	STRONGLY AGREE AGREE UNCERTAIN DISAGREE STRONGLY DISAGREE

or

How important is European unification to you, personality?	EXTREMELY IMPORTANT VERY IMPORTANT MODERATELY IMPORTANT NOT VERY IMPORTANT NOT IMPORTANT AT ALL

Figure 11.2 Common rating scale response formats

separate responses: one for whether apples were purchased, one for pears and one for oranges.

rating scales *Rating scales.* Examples of **rating scales** may include those in Figure 11.2. Note that here the respondent is asked to circle one of the five alternative responses. It is perfectly possible to present the response options as in Figure 11.3. Having numbered each option, respondents can be asked to write in the number that corresponds to their chosen option in a box next to the question statement or to tick boxes laid out so that the response options form columns. Box 11.1 deals with some issues to do with labelling these response options.

ranking scales *Ranking formats.* Examples of **ranking scales** may include those in Figure 11.4.

Alternative A

Using the scale below, please tell us how much you agree or disagree with the following statements by placing a number in the box provided.

1	2	3	4	5
Strongly agree	Agree	Neither agree nor disagree	Disagree	Strongly disagree

1 Government policy on public transport will be good for the environment in the long term ☐

- -

Alternative B

Please tick one box for each question.

	Strongly agree	Agree	Neither agree nor disagree	Disagree	Strongly disagree
1 Government policy on public transport will be good for the environment in the long term	☐	☐	☐	☐	☐

Figure 11.3 Alternative layouts for rating scale responses

Which of the following do you feel are the most important factors to consider when choosing a new car?

Please rank the following in order of importance. Number them so that 1 = most important, 2 = next most important, through to 6 = least important.

Fuel consumption ____
Maximum speed ____
Quick acceleration ____
Having a safety cage/cell ____
Servicing costs ____
Status/prestige ____

Figure 11.4 An example of a ranking response format

Box 11.1   Using 'don't know' and 'no opinion' response options

In a great many questionnaire surveys you will find questions which offer 'don't know' or 'no opinion' as one of the possible responses. This is usually done, particularly in studies on people's attitudes and opinions, to get over what is called the **non-attitude problem**. This was first identified in a now classic work by Philip Converse (1964) which raised the possibility that when surveyors ask questions in surveys people may make up their responses on the spot so as to provide an answer and

(Continued)

non-attitude problem

to avoid looking foolish. The problem with this, he suggested, was that it was unlikely in such cases that the response really meant anything at all. If you asked people the same question again they might well say something different and the responses were very unlikely to be predictive of any future behaviour (often the main reason why we are interested in people's attitudes in the first place).

To deal with non-attitudes, the argument runs that we should give people the option to say that they have no opinion and they can indicate the lack of opinion without feeling inadequate in any way. This should improve the quality of the data and there will be less 'noise' in it to mess up our analyses. For many years this has been the accepted wisdom, but in a recent series of studies by Jon Krosnick and colleagues (Krosnick *et al.*, 2002) this has been seriously challenged. Without going into the details of the quite elegant studies here, they conclude that there is very little evidence that offering 'don't know' or 'no opinion' options improves the quality of the data at all. They show that many respondents will adopt what they call **satisficing** response strategies and will use the 'no opinion' options even when they have a real opinion which they could express. Some of this will be due to a lack of motivation to reflect on their attitudes and some due to time pressures and fatigue among other factors. While they do not go so far as to claim that excluding 'no opinion' options would improve data quality, they seriously under-mine claims that including them improves data quality at all.

satisficing

These findings, while not especially helpful in telling you as a questionnaire designer what to do, should at least give you reason to challenge claims from others who want you to include 'no opinion' options that doing so will improve data quality.

11.5 COMMON WORDING PROBLEMS

In this section I have grouped together a range of common wording problems that you should be aware of. Oppenheim (1992) and Sudman and Bradburn (1982), among other texts, provide more examples of these types of wording problem.

Vague/ambiguous terminology. If you are vague in the phrasing of your questions you cannot be sure what responses to the items mean. An example is in the word-ing of frequency response options for behavioural report items, as in Figure 11.5. Just what does 'frequently' mean here? Every hour? Twice a fortnight? Such a term is sometimes referred to as a vague quantifier. Respondents will try to guess what you mean by 'frequently' but they may not all make the same guess, leading to hidden ambiguity in the data.

Another problem under this heading concerns ill-defined terms. In sexual behaviour research, for instance, researchers were initially keen to ask people if they felt they were promiscuous or not. Unfortunately, research has shown (Spencer, Faulkner & Keegan, 1988) that the public are unsure what 'promiscuous'

How often do you clean your teeth?	FREQUENTLY
(please circle one answer)	OFTEN
	INFREQUENTLY
	NEVER

Figure 11.5 Example of vague quantifier response format wording

means in terms of absolute numbers of sexual partners. Indeed, some people believe promiscuity is a term that applies to anyone who has had more partners than they have. Beware inherently ambiguous terms.

Technical terminology. It might seem like a good idea to use technically correct terminology to get over problems of the ambiguity of day-to-day language. For some research topics this may be appropriate, but you should pilot your form carefully to be sure that respondents will understand the terms. If appropriate you can give both a technical and a lay explanation for problematic terms in the introduction to the questionnaire. You should seek to use plain English wherever possible.

Hypothetical questions. In many research areas you are interested in asking people 'What would you do if …?' types of question. Such questions about hypothetical future situations must appear reasonable to respondents if their answers are to be meaningful. If you were to ask, say, 'If it appeared that the Liberal Democratic Party could win the next election, would you vote for them?', the meaning of the response would depend on the respondent accepting that the Liberal Democratic Party being in a position to win the election was a realistic premise. You might think it was, and some respondents might agree with you, but others might not. Responses from these two groups may not be comparable and there is little you could do about this unless you also asked whether this premise was acceptable first.

Leading questions. Questions such as 'Would you agree that the government's policies on health are unfair?' will suggest to some people that you would like them to agree with you. Similarly, the question 'Do you agree that Brand Z washes whiter?' might be harder to disagree with than a more neutrally worded item. In such cases you may be indicating something about what would be regarded by some as a 'right' response. Avoid leading questions.

Value judgements. Item wordings should not contain implicit value judgements. In a similar way to leading questions, you should not express your own views, or those of the research sponsor, in question items.

Context effects. These are somewhat more subtle effects on responses that are dependent on the nature of the rest of the questions on the form. Take the following question as an example: 'How many pints of beer did you drink last week?' In the context of a survey into young people's lifestyles and leisure activities this seems like a reasonable question, and young males in particular might give relatively high figures in response. If you had asked the same question in the context of a questionnaire on health behaviours and heart disease, responses might well be lower. You should be aware of the potential impact of surrounding questions on your target item. Box 11.2 looks in more detail at another kind of context effect, that due to question order.

Box 11.2   More on question order effects

Schuman and Presser (1996) report a series of studies that highlight just how sensitive respondents can be to the order in which questions are asked. They noticed that the following general question about abortion had been used in two US surveys, one in 1978 the other in 1979. The question asked 'Do you think it should be possible for a pregnant woman to obtain a legal abortion if she is married and does not want any more children?' In the 1978 survey 40.3% said 'yes' to this question, while in the 1979 survey 54.9% said 'yes'. This was a major change in public opinion if taken at face value, as it suggested that in 1979 a majority now supported legalized abortion whereas that was not the case a year before. As you will be expecting, rather than appealing to a real change in public opinion Schuman and Presser took a closer look at the adjacent items in the surveys and decided to run some experiments to see whether another question on abortion in the 1978 survey had influenced subsequent responses to this more general question.

In the experiment they used two questions: the 'general' question above and a more 'specific' one which asked 'Do you think it should be possible for a pregnant woman to obtain a legal abortion if there is a strong chance of serious defect in the baby?' The questions were presented in the context of a larger survey, with the general question either immediately preceding or following the specific question. The other questions adjacent to these items were about labour relations and not concerned with abortion. The table below presents the percentages agreeing with each item.

Order		Specific/General					General/Specific		
		General item					General item		
		Yes	No				Yes	No	
Specific	Yes	47.1	36.9	84.0	Specific	Yes	57.4	25.6	83.0
Item	No	1.0	15.0	16.0	item	No	3.3	13.8	17.1
		48.1	51.9	100%			60.7	39.4	100%
				(293)					(305)

The table shows clearly that while the endorsement levels for the specific abortion question remain the same, the question order had a major impact on the numbers agreeing with the general question.

Schuman and Presser (1996) provide a number of possible mechanisms to explain why this effect might occur, and there is not space here to go into these in detail. However, this example is one of the better-known examples of question order effects and there are many others of varying types, and it is impossible to be sure that subtle order effects are absent from questionnaire surveys. The only real checks are to do experiments like those above, though naturally these are expensive and even then may still leave you uncertain about exactly how many people really agree with the item!

Double-barrelled questions. Items that involve multiple premises are to be avoided as the meanings of responses are unclear: for instance, 'Do you believe the training programme was a good one and effective in teaching you new skills?' If someone disagreed with this item it could be because they thought the programme was generally good but ineffective for them personally, or bad and ineffective, or even effective for them despite being of poor quality. Here it is not clear exactly which premise is being disagreed (or agreed) with.

Hidden assumptions. Items should not contain hidden assumptions. The classic example of this sort of problem is contained in the item 'When did you stop beating your wife?' This assumes you used to beat your wife and, indeed, that you have a wife to beat.

Social desirability. Whilst it might seem a source of irritation to the questionnaire researcher, people like to present themselves in a positive light when answering questionnaires. If you were asked if you ever gave to charity, for instance, then saying 'no' (assuming this to be the correct answer) says something about you that you may not want to convey to the researcher. Many apparently innocuous questions have response options which, if selected, might indicate something negative about the respondent. This leads to potential biases in response patterns which you would usually wish to avoid.

Sometimes social desirability phenomena can be quite subtle. For example, Krosnik and Schuman (1988) have shown that people are more prepared to agree 'not to allow' something than to 'forbid' the same thing. Though these responses are logically equivalent, the latter one is thought to carry with it undesirable authoritarian overtones, making some people in favour of forbidding things less likely to tell you, the researcher.

On some occasions it can be useful to use items with certain socially desirable responses since this is of some theoretical or analytical use to you. The

Crowne–Marlowe Social Desirability Scale (Crowne & Marlowe, 1964) is sometimes used for this very purpose. Box 11.3 also looks at social desirability in the context of cross-cultural research.

Box 11.3   Using questionnaires for cross-cultural research

The apparent simplicity of the questionnaire makes it very attractive to researchers who want to collect data in a number of different countries and want to use country or culture as an explanatory variable. Simple examples might include asking whether people in country A are more satisfied with their jobs than people in country B, or whether people from southern European nations are happier and less depressed than their northern European counterparts.

back-translation

The standard advice when attempting to use a questionnaire in more than one country is to get the questionnaire back-translated. **Back-translation** involves having your questionnaire translated into the target language and then having a separate, independent individual translate the questionnaire back into the original language. The task is to ensure that the original and back-translated versions of the questionnaire are equivalent in meaning. In practice it is rare for the two versions to be absolutely identical, but most researchers are prepared to use the translation if the two versions are 'close enough' in meaning.

While this procedure has some rigour about it, it does not ensure that scores can be meaningfully compared. Many cultures differ in the degree to which filling in questionnaires is a normal everyday occurrence. In some countries questionnaires are only usually encountered when the government or other authority sponsors them. People in these countries are unused to the Western concept of research and scientific inquiry and will respond as if responding to the government or authority, with all the attendant biases that that might bring with it. More subtly, Hui and Triandis (1989) point out that in some cultures expressing moderate positions on questionnaire items is valued and in other cultures there is a

acquiescence bias

tendency to say 'yes' or 'agree' with questions – also called an **acquiescence bias**. Clearly data from such countries are not easily compared as mean scores in the former country will tend towards mid-scale values while the latter country will generate more extreme values *even though* there may be no meaningful differences between the countries on the construct being measured. One solution to this is to attempt standardization by expressing item scores relative to each individual's average score across items. Another strategy is to avoid using response scales with mid-points and/or to reduce the number of response options on the scale.

Despite these remedial options, achieving cross-cultural equivalence of measures is very difficult and researchers are well advised to attempt to demonstrate the cross-cultural equivalence of their measures (e.g. by using multi-group confirmatory factor analyses – see Chapter 21) before assuming comparisons or contrasts can be legitimately made.

Sensitive issues. You should be wary of assuming that all your respondents find your questions as acceptable as you do. When you are engaged in research on sensitive issues (e.g. death, sex, religion) you should be aware that your items may cause offence to certain groups. It is good practice to ask about sensitive issues as directly, yet with as much sympathy for your respondents, as is possible. Do not try to get at sensitive information indirectly by attempting to deceive respondents. If you cannot ask something fairly directly, then you should think about approaching the issue via an alternative method to the questionnaire.

11.6 TYPES OF INFORMATION GLEANED FROM QUESTIONNAIRES

Questionnaires can be used to gather a variety of types of information. You can ask about people's background and other factual, demographic information. You can ask about their behaviours, their attitudes or beliefs, their knowledge or their intentions and aspirations. Each sort of information is associated with particular difficulties, which are discussed below.

11.6.1 Background and demographic data

Most questionnaires will ask for some information about the respondent's background. Numerous texts deal with how to ask for this demographic information (e.g. Sudman & Bradburn, 1982), and it is well worth the time consulting such books if in doubt about how to phrase certain items. Although these types of information are readily accessible to the respondents themselves, it is surprising how often people resist giving this information. You should consider some of the following issues.

Age. How accurately do you need to know a person's age? Some respondents may not want to declare their age exactly, so it may be appropriate to ask people to indicate their approximate age in a series of age bands (e.g. 18–25, 26–35, 36–50, 51+). How many bands you need will depend on how crucial it is to distinguish between respondents on the basis of age. If you need to know ages more accurately, then you should ask directly, making it clear how accurate you want the answer to be. You can ask for ages in years, or in years and months. It is possible to ask for dates of birth as an alternative. Requesting greater precision runs the risk of some respondents failing to answer at all.

Biological sex. It is good idea to make this a forced-choice, male/female item. If you leave the response category open-ended someone will put something inappropriate in. Although social scientists draw a distinction between biological sex and gender and often wish to classify the respondent's gender, the term 'gender' is not well understood by lay respondents and may serve to confuse some people. Unless it is central to your research it is probably easiest to use an item like question 2 in Figure 11.1. A question asking 'What is your gender?' can annoy certain sections in society and thereby produce unusable responses.

| What is your *nationality* (e.g. British, French)? | _____ |
| What is your *ethnic origin* (e.g. Caucasian, Afro-caribbean, Asian)? | _____ |

Figure 11.6 Example questions to assess nationality and ethnicity

Ethnicity and nationality. Ethnicity and nationality are two bits of information about respondents that you may need to ask about, despite the fact that the very act of asking for this information is heavily laden with political baggage. Many people confuse nationality with ethnicity and, as a researcher, you should be absolutely clear what information you need *and why*. Remember that being 'British' is a statement about nationality, not ethnicity. Respondents may reasonably want to know why their ethnicity or nationality is relevant to your study and what use you will make of this information. Research that may reveal important differences between ethnic groups may be regarded as politically suspect by whichever group is likely to come out worst in the survey. If you must ask about nationality and/or ethnicity you should be sure that such information cannot be used to systematically disadvantage any group. Indeed this applies to all demographic data. If you wish to ask about this, the items in Figure 11.6 may help reduce confusion.

Social class or socio-economic status. Social stratification is a topic on which so much has been written it is difficult to provide simple guidance on good practice. There are several systems of classification, of which the Standard Occupational Classification is the best known and the one used by the UK Office for National Statistics. Most systems involve defining class on the basis of the nature of the person's occupation. This means obtaining enough information about someone's job to permit accurate classification. A common problem is that if someone says they are an 'engineer' this could mean anything from someone who repairs TVs to someone who designs nuclear power stations. You need more information such as that provided by the items in Figure 11.7 (adapted from the Economic and Social Research Council 16–19 Initiative: Banks *et al.*, 1992).

When studying women it is difficult to know *whose* social class/status should be assessed. There is a debate (e.g. Dale, Gilbert & Arber, 1985) about how women's social class should be measured, particularly as women's jobs tend to carry a lower occupational status than men's jobs in some classification systems. Basing a woman's class/status on her husband's occupation is common practice but is probably unsound and ignores those who are not married.

Difficulties also occur when trying to classify young people's occupations. Occupations common among people at the beginning of their careers tend to carry low status, yet they may still lead to high-status careers in later life. Using parental class/status is one possible solution, but it is unclear at what age a person's occupation should be regarded as a good indication of class/status. Classifying students and the unemployed also remains problematic.

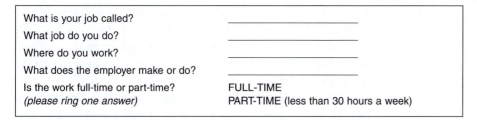

What is your job called?	_____
What job do you do?	_____
Where do you work?	_____
What does the employer make or do?	_____
Is the work full-time or part-time?	FULL-TIME
(please ring one answer)	PART-TIME (less than 30 hours a week)

Figure 11.7 Example occupation questions

When asking about social class/status you should be clear in your mind what it is you really want to know about the respondent. Sociologists have spent decades theorizing about what constitutes our social status, and even a cursory dip into the literature will make it clear that such concepts as 'class', 'status' and 'advantage' are complex and very slippery things: psychologists should beware the temptation to accept measures of 'status' unconditionally. For many psychological applications it might be more appropriate to simply ask about factors such as income and educational history, since it may be these variables you are really interested in rather than a stratification based on occupations.

Income. A person's income is perhaps one of the most sensitive issues you can ask about in social research. Requests for exact amounts are often regarded with suspicion, and common practice in market research is to provide income bands (e.g. £0–£5000 p.a., £5001–£10,000 p.a., …) and ask respondents to select one band only. Respondents need to be assured that their responses will not be handed over to the Inland Revenue or other government agency.

With many factual types of responses it can be useful to ask respondents to tick a box if they do not wish to provide certain bits of information. This helps you distinguish between data that are missing because people did not want to provide some information, and data that are missing because people simply neglected to fill in the form completely. Providing an option not to respond like this may help to make people feel more relaxed about providing other sorts of information. Making people feel they have to answer absolutely everything may make some feel they would rather not respond at all. Obviously, you should not do this with items that are crucial to your study's design.

There is a useful discussion of alternative ways to ask for social stratification information (including examples) on the CASS Web page (see Section 11.10).

11.6.2 Behavioural reports

By their very nature, questions asking about past behaviours assume accurate memory for events as well as a willingness to report these to a researcher. Both assumptions need to be considered afresh for each new item you generate.

It should come as no surprise that sensitive and socially undesirable behaviours are often misreported if reported at all. Questions about sexual activities are thought to produce overreporting in some groups and underreporting in others (see Boulton, 1994). Reports of involvement (or not) in illegal practices are also likely to be prone to error.

It would be a mistake to assume that biases apply just to the reporting of private and/or undesirable acts. Sudman and Bradburn (1982) report studies that suggest overreporting biases also apply to socially desirable behaviours too (e.g. charity donations, library use). Given these problems, the best solution in the absence of corroborative data is to introduce additional items elsewhere in the questionnaire to test for consistency in reporting. If someone is going to misrepresent their behaviour to you, then if they are inconsistent at least you can have clear grounds to exclude their responses from your analyses.

In some circumstances it may be possible to make respondents believe that you will have an alternative way to find out about their behaviour. This tactic is **bogus pipeline** called the **bogus pipeline**. In a questionnaire study on children's smoking behaviour, Evans *et al.* (1978) took saliva samples at the time of questioning and led respondents to believe that the saliva would be used to confirm their behavioural reports on the questionnaire. In fact, the cost of saliva testing was too high to permit all samples to be tested but, compared with a control group, the group who thought their behaviours could be monitored reported higher levels of smoking. Where appropriate, this strategy seems likely to improve the quality of behavioural report data, though you should be wary of deliberate attempts to deceive respondents, especially if you will be unable to fully debrief them.

Assessment of the frequency with which behaviours have been done in the past is an area where there is much research activity (see Gaskell, Wright & O'Muircheartaigh, 1993). What is clear is that you should avoid vague response categories (such as 'regularly') as discussed above. When asked about very regular, mundane events people may find it easier to estimate how often they have done the act in a given time period since they are unlikely to remember every time they did the act. When asking about more memorable, major life events, more specific recall can be requested.

11.6.3 Attitudes and opinions

People's attitudes and opinions are often of great interest, but there is little consensus on how best to measure them. The commonest procedure is to present a statement and ask people to rate on a scale (of usually five or seven points) how much they agree or disagree with the statement (see Figure 11.3). It is possible to use more than five or seven points. You can provide a line with the ends labelled 'strongly agree' and 'strongly disagree' and ask respondents simply to mark their preferred position on this agreement dimension with a cross. This procedure requires the researcher to use a ruler or template on each response to retrieve a usable score for computational purposes.

An alternative to the rating scale is the forced-choice design where two opposing statements are presented and the respondent must choose to endorse one or the other. This procedure is less common as it does not give information about the extremity of agreement/disagreement. However, five- or seven-point rating scales can suffer from people's overreliance on the neutral response ('neither agree nor disagree') rather than committing themselves to expressing an opinion.

All pen-and-paper attitude measurements make a number of assumptions. The first is that people actually have attitudes towards the issues and that they have ready access to them. The second is that these can be adequately reflected in simple ratings or forced-choice judgements. Sometimes you will see the type of rating scale presented in Figure 11.3 referred to as a Likert scale. This is only technically true if the item has been developed following Likert's standardized procedure, and this may not always be the case.

Given these kinds of problems it is common to ask multiple questions about the same attitude object in the hope that greater accuracy will be achieved. Multiple-item measures of attitudes allow for the possibility of measuring the internal reliability of the items and thus how much 'error' there is in the measurement of the attitude (see also Chapter 10).

11.6.4 Knowledge

Quite often it would be useful to assess factual knowledge in a questionnaire survey. Such 'tests' can be carried out, but the validity of responses and thus the knowledge scores have to be considered to be in some doubt. Unless you can be present at the time of testing you cannot be certain who answered the test. This could apply to the whole questionnaire, of course, but people may simply ask someone else for help with the difficult questions so that they do not appear ignorant. Tests of this sort can be used reasonably successfully in non-survey settings on populations such as school pupils and employees where you can exert some control over the testing conditions.

11.6.5 Intentions, expectations and aspirations

Many social psychological theories are concerned with accounting for intentions, expectations and aspirations which are fairly easily assessed via questionnaires. You should be careful to specify an appropriate time frame for such items as vague specifications can lead to vague responses. For instance, if you were to ask 'Do you expect to travel abroad in the future?', respondents could quite reasonably say 'Who knows?' A much better form would be to ask 'As far as you can tell, do you expect to travel abroad in the next year?'

11.7 EXISTING SCALES AND MEASURES

When using established measures it is often tempting to alter the wording of some items to make them sound better or to clarify them a little. It is quite surprising how many published and well-established measures contain wording errors like those outlined in the earlier sections of this chapter. It is also the case that scales developed in other countries can contain culturally specific phrases or assume some familiarity with cultural norms that would be somewhat inappropriate for your sample. Should you change item wordings or leave them as they are?

It is not possible to answer this with a categorical 'yes' or 'no'. One side of the argument says that any tampering with item wordings will change the nature of the scale so that it is no longer equivalent to the original. Hence, comparability of scores between your study and existing research using the scale is no longer appropriate. You might be tempted to make minor changes in the hope that scale scores will still be comparable but, in the absence of supporting validity data, this cannot be assumed.

The other side of the argument says that it is poor research practice to administer questionnaires that contain phrases or assumptions that your respondents are unlikely to be familiar with. It may alienate them or make them think the items are silly or not serious. As an example, early versions of the Wilson–Patterson Conservatism Scale (Wilson & Patterson, 1968) contained items asking people to endorse (or not) chaperones, pyjama parties and beatniks among other potential indicators of conservative attitudes. At the time (the 1960s) chaperones, pyjama parties and beatniks were topical and made sense in such a questionnaire, but today these items would raise eyebrows.

The point about the latter example is that the scale would presumably no longer be particularly valid (indeed, Wilson subsequently updated the scale). Even though you might wish to compare current levels of conservatism with those found in the 1960s and 1970s by using an equivalent measure, it is doubtful that such a comparative study would be very informative. You should always consider this potential lack of validity when thinking about using an existing measure that was not validated on the type of sample that you are going to study. You may need to consider attempting to establish validity yourself (e.g. via a criterion groups approach; see Chapter 10).

11.8 QUESTIONNAIRE LAYOUT

This section deals with issues regarding the presentation of your questionnaire. There is always a trade-off between on the one hand better presentation, and thus, one hopes, better-quality data and higher response rate, and on the other, increased cost. This is important even if you are going to be present when the questionnaire is administered.

Respondent motivation. Unless you will be present at the administration, explanatory notes should always be provided. These should spell out the broad aims of the study and why the individual's compliance is important. The individual must be encouraged to feel that the responses are valued by you and that you will treat them with respect. Wherever possible, you should ensure anonymity for respondents. If the research design is such that you need to be able to identify individual respondents, acknowledge this and ensure confidentiality (and, of course, mean it). If you intend to keep computerized records of responses that could identify respondents, you should seek to be registered under the Data Protection Act as a holder of such information. Tell respondents that you have done this.

Provide feedback to respondents (which is always good practice), and explain how this is to be achieved. Compliance is likely to be higher if respondents can find out what happened to the research and what benefits may have come from it.

You should always thank respondents for their help in the introductory notes *and* at the end of the form.

Case identifiers. It is good housekeeping practice to be able to identify individual questionnaires (though not necessarily individual respondents) so that when you find problems with the data later on you can use the computer to tell you which questionnaire the problem is associated with. Fail to do this with a large survey and it will be very difficult to make valid corrections to the data.

Length. There are no rules to guide you on the optimum length for a questionnaire since this depends so much on the topic of the study, the method of distribution (e.g. postal, face-to-face) and the anticipated enthusiasm of your respondents. There are some rough guidelines that can be given, however.

The problem facing most researchers is how to ask all the questions they want to ask without tiring or boring their respondents. How long it takes to answer a questionnaire can only really be assessed via pilot work, and efforts should be made to pilot the form on people who are likely, on a priori grounds, to have difficulty with it. Experience would suggest that forms that take more than 45 minutes to complete are only appropriate where the respondent can be assumed to be very highly motivated to help you.

Very short questionnaires (one or two pages) have the virtue of not taxing respondents unduly, though they may not be taken very seriously either. It would be rare to have a substantive research issue that could be dealt with in such a small questionnaire, and some respondents may think the exercise can only be superficial and thus adopt a less than serious attitude towards answering.

Question order. There seems to be a growing convention in social research to collect information about respondent demographics (age, sex, etc.) at the end of

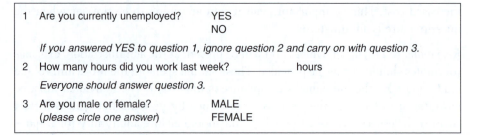

Figure 11.8 An example of a filter question

a questionnaire. This is information that people have ready access to and, if asked appropriately, they will have little difficulty in providing it. As they tire of your questionnaire they get asked the less taxing questions.

It is also rare to place extremely sensitive questions right at the beginning of a form. People need time to get accustomed to the types of issues you are interested in, and starting off with your equivalent of 'When did you stop beating your wife?' will not make the respondent feel at ease.

Question density. You may be tempted to cram lots of questions into a small number of pages so that the questionnaire booklet does not appear too large and daunting. This is generally counterproductive as squashing lots of items into a small space makes the form look complex and raises the possibility that respondents will get confused and put their responses in the wrong places. Clear, self-evident layout will enhance the possibility of getting valid information from your sample.

Questions that do not apply to everybody. It is often the case that you are forced to use a single form to ask questions and some of these will not be applicable to some people. For instance, you may not wish to ask unemployed respondents about how many hours they work. If you cannot provide a separate question-naire for the unemployed, you will need to use **filter questions**. An example is shown in Figure 11.8.

filter questions

Typeface and size. Some people will find small, densely packed text difficult to read. Pick a clear font (typeface) and make it reasonably large (12 point or bigger). Use a different font or colour for instructions and bold or italic lettering for filter questions if you have such a facility.

The use of graphics in response options. Most respondents either have no idea, or do not need to know that their carefully thought through responses to our questions will be turned in to numbers for statistical analysis. Indeed, they may not like the idea that their heartfelt agreement with a statement on an issue will most probably be turned into a single number later to be aggregated with a range of other responses in a composite index (see Chapter 10).

Although often used, asking people to respond by circling a number on a scale carries with it certain threats to the validity of the data. Firstly, there will be those who mistakenly assume that bigger is perhaps better and misunderstand the nature of the response scale. There will also be some who do not understand numbered scales at all and would not be able to make the conceptual leap to link the numbers with a latent agree/disagree dimension. There are various ways around this. One is to abandon numbers and use tick boxes laid out in a line that implies the relevant response dimension (most often agree/disagree). Another is to use graphics such as 'smiley' faces which can convey happiness/sadness with regard to the questionnaire item. This is a particularly useful approach with children.

11.9 CONCLUSION

This chapter has attempted to alert you to many common problems in questionnaire design. The solutions proposed here are intended as guides to good practice but you should not feel that these are the only possible solutions to these difficulties. A lot more inventive use could be made of questionnaires than is currently the case. Guides such as this necessarily deal with common problems, but you should not limit yourself to asking about the broad general topics covered here. Breakwell and Canter (1993), for example, illustrate a number of possibilities for alternative questionnaire approaches to the social psychological topic of social representation; such experimentation should be encouraged in other research domains too.

11.10 FURTHER READING

Oppenheim's (1992) text is a good and clear introduction to questionnaire design, as is the older Sudman and Bradburn (1982) book. Schuman and Presser's (1996) book reports an intriguing series of experimental studies with survey data which highlight the sensitivity of respondents to quite minor wording changes in questionnaire items. Those wishing for a contemporary angle on some of these effects should take a look at the work of Gaskell et al. (1993). Information on how to ask questions about demographic issues can be found at the Centre for Applied Social Surveys (CASS) Web page (at http://www.socstats.soton.ac.uk/CASS). This gives information on the way in which such questions have been asked in major social surveys, and one hope is to promote best practice in this area and seek some standardization where possible.

12

Interviewing Methods

Glynis M. Breakwell

12.1   Introduction
12.2   The interview structure
12.3   Piloting the interview
12.4   Conducting the interview
12.5   Medium of the interview
12.6   Interviewing children
12.7   Validity and reliability of interview data
12.8   Analysing interview data
12.9   Reporting interview research
12.10 Conclusion
12.11 Further reading

AIMS

This chapter will introduce the reader to the design, conduct, analysis and reporting of interviewing used as a research method. It will discuss the issues to consider when selecting samples of participants to be interviewed, structuring data for interpretation, and using computer-assisted data collection. Factors affecting the validity and reliability of information collected through interviewing will be examined. Some common pitfalls which need to be avoided when using interviewing will be highlighted.

Key terms

acquiescence	interviewer effects
response bias	interview protocol
debriefing	interview schedule
differential dropout	researcher effects
fully structured interviews	unstructured interviews
inter-rater reliability	

12.1 INTRODUCTION

Interviewing is an essential part of many types of social research. This chapter describes how interviewing is done in a research context. The skills needed are similar to those required when interviewing is used in other contexts such as selection or appraisal procedures, but there are differences. Research interviews require a very systematic approach to data collection, analysis and description that allows you to maximize the chances of achieving meaningful, valid and reliable conclusions.

Interviews can be used at any stage in the research process. They can be used in the initial phases to identify areas or issues for more detailed exploration. They can be used as part of the piloting and validation of other instruments. They can be used as the main vehicle of data collection. They can be used once findings have been compiled to check whether your interpretations of other types of data make sense to the participants who were involved.

The interview is an almost infinitely flexible tool for research. It can encompass other techniques (e.g. as part of an interview, a self-completion questionnaire can be administered or psychophysiological measurements can be taken). Also it can be placed alongside other data elicitation procedures (e.g. it can be used in tandem with ethnography or participant observation).

Interviewing is relatively unusual as a research tool in that it is not tied to any one theory, epistemological orientation (whether constructivist or positivist), or philosophical tradition. Researchers from virtually all approaches will use interviewing at some time. This may be because interviews are the vehicle for deploying many more specific data collection methods. It is also because interviews are flexible in format and function. They can be configured to generate many types of information and, perhaps more importantly, the data they generate can be interpreted and represented in myriad different ways. Section 12.9 on reporting interview data emphasizes the variety that exists in the approaches to interview data. It is also evident in other chapters in this book (e.g. Chapters 15, 16 and 18) that interviewing is the basic building block of far more specific and elaborate methods.

In the context of this ubiquitousness of interviewing and the variety of its forms, you may be wondering what is the distinctive feature of this method. Quintessentially, the distinctive feature of this method is that it involves a direct interaction or exchange, usually verbal, between the researcher and the participant or participants who are researched. The interaction does not need to be face-to-face, although often it is. It does not need to be one-to-one, although often it is. It does not need to be verbal (i.e. involving words), although almost invariably it is. It does not need to be vocal, although regularly it is.

It should be acknowledged that interview questions do not have to be addressed to one person at a time. It is possible to conduct group interviews. Chapter 14 addresses some of these issues with regard to focus groups and the peculiarities of group interviewing, so they will not be considered here.

It is important to note that no method of collecting information is free of pitfalls. This chapter will present both the strengths and the weaknesses of the interview method. When all the problems surrounding question construction, the biases introduced by the researcher and the interviewee, and the inadequacies of the available media of communication and recording mechanisms are taken into account, the method still has much to recommend it. Like any method, it has to be used with care and in the full knowledge of its limitations.

12.2 THE INTERVIEW STRUCTURE

Chapter 1 emphasized the significance of adequate specification of your research questions. Having specified the research questions, you need to translate them into a form that can be used with your interviewees. This translation process is often troublesome because the way the research question can be operationalized in a series of questions posed to a sample is severely limited by the complexity of the research question and level of the capacities and extent of co-operation of the respondents.

The nature of the research questions will also determine the selection of participants: see Box 12.1.

Box 12.1   Selection of participants

There are no simple absolute rules that determine the appropriate selection of participants for interview studies. Such studies are very diverse (ranging from the single case study to surveys conducted by telephone involving thousands of interviewees). The size of the sample should be determined by the extent to which the research question demands responses from a number of people who could be said to be representative of a specific population. The diversity within that population will then determine what constitutes a representative sample. It is the research issue that you wish to study. There is no problem with the use of small, highly targeted samples that possess the characteristics you believe salient to your research question. However, you should remember that the smaller the sample and the more narrowly defined their target characteristics, the less it is possible to generalize your results beyond that specific sample.

Ideally, sample size should not be determined by resource considerations. Often, however, it is. Samples are constrained by the time available for the research, the money available to do it, the availability of willing participants, and so on. These are factors that affect all research approaches.

It is often supposed that sample size is traded off against the amount of data collected from each individual. It is suggested that small samples lend themselves to more in-depth interviewing. This is, of course, merely a practical outcome of resource constraints, not a logical necessity.

(Continued)

Box 12.1 (Continued)

The issue of refusal

Sometimes people refuse to be interviewed. It is important to record how many refuse and any details you know about them. If it is possible, you should find out from them why they do not want to participate. This information should be included in your final report of your study.

There are two main ways of handling refusals.

- You can substitute other people into the sample in a second round of approaches to potential participants on the assumption that they share with those who refuse the target characteristics for the research. The result is effectively a quota sample. This approach maintains the integrity of the sample size but does not eliminate the possibility that those who refused would have offered very different information during the interview. Thus the details of refusal must be reported.
- You can proceed with a reduced sample size and seek to analyse differences between the participants and 'refusers' on baseline characteristics, then assess whether variability in the interview sample on any characteristics on which they differed from the refusers is associated with variability in responses during the interviews. With large samples this can be an illuminating approach.

12.2.1 The introduction

Interviewees will require an introduction to the interview. The participants should be given information appropriate for them to be able to give their informed consent to their participation. However, the researcher must ensure that the context of this introduction does not compromise the validity of the participants' subsequent answers to questions. For instance, it is not good practice to explain to a participant the hypothesis or proposition you hope to examine in the research. So, for example, if you are proposing that there is no strong relationship between environmentally concerned attitudes and environmentally concerned patterns of behaviour, it would not be appropriate to explain this to a participant prior to asking a series of questions on environmental attitudes and behaviour. The fact that the participants have been informed of your proposition or hypothesis may mean that they provide answers that they would not otherwise have provided. Sometimes cover stories are used to frame the research so that hypotheses are not manifest.

Introductions and explanations should be designed to encourage participation and confidence in the interview but should not reveal the central research agenda. For example, the interviewer can explain the general area of the research (this is a study of environmental attitudes and behaviour). The interviewer could also explain that it is important for the participant to give honest and full answers. The interviewer might explain why the individual was chosen for interview, but again, only in general terms.

12.2.2 The form of questions and responses

In its entirety, the series of questions asked in an interview is usually called the **interview schedule**. Interviews use many question-and-answer formats which range from the totally structured to the totally unstructured. Structure can be imposed either through the fixed nature of the questions and their sequence or through the fixed (i.e. constrained) nature of the answers allowed. The most structured interviews involve constraint of both questions and answers. In these, the researcher is usually examining highly specified hypotheses or propositions. Few actual interviews fall at either of the poles of this continuum between fixed and absent structure.

interview schedule

Fully structured interviews involve a fixed set of questions which the researcher asks in a fixed order. Commonly, respondents are asked to choose an answer from a fixed series of options given by the researcher. The options may include options given in any format (e.g. rating scales, sorting exercises or multiple-choice alternatives). This type of interview structure yields information which is easily quantified, ensures comparability and consistency of questions and response elements across respondents, and makes certain that the necessary topics are included. It is often used when large numbers of participants are required in a study to address the research question. However, like all prestructured data elicitation techniques, it leaves little room for unanticipated discoveries. People often feel constrained because they are not free to give the information that they feel is important. You may miss very salient issues in this way.

fully structured interviews

In **unstructured interviews**, the researcher has a number of topics to cover but the precise questions and their order are not fixed; they are allowed to develop as a result of the exchange with the respondent. Open-ended answers allow the interviewees to say as little or as much as they choose. Comparability across respondents is sacrificed for the sake of individual relevance. It would be wrong, however, to think that the flexibility of the unstructured interview of necessity permits a deeper analysis than the structured interview. In both cases, the richness of the data is determined by the appreciation that the researcher has of the topic and the extent to which the research question is properly addressed.

unstructured interviews

Analysis of unstructured interviews is time-consuming and difficult but not inevitably purely qualitative. *Post hoc* content analysis of unstructured responses will provide categorical data which are open to quantification (Chapter 14 contains a description of how to conduct a content analysis). There are now sophisticated software packages which, given the word-processed transcript of an interview, will count the incidence of certain phrases or words for you, taking some of the pain out of content analysis. This issue of analysis of interview data is explored further in Section 12.8 and Box 12.4. However, it should be noted here that many researchers who use unstructured interviews shun all quantification. They believe that by immersing themselves in the data they can understand the key themes which emerge. These they believe can be illustrated through taking direct quotes from transcripts and linking these in a coherent description of the themes. Ideally, the quotes allow the interviewees to speak for themselves, telling their own story. The researcher acts as the editor only in so far as quotes must be chosen. Chapters 16 and 17 describe some of these approaches further.

Whether you use structured or less structured interviews, there are a number of guidelines to follow in formulating questions and in asking them (see Box 12.2). Avoiding these traps in formulating the questions may seem relatively easy. However, a surprising number of experienced researchers fall into them.

Box 12.2 Question formats that should not be used

Things questions should not do.

- Be double-barrelled. (Example: 'Do you think whaling and seal culling should be banned?' A 'no' answer could mean no to either whaling or seal culling or both.)
- Introduce an assumption before going on to pose the question. (Example: 'Do you think that the terrible cruelty of whaling has been adequately reported in the press?' This question assumes that whaling is seen to be cruel by the respondent. The assumption may or may not be true and makes interpretation of any response indeterminate.)
- Include complex or jargon words. (Example: 'Do you think you are eco-conscious?' This might be inadvisable unless you checked that the respondent shared your definition of eco-consciousness.)
- Be leading. (Example: 'I suppose you know what eco-consciousness is?' Some people might say 'no' to the question in that form but the pressure is on them to say yes.)
- Include double negatives. (Example: 'Do you think now that not many people would not understand the term eco-consciousness?' Could you be sure what a 'no' response meant?)
- Act as catchalls. (Example: 'Tell me everything you know about the Green movement and how it has influenced you?' After the silence which the question is likely to engender, it is unlikely you will get anything useful without a series of further prompt questions.)

12.2.3 The sequence of questions

There is a further set of problems which also need to be tackled. An interview schedule needs to be looked at in its entirety. Getting the individual questions right is vital but they also have to be ordered appropriately. A good interview schedule has a rhythm to it which takes the respondent through what appears to be a set of issues which are sensibly related. Interviews should not jump, without explanation, from one topic to another. Even if it is not the complete rationale for the research, the respondent has been given some notion of why the questions are being asked and must feel that the sequence of questions makes sense. If the schedule fails to do this, respondents can become confused, suspicious and, sometimes, belligerent. Necessary jumps between topics can be covered by short but apparently reasonable explanations. For instance, often at the end of an interview it is necessary to get data that will allow socio-economic status to be assessed. Respondents sometimes fail to see why this is relevant to the views they have just been offering you. The switch to questions about their occupational status or educational qualifications can be made if you use a link explanation such as: 'As a matter of routine we collect information on what jobs our interviewees do. I hope you do not mind me asking you ...'. If the respondent then queries the relevance of the questions, it can be helpful just to add 'Occasionally, we find differences between the views of people who have different jobs'. The key thing in constructing link explanations is that they should not suggest what you expect people to say in answer to the next set of questions.

12.2.4 Concluding the interview

When designing the interview, you should also include clear guidelines on how to conclude it. Some **debriefing**, involving a more comprehensive explanation for the questions asked or the way the research will be used, may be needed. Often respondents want the interviewer to tell them immediately what their answers reveal about them. The interviewer has to be ready with a response which is non-committal and not likely to cause offence. It is best to anticipate this request for immediate analysis by stating at the end that you cannot say anything about individuals or that the findings will take a long time to produce. Whatever strategy you choose to adopt at the end of the interview, it is good practice to be consistent across respondents. Sometimes interviews trigger highly emotional responses in interviewees. This obviously depends on the subject matter of the interview, but it is always useful to have decided how to deal with interviewees who become upset as a result of your interview. Usually, having clear referral routes to experts in the area of concern is preferable. You might even provide information about such experts to all interviewees as a matter of course if you anticipate any possibility of distress being initiated by the interview.

debriefing

12.3 PILOTING THE INTERVIEW

Since there are so many problems in getting the individual questions, the order in which they are asked and the links between them absolutely right, interview schedules need to be piloted. In the same way that you would pilot a questionnaire (see Chapter 11), an interview schedule must be tested and refined. There is no required routine for piloting an interview schedule. The following stages are, however, frequently used.

Stage 1. Test whether your explanation for the interview is understood by a small sample drawn from the same population as the people you intend to interview. Normally, understanding in this context is ascertained by having this pilot sample explain the interview back to you in their own words. They can also be asked to tell you about any doubts or queries they might have about the interview. Getting the explanation for the interview right is fundamentally important. Not only will it influence the data you get from the people you manage to interview, it is very likely to have a big impact upon whether people are willing to be interviewed at all. The most successful explanations are those which emphasize the significance of the research, the significance of the particular individual's participation in it, the confidentiality of all data, and the possibility of withdrawing from the interview if at any point the person wishes to do so. At the pilot stage, you may wish to try alternative types of explanation in order to test if they will influence willingness to participate or indeed responses given during the interview itself.

Stage 2. Use the same pilot sample to test comprehension of particular questions which you know have not been used with this population before or which you feel are difficult (e.g. possibly ambiguous, lacking relevance, or involving too advanced vocabulary).

Stage 3. Amend the introduction and questions in the light of stages 1 and 2. Surprisingly, researchers often go through the motions of piloting and then ignore what they find. This is a form of intellectual arrogance and research hypocrisy. There is no point in doing the pilot work if you do not respond to the information it gives you and then check by further piloting that your changes were the right ones.

Stage 4. With a new subsample, test the revised explanation and all questions for comprehension. This should be a complete run through of the entire interview schedule. It is still possible to make changes at this point. It is better to fine-tune the questions in the course of the pilot work at this stage than to get into a never-ending cycle of resampling in order to test out small refinements of the schedule.

Stage 5. With a new subsample, use the interview schedule to establish whether the answers which you are getting are the ones which interest you. This stage moves away from testing comprehension to being genuine data collection. Nevertheless, even if the schedule is working as you wished, the data from this stage should not be collapsed with data later collected from the main sample since this would change the sample structure (obviously, this warning only matters if your sample structure is important to you – see Box 12.1). Assuming that the schedule is performing as you expected, it is possible at this point to proceed to the main study.

Properly conducted pilot work pays off: it minimizes the chances of finding midway through the study that a vital issue has been ignored or that certain parts of the participant group cannot understand batches of questions. Of course, to be maximally useful, the pilot work must be conducted on a subsample which is thoroughly representative of the sample you will ultimately use. Rigour in choosing the subsample for pilot work is important and often missing. It should be noted that piloting is just as important for unstructured interviews as it is for structured interviews. The unstructured interview, despite not having a fixed list of questions in a fixed order, must be informed by a thorough appreciation of which routes of questioning are likely to be productive, what sorts of questions make sense, and so on. It is impossible for the researcher to achieve that understanding without preliminary pilot work. In the absence of good piloting, unstructured interviews can all too easily lose sight of the main research issue they were addressing. Chapter 16 gives an excellent description of the way piloting should be done when small numbers of participants are involved in relatively unstructured and in-depth interviews.

12.4 CONDUCTING THE INTERVIEW

Piloting should result in an interview protocol that can be used with ease. Yet the conduct of the interviews must also be very systematic as you move into the main formal part of the study.

While there are traps lurking for you when you formulate questions, there are also traps waiting for you when you ask them. In order to avoid them, there are a few golden rules that should be followed. Firstly, be thoroughly familiar with the interview schedule before you start. Secondly, ask all questions of all respondents, even if you think you know what some of them will say. Give all respondents an equal hearing. Thirdly, know what each question is meant to tap and, if you are failing to get relevant material, probe further. Probes (e.g. non-committal encouragements to extend answers using eye contact, glance, repetition of the answer, gentle queries like 'I'm confused here') should be non-directive. Prompts (which suggest possible answers to the interviewee) should only be used if they are deployed consistently to all. In pursuing a point it is important not to seek or give unrelated or irrelevant information. It is essential to avoid offering advice or counselling as part of a research interview unless this has been explicitly agreed in advance. If the interviewee does become upset or aroused the researcher should ensure that this is acknowledged and normally should not leave until the interviewee is calmed or other support arranged. The researcher handling sensitive subject matter should be sure to have information ready which will tell the interviewee where advice can be found. Fourthly, whatever technique for recording you use, be consistent in recording answers (see Box 12.3 on recording techniques). Fifthly, an answer in a face-to-face interview has both verbal and non-verbal components. It is sometimes useful to encode non-verbal aspects of the answers even when visual recording is not used. They can change the underlying message substantially. Bull (2004) illustrates the value of analysing both verbal and non-verbal components of interviews in his insightful exploration of equivocation by politicians in media interviews. Chapter 7 in this book also has further details on this.

Box 12.3   Recording techniques

Where interviews are recorded on audio or videotape it is possible to transcribe the tapes and use these transcriptions as the basis for analysis. Usually, it is easier to carry out content analysis from the transcripts since moving backwards and forwards in the text is easier than doing so on the tapes. The transcripts can include systematic records of the non-verbal communication involved (Rich & Patashnick, 2002; Auerbach & Silverstein, 2003). Transcription is a slow and expensive business and it may be necessary to be selective about which elements of the interviews you choose to get transcribed fully (it usually takes about seven hours to transcribe one hour of speech). Selection can be driven by theoretical concerns. Initial selections can always be revised later. The tapes should always be available as the complete and permanent record, and they can always be re-examined.

Semi- or unstructured interviews require careful consideration of the way in which interviewees' responses to questions will be recorded. Note that any method of recording should only be used with the explicit permission of the interviewee. There are three prime recording methods.

Note-taking during or immediately after the interview. Note-taking is low-cost, can be selective and facilitate quick analysis if pre-structuring of response categories has been done (e.g. following piloting). However, it is partial and can lose significant information from the interview. It can reinforce interviewer biases.

Audio-recording of the interview. Audio-recording provides a comprehensive (but not visual) record. However, the audio record must be translated to a written record to some degree. Complete transcription of tapes is time-consuming and costly. If total transcription is not conducted, then partial transcription is open to some of the same criticisms of researcher bias as note-taking. Total transcription is now regarded as good practice.

Audio-visual recording of the interview. Audio-visual recording equipment is now low cost and unobtrusive in the interview context. However, audio-visual recordings require very complex transcription to capture and analyse the visual elements of the interviewees' responses (Bull, 2004), and analysts have yet to develop shared systems for reporting and interpreting the visual components of the interview. Few interviews are structured to take advantage of the extra data generated in the visual medium. There is no commonly shared system for codifying visual interview data.

12.5 MEDIUM OF THE INTERVIEW

Interviews do not have to be face-to-face. Increasingly, researchers are using telephone interviewing. Telephone interviewing seems to yield similar data to face-to-face interviews, though perhaps inevitably not so rich since non-vocal data cannot be captured. Telephone interviewing is cheaper and faster than other methods. Since interviewers can be all located in one place using a bank of telephones, it is easier to monitor their performance and to assess problems with the interview schedule. The telephone interview does have its drawbacks. It is difficult to predetermine who in a household will answer your call. Women in the UK are apparently more likely to pick up the phone at most times of the day, and this results in telephone interview samples containing more women unless steps are taken to ensure gender equality in the sample. 'Cold calling' for interviews (i.e. without any prior warning or agreement) is likely to mean that the interviewee is pulled away from some other activity to answer your questions. When this happens, it is difficult to ascertain whether the context (e.g. what they were doing immediately previously) is important in determining their responses. People are unwilling to talk on the telephone for very long periods. A maximum of 15 minutes has been suggested for the standard interview. Anything longer needs to be timetabled in advance. Answers to open-ended questions also seem to be truncated on the telephone. People are faster in their responses and silences seem to be avoided. Complex questions (or those with a large number of response options) prove more difficult to understand on the telephone and this means that question structuring needs to be tailored for the telephone administration specifically. Response rates achieved by telephone contacts vary according to subject matter of the interview and by national group (Reuband & Blasius, 1996). They are said to be worse on evening and weekend calls (perhaps because people who are at home are busier at these times). The effect of gender of interviewer on the telephone might be expected to interact with the subject of the interview in determining response rates achieved from telephone contacts. For instance, Hutchinson and Wegge (1991) found no interviewer gender effects on sample demographic characteristics, but they did find that male participants provided different information on their political views when interviewed on the telephone by a female. Caution should be applied when summarizing the effects on information collected that might emerge as a result of the medium of the interview. Thus far there has been no comprehensive empirical examination of the effects of the medium of the interview. Now that the vast majority of households in industrial societies have telephones, one of the problems that used to militate against the use of telephone interviewing, namely the exclusion of lower-income households from the sampling frame, has been removed. On balance the scales weighing the pros and cons of telephone interviewing seem nowadays to be tipping increasingly in its favour – particularly for short, well-structured interview schedules.

With the increasing availability of online electronic access through the Internet, researchers have sought to move beyond telephone interviewing to Web or e-mail interviewing. Indeed, the Web is already regularly used for surveys involving questionnaires (see Chapter 6). It seems fair to say that currently both telephone and Web-based media methods are less amenable to exploratory, extended, semi- or unstructured interviews. They are primarily advantageous if the researcher requires large, geographically disparate samples.

Computer-assisted administration of interview schedules is also now frequently used. Computer-assisted telephone interviewing (CATI) involves the interviewer being linked to a computer which cues the questions to be asked and allows answers to be immediately coded and inputted directly. Some researchers have taken this one step further and have replaced the interviewer with an auto-mated interactive voice response (IVR) system. Corkrey and Parkinson (2002) showed that the use of IVR systems could improve self-report of sensitive behav-iours (e.g. consumption of alcohol or marijuana) because they induce greater per-ceived confidentiality. They also found that there were no differences in response rates between CATI and IVR.

Computer-assisted self-interviews (CASI) and computer-assisted personal interviews (CAPI) are also often used. CASI entail the interviewee providing responses directly to the questions delivered on screen by the computer. CAPI involve the researcher relaying the questions from the computer to the intervie-wee and the answers back to the computer. These approaches are likely to become increasingly available as communications technologies grow more sophisticated. Two things particularly should be remembered when using them. Firstly, they represent a mechanism for collecting information; they require the researcher to do all the background specification of the research question, sampling, question structuring, and so on that are required for non-computerised data capture. Secondly, the medium of data collection may interact with the nature of the sub-ject matter and with the characteristics of the sample studied; this should not be ignored, it should be examined.

12.6 INTERVIEWING CHILDREN

There are some categories of people who are particularly difficult to interview effectively. These include children and the very elderly. There are a number of hazards to watch out for especially when dealing with children. Some of them clearly apply when dealing with other respondents who may feel themselves to be in a less knowledgeable or powerful position relative to the researcher (e.g. in cross-cultural exchanges). There are also ethical questions that must be addressed when dealing with participants who may not fully understand the process in which they are asked to engage (see Chapter 2).

Young children are often unwilling to assert themselves or to contradict an adult. They will, therefore, answer questions in a way they think you want them answered. Of course, teenagers may relish contradicting adults, which results in a totally opposite bias in information derived from interviews. Either way, it is important to guard against giving the interviewee clues about what you expect them to say. They have to be encouraged to disclose their own opinion. This can be achieved by reassuring them that you are really only interested in what they think and that there are no right or wrong answers. Any approach which looks like a test should be avoided since this will either silence them or release a store of responses which they think people like you (e.g. of your age, class, ethnicity) would like to hear. There is a strong **acquiescence response bias** in children: children tend to say 'yes', irrespective of the question or what they think about it (Wilson & Powell, 2003). Questions should be posed so that they are not open to a yes/no response. For instance, 'Did you want to do that?' would become 'How did you feel about doing that?'.

Besides the acquiescence bias which is most marked when they are eager to please, children exhibit a preference for 'don't know' responses. Children say 'don't know' for a variety of reasons: they aren't interested in answering; they do not understand the question either conceptually or in its vocabulary; they think you expect them not to know; they do not wish to admit what they know; they are too shy to say more; they do not know how to explain what they know; and they really do not know. Consequently, 'don't know' is a response which needs cautious treatment. It is sensible never to base a conclusion on 'don't knows', especially the conclusion that children actually 'don't know'.

Children may be relatively easily distracted. They pay attention to unpredictable aspects of the interview situation or the questions. They can become fascinated by your pen, the lorry loading outside the window or an itch in their nose. Besides being disconcerting to the interviewer, it can result in time-wasting and irrelevant information. To retain their attention, an interview must be full of different topics and changes of pace, with verbal questions giving way to visual materials (e.g. cartoons or objects) and responses perhaps being in the form of some physical activity (e.g. the child illustrates what she did in the situation you are talking about or draws a picture which depicts her feelings). Cappello (2005) describes the use of photographs in interviews with children. Nigro and Wolpow (2004) examine the use of props in interviews. Lewis and Porter (2004) illustrate how to interview children with learning disabilities using varied tools for engagement. A quiet location, not overlooked, and free of strong emotional connotations (e.g. not the headteacher's office where the child was recently severely reprimanded) can improve concentration. However, it would be foolishly optimistic to expect to get more than 15 minutes' worth of good answers from young children even in optimal conditions. Therefore, it is important to keep the interview short.

Young children, like any novice to a linguistic community, tend to interpret questions literally. Metaphors, similes and analogies should all be excluded from questioning. Any phrasing of the question which relies upon an underlying set of assumptions about cultural or social mores must be carefully checked so as to ensure that children of the age group actually understand these assumptions. Essentially, any question such as 'When do you think your sister has been as good as gold?' tells you as much about what the child knows of the aphorism as what she thinks about her sister's activity.

Children have quite different priorities from those of adults. They may not understand that the implicit rule of the interview is that one person asks questions and the other person answers. They may wish to ask as well as answer questions. Particularly, they are likely to be curious about you, whether you are new, why you are there, all sorts of personal details. Responding to these questions briefly, without showing any exasperation, is the best tactic. For children who get into the infinite regress of 'Why?' questions, the best strategy is to distract them with a new topic.

Very often children explain what other people do in terms of their own feelings or characteristics. They find it difficult to see the world through another person's eyes (what is called taking the role of the other). This is one aspect of childhood egocentricity (something which returns in another form in some very elderly people). It means that it is important that you check when accepting an answer that the child is actually focusing upon the right subject. For instance, you might ask a child 'Why did your mother shout at you last night?' The child might say 'She was sad.' It would be necessary to check whether the sadness mentioned referred to the feelings of the mother or the feelings that the child experienced.

Children, and other categories of people who have some vocabulary deficits, may hesitate in answering questions. The pauses which ensue introduce a pressure upon the researcher to jump in to offer suitable words. In essence, this means that the researcher answers for the respondent. This is a temptation which must be resisted.

Some groups of people, and children and the elderly are amongst these, are often interviewed in an institutional setting (e.g. the school or hospital). This entails taking them away from the normal activities of the institution, interviewing them, and then returning them. Once back, they are liable to talk about the interview with other inmates who will subsequently be interviewed. This introduces the possibility of a feedback loop with early interviewees acting as informants for later interviewees. There is a very real prospect for the gossip about the interview to result in rumour and to a distorted expectation of what the interview entails. The later interviewees may develop a distorted picture of what you are doing. This needs to be controlled. You can ask later interviewees what they have heard and what they expect and then clarify any misconceptions. The possibility of feedback between interviewees is not peculiar to institutional settings; it can happen elsewhere. It is a possibility to which the researcher should always be alert.

It can be especially difficult to keep accurate records of what an interviewee is saying if you are reliant upon note-taking when the responses are perhaps self-contradictory and the interviewee requires coaxing. The note-taking is also disruptive since a child interviewee may lose interest in the time it takes you to get your notes in order. It is best to have someone else record the interaction or, if possible, use audio-taping or videotaping.

To summarize, the chief hazards in interviewing children, amongst other difficult types of people, are: the tendency to say 'yes'; the tendency to say 'don't know'; susceptibility to distraction; literal-mindedness; different priorities; egocentricity; the urge to prompt; feedback loops; and recording problems.

12.7 VALIDITY AND RELIABILITY OF INTERVIEW DATA

There is no evidence to suggest that in any generic manner interviewing as a data elicitation technique yields data which are less valid or reliable than other methods. There are artefacts intrinsic to the interview method which affect the validity and reliability of the data it produces, but these tend to be common to many methods.

Like any self-report method, the interview approach relies upon respondents being able and willing to give accurate and complete answers to questions posed, no matter what their format. Yet respondents may be motivated to lie. They may dislike or distrust the researcher. They may wish to sabotage the research. They may be too embarrassed to tell the truth. Even if they wish to co-operate, they may be unable to answer accurately because they cannot remember the details requested or because they do not understand the question.

You can overcome some of these difficulties by constructing a systematic set of questions which, at the same time as helping the respondent to remember or to understand, will provide evidence of consistency (or not) across responses. Having a pattern of questions which allows for internal consistency checking offers you one way of assessing the validity of the data. If a respondent is inconsistent in the pattern of answers, you may wish to extend the questioning to achieve clarification or you may choose to exclude that data from the analysis. Of course, consistency of response does not guarantee accuracy, but inconsistency certainly entails some inaccuracy. The other way to establish the validity of interview data is by complementing it with other types of data. You might use observation, diary techniques, or experimental procedures in addition to the interview. Collecting such ancillary data may not be necessary for the entire sample. To assure you that the interview is effective, it may be sufficient to take additional evidence from only a subsample of respondents.

There is a common belief in the research community that the validity of data collected in interviews improves if you can talk to the participant repeatedly. It is thought that interviewing someone on several occasions increases openness and honesty. Of course, since only people who have a positive attitude towards the research are likely to agree to be interviewed repeatedly, it is possible that the apparent power of repeated interviewing to induce frankness is an artefact of the sample bias which develops in any panel study because of **differential dropout**.

differential dropout

Like any method where the researcher is an overt participant in the data collection process, interviewing involves **researcher effects** (elsewhere labelled experimenter effects). In an interview the characteristics of the researcher (e.g. demeanour, accent, dress, gender, age, power) will influence the respondents' willingness to participate and the nature of their answers. Various effects have been catalogued in the past, and not all of these will still apply today: for example, people have been shown to engage in more self-disclosure to an interviewer who they think is similar to themselves; people of both sexes and of all ages have been shown to be more likely to be willing to talk to a middle-aged woman about sexual matters than to a man, irrespective of his age; and people were shown to be more likely to comply with requests for information from someone who speaks with a Received Pronunciation accent than a regional accent. The specifics of these biases will doubtless change over time. Also, it is evident from the research which has focused on interviewer effects that the characteristics of the interviewer interact with the subject matter of the interview to determine how the interviewee will respond. An interviewer characteristic which is not salient in one interview will become important in another. For instance, the fact that the interviewer and interviewee are of different religious backgrounds may be unimportant when the topic of the interview concerns responses to traffic noise, but such difference may encroach if the topic is responses to the conflict in a province torn apart by religious rivalry.

researcher effects

Such **interviewer effects** cannot be eliminated, but steps can be taken to control for them. One way to do this entails having the same interviewer conduct all interviews. This serves to hold the stimulus provided by the interviewer constant. This will not wipe out the possibility that the same interviewer has different effects across interviewees as a result of some complex interaction between their characteristics and those of the interviewer. In any case, using a single interviewer may be impractical in any large-scale study. Another way to tackle the problem is to use many interviewers and randomly allocate them to respondents. This allows you to eradicate any strong effects of any one interviewer. It also allows you to analyse the extent of interviewer differences. The interview data collected by each interviewer are compared with those collected by others. Any systematic differences can be identified, attributed to some characteristic of the interviewer, and, if sensible, some weighting procedure can be used to moderate the data. This approach is obviously only practicable if the sample size is large. Sometimes, interviewer effects are countered in a different way which uses

interviewer effects

matching procedures. For instance, if interviewer gender is thought to be the biggest potential bias, the research director might use a pool of interviewers who were all female or all male. Alternatively, in such a situation, interviewer gender might be matched to interviewee gender. The matching approach can only be used if you know which interviewer characteristics are likely to have a significant effect upon the interviewees.

Interviewer effects do not simply occur because the respondent reacts to some attribute of the interviewer. It is also possible that they occur because the interviewer reacts to some characteristic of the respondent and this influences how questions are asked or how responses are recorded. Since the interviewer may be completely unaware that this is happening, controlling it is notoriously difficult. Clearly, following the guidelines described above, which emphasize consistency in question presentation, will reduce the problem, but in unstructured interviews the effect can be considerable. In large samples, with large numbers of interviewers and assuming the bias is randomly distributed relative to the research question, the effect could become statistically unimportant. It is where the bias introduced by the interviewer is pertinent to the research issue or where the interviewer conducts large parts of the study that the problem is significant. Good initial training of the interviewers will serve to heighten their awareness of their own prejudices or other characteristics that are relevant to the research topic. This may reduce the likelihood that they will be completely oblivious to biases which they are introducing. Therefore, it makes sense, when using a team of interviewers, to include a procedure for debriefing the interviewers. This would include a component which allowed them to express any doubts which they had about their conduct of particular interviews in a systematic manner (perhaps as a written comment required after each interview). Where any doubt was expressed by the interviewer, that interview or set of interviews could be compared with data from interviews with other similar individuals in the sample to explore if there were apparent inconsistencies. This process might result in some interviews being excluded from subsequent analysis. Some epistemological approaches (reflected in Chapters 17 and 18) would also argue that the researcher must always analyse in a reflexive manner their own position with regard to the research topic and participants. They are expected to report their position fully and frankly (as far as they can ever be aware of it). Such traditions suggest that attempts to control for researcher effects are bound to fail. The effects need to be acknowledged, and this becomes part of the conclusions of the research.

The best way to exclude interviewer bias from the recording of responses (as opposed to eliciting responses) is to use some mechanical method for recording them. Audio-taping is cheap and easy. Videotaping captures the fuller range of information (e.g. non-verbal communication). Either way, the record is permanent and open to verification by other researchers. There is no good evidence to show that audio-taping constrains what respondents are willing to say. Even video-recording has now apparently lost its power to intrude as many people have access to the technology.

12.8 ANALYSING INTERVIEW DATA

People using interviews as a research tool often find that they collect an enormous amount of information and then do not know how to interpret it. The problem is obviously less acute if you use fully structured interview schedules since then the response variety is constrained. In a structured interview the data are usually already framed ready for analysis. With unstructured or semi-structured interviews, there are some guidelines below which could focus your activity.

Firstly, allow your research questions to act as a prism through which you view the data collected. Content analysis (described also in Chapter 13) can be used to reduce the data to a manageable scale. Content analysis can be supplemented with systematic quotations from the interviews to illustrate conclusions. There will be problems in deciding what categories to use in the content analysis. You are trying to generate slices of meaningful information and knowing where to cut into the flow of information is tricky. It may be necessary to try out several cutting positions before you find one which reveals relevant results for your research question. Also, remember that some of the best researchers rely on spotting what is omitted from what the respondent says in order to draw conclusions. It is sensible to stand back occasionally from the attempt to impose order (which is essentially what a content analysis does) and search for the disorderly elements, the discord which shows important differences. Look for themes which you expected to find but which are surprisingly absent. This may guide you to a new perspective. Sometimes people fail to say what they treat as common knowledge or very obvious. Many of the most central understandings in a community are unspoken because they are taken for granted. If you are driven by a simplistic approach to your content analysis you will misinterpret these apparent absences. (See Box 12.4 for principles of structuring content analysis.)

Box 12.4   Principles of structuring data content analysis

Pre-interview

You can set up prior to the interview a content analysis category system that allows responses to be coded. A priori category systems for content analysis tend to be more useful if the questions used are highly structured (even if open-ended responses are allowed). A priori systems are more likely to be feasible where an area of research is relatively mature and other researchers have provided substantial prior data on the topic. This allows new researchers to anticipate the form

(Continued)

Box 12.4 **(Continued)**

and content of interviewee responses, and this generates relevant a priori category systems. Even without substantial earlier research in an area, it is possible to decide prior to the interviews what information will be valuable for your research question and choose to record and analyse only that.

Post-interview

There are many approaches to post-interview data interpretation and all require some form of data structuring. However, conceptually there are four broad types of approach to structuring data post-interview.

Categorical. This approach looks at the content of the interview responses, establishing 'units', 'categories' or 'elements' that are salient in the responses from a repeated examination of the interviews' contents. This approach has been computerized and computer-assisted qualitative data analysis software is now available (e.g. QSR*NVIVO software: Bringer, Johnston & Brackenridge, 2004). Typed transcripts can be electronically interrogated to determine when and where the elements occur and patterns across interviewees. These elements, once established, can be cross-tabulated with any other sample characteristic, allowing many forms of analysis.

Thematic. This approach repeatedly examines interviews for quite complex, elaborated statements, not easily open to conversion into simple elements or categories. These can be regarded as themes emerging from what respondents say. Each usually involves a number of different elements (that might be evident from the categorical content analysis) that are habitually or frequently linked together. This technique is often used with information from focus groups (Wilkinson, 2004a).

Network. This form of data structure content analysis is concerned with the linkages between constellations of elements or between themes. It results in descriptions of patterns across the interviewee's overall responses. These linkages are often depicted in terms of hierarchies or clusters with subclusters within them. So for instance, the interviewee may attest to a particular value, the behaviour implications of holding that value may form a subcluster, the attitudinal association may form another subcluster. This approach is illustrated in the laddering technique (Miles & Rowe, 2004) and in cognitive mapping methods (Farsides, 2004).

Holistic. This approach seeks to summarize in a coherent way the overall content, meaning and implications of the interviewee's responses. It can be seen to operate in some forms of narrative analysis where the researcher is primarily trying to describe in its entirety the story which the interviewee has told during the interview. Chapter 13 examines this approach further.

Secondly, your analysis should be open to verification as far as possible. You should provide a description of the data on which you base your conclusions which is good enough for someone else to repeat what you have done and check your conclusions. It is advisable to include estimates of **inter-rater reliability**

inter-rater reliability

(Chapter 10) to establish that your interpretations of the data are not idiosyncratic. In the interests of verification, you should always keep raw data for a significant period after you publish or report on them. Nowadays, digitized data recording makes this relatively simple.

'Authenticate interpretations' is a dictum which has helped many researchers. Taking the conclusions back to the interviewees (or some subset of them) to check whether they make sense has become frequent. There are, of course, difficulties in knowing what to do when the interviewees do not agree with your conclusions. Who is right and at what level becomes an interesting issue. It is not necessarily the researcher who is wrong.

Following these guidelines will help you to produce a relevant and focused analysis of the interview material. If there is a single thing to remember when using interviewing, it is that it is a data elicitation technique which can deliver the broadest possible variety of data types. The analysis you choose must match the measurement level of the data you collect and be sensitive to your sample structure, but there is usually more than one way to examine the data. Try multiple techniques in the analysis. See whether they lead you to the same conclusions. Stop the analysis only when you are satisfied that you understand the data fully.

12.9 REPORTING INTERVIEW RESEARCH

Box 12.5 summarizes the key elements that should be included in the formal report of a piece of research using interviews. It should be evident that reporting of an interview study shares many characteristics with reports required by other methods. The most important requirement for any research report is that is should be accurate and comprehensive. The guidelines in Box 12.5 act as a template for achieving this.

Box 12.5   Key elements in a report of research using interviewing

The report format used will depend upon the theoretical orientation of the research and the place (journal article, book, monograph, etc.) where it will be published. However, good practice typically requires certain key elements.

- Clear statement of the research question or reason for the study and its objectives.
- Characteristics of the sample: number, relevant socio-demographic background (e.g. age, gender, educational status), etc.
- Details of how the sample was located and invited to participate.
- Level of refusal to participate (with reasons if available).

(Continued)

Box 12.5   (Continued)

- Description of context in which interviews took place (e.g. location, date, time of day, etc.) with details of variation across interviews which might be pertinent to analyses.
- Details of the interviewer(s) involved (if more than one, including how they were trained to achieve a common approach to the interview).
- Details of the interview protocol and schedule.
- Details of response-recording methods.
- Details of data-structuring techniques used.
- Specification of any data analysis verification (e.g. inter-rater reliabilities).
- Summary of main findings (style will depend on approach to data structuring, but will often be enhanced by illustrative verbatim quotations from the interviewees).
- Description of how raw data are being stored and accessibility for other analysts.
- Discussion of implications of the findings for the research question originally posed.
- Consideration of the methodological weaknesses (including any researcher effects identified) and strengths of the study design and analysis.
- Conclusions for future research in the area.

12.10 CONCLUSION

This chapter has introduced the reader to the design, conduct, analysis and reporting of interviewing used as a research method. It has discussed the issues to consider when selecting samples of participants to be interviewed, structuring data for interpretation, and using computer-assisted data collection. Factors affecting the validity and reliability of information collected through interviewing were examined. Some common pitfalls which need to be avoided when using interviewing were highlighted.

12.11 FURTHER READING

Fielding's (2003) book is a comprehensive guide to the ways in which interviewing can be used in research. It is a good guide to the common errors of interpreting interview data and good on the recent developments in computer software for analysing interview data. Holstein and Gubrium's (2003) text provides a broader perspective on the approaches to interviewing used by non-psychologists. Finally, Wengraf's (2001) book is especially useful as a detailed account of the use of narrative methods in interviewing.

13

Using Self-recording: Diary and Narrative Methods

Glynis M. Breakwell

13.1   Introduction
13.2   What are diary techniques?
13.3   What sorts of data are suitable for diaries?
13.4   The pros and cons of the diary approach
13.5   Getting the best out of diary techniques
13.6   What are narrative techniques?
13.7   Eliciting the narrative
13.8   Analysing diary and narrative records
13.9   Conclusion
13.10   Further reading

Aims

This chapter will introduce two data elicitation methods that both rely upon the research participant producing self-records. The term 'self-record' is used to mean that the participants are producing their own record of themselves. Often this is a record not just of and by themselves but for themselves and in this sense is more than what is normally associated with the term self-report, where there is an inevitability about the existence of an audience in addition to the self. The two self-record approaches described here are diary and narrative methods. The chapter will illustrate how and when these two methods may be used, examining their strengths and weaknesses. Techniques for analysing data generated from these two methods will be outlined.

Key terms

archetypal narratives
co-construction
narrative
overreporting
sample maintenance

self-record
self-selection of material
thematic analysis
underreporting

13.1 INTRODUCTION

Many research methods in psychology use some form of self-reporting. Questionnaires and interviews rely on the research participant reporting verbally, textually or pictographically something of what they think, feel or do. The self-recording methods can be regarded as a subset of the self-report genre. Self-recording specifically entails the participant describing, and sometimes explaining, aspects of their own life and often of their personal history. Self-recording is a particularly useful tool in exploring identity structure and processes.

There are two popular methods for self-recording: the diary and the narrative. These are described in turn below. It should be noted that since diaries and narratives are simply data collection techniques they can be used as part of any type of research design. Both techniques have been used in experimental and quasi-experimental research designs as well as in single case studies, large-scale surveys and ethnographies.

13.2 WHAT ARE DIARY TECHNIQUES?

The diary record is one of the oldest methods used by psychologists. Neugebauer (1929) constructed a model of three phases of emotional and volitional development (capacity for joy and happiness, delicacy of feelings, and capacity for perseverance) based on a diary record of the growth of her son. Any data collection strategy which entails getting respondents to provide information linked to a temporal framework is essentially a diary technique. The record of information in relation to the passage of time is referred to as the diary. In fact, this record may be unlike anything that would be recognized as a traditional diary purchased in a stationery shop and would not necessarily involve a *daily* record of events: the frequency of entries differs according to the research purpose. Diaries can involve various media of report (most obviously verbal or written records, but also photographic or video images). Nowadays researchers might use multimedia diary records. The diary techniques allow the medium of the record to be chosen so as to best suit the topic and the type of respondent studied. One study, for example, used the original idea of a *postcard* diary for tracking health care utilization (Reuben, Wong, Walsh & Hays, 1995). In this study, participants sent the researcher a postcard with a description of their health care uptake on the day they used it. This meant that the respondents did not have to maintain the physical diary record themselves and meant that the researcher had real-time data to analyse. Electronic diary collection is sometimes used to ease the burden for participants who may be experiencing pain or discomfort (Peters *et al.*, 2000).

The reports required can differ substantially in the amount of structure imposed by the researcher and the flexibility permitted the diarist. Some demand very detailed accounts of one type of behaviour. For instance, consumer researchers may wish to know how often certain groups of people purchase eco-labelled products. They can find out something about this by asking samples from those groups to keep shopping diaries in which they simply have to tick against a checklist what they purchase on a daily or weekly basis. In such diaries, entries are carefully prestructured. If, however, the object was broadly to understand more about eco-friendly behaviour, the research might ask each individual to describe in the diary what they thought they had done during that period which had some bearing on environmental conservation.

The time period over which the diary is kept can vary widely from a few hours to several years, and this is echoed in variability in the periodicity of entries, which can range from every few minutes to every few months.

Diary studies can use reports which are specially elicited or can be analyses of spontaneously generated records of information over time. So, for instance, a researcher attempting to identify the way military leaders make decisions under stress may ask a sample of such leaders to produce diaries during an operation specifically for the study or may consider it more useful to analyse the published diaries of senior army commanders. The value of historical diary material has recently been more accepted by psychologists, some of whom now argue that this is one route to test claims that psychological processes are socioculturally and temporally specific. However, comparing diary accounts generated in different historical periods is obviously fraught with difficulties, since the writers will reflect in some way the literary mores of their era and these may obscure the possibly more specific differences between writers. It will always be uncertain whether there were changes in psychological processes over time, changes in the norms of self-report over time, or differences between the specific writers chosen.

There is, of course, a problem that arises when using published material. Publication usually entails some form of editorial control that may change the substance of the diary. Also, diaries written for publication may have different emphases from those written for private purposes. Anticipation of publication may result in the elimination or addition of some forms of information. Diaries produced for a research study may be subject to some of the same self-censorship. Researchers have considered this possibility and it is examined in Section 13.4. Diaries produced initially neither for publication nor a research study might be a particularly valuable source of data. There is, however, no recent published research that has used such private spontaneous self-records listed in the most comprehensive abstract databases.

It should be noted that requesting a research participant to produce a diary record can be used as an intervention in itself. The requirement to produce the diary can be the manipulation that the researcher is introducing in the study. This is based upon the recognition that the act of recording that the behaviour has occurred can change the subsequent likelihood of the behaviour. For example,

Kiernan, Cox, Kovatchev, Kiernan and Giuliano (1999) found that the driving behaviour of senior drivers could be improved when they were asked to self-monitor their driving behaviour using a driving diary.

13.3 WHAT SORTS OF DATA ARE SUITABLE FOR DIARIES?

Diary techniques can be used with virtually any type of data. The breadth of subject matter is as large as the imagination of the researcher. They may entail reports of actions, thoughts or feelings as well as accounts of physical or social context. An interesting example of unusual subject matter for a diary comes from the work of Freud on the interpretation of dreams. He compiled records of his own dreams by writing down what he remembered of them as soon as he awoke each morning. Dream researchers still use this method. More conventional early uses of diaries tended to concentrate on such issues as consumer buying patterns, household work activities or TV viewing patterns. However, their usage has spread to a much greater range of psychological issues. Some examples drawn from the psychological literature utilized the technique to study social interaction (Nezlek, 1991), cognitive therapy (Campbell, 1992), illness behaviour (Dworkin & Wilson, 1993), mood or emotional states (King & Wilson, 1992), stressful events and HIV/AIDS (Coxon, 1994).

Diary records are commonly used to assess changes over time in subjective physical state; for example, Ray and Page (2002) used a diary record of pain to assess the impact of a single session of hypnosis upon the experience of chronic pain. In fact, diary measures are frequently used to assess the impact of treatment upon people with illness (Sherliker & Steptoe, 2000). Diary records are also frequently used to monitor food intake (e.g. Legg, Puri & Thomas, 2000; Bellisle, Dalix & De Castro, 1999; Conner, Fitter & Fletcher, 1999; Steptoe & Wardle, 1999).

In addition, diaries are now often used in combination with other psychological methods, such as questionnaires (see Chapter 11), interviewing (see Chapter 12) or psychometric testing (Chapter 10), to provide a more rounded picture, or as part of the process of triangulation. This diverse list is by no means comprehensive, but clearly illustrates how ubiquitous the diary technique has become. Diary records are a good way to access responses to diverse social experiences (i.e. ones where there are likely to be big differences between individuals or big differences for one individual across time such that anticipating the nature of the events might prove difficult and make more structured elicitation methods – such as checklists – less viable). However, if the breadth of the diary method can be linked to other more limited techniques, the researcher may enhance the effectiveness of both approaches. Lundh and Sperling (2002), for instance, used diary records to study the relationship between social anxiety and socially distressing events. Their study is an interesting exemplar in that they paired the diary record of socially distressing events with a standardized questionnaire assessment of social anxiety. Linking methods in this way can be very valuable.

Sometimes, diary records are compared with other sources of information about the same behaviour. For instance, Wolke, Meyer and Gray (1994) compared maternal responses to the Crying Pattern Questionnaire (CPQ) with a 7-day, 24-hour systematic diary record by parents of crying behaviour of their infants. They found moderate to good convergence between maternal reports in the CPQ and the diary. Similarly, Libman, Fichten, Bailes and Amsel (2000) compared a sleep questionnaire with a sleep diary. Frequently, these comparison studies are conducted to validate the questionnaire rather than validate the diary record. In fact, of course, to assume the greater veracity of the diary record may be an error. Rather than on an a priori basis treating one method as more likely to yield accurate recording, it may be more useful to explore the discrepancies in the records generated by different methods. For instance, researchers concerned with sexually transmitted diseases are seeking valid records of sexual behaviour and there has been much debate about the relative merits of diary and questionnaire recording (Coxon, 1999). In the absence of any absolute evidence that diary records are more or less valid, it is important to acknowledge their possible limitations and to use them as far as possible in conjunction with other methods that will reveal the range of discrepancies in self-records.

We might assume that the diary technique would be restricted to a single individual making self-reports about some aspect of themselves or their life. However, this is not necessarily the case. Numerous studies involve respondents completing diaries on themselves and others (e.g. in studies of social interaction), or pairs of respondents completing diaries about the same events (e.g., husband and wife); see Dunn, Seithamer, Jacob and Whalen (1993). There is no rule that the self-record has to be individualized. It can be a negotiated construction with the investigator prompting the participant, or it can be collaborative with other research participants who can challenge or corroborate or improve the self-description. However, to the extent that others are significantly involved, the method moves closer to other forms of data elicitation described in this book – such as the interview (see Chapter 12), the focus group (see Chapter 14), or the capture of discourse (see Chapter 18).

13.4 THE PROS AND CONS OF THE DIARY APPROACH

Since diary techniques have no simple uniform guise, it is not easy to draw up simple lists of the pros and cons associated with them as a research method when exploring psychological processes. It is, however, possible to give general indications of the strengths and weaknesses of this approach to data collection.

The diary approach can be used to great effect because respondents are typically familiar with the notion of what a diary is. When you ask someone if they will keep a diary of activities of a specific kind every day over a fortnight, the person understands the task. You may need to refine that understanding through careful instructions, but you have the advantage of the respondent having some initial appreciation of what you want. This may be very helpful if you are dealing with individuals who are especially anxious, suspicious or ignorant about psychological assessments. Having said this, one should bear in mind that when we draw a sample for any type of psychological study, the characteristics of the volunteers may differ from those of non-volunteers. There is some evidence that even when using essentially non-threatening diaries, those who volunteer are likely to be more stable and have less anxious personalities than those who do not (Waite, Claffey & Hillbrand, 1998).

The diary approach can be particularly useful and cost-effective when you want data from the same person over a considerable period of time and/or very frequently. Given appropriate instructions, respondents can be generating information often for long periods without the need for the researcher to be in contact. They can be given the diary to complete and only recontacted at the end of the study. It should be noted, though, that respondents who are not in regular contact with the researcher may cease to complete the diary in the prescribed manner and may just stop participating in the research.

Of course, the greatest advantage of the diary approach is that it yields information which is temporally ordered. It tells you the sequence of events, giving you the profile of action, feelings or thoughts across time. There are other ways of doing this, but they tend to involve greater intervention by the researcher and consequently higher potential interference with the sequence under consideration. This makes the diary method a valuable tool when first formally exploring an area of psychological processes. The method can be used to open areas of investigation and to identify the broad parameters of the issues involved that may need to be explored later in greater detail with more intrusive techniques.

Diaries are often used in order to access so-called 'intimate' information (e.g. as indicated above, about sexual behaviour), in the belief that iterative self-reporting, mostly without any interpersonal interaction, will engender self-revelation and honesty. Whether this assumption is valid or not has not been fully established: however, it seems likely that respondents may be prone to **underreporting** events or behaviour they believe may be disapproved of, and conversely **overreporting** things they think people will approve of. In some cases this common social desirability bias can be allowed for and factored into the interpretation of data. It also remains the case that the range and variety of personal information elicited in a diary can be very great and this suggests that social desirability and conformity effects are not eliminating diversity in individual responses.

underreporting

overreporting

Diaries can be used to map the variety of human experiences salient in a domain. In doing this, it is sometimes useful to use spontaneously generated diaries. The fact that a diary was not produced specifically for your research does not mean that it is not useful to your research. There are essentially two types of spontaneously generated diaries, as mentioned earlier: those produced for private consumption and those produced for public consumption through publication. There is some evidence that women are more likely to keep private diaries than men, but this is hard to prove. It has been suggested that the act of diary keeping may be interpreted as a self-initiated coping strategy for life's hassles, involving reflection and aiding the management of emotions.

Both types of diary can be useful for the psychological researcher. They differ significantly in two ways: their accessibility and their probable veracity. The accessibility difference is evident. Getting hold of diaries which have not been produced for publication can be difficult for obvious reasons: you are unlikely to know of their existence and, even if you do, you are unlikely to get permission to use them. The veracity difference is more contentious. Diarists writing for public consumption are subject to a variety of pressures which may lead to misrepresentation of events or their sequencing. In the simplest terms, diarists who seek publication of their diaries are unlikely to wish to represent themselves negatively. They will wish, most probably, to justify or excuse themselves. Questions concerning their accessibility and veracity obviously limit the real usefulness of spontaneously generated diaries for psychological researchers. They will, nevertheless, remain attractive sources of information because they provide access to a range of people who might never ordinarily agree or be able to participate in a psychological study (e.g. the rich, the powerful, the isolated, the dead).

The debate concerning the usefulness of diaries from different historical periods to provide evidence of changes of psychological significance over time will doubtless continue and is unlikely to be reconcilable. Irrespective of their capacity to evidence changes in underlying psychological processes, the diaries of different eras can provide important clues about the social priorities and attitudinal structures of different historical periods. Comparative analysis of such diaries could be interesting but would need to be undertaken with great care. Comparing the diary of a wealthy, well-educated, upper middle-class Victorian wife and mother in her thirties living in a London suburb after the early death of her first husband with that of a similarly wealthy, well-educated, upper middle-class twenty-first-century wife and mother in her thirties living in a London suburb after the early death of her first husband might yield some useful insights into the historical differences. However, the significant practical task lies in matching for characteristics other than period before coming to conclusions about the effect of period.

The advantages of the diary approach can be summarized therefore by a few key words: familiarity; cost-effective sampling of information; sequencing data; intimacy; exploration; spontaneity; access to usual participants; and historicity.

The potential disadvantages of the diary approach can be ameliorated and are not inevitable. They should nevertheless be summarized before examining the ways to overcome them. Most importantly, control over the data elicited is always difficult to achieve. Clearly, if you use spontaneously generated diaries you have no real control over what data are provided. These diaries inevitably involve **self-selection of material** by the diarist. Even if you use diaries which you request, your level of control is suspect. You can, of course, ask for specific categories of information. However, getting people to remember to make entries at the right time about the right things can be difficult, even when they have goodwill towards the research and every intention of complying with your instructions.

self-selection of material

One of the possible advantages of the diary technique is that it can represent contemporaneous reporting of events or experiences. One of the possible disadvantages is that the diary may be constructed retrospectively. With spontaneous diaries, this retrospective construction could be a considerable time after the actual events took place. Even with research-initiated diaries there may be some temptation to leave the task for a while and then catch up later. Any doubt about whether the record is contemporaneous is a weakness in the data.

The diary technique is plagued by a further lack of control. Diary studies suffer significant problems with dropout: respondents do not continue to provide information throughout the designated period. This problem of **sample maintenance** often can be exacerbated by poor initial recruitment into the study. Completing a diary (especially over any lengthy period) can be seen as onerous and will result in people being unwilling to join the study in the first place. This, combined with subsequent potentially high dropout rates, is likely to mean that the sample is highly biased by the end of the study. This suggests that any research question that requires a good representative sample would be difficult to address using a diary method.

sample maintenance

There is another sampling issue that affects the value of diaries. The individual asked to generate the diary must be capable of reflecting upon themselves (minimally upon their behaviour but probably also upon their thoughts and feelings) and recording their conclusions in the manner required in the study. This means that the method cannot be used with people who are incapable of such self-reflection. This may mean that the method cannot be used effectively with young children, or indeed with some older people or people with certain illnesses. There is also the problem of ascertaining whether a potential participant is capable of the required self-reflection or not. It may not be immediately obvious that someone is not capable of the self-recording task involved. This suggests that before embarking on a study using diary methods, it is important to assess the participant pool to determine not only their willingness but also their ability to do the task required.

Another disadvantage of the diary approach harks back to the issue of veracity. Getting the respondent to tell you the truth may be difficult but, more importantly, you may never be able to ascertain whether they did or not. It may be necessary, if you are very concerned with verifiability of data, to use other methods alongside the diary approach. As indicated earlier, a number of such studies have been conducted to establish the validity of diary data by comparing them with such methods as checklists, interviews, questionnaires, observation and mechanical recording methods. By and large the results have been encouragingly positive, although reporting biases have been shown to occur in some cases, as mentioned earlier.

Like any intrusive research technique, the diary when initiated by the researcher may produce data affected by 'reactance'. The very fact of having to produce the diary may alter the behaviour, thoughts, feelings, and so on, that are recorded. An example of this effect comes from Freud's dream diaries. As he got into the habit of recording the dreams, he found that he 'dreamed more often' (i.e. tended to wake at a point in the sleep cycle when he was more likely to recall his dreams). The extent of reactance is essentially not assessable and may vary over time throughout the period of the research, thus influencing results in a non-constant fashion. It is clear, however, that if we require individuals to make large numbers of entries, or write extensively about events, then the action 'diary filling in' becomes a significant element of everyday behaviour. Whilst in general we look for psychological methods that have low reactance, occasionally the process of conducting the study can be deliberately planned so as to have positive effects. At least one such study involving the diary technique has used this approach. In this case, the research was concerned with the management of information systems development, and it was found that the act of filling in the diaries supported reflection and changed work habits by the respondents.

The disadvantages of diary techniques can be summarized in a few key words: control of content; achieving contemporary recording; dropout; poor recruitment; demands on participant ability; veracity and verifiability; and reactance.

13.5 GETTING THE BEST OUT OF DIARY TECHNIQUES

The advantages of the diary approach can, obviously, be enhanced and the disadvantages minimized by careful construction of the research. In the case of diaries initiated by the researcher there are certain key guidelines to follow.

Firstly, it is important to choose the right recording medium for your type of respondents. Respondents lacking the necessary level of literacy should not be asked to produce written diaries (this might include the young, the poorly educated, and anyone who for physical reasons – e.g. poor eyesight – might find the task impossible). Alternative recording forms such as audio-taping or videotaping should be considered.

Secondly, respondents should be given very comprehensive and comprehensible instructions on how to complete the diary. Pilot work should be used to establish that the instructions are understandable. These instructions should emphasize the importance of accuracy and offer assurances of confidentiality and anonymity where appropriate. They should be explicit that the researcher has no brief to evaluate the appropriateness or otherwise of the behaviour, thoughts or feelings described in the diary. They should indicate that entries need to be made regularly at the times specified and explain that entries made retrospectively, relying on memory, are subject to distortions which detract from the value of the information. The possibility of reactance should be described to the respondents in simple terms so that they are on guard against it.

Box 13.1   Example page of a diary

MONDAY
Please enter today's date here:
Please enter in the table below how much time (in minutes) you spent in the 24 hours between 12 midnight Sunday and 12 midnight Monday doing each of the things listed.

                                                              Number of minutes

Sleeping
Physical exercise (e.g. walking, football)
Doing housework (e.g. cooking, cleaning)
Looking for a job
Watching TV
In the pub
House maintenance (e.g. painting, repairs)
Gardening
Shopping

Thirdly, the diary format should be straightforward and uncluttered. With written diaries, the print quality of the booklet is important as a cue to the professionalism of the research. Layout is vital for the written diary. Respondents have to be given enough room to provide their answers. Box 13.1 is an example of a diary layout which might be used in a piece of research designed to establish how unemployed men spend their time. The format imposes a clear structure on the record, indicating which types of activity should be reported and what the unit of report is to be (i.e. length of time).

Fourthly, no matter how clear the diary format and instructions are, there will be respondents who fail to understand. It helps to give respondents an example of a completed entry to the diary so that they can see what they are supposed to be doing. Also part of the procedure for diary administration, whenever possible, should include talking the respondent through the diary. This will allow you to cue and target appropriate recording. As a general rule, therefore, diary placement would normally involve a personal contact by a member of the research team, rather than sending diaries by post.

Fifthly, problems with sample maintenance are reduced if you can ensure relatively frequent contact with respondents. This is particularly important in the early stages of a diary study. There will inevitably be queries about category definitions (what, for example, constitutes a 'leisure activity'?), the boundaries between various activities, the level of detail required and so on. It may be useful to provide respondents with a telephone number, so that they can contact you to resolve such queries fairly quickly. If this is not done then they may abandon the recording because they are in a state of uncertainty about what to record, or, perhaps even worse, make their own decisions about what should be recorded and thus provide large numbers of entries that are useless for your analysis.

A postcard or telephone call occasionally (e.g. birthday or Christmas cards) for long-term diary studies have been shown to improve sample retention. Requiring diaries to have frequent entries made also seems to improve sample maintenance. Material incentives (such as small payments) tend to have a good effect upon retention. Along these lines, researchers have used lotteries to encourage both joining and remaining in studies. The prospect of winning something has been shown to incite initial interest but, once the outcome of the lottery is known, some researchers have found large-scale dropout. One answer seems to be to operate with repeated lotteries, but this practice is now less effective as the general public have become sensitized to the technique.

Sixthly, in order to maximize initial response rates and to retain the sample subsequently, it has been shown that it is best to start with relatively brief diaries. If you need to collect lengthy diaries, it seems to be most effective to introduce the respondent to the process initially using a short diary. They can be transferred from the short to the long version more easily than persuading them to start from scratch on a lengthy diary.

Finally, there have been various ingenious techniques used to ensure that people remember to make entries when they are supposed to do so. It is now not uncommon to give respondents electronic paging devices and ask them to make their entries when the devices bleep. Alternatively, researchers may enlist the help of other members of the family to remind the respondent at meal times. Some studies have used computer-assisted diaries (Baumann, Laireiter & Krebs, 1996), whilst others have used electronic devices for a time-use diary (Kalfs & Willem, 1998).

13.6 WHAT ARE NARRATIVE TECHNIQUES?

The concept of narrative has come to play an important role in a variety of disciplines – literary theory, linguistics, historiography, psychotherapy, ethnology, philosophy, and psychology. What is narrative? As used in psychology, a **narrative**, at the most simplistic level, is an individual's story or account of their experience of events or people from the present or the past. It is diary-like in that it may recount events in a time sequence (McAdams, 1999), but not necessarily so. A narrative may have a disjointed temporal frame. It can vary in the extent to which it includes not only descriptions of the subject matter (such as events, feelings, thoughts) but also explanations or interpretations of that subject matter. A narrative record can allow the participant full reflexivity: to describe, explain and evaluate their own explanation.

narrative

Narrative techniques have now been used in many types of psychological research. For instance, Ussher and Mooney-Somers (2000) studied the life narratives of young self-styled 'lesbian Avengers' that operated as an inner city gang; Dickinson and Poole (2000) examined eye-witness narratives of particular crimes; and Ewing (2000) conducted a cross-cultural comparison of dream narratives to explore the role of cultural myths in dream memory. Narrative techniques are used a lot with children (e.g. Ely, Melzi, Hadge & McCabe, 1998).

The use of the capture of self-narratives to study identity has gathered momentum in recent years following the theoretical work of Ricoeur (see, Ezzy, 1998) and Bakhtin (see Bell & Gardiner, 1998). It has been tied to a way of seeing the self or identity as a work of memory that relies upon narratives to achieve coherence over time and social relevance and understandability (Singer, 2004; Beike, Lampinen & Behrend, 2004; Teichert, 2004). Renegotiation or restructuring of narratives is thus seen to allow development of the identity.

As a source of data, narrative records can be very complex. They can have many layers of information. The method allows the researcher to ask the participant to talk about long periods of their life and the relationships between what they did or what happened to them over these different times. The method has enormous potential to explore complicated research questions. By the same token, it is easy to become so immersed in the richness of the narratives that the research question is not addressed (see the advice on focusing upon answerable research questions in Chapter 2).

Box 13.2 provides a narrative record constructed solely for the purpose of illustrating the type of structure a narrative record often has. This narrative clearly has no simple linear structure. There is no start-middle-end sequence such as might be found in a formal story. The narrative record builds a picture of the experience, but through fragments of information. Some elements of that information seem to hang unresolved (e.g. the planes that fired on the tank) and not integrated in the account. The narrator jumps backwards and forwards in time. There is reference to a broader range of experience that informs the narrator's interpretation of the events (i.e. the family connections and the 'old man'). Amidst all of this, a theme emerges: the overwhelming importance of being tired during this experience.

Box 13.2 Illustrative narrative record

From a soldier asked to talk about his part in an invasion army:

I was in the lead tank and we had been going for 54hrs straight, barely a break. I had never been on any operation like this one before. No exercise prepares you for it. The smoke was bad but the sand was worse. We got into a minefield. That was after we had taken some prisoners further down the road. They had just given up, not a fight. Well, the minefield was just suddenly all round us. Then these planes appeared from nowhere, firing at us. I had been scared for days. First, waiting for the call and then for the go. All the time expecting a NBC (nuclear, biological or chemical) attack. My family has a tradition of soldiering and I had been told what to expect. In the minefield, I just knew we had to go East. The co-ordinates we got from command were telling us to go North. My old man had always said ignore your instincts at your peril but ignore your commander and you've had it. Later, after we had been going another 20-30hrs, it might have been different. Then, we were totally done in.

The narrative in Box 13.2 illustrates some of the common characteristics of a narrative record that is collected about a recent experience or about an experience that the participant has not recorded often before. It has a rawness or lack of resolution typical of initial narrative records collected just after an event. There seems to be a tendency for the refinement of the narrative if there is iterative retelling. This results in narratives that have a more traditional story-like structure, that incorporate more acknowledgement of socially acceptable or expected descriptors, and that provide more opportunity for self-justification. Schuetz (1998) showed that narratives introduced more defensive and favourable self-descriptions as their authors' self-esteem needs were increased. In effect, Schuetz described a process where narratives were refined and reshaped to exaggerate certain aspects of the experience of the self and to minimize other aspects in such a way as to redirect attention to the more positive and distract from the negative. The transformation of the narrative record over time and for particular self-presentational purposes is probably to be expected. The narrative record may be a form of self-defence.

13.7 ELICITING THE NARRATIVE

Narrative collection can be located within a wide range of research vehicles (the interview, the postal request, the focus group, and so on). Narratives, like diaries, can be captured in many media: text, verbal, visual (Ziller, 2000, used photo-self-narratives), and performative (Brockmeier & Carbaugh, 2001, asked participants to act out their narrative). Use of alternative media can broaden the participant pool for research beyond the literate. Visual media are a particularly flexible **self-record** mechanism for **self-record**. However, interpretation of such visual narrative records is especially difficult (Minami, 2000).

Like diaries, narrative records can be spontaneously generated (e.g. in autobiography or in the accounts people produce of momentous events in which they have participated – like scaling a mountain or single-handedly sailing across the sea). Such narratives can be used in psychological research but carry the same advantages and disadvantages as spontaneously generated diary material.

Approaches to eliciting narratives specifically to address a particular research question differ greatly. However, the same guidelines that apply to getting the best out of diary techniques can be applied when using narrative techniques. Choose the medium for recording the narrative that suits the participant pool and the subject matter. Participants should be given clear instructions about the nature of the task. The same instructions should be used with all participants. The subject matter for the narrative should be clearly stated. The nature of the subject matter will differ. Box 13.3 describes various categories of subject matter. Specification of the subject matter should be closely tied to the research question. If production of the narrative involves the participant in more than one session, measures must be taken to ensure continuing commitment to the study.

Box 13.3   Narrative subject matter categories

Typically, requests for narrative records fall into three categories or types:

1   narratives about a specified time period (and this can be very short, e.g. a day in the life of, or can be very long, e.g. the school years);
2   narratives about a particular type of event (and these can be any sort of event, e.g. deaths in the family, sporting successes, the first kiss);
3   narratives about certain relationships (and these can be from the fleeting, e.g. an encounter on a train with a stranger, to the very long-term, e.g. with parents).

Within these categories, the researcher may well be expecting to elicit information on particular thoughts or emotions characteristic of the individual. Sometimes the researcher will ask directly for a narrative about the individual feelings or thoughts, and this could be said to be a fourth category of narrative. However, such narratives are usually tied to one of the other three categories.

Narratives as rich individual records can be used in single-case studies. They can also be co-constructed (Gergen, 1998; Ellis, 1998) by two or more people. The **co-construction** of a narrative can be used in various ways. The process of con- **co-construction** structing the narrative itself can be the object of the research. This would entail careful recording of how the narrative was produced (the role of all participants, the contributions made at what points, the nature of any debate or disagreement, the changes imposed on initial drafts of the narrative, etc.). Of course, the outcome of this process may be the sole object of the research. If so, it can be subjected to the same analyses as any other narrative record. Usually, with a co-constructed narrative the researcher will want to understand the relative contributions of all the participants to the narrative.

13.8 ANALYSING DIARY AND NARRATIVE RECORDS

Since the forms of data yielded by diary or narrative studies vary widely, many analytic approaches are possible. The decision that you take concerning the amount of structure which you impose upon the record will affect all subsequent decisions. If you leave the diarist or narrator free to choose what is recorded you are virtually sure to need to conduct a content analysis before doing any further data processing. The procedures involved in content analysis are described in Chapters 12 and 14. Having done the content analysis, you can subject the data to either a qualitative or a quantitative description.

Content analysis, when tied to simple quantification, is most likely to result in a matrix which tells you how many people report each category of behaviour or event and how often these occurred. This may be all you need to do, but that is unlikely. A major feature of a diary technique is that it gives you data which are ordered over time. To take advantage of this you need to use analyses which allow you to map sequences or patterns in the data across time.

One way to do this with non-parametric data is to use an analysis which identifies whether within the sample there are groups of respondents whose sequences of entries are similar to each other and different from the patterns of other groups. So, for instance, in a sample of 25 men completing diaries for the first 3 months of a period of unemployment, there might be 10 who spend most of their time in job search for the first month, house maintenance for the second and watching TV for the third. Another ten might focus on housework in month 1, job search in month 2 and TV watching in month 3. The remaining five might concentrate on TV watching in month 1, job search in month 2 and TV watching again in month 3. The analysis would show the range of profiles that exist in the sample. It would also show whether the distribution of individuals across the profiles is not statistically significant and might be expected by chance. Profiles exemplified by either more or less of the sample than would be expected by chance are worth exploring further since these may be indicative of 'types' or 'anti-types' of response. The task of the psychologist would then be to explain the origin of these 'types'. One statistical technique which will allow you to identify these profiles is called configural frequency analysis (e.g. von Eye, 1990). There are, of course, many other mechanisms for structuring qualitative data (e.g. see Chapter 12).

When you use highly structured entry formats in the diary the range of analytic approaches available is very broad. There is no reason why the diary should not include standard questions with response categories such as those used in a questionnaire. In this case, you would be able to use all of the techniques described in Chapter 11.

Research using a single-case design will sometimes mean that the analysis of a narrative record entails the detailed exploration of material generated by one participant. The same principles of content and thematic analysis can be used. More often, narrative records are subjected to cross-individual analysis. For instance, Van der Molen (2000) examined the narratives of six cancer patients who provided accounts of their illness and conducted a thematic analysis, looking for commonalities of theme or emphasis across their narratives. She showed that all six shared a belief that they had been given or had available to them too **thematic analysis** little information concerning their disease. A **thematic analysis** will emphasize both commonalities and differences between participants concerning the dominant themes. It is important when analysing narrative records to capture both the similarities and the differences between people.

Understanding the meaning of a narrative is not without difficulties. Narratives depend upon shared understandings of symbols and icons for their interpretation. The researcher who is not part of the community of shared meanings may not 'receive' the full implications of the narrative. For instance, Banks (2004) looked at the identity narratives of Americans who retired to Mexico and showed these narratives to be very complex with apparently contradictory stories about their host culture being presented simultaneously. The host population was characterized as happy, friendly, helpful, polite, and enterprising, but also as untrustworthy, inaccessible, lazy and incompetent. Banks argued that the apparent inconsistencies served an important identity purpose for the retired ex-pats, showing them to be culturally tolerant and pragmatically adaptable. To make and support this argument, Banks needed to understand the broader value system and cultural stereotypes of those creating the narratives.

archetypal narratives Some argue that there are **archetypal narratives** (McAdams, 2004) that we all have access to and can use as appropriate to reflect our own condition when called upon to describe and explain ourselves. McAdams refers to the 'redemptive self' narrative manifest in the USA in life stories that characteristically focus upon the transformation of personal suffering into positive-affective life scenes that serve to redeem and justify one's life. Narratives of national identity appear to be particularly high in impact upon individual autobiographical narratives (Feldman, 2001). Other researchers have also shown the importance of archetypal narratives, not through their adoption but through their vehement rejection. For instance, May (2004) found that lone mothers in Finland constructed a counternormative account of their status, focusing upon the value of their independence. Analysis of the narrative record must acknowledge the existence of these archetypal or stereotypical narratives where they can be shown to exist in so far as they provide an interpretive frame for the content of the individual narrative. The problem for the researcher lies in establishing that they actually do exist.

The approach to the analysis of narrative research has been affected by the implications of the 'recovered memory' debates. Recovered memories refer to those memories of early life events (normally traumatic) remembered during psychotherapy or hypnotic trance. There has been extensive argument about the possibility that these are false memories, reconstructed as a result of the therapeutic intervention. The significance of these phenomena for narrative research cannot be ignored, particularly as they might affect the interpretation of narrative identity data. Singer (1997) argues that the phenomenon may provide some clues as to the way that narrative identity is constructed and suggests that the relation of narrative identity to objective truth is unspecifiable. Rather more importantly, the phenomenon suggests that, as a method, use of the narrative record should be concerned only with the narrative itself, not in some simplistic way with the assumed underlying truth that it represents. Narrative can thus be analysed for its structure, even its purpose, but not sensibly for its relationship to historical facts (except in so far as these can be ascertained independently of the narrative). The significance of the phenomenon for diary techniques is less debated in the literature, but could be argued to be parallel.

In choosing analytic approaches to any self-record technique the vital thing to remember is that you are using them merely as tools that will give you answers to the questions you posed at the start of the research. Amid the flood of data which a diary or narrative technique can generate, it is easy to lose sight of your original objectives for the research. You can get lost in the minutiae of the specific life stories. The process of analysis should be one which allows you to see genuine patterns within these data. Thus it is vital to choose analytic tools which give you relevant answers and which are appropriate for the type of data you have.

13.9 CONCLUSION

The two self-record approaches described here are diary and narrative methods. The chapter illustrates how and when these two methods may be used, examining their strengths and weaknesses. Techniques for analysing data generated from these two methods have been outlined. It should be clear that the diary technique and the narrative technique are potentially extremely useful as means of collecting psychological and behavioural data. As with other methods, they have both advantages and disadvantages. Before embarking on a diary study you should ask yourself: 'Do I *really need* to collect data on a continuous basis over time?' Before using either diary or narrative techniques you must have a very clear idea of your research objectives. The reason for this was mentioned earlier. Diaries and narratives can be a very rich source of data, and unless we have a clear view of the purpose of the study, the volume of data generated can overwhelm the unwary researcher. Finally, do not be seduced by the apparent simplicity of these techniques. The quality of the data will be directly related to the quality of the data elicitation design and execution. Above all, know how you intend to analyse the data before you collect it.

13.10 FURTHER READING

Any of the articles referred to in the text would be a useful additional source of understanding about these two techniques. However, of particular value would be Coxon's (1999) and Lundh and Sperling's (2002) texts on diary methods; and McAdams's (2004) and Singer's (2004) books on narrative methods.

14

Focus Groups

Lynne J. Millward

14.1   Introduction
14.2   The appropriateness of the focus group method
14.3   What type of evidence do focus groups yield?
           14.3.1   The essentialist position
           14.3.2   The social constructionist position
14.4   The focal stimuli
14.5   Focus group design and planning
           14.5.1   Sampling and recruitment of subjects
           14.5.2   Sample size
           14.5.3   Group size
           14.5.4   Location, setting and length of session
14.6   Focus group implementation
           14.6.1   Moderator style and skills
           14.6.2   Topic guide
           14.6.3   Listening and questioning skills
14.7   Recording the data
14.8   Transcription
14.9   Analysis of focus group data
           14.9.1   Content analysis
           14.9.2   Other analytic techniques
14.10   Feedback of results/findings
14.11   Future developments in focus group research
           14.11.1   The 'e-focus group'
           14.11.2   The study of social interaction in context
14.12   Conclusion
14.13   Further reading

AIMS

The aim of this chapter is to provide an overview of the focus group method from a distinctly psychological perspective. This will enable the reader to make an informed epistemological judgment about whether to use focus groups as a tool of investigation and/or as a means of analytic investigation in its own right; manage a focus group investigation (including design and implementation); and handle the data appropriate to the nature of the evidence being sought.

Key terms

content analysis
discourse analysis
discursive analysis
e-focus group
essentialist
fantasy theme analysis
focus group
grounded theory
group process

interpretative phenomenological
  analysis
intragroup
intrapersonal
moderator
qualitative
sense-making
social constructionist

14.1 INTRODUCTION

focus group

group processes

qualitative

The **focus group** is a discussion-based interview that produces a particular type of qualitative data generated via group interaction. It is the 'focused' (i.e. on an 'external stimulus') and relatively staged (i.e. by a 'moderator') nature of the focus group method that separates it from other types of group interviewing strategy. Whilst the study of **group processes** has a rich and substantial research history, the focus group method nonetheless challenges the epistemological assumptions underlying much research in psychology. This lends it a rather more controversial flavour.

The earliest known scientific use of the focus group method can be traced to the work of Bogardus (1926), testing his social distance model with groups of schoolboys. However, a more formal articulation of the method is attributable to Merton and Kendall (1946) from their research into the social effects of mass communication (most notably wartime propaganda). Yet its evolution as a viable research tool is less rooted in this sociological tradition than in what Berg (1995) has called the 'vulgar world of marketing'. For decades, marketing research has relied on the untested assumption that focus groups are the quickest and most cost-efficient means of obtaining consumer-relevant information. Hence the method largely evolved as a 'quick and dirty' means of generating a lot of data quickly rather than as a sophisticated research tool.

Morgan (1988: 75) noted that 'the contribution of focus groups to social science research ... is more potential than real'. Since then, there has been an exponential rise in the number of published works legitimizing the method (e.g. Barbour & Kitzinger, 1998; Greenbaum, 1998; Krueger, 1994; Morgan & Krueger, 1997). Within psychology alone, the method has gained a substantial foothold as a means of distinctively '**qualitative** research' (Breakwell, 2004; Silverman, 2004; Smith, 2003; Wilkinson, 2003, 2004b). In the decade between 1995 and 2004, the rise in use of the focus group method (either for primary or secondary data gathering) was substantial, with 2367 papers extracted from PsychInfo, compared with only 138 publications between 1985 and 1994, and a mere 7 recorded between 1975 and 1984. The method is seen to be especially popular within applied psychology, particularly consumer psychology, and in recent years the uptake of the focus group method in health psychology is note-worthy (Wilkinson, 1998).

Despite this, 17 years on, many still maintain that the 'real potential' of focus groups has yet to be realize and as such should be a matter of 'crucial concern' to the social scientist (e.g. Hollander, 2004). This chapter highlights some of this relatively untapped potential, demonstrating, I hope, how focus groups can not only enhance the ability of psychologists to answer their research questions but also, more importantly, generate questions from new angles and perspectives. In the words of Wilkinson (1998: 182), the focus group method is 'distinctive not for its mode of analysis, but rather for its data-collection procedures, and for the nature of the data so collected'. To this end, some additional practical issues will also be addressed, including use of the Internet to generate discussion across participants distributed in both space and time, and also issues of analysis arising from the use of focus groups as a forum for investigating **social interaction**.

social interaction

It will be argued that the future of focus group research in psychology depends not only on the quality and rigour of its use (Krueger, 1993) but also an appreciation of its full potential as a means to obtain 'tiny glimpses of the world' (Hollander, 2004: 605) one might not normally get access to. By skillfully managing the group dynamic, it is possible to cultivate 'natural' conversation and discussion (through 'synergy, snowballing, stimulation and spontaneity') as a focus of investigation in its own right (Catterall & Maclaran, 1997; Jovchelovitch, 2000; Linell, 2001). For example, Kitzinger (1994) describes a major shift she witnessed in her research on illness explanations from personal and self-blaming (e.g. 'I should have been stronger') to structural/systemic (e.g. 'If we all felt confused a leaflet would have helped us deal with it better') as a function of a focus group dynamic. She concludes, from this and other similar findings, that people's attitudes are 'not necessarily neatly encapsulated in reasoned responses to direct questions' (1994: 108); they are more likely in fact to be constructed through discussion and interaction. In other words, focus groups have a relatively untapped potential to explore answers to 'how' and 'why' (i.e. process) questions as well as 'what' (i.e. content).

14.2 THE APPROPRIATENESS OF THE FOCUS GROUP METHOD

Used alone or in combination with other methods, the aim of focus groups is to capture understandings, perspectives, stories, discourses, and experiences 'not otherwise meaningfully expressed by numbers' (Berg, 1995: 3; see also Hoepfl, 1997). It is not geared to the formal testing of hypotheses in the traditional hypothetico-deductive sense, although it can be used for hypothesis formulation and/or construct development. The focus group can be used either as a self-contained means of data collection (i.e. a primary research technique) or as a supplement (i.e. a supplementary research technique) to other methods, depending on how it fits into the overall research plan and also on its epistemological basis (i.e. essentialist, social constructionist – see Section 14.3). Secondary, more 'strategic' uses of the focus group with a psychological 'edge' to them (e.g. for decision-making, intervention, collective empowerment and social change), for obtaining some end other than research (e.g. attitude change, problem-solving) do not fall strictly within a research remit.

In practice, the focus group method is most commonly used as a forum in which to develop and/or operationalize, constructs (e.g. Strong & Large, 1995), as a first step in questionnaire construction (Strong & Large, 1995), to test the viability of a conceptual model (e.g. Stanton, Black, Laljee & Ricardo, 1993), to supplement a more traditional method (e.g. Winborne & Dardaine, 1993), to elicit a uniquely different perspective on an issue (e.g. Michell, 1998; Michell & West, 1996) and to generate dialogue worthy of analysis in its own right (e.g. Lunt, 1996). For instance, Strong and Large (1995) explored the 'coping' construct in the context of chronic pain and then used this as the basis for questionnaire construction, whilst Stanton *et al.* (1993) used constructs provided by 'protection motivation theory' to both 'focus' and 'frame' a focus group discussion examining risk protection in the context of adolescent sexual behaviour. Winborne and Dardaine (1993), on the other hand, used the focus group to generate additional, more open-ended dialogue around issues arising from a survey on 'at risk' children in an educational setting.

Michell (1998) found that focus groups afforded a completely different sort of data on peer group structures than possible using other methods, and likewise Michell & West (1996) found unexpectedly that teenagers in their study came across as more self-determined than they are ordinarily given credit for, being actively involved in the decision to smoke or not (rather than easily coerced or bullied into smoking by peers). The potential for focus groups to yield an alternative and equally valid perspective on an issue than that afforded by other more traditional techniques is thus illustrated (see also Bloor, Frankland, Thomas & Robson, 2001, for other examples).

More unusually, focus groups may be used to generate dialogue of interest in its own right. Exploration of this kind is of particular interest to researchers operating within the qualitative epistemological tradition such as discourse analysts (e.g. Lunt, 1996; Myers, 2000), **social constructionists** (e.g. Linell, 2001), narrative psychologists (e.g. Barker & Rich, 1992) or advocates of the phenomenological approach (e.g. Michell & West, 1996). For instance, Lunt (1996) used the focus group to elicit and unpack tensions in discourses of 'savings' (e.g. between discourses of cash and credit, between budgeting and borrowing, between necessity and luxury, and between prudence and pleasure), linking these tensions to discourses of social and economic change.

social constructionists

14.3 WHAT TYPE OF EVIDENCE DO FOCUS GROUPS YIELD?

14.3.1 The essentialist position

essentialist

Conventional uses of the focus group fit squarely into an **'essentialist'** framework, an approach to research that assumes a 'truth' to be accessed and that some methods are better than others at getting closer to it. The advantage of focus groups is that in principle, they can elicit a broader as well as more in-depth understanding on an issue or topic, because the *interaction process* stimulates memories, discussion, debate, and disclosure in a way that is less likely in a one-to-one interview (Wilkinson, 2003). The emphasis within this framework is thus on content (i.e. thoughts, feelings, beliefs, values, knowledge, ideas and so on) and on being skilled enough to moderate the interaction process to optimize both the *quantity* and *quality* of the content generated by the focus group (Krueger & Casey, 2000).

Accordingly, all the usual guidelines on how to conduct a focus group study are underwritten by a requirement to harness the group process to maximize disclosure and minimize the likelihood that the truth will be 'clouded' by problems of inhibition (i.e. silence) and self-presentation (manifest, for example, in exaggeration or invention) arising from dysfunctional group dynamics (e.g. groupthink/conformity, status dynamics and polarization) (Catterall & Maclaran, 1997; Morgan, 1997). In Hollander's (2004) words, 'even when there is a "truth" to be told, people may choose not to tell it'. Debates centre on whether homogeneous groups that have something in common facilitate disclosure more than groups comprised of divergent individuals with no obviously shared interests or experiences, and whether members who already know each other generate better-quality data than a group of strangers (e.g. Wellings, Branigan & Mitchell, 2000; see below for a more detailed discussion of these kinds of 'sampling issues' arising in association with focus group research). What the focus group cannot do is to measure attitudes in the conventional sense of a survey (Wilkinson, 2003).

14.3.2 The social constructionist position

Hollander (2004) points out that focus groups are actually very limited in their potential for understanding individual thoughts, feelings and experiences but are excellent for 'analysing processes of social interaction'. Given that the former is the most common use of focus groups (Wilkinson, 1998), it is important to appreciate that no matter how skilled or experienced the moderator, they cannot and do not provide a 'transparent window on reality' (Frith & Kitzinger, 1998: 304). On the contrary, it can be argued that the 'reality' represented by focus groups is collaboratively produced via a process of context-specific **sense-making** (Wilkinson, 2003). Of particular interest here is not so much the 'reality' itself (or the co-constructed meanings afforded by the discussion process) but the way this reality is 'constructed, defended and modified' (Wilkinson, 2003), particularly if group members are empowered to guide the direction and flow of the discussion (Glitz, 1998).

From this so-called '**social constructionist**' position, the focus group is much more than a tool for accessing cognitions and meanings – it is 'by definition an

social constructionist

exercise in group dynamics and the conduct of the group, as well as the interpretation of results obtained, must be understood within the context of group interaction' (Stewart & Shamdasani, 1990: 7). Formally stated, then, two interrelated forms of evidence are in principle derived from focus groups: the group process (the way in which people interact and communicate with each other) and the content around which the group process is organized (the focal stimulus and the meanings arising from it).

Analytically speaking, the group process can be understood on two different levels: the **intrapersonal** (i.e. the thoughts, feelings, attitudes and values of the individual) and the **intragroup** (i.e. how people communicate and interact with each other within the group). With regard to the 'content' of the discussion, one advantage of using the group as opposed to the individual as the medium of investigation is its 'isomorphism to the process of opinion formation and propagation in everyday life' in so far as 'opinions about a variety of issues are generally determined not by individual information gathering and deliberation but through communication with others' (Albrecht, Johnson & Walther, 1993: 54).

intrapersonal
intragroup

Focus groups are communication events in which the interplay of the personal and the social can be systematically explored. Gervais (1993), for instance, used focus groups (among other qualitative methods) involving Shetlanders to analyse their processes of social representation in the wake of an oil spill. Each focus group comprised a natural social unit (a family, a fisherman crew, fish farmers, local council members and a group who had got together after the spill to act on behalf of the community). Evidence revealed the evolution of a collective rhetoric which maintained community integrity by minimizing the impact of the crisis despite it being experienced 'like a death in the family' (engendered by the intimate relationship that Shetlanders have with their land). The rhetoric was derived from Shetlanders' representations of their identity as 'resilient' and of the archipelago as 'the Old Rock'. The focus groups thus provided the ideal forum in which the collective mobilization of community resources and traditions could be captured and analysed in the face of crisis.

On the issue of 'process', one way of investigating how meanings arise in context is to look at what happens when people are confronted with active disagreement and are prompted to analyse their views more intensely than during the individual interview. Jarrett (1993), for instance, describes how, in her study involving low-income black Americans, participants were inclined to 'perform for each other'; a climate was established in which they were encouraged to discuss things with greater licence than they would otherwise. The reality created within this forum was tempered by peer pressure to 'tell it like it is' whenever idealism prevailed. In this way group pressure inhibited people from providing misleading information.

This example illustrates how attempts to resolve differences provide leverage on the basis of which participants build comprehensive accounts to explain their various experiences, beliefs, attitudes, feelings, values and behaviours. The challenges that group members can level at each other (e.g. pointing out discrepancies between what is said and assumptions made) during a member-'empowered' focus group discussion may not be the kind that are possible or even ethical for a researcher (Hyden & Bulow, 2003), highlighting the potential of this method to provide unique insights into 'the complex and varying processes through which group norms and meanings are shaped, elaborated and applied' (Bloor *et al.*, 2001: 17).

There is a growing and increasingly apparent tension between the essentialist and social constructionist perspectives on focus group research. Until recently, few had taken up the potential within focus group contexts for examining communication processes *per se* and the impact of these on the way meanings are constructed *in situ*. However, examples are beginning to emerge in the shift towards investigating these processes at work in focus groups comprised of naturally occurring groups (e.g. Lunt & Livingstone, 1996), including work groups consistent with an emerging interest in 'organizational ethnography' involving the investigation of cultural processes (e.g. Steyaert & Bouwen, 2004).

One rare early example of this potential for focus groups to investigate sense-making processes is provided by Delli-Carpini and Williams (1994) who examined the relationship between television and the formation of public opinion. The focus group was seen as a vehicle (a 'conversational metaphor') for examining the way opinions are formed via discourse generated by television. This conversational metaphor for examining the influence of the media contrasts radically with the idea that the media operate like a 'hypodermic' syringe, 'injecting' people with opinions.

14.4 THE FOCAL STIMULI

The 'focusing' component of focus group research – i.e. its distinguishing characteristic – refers to the concrete and specific character of the discussion in relation to a particular stimulus object, event or situation. Originally the stimulus object was a form of mass media communication (e.g. a film or a pamphlet). In marketing, the focus of research might be people's reactions to a particular advertising campaign or consumer product. In the social sciences, the stimulus might be a behavioural scenario (e.g. a sexual encounter as a way of accessing attitudes towards safer sex: O'Brien, 1993), a concrete event (e.g. driving and young people's risk taking: Basch, 1987), or even a concept (e.g. household crowding and its effects on psychological well-being: Fuller, Edwards, Vorakitphokatom & Sermsri, 1993). The range of possible stimuli is in fact quite broad, extending to the use of projective techniques, role-play scenarios, word association exercises, sentence completion and fantasy themes – which have proved especially effective in eliciting responses from children.

One suggestion put forward by Stanton *et al.* (1993) is to use 'theory' as the focusing vehicle especially if the topic or issue is highly complex and/or potentially sensitive (personally or politically). Hilder (1997) likewise used Schein's model of organizational culture – an otherwise complex and multi-faceted construct – to frame employee discussion in a series of focus groups conducted in organizational settings. Culture is a topic that employees may not have thought much about before, and even if they had, they may not have be able to comment on it easily without being provided with some kind of discussion context.

Using theory, however, as a focusing device, the researcher is faced with a dilemma. If the discussion is framed using constructs from a model, there is an obvious risk of prejudicing the information gained. 'Advance organizers' of this kind may eliminate other avenues that would otherwise be explored by participants with respect to the topic of culture, which thus risks loss of useful information. On the other hand, participants may not know where to start or what to say, and may end up talking endlessly about quite superficial aspects of the phenomenon in question or using the focus group as an 'offloading' forum. Since some kind of 'focus' is necessary and limitless time is not available, it may be more sensible, Hilder (1997) recommends, to scene-set so as to gain quality input on the preferred topic within an agreed time-span.

In general, research objectives guided by substantive issues (i.e. theoretical concerns) are not likely to be exactly the same as the aims presented to participants and which are used to frame the discussion process. In the research conducted by Stanton *et al.* (1993) it is unlikely that the participants were told that the aim of the focus group was to enable the researchers to 'explore developmental, socio-historical and cultural concepts' influencing sexual behaviour! Participants would be informed more concretely that the aim is to find out what they think or how they feel about particular sexual behaviours. Likewise, for an investigation of 'processes' the aim of the focus group will be the research objective translated into a concrete set of questions or issues for exploration. For instance, a study into the effects of certain contextual factors (e.g. gender) on both the process and the content of discussion may employ a topic of conversation that is most likely to throw up gender issues (e.g. experiences of violence) (Hollander, 2004). The onus is then on the researcher to translate this into an aim that will both focus and facilitate group dialogue around this issue in anticipation of being able to witness gender differences in both process and content (e.g. 'the aim of the discussion is to find out what your feelings are about …'). Where focus groups are guided purely by pragmatic rather than substantive concerns (e.g. to find out what clients think about the quality of a particular hospital service), the aims are rather more translucent.

The issue of what to tell participants about the research aims generally is likely to become particularly salient in an organizational context where political sensitivities may arise. Participants may become suspicious and apt to withhold information or to say only what they feel is expected of them, if they perceive that they are not being properly informed. Participants may suspect a 'hidden agenda' and will need to be reassured that this is not so. Gaining participation in defining the nature and scope of the subject for discussion is one way of achieving a sense of group ownership of a topic and thereby opening people up to further discussion (Hilder, 1997).

14.5 FOCUS GROUP DESIGN AND PLANNING

The preferred epistemological approach combined with the research question framing the investigation will heavily influence decisions about how to design and manage a focus group study, including the style of moderation that is most appropriately suited to generating the evidence being sought. The very first step in the design and planning process is to define and clarify the issues to be investigated in terms of the exact nature of the evidence required. Both substantive and practical considerations will influence this.

14.5.1 Sampling and recruitment of participants

It is not the intention of focus group methodology to yield generalizable data, so random sampling is not necessary. Nonetheless, it is important to employ a systematic strategy when deciding on group composition. The sample should be chosen on theoretical grounds as reflecting those segments of the population who will provide the most meaningful information pertinent to the project objectives. Participants should have something to say about the topic of interest or something to demonstrate when using focus groups to understand processes.

Recruitment strategies have important consequences for the degree of co-operation and commitment generated amongst respondents. The time and energy invested in meeting with 'local' people and making personal contact with potential participants at the outset can facilitate group rapport and contribute substantially to this.

Focus group researchers disagree on whether it is necessary to use screening procedures during the recruitment process. One argument in favour of screening alludes to differences in participant background and/or lifestyle that might inhibit the flow of discussion due to lack of common ground. Others argue to the contrary that if all participants were to share virtually identical backgrounds the discussion would be flat and unproductive. The general rule of thumb is that group members should exhibit at least some common characteristics (e.g. same socio-economic class, same age group) to facilitate disclosure because of the rapport it creates among people who are otherwise unknown to each other (Box 14.1).

Knodel (1993) advocates conducting separate focus group sessions with homogeneous but contrasting subgroups defined in terms of break characteristics. Break characteristics are selected on substantive grounds and involve the subdivision of groups according to their potentially contrasting views and experiences concerning the issues being investigated. For example, the sample may comprise females who are subdivided by role – e.g. 'housewife and mother' and 'career woman' – in an investigation of social representations of women in connection with female identity. Another pertinent break characteristic might be socio-economic class. There is a limit to the number of break characteristics that can be incorporated into any one study. Knodel suggests that they should be kept to a minimum, otherwise both the sampling and the analysis process will become unwieldy and also very costly given, at the very least, one focus group will need to be conducted for each combination of break variables.

One caveat to the use of break characteristics is that having something in common is by no means a guarantee of increased disclosure and in some cases may inhibit it – e.g. males disclosing experiences of fear in a study of violence are less likely in all-male groups (Hollander, 2004; Wellings *et al.*, 2000).

Another argument in support of screening is based on the principle of reactivity. Ordinarily, the reactivity arising from the screening process is seen as a liability: participants are given the opportunity to familiarize themselves with the research issues and may therefore enter the focus group situation with prejudice and bias. Alternatively, the reactivity created by screening procedures may afford people the opportunity to mull over the topic in advance, but this can enhance rather than undermine the validity of the content generated by the discussion. The issue of bias, however, is only problematic if the aim is to get 'closer to the truth' of something.

If, on the other hand, the aim of the focus group is to investigate the interrelationship between various contextual factors (e.g. gender, socio-economic status, extent of acquaintance, topic context, and so on), interaction and discussion processes, and the content of what is discussed, the question of bias is irrelevant. The important consideration in this respect is to be aware of all relevant 'contextual factors' including moderator characteristics and preconceptions. From this perspective there is no absolute truth to be accessed: 'what' is said is entirely relative and must be appropriately contextualized (Hollander, 2004).

For instance, in a discussion about experiences of violence, men in predominantly male focus groups downplay their victimization stories and exaggerate their role as perpetrators; women do the opposite. Hollander (2004) put this down to norms of masculinity becoming salient in predominantly male groups (i.e. where men are motivated to strategically present themselves with strength and bravado in relation to their male peers), especially in groups where 'what one says' in the group discussion could have ramifications for maintaining valid masculine identities back in the real world. In other words, if participants know each other, what they say may have longer-term consequences. The issue here is not so much 'what' was found (which was different to data obtained from surveys) but why, and what self-presentational purposes are being served (Michell, 1998).

Ultimately the decision rests on determining the composition of the group which will maximize the probability of obtaining the most theoretically relevant information. There is mounting evidence that males and females interact differently in mixed-sex as opposed to same-sex groups, and this has prompted some to suggest that focus group sessions should be homogeneous in terms of gender (Stewart & Shamdasani, 1990) but this assumes a focus on content only rather than process or both content and process (Hollander, 2004). Some would argue that the dynamics of gender in a focus group context is interesting in itself.

Social scientists argue that there are many occasions when participants have not only something in common but also a shared history. Not only can a shared history facilitate openness by offering validation via the sharing experience but it may in itself be of interest to the investigation (Frith, 2000). There are many examples of focus groups being successfully conducted with naturally occurring communities of people (e.g. Gervais, 1993; Taylor *et al.*, 1991). Taylor *et al.* (1991), for instance, used 'natural' focus groups to examine the psychosocial impact of solid waste facilities within exposed communities.

14.5.2 Sample size

Sample size (not group size, note) varies widely from as small as 21 (e.g. occupational therapy practitioners in Llewelyn, 1991) to one rare exception of 744 (e.g. parents, adolescents and educators in Croft and Sorrentino, 1991). The number of focus group sessions conducted will be a function of both sample and group size. Some researchers have noted that the data generated after about ten sessions are largely redundant. The decision rests on the type of evidence required and from whom, as well as considerations of cost in terms of time and resources.

14.5.3 Group size

A systematic review of recent focus group research in psychology yields an average of nine participants per session as conventional, with a range of six to twelve. This conclusion is consistent with the figures quoted in the focus group literature, although some would advocate between six and eight participants as ideal (Albrecht *et al.*, 1993; see also Wilkinson, 2003).

There are several reasons why it is advisable to keep the groups as small as possible whilst still being able to elicit the breadth of responses required. Large groups are unwieldy to manage, afford free-riding and can be apt to fragment as subgroups form. Also it may be hard to obtain a clear recording of the session:

people talk at different volumes and at different distances so the discussion may be difficult if not impossible to track. It is common practice to over-recruit for each session by 20% since it is inevitable that not all will actually turn up. The group size on the day will therefore vary.

14.5.4 Location, setting and length of session

Choice of location will need to balance the needs of the research with those of participants. It should set the tone of the research as professional and, where possible, be on neutral ground. However, there are times when the sample will be hard to reach unless the research is conducted on home territory (e.g. a hospital), or it may be of particular interest to frame the research in a particular context. Two prime considerations for participants are convenience and comfort. The location should be easy to reach and the research schedule should not pose any difficulties for them (e.g. child care and transportation problems). Once there, the conditions of the room itself should be conducive to a smooth-flowing discussion and basically comfortable (e.g. appropriate ambience of informality, availability of refreshments, nearby toilets, suitable seating and table arrangements). It is also usual to supply name tags. Most focus group researchers agree that between one and two hours is the standard duration for each session involving adults, and a maximum of one hour for sessions involving young people.

14.6 FOCUS GROUP IMPLEMENTATION

At its most basic level, the successful implementation of a focus group study depends on two key factors: preparation and good people skills (Greenbaum, 2000; Wilkinson, 2003). The exact nature of the preparation and the skill involved will, however, depend on epistemological stance, perhaps even more so than the question(s) being asked.

Broadly speaking, an investigation of content will necessitate a very different kind of preparation and moderation (e.g. active process facilitation) than an investigation of processes of meaning construction and negotiation in a natural group (e.g. strategic retraction from both group content and process). In the content-oriented scenario, the aim is to maximize disclosure by actively engaging all participants in the discussion, minimizing group biases and status dynamics. The discussion will perhaps be guided in this instance by a fairly strict topic guide (see below), the intention being to elicit and record as many individual utterances as possible.

In the more process-oriented investigation, the idea is to create a situation where participants direct their conversations to each other in as natural a way as possible (Hollander, 2004): group members are effectively *empowered* to direct the flow and direction of the dialogue that ensues (Wilkinson, 1998). Here the focus of interest is the 'interaction process'.

14.6.1 Moderator style and skills

From the above it is clear that the style and skills of the moderator are fundamental to the effectiveness of the focus group (Box 14.2). In some instances also the moderator must be someone with whom the participants can identify so as to be able to gain their trust and commitment (e.g. members of low-income ethnic minority groups). In practice people will talk surprisingly freely about a wide variety of personal topics so long as the climate is permissive and non-critical.

From an essentialist perspective, the best **moderator** guides the proceedings in an unobtrusive and subtle way, intervening only to the extent of maintaining a productive group. For example, one or two of the more dominant group members may be engaged in a heated exchange at the expense of others in the group who are obviously experiencing some discomfort. In this case the moderator would need to take active steps to defuse the situation, refocus the group and balance out the discussion process (Box 14.2).

moderator

Box 14.2   Moderator Styles

There are two basic styles of moderation most appropriate to the implementation of focus groups: process facilitation and role retraction. Which is used will depend on whether the investigation is content- or process-focused.

Process facilitation.   This moderator style requires low content (i.e. what is discussed) control but high process (i.e. interaction) control, with a view to maximizing involvement. The moderator facilitates interaction by ensuring that the discussion is productive (i.e. all the relevant issues are covered and in sufficient depth). Only the issues to be focused on are determined in advance. However, there will be occasions when the research objectives are revised in accordance with the findings derived from focus group sessions, in which case the moderator should allow mainly the participants to determine the agenda. A pose of 'incomplete understanding' but not ignorance (which will appear insincere) is recommended; the moderator makes it clear that she or he is there to learn from the participants. The moderator will need to balance the 'requirements of sensitivity and empathy on one hand, and objectivity and detachment on the other' (Stewart & Shamdasani, 1990: 69).

Role retraction.   This moderator style involves minimal direction and control of content and process. The moderator may introduce the focus group session in the process facilitation mode and then work to empower the participants to take progressively more responsibility for the process as well as the content of the discussion. It therefore provides the opportunity to see how participants naturally organize their discussions of certain issues. The climate is then also ripe for the discussion of controversial or sensitive topics that would otherwise threaten rapport if the researcher introduced them. The main disadvantage for the essentialist stance is the complete absence of standardization, thus rendering it difficult to compare findings across different focus groups within the same research project. Without prompting, some topics may never come up.

If the interest of the study is the content of the discussion, there are three additional criteria for ensuring that 'focus' is maintained: specificity, range and depth. The first requires that minute detail is sought in people's responses and reactions to the stimulus object or event. It is the moderator's task to elicit meanings and differential responses. The second concerns coverage, the issue for the moderator being one of facilitating transitions from one area of a discussion to another. The third concerns the personal context of the response or reaction elicited by the stimulus. Eliciting in-depth responses involves expanding on responses beyond limited reports of 'positive' or 'negative', 'pleasant' or 'unpleasant' reactions. The moderator's task is to diagnose the level at which participants are operating (i.e. ranging from superficial description to detailed elaboration) and where necessary to deepen it. All these criteria can be met by the moderator who is skilled in listening and questioning techniques.

There are some instances where group members may themselves *spontaneously* take responsibility for the flow as well as the content of the discussion. This would occur when, say, someone in the group tries to reorient a discussion that has gone off track or who frequently asks others for clarification. From a social constructionist perspective this will be a phenomenon of interest in its own right. Jarrett (1993) describes how the low-income African-American women in her study challenged each other's 'idealized accounts' (e.g. as strong women who have to manage errant husbands, disobedient children and meddlesome mothers) of their housewife role.

The extent to which self-management of this kind occurs depends on the climate established by the moderator at the very outset. Overall, the smaller the degree of external control, the smaller the opportunity for moderator influence (e.g. unwittingly leading participants into a particular area of discussion that provides validation for previous work), thereby increasing the external validity of the information derived (Box 14.2).

14.6.2 Topic guide

A topic guide is necessary only to the extent that content is of particular interest to the moderator. The guide should nonetheless be no more than suggestive, affording the moderator considerable latitude to improvise fruitful questions and pursue unanticipated lines of enquiry as the discussion progresses. The guide should not be used in the form of a questionnaire or interviewing straitjacket. Reliance on fixed questions may undermine the ability of the moderator to listen analytically to the content of the discussion, thereby overlooking the implications of what is said. Sometimes the feelings being expressed in people's comments are cloaked in abstractions and rationalizations. The moderator might form a hunch about the nature of the undercurrent and raise it in the form of tentative questions, thus creating a climate in which people are encouraged to articulate their feelings. To ward against using the guide as a script, some have advocated that the issues to be covered are instead committed to memory. The number of issues raised will depend on the extent to which the group identifies with the topic as a whole and the type of thinking they are required to engage in (e.g. highly sensitive topics may lead quickly to emotional fatigue). It may be advisable to pre-test the 'tone' of the discussion to derive clues about the appropriateness of the focus group method for how easily or openly a topic is discussed and the range of emotions elicited.

14.6.3 Listening and questioning skills

Whatever the epistemological stance, the listening and questioning style of the moderator is key to determining the nature of the discussion. This will reflect in the sequence of questions as well as how the questions are worded (Box 14.3).

Box 14.3 Questioning skills

Merton and Kendall (1946) distinguish questioning styles according to their degree of structure: unstructured, semi-structured and structured. The unstructured question is one which is free of stimulus and response (sometimes called an *open question*); the respondent is not guided either on which stimulus or aspect of a stimulus to respond to or on the type of response that is required (e.g. `What are your thoughts on recent health education campaigns emphasizing safer sex?', 'Tell me something about ...'). There are two types of semi-structured questions: stimulus-structured and response-free (sometimes called a probing question); and stimulus-free and response-structured (sometimes called a leading question). In the former, the particular focus of the question is specified but the nature of the response is left completely open (e.g. 'How do you feel about the emphasis on condom use in campaigns on safer sex?') In the latter, the focus of the question is unspecified but a particular kind of response is requested (e.g. 'What did you learn from the campaigns on safer sex?')

In the structured question, both the stimulus and the response components are rigidly specified (e.g. 'Do you think that sticking to one sexual partner is a better means or as good a means or a poorer means of practising safer sex than the regular use of condoms?') Such questions prompt people to agree or confirm something they have not actually said (e.g. 'Would you agree that ...?') Within the current framework of creating a climate of openness and disclosure or of empowering focus group members to direct the flow and direction of the discussion, it is clear that this type of questioning would be inappropriate. Leading questions can also provoke a defensive reaction or withdrawal. There is a fine balance also to be struck when people need help articulating a response (e.g. 'Are you saying that you feel ...?')

Overall, question wording should facilitate openness. For instance, rather than direct people to say either 'yes' or 'no' without elaboration ('Are you happy with …?'), a question should invite a disclosure and elaboration (e.g. 'What are your thoughts about …'). Consistent use of open or probing questions helps create a climate of attentiveness and listening where people feel able to respond in any way they like (Box 14.3). Probing questions like 'Tell me more about …' can also help to funnel people to respond on a more concrete and specific level if necessary whilst maintaining openness.

Questions need to be strategically and sensitively used by a moderator when initiating transitions in the discussion perhaps cued by something said or alluded to by a respondent or by a more strategic desire to revisit an issue that was sidestepped, discussed superficially or not mentioned at all. However, cues for transition originating from the respondents help maintain the flow of the discussion, whereas the more stylized kind of moderator-initiated moves can interrupt the flow if not managed carefully. Other requirements for moderator intervention may arise from 'difficulties' with particular people (Box 14.4).

Box 14.4   Managing 'difficulties' in the discussion

The attribution of 'difficulty' within a focus group discussion depends on the purpose of the investigation. If the intention is to engage everyone on a fairly equal level without inhibition, the 'domination' of one member in dictating both the content and the process of the discussion would be considered difficult. If, on the other hand, the focus is on process, this pattern of domination may be highly informative if read in context (i.e. an interrelational and/or status context). Lakoff (1990: 45) shows how the first person to speak at length in a discussion can set the tone and direction of the conversation, legitimizing some topics as the focus of conversation over others. This is 'difficult' for a discussion in which the intention is to increase the breadth and depth of discussion about a range of preplanned topics, but a rich source of data for those interested in looking at status dynamics in context. A slight caveat to the latter is posed by the ethics of allowing someone not only to inhibit the contributions of others but also potentially to upset them.

Silence is also a powerful way of getting people to talk, allowing them time to think about and formulate a response. Moderators should not be tempted to fill every single void with a question, and certainly, within a framework of interest in the process of interaction, silence in terms of what is not being said and why is a relational issue and thus an important form of data in itself (Michell, 1998).

Skilled use of questions in particular requires double hearing or the ability to read between the lines of a discussion in order to 'ferret' out what is only implied (e.g. in linguistic derivatives) rather than relying totally on what is made explicit. By explicating the implied (e.g. tentatively playing it back to respondents in the form of a clarificatory question), it is rendered legitimate (e.g. it is acceptable to talk about this) and respondents may thus feel able to elaborate.

14.7 RECORDING THE DATA

Focus groups generate data in the form of transcripts produced from audio or videotape. By videotaping the focus group sessions, observational data can be extracted (e.g. non-verbal communication) as well as the content of the discussion. However, this might be outweighed by the effects on the interaction and communication process (i.e. possible inhibition) created by the presence of closed-circuit TV equipment. The audio tape limits the form of data to the content of the discussion but can be supplemented by moderator observations of the process. Most researchers, however, rely on audio-taped recordings of the discussions supplemented by a few general field notes to minimize the burden imposed by having to simultaneously observe, listen and moderate.

It is crucial to first obtain the informed consent of the participants and to give assurances of confidentiality. Note that the larger the group the less easy it is to get a clear recording using one tape recorder alone, so it is important to carefully plan and trial the logistics of recording.

14.8 TRANSCRIPTION

Transcription is a primarily mechanical task. Its time-consuming and laborious nature, however, has often led researchers to analyse the content directly from the tape, which entails transcribing only the most illustrative comments. Since the purpose of a focus group is to gain insight into how respondents represent a particular issue as a whole and on a collective rather than an individual basis, it is important to capture the entire character of the discussion, warts and all. Any form of short-circuiting of the transcription process or selective editing is therefore undesirable.

14.9 ANALYSIS OF FOCUS GROUP DATA

It is clear, as Wilkinson (2003: 203) succinctly puts it, that there is 'no single canonical – or even preferred – way of analyzing (focus group) data'. The practicalities are, she recognizes, that focus group data are 'voluminous, relatively unstructured and not easily analysed'. The form of analysis, moreover, will depend fundamentally on whether it is the 'content' or the 'process' (i.e. group dynamic) that is the 'data' of interest. The social constructionist perspective is underwritten by the assumption that process and content are inextricably linked, but an essentialist perspective in which 'content' is primary may or may not involve a consideration of process. Conventionally, then, it has been most usual to deal with 'content' using some means of formal 'content analysis'.

14.9.1 Content analysis

content analysis   This discussion of **content analysis** as it is used to analyse transcription data is equally applicable to other types of data that can be reduced to textual form (e.g. discourses and historical materials). Content analysis can even be used to analyse non-textual data such as works of art and architecture. However, most psychological applications are concerned with analysing material that can be presented to content analysts as text (Holsti, 1969).

Content analysis comprises both a mechanical and an interpretative component (Krippendorf, 1980). The mechanical aspect involves physically organizing and subdividing the data into categories whilst the interpretative component involves determining what categories are meaningful in terms of the questions being asked. The mechanical and interpretative are inextricably linked in a cycling back and forth between the transcripts and the more conceptual process of developing meaningful coding schemes (see also Chapters 12 and 13).

quantitative content analysis   There are three main forms of content analysis: quantitative, qualitative, and structural content analysis. **Quantitative content analysis** generates numerical values (frequencies, rankings, ratings) from the verbatim text. However, the process by which these values are generated may include elements of qualitative analysis, making the qualitative–quantitative distinction far from clear-cut. Quantitative content analysis is slightly mislabelled anyway, as it is less a type of analysis than a way of producing data which can then be statistically analysed, i.e. the output of the content analysis is not the end of the analysis as a whole (Box 14.5).

Box 14.5   Quantitative content analysis

Stage 1. In the case of transcripts of focus groups, this will be all the material that has been collected while running the groups.

Stage 2. The selection of some 'unit of analysis' which pertains to the discrete bits of information that will be assigned to categories in the subsequent analysis (or coding unit). This may be a word, a theme, a character, an item, time spent on a topic, etc. When the unit of analysis is the word, then content analysis may become a relatively simple exercise of counting the occurrences of particular

(Continued)

Box 14.5   (Continued)

words or types of words (e.g. active versus passive constructions). Although this approach has some advantages, in particular that it can be easily computerized, it is limited in that the meaning of a word can change depending upon the context. A more subtle, though potentially less reliable, approach is to identify themes.

A theme is a statement or proposition about something. Sometimes themes can be identified by the presence or absence of specific words (e.g. self-referential statements may be identified by the presence of 'I' and 'me'). However, the identification of themes will inevitably require some interpretative action on the part of the coder(s) (Smith, 2003; see Chapter 16).

In order to conduct a thematic content analysis one needs to generate a coding frame. The coding frame is a set of categories into which instances will be allocated. The categories should be exhaustive (i.e. all instances can be assigned to a category) and exclusive (i.e. all instances should be assigned to only one category). The coding frame can be developed either on the basis of the substantive content of the target material (e.g. categories could be different types of environmental issue) or on the basis of theoretically determined categories (e.g. internal and external attributions). To some extent, a theoretically derived coding frame is more analytic, whilst a content-derived coding frame is more descriptive. Of course, different coding frames can be applied to the same material.

Regarding quantification of the material, the output of a content analysis is often the frequency of occurrence of the different coding categories – for example, how many times a particular coding category appears in a transcript (or text, etc.). Comparisons between different source materials may then be assessed. However, it is possible to evaluate the content along one or more ordinal dimensions. This increases the scope for statistical analysis of the data. Ranking may be used when a number of instances are being analysed – for example, one could rank focus groups on the degree to which group members used personalized examples to illustrate points in their arguments. Rating scales may also be used in some cases.

Qualitative content analysis tends to be more subjective and less explicit about the processes of interpretation: the emphasis is on meaning rather than on quantification. Initially the system of classification may be derived from the research question and the topic guide used by the moderator during process facilitation. Additional conceptual codes may arise from a closer examination of the data as a whole. Coded segments may include long exchanges, phrases or sentences. Codes can also be developed to signal useful quotations. Following this, a grid which tabulates code on one axis and focus group identifier on the other is developed that provides a descriptive overview of the data. The aim is to be able to find quotations to illustrate particular themes or strands of meaning within the transcript. With this form of content analysis the aim is not normally to put numbers to the data.

qualitative content analysis

Computer-assisted approaches to data reduction which are designed to organize textual data can make at least the mechanics of the task much more manageable (e.g. The Ethnograph: Seidel, Kjolseth & Seymour, 1988).

Structural content analysis involves the development of a representation of the relationships between elements in the target material. To do this both qualitative and quantitative aspects of the data have to be considered. Structural content analysis is appropriate for the analysis of complex systems, of which naturally occurring focus groups are an excellent example. Variants of this approach, such as cognitive mapping (Axelrod, 1976), have often been applied to aspects of decision-making. As well as being relevant to decision-making, this approach is useful for investigating belief systems and social representations. Structural content analysis involves some of the same processes and techniques as are used in quantitative (and qualitative) content analysis. However, the rules governing the relationships between response categories also need to be defined. These relational rules will vary depending upon the research aims. Research on political decision-making, for example, might examine belief systems about crime and what should be done about it. As well as being able to examine the effects of group contexts on the expressed beliefs, one can compare the belief systems of members of different parties (or other groups) and explore change in the belief systems over time. Relational rules would concern covariation and potential causality (e.g. whether the political make-up of the group influences the way crime is discussed).

Content analysis is not without its problems. It is heavily reliant on the multiple judgements of a single analyst. As the analyst may be (unknowingly or otherwise) keen to find support for a particular view of the data, it is advisable to independently involve two or more people in the coding of the transcripts so that the reliability of the analysis can be systematically assessed. Inter-rater reliability is then assessed by computing an agreement index such as Cohen's kappa.

Other problems include concentrating only on what is mentioned. Sometimes what is not mentioned or strategically side-stepped by the group may be as important. This is where it would be important to look at process as an integral part of the 'content' analysis (or how the content is produced). However, in practice, if something does not appear in the transcript it tends not to be subjected to content analysis. Thus, talking about themes in the data in isolation may side-step the complex totality in which 'themes' are embedded. Structural content analysis may go some way towards dealing with this problem, though the techniques of structural analysis are relatively underdeveloped.

14.9.2 Other analytic techniques

Other techniques for analysing focus group material include discursive analysis, fantasy theme analysis, interpretative phenomenological analysis (IPA) and grounded theory.

Fantasy theme analysis is a variant form of discourse analysis concerned with how communication affords dramatization (e.g. story telling) which in turn creates social realities for people (Bormann, 1972). Dramatization is of interest only in the collective sense as providing insights into the cultural, emotional and motivational style of a particular community or population of people. The focus group method provides the ideal forum for the investigation of 'dramatized communication'. A detailed consideration of how to conduct fantasy theme analysis can be found in Bormann (1972).

fantasy theme analysis

Discursive analysis is a particular form of discourse analysis based on the epistemological assumption that what people say is a form of purposive social action which has a function to serve in a particular interactional context (see Chapter 18). In this instance, the focus group is the interactional context in which statements are made. In Wilkinson's (2003: 203) words, 'if video (rather than audio) data are available, a broader analysis of the group dynamics within which particular conversations are located becomes a real possibility'. Wilkinson (2003: 202) illustrates this using a data extract from a discussion between two pub landladies where they collaboratively produce ideas about the role of their profession in 'causing' breast cancer. However, only a very small proportion of the focus group data can be handled using discursive analysis; it does not furnish the researcher with the potential to summarize the data in any general way.

discursive analysis

Interpretative phenomenological analysis is a form of qualitative analysis which explicitly acknowledges that the process of analysing experiences and the meaning of these experiences will necessarily involve 'interpretation' on the part of the researcher (Smith, 2003; see Chapter 16). As a fundamentally idiographic approach to investigation and analysis, IPA is concerned with the exploration of *intrapersonal* rather than group experiences. However, there may be instances where people find it easier to talk openly about their personal perceptions and experiences in a context in which these experiences can be shared with similar others. Alternatively, there may be good practical reasons why focus group interviews are being used to explore individual experiences – including cost and time considerations. In such instances, the *individual perceptions and experiences* will need to be parsed out from the group discussion (and to an extent, this will only be possible if the facilitator has engaged each and every individual at an experiential level in the discussion process).

interpretative phenomenological analysis

Another means of qualitative analysis more pertinent to the capturing of shared experiences is furnished by techniques associated with **grounded theory**. Grounded theory's theoretical background is in sociology, underpinned by the assumption that meanings are made sense of in social interaction (see Chapter 17). Grounded theory should be used when the researcher wants to explore complex issues or processes and create a theory. It involves the progressive identification and integration of categories of meaning from textual data. Researchers often look for negative cases – instances that do not fit with the identified categories – to ensure they have understood the full intricacy of the data.

grounded theory

14.10 FEEDBACK OF RESULTS/FINDINGS

Feedback to participants or an organization raises a dilemma for the researcher. It is unusual for access to be granted within a company without some expectation of feedback. However, some of the information arising out of the focus group may not be what the sponsor wants to hear and may even be personally compromising. One also has to consider that what people have talked about in the group may be not what they would wish to pass on, and not pleasant to receive. The decision as to how much, if any, of the information and analysis to discuss with the company sponsor has to be an individual one. Clearly no attributable information should be given: the confidentiality agreed with the group members must be absolute. However, if the focus groups are part of a potentially long-term relationship between you, the researcher and the company, then the relationship with the sponsor is also an important one. Thus, while diplomacy in the analysis given may be appropriate, there is little point in hiding non-attributable information which will form part of the longer-term study (Hilder, 1997).

14.11 FUTURE DEVELOPMENTS IN FOCUS GROUP RESEARCH

14.11.1 The 'e-focus group'

Advances in technology and the 'globalization' of real-time communication open up the possibility for focus groups (crossing cultural, spatial and temporal boundaries) to be run 'online' (Greenbaum, 1998; Markham, 2004). As Markham (2004: 95) puts it, as 'a communication medium, a global network of connection, and a scene of social construction, the Internet provides new tools for conducting research and new means for understanding the way social realities get constructed and reproduced through discussion behaviours'. In particular, the opportunity via an online medium to 'witness and analyze the structure of talk, the negotiation of meaning and identity, the development of relationships and communities' (Markham, 2004: 97) is one that researchers could capitalize on in the pursuit of their interest in using focus groups to study the process of sense-making.

Two types of online global focus groups can be envisaged: real-time focus groups who log on to the network at a set time for a set period to discuss a topic or issue, and ongoing focus groups whose members sign on and off whenever they wish, and contribute whenever convenient and/or appropriate (Box 14.6). In the real-time version a focus group could be run in the traditional fashion with a facilitator keeping the discussion on track, probing wherever necessary and so on. In the ongoing version a discussion is not easily managed or facilitated, the group itself being responsible for determining the shape and direction of the dialogue that ensues. Real-time 'virtual' focus groups are staged, whilst ongoing focus groups are not and exist irrespective of whether all their members are signed on at any one time.

Box 14.6   Interaction in cyberspace

The concept of 'global focus groups' opens up a whole realm of research possibilities, but also brings with it potential logistical problems and issues of 'virtual' facilitation. Kenny (2005) used a computer program called WebCT© to facilitate online engagement and interaction among a group of nurses brought together (from any location at any time) to explore certain nursing issues. She describes the experience as positive, enabling her to 'collect richly detailed research data' (2005: 414). Whether the unmanaged and ongoing aspects of online discussion groups mean that they can no longer be called focus groups is yet to be contemplated. One problem with the real-time discussions is ensuring that everyone knows what time to sign on and that the timings are co-ordinated exactly across time zones (see Greenbaum, 1998, for more on this).

14.11.2 The study of social interaction in context

The potential to use focus groups to study processes is a relatively recent realization, despite Stewart and Shamdasani's (1990) efforts to encourage the application of theoretical insights to group processes. Now, coincidental with the increased use and legitimacy of a more social constructionist approach to psychological investigation, questions about 'process' have become core to the qualitative research agenda. One of the impediments to using focus groups to pursue this kind of research, however, is the question of how to systematically explore content whilst also capturing interactivity in sense-making processes (Linell, 2001). As cautioned by Hollander (2004), the data collected from one participant cannot be considered separate from the social context in which they were collected, including relationships among participants, between participants and facilitators, and larger social structures.

14.12 CONCLUSION

This chapter has described and explained the potential of the focus group method to generate both content and process data depending on which epistemological approach is used to underwrite the choice of method. Design and implementation of a focus group study is discussed according to which of these two foci of investigation – if not both – is of primary research interest. Accordingly, various analytic approaches are also introduced including basic content analysis, as well as the application of more sophisticated qualitative approaches underpinned by a particular analytic approach such as discursive analysis, interpretative phenomenological analysis and grounded theory. Innovative uses of the focus group in an online capacity as well as to investigate active sense-making processes in context are noted.

14.13 FURTHER READING

There is now burgeoning literature on the focus group method. Some of the more recently published handbooks include Greenbaum's (1998), which introduces the idea of 'global focus groups' and also examines the relevance of technological advances for the focus group method; Bloor *et al.*'s (2001); Edmunds's (1999); and Morgan and Krueger's (1997), which comprises a set of six books each devoted to a particular aspect of the focus group method, from design and planning through to implementation and analysis. Greenbaum's (2000) is a must for advancement in uses of the focus group method for different types of purposes. Krueger and Casey's (2000) text addresses problems likely to be encountered during focus group research, providing a down-to-earth set of guidelines on how to optimize the potential of the focus group method. Other recommended books include Stewart and Shamdasani's (1990), which has now acquired the status of a theoretical classic on the focus group method, and Morgan's (1997). Last, but by no means least, for a distinctively psychological perspective on focus groups and, in particular, on how to handle the data analysis, Sue Wilkinson's (1998, 2003, 2004b) work is an inescapable must.

15

Ethnographic and Action Research

David Uzzell and Julie Barnett

15.1   Introduction

15.2   What is ethnography?

15.3   Problems in ethnography

15.4   Measuring quality in ethnographic research

15.5   Action research

15.6   Distinguishing criteria of action research

15.7   Conclusion

15.8   Further reading

This chapter aims to provide an introduction to two approaches to research that challenge traditional empirical positivist assumptions: ethnographic research and action research. Both seek, through largely qualitative approaches, to uncover and reveal the complexity of social processes. Although similar in some respects, the important ways in which these approaches differ from each other are outlined along with the challenges that working within this kind of research framework provides the researcher. These approaches are increasingly relevant to policy-makers, and a range of current illustrations and examples are provided.

Key terms

anthropology	naturalistic
change	observation
co-construction	participation
context	phenomenological
culture	power
description	qualitative
interpretative research	significance
intervention	

15.1 INTRODUCTION

In this chapter we discuss two approaches to research, both of which try to uncover and reveal the complexity of social processes. Although both approaches seek to explore in depth the meaning the world has for a particular group of people and recognize that the researcher, rather than being seen as a disinterested and neutral observer of the social scene, is in fact an integral part of it, they are in quite important respects different from one another. Ethnographic research is an **interpretative** example of **interpretative research**. In this, the researcher is engaged in a process **research** of interpretation and (re)construction of reality, that is to say, it is the role of the researcher to understand the constructed realities of those interviewed or observed: the research is concerned with 'constructions of reality – its own constructions and in particular those constructions it meets in the field or in the people it studies' (Flick, 1998: 11). On the other hand, action research works with **participation** co-constructed or participatory realities. At the heart of this process is the **partic- change ipation** of those directly involved in a **change** situation (Hart & Bond, 1995).

Both approaches tend to be holistic in as much as they recognize the complexity of social life and seek to understand beliefs, attitudes and action in context. The aim of ethnography has been described as to understand 'the social world of people through immersion in their community to produce detailed descriptions of culture and beliefs' (Spencer, Ritchie, Lewis & Dillon, 2003). Whereas in action research the **co-construction** researcher is part of a process of change, having a responsibility for **co-construction** of narratives, in ethnographic research he or she is there as an observer, a chronicler and an interpreter (Uzzell, 1979). Both of these approaches to research often result **qualitative** in the analysis of **qualitative** data. Consequently, we need to question whether the criteria typically employed to assess quantitative research (e.g. validity, reliability and objectivity) are in themselves valid for assessing qualitative methods such as those employed by ethnographers and action researchers. The chapter concludes with a brief discussion of why these two approaches are assuming more significance in informing government policy-making.

15.2 WHAT IS ETHNOGRAPHY?

Ethnographic research provides descriptive and interpretative analyses of the symbolic, connotative and denotative meanings that inform the routine practices **culture** of everyday life. Ethnographic studies within one's own **culture** or subculture are not without difficulty because they require that we 'make the familiar strange', or make visible what otherwise are implicit and taken-for-granted aspects of **anthropology** social life. As Jordan and Roberts (2000: 1) express it, 'both traditional **anthro-pology** which involved making the strange familiar, and modern urban ethnography which involves making the familiar strange are the two perspectives that allow us to gain a better understanding of the nature of cultural patterns and practices'. Goetz and LeCompte (1984: 2) have defined ethnography as the 'analytic descriptions or reconstructions of intact cultural scenes and groups. Ethnographies recreate for the reader the shared beliefs, practices, artefacts, folk knowledge, and behaviours of some groups of people'.

Ethnography has often been associated with the study of exotic cultures. This is not surprising given its association with anthropology; its beginnings are usually traced to the research of Malinowski's fieldwork on the Trobriand Islanders of the Western Pacific in the 1920s and Franz Boas's studies of Kwakiutl Indians from Northern Vancouver. Both these pioneers established some of the critical identifying characteristics of ethnographic research: the role of participant observation, that is, participating as well as observing the group's social life; the meticulous collection of data; the identification of differences and particularities of cultural groups; long-term immersion in a culture or subculture; and learning the language of the cultural group. But ethnographers' attention to the distant and exotic is being replaced by an interest in social life and everyday cultural settings.

The essence of ethnography is to understand the culturally specific patterns of behaviour and attitudes that give people the feeling of being members of a group. This not only requires the researcher to study cultures without prejudice, but also involves the ethnographer being aware of his or her own culturally specific beliefs, attitudes, behaviours and how they might influence the interpretation of what is under study. This has led to a debate within ethnography: are ethnographic studies best conducted by someone from outside the culture so that a dispassionate and objective view can be taken? Alternatively, are 'native ethnographers' better as they can provide insider accounts of the culture under investigation?

Ethnography is a process, a way of studying human behaviour. Goetz and LeCompte (1984) suggest that ethnographic methodologies have four characteristic features. Firstly, they aim to elicit **phenomenological** data – that is, they aim to represent the world-view of those individuals or groups under investigation. Although other methodologies in psychology seek to do this, where ethnography differs from other methodologies is that the representations of the world are structured by the participants, not by the researcher. It is the participants' structuring of the world in which the researcher is interested.

phenomenological

Secondly, ethnographic techniques are empirical and almost without exception employed in **naturalistic** settings. The researcher is interested in how individuals and groups behave in their own real-world setting unmanipulated by the researcher. Ethnographic research has been undertaken in an extensive range of settings (Hobbs & May, 1993) and has been concerned with a substantial number of social issues (Burawoy *et al.*, 1991).

naturalistic

Thirdly, ethnographic research attempts to present the totality of the phenomenon under investigation. The **context** is as important as the action. The temporal

context

and environmental factors and the social/cultural and economic context are not noise but fundamental contributory explanatory variables. Behaviour is seen to have a history and an anticipation of the future. Finally, given the kind of picture painted here of ethnographic research, it will not come as a surprise to find that not only does one find a variety of methods and techniques used in ethnographic research but any one study may use more than one method.

Ethnography is a research process whereby the researcher tries to enter the culture of a particular group and to report on its activities and values from the inside. There is not a single way of 'doing ethnography' – indeed, one should not think of or refer to ethnography as a methodology, as if it were a single data-collection procedure equivalent to questionnaires or interviews. Ethnography comprises many 'methods' or tools for gathering data; these might include participant observation, making field notes or interviewing. Many of the methodologies described in this book are used by the ethnographic researcher, such as direct observation (Chapter 7), interviewing (Chapter 12), discourse analysis (Chapter 18) and diary techniques (Chapter 13). What distinguishes ethnographic research is its purpose – cultural description. Spradley (1979: 10–11) defined ethnography as a 'culture-studying culture. It consists of a body of knowledge that includes research techniques, ethnographic theory, and hundreds of cultural descriptions. It seeks to build a systematic understanding of all human cultures from the perspective of those who have learned'. This last point is crucially important for it stresses that, unlike other areas of social science research where the researcher attempts to explain human action in terms of psychological theories such as attribution theory, ethnographic research lays emphasis on the actor's understanding of and theorizing about their actions. In other words, the view is not the outsider looking in, but the insider looking around.

It might also be useful to think of the distinction between the ethnographic approach and other types of research in psychology as a distinction between a quest for questions and a quest for answers. Within psychology, the questions we seek to answer are typically determined by the theoretical propositions we seek to test, and these are clearly stated at the outset of any investigation. In ethnographical research we are interested in the questions people are answering themselves about their life, their relationships and their environment by their actions. They may be questions which are unarticulated because they are part of the taken-for-granted world. Nevertheless, by their actions people are responding to the situations, rules and relationships in which they find themselves. **observation** **description** Ethnographic research often starts with **observation** and **description**, for it is in the process of observing that situation-specific questions emerge. In Spradley and Mann's (1975) closely observed study of life in Brady's Cocktail Bar, they found that cocktail waitresses learned very quickly that a good waitress is not one who serves customers well but one who knows how to please the bartenders. Because of the status hierarchy the waitresses need the approval and praise of the bartenders, and making the bartenders' job easy is essential to ensure a trouble-free life.

Although distinguishable in many ways from ethnography, the ethogenic approach within social psychology has related aims and intentions; ethogenics is concerned to explore the underlying structure of behavioural acts by investigating the meaning people attach to them. Thus, the researcher is interested in how participants theorize about their own behaviour rather than imposing theory on the behaviour. Marsh, Rosser and Harré (1978: 21) write that the ethogenic approach 'is based on the idea that human social life is a product of an interaction between sequences of actions and talk about those actions. Everything can be redone by talk.' They argue that since the same skills and social knowledge are involved in the creation of both action and accounts of that action, then the researcher has two mutually supporting and confirmatory ways of revealing the underlying system of social knowledge and belief. Marsh *et al.* go on to argue that the best (but not the only) authorities as to what action is and means are the actors themselves. This is not to say that such accounts are in any sense 'true'. Marsh *et al.* demonstrate quite clearly in their multi-method study of football hooligans that the rhetoric and ritualization of aggression do not reflect 'reality' in any documentary sense, but the accounts by the football supporters serve to confer on the football supporter's world structure, meaning and status. 'Hooliganism', rather than being seen as mindless and irrational aggression, can be reinterpreted as rational and rule-bound from the perspective of the 'hooligans'.

Another important aspect of Marsh *et al.*'s (1978) study is that it demonstrates that the social situations or context in which action takes place are fundamental to the analysis of the behaviour, illustrating Spradley's comment above. The social context is not ignored as if it was irrelevant or interfering noise but is crucial to the explanation of behaviour by both the researcher and the actors themselves. For this reason some ethnographers distinguish between 'thick' and 'thin' descriptions. A 'thin' description only details events, whereas a 'thick' description provides an account of the context in which observed actions take place and can be interpreted.

15.3 PROBLEMS IN ETHNOGRAPHY

So much of what is cultural is hidden and is rarely made explicit. It exists between the lines and in the assumptive world of both the researcher and the researched. Parkes (1971: 104), describing the concept of the assumptive world, writes that a person is 'tied to their assumptive world. By learning to recognize and act appropriately within their expectable environment a person makes a life space of their own ... the assumptive world not only contains a model of the world as it is ... it also contains a model of the world as it might be'. Young and

Kramer (1978: 239) describe the assumptive world as 'multidimensional; it includes perceptions of the world, evaluations of its aspects, a sense of relatedness to them, and recurrent demands that they are acted upon. These dimensions interact to generate preferred states of the world and "calls to action".'

Ethnographic approaches present a particular set of problems for the researcher. In the process of trying to understand the assumptive world of individuals and groups we have to try and break free from our own assumptive world or subculture. In the process of description and interpretation there is always a danger that our viewpoint will be ethnocentric. However hard we try, it is difficult to describe or analyse outside our own cultural references and world-view. Culture, of course, includes social background, age, religion and ethnicity. Werner and Schoepfle (1987) suggest that we should keep two separate records: the *journal*, which is the ethnographer's account (i.e. texts that are the product of the ethnographer's mind), and the *transcript* text, which is the product of the respondent's mind. Although the term 'respondent' is used here, it denotes the person providing ethnographic data in whatever form. It is not necessarily interview data as typically implied by that term: it could be text material. Some psychologists often use the generic term 'subjects', but this implies a power relationship between researcher and researched which is questionable. Some ethnographers use the label 'natives', but outside certain contexts this may be equally inappropriate.

Allied to this problem is the reduction of what Werner and Schoepfle (1987) call 'semantic accent' – the confusion of respondents' meanings with the ethnographer's meanings. One word may be the same but the meanings may be different. Therefore we think we know what an individual means when in fact they may mean something very different. Of course, the ethnographer does not always rely on words. The observation of behaviour provides important evidence of a group's perceptions, attitudes and behaviour – the actions of people are the vestigial indicators of attitudes, emotions and intentions. In terms of data collection, the ethnographer is likely to observe the social interactions between people, but he or she is then likely to ask those people what their interpretations of the events/interactions are, and then with these two sets of information synthesize and analyse these interpretations in the context of the ethnographer's knowledge of the interactions.

The attraction of the ethnographic approach is that it reduces the distance from respondents' meanings, understandings and world-view to our own understandings. With each description and analysis we inevitably translate others' meanings and world-views into our language – the language of the social scientist. However hard we try to retain the fidelity and verisimilitude of the original, there is not only a mutation in meaning, but probably also in richness and complexity. This can be illustrated if we think of the problem of research methods which attempt to understand the past.

No historical account can ever capture what is the infinite content of an event. Most of the information generated by an event – whether it is at the individual or group level, or whether it is cognitive, affective or behavioural information – is not recorded. That which is recorded is also only a record of the past and can only be verified through other accounts of the past. Lowenthal (1985) argues that what is now known as the past was not what anyone experienced as the present. There is a sense in which we know the past better than those who experienced it. We have the benefit of hindsight and we know the outcome of the story: 'Knowing the future of the past forces the historian to shape their account to come out as things have done'. Historical knowledge, however well authenticated, is subjective and subject to the biases of its chronicler who is in turn subject to the psychological processes of selective attention, perception and recall. Finally, there is the temporal equivalent of the problem of ethnocentricity. It is very difficult to view and understand the world outside the framework of our twenty-first-century beliefs, values and attitudes.

Writing ethnography in order to capture an authentic 'voice' is a skill. Reference was made above to the pros and cons of the objective and neutral outsider as opposed to the involved insider. Des Stockley, a researcher at the University of Surrey, undertook research on rough sleepers in London (Stockley, 1998; Moore, Canter, Stockley & Drake, 1995). He was able to capture life in 'cardboard city' because he had been homeless himself and while doing the research lived with those sleeping in subways and on benches. When such faithfulness is not possible, then the researcher should at least take a collaborative approach to ethnographic analysis, drawing on the interpretative insights of those who are immersed in the culture of interest.

Writing ethnographic reports or accounts has been subject to debate in recent years. The classic way of writing ethnographic accounts has been to adopt a quasi-scientific approach in which there is an emphasis on the structure of the culture or group, the story is told in the present tense and there is a single authorial voice. There is a growing trend in ethnographic writing, however, to include multiple voices which permit contrasting points of view and convey the complexity of social life. Some researchers have sought to take a more reflexive approach by including their own personal experiences, reactions and attitudes within the account and discuss how they accommodate and reconcile these. For example, Les Back has undertaken research on racism among young males in South London, and in his account includes a discussion about his own feelings on researching what he saw as abhorrent attitudes and the emotional conflicts it caused him (Back, 1993).

There is one further issue about which psychologists need to be aware. In the example cited in Box 15.1, Amparo Lasen (no date: 10) stated: 'I restricted the filming to open spaces where there was less risk of being noticed by the users. Filming and observing people, perhaps covertly, present some problems. First, there are ethical considerations about taking images of users without their permission. Also there is always the possibility of an unfriendly reaction if the person realizes that he or she is being filmed'. The British Psychological Society's *Code of Conduct, Ethical Principles and Guidelines* (September 2004), which was clearly written with conventional experimental research in mind, is not particularly helpful when it comes to research approaches and methods of this kind. It states:

intervention

Psychologists shall normally carry out investigations or **interventions** only with the valid consent of participants, having taken all reasonable steps to ensure that they have adequately understood the nature of the investigation or intervention and its anticipated consequences.

Specifically they shall: …

where it is necessary not to give full information in advance to those participating in an investigation, provide such full information retrospectively about the aims, rationale and outcomes of the procedure as far as it is consistent with a concern for the welfare of the participants.

Box 15.1 Making sense of life on the streets

In the second volume of Philip Pullman's trilogy, his *Dark Materials* (1998), Will Parry is given what is called the 'subtle knife', after which the second volume is named. Will is told that by gently feeling with the tip of the knife, he can detect 'a snag in the empty air….. the smallest little gap in the world'. He can then cut his way through – open a window in the air – and move from one universe to another. Pullman is suggesting that universes coexist in the same space – we cannot see them but they are there, adjacent to 'our universe'. It is the job of the ethnographer to see and make sense of these parallel universes. One of the ways in which these parallel universes become visible is evidenced by people's use of space; they seem to share our space but at the same time they are in another world. People's use of mobile phones mimics in many ways Will Parry's use of his subtle knife; every time people take out their phone in a public place they seem to step into other spaces and universes of interaction. Amparo Lasen from the Digital World Research Centre at the University of Surrey conducted an ethnographic study of mobile phone use in London, Madrid and Paris, examining social action and technology use in the context of culture and place. Lasen's paper illustrates well how the use of technology not only alters the way we interact with others but also changes the way we relate to our surrounding environment.

In Madrid and Paris young mobile phone users are more willing to talk in the middle of the pavement than in London, where streets are mainly transient places; the younger the users, the less they are bothered about being overheard. But Lasen notes that in London mobile phone users seem to create temporary phone zones, improvised open-air wireless phone booths, where several people, unaware of each other, stop in the same place to make a call. Despite the willingness to

(Continued)

Box 15.1 (Continued)

occupy the central spaces in pavements, French users are more exercised by hearing other people's [private] conversations as they feel forced to know things they do not wish to be a party to; mobile phone users seem to forget there are other people around, in other words, they occupy their own universe oblivious to the presence, needs and sensibilities of others. This, of course, extends to the intrusion of ringtones into public spaces; mobile phone sounds, both ringtones and conversations, are a part of the new urban soundscape of public transport, restaurants, cinemas and shops. The technology has led to new behaviours and a changed relationship between people and their physical surroundings. The etiquette of place is continually evolving and can often only be understood by means of ethnographic methodologies (see Lassen (nd)).

15.4 MEASURING QUALITY IN ETHNOGRAPHIC RESEARCH

There is a long tradition of ethnographic research in the social sciences, with many notable studies dating back to the 1920s and the Chicago School of Human Ecology, among them Zorbaugh's (1929) *The Gold Coast and the Slum*, Wirth's (1928) *The Ghetto* and, later, Whyte's (1943) *Street Corner Society*. Park (1967) believed that urban areas and communities constituted large-scale social laboratories and could be studied like any scientific phenomena. Thomas (1993: 16) argues that 'Ethnography ... respects the same basic rules of logic, replication, validity, reliability, theory construction, and other characteristics which separate science from other forms of knowledge'.

How appropriate, though, are these criteria for evaluating the integrity of a piece of ethnographic research? Most of the criteria for evaluating the quality of a piece of research are derived from the quantitative research tradition. These criteria are not always appropriate, or they may need to be translated into a terminology more sympathetic to the epistemology and objectives of action and ethnographic research.

The touchstone of scientific endeavour is reputedly the replicability of the investigation. When one is working within a naturalistic setting with social groups engaged in everyday actions, one cannot guarantee that a research exercise and its results can be repeated. Reality is not stable. As the Greek philosopher Heraclitus argued 2500 years ago, the essence of the universe is change – you cannot step into the same river twice, for the second time it is not the same river. It is doubtful whether you can even step into the same river once as it changes while one is stepping. This would suggest that the object of investigation never *is* because it is always changing into something else.

In ethnographic (and action research) it is impossible to replicate naturally occurring events in all their complexity and their history because the river has flowed on; this does not, however, invalidate the findings. One should remember that many important events take place on unique occasions and for this reason one must separate statistical or scientific **significance** from behavioural significance. The significance of an event is independent of its probability of occurrence. Events are behaviourally significant when something happens which makes a difference to the values and behaviour of the individuals or groups affected, or when behaviour departs significantly from a previous steady state. There have been many one-off events which have brought about behavioural changes for individuals and the communities in which they live. In the absence of replication, multi-method and confirmatory data sources become all the more important.

In experimental psychology the researcher attempts to control as many of the experimental variables as possible. Any change in the dependent variables can be attributed to purposeful manipulation of the independent variables. But in naturalistic or field settings there may only be very limited opportunities for the researcher to manipulate the independent variables, even if this is seen as desirable. Furthermore, the contextual variables such as place and time (what in many experimental situations would be called 'noise') are not only equally likely to have an effect, but one is also interested in them in their own right. They may be an important source of data contributing to the explanation of behaviour.

How does one measure quality? What are the criteria for assessing the quality of ethnographic and action research? One place where we can look is those writings which have sought to identify the criteria for evaluating the quality of qualitative research generally. There is substantial literature on the assessment of qualitative research (Lincoln & Guba, 1985; Spencer *et al.*, 2003); see also Box 15.2.

Box 15.2   Evaluating qualitative research

The National Centre for Social Research, on behalf of the Strategy Unit of the UK Government Cabinet Office, has developed a framework to guide assessments of the quality of qualitative research evaluations (Spencer *et al.*, 2003). The framework is based on four guiding principles, which state that research should be:

1   contributory in advancing wider knowledge or understanding;
2   defensible in design by providing a research strategy which can address the evaluation questions posed;
3   rigorous in conduct through the systematic and transparent collection, analysis and interpretation of qualitative data;
4   credible in claim through offering well-founded and plausible arguments about the significance of the data generated.

(Continued)

Box 15.2   (Continued)

In the light of these principles, researchers and users of research are encouraged to address 18 appraisal questions.

1 How credible are the findings?
2 How has knowledge or understanding been extended by the research?
3 How well does the evaluation address its original aims and purpose?
4 How well is the scope for drawing wider inference explained?
5 How clear is the basis of evaluative appraisal?
6 How defensible is the research design?
7 How well defended are the sample design/target selection of cases/documents?
8 How well are the eventual sample composition and coverage described?
9 How well was the data collection carried out?
10 How well has the approach to, and formulation of, analysis been conveyed?
11 How well are the contexts of data sources retained and portrayed?
12 How well has diversity of perspective and content been explored?
13 How well have the detail, depth and complexity (i.e. richness) of the data been conveyed?
14 How clear are the links between data, interpretation and conclusions – i.e. how well can the routes to any conclusions be seen?
15 How clear and coherent is the reporting?
16 How clear are the assumptions/theoretical perspectives/values that have shaped the form and output of the evaluation?
17 What evidence is there of attention to ethical issues?
18 How adequately has the research process been documented?

15.5 ACTION RESEARCH

Action research marries thinking, research and action in changing things. It emerged specifically from attempts to 'bridge the gap between theory, research and practice' (Holter & Schwartz-Barcott, 1993). Action research does not involve a clear set of steps. Although it can be conceptualized as involving 'looking, thinking and acting' (Stringer, 1999) or 'planning, acting, observing, reflecting' (Kemmis & McTaggart, 1988), this process necessarily involves revision, repetition and changed directions. Action research does not mean a linear process of accumulation of information; it is a dynamic process where research, action, participation and evaluation interact. The participation of those directly involved in a change situation (Hart & Bond, 1995) is one of the key ways in which action research can be distinguished from other approaches such as participant observation: researcher involvement is high for both approaches but in action research *active* participant involvement is also integral, and the relationship of researcher to researched is fundamentally different, in theory, method and practice.

Greenwood and Levin (1988) argue that action research is not applied research as there is no distinction between thought and action. It is not tied to particular social research techniques. Although perhaps mainly associated with qualitative methods there is no reason why quantitative methods cannot be used. According to Greenwood and Levin (1988: 7), the litmus tests for acceptable methods is that the 'the reason for deploying them has been agreed by the action research collaborators'.

Action research initially emerged as a way of providing practical resolution to social problems. Paradoxically its popularity declined in the 1960s as it became heavily identified with radical political activism. During the 1990s, responding to both pragmatic pressures and a discontent and questioning with positivist approaches to social science, it re-emerged. Its popularity is such that its language and approach are often the choice of large and powerful institutions (Gaventa & Cornwall, 2001). One reason for this is the growing importance of evidence-based policy (see Box 15.3).

Box 15.3   Evidence-based policy

Despite John Maynard Keynes' view that 'there is nothing a government hates more than to be well-informed; for it makes the process of arriving at decisions much more complicated and difficult' (Skidelsky, 1992), it has long been recognized that government departments need scientific support for policy and decision-making. While this goes back to the beginning of the twentieth century with the establishment of the UK Medical Research Committee, a forerunner of the Medical Research Council, it was the publication of the Rothschild Report in 1971 that articulated the relationship even more strongly:

> However distinguished, intelligent and practical scientists may be, they cannot be so well qualified to decide what the needs of the nation are, and their priorities, as those responsible for ensuring that those needs are met. This is why applied R&D must have a customer. The customer says what he wants; the contractor does it (if he can); and the customer pays. (Rothschild, 1971: 4, para. 8; 3, para. 6)

The link between research (or, more accurately, research funding) and policy has probably never been stronger as government departments, the research charities and the research councils themselves have seen academic research as an important instrument in social and economic development and policy-making (Solesbury, 2001). Furthermore, there has been 'a commitment to make research not just useful but useable' (Solesbury, 2001: 5).

The 1999 White Paper on *Modernising government* stated that 'This Government expects more of policy-makers. More new ideas, more willingness to question inherited ways of doing things, better use of evidence and research in policy making and better focus on policies that will deliver long-term goals' (Cabinet Office, 1999: Ch. 2, para. 6). Policies need to be informed and developed on the basis of evidence.

(Continued)

Box 15.3 (Continued)

Action research approaches on a national scale are relatively rare. One potential danger of this is that powerful interests use participation instrumentally to achieve their own ends rather than truly allowing for the co-construction of narratives. However, Chambers (1998) suggests that such action research approaches create the possibility of substantial and far-reaching changes, even at a national level. The increasing openness to action research approaches also links with changes in how the policy process itself is viewed (Performance and Innovation Unit, 2001): it is increasingly recognized that traditional models of delivery may not link well with the real world and that successful policy delivery involves a shared and widely held vision and policies that draw on experience of what works.

Bearing in mind the level of participation by stakeholders that is increasingly a hallmark of action research, one of the key issues that emerges and that is rarely explicit around other social science approaches is that of **power**. The possibilities for action research being part of bringing about change are affected by the value systems of the sponsors, their openness to change, willingness to approach the issue openly and the funding arrangements (e.g, how tightly funding is tied to time). Hart and Bond (1995: 10) suggest that in the face of the way in which power differentials have the ability to affect the course of the research, the most important lesson is that 'the process of defining the problem and formulating research questions arising from it needs to be collaborative'.

Looking across the history of action research, it is possible to discern different (albeit overlapping) types. Rapoport (1972) identifies four types – diagnostic, participant, empirical, experimental. Carr and Kemmis (1986) distinguish between three types of action research – technical, practical and emancipatory – with the authors arguing that only the last is 'true' action research. Hart and Bond (1995) distinguish between the *experimental* approach associated with Lewin, the *organizational* approach associated with the Tavistock Institute, the *empowering* approach associated with community development, and the *professionalizing* approach associated with education and nursing. This system provides one useful way of summarizing the history of action research.

1 *Kurt Lewin and the emergence of experimental action research.* Action research was initially developed as 'a form of research which could marry the experimental approach of social science with social action in response to major social problems of the day' (Hart & Bond, 1995. 15). Kurt Lewin (1948) is often considered to be the founder of action research or 'rational social management' as he also called it. Lewin is perhaps best known for exploring the nature of group dynamics and the power of groups, and it was a concern

to understand when groups were most productive that underlay the development of his thinking on action research. Lewin is credited with two well-known maxims that encapsulate key elements of action research: 'nothing is as practical as a good theory' and 'the best way to understand something is to try and change it'.

2   *Organizational action research.* Continuing the industrial focus of Lewin's work the concept of action research was developed in Britain by the Tavistock Institute of Human Relations albeit drawing on psychoanalytic rather than experimental models (Holter & Schwartz-Barcott, 1993). One of the distinctive features of much modern day action research – the involvement of participants – first evolved within research in organizations (Whyte, 1991).

3   *Empowering action research and community development projects.* Community development projects emerged in the UK in 1969 as part of a government programme to explore causes of poverty and other social problems. Research and action were linked in teams of research academics and community workers. This liaison between research and action also emerged in the context of the health services (Hart & Bond, 1995).

4   *Action research in education and nursing.* Action research in relation to the education and nursing professions has emerged as a means of closing gaps between theory and practice, seeing theory emerging from practice, and empowering teachers and nurses as researchers. Latterly of interest in both fields is 'new paradigm' research (Reason, 1988). Here distinctions between researcher and participant can blur to the point of disappearance: 'all who participate are both co-researchers and co-subjects' (Reason, 1988: 1).

Of course this simple classification system cannot remotely do justice to the many and complex ways in which action research has evolved (Reason & Bradbury, 2001a), but it helps to align us to the broad direction of change over the last 70 years or so. As we might expect against this diverse and multidisciplinary background, action research has been carried out in many different areas of social investigation. A recent four-volume overview of action research in theory and practice (Cooke & Wolfram Cox, 2005) provides details of action research in a wide range of domains, including industry, education, organizations, health and social care, the military, international development, community development, disabled communities, and feminist action. Action research has been used in a variety of different cultural settings. One variant of action research – participatory action research – has been particularly associated with cultures where the desire for empowerment and democracy have been paramount (Fals Borda, 2001; Swantz, Ndedya & Masaiganah, 2001).

Action research is sometimes distinguished from other 'action inquiry strategies' such as participatory action research, action learning and action science (Ellis & Kiely, 2005). For our present purposes it is sufficient to note that they each have common threads (noted below) of cycles of action and reflection, intervention and collaboration.

15.6 DISTINGUISHING CRITERIA OF ACTION RESEARCH

What are the distinguishing features of action research? As might be expected from the many roots and fields of application of action research, there is no simple consensus. However, Hart and Bond (1995) draw attention to several different ways of cutting the cake and suggest a useful set of seven criteria that distinguish action research from other approaches. Obviously the exact nature of the criteria will vary depending upon the 'type' of action research involved (see above). It is valuable to identify these criteria in order to guard against the criticism that action research is by definition sloppy or that the label is meaningless.

1 Action research is educative. In the early models of action research re-education was linked with social management. For example, one of the 'social experiments' of Lewin in the context of a scarcity of beef was to explore how American housewives could be encouraged to use tripe instead of beef in their cooking (Lewin, 1943). Latterly the educative focus has moved to 'awareness-raising' and empowering professional groups or oppressed groups. Reason and Bradbury (2001b: 10) say that at its best action research is a process that 'explicitly aims to educate those involved to develop their capacity for inquiry both individually and collectively'.

2 Action research deals with individuals as members of social groups. These may be selected by the researcher or may be self-selecting; they may be closed groups or open to admit participants after the research process has begun.

3 Action research is problem-focused, context-specific and future-oriented. The researcher is directly and immediately involved in a real-life problem situation. 'Problem' does not imply there is anything wrong; it is, rather, about the need for change. Of course, this raises the issue of who identifies the need (e.g. academic or management interests or the group members themselves) and whether the other parties think that there is an issue or problem with which to be involved. These criteria for action research help us understand why action research is not an appropriate framework for comparing different cultures.

4 Action research involves a change intervention. Interventions may be identifiable real-world actions – as in the 'change experiment' of Lewin. In other models of action research the interventions may be less distinct, for example they may consist of changing the way things are discussed or opening up different lines of communication.

5 Action research aims at improvement. This immediately begs the question of who defines what constitutes improvement. In early models of action

research this was generally assumed to be consensual; later models may involve taking into account multiple perspectives and negotiating what this means.

6 Action research involves a cyclical process in which research, action and evaluation (see Box 15.4) are interlinked. Different components may dominate at different stages. Lewin (1948) articulates a cycle of activities that continues to be the crux of action research: a 'cycle of planning, action and fact finding about the result of the action'.

7 Action research is founded on a research relationship in which those involved are participants in the change process. Early models of action research differentiated between the researcher and the researched. Latterly these differentiated roles are more commonly merged or even shared.

Box 15.4   Action research and evaluation

Because organizations are increasingly accountable for their resources, evaluation is increasingly used to (for example) justify funding decisions, continuation of programmes and to assess the success of projects. Often such evaluations are done by 'objective outsiders' at key points in the life of a project or, more commonly, at the end.

Action research provides a very different perspective on evaluation. The process of evaluation is integral to action research. As noted above, 'fact finding as a result of the action' and discerning whether an action has led to an improvement is an integral part of the cycle of ongoing action research activity. Thus evaluation is never a 'bolt-on', rather it is how the ongoing development of the project is generated. Beattie (1991, cited in Hart & Bond, 1995) outlines practical ways in which this ongoing evaluation can be conducted.

Where the evaluation is itself participatory or 'co-produced' it can offer further benefits, for example, building community capacity, networking, providing an opportunity to strengthen and consolidate project achievements, further participation by those involved and an expansion of the criteria for evaluating success (Walker, Lewis, Lingayah & Sommer, 2000).

The focus of evaluation in action research is upon having a positive effect on (improving) the ongoing project rather than proving at the end the negative and positive effects of the project.

It should be clear from this overview of the development of action research that some have seen it as a type of experiment; others as the antithesis of experimental research. Greenwood and Levin (1998) suggest that repeated 'action–reflection–action' cycles of action research actually reflect true scientific method better than conventional social science where thought is separate from action. Conventionally social scientists are often concerned that their research results are reliable and valid. Lincoln and Guba (1985, cited in Stringer, 1999) suggest that researchers should report on the following three criteria to establish the trustworthiness and rigour of their research

- *Credibility*. This is established through prolonged engagement with participants, triangulating multiple data sources, incorporating ways that participants can check accuracy of information and including processes for peer reflection.
- *Transferability*. This is achieved by allowing decisions to be made about other contexts in which the research might be applicable. 'Thick' (i.e. detailed) description assists in identifying other contexts and settings where the research may be applicable.
- *Dependability and confirmability*. This is achieved by providing a clear description of how data have been collected and analysed and helps the readers align themselves appropriately to the raw data.

Greenwood and Levin (1998) suggest specifically in relation to action research that 'the results of an action research process must be judged in terms of the workability of the solutions arrived at. Workability means whether or not a solution resolves the initial problem' (p. 77). Interestingly, McTaggart (2005) argues that action research, rather than rejecting the notion of validity, should expand the concept such that it means meeting criteria of defensibility, educative value, political efficacy and moral appropriateness. Box 15.5 provides an example of an action research project in a policy context. It illustrates the seven criteria of action research noted by Hart and Bond (1995) above.

Box 15.5 Action research in action: addressing environmental inequalities in UK policy (adapted from Chalmers and Colvin, 2005)

The Environment Agency in the UK has recently been exploring the value of action research in fostering evidence-based policy-making in relation to environmental inequality. The Environment Agency is the body with primary responsibility in the UK for improving and protecting the environment and so has to consider how the environment impacts upon human health. In 2002 a two-year project was commissioned, the overall aim of which was to develop a policy position for the Environment Agency on environmental equality. There were several reasons why an action research approach was felt to be inherently suited to addressing this. The Environment Agency wished to learn from the practical experience and knowledge of both Environment Agency staff and external policy-makers, researchers and practitioners who would be involved in implementing any change,

(Continued)

Box 15.5 (Continued)

to be sensitive to processes of organizational change within the Environment Agency and to be enabled to take timely action. An action research perspective thus seemed to provide a credible alternative to linear and rational models of project management more common within the Environment Agency.

The approach to action research taken by the Environment Agency practitioners was adapted from Reason and Bradbury (2001b). In this approach, action research is aimed at worthwhile purposes (environmental justice); it aims to create knowledge that is practically valuable to those who will use it (i.e. Environment Agency staff and external stakeholders); it recognizes the many ways of knowing that reside both within current research understandings (both qualitative and quantitative) and within different stakeholders; participation is central; and finally, the emergent form of action research was thought well suited to being sensitive to, and yet challenging, processes of organizational change in the Environment Agency.

Four main stages made up a single cycle of enquiry.

1 *Framing the research questions.* Policy developments in government and the Environment Agency's directors' thinking clearly located environmental equality issues on the Environment Agency's research agenda.
2 *Gathering the evidence.* Four different groups that varied in their composition, remit and links with wider stakeholders were created. An empirical review of the environmental justice literature was mapped against the knowledge of a range of stakeholders. This in turn shaped the commissioning of research by one of the four teams that analysed the relationship between deprivation and environmental hazards.
3 *Developing a joint policy narrative.* This involved discussions of research results from an early stage by a range of stakeholders. This also involved providing Environment Agency staff with the opportunity to explore and define their commitment to tackling environmental inequalities. Further evidence emerged in this process and in working with other government departments, and over time a policy narrative emerged.
4 *Seeking policy commitments.* A draft policy framework was presented to Environment Agency directors, and several months later, in the context of media attention and the acknowledgement by relevant government departments of their willingness to act, the Environment Agency's policy position was agreed.

In the practitioners' evaluation of this process, firstly, the action research approach was seen to have value in developing the Environment Agency's understanding of environmental inequalities and to have done this through a collaborative form of inquiry that was relatively untried within the Agency. Secondly, the high-level policy commitment within the Environment Agency was matched by developing staff awareness of environmental inequalities. The value of participation was clearly seen, though this was matched by an awareness of the care that is needed when participation is initiated by the powerful. A key challenge emerging from this action research is how to link such 'national' level initiatives with local action research involving deprived communities themselves.

There are particular challenges for students wishing to carry out action research as part of achieving an academic qualification. Completion of projects within a particular time scale that are in some large part to the benefit of the students raises challenges about the relationship of the researchers to the groups of participants with whom they are working. Needing permission to gain access to particular populations may mean that to some extent the researchers have to link with the agenda of powerful groups. Much as the research questions are generated and shaped by the questions and concerns of the researchers and participants in the research, the analytic strategy is also generated in this way: there is no 'how to' manual. The core task in analysis is for researchers, co-researchers and participants to develop agreed ways of documenting the cycles of action and reflection that they have made. Stringer (1999), focusing on community-based action research, provides some guidelines for those writing formal reports, theses and dissertations about translating action research projects into appropriate written outputs. He outlines frameworks that are relevant to interpretative, action-oriented inquiry and explains how and why they differ from more traditional research reports.

The introduction explains the purpose of the research, its focus, the context in which it occurs and details of the participants. It might also usefully contain an overview of and rationale for the way in which the remainder of the report/dissertation is structured. Next, the results section contains accounts that reveal the ways in which participants describe and interpret their experience of the issue studied. Unusually for research reports, this section is not prefaced by a review of the literature. Reserving this for the next chapter rather stresses the priority of the participants in framing the research perspectives. The literature can then be reviewed in the light of these perspectives. Stringer terms the final section of the report 'Contextualization'. Here the differing perspectives presented in the literature review and the results sections are explored and the implications of these for changed policy or practice outlined. Within this format the research procedure and methods sections are included within an appendix so that it is available for scrutiny without potentially distracting from the core presentation of the research results.

15.7 CONCLUSION

Research is a social process and, however hard they try, researchers are necessarily part of a social engagement. Flick (1998: 5) argues that one of the defining characteristics of interpretative research is the integration of the 'perspectives of the participants and their diversity'. While this statement is made with reference to ethnographic research, it is no less relevant to action research. Furthermore, both ethnographic and action research approaches are self-reflexive as they require the researcher to consider their own role and influence within the research process. Our consideration of ethnographic and action research approaches to research has tried to stress that research is not necessarily flawed because of the researcher's involvement: indeed, are we not deluding ourselves into believing these same processes are not operating in other, more conventional research strategies? The reader should now be alert to the dangers of assuming that there is only one appropriate model of scientific activity and one appropriate role for the researcher.

Our brief introduction to ethnographic and action research has examined two approaches that some would consider to be uneasy bedfellows (Reason & Torbert, 2001). While we have tried to make clear important differences between ethnography and action research, a key goal of this chapter has been to demonstrate that alternative approaches are open to the researcher which challenge the more traditional and dominant research strategies associated with empirical positivist assumptions, assumptions which have increasingly been called into question.

15.8 FURTHER READING

Whyte's (1991) and Stringer's (1996) books both give an excellent introduction to action research. The website of the Centre of Action Research in Professional Practice provides access to a detailed range of action research resources (http://www.bath.ac.uk/carpp/papers.htm). Most recently, the four volumes by Cooke and Wolfram Cox (2005) provide an extensive overview of the history of action research as well as a wealth of examples. For detailed 'how to do' accounts of ethnography, Hammersley and Atkinson's (1995), Atkinson, Coffey, Delamont, Lofland and Lofland's (2001) and O'Reilly's (2004) texts are worth consulting. Hobbs and May's (1993) book provides examples of the varied contexts in which ethnographic strategies have been used, but also highlights the difficulties and dilemmas which may emerge when undertaking ethnographic research.

PART 3
DATA TREATMENT

16

Interpretative Phenomenological Analysis

Jonathan A. Smith and Virginia Eatough

16.1   Introduction
16.2   IPA and psychology
16.3   Suitable research questions for IPA
16.4   How many participants?
16.5   Data collection methods
16.6   Stages of analysis
16.7   Writing up an IPA study
16.8   Conclusion
16.9   Further reading

This chapter will describe interpretative phenomenological analysis as a distinctive qualitative approach to psychological research. It will briefly discuss its epistemological orientation and the sorts of research questions to which it can be applied. This will be followed by a description of suitable methods of data collection, in particular the semi-structured interview and how to develop an appropriate interview schedule. A set of guidelines for the stages of analysis will be described in detail using examples. Finally, we will offer some suggestions for how to write up an IPA study.

Key terms

case study	interpretation
cool cognition	interview schedule
double hermeneutic	lifeworld
hermeneutic	meaning-making
homogeneous sample	narrative
hot cognition	phenomenology
identity	semi-structured interviews
idiographic	themes
inductive	

16.1 INTRODUCTION

At the heart of interpretative phenomenological analysis (IPA) is the notion of people as 'self-interpreting beings' (Taylor, 1985). By this we mean that individuals are actively engaged in interpreting the events, objects, and people in their lives, and this interpretative activity is captured by the phrase 'sense-making'. Thus the central concern for IPA is the analysis of how individuals make sense of their lived experiences. It aims to provide a detailed exploration of these personal lived experiences as well as a close examination of how participants make sense of them. The main currency for an IPA study is the meanings particular experiences, states, events and objects have for participants.

phenomenology hermeneutic

Phenomenology and **hermeneutic** inquiry form the dual epistemological underpinnings of IPA. Phenomenology is concerned with attending to the way things appear to us in experience: how, as individuals, we perceive and talk about objects and events. This is in contrast to an attempt either to produce an objective statement of the object or event in itself or to examine the object or event in terms of pre-existing conceptual and scientific criteria. Contemporary hermeneutic inquiry draws attention to how we are interpreting and sense-making individuals. From this perspective, IPA's aim is achieved through interpretative activity on the part of the researcher. This is a familiar and human activity carried out empirically and systematically. Thus, IPA emphasizes that research is a dynamic process with an active role for the researcher in that process. In part, the researcher attempts to assume an insider's perspective (Conrad, 1987), trying to understand what it is like to stand in the shoes of the participant whilst recognizing this is never completely possible. For more on phenomenology, see Moran (2000); for hermeneuetics, see Palmer (1969).

double hermeneutic

Access to the participant's experience depends on, and is complicated by, the researcher's own conceptions, and these processes are necessary in order to make sense of that other personal world through a process of interpretative activity. This is described as a **double hermeneutic** or dual interpretation process in which 'the participants are trying to make sense of their world; the researcher is trying to make sense of the participants trying to make sense of their world' (Smith & Osborn, 2003: 51). 'Reality' as it appears to and is made meaningful for the individual is what is of interest to the IPA researcher, and she or he recognizes her or his dynamic role in making sense of that reality.

It is possible to think of this double hermeneutic in another way as one which combines both an empathic and critical hermeneutics (Ricoeur, 1970). Thus, consistent with its phenomenological origins, IPA aims to understand what an experience, an event, an object is like from the point of view of the person. Yet at the same time IPA can assume distance from the participant, asking interested and critical questions of the accounts: 'What is the person trying to achieve here? Is something leaking out here that wasn't intended? Do I have a sense of something going on here that maybe the person is less aware of?' Both modes of interpretation can be part of sustained qualitative inquiry, and IPA studies will often contain elements of each. Permitting both aspects of inquiry is likely to lead to a richer analysis and do greater justice to the totality of the person's **lifeworld**. In sum, IPA synthesizes ideas from phenomenology and hermeneutics, resulting in a method which is descriptive because it is concerned with how things appear and letting things speak for themselves, and interpretative because it considers there is no such thing as the uninterpreted phenomenon.

lifeworld

16.2 IPA AND PSYCHOLOGY

Interpretative phenomenological analysis locates itself firmly within the discipline of psychology, seeing opportunities for a useful dialogue between the various traditions, which can contribute to the debate as to what constitutes a viable mode of inquiry for psychology. First, IPA's emphasis on sense-making by both participant and researcher means that cognition can be usefully seen as a central analytic concern, and this suggests a compelling theoretical alliance with the dominant cognitive paradigm in contemporary psychology. IPA shares with cognitive psychology and social cognition a concern with unravelling the relationship between what people think (cognition), say (account) and do (behaviour). However, notwithstanding this shared concern, IPA differs when it comes to deciding the appropriate methodology for such questions. Cognitive psychology generally continues to be committed to quantitative and experimental methodology, whilst IPA employs in-depth qualitative analysis. Thus IPA shares with Bruner (1990) a vision of cognitive psychology as a science of meaning and **meaning-making** rather than a science of information processing. See Smith (1996) for more on this.

meaning-making

IPA is one of several closely related approaches described as phenomenological psychology (Smith, 2004). These approaches share a commitment to the exploration of personal lived experience but have different emphases or suggested techniques to engage in this project. For example, Giorgi and Giorgi (2003) describe a method for conducting empirical phenomenological inquiry which aims to ascertain the underlying essential structure of psychological experience. Ashworth (2003a) is particularly interested in identifying the elements of the 'lifeworld' in participants' accounts: selfhood, sociality, embodiment, temporality, spatiality, project, discourse. However, he stresses that these fragments are no more than the 'perspectives or analytical moments of a larger whole which is the situated embodiment of the human individual' (Ashworth, 2003b: 151).

idiographic case study

A particular characteristic of IPA is its commitment to an **idiographic, case study** level of analysis. In contrast to the nomothetic principles underlying most psychological empirical work, IPA is resolutely idiographic, focusing on the particular rather than the universal (Smith, Harré & Van Langenhove, 1995b). In nomothetic studies, analysis works at the level of groups and populations and the researcher can only make probabilistic claims about individuals, e.g. there is an 85% chance that person X will respond in a given way. In idiographic studies, it is possible to make specific statements about those individuals because analyses are derived from the examination of individual case studies. For IPA, these two ways of acquiring knowledge do not require an either/or stance. Rather, it argues for (a) the intensive examination of the individual in her or his own right as an intrinsic part of psychology's remit, and (b) that the logical route to universal laws and structures is an idiographic–nomothetic one (Harré, 1979).

Thus for IPA the analysis always begins with a detailed reading of the single case. One can then write that case up as a case study or can move to an equally attentive analysis of the second case, and so on. Supposing that the analysis is of a group of individuals, a good IPA study will at all times allow itself to be parsed in two different ways – it should be possible to learn something about both the important generic themes in the analysis and the narrative lifeworld of the particular participants who have told their stories. It is the case that, even among qualitative methodologies, IPA is unusual in having this idiographic commitment.

Qualitative research is characterized by epistemological diversity, and recently researchers have begun to reflect on the ways in which the various approaches converge and diverge. Commenting on Elliott, Fischer and Rennie (1999), Reicher (2000) distinguishes between *experiential* research (a focus on understanding, representing and making sense of people's ways of thinking, motivations, actions and so on) and *discursive* research (a focus on the ways in which language constructs people's worlds). At the simplest level, one might say that IPA clearly fits in the former category, while discourse analysis (see Chapter 18) clearly fits in the latter. Yet, IPA recognizes the importance of language in influencing how individuals make sense of lived experiences and then in turn researchers make sense of participants' sense-making. However, IPA would disagree with a claim that language is the sole or primary constructor of reality.

16.3 SUITABLE RESEARCH QUESTIONS FOR IPA

inductive

Interpretative phenomenological analysis not only studies people idiographically, but also emphasizes the strength of an open **inductive** approach to data collection and analysis, what has been referred to as 'big Q' research (Kidder & Fine, 1987). Qualitative research rejects hypotheses in favour of open-ended questions, which for IPA aim to generate (at the minimum) rich and detailed descriptions of the phenomenon under investigation. IPA's concern with the in-depth exploration of the participants' lived experiences and with how they are making sense of those experiences helps define the type of question which is suitable for an IPA study. Below are some examples of the sorts of questions which might guide an IPA project.

- How do people make the decision whether or not to have a genetic test?
- What does jealousy feel like?
- How do people view voluntary childlessness?
- How does redundancy affect the individual's sense of self?
- How do parents manage the challenge of living with an autistic child?

Thus, IPA studies are more often than not concerned with big issues, issues of significant consequence for the participant either on an ongoing basis or at a critical juncture in her or his life. These issues are frequently transformative, often they are about **identity** and a sense of self, because thorough, in-depth, holistic analyses of individual accounts of important experiences or events almost always touch on self and identity. Research questions can be specific and well defined (How does a person decide whether to have a genetic test or not?) or much wider ranging (How does bringing up a child influence a parent's anger expression?) IPA's concern with the participant's sense-making generates questions which can tap into **hot cognition** – those issues in a person's life which are current, emotive and dilemmatic – or those involving **cool cognition** – involving longer-term reflection across the life course. The common thread running throughout IPA studies and the questions they pursue is the meticulous exploration of the lived experience of the participant.

identity

hot cognition
cool cognition

16.4 HOW MANY PARTICIPANTS?

Usually, IPA studies have small sample sizes. The main concern is to do justice to each participant's account (case), and detailed case-by-case analysis is time-consuming. This means that, early on, careful choices have to be made: whether to give an exhaustive and nuanced account about a particular participant's experiences, or to say something more general about a group or specific population. How these questions are answered determines the subsequent methodology and research design. Importantly, not least because of time limitations with most research, it is rarely possible to do both. Having a larger sample size simply because that is more common in psychological studies means that one can end up in the trap of being swamped with data, with the end result being a superficial qualitative analysis.

So how many participants should one include? There is no *right* answer to this question. In part it depends on:

- one's commitment to the case study level of analysis;
- the richness of the individual cases;
- how one wants to compare or contrast cases;
- the pragmatic restrictions one is working under.

Published IPA studies include sample sizes of 1, 4, 9, 15 and more. There seems to have been some convergence in clinical and health psychology postgraduate programmes that six to eight is an appropriate number for an IPA study (Turpin *et al.*, 1997). This gives enough cases to examine similarities and differences between participants, but not so many that one is snowed under by the amount of data generated. With respect to undergraduates wanting to use IPA, three or four participants would seem appropriate. However, it is important that a certain figure or band does not become reified. As we will argue below, in certain situations, a case can be made for a sample size of one; at other times, a comprehensive examination of convergences and divergences within a set of three cases would be the best way to proceed. See Brocki and Weardon (2006) and Reid, Flowers and Larkin (2005) for more on this.

We have recently been arguing the case for a sample size of one (Bramley & Eatough, 2005; Eatough & Smith, in press; Smith, 2004). Psychology has largely passed over the single-person case study (Radley & Chamberlain, 2001; Smith, 1993; Yin, 2003), but we would argue that it is often the logical choice for a psychological understanding of the subjective and richly patterned lived experiences of the person. Of course, if one is submitting work for a degree, then the decision to carry out a single-person case study should be carefully thought through. A high level of commitment and some confidence are required to sustain an exclusive focus on one person, and one needs to be cautious in the selection of the case put under such intense scrutiny. Furthermore, it remains true that some examiners will be uncomfortable with a case study approach. Nevertheless, postgraduate students who pursue this option discover the merit of staying with an absorbing, complex case and attempting to do justice to it in its own right.

There are two key advantages of carrying out a single-person case study. Firstly, a great deal is learnt about that particular person and their lived experiences of the phenomenon under investigation. It is also possible to focus on connections between different aspects of the participant's account. However, Warnock (1987) makes the valuable and insightful point that probing deeper into the particular also takes us nearer to the universal. The study of the individual can illuminate and affirm 'the centrality of certain general themes in the lives of all particular individuals' (Evans, 1993: 8), bringing the researcher closer to noteworthy aspects of the general by connecting the individual unique life with a common humanity.

Typically, IPA researchers aim for a fairly **homogeneous sample**. Very simply, usually it is not helpful to think in terms of random or representative sampling if one is interviewing, for example, six participants. Rather, through purposive sampling IPA studies aim to find a more closely defined group for whom the research question will have relevance and personal significance. How the specificity of a sample is defined can depend on a number of factors; the subject matter to be investigated may define the boundaries of the relevant sample (e.g. if the topic is rare). Alternatively, if the topic is more commonplace the sample may be made up of individuals with similar demographic/socio-economic status profiles.

In this respect, the IPA researcher is emulating the social anthropologist who carries out ethnographic research in one particular community. The anthropologist provides detailed descriptions and commentary about that particular culture but does not profess to say something about all cultures. Over time, later studies can investigate other groups and generalization becomes possible through a steady accumulation of similar cases (Hammersley, 1992; Smith, Harré & Van Langenhove, 1995b). Researchers can also think in terms of theoretical rather than empirical generalizability. Theoretical propositions can be refined and modified through comparison with other cases, other conceptual claims in the extant literature, and the personal and professional experience of the researcher or reader. The strength of the IPA study is then evaluated in terms of the insights it gives concerning the topic under investigation.

However, it must be remembered that a pragmatic approach to these issues is essential. Inevitably, the research sample selects itself in the sense that potential participants are or should be free agents who choose to participate or not. So it is not unusual to have to adapt or redraw the criteria for inclusion if it transpires that not enough of the originally defined group agree to take part in the study.

16.5 DATA COLLECTION METHODS

IPA studies require a flexible method of data collection, one which gives experience a central place whilst recognizing the multiple influences on any experience: its historical and cultural situatedness, including language and social norms and practices. The vast majority of IPA studies have been conducted on data obtained from face-to-face **semi-structured interviews**, and this method of data collection might be considered the exemplary one for IPA. Chapter 12 provides an overview of the interview in psychological research, and in this section we simply try to give the reader a flavour from the perspective of the IPA researcher. As discussed above, IPA attends to the experiential world of the participant attempting to understand it from the perspective of that person. Thus, an appropriate metaphor for an IPA study is that of the researcher as a traveller who:

homogeneous sample

semi-structured interviews

> wanders along with the local inhabitants, asks questions that lead the subjects to tell their own stories of their lived world, and converses with them in the original Latin meaning of conversation as 'wandering together with'. (Kvale, 1996: 4)

At the same time, the interpretative focus of IPA means that the researcher adopts a probing stance towards the meaningful worlds offered by the participants. This dual focus requires the semi-structured interview for the IPA study to be participant-led in the fullest sense, yet guided by the researcher; and for the researcher to be empathic but also where necessary questioning. Both are needed to produce meaningful and useful theoretical and conceptual accounts of the phenomenon under investigation.

Interviewing is one of the most powerful and widely used tools of the qualitative researcher, and the advantage of the semi-structured format for IPA is that the researcher is, in real time, in a position to follow up interesting, important and even unexpected issues that emerge during the interview. However, it is important not to be exclusionary about this because rich verbal accounts can be collected by other means. For example, participants can be asked to write autobiographical or other personal accounts, to take part in online interviews (Weille, 2002) or to keep diaries over a designated time period (Smith, 1999). See Chapter 13 for more on some of these types of methods.

Semi-structured interviewing lies on a continuum from unstructured to structured, but just what researchers mean by these terms can vary considerably. The IPA researcher develops a set of questions which address the topic of interest, but these are used to guide rather than dictate the course of the interview. If the participant opens up a novel and interesting area of inquiry then this should be pursued. The researcher using a semi-structured format treats people as experiential experts on the topic under investigation (Smith & Osborn, 2003). The aim is to facilitate the giving and making of an account in a sensitive and empathic manner, recognizing that the interview constitutes a human-to-human relationship (Fontana & Fry, 2000).

Box 16.1 presents some illustrative interview questions from a project of the authors on women's experiences of anger and aggression (see Eatough & Smith, in press, for more details). The interviewer starts with a very general question and hopes that this will be sufficient to enable the participant to talk about the topic. Individuals tell their stories with varying degrees of ease, not least because they do not always view them as interesting to an outsider. Starting at the outset with questions about anger and aggression episodes and nothing else might have narrowed down the topic too prescriptively too early, telling us little about how such events influence and shape the totality of their experiences. Starting too quickly with a potentially sensitive topic might also have made the participant uncomfortable and reluctant to talk. We hoped, therefore, that the more open question would enable both participant and researcher to relax into the interview and to begin establishing trust and rapport. However, it is important to realize that there are no fixed rules about these decisions – they must be made in the context of the particular topic being discussed and the particular type of person being interviewed.

Box 16.1 Illustrative interview questions

1 Can you tell me about what your life was like as a child and when you were growing up?

  Prompt: might want to focus child/teenager/young adult family/school/college/work relationships

  Follow-on: What about more recently?

2 Can you tell me about times when you've been angry when you were growing up?

  Prompt: maybe focus on particular age points/contexts such as friendship groups, family

    Description/cause/protagonist/actions/affect/cognitive response

  Follow-on: What about more recently?

3 Can you tell me how you have acted on that anger?

  Prompt: focus on age points/contexts

4 Can you tell me what the word 'aggression' means to you?

  Follow-on: Do you think anger and aggression are related in any way?

5 Can you tell me about any times growing up when you have been aggressive?

  Prompt: focus on particular age points/contexts such as friendship groups, family

    Description/cause/protagonist/actions/affect/cognitive response

  Follow-on: What about more recently?

Questions 2 and 5 are more specific and are there to help the conversation where a participant needs more assistance in moving from the general to the more particular. Typically, a successful interview will include both specific and general questions and will move between the two types fairly seamlessly. Constructing an **interview schedule** takes time and thought and will usually require a couple of drafts. Having constructed it, our suggestion is that you learn it by heart so that

interview schedule

at the interview it acts as a mental prompt, if needed, not something to which you are constantly referring.

The interviewer does not have to follow the sequence on the schedule, nor does every question have to be asked, or asked in exactly the same way of each participant. Thus the interviewer may decide that it would be appropriate to ask a question earlier than it appears on the schedule because it follows on from something the participant has just said. Similarly, how a question is phrased, and how explicit it is, will partly depend on how the interviewer feels the participant is responding.

The interview may well move away from the questions on the schedule. It is quite possible that the interview may enter an area that had not been anticipated by the researcher but which is extremely pertinent to, and enlightening of, the project's overall question. Indeed, these novel avenues are often the most valuable, precisely because they have come unprompted from the participant and, therefore, are likely to be of especial importance for her or him. On the other hand, of course, the researcher needs to ensure that the interview does not move too far away from the agreed topic. In essence, you are aiming for a conversational and participant-led style of interviewing that allows the participant's perceptions of and stories about the topic to come to the fore.

It is necessary to tape and transcribe the whole interview, including the talk of the interviewer. Leave a wide enough margin on both sides of the page to make your analytic comments. However, for IPA one does not need the more detailed prosodic features of the talk which are required in conversation analysis (Drew, 2003). Transcription of the tapes is a lengthy process, depending on the clarity of the recording and one's typing proficiency. As a rough guide, allow seven hours of transcription time per hour of interview for the type of transcript required for IPA.

16.6 STAGES OF ANALYSIS

Before we take you through the various analytic stages, it is worth pointing out that the novice qualitative researcher should feel positive about dealing with the data. At the outset it is sometimes difficult to imagine that you will be able to make sense of the many pages of interview material. However, if you are careful, systematic, and *take your time* with each analytic stage, you will begin to develop confidence.

It is useful to think in terms of totally *immersing* yourself in the data, as far as is possible stepping into the participant's shoes. You are aiming to give evidence of the participant's sense-making with respect to the topic under investigation, and at the same time document your own sense-making as the researcher.

The latter involves looking at the data through a psychological lens, making sense of it by applying psychological concepts and theories.

IPA is not a prescriptive approach; rather, it provides a set of flexible guidelines which can be adapted by individual researchers in light of their research aims. This is particularly true when it comes to the analysis. This section describes the analytic steps we went through in the anger and aggression study in order to help the reader see how the analysis unfolds, but this should not be treated as a recipe, the only way of doing IPA. Rather, it is an illustration of one way of doing it. The study is an idiographic in-depth case study which examines one woman's lived experiences of anger and aggression, how she made sense of her emotions and behaviour, and the contexts in which they happened. The interviews were carried out by the second author.

In brief, the analytic stages were as follows.

- Several close, detailed readings of the data were made, to obtain a holistic perspective so that future interpretations stayed grounded within the participant's account.
- Initial themes were identified and organized into clusters and checked against the data.
- Themes were then refined and condensed, and examined for connections between them.
- A narrative account of the interplay between the interpretative activity of the researcher and the participant's account of her experience in her own words was produced.

Here we describe these stages in more detail and give a worked example – see also Smith and Osborn (2003) for another detailed treatment of this process.

Firstly, during transcription, the interviewer kept a record of initial thoughts, comments, etc. It was felt they might be useful to return to and check against later interpretations during the analysis. Then the first transcript was read several times and the left-hand margin used to make notes on anything that appeared significant and of interest. With each reading, the researcher should expect to feel more 'wrapped up' in the data, becoming more responsive to what is being said. The extract in Box 16.2 demonstrates this stage of analysis for a small section of the interview with Marilyn (name changed).

The next stage involved using the right-hand margin to transform initial notes and ideas into more specific **themes** or phrases which call upon psycholog- **themes** ical concepts and abstractions (Box 16.3). Caution is essential at this point, so that the connection between the participant's own words and the researcher's interpretations is not lost. These early stages of analysis require the researcher to be thorough and painstaking.

Box 16.2   First stage of analysis

V: Can you tell me about your life from as far back as you can remember?

First significant memory

M: I think the first memory, memory that I have is when I was six. I can't remember anything before that. It was when my mum and dad divorced. I remember the

Divorce

argument, picturing the argument and my

Physical aggression
Separation from father
Temporary home

dad hitting my mum, erm, then my mum walked out with me and my brother. And we went to live with my auntie for a short while

Second temporary home

and then we moved in with my stepfather's parents for a long while and, erm, in between that time, while they were splitting up type of thing, I was admitted into

Hospitalization – separation
Vague memories of childhood

hospital for tonsillitis, I had my tonsils removed. And erm, it's quite vague really I can't remember a lot about my childhood previous to that and it's quite vague after that until my teens. Erm, I remember my

Mother–brother connection

mum was always with my brother, he was always you know the lad and my mum used

Negative comparison to father

to be like, say that I used to look like my

Mother's dislike of father
Perception of mother's dislike of her

dad and she didn't like me dad so I always thought she didn't like me. What can I remember before, after that. Erm.

V: Do you remember it being happy?

Feels hatred – unspecified
Unhappiness
Unhappiness attributed to mother
Happy child/unhappy child

M: I think ten onwards or perhaps just a bit before ten, er I hated, I wasn't very happy at all, not at all but I think a lot of that was between me and my mum and erm but I think I was a happy child or seemed to everybody else I was a happy child but I wasn't, I think deep down. Erm.

V: So can you tell me about your relationship with your mother, it might be easier to talk about your relationship with your mum as a child.

Mother–brother connection
Brother perfect in mother's eyes

M: Yeah, erm, I mean like I said she was always my brother. I mean my brother could never do anything wrong but I think that was because she was in two minds whether

Box 16.2   (Continued)

	he was my stepfather's. She, I think she'd been having an affair with him and I think she might have thought he was my
Different father from Marilyn	stepfather's and not my real dad's. She used
Comparison to father	to always compare me to my dad in my ways and my looks and my actions and that and it just wasn't, I mean there was never any
Perceived lack of affection	affection. I mean I can't remember ever her
No memories of physical closeness	putting her arm around me and kissing me. Erm, my stepdad he used to but my mum
Father loving/mother not loving	never. My dad was very loving, I remember that, he really was.
	V: Not even as a teenager? Did it improve at all at any time?
Deteriorating situation with mother	**M:** Got worse as a teenager because I started on my own now, on me own and she
Separateness poss. Independence	wanted me to be there for her in a pretty pink
Self-perception – overweight	dress with lovely pigtails and I was too big
Mother's preference for cousin	for that (laughs). And she used to think more
Physical comparison with cousin	of my cousin who was a dainty, she was the same age as me, there were two weeks
Negative comparison – size	between us but she was small, she was
Negative comparison – prettiness	petite you know, prettier looking and I think
Mother–cousin connection	she was more with her, she was how can I
Mother showed more emotion for cousin	say it, she showed her more emotion than she did me. Well, I mean, I've lost myself now.

The next stage consists of further refining the data by establishing connections between the preliminary themes and clustering them appropriately. Ordinarily one would compile themes for the whole transcript before looking for connections and clusters. In Box 16.4 we have shown how this works for a small piece of text so the reader can see how it is done. The clusters are given a descriptive label which conveys the conceptual nature of the themes therein. To help with this, 'imagine a magnet with some of the themes pulling others in and helping to make sense of them' (Smith, 2004: 71). At this point, some of the themes may be dropped, either because they do not fit well with the emerging structure or because they have a weak evidential base.

Box 16.3   Turning initial notes into themes

V: Can you tell me about your life from as far back as you can remember?

M: I think the first memory, memory that I have is when I was six. I can't remember anything before that. It was when my mum and dad divorced. I remember the argument, picturing the argument and my dad hitting my mum, erm, then my mum walked out with me and my brother. And we went to live with my auntie for a short while and then we moved in with my stepfather's parents for a long while and, erm, in between that time, while they were splitting up type of thing, I was admitted into hospital for tonsillitis, I had my tonsils removed. And erm, it's quite vague really I can't remember a lot about my childhood previous to that and it's quite vague after that until my teens. Erm, I remember my mum was always with my brother, he was always you know the lad and my mum used to be like, say that I used to look like my dad and she didn't like me dad so I always thought she didn't like me. What can I remember before, after that. Erm.

Father absent

Lack of stability (home life)

Family absent

Mother–brother bond

Marilyn–father connection

V: Do you remember it being happy?

M: I think ten onwards or perhaps just a bit before ten, er I hated, I wasn't very happy at all, not at all but I think a lot of that was between me and my mum and erm but I think I was a happy child or seemed to everybody else I was a happy child but I wasn't, I think deep down. Erm.

Unhappiness
Unhappiness attributed to mother
Happy child/unhappy child

V: So can you tell me about your relationship with your mother, it might be easier to talk about your relationship with your mum as a child.

M: Yeah, erm, I mean like I said she was always my brother. I mean my brother could never do anything wrong but I think that was because she was in two minds whether he was my stepfather's. She, I think she'd been having an affair with him and I think she might have thought he was my stepfather's and not my real dad's. She used to always compare me to my dad in my ways and my looks and my actions and that and it just wasn't, I mean

Brother perfect in mother's eyes

Negative comparison to father

(Continued)

Box 16.3   (Continued)

there was never any affection. I mean I can't remember ever her putting her arm around me and kissing me. Erm, my stepdad he used to but my mum never. My dad was very loving, I remember that, he really was.

Perceived lack of affection
Lack of physical closeness

Father loving/mother not loving

V: Not even as a teenager? Did it improve at all at any time?

M: Got worse as a teenager because I started on my own now, on me own and she wanted me to be there for her in a pretty pink dress with lovely pigtails and I was too big for that (laughs). And she used to think more of my cousin who was a dainty, she was the same age as me, there were two weeks between us but she was small, she was petite you know, prettier looking and I think she was more with her, she was how can I say it, she showed her more emotion than she did me. Well, I mean, I've lost myself now.

Alienation from mother

Mother's preference for cousin

Negative self–other physical comparison

Mother–cousin bond

Box 16.4   Clustering of themes

Superordinate theme: 'Disconnection from mother'

Mother's connection with other

Mother's preference for cousin
Brother perfect in mother's eyes
Mother–brother bond
Mother–cousin bond

Mother's rejection

Alienation from mother
Perceived lack of affection
Lack of physical closeness
Father loving/mother not loving

Instability

Father absent
Family absent
Lack of stability (home life)

Unhappiness

Unhappiness
Unhappiness attributed to mother
Happy child/unhappy child

Negative comparisons

Negative comparison to father
Negative self–other physical comparison
Marilyn–father connection

In the worked example given here, there is a strong interrelationship between the clusters. In order to emphasize these connections, rather than considering each cluster as a separate superordinate theme, we have regarded them as a set of subthemes nested within a single superordinate theme we have named 'Disconnection from mother'.

More typically, each superordinate theme stands more separately. A final table might comprise a number of superordinate themes. When working with more material, a brief illustrative data extract is usually presented alongside each theme. It is also useful to add identifying information such as interview and page number.

For the researcher, the final superordinate themes are the outcome of an iterative process in which she or he has moved back and forth between the various analytic stages, ensuring that the integrity of what the participant said has been preserved as far as possible. If the researcher has been successful, it should be possible for someone else to track the analytic journey from the raw data through to the end table. As we have done with this study, a single participant's transcript(s) can be written up as a case study. Alternatively, if your study has several participants then each case should be analysed in a similar way to the first case. Then one can look for patterns across the different tables of themes. During this process one is aiming to respect convergences and divergences in the data – recognizing ways in which accounts from participants are similar but also different. For more on this cross case analysis, see Smith and Osborn (2003).

On a practical note, researchers adopt various strategies to organize and condense the themes. For example, clustering the themes can be done on a computer by 'cutting and pasting'. Alternatively, write each theme on a piece of paper and use a large space (e.g. floor or wall) to place them into clusters. This has the advantage of giving a bird's-eye view and makes it easy to move themes around. The final table of themes forms the basis and structure of the write-up of the analysis.

16.7 WRITING UP AN IPA STUDY

narrative

Analysis continues into the formal process of writing up a **narrative** account of the interplay between the interpretative activity of the researcher and the participant's account of her experience in her own words. The aim is to provide a close textual *reading* of the participant's account, moving between description

interpretation

and different levels of **interpretation**, and at all times clearly differentiating the participant's words from the researcher's analysis.

This section briefly illustrates how writing up the analysis involves moving between description and low-level interpretation of the data to a more highly nuanced, interpretative and theoretical level. This quality of moving between levels reflects the multifaceted nature of psychological process and gives qualitative psychology its imaginative force (Smith, 2004). A first-level description may involve producing a rich, full description of the topic under investigation – for example, how anger is experienced by the participant:

> Marilyn's portrayal of what her anger feels like describes an intensely felt emotion which is depicted through images of boiling heat, rage, and the colour red. She feels her anger as transformative.

Enough data should be presented for the reader to assess the usefulness of the interpretations. IPA's iterative process means that the interpretative levels acquire more depth as the researcher moves beyond a description of the phenomenon to interrogating the participant's sense-making. For example, Marilyn attempts to make sense of her anger and aggression by making causal attributions:

> I think a lot of it is hormonal my aggression and things like that.

Here, the researcher can demonstrate a hermeneutics centred in empathy and meaning recollection (Smith, 2004) and is more or less accepting what the participant says at face value. However, the researcher can engage more critically and ask questions of the accounts which the participant might be unwilling or unable to do. At this level, the empathic reading is likely to come first and may then be qualified by a more critical and speculative reflection.

Interpreting the data at a more subtle and conceptual level involves the researcher building an alternative coherent narrative from the messy sense-making of the participant – a messiness which is only revealed when the researcher examines closely what the participant is saying. For example, in the worked example Marilyn says 'My mum was always *with* my brother'. At its simplest level, this can be seen as indicating Marilyn's belief that her brother was her mother's favourite. However, the researcher might want to critically reflect on Marilyn's use of the word *with* and offer a tentative reading that mother and brother have a shared identity that excludes Marilyn and places her outside. To strengthen this interpretation, the researcher can look for examples elsewhere in the data. At a later point, Marilyn says 'I mean like I said she was *always my brother*'. This corroborates the shared identity reading and at the same time pushes the interpretation further: the identification between mother and brother appears to be experienced by Marilyn as not simply shared but merged.

Finally, two broad presentation strategies are possible. In the first, the 'results' section contains the narrative account of the analysis with the researcher's descriptions and interpretations interspersed with verbatim extracts from the transcripts, and the separate 'discussion' examines that analysis in light of the extant literature. A second strategy is to discuss the links to the literature as one presents each superordinate theme in a single 'results and discussion' section. Box 16.5 shows a very short piece from the final write-up of the anger and aggression study. In this case we used the former writing strategy.

Box 16.5   Writing up an IPA study – a brief illustration

Below Marilyn offers an explanation as to why her mother preferred her brother:

I mean like I said she was always my brother [*sic*]. I mean my brother could never do anything wrong but I think that was because she was in two minds whether he was my stepfather's. She, I think she'd been having an affair with him and I think she might have thought he was my stepfather's and not my real dad's. She used to always compare me to my dad in my ways and my looks and my actions and that and it just wasn't, but I mean there was never any affection. I mean I can't remember ever her putting her arm around me and kissing me.

Not only does this extract illuminate the complicated nature of the family nexus, it is a potent display of how Marilyn experiences the relationships. The opening sentence, 'I mean like I said she was always my brother', carries tremendous symbolic force; her mother and brother do not simply have a close bond, rather they have psychologically merged for Marilyn into 'one' person. Similarly, Marilyn and her father have become 'one', and it is a 'one' that is hated by her mother. From Marilyn's perspective, there is a clear division between herself and her father who looked and behaved the same (the old family); and her mother, brother and stepfather (the new family). The affection Marilyn received from her father and stepfather was not enough to compensate for her mother's lack of it.

16.8 CONCLUSION

This chapter has aimed to provide a clear exposition of the theoretical underpinnings of IPA, as well as explaining the practicalities of carrying out an IPA project. IPA is committed to understanding phenomena from the perspective of the individual's lived experiences but recognizes that this is an interpretative process. It attempts to be scientific in being systematic in its procedures, but also involves the application of creative personal skills as part of the endeavour of understanding those participants' experiences. We hope these dual aspects of the approach are both clear to, and resonate with, the reader.

16.9 FURTHER READING

For more on the theoretical basis for IPA, see Smith's (1996, 2004) texts. For detailed descriptions of how to do IPA, see Smith and Osborn's (2003) or Willig's (2001). Discussion of various aspects of the method can be found in Brocki and Wearden (2006) and Reid *et al.'s* (2005) books. There are now many examples of studies using IPA. Here are just a few suggestions. Eatough and Smith (in press) present's a case study from the women's anger and aggression study; Smith (1999) describes identity change during the transition to motherhood. Chapman (2002) discusses the social and ethical implications of changing medical technologies. Golsworthy & Coyle's (1999) paper is concerned with the role of spiritual beliefs in the sense-making process in older adults after the death of their partners. The IPA website gives lots of useful information: http://www.psyc.bbk.ac.uk/ipa

17

Grounded Theory

Karen Henwood and Nick Pidgeon

17.1 Introduction
17.2 Emergent design, flexibility and iteration
17.3 The origin point and use of the prior literature
17.4 Theoretical sampling
17.5 Storage: the research record
17.6 Open coding and constant comparison
17.7 Theoretical memos
17.8 Core analysis I: refining and saturating categories
17.9 Core analysis II: building theory and models
17.10 Writing and evaluating grounded theory studies
17.11 Conclusion
17.12 Further reading

This chapter describes the intellectual background to and methodological strategies of grounded theory, a core approach to qualitative data analysis used within psychology and the social sciences today. We describe how this differs from traditional hypothetico-deductive research, and in particular the flexible and iterative nature of 'emergent design' alongside the core commitments of theoretical sampling and constant comparison. A number of specific data analysis strategies are outlined, including: open coding, memo writing, category refinement, and building conceptual models. The chapter concludes with a discussion of writing and evaluating grounded theory studies.

K ey terms

axial coding	member validation
code and retrieve	open coding
constant comparison	openness of inquiry
disciplinary knowledge	reflexivity
emergent design	relabelling categories
external auditing	researcher categories
fit and work	splitting categories
flexible and iterative	theoretical agnosticism
flow of work	theoretical memos
focused coding	theoretical sampling
indexing system	theoretical saturation
integrating categories	theoretical sensitivity
interpretative thematic analysis	theory-building
member categories	triangulation

17.1 INTRODUCTION

The idea that understanding, explaining and theorizing should be well grounded in the processes and products of empirical inquiry is now well established within social, psychological, health and clinical research. The methodology of qualitative research and analysis which has come to be labelled grounded theory explicitly codifies the ways in which theoretical accounts can be generated through the close and detailed inspection and analysis of qualitative data, in ways that hold a clear relevance to real-world problems and phenomena.

The term 'grounded theory' itself has two interrelated meanings in the literature. Firstly, it refers to a type of theory; specifically, one can talk of a grounded theory when this has been generated from (hence is grounded in) a close inspection and analysis of a corpus of complex qualitative data. Secondly, it refers to a method of analysis; specifically, the commitments and procedures for data analysis first advocated by the sociologists Glaser and Strauss (1967) for achieving this goal, and developed in subsequent years by researchers from a range of social sciences disciplines, particularly in the health and practitioner domains. One of the major reasons why grounded theory has gained contemporary widespread appeal is that it is often read as describing a generic set of techniques for con-

theory-building

ducting and gaining credibility for qualitative inquiry, through **theory-building** from qualitative data. In particular, we view grounded theory as exemplifying some of the core 'strategies' of qualitative inquiry that involve the creative interplay of theory and method during the integrated processes of social research.

Conceptually, grounded theory has an especially long-standing association with the pragmatist and symbolic interaction philosophical traditions which emerged in America in the 1920s and 1930s (see Blumer, 1969). These served to frame several generations of researchers' theorizing, questions and inquiries, especially within social psychology and micro-sociology. The symbolic interaction tradition holds an important historical place in the development of qualitative research practice as it is today, providing an early and coherent alternative to quantitative approaches that measured essential properties of events, objects and people's perceptions of them. Symbolic interactionism presented a case for studies that both explored the activities and interactions involved in the production of meaning, and used these as a platform to illuminate people's complex social worlds.

When grounded theory first emerged on the scene in mainstream UK psychology in the early 1990s, the main focus of methodological discussions was upon how it offered a different approach to quantitative research, and especially the challenge it posed to orthodoxy in the form of the experimental method and quantitative research (Henwood & Pidgeon, 1992). Historically, psychology has privileged the use of experiments, measurement and statistical methods. But in so doing psychological researchers have been denied the opportunities that could be offered to them by a wide variety of naturalistic, real-world and qualitative enquiry methods. Accordingly, grounded theory offers much-needed resources to psychologists wishing to develop their methodological skills in a number of areas: handling and analysis of large volumes of ill-structured qualitative data; conceptual development and theory generation; and **interpretative thematic analysis** of the meanings of qualitative data. These remain equally relevant today, but do have to be viewed in relation to the availability of a far greater range of qualitative methodologies across the social sciences. There has been a rapid expansion in psychologists' familiarity with and proficiency in using qualitative approaches and methods, among them content and thematic analysis, grounded theory, case studies, ethnographic/fieldwork methods, individual interviews and focus groups, participatory and action research, and specialist methods for the analysis of talk and text (such as discourse analysis, narrative analysis and semiotics) as well as use of analysis tools such as computer-assisted qualitative data analysis software (CAQDAS) packages.

interpretative thematic analysis

Among the types of projects and questions addressed by grounded theorists are the following.

1 The meaningful patterns and processes of action, interaction and identity within many different time, space and culturally bounded settings, organizations and other kinds of 'social worlds' – including those of health and illness, adults and children, and public and private spheres.
2 The interpretative analysis of peoples' subjective meanings. These might include actors', participants', patients' and professionals' understandings, phenomenological points of view or perspectives – to characterize either detailed 'structures of experience' or taken-for-granted, routine or skilled knowledge and practices. Linking grounded theory and phenomenology in this way usefully reflects the current situation in health and clinical psychology, and some other health care studies, where interpretative approaches are often used to investigate people's lived experiences and 'lifeworlds'.
3 The complexity, fluidity and multiplicity of meanings and accounts as they relate to social contexts and settings, in order to bring the micro-social, symbolically, textually or discursively organized character of roles, identities, cultures and power relations into view. Grounded theorists often use detailed case studies here, since these provide a resource for the holistic analysis of processes in specific settings.

It is important to note, however, that grounded theory studies have always been part of a broad qualitative and interpretative inquiry tradition. Grounded theory is sometimes inappropriately portrayed, in psychology at least, as being solely associated with the collection and analysis of interview data. Nothing could be further from the truth. Although interviews are indeed the main material of analysis in a range of phenomenologically based studies, the analytic strategies which we go on to describe have been used with a variety of source materials, as illustrated in Box 17.1.

Box 17.1 Materials typically analysed using grounded theory

Transcripts from one-to-one interviews

Transcripts from focus groups

Researcher's notes of interviews or focus groups

Observational field notes (perhaps of an organization or other social setting)

Documentary sources (such as inquiry reports, printed media, historical records)

Secondary interaction or verbal data (television programmes, political speeches)

Accounts of other research studies

Multiple data sources (from any of the above)

17.2 EMERGENT DESIGN, FLEXIBILITY AND ITERATION

As noted earlier, although grounded *theory* indicates a property of a conceptual system (strictly an outcome of research), the term has over time become associated with the *methodological strategies* used to achieve that outcome (a set of **flow of work** processes). The core **flow of work** in a grounded theory study is shown in Figure 17.1. In overall terms the analyst typically works from an initial topic or research question(s), to data gathering, through initial treatment of unstructured materials (using the varied analytic operations listed), possibly more data gathering and analysis, and on to a set of theoretical categories, interpretations, models, and written accounts of theory. This flow is accompanied by a gradual development of the conceptual focus away from local descriptions inherent in the data towards more ordered and analytic (i.e. theoretical) concepts and categories.

Some writings on the topic, often in order to contrast grounded theory with the traditional hypothetico-deductive method common to experimental psychology, describe the general approach as one of classical induction. Certainly the original writings by Glaser and Strauss give this impression. However, a risk here is that grounded theory might then be followed as if it were a prescriptive method – a standardized procedure for guaranteeing 'true' representations of the psychosocial world. Philosophically speaking, theory cannot 'emerge' from or reflect data in any simple manner. Interpretation and analysis are always conducted within some pre-existing conceptual framework brought to the task by the data analyst.

In this respect grounded theory shares some elements with more constructivist interpretative approaches such as discourse analysis (see Chapter 18). This way of thinking about grounded theory also captures more nearly the essential characteristics of its combination of systematic rigour in analysis with the essentially creative and dynamic character of the interpretative research process. For this reason we prefer to use the term 'generation' of theory, rather than discovery, as it more accurately describes both the epistemological *and* practical realities of the approach. In particular, rather than theory being discovered or emerging from a purely inductive process, grounded theory always involves a constant two-way process, a back and forth or 'flip-flop' between raw data and the researcher's emerging conceptualization of that data.

In actual practice, the core processes of generating grounded theory exhibit both linear and iterative qualities. Figure 17.1 illustrates the interrelationships between the core stages, with the flow of intellectual work, in very broad terms, a linear one. The analyst works from an initial topic or research questions towards more ordered analytic (theoretical) concepts and categories. However, in its detailed execution the flow of work is also **flexible and iterative**, reflecting the ongoing 'flip-flop' between data and conceptualization. This also means that research design decisions such as sampling, which aspects of the data to concentrate upon, even the very research question itself, are likely to be emergent (i.e. modified as the analysis proceeds) rather than fixed indelibly in advance.

flexible and iterative

Hence, Figure 17.1 indicates pathways through which the researcher will move from later back to earlier operations as necessary, and as the analysis proceeds. For example, the research question itself, which may only be tacitly understood at the outset of the enquiry, is often sharpened and refined – sometimes changed entirely – by the process of data analysis. In a similar way, a recategorization of codes can follow the development of the emerging theoretical analysis, or a realization by the analyst that initial terms and concepts used do not in fact fit the data in the ways originally assumed. And data analysis may prompt a new round of data collection, in order to check out emerging ideas or to extend the richness and scope of the sample and theory.

It is the intertwining of data gathering and analysis in classical accounts of grounded theory methodology which most clearly distinguishes the approach from the principles and practices of experimental method. Clearly, in the experimental model, if data are being gathered to specifically test prior hypotheses it would be anathema to change the data to fit the hypotheses, since this would undermine the logic of that mode of enquiry. However, in grounded theory the mode of enquiry is quite different. The researcher seeks to work creatively but systematically with rich, relevant and possibly wide-ranging sources of data, so as to *generate* understandings and explanations of the phenomena under investigation that are most plausible and credible in the circumstances.

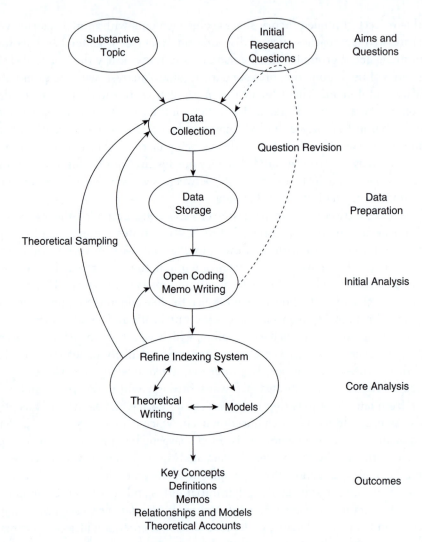

Figure 17.1   The flow of work in grounded theory studies
Source: Pidgeon and Henwood (2004: 631)

17.3 THE ORIGIN POINT AND USE OF THE PRIOR LITERATURE

Figure 17.1 depicts what is, in some ways, an unremarkable design dilemma: envisaging a set of clearly planned choices while simultaneously acknowledging that, because grounded theory research has a contingent and unfolding character (**emergent design**), in the search for appropriate theory, some of those decisions at least are likely to change. It is important to recognize that *all*

emergent design

research projects inevitably have to start from somewhere: and this will involve developing some form of guide, plan or protocol of how the study is designed at the outset, if the researchers' chances of being able to arrive at a successful set of results, interpretations or conclusions are to be maximized. Our own experience of teaching grounded theory to students is that new researchers often struggle to put into practice the ideal (which they readily and enthusiastically glean from the classic writings on the topic) that they should approach fieldwork without any prior preconceptions. In our view this does *not* mean that the prior literature should be ignored when designing and beginning to analyse a grounded theory study (as discussed below).

It would be fair to say that many writings in the grounded theory tradition are less than helpful on, and in some instances muddle, the issues surrounding study origin and (at least initial) research design. Many studies that report adopting a grounded theory methodology are indeed often prompted by quite general research interests at the outset. Initial research goals might be: to identify actors' perspectives on a topic; to investigate social processes or phenomena of interest within their local contexts and settings; to devise explanatory schemes relevant to locally situated, real-world problems; or explore an underresearched topic where a clear gap in existing knowledge exists. The suggestion that *questions* must be developed early on to guide the subsequent course of an investigation brings grounded theory more closely into line with other accounts of qualitative research design and widely read resource books on qualitative methods. All of these caution against the dangers of too loose initial research designs, so as to avoid researchers becoming personally overwhelmed by too much data and studies becoming conceptually diffuse. New researchers, in particular, may be unable to focus sufficiently to provide insights, accounts or explanations of important or relevant issues (or commence effective data gathering) if they do not make explicit what interests them about their chosen topic area, and state these interests as tentative research questions fairly early on in their investigations.

Giving at least some priority to question formation in study design goes beyond the practical issue of asking manageable and answerable questions, but also begins to delimit the conceptual scope of subsequent analysis. By thinking ahead to what is likely to be relevant in a particular topic and investigation, researchers will also be able to deploy their background or **disciplinary knowledge** so as to refine their research questions, avoid merely repeating studies that have been done before, move knowledge and theorizing about a problem or issue forward, and build into projects the capacity to benefit fully from the exercise of **theoretical sensitivity**. Whether this then forecloses upon possible creative insights about the data is a point of issue in the methodological literature on grounded theory.

Embedding projects in background and disciplinary knowledge in order to formulate not just workable but maximally useful research questions early on when designing a study brings the role of the theoretical literature into question. The

disciplinary knowledge

theoretical sensitivity

principle that people new to grounded theory often read into descriptions of the approach – of completely setting aside the literature at the start of the project so as to maintain sensitivity to relevance in the data – is displaced by a more discriminating strategy of using the literature early on in specific ways. We would recommend here using the theoretical literature prior to entering the study to promote clarity in thinking about concepts and possible theory development. Others have advocated an early skimming of the literature to provide a partial framework of local concepts that identify a few main features of the situations that will be studied (actors, roles, organizational goals, etc). This position reflects an awareness that researchers, far from approaching analysis as a *tabula rasa*, sometimes can use a first pass at the existing literature (necessary even if the objective is to address a significant *gap* in that literature), alongside their own existing theoretical sensitivities, to support what might otherwise remain a tacit orientation towards the investigative process. The special counsel that remains within grounded theory is to avoid being tied to particular theoretical positions and key studies in the literature in ways that overly direct ways of looking and stymie the interactive process **theoretical agnosticism** of engagement with the empirical world being studied. **Theoretical agnosticism** is a better watchword than theoretical ignorance to sum up the ways of using the literature at the early stages of the flow of work in grounded theory.

17.4 THEORETICAL SAMPLING

Theoretical sampling is the process of data collection for generating theory whereby the analyst jointly collects, codes, and analyses his [*sic*] data and decides what data to collect next and where to find them, in order to develop his theory as it emerges. This process of data collection is *controlled* by the emerging theory. (Glaser & Strauss, 1967: 45)

theoretical sampling
Grounded theory shares with much qualitative research the use of non-probability sampling and, in particular, the use of **theoretical sampling.** In this respect the aim of sampling is not guided by the overriding need to ensure precisely comparable experimental groups, as in experimental studies, or to generate a demographically representative subset of the population, as in much survey research. Rather, theoretical sampling involves specifying new samples of data as the analysis proceeds, in order to elaborate and build up emerging insights and theory. Typically, one might recognize a clear gap in the initial sample (perhaps a group of individuals with clearly contrasting views to those studied already, or a different context in which the phenomenon of interest might be manifest) which needs to be filled to achieve theoretical closure. For example, in an environmental psychology study of the meanings and values that woodlands and trees hold for people in Wales, the current authors initially convened five community focus groups (Henwood & Pidgeon, 2001). As we wished to access a

broad spectrum of beliefs and values amongst the local community where the study was being conducted (Bangor, North Wales) the overall sample of groups was designed to include a mix of genders, ages and socio-economic group. In effect, this represented a stratified purposive sample. However, once initial coding and memo writing for this set of data had commenced (see also Section 17.7) it became clear that individuals' perceptions of their local environment were dependent upon not only the *physical* nature and extent of woodlands experienced in their locality, but also an area's *social* geography (e.g. with respect to the extent to which Welsh was spoken in the area) as well as whether participants had been born in the area or not. None of these criteria had featured in our sampling decisions at the outset of the study. Accordingly, we decided to extend the study by sampling from four further socially and geographically distinct areas of Wales, giving particular consideration also to explicitly including groups of locally born and incomer residents in the new focus groups.

As this example suggests, subsequent stages of data collection are controlled by the emerging account. This process continues until nothing new is being said about the concepts and ways of theorizing being explored (the analysis reaches 'theoretical saturation'). Theoretical sampling is central to the successful prosecution of an iterative data–theory interaction, and hence the generation of theory. There is now a wealth of guidance upon the types of sample that might be selected on theoretical grounds. Box 17.2 lists some of the most important examples for grounded theorists, many of which would be useful for psychologically based projects.

Box 17.2 Illustrative types of theoretical sampling

1   Extreme or deviant cases (which may prove to be troublesome, counter to, or enlightening in relation to emerging theory)
2   Theory-based selection (elaborates and examines an important theoretical construct)
3   Typical cases (highlights what is average or 'normal', and to avoid claims that theory is grounded in atypical cases)
4   Maximum variation sampling (to encompass the range of variations, or extremes, that emerge in relation to different conditions)
5   Critical cases (which permit maximum application of findings to other cases)
6   Politically important or sensitive cases (as a focus for drawing attention to the findings or study, perhaps for policy purposes)
7   Confirming and disconfirming cases (elaborating initial analysis, seeking exceptions, looking for variation)
8   Stratified purposeful sampling (illustrates subgroups, facilitates group comparisons)
9   Rich response sampling (to provide the richest or most explanatory data sources)

Many grounded theorists would claim that one can only identify truly 'extreme', 'typical', 'sensitive' or 'subgroup' cases through the process of at least some initial data analysis and conceptualization. Similarly, 'maximum variation' is bound up with the principle of theoretical saturation: only through some initial comparative data analysis can the researcher judge whether maximum theoretical variation (or saturation) has been achieved, or alternatively whether new cases need to be sampled to build further theoretical density.

However, the question can also be raised: what guides sampling before the initial emergence of theory begins to prompt theoretical sampling? Here one can argue that initial data collection does not differ from later selection in the need to be guided by relevance and appropriateness. But this needs to be balanced against the very real danger of becoming prematurely locked into a (possibly costly) data collection strategy that does not ultimately yield dense conceptualization. In pragmatic terms, in grounded theory studies it is often appropriate to commence data collection with a small number of 'rich response' cases or sources, such as a key 'gatekeeper' with the most experience of the topic. In other instances initial sampling can be prompted by a first pass at the available literature (albeit disciplined by theoretical agnosticism, and the need to develop a theoretical sampling strategy as data analysis proceeds). In practice, then, research using grounded theory commences inquiry from a number of starting points.

An important final consideration, as shown in Box 17.1, is that grounded theorists treat any relevant medium or combination of media as data. In this respect theoretical sampling can be viewed more generically as the activity that treats 'everything as data'. If the goal is to maximize the possibilities of being able to make conceptual comparisons and developing theorizing through emergent fit, then the researcher must be constantly alert to any data resource that might achieve this.

17.5 STORAGE: THE RESEARCH RECORD

For grounded theory work to proceed, the data must first be assembled in some form of permanent record that allows ready access during analysis. When working from documentary or archival data sources, photocopies have traditionally formed this permanent record (leaving sufficient space in the margins for jotting the theoretical codes generated). Alternatively, with interview, observational or interactional (e.g. focus group) studies tape recordings can be treated as the record (thus preserving a range of paralinguistic features of talk). More typically, though, the full data from taped interviews or other verbal interactions are transcribed verbatim. Transcription itself is highly labour-intensive, taking a minimum of six hours per hour of tape (and significantly longer if interactional or paralinguistic features are also transcribed). However, as Chapter 12 on interviewing notes, transcription is becoming normal practice with much contemporary qualitative research.

A frequent next step in handling each discrete data set (from a single document or interview, say) is to provide it with a label (e.g. indicating date, source and topic). A second is to allocate a numerical reference to segments of the text, typically numbering pages, paragraphs or sometimes lines in the record. The level of coarseness at which this initial segmentation is conducted is, in some respects, a matter of judgement. Our own preference when working manually has always been to segment text into naturally occurring paragraph breaks or, where interaction is involved, into individual turns in talk. There is a sense in which very fine segmentation and subsequent coding (say, at the level of sentences or even individual words) runs the danger of losing sight of overall context, or the contrasts and continuities in individual or group discourses, when text segments are subsequently accessed. Also, too fine a segmentation might restrict the possibility for potentially fruitful multiple codings on a single segment. On the other hand, too large a segment (a page or above) will mean that a code's precise referent in the text may be hard to identify later. The aim here is to provide a systematic labelling system through which any particular segment of raw text can be quickly identified, accessed, compared to other segments, and interrogated on the basis of subsequent coding operations. It can also help in maintaining the anonymity of participants, so is a way of implementing one of the standard ethical practices in the conduct of qualitative research.

It is accordingly no surprise to find that today many CAQDAS packages, such as Ethnograph, HyperResearch, N6 (formerly NUD*IST) Atlas-TI and NVivo, are founded upon the theory generation approach, and some explicitly reference grounded theory as their source of analytic logic. Such software is invaluable where a project involves large and complex data sets, which the analyst needs to organize, sift and sort for complex comparisons and emergent relationships, or for organizing the database for access by teams of researchers. In our experience CAQDAS programs greatly simplify the mechanics of open coding, although this may be outweighed by the effort to properly set up a database in ways that fully exploit a particular program's capabilities. Even more importantly, it is still the researcher who must provide the *interpretative* work which generates the label, and who decides which segments of data to compare. Accordingly, our general recommendation is that such software should be utilized by the beginning grounded theorist only with care.

17.6 OPEN CODING AND CONSTANT COMPARISON

The analytic steps in conducting grounded theory are shown in Box 17.3. Having collected and recorded a sufficient quantity of material, the next task is to build an **indexing system** for the data through 'open' (or 'substantive') coding, as soon as practical after the first round of data collection. The indexing system will subsequently allow the researcher to compare and reorder the data collected as interpretations develop, traditionally by highlighting, cutting, pasting and re-sorting photocopies of documents or transcripts. In the language of CAQDAS analysis

packages, the basic indexing amounts to a **code and retrieve** paradigm. The technique we describe here involves building an indexing system manually on file cards, using the term 'file card' interchangeably to represent both manual and virtual devices.

Box 17.3   Core steps of data analysis

1 Open coding to capture the detail, variation and complexity of the basic qualitative material (sometimes also referred to as substantive coding)
2 Constantly comparing data instances, cases and categories for conceptual similarities and differences (the method of constant comparison)
3 Sampling new data and cases on theoretical grounds as analysis progresses (theoretical sampling) to extend the emergent theory by checking out emerging ideas, extending richness and scope, and in particular to add qualitative variety to the core data included within the analysis
4 Writing theoretical memoranda to explore emerging concepts and links to existing theory
5 Subsequently, engaging in more focused coding (including focused, axial and theoretical coding) of selected core categories
6 Continuing to code, make comparisons, and sample theoretically, until the point at which no new or further relevant insights are being reached (theoretical saturation)
7 Further tactics to move analysis from descriptive to more theoretical levels: for example, grouping or reclassifying sets of basic categories; writing definitions of core categories; building conceptual models and data displays; linking to the existing literature; writing extended memos and more formal theory

---

Open coding proceeds by means of the tentative development and labelling of concepts in the text that the researcher considers of potential relevance to the problem being studied. To construct such a set of codes we start with the first paragraph of the transcript and ask: 'what categories, concepts or labels do I need in order to account for what is of importance to me in this paragraph?' Clearly, the facets of the data that are coded will vary depending upon the aims of the study and the theoretical sensitivities of the researcher. Even when using CAQDAS programs, it is the researcher who must provide the difficult interpretative work which generates the label.

When a label is thought of it is recorded as the header on a file card. A précis of the data of interest, together with a reference for accessing the specific transcript and paragraph, is noted on the card, with the latter filed in a central record box. This initial entry then serves as the first indicator for the concept (or category) described by the card header. Open coding continues by checking whether further potentially significant aspects of the paragraph suggest different concepts (almost certainly they will), and continues in this way with subsequent paragraphs.

At this stage, the labels used may be long-winded, ungainly or fanciful, and they may be formulated at any conceptual level that seems to be appropriate. Indeed, later success in moving the analysis from initial coding on to a greater level of abstraction will depend in part upon choosing an appropriate level of abstraction for the concepts in question. The use of highly particular terms (**member categories** or *in vivo* codes) that are a direct précis of the data will tie the analysis to the specific context of that interview or document. Other terms (**researcher categories**) may refer to more generalized theoretical ideas. A particularly difficult judgement for beginners to make here is the level of coding to be adopted: a common trap is to generate mainly member categories with few researcher categories.

member categories

researcher categories

When conducting open coding it is crucial that the terms should 'fit' the data well – that is provide a recognizable description of the item, activity or discourse under consideration. As coding continues, not only will the list of concepts (and hence store of file cards) rapidly expand, but also concepts will begin to recur in subsequent paragraphs or data segments. For the purposes of subsequent analysis, it is important to recognize that the aim is not principally to record *all* instances of a particular concept, but to record *different* instances which highlight significant variations on that concept. In this way the aim of open coding is to seek similarities and diversities, using the indexing to collect together a range of indicators that point to the multiple qualitative facets of a potentially significant concept. The active flip-flop between the data and the researcher's developing conceptualizations also demands a dynamic process of changing, rechanging and adjustment of terms used where fit can be improved. For example, in a study of adult mother–daughter relationships one of the authors (Henwood, 1993) conducted 60 interviews with mother–daughter dyads. The initial coding led to the development of a long and varied, but highly unwieldy, list of instances under the label 'relational closeness'. The attributes that had been coded on the card were initially glossed as attaching global value to the relationship. However, closer reading and comparison of the individual instances indicated a much more mixed view of the emotional intensity of the relationships, ranging from a welcome but painful sense of gratitude and debt to a stance of hypersensitivity and a desire to flee from a relationship which involved 'confinement' or 'smothering'.

The exercise of coding to explore similarities and differences is basic to implementing the analytic method of **constant comparison**, upon which the generation of grounded theory is founded. The method of constant comparison involves continually sifting and comparing elements (basic data instances, emergent concepts, cases, or theoretical propositions) throughout the lifetime of the project. By making such comparisons the researcher is sensitized to similarities and nuances of difference as a part of the cognitive exploration of the full range and complexity of the data, as well as to further cases to sample. In short, similarities and differences are central to promoting dense conceptual development. Taken together, the commitments of constant comparison and theoretical sampling define the analytic dynamic of the grounded theory process, which involves the researcher, as we have suggested, in a highly interactive and iterative process.

It is particularly important for researchers to be aware of the differences between the practices and aims of coding and analysing data in grounded theory and those of 'objective' coding methods such as content analysis. Content analysis involves arriving at definitive criteria prior to data coding and analysis of the precise categories that will be used (specifically, what they will, and will not, contain). Subsequently, the frequencies with which data units are coded into the categories will be tabulated or analysed statistically. It is assumed that this kind of process will make the quality of the analysis easier to judge as any inferences should be made systematically. This is different to grounded theory since, here, the researcher seeks to develop a meaningful understanding of the data by generating and refining codes and categories (or themes) in the course of data analysis, and uses various strategies to shift that understanding to a more abstract or conceptual level. While it would be possible to use the categories generated by a grounded theory study as the prior coding scheme for a subsequent content analysis study, typically knowledge is built up in a very different way.

The contrast between grounded theory and content analysis is important in highlighting the characteristic features of an interpretative qualitative approach to thematic coding and analysis (Chamberlain, Camic & Yardley, 2004). Such an approach does not assume that meanings inhere within the data or that boundaries between data segments that have been coded similarly are fixed (as is assumed in 'objective' coding methods such as content analysis). Rather, it is assumed that codes or themes that have been identified in the data contain meanings that can be analysed at multiple levels. In interpretative approaches to qualitative thematic analysis there is an important distinction to be made between manifest meanings (viz. observable meanings in the data) and latent meanings (which have to be inferred by the researcher). As latent meanings require referring to other parts of the data to discern what they signify, their analysis involves a process of 'contextualization', a key element of interpretative practice. Analysis of latent meanings is, therefore, a different approach than content analysis, as the latter involves fixing meaning by applying a standardized coding frame to the data.

17.7 THEORETICAL MEMOS

As the list of open codes builds up, some indexed to many incidents across the data corpus, some indexed to few, the analysis begins to involve other operations with the explicit aim of taking conceptual development forward. **Theoretical memos**, in particular, are often stimulated by the intellectual activity of coding, and many researchers build up a separate record system (or 'memo fund') for them. Unlike categories (which have to 'fit' the data), the contents of memos are not constrained in any way and can include: hunches and insights; comments on new samples to be checked out later; deliberations about refinements of file cards; and explanations of modifications to categories. Memos serve both as a means of stimulating theoretical sensitivity and creativity, and as a vehicle for making public the researcher's emerging theoretical reflections. Indeed, memoing can be at the heart of the whole theory generation process, as they provide a publicly available trace of the set of ideas about codes and their relationships as they occur to the researcher. In short, memoing leads naturally to abstraction of theory.

theoretical
memos

Memos can subsequently be used: to discuss the emerging analysis with colleagues; as a part of a 'reflexive account' charting the course of interpretation; as core material during the writing up of the research; or to make connections to the existing literature. Conducting memoing and open coding as parallel operations allows sensitivity to existing literature and theory to be combined with a commitment to grounding in data. In the environmental psychology study mentioned in Section 17.4, our initial coding of the talk about woods and trees was accompanied by a series of short memos noting: firstly, an initial hunch that some individuals were expressing an 'insider' view of the environment; secondly, that such participants also at times resisted having a 'nationalist' discourse imposed on them in the group discussions; and finally, that in places there were clear contrasts between the environmental discourses of ex-city dwellers who had moved into the area from elsewhere, and those of participants who had been born as well as lived in North Wales itself (Henwood & Pidgeon, 2001). These tentative observations in the memos then led to the conclusion that an important conceptual distinction should be made between those members of the community who were locally born and those who could be classed 'incomers'. They also led us to consider the literature from rural studies in Wales, which had previously discussed and categorized such differences in terms of local identity, power and rural economic factors.

Memo writing as an activity is, of course, only one of several ways in which grounded theorists raise the conceptual level, albeit one that is likely to continue throughout the lifetime of a project (as analysis develops, the content will shift from being 'memos on data' to 'memos on memos'). Also, there is no simple distinction one can make between memo writing and the assembly of a final account. The latter (as a first draft to, say, a thesis chapter, research report or journal article) would expect to draw upon some earlier memos, but also to continue with the process of conceptual development started in these early memos. Grounded theories are always provisional and contingent, never complete.

17.8 CORE ANALYSIS I: REFINING AND SATURATING CATEGORIES

Open coding leads to categorization through fragmentation of the data. However, over time the analysis increasingly involves other core activities (see Box 17.3 and Figure 17.1) designed to both raise the conceptual level and (re)construct an orderly theoretical account. The early phases of grounded theory (open coding and initial memoing) can be likened to stepping deeper into a maze, a place of uncertainty (and some anxiety), particularly for the new researcher. During the core analysis phase the researcher has to find suitable routes out of this maze. In this section we briefly discuss a number of strategies we have used for conceptual development.

Alongside further analytic memo writing, core analysis typically involves a refinement of the indexing system through category splitting, renaming and integration, often as a direct product of the application of constant comparison at the level of data (i.e. with respect to instances collected under a single index card or category). As described in Section 17.6, in the adult mother–daughter study an initial category of 'relational closeness' was generated with many entries (Henwood, 1993). Constant comparison of the individual instances subsequently indicated a much more mixed view of the emotional intensity of the range of relationships described on the concept card. This eventually led the researcher to subdivide the concept and entries under two new codes, with the inextricable link between the two concepts resulting from this subdivision retained and coded through their respective labels 'closeness' and 'overcloseness'. This link then became a key stimulus and focus for conceptual development and reflection, in turn mediated by the writing of theoretical memos.

splitting categories
integrating categories
relabelling categories

Operations such as **splitting categories**, **integrating categories** and **relabelling categories** to adjust fit are likely to occur repeatedly during the early phases of the core analysis. However, there comes a point at which the collection and coding of additional data no longer contribute further insights to a specific category or categories; that is, the researcher perceives nothing new – no more conceptual variation – as new data are coded. At this point a category may have become

theoretical saturation

'**theoretically saturated**', to use Glaser and Strauss's term. The researcher's task then is to try to make the analysis more explicit by summarizing why all of the entries have been included under the same label. One way of commencing this process is to write a definition for the concept that explicitly states the qualities that were already recognized in an implicit manner when a new entry was classified.

This is a demanding task (and is typically comparative at the level of both data and concepts), but one which can nevertheless be crucial to the analysis. It often leads to a deeper and more precise understanding of central categories.

Alongside saturation of key categories, the research process also involves category integration – typically, through clarifying the relationships between emerging categories by linking, by reclassifying under higher-level concepts, and by conducting conceptual sorting exercises on both file cards and on theoretical memos. This might eventually involve drawing up various forms of diagrammatic, network or tabular representation. Alternatively, even in this age of computer support, there may be no substitute to sorting paper memos, file cards and concepts into piles, perhaps returning several times to re-sort these, in order to develop a deeper understanding of basic classes and relationships.

Finally, it should be noted that as the indexing system grows, many cards will hold only one or very few instances. This does not necessarily mean such categories are unimportant. However, processes of 'forgetting' (about less relevant cases, instances or categories) are as much a part of the cognitive processes involved in generating grounded theory as is the explicit narrowing of focus upon a set of core or particularly well-saturated categories.

17.9 CORE ANALYSIS II: BUILDING THEORY AND MODELS

Perhaps the most critical stage of the whole analysis comes at the point of theoretical saturation, where the researcher focuses on important core categories (**focused coding**) and relationships between them and more formal theory. In the spirit of theory generation, maximum flexibility in theoretical coding is also desirable here. Glaser, for example, argued that one should think in terms of families of theoretical codes expressing broader social and social-psychological constructs, at differing levels of analysis. A researcher could use any family or combination of such to integrate an account. He lists 18 generic families, 3 examples of which are the 6 Cs (causes, contexts, contingencies, consequences, covariation, conditions), process families (stages, phases, progressions, passages) and identity families (self-concept, social worth, identity loss).

focused coding

Integrating elements of generic social science concepts with those more directly derived from the data is often achieved using models. The simplest of models are skeletal organizing schemata that mainly serve to catalogue the features of codings and categories, and are more implicit in suggesting relationships between them. Many qualitative studies (within and beyond grounded theory) report their findings in this way, and so the usefulness of this simple representational device must not be understated. Models can also depict, explain or otherwise account for time-event sequences, patterns of action and interaction, or 'processes' of (for example) transition and change, typically by assuming some variant of a representational theory of meaning. Visual displays of the relationships and conceptualizations specified in a model are frequently used as devices to immediately convey its particular kind of analytic message (e.g. flow charts, concept maps, matrices, typologies, taxonomies and other sorts of ordering and pattern template diagrams). For example, in a study of the human and organizational preconditions to major industrial accidents and disasters that uses time as one of its central dimensions, Turner and Pidgeon (1997) develop the core analytic category of the 'disaster incubation period'. Here a series of seemingly unrelated events and human errors combine over time to produce an unnoticed unsafe situation. They illustrate this idea through event sequence diagrams which allow the contributory causes and their interactions to be concisely displayed in visual form for any specific case study accident, while at the same time clearly illustrating the processual nature of the higher-level theory.

A further classic example of grounded theory research resulting in an explanatory model is Kathy Charmaz's study of how people with serious chronic illness struggle to have valued lives and selves (Charmaz, 1990, 2000). The study revealed two interrelated issues for studying identities in this context: the role of 'preferred identities' and the development of 'identity hierarchies'. Preferred identity refers to an individual's choice of identities through outlining plans and assessing choices. They symbolize assumptions, goals, hopes, desires and plans for a future that can no longer be realized. The model specifies four different types of preferred identity, and how they also constitute particular levels in an identity hierarchy reflecting relative difficulty in achieving specific objectives and aspirations. Specifically, a 'super-normal identity' refers to an identity demanding extraordinary achievement; a 'restored self' to a reconstruction of previous identities before the illness; a 'contingent' self to a hypothetically possible but uncertain identity because of possible illness progression; and a 'salvaged' self to a retained past identity based on a valued activity or attribute while becoming physically dependent. The explanatory value of the model lies in its portrayal of people's experiences of chronic illness as often resulting in a reduction of identity goals and aiming for a lower level in the identity hierarchy where the illness becomes more debilitating. Living with chronic illness, by this model, means shifting identity goals and aiming for a more or less preferred identity depending upon difficulties primed by the illness.

axial coding

One important means to (re)assemble substantive codes, developed by Strauss and Corbin (1990), involves an intermediate process called **axial coding**. This is both a heuristic analytic device and a theoretical commitment, in that it is closely aligned with a concern for how socio-structural conditions inform interaction and meaning. In essence, they recommend the exhaustive coding of the intersecting properties of core conceptual categories along important dimensions or axes. They also describe axial coding along multi-space typologies, whose axes are defined by the dimensions to important concepts, and the way in which axial coding can be fruitfully used to link socio-structural conditions with contexts and consequences, as well as to elaborate emergent hypotheses.

Our own view is that axial coding is only one amongst many potential pathways to theoretical development (and, indeed, not all psychology projects will be centrally concerned with underlying socio-structural causes of behaviour and meanings), and like any other path is unlikely to guarantee a straightforward or simple route. The most appropriate way of displaying or modelling information, ideas, concepts, processes and events needs to be found for the particular project and the stage it has reached, for its targeted audience, and to reflect the researcher's varied interests in describing, explaining and understanding aspects of the human and social world.

17.10 WRITING AND EVALUATING GROUNDED THEORY STUDIES

One final, interlinked set of considerations remains outstanding. How is the quality of research likely to be judged and by whom? How is it possible to foster informed appreciation and criticism of its credibility, quality or validity? What strategies are best used when presenting study outcomes or findings? While pertinent from the outset, these considerations tend to gain primacy as a project moves towards completion. This is also an important consideration when writing up a grounded theory study. Considerations to be taken into account when doing this are shown in Box 17.4.

Box 17.4 Writing up grounded theory studies

At the outset of the account elucidate the context of the research.

State how sampling decisions were initially made. Did they change over time as the analysis developed?

Document the process of analysis in as transparent a way as possible.

Fully describe and/or define key categories.

What negative examples are there that do not fit the emergent theory?

Try to reflect the complexity of the account (however messy this might seem).

Use diagrammatic, network or tabulated representations to summarize linkages and key concepts.

Document whether respondent validation was attempted, and to what effect.

Document the analytic and personal commitments of the researcher (reflexivity).

Some guidance on these issues can be found in the dedicated grounded theory literature, where they appear as integral to the task of building conceptual schemes and explanatory models out of the core grounded theory operations. Typically notions of 'credibility', 'plausibility' or 'trustworthiness' of qualitative analyses (as viewed both by researchers and readers) are used within their narratives of the ways in which grounded theory projects are brought to a close, and why discovery methods are as important in social inquiry as verificationist ones (rather than being a mere prerequisite to subsequent, more rigorous testing). At the point of theoretical saturation, at which systematic efforts at coding data and constantly making conceptual comparisons no longer produce new insights, and when a high level of conceptual density and integration has been reached, enquirers will deem it appropriate to disseminate their work based on a belief that the account will both fit (provide a recognizable description) and work (be of use to other researchers and

fit and work   practitioners). The terms **fit and work**, as coined by Glaser and Strauss, signal such plausibility and credibility: conveying a strong analytic logic, its underpinnings in the systematic use of data, and a meaningful picture that can be grasped by people (because its theorizations remain grounded in the actions, interactions, symbolism, common-sense knowledge and human experience making up actual social worlds).

Proposed sets of criteria for use in the evaluation of qualitative studies more generally now exist in a number of disciplines, each with slightly different emphases. Tensions still remain in some guidelines. It is not uncommon in some disciplines, for example, for users of grounded theory to interpret the proposal to eliminate 'researcher bias' as signalling the need for researchers to demonstrate credibility of coding schemes by having senior researchers check junior researchers' codes for their 'accuracy', or by calculating inter-rater reliability scores. However, this quantitative technique lacks consistency with the approach of grounded theory and other similar forms of qualitative enquiry that use coding and categorizing where quality concerns are met by demonstrating links between data and conceptualization and, ultimately, the conceptual clarity of categories. As important as it may be to demonstrate credibility of categories and codes, this needs to be done without losing sight of the principle that they should capture the subtlety and complexity of contextual and/or experiential meanings. In some studies, where the stated goal of a study involves illuminating participants' phenomenological experiences and worlds, very tightly formulated conceptualization may be read as overwriting participants' meanings with externally imposed frameworks in overly controlling ways. The technique of

member validation   **member validation** commonly exists in lists of quality criteria for qualitative studies. Demonstrating that the categories derived from the research process are recognizable and acceptable to study participants represents a 'validity' criterion, however, only when there are grounds for believing that participants have special insights into the social worlds and issues under study. More typically, such commentaries work best if they are also treated as additional data.

Two further techniques – external auditing and triangulation – are often also deemed to overlap with quality concerns within grounded theory. **External auditing** can be appropriate where projects attach special importance to the transparency of the definitions of categories or systems of meaning, for example, in multi-site studies, or in multi- or interprofessional working teams. **Triangulation** is feasible to use in studies using multiple sources of observations and data, and can be conceptualized so that practising it is consistent with 'subtle realism' and even constructivist theories of meaning. It is possible to set aside the traditional navigational metaphor (where multiple measurements are taken because a single one would not determine an object's unique position in a dimensional space) and see triangulation as a way of opening up different facets of complex phenomena to view.

external auditing

triangulation

When seeking to build in a concern for research quality in a grounded theory study, it is above all important to bear in mind the key tenets of the approach. **Openness of inquiry** is one such issue, as is the aim of studying the research subject in its full complexity and *in situ*. Taking into account and documenting, as far as possible, the role of multiple perspectives of both the researcher and researched (sometimes referred to as **reflexivity**) is another. Putting these sorts of principles into practice offers its own kind of precision in much of contemporary qualitative inquiry, but especially that which is based on grounded theory.

openness of inquiry

reflexivity

17.11 CONCLUSION

The grounded theory approach provides a set of rigorous and creative strategies and methods for the analysis of diverse kinds of unwieldy, initially unstructured qualitative data. In this chapter we have emphasized how its logic of enquiry is markedly different from the hypothetico-deductive tradition that remains pervasive within many areas of psychology, and which underpins the majority of teaching of undergraduate and postgraduate research methods. We recognize that some writers about grounded theory take a different view, explicating closer parallels with the logic and strategies of quantitative research. More typically, when grounded theory is embraced in psychology, it is as a means of taking forward the interpretative thematic analysis of meanings. As such, it tends to be linked with key concepts that signal the important characteristics of interpretative approaches to qualitative research. Intense intellectual work is involved in grounded theory studies, along with a good deal of uncertainty which has to be channelled productively throughout the research process. The products of such efforts can have high impact when they meet the applied aims of using the approach: intelligibility to research users and interested readers, and relevance to the important practical and policy problems at hand.

17.12 FURTHER READING

The original work on grounded theory, by Glaser and Strauss (1967), is still worthy of a close read. Henwood and Pidgeon (1992) make the general case for using qualitative research – and grounded theory in particular – in psychology. Strauss and Corbin (1997) give good examples of a range of grounded theory projects. Marshall and Rossman's (1999 third edition) text is very useful for help with initial research design questions. Miles and Huberman (1994) give examples of integrating and data display techniques when building theory.

Lincoln and Guba (1985) give a general discussion of qualitative epistemology and approaches. Blumer's (1969) text is a classic on the symbolic interactionist tradition.

Henwood and Pidgeon (2003) explore the notions of coding, memoing and theoretical sensitivity through a closely worked example.

Finally, for a discussion of various software tools for qualitative analysis, see Lee and Fielding's (2004) work.

18

Discourse Analysis

Adrian Coyle

18.1 Introduction

18.2 Discourse analysis: assumptions, approaches and applications

18.3 Sampling discourse

18.4 Techniques of discourse analysis

18.5 Working with data

18.6 Evaluating discourse analytic work

18.7 Problems in discourse analytic work

18.8 Conclusion

18.9 Further reading

AIMS

This chapter aims to provide an account of discourse analysis which attends not only to the practicalities of the approach but also to the assumptions which underpin it. The process of subjecting data to discourse analysis is illustrated through an analytic engagement with some relatively brief data excerpts. Readers should emerge with a basic informed understanding of what discourse analysis involves, together with a critical appreciation of the approach.

Key terms

action orientation
coding
critical discursive psychology
discourses
discursive psychology
epistemology

Foucauldian discourse analysis
functions
positioning
social constructionist
texts
variability

18.1 INTRODUCTION

Discourse analysis is a field of enquiry that traces its roots to various domains such as speech act theory, ethnomethodology, conversation analysis and semiology. It owes a particular debt to post-structuralism which holds as a central tenet that meaning is not static and fixed but is fluid, provisional and context-dependent. However, discourse analysis does not fit easily within any particular disciplinary boundaries. Indeed, it does not even fit within a unitary framework as the term 'discourse analysis' has been applied to diverse analytic approaches that are often based upon different assumptions and have different aims. This makes it difficult to provide an account of the commonalities of discourse analysis except in the broadest terms, and any representation of the field will inevitably satisfy some and irritate others.

The popularization of discourse analysis within social psychology can be dated to the publication in 1987 of Jonathan Potter and Margaret Wetherell's classic text *Discourse and Social Psychology: Beyond Attitudes and Behaviour*. This work urged a radical reformulation of the issues that social psychology has traditionally addressed. Social psychologists have long worked with linguistic and textual material in the form of spoken responses within interview settings and written responses to questionnaire items. The question then arises as to what status should be accorded to this material. It is generally assumed that language is a neutral, transparent medium, describing events or revealing underlying psychological processes in a more or less direct, unproblematic way. The possibility of self-presentational and other biases occurring within this material may be acknowledged, but it is assumed that these can be eradicated or at least minimized by refining methods of generating and collecting data.

18.2 DISCOURSE ANALYSIS: ASSUMPTIONS, APPROACHES AND APPLICATIONS

Within a discursive approach to psychology, language is represented not as reflecting psychological and social reality but as *constructing* it. There are no objective truths existing 'out there' that can be accessed if only the appropriate scientific methods are employed. Instead, language in the form of **discourses** constitutes the building blocks of 'social reality' (note that it is common practice to use inverted commas to draw attention to the constructed nature of taken-for-granted 'things'). The analysis of discourse emphasizes how social reality is linguistically constructed and aims to gain 'a better understanding of social life and social interaction from our study of social texts' (Potter & Wetherell, 1987: 7).

discourses

social constructionist

Discourse analysis can therefore be classed as a **social constructionist** approach to research (although exactly what this means varies across discourse analytic approaches). Social constructionism represents its **epistemology** – its core **epistemology** assumptions about the bases or possibilities for knowledge. In broad terms, the social constructionist perspective adopts a critical stance towards the taken-for-granted ways in which we understand the world and ourselves, such as the assumption that the categories we use to interpret the world correspond to 'real', 'objective' entities (Burr, 2003). These ways of understanding are seen as having been built up through social processes, especially through linguistic interactions, and so are culturally and historically specific (see Box 18.1 for an example).

Box 18.1   The social construction of sexuality categories

The categories 'gay man', 'lesbian' and 'homosexual' are now a taken-for-granted part of how we talk about sexualities. It is easy to forget that defining people in terms of their preference for sexual partners of the same gender as themselves only began in the eighteenth century. Before then there were terms that referred to sexual activity involving people of the same gender but these terms did not denote a particular kind of person. Furthermore, the ways in which these behaviours were socially organized, regulated and responded to varied across cultures. The term 'homosexual' was not coined until the mid-nineteenth century with the increasing medicalization of sexuality. Terms such as 'gay man' and 'lesbian' were only adopted in the 1960s and 1970s in line with the political concerns of the gay liberation and women's movements (for detailed analyses of the social construction of 'the homosexual' up to that point, see Plummer, 1981). And with the postmodern trend within 'queer theory', concepts of 'the gay man' and 'the lesbian' have been subjected to critical scrutiny (Sedgwick, 1990; Simpson, 1996). So, from this one example, it can be seen that there is nothing fixed or inevitable about what may appear to be common-sense ways of representing the world: they are socially constructed.

The emphasis on language as a constructive tool is one of the core assumptions of discourse analysis. The language user is viewed as selecting from the range of linguistic resources available and using these resources to construct a version of events, although not necessarily in an intentional way. The person may not be able to articulate the constructive process in which he or she is engaged, but this does not mean that it does not exist. It simply highlights the extent to which the constructive use of language is a fundamental, taken-for-granted aspect of social life.

Discourse analysis does not use people's language as a means of gaining access to their psychological and social worlds. As Burman and Parker (1993a: 1) have contended, 'Psychological phenomena have a public and collective reality, and we are mistaken if we think they have their origin in the private space of the individual'. Instead, discourse analysis focuses on this 'public and collective reality' as constructed through language use. It examines how people use language to construct versions of their worlds and what is gained from these constructions.

It can be difficult to specify exactly what discourses are because, although they are generally represented as broad patterns of language use within spoken or written material, a variety of meanings have been ascribed to the term. It may be useful to consider various definitions of 'discourse' and of related concepts in order to divine some basic commonalities. Parker (1992: 5) emphasized the constructive potential of discourses and defined a discourse as 'a system of statements which constructs an object'. In their classic text, Potter and Wetherell (1987) preferred the term 'interpretative repertoires' rather than 'discourses' because the idea of 'repertoire' implies flexibility in the ways in which the linguistic components of the repertoire can be put together. They regard these interpretative repertoires as linguistic phenomena which have coherence in terms of their content and style and which may be organized around one or more central metaphors. In a similar vein, Burr (2003: 202) defined a discourse as 'a systematic, coherent set of images, metaphors and so on that construct an object in a particular way'. This definitional survey is hardly exhaustive but, amalgamating these and other related ideas, discourses can be defined as sets of linguistic material that have a degree of coherence in their content and organization and which perform constructive functions in broadly defined social contexts. Different discourses can be invoked to construct any object, person, event or situation in a variety of ways.

texts Discourses are identified through the examination of **texts**. All spoken and written material (and indeed the products of every other sort of signifying practice too) can be conceptualized as a text and subjected to discourse analysis, in the same way that, within traditional scientific paradigms, almost anything can be construed as data and analysed. Indeed, the post-structuralist philosopher, Jacques Derrida (1976: 58), held that 'Il n'y a pas de hors-texte' ('There is no outside-text' or 'There is nothing outside the text'), meaning that everything is part of the context of a signifying system. This raises the question of whether discourse analysts hold that there is a real world outside texts or discourse: we shall return to this issue shortly.

action orientation Discourse analysis assumes that linguistic material has an **action orientation**, that is, that language is used to perform particular social functions such as justifying, questioning and accusing, and it achieves this through a variety of rhetorical strategies. Key tasks that discourse analysts within this action-oriented approach set themselves are to identify what functions are being performed by the linguistic material that is being analysed and to consider how these functions are performed and what resources are available to perform these functions. This entails a close and careful inspection of the text. In this process, some discourse analysts are concerned with the fine grain of talk. These writers tend to adopt and adapt the approaches of conversation analysis in their work (see Atkinson & Heritage, 1984), recursively moving between a micro-level focus on textual detail and a consideration of the rhetorical functions towards which the text is oriented. Generally, though, discourse analysis is concerned more with the social organization of talk than with its linguistic organization. This approach involves looking at what discourses are shared across texts and what constructions of the world the material can be seen as advocating, rather than focusing on the details of how utterances relate to the conversational sequences to which they belong and the interactional work accomplished by these utterances and sequences.

Exploring this issue of different approaches further and returning to a point made at the start of the chapter, it is worth noting that there are two main approaches to the study of discourse within UK psychology. The approach known as **discursive psychology** views language as a form of social action, addresses the social functions of talk and considers how these functions are achieved. It is particularly attentive to the ways by which 'factual accounts' and 'descriptions', which might be interpreted by other research approaches as straightforward 'objective' representations of internal or external psychological and/or social realities, are made to appear as such. Recently, its focus has encompassed linguistic interaction in everyday settings (e.g. Wiggins, 2004) and institutional contexts (e.g. Hepburn & Wiggins, 2005). Discursive psychology is most closely associated with the work of writers such as Jonathan Potter and Derek Edwards (Edwards & Potter, 1992; Potter, 1996). Work conducted within this tradition adopts a thoroughly social constructionist position: writers do not necessarily deny that a material reality exists, but they do not see it as reflected in our language use and they query the possibility of obtaining direct knowledge of material reality.

This approach has been represented as politically limited by other practitioners who are more concerned with issues such as identity and selfhood, ideology, power relations and social change. This perspective has been termed **Foucauldian discourse analysis** as it owes a particular debt to the work of the philosopher Michel Foucault. Writers within Foucauldian discourse analysis see the world as having a structural reality, which they usually describe in terms of power relations; these are viewed as underpinning how we understand and talk about the world (Burr, 2003). The Foucauldian approach holds that discourses 'facilitate and limit, enable and constrain what can be said, by whom, where and when' (Willig, 2001: 107). Hence, dominant discourses privilege versions of social reality that accord with and reinforce existing social structures and the networks of power relations associated with them. Analysts study the availability of discursive resources within a culture and the implications that this carries for those living within that culture. This form of discourse analysis is most closely associated with the work of Ian Parker, Erica Burman and Wendy Hollway (e.g. Burman, 1992, 1995; Burman & Parker, 1993b; Hollway, 1989; Parker, 1992; Parker, Georgaca, Harper, McLaughlin & Stowell-Smith, 1995).

discursive psychology

Foucauldian discourse analysis

As we can see, although Foucauldian discourse analysts agree with the discursive psychology emphasis on the linguistic construction of social reality, one major difference is that they advocate a need to hold on to some idea of language representing things that have an existence independent of language. Parker (1992) has suggested that 'things' should be represented as having different statuses as objects. Some objects are said to exist independently of thought and language – those that are needed for thought to occur (such as our brains and bodies) and around which thinking can be organized (such as the physical and organizational properties of the environment). Yet, we do not have direct knowledge of these objects because thinking is a constructive, interpretative process. Other objects are constructed through language but are treated in language as if they had an enduring reality.

positioning   One feature of discourse analytic research that is associated with Foucauldian discourse analysis is **positioning**, which comes from the work of Davies and Harré (1990). This represents one discursive interpretation of the social psychological concept of identity. When an individual is constructed through discourse, they are accorded a particular subject position within that discourse, which brings with it a set of images, metaphors and obligations concerning the kind of response that can be made. For example, within a biomedical discourse, people who are ill are placed in the subject position of 'the patient', with its obligation to act as a passive recipient of care from those who are placed in the subject position of 'medical expert'. In their linguistic response to that positioning, the individual can accept it (and fulfil the obligations of their position) or they can resist it. Of course, people can also position *themselves* within a discourse and their audience can accept or reject this positioning. Any individual may assume some positions fairly consistently within their talk while other positions are more temporary, giving rise to variability. As Davies and Harré (1999: 35) have commented, the question of 'who one is ... is always an open question with a shifting answer depending upon the positions made available within one's own and others' discursive practices'. Some exponents of Foucauldian discourse analysis have dealt with self and subjectivity by drawing upon particular versions of psychoanalytic theory to introduce into their analyses a notion of the person as motivated and as having agency, that is, as acting upon their environment (Frosh, Phoenix & Pattman, 2003; Parker, 1997). The necessity of invoking psychoanalytic theory to develop analyses of self and subjectivity is, however, open to debate.

critical discursive   In addition to the two approaches outlined so far, a third approach has emerged
psychology   which has been termed **critical discursive psychology** and which attempts to synthesize discursive psychology and Foucauldian discourse analysis. The tenets of this approach are expounded in Margaret Wetherell's (1998) paper, although it can also be seen in action in her work on masculinities with Nigel Edley (e.g. Edley & Wetherell, 1999).

Moving on to consider the issue of research questions, although discourse analysis has been used to investigate a wide variety of research topics, it is only appropriate for the exploration of particular types of research questions. Many research questions from elsewhere in psychology are based on a logic of factors and outcomes, whereas discourse analytic research questions focus on construction, rhetoric, ideology and action (see Box 18.2). With these critical and analytic foci, it is not surprising that discourse analysis has been taken up with enthusiasm by those who wish to give psychology a radical, political edge. Some analysts choose to focus on discourses which reproduce social relations of dominance and oppression and/or which include oppressive aspects that are often glossed over. Discourse analysis can be used to indicate that alternative discourses could be constructed in their place. Yet it is important to acknowledge that the supplanting of oppressive discourses is a complex and lengthy process and there is no way of predicting with confidence what the social implications of discursive change might be.

Nevertheless, the critical and analytic focus counteracts the accusation sometimes levelled at discourse analysis that it is far removed from 'real-life' concerns and threatens psychologists' aspirations to influence practices and policies outside the research domain (Abraham & Hampson, 1996). Given that 'Language (organized into *discourses*) … has an immense power to shape the way that people … experience and behave in the world' (Burman & Parker, 1993a: 1, emphasis in original), discourse analysis *does* have considerable practical potential. Indeed, Willig (1999) produced an edited volume entitled *Applied Discourse Analysis* which demonstrated how discourse analysis can inform social and psychological interventions on issues such as smoking, sex education and psychiatric medication.

Box 18.2 Discourse analytic research questions

Potter (2003) identifies four foci in discourse analytic research questions.

- How specific actions and practices are linguistically done in particular settings. For example, Barnes, Auburn & Lea (2004) explored the question of how people claim citizenship and to what ends by analysing letters of complaint written to council officials concerning the use of rural space by travellers.
- How particular accounts of things are constructed and made to seem factual and objective or how seemingly factual accounts are challenged. For example, Wallwork and Dixon (2004) examined how fox hunting was constructed as a national issue in Britain in pro-hunting newspaper and magazine articles.

(Continued)

- Psychological practice: this involves reframing psychological concepts in discursive terms. For example, Harper (1994) examined the resources used by mental health professionals to construct and identify 'paranoia'.
- Exploitation, prejudice and ideology: this involves examining how racism, sexism, homophobia and other oppressions are expressed, justified or rendered invisible. For example, see Wetherell and Potter's (1992) extensive study of racist language and practice in New Zealand and Forbat's (2005) examination of themes of care and abuse in talk about informal care relationships.

18.3 SAMPLING DISCOURSE

In order to conduct an analysis of discourse, texts are required in which discourses may be discerned. These texts may take many forms. The preferred form of text is a naturally occurring one, although transcripts of interviews (preferably focus group interviews) conducted on the research topic or excerpts from writing on the topic are also acceptable. Accurate transcription is a lengthy process which is made even more laborious if the transcriber wishes to include every 'um' and 'uh' uttered by the speakers and to measure pauses in speech production. This sort of detailed approach is less often seen in discourse analysis than in conversation analysis, although Wooffitt (2001: 328) has rightly observed that 'it is a good methodological practice always to produce as detailed a transcription as possible'.

Within traditional approaches to sampling in psychological research, the emphasis is placed upon securing as large and representative a sample as possible. Within discourse analysis, if interview material is used as a source of data, there is no necessity to sample discourse from a large number of people. If newspaper reports of a particular event are to be used, it is not necessary to collect all reports from all newspapers on that event. The analysis stage of qualitative data is almost always more laborious and time-consuming than the analysis of structured data, so the researcher must beware of ending up with an unmanageable amount of unstructured data to sift through. What is important is to gather sufficient text to discern the variety of discursive forms that are commonly used when speaking or writing about the research topic. This may be possible from an analysis of relatively few interview transcripts or newspaper reports, especially where common discursive forms are under consideration. In this case, larger samples of data add to the analytic task without adding significantly to the analytic outcome. Where an analysis is purely exploratory and the analyst has little idea in advance of what the analytic focus might be, larger samples of data are required.

18.4 TECHNIQUES OF DISCOURSE ANALYSIS

While it is relatively easy to expound the central theoretical tenets of discourse analysis, specifying exactly how one goes about doing discourse analysis is a different matter because there is no rigid set of formal procedures. It has been contended that the key to analysing discourse is scholarship and the development of an analytic mentality rather than adherence to a rigorous methodology (Billig, 1988). The emphasis is placed upon the careful reading and interpretation of texts, with interpretations being backed by reference to linguistic evidence in the texts. The first step is said to be the suspension of belief in what is normally taken for granted in language use (Potter & Wetherell, 1987). This involves seeing linguistic practices not as simply reflecting underlying psychological and social realities but as constructing and legitimating a version of events.

However, one cannot help feeling that a more systematic methodological approach would be beneficial to those entering the field for the first time. It is all very well to suggest that to conduct discourse analysis, one needs to develop 'a sensitivity to the way in which language is used', especially to the 'inferential and interactional aspects of talk' (Widdicombe, 1993: 97), but it is unclear exactly how this sensitivity is developed and systematized. In an attempt to provide some pointers, Potter and Wetherell (1987) suggested a loose ten-stage approach, with two stages devoted to the analytic process. This process begins with what is termed **coding**. By this is meant the process of examining the text closely. With **coding** a large data set, it may be worth using appropriate software to help organize and code the data, such as NVivo (Richards, 2000; Gibbs, 2002). If the research focus has been specified in advance, instances of the research focus are identified at this point. It is worth being as inclusive as possible and noting what appear to be borderline instances of the research focus. This makes it possible to discern less obvious but nonetheless fruitful lines of enquiry. The coding process is more complex if the research focus has not been determined in advance. In this case, it is necessary to read and reread the text, looking for recurrent discursive patterns shared by the accounts under analysis. It is at this stage that Widdicombe's (1993) notion of sensitivity to the way in which language is used is important. Hypotheses about which discourses are being invoked in the text are formulated and reformulated. This can be a very frustrating stage as hypotheses are developed, revised or discarded as the linguistic evidence needed to support them proves not to be forthcoming. It is important that the analyst should remain open to alternative readings of the text and to the need to reject hypotheses that are not supported by the text.

A useful strategy for the next stage of analysis involves reading the text mindful of what its **functions** might be, especially when using a discursive psychology **functions** approach. Any text is held to have an action orientation and is designed to fulfil certain functions, so the question is what functions this text is fulfilling and how it is fulfilling them. The formulation of hypotheses about the purposes and consequences of language is central to discourse analysis. However, identifying the functions of language is often not a straightforward process because these functions may not be explicit. For example, when someone asks you to do something, they may phrase it not as an order or command ('Do the washing up') but as a question to which the expected answer is 'Yes' ('Would you like to do the washing up?')

In seeking to identify discursive functions, a useful starting point is the discursive context. It can be difficult to divine function from limited sections of a text. A variety of functions may be performed and revisited throughout a text, so it is necessary to be familiar with what precedes and follows a particular extract in order to obtain clues about its functions. Although Foucauldian discourse analysts also emphasize context, they mean something quite different by the term. Parker and Burman (1993: 158) have stated that the analyst needs to be aware of broader contextual concerns such as cultural trends and political and social issues to which the text alludes: 'If you do not know what a text is referring to, you cannot produce a reading'.

Another analytic strategy that may be helpful is to examine a text in a situated way, mindful of what version of events it may be designed to counteract. Any version of events is but one of a number of possible versions and therefore must be constructed as more persuasive than these alternative versions if it is to prevail. Sometimes alternative versions will be explicitly mentioned and counteracted in a text, but on other occasions they will be implicit. If analysts are sensitized to what these alternative versions might be, they may be well placed to analyse how the text addresses the function of legitimating the version constructed therein.

In analysing function, it is useful to become acquainted with the ways in which various features of discourse are described in the discourse analytic and conversation analytic literatures. These discursive features frequently perform specific rhetorical functions. Therefore, if analysts are able to identify these features, they can examine the text mindful of the functions that these features typically perform. For example, the use of terms such as 'always', 'never', 'nobody' and 'everyone' may represent what have been called 'extreme case formulations' (Pomerantz, 1986). These take whatever position is being advocated in the text to its extreme and thereby help to make this position more persuasive. For those interested in becoming acquainted with these technical features of discourse, Potter (1996) has outlined a wide range of strategies but the best one is to examine studies which have used discourse analytic and conversation analytic approaches.

According to Potter and Wetherell (1987), one means of elucidating the functions of discourse is through the study of **variability** in any discourse. The fact that discourse varies appears to be a common-sense statement. If we were

variability

analysing discourse from different people about a particular object, we would expect variations related to whether individuals evaluated the object positively or negatively. However, variation also occurs *within* an individual's discourse, dependent upon the purposes of the discourse. Indeed, this was a key feature of Harper's (1994) study of mental health professionals' talk about diagnosing 'paranoia' (see Box 18.2). It has been claimed that, in their search for individual consistency, mainstream approaches to psychology have sought to minimize or explain away intra-individual variation (Potter & Wetherell, 1987). Discourse analysis, in contrast, actively seeks it out. As variability arises from the different functions that the discourse may be fulfilling, the nature of the variation can provide clues to what these functions are. The process of discourse analysis therefore involves the search for both consistency (in the identification of discourses) and variability (in the analysis of discursive functions).

18.5 WORKING WITH DATA

In this section, the practicalities of conducting discourse analysis are explored, taking as an example a study conducted by the author which examined an attempt to construct an alternative to the traditional condemnatory Christian discourse on homosexuality in a workshop for members of a predominantly lesbian and gay church. This discourse is grounded in interpretations of Biblical texts and centres on notions that same-sex sexual activity is sinful and unnatural. One denomination that has tried to counter and reinterpret that is the Metropolitan Community Church (MCC). The majority of MCC's clergy and congregations in Europe and North America are gay or lesbian. This denomination has reinterpreted those Biblical passages that are customarily seen as referring to and condemning homosexual activity and, by extension, gay men and lesbians. The essence of the alternative discourse it offers is that the Bible contains no unequivocal prohibitions against same-sex sexual activity and that a belief in God, the authority of the Bible and homosexuality are entirely compatible. MCC has attempted to propagate its alternative discourse through its congregations and publications and by offering courses and workshops on its Biblical reinterpretations. The following analyses are based on a transcript of one such workshop conducted at MCC in East London by a senior figure in MCC's theological college in Europe, an American who will be referred to as 'David'. The text was obtained through tape-recording and transcribing workshop proceedings, having obtained the permission of the workshop facilitator and participants. Various factors meant that it was only possible to produce a basic transcript of the proceedings.

Given that the workshop ran for an entire day, the transcript of the proceedings was very lengthy. As there was no predetermined analytic focus, this transcript was read and reread closely, looking for broad recurrent discursive patterns. One which was discerned was the establishment of legitimacy or warrant by the facilitator for his reinterpretation of the traditional discourse. As we have noted, the attempt to ensure that one's version of events prevails against competing versions is a common feature of accounts. This aspect of the proceedings was therefore selected as a potentially interesting analytic focus. The analysis that follows is not designed to be comprehensive but, rather, to demonstrate some fundamental aspects of the analytic process in simple terms. It draws chiefly but not exclusively upon a basic discursive psychology approach. Although some positioning is identified, in a text which mostly consists of a monologue (David only took questions from his audience occasionally) it is impossible to demonstrate the cut-and-thrust of positioning where positions are assigned, negotiated and accepted or rejected. For examples of more complete and complex analyses, the reader is referred to the journals *Discourse & Society*, *Discourse Studies* and the *British Journal of Social Psychology* and to the discourse analytic research articles that have already been cited. In the extracts of text that are cited in the following analysis, empty square brackets indicate where material has been omitted.

The principal strategies that David used during the workshop to establish warrant were positioning himself as an expert through expositions of his scholarship; positioning himself as a benign teacher or guide; tales of his personal experiences with the traditional discourse; and assurances of his honesty. These were juxtaposed and interwoven to create a powerful cumulative warranting effect.

At several points during the workshop, David emphasizes his Biblical scholarship, particularly his skills in Biblical languages. For example, at different points he says:

> What I'm going to say to you has very sound academic structure – foundation. I don't intend to overwhelm you with the academics of it which can be quite boring. I do have the academic background and the study in the original languages to support what I'm going to say.

> The Bible was written in ancient languages. The Old Testament is written in Hebrew with some Aramaic in the Book of Daniel and one of the other prophets. The New Testament is written in Greek – in koine Greek which was the common language of the people. Greek is a very complex language with balanced clauses and classic literary Greek is great fun to translate which is where I started my Greek studies. The New Testament Greek is sort of common street slang language sometimes and is great fun – the koine Greek.

The use of this strategy establishes credibility and validity specifically for the reinterpretations of Biblical passages that he will expound later and generally for any other pronouncements that he will make (although note that we make no assumptions about whether David used this strategy intentionally). If his views are regarded by his audience as informed opinions, underpinned by scholarship and expertise, they are more likely to prevail than if they are seen as uninformed speculation. However, a heavy emphasis on scholarship may risk alienating the audience if they are made to feel inadequate in comparison or if they assume that what will be said will be 'over their heads'. This possibility is counteracted by the way in which David constructs his learning. He reassures his audience that 'I don't intend to overwhelm you with the academics of it which can be quite boring'. One could draw out his positioning of his audience here by filling in the implied 'to the layperson' at the end of this utterance, which positions David as an expert, the possessor of privileged insight into the material he is about to address.

Within the second extract ('Greek is a very complex language ... the koine Greek'), he also creates the impression that he wears his learning lightly and points to the enjoyment he derives from it. The juxtaposition of the account of the complexity of classic literary Greek (complete with the introduction of the quasi-technical term 'balanced clauses') and the description of it as 'great fun' further stresses David's scholarship. Note how the notions of complexity and fun are accompanied by terms of emphasis ('very complex', 'great fun'). Their presence draws attention to the possibility that these notions are carrying out important work in this extract. Whatever the public perception of classic literary Greek might be, it is unlikely that fun features significantly. While it takes a high level of intellectual capacity to become proficient in as complex a language as Greek, one would imagine that an even more rarefied level of operation would be required to find it 'fun'. Note also how the range of David's learning is stressed here. Not only is he skilled in 'classic literary Greek' but also in the 'common street slang language ... the koine Greek', which is again described as 'great fun'. Mark the judicious use of the technical term 'koine Greek'. David provides a description of what this means, so one could ask what function the use of the technical term serves. It adds nothing in terms of meaning and could easily have been omitted, so it may be seen as performing an explicitly rhetorical function. This is an example of an occasion when the analyst needs to be mindful of potential alternative versions of the text. It may be that the use of the term again stresses David's expertise by giving an example of the privileged knowledge to which he has access. So we can see that in these extracts, David positions himself as an expert and subsequently reinforces that positioning.

Although David bases his warrant largely on his scholarship, he appears to belittle this scholarship at one juncture. However, the way in which he elaborates his point means that he ends up emphasizing his scholarly skills and further reinforcing his position as expert. He says:

At that point there came in hand [ ] a book by an Anglican clergyman called *Homosexuality and the Western Christian Tradition* by Derek Sherwin Bailey. He wrote this as a part of the Wolfenden report and it was published as you see in 1955

> and he was saying only with all the basic academic apparatus that I didn't have and with all of the scholarly qualifications the very same thing that I had discovered and I was quite bowled over by it.

This is a clear instance of variability in the account that David is providing of himself. We have seen how earlier he assiduously emphasized his scholarship, yet here he actively denies it. What clues does this variability provide about the function of this description? Although he underplays his 'academic apparatus' and 'scholarly qualifications', he claims that, independently, he reached the 'very same' conclusions (note the emphasizing 'very') as Bailey. He exalts Bailey's standing by associating him with the Wolfenden report, on which was based the 1967 law reform decriminalizing consensual private sexual activity between men aged over 21 years. This interpretation is founded on an understanding of the context which David is evoking, which underlines how important it is for the analyst to be familiar with the context in which the text under analysis is located. The rhetoric in the extract implies that, underlying whatever formal academic training David has, is an inspired mind that enabled him to reach the same conclusions as such an intellectually esteemed figure as Bailey. His humility at this discovery is conveyed by his reaction to it ('I was quite bowled over by it'). That this reaction is expressed in folksy terms again underlines his construction of himself as an ordinary person. He is thus simultaneously positioned in conflicting ways. The function these positionings serve is to reassure the audience that David possesses the formal scholarship and the creative thinking necessary for the expression of informed opinions, while downplaying any threat that this scholarship may present.

The theme of not overwhelming the audience with scholarship recurs at several points in the text. Having constructed himself as gatekeeper to a privileged realm of knowledge, David proceeds to represent himself as cutting a careful path through academic irrelevancies for the workshop participants. For example, while distributing handouts on principles of Biblical interpretation, he says:

> These are just some basic a basic approach for example. It's very helpful to have access to the original languages either directly or through the work of others. There are very fine books where they are attempting to-to interpret the Greek and the Hebrew in a popular way without overwhelming you with technical things and to have access to that scholarship is very helpful if you can't do it yourself.

This extract constructs the audience as lacking knowledge of and scholarship in Greek and Hebrew and so they need to be directed to popularized texts that will not overwhelm them. Such a positioning is not without risk, as it may appear condescending to the audience who may subsequently resist it. This possibility is offset somewhat by the use of the phrase 'if you can't do it yourself'. Although the audience's lack of knowledge and competence is strongly implied, the use of this conditional phrase hedges the implication to some extent. The extract also implicitly positions David as a knowledgeable and benign teacher or guide, furnishing his audience with the tools necessary for reinterpreting the traditional discourse but not overwhelming them. The way in which a previous extract was constructed tallies with this interpretation of David as teacher:

> The Bible was written in ancient languages. The Old Testament is written in Hebrew with some Aramaic in the Book of Daniel and one of the other prophets. The New Testament is written in Greek – in koine Greek which was the common language of the people.

The extract is constructed in a didactic fashion. It begins with a straightforward statement of 'fact'. David then elaborates this statement in a more specific way, incorporating technical terms ('Old Testament', 'Hebrew', 'Aramaic', 'Book of Daniel') and introducing and explaining a more inaccessible term ('koine Greek').

As Gergen (1989: 74) put it, 'one may justifiably make a claim to voice on the grounds of possessing privileged ... experience'. David invokes this warranting strategy when he uses various powerful rhetorical devices to construct an emotive testimony of his personal involvement in the arguments that he will advance, saying:

> I have a very personal stake in this material. I came out of a church which taught me that God does not love gay and lesbian people – that God condemns us out of hand and it was a very conservative church in the United States. I was married. I have three children. When my wife and I separated the minister who succeeded me at that church used the scriptures to take my children away. I mean to take their minds away convincing them that I was going to go to hell because I'm gay and I haven't seen two of my three children in twelve years and I have a very personal stake in what the Bible says.

The deeply personal emphasis within this extract acts as a counterbalance to any connotations of objectivity that the emphasis on scholarship may have created. This extract sees David's first explicit statement of his sexual identity, which may be viewed as another convention of warrant. He establishes warrant for his deconstruction of the traditional Christian discourse on homosexuality and for the need to offer an alternative discourse because he, as a gay Christian, has suffered personally and grievously at the hands of those who wield the traditional discourse. Furthermore, David's disclosure of his sexual identity positions himself alongside his audience, most of whom had earlier presented themselves as gay or lesbian. This positioning is achieved through the statement 'I came out of a church which taught me that God does not love gay and lesbian people – that God condemns us out of hand'. The clause 'that God condemns us out of hand' restates and emphasizes the point made in the clause 'that God does not love gay and lesbian people'. However, its more important function is that, in replacing 'gay and lesbian people' with 'us', David explicitly presents himself as gay and constructs a commonality of oppression between himself and his audience. The workshop participants are thereby incorporated into his personal testimony of having been oppressed by the traditional discourse, which imparts legitimacy to the need to rework it, not just for David's sake but for the sake of all present.

Powerful though the relating of personal experience may be as a warranting device, it may also have the opposite effect. As a gay Christian, David may be seen as having a vested interest in seeking to alter the traditional Christian discourse on homosexuality. This unspoken version of events is counteracted by a fourth strategy that he uses to establish warrant, namely his self-construction as 'honest David'. He employs this device at the beginning of the workshop and again when discussing a gospel text. At the outset, he says:

> Whatever your questions are if I don't have an answer I won't try to bluff you. I'll tell you I don't know cos I'm not in the business of trying to sell you a bill of goods that I can't support.

Later, he examines two verses from Matthew's Gospel and two from Isaiah which refer to eunuchs. He talks of how these passages have been unjustifiably used by gay apologists to assert that sexual outcasts in general and gay men and lesbians in particular will have their place in the kingdom of heaven. He claims that there is insufficient evidence to support such an assertion, saying:

> It's far more honest to say we're not really sure than to try to sell a bill of goods or try to read into it. [ ] If we could make a case that based on the Isaiah prophecy that these people who were sexual outcasts would be gathered in and we could make that connection and jump to Matthew and then to us it would be wonderful [ ] but if we're really going to be honest it's not there and I don't I don't see an honest connection.

The strategy of taking material that appears to support his argument and rejecting it on the basis of its unjustified interpretation is a powerful warranting device. It suggests that he has not simply amassed material regardless of how tenuously it supports his argument. Rather, it suggests that he has applied his scholarship to Biblical material and has selected those passages that can justifiably be interpreted as indicating that same-sex sexual activity is not prohibited by the Bible. The biblical interpretations that he will offer are thus warranted in advance. David is positioned as a rigorous and honest interpreter, thereby offsetting any accusation of bias in the interpretations that he will provide.

18.6 EVALUATING DISCOURSE ANALYTIC WORK

The discourse analyst is sometimes accused of 'putting words into the mouths' of those whose discourse is being analysed and of unnecessarily complicating apparently straightforward speech acts. Yet, post-structuralist writers, with their contention that meaning is not fixed or stable, have noted how language use may have consequences that the speaker did not intend. For example, in their analysis of talk about community care policies, Potter and Collie (1989) pointed out how the notion of 'community care' invokes a reassuring community discourse, centred on images of neighbourliness, close ties and social support. This poses problems for those who wish to criticize community care, as, in naming it, they end up invoking these positive associations and thereby undermining their arguments. As individuals may not be aware that their language creates such effects, the method sometimes advocated for evaluating qualitative analyses which involves asking those who produced the data to comment on the analyses is inappropriate for discourse analysis. In relation to our analysis here, David might protest 'But I never meant that', yet this does not invalidate the analysis. The analyst is engaged in elaborating the perhaps unintended consequences of the language that was used, tracing the ripples that discourses create in the pool of meaning into which they are tossed.

This does not mean that analysts are free to posit whatever interpretations they please. For discourse analysis to be taken seriously, there must exist criteria which allow the quality of an analysis to be evaluated. Discussions about the evaluation of psychological research generally focus on success in hypothesis testing and concerns about reliability and validity. It is inappropriate to evaluate discourse analytic work within such a framework because discourse analysis is positioned outside this tradition. Criteria such as reliability and validity are based on the assumption of scientific objectivity, which in turn assumes that researcher and researched are independent of each other. With discourse analysis this cannot be the case. Analysts who demonstrate the contingent, socially constructed, rhetorical nature of the discourse of others cannot make an exception for their own discourse. Like the person whose talk or writing they are analysing, analysts construct a purposeful account of their texts, drawing upon their available and acknowledged linguistic resources and ideological frameworks. In the analysis offered in this chapter, factors such as my training as a psychologist, my familiarity with existing work relevant to the research topic and my position as a gay man all influenced the ideological framework which I brought to bear on the analysis – my speaking position. Acknowledging this should not be seen as undermining the analysis because no one can adopt a perspectiveless, utterly 'objective' stance on the world. Instead, it should be seen as part of a process of making research more accountable, more transparent and easier to evaluate.

This reflexivity bridges the chasm that more traditional research approaches create between researcher and researched and makes it impossible to assess an analysis of discourse using traditional evaluative criteria. Yardley (2000) has suggested four alternative criteria for the evaluation of qualitative research, namely sensitivity to context, commitment and rigour, transparency and coherence and impact and importance. With some modifications and caveats, these criteria can assist in the evaluation of discourse analytic work. However, the method of reporting discourse analytic studies potentially provides the most useful means of evaluating them. Alongside interpretations, the analyst should try to present as much of the relevant text as possible, demonstrating how analytic conclusions were reached with reference to the text. Readers can then judge for themselves whether the interpretations are warranted. They can offer alternative readings of the text so that, through debate, coherent and persuasive interpretations can be achieved. The only problem with this is that the submission guidelines of most academic journals make it difficult to present large amounts of raw data in research reports. However, with the advent of the Internet, it should become standard practice for discourse analytic (and other qualitative) researchers to include in their articles the address of a website where they have made their raw data available for inspection.

18.7 PROBLEMS IN DISCOURSE ANALYTIC WORK

Since it was formally introduced to social psychology, discourse analysis has made tremendous strides in terms of its theoretical and conceptual development and its influence on the discipline – and not only on social psychology. Discourse analytic work has also appeared in British journals in health psychology, counselling psychology and developmental psychology, among others. However, it is not without its problems and pitfalls.

One pitfall sometimes seen in the work of novice discourse analysts is the tendency to reify discourse. One sometimes gets the impression that discourses are somehow embedded in the text and that the analyst plays the role of the linguistic archaeologist, simply chipping away the surrounding linguistic material to excavate and reveal the discourses (and, in the case of interview texts, often ignoring their role as interviewer in constructing the texts). As Parker and Burman (1993) have noted, this reifying tendency leads to discourses being represented as static and unchanging. To counteract this, they urge discourse analysts to study the fluctuations and transformations of discourses. Furthermore, the archaeological model of discourse analysis is inappropriate because any discourse analysis involves interpretation by the analyst and is constructed from the analyst's reading of the text. As has already been noted, this means that a discourse analytic report can itself be seen as a text which attempts to construct a particular version of social reality and which can itself be subjected to discourse analysis (to practise using discourse analysis, consider how my analysis of David's language use is itself legitimated).

The discourse analytic stance on personal agency, motivation and intention has also been subject to criticism. Madill and Doherty (1994) have claimed that, despite the refusal of discourse analysis to speculate about what might be going on inside a person's head, the approach is based on an implicit model of the person as an active, creative and strategic user of language, thereby connoting motivation and intention at some level. The idea that language has an action orientation and is performing particular social functions could be interpreted as implying a language user who is motivated to have these functions performed. Yet, these criticisms could be seen as a reflection of the difficulty of escaping from culturally pervasive mentalist discourse when reading a text. Madill and Doherty (1994) have themselves noted that, because discourse analysis says nothing about the 'inner life' of the speaking subject, audiences may tend to fill this gap using familiar mentalist discourse. Also, when presenting discourse analytic research, it is difficult for researchers to avoid producing a text that could not be read as having mentalist implications. It is therefore a relatively simple matter to trawl through studies which lay claim to an agnostic stance on the 'interior world' and find passages which can be read as contradicting this, as Madill and Doherty (1994) have done with the work of Wetherell and Potter. Indeed, in the analysis offered in this chapter, an attentive reader could find many instances where motivation, intention and other mental states and qualities seem to be implied. Pointing this out is not a criticism of discourse analysis *per se*. Rather it acts as a reminder of the continual need to convey clearly the epistemology of the approach and the way in which it constructs the speaking subject.

One notable technical problem within discourse analysis is the difficulty it has in dealing effectively with some data that are not spoken or written. While photos and other visual images *can* be treated as text and examined, it is more difficult to incorporate gestures, facial expressions and analogous non-verbal data within an analysis in a way that accords these data equivalent status to verbal data. There may in the past have been insufficient motivation to develop strategies for analysing such data, given the difficulties of conveying these data and their nuances in printed journal articles or books. The development of online journals and advances in digital technology mean that it is now possible to include sections of relevant footage from interviews or real-life situations in analyses. It is to be hoped that this provides a spur to develop sufficiently sophisticated ways of analysing such data that, where appropriate, the interpretation of spoken data is routinely elaborated by insights gained from the analysis of non-verbal data.

Looking at the discourse analytic field more broadly, the diversity of discourse analysis is also a matter of some concern, especially as positions become entrenched. It remains difficult for psychological researchers to conduct qualitative research and to have this regarded as credible in some quarters of the discipline; discourse analysis, in particular, is still subjected to routine critique (e.g. Archer, 2004; Campbell, 2004). In these circumstances, some discourse analysts may find it difficult to be working within a research approach that is also marked by debate and dissent over some fundamental issues which may further undermine its credibility (see Wetherell, 2001, for an overview of the main areas of debate). The fragmentation of the area can make it difficult for outsiders to understand what discourse analysis is about and what it offers to psychology. Debate and dissent are not undesirable in themselves because new developments and advances can arise from debate conducted in an appropriate spirit. Nevertheless, further coherent attempts at synthesis are required and the outcome of the most notable existing attempt, critical discursive psychology, needs to be further refined in light of lessons learned through its use in exploring a range of research topics.

These problems are not life-threatening for discourse analysis. They merely represent the developmental troubles of a domain which, while no longer in its infancy, still has work to do on its theory and practice. As discourse analytic specialists within psychology extend and refine their ideas and as the body of research work grows as more psychologists from various branches of the discipline turn to discourse, there is every reason to believe that the necessary developmental work will be forthcoming. Indeed, in the relatively short time between the first and current editions of this book, advances have been made, positions clarified and new debates initiated within the field. During this process, it is to be hoped that discourse analysis will continue to develop and to offer a radical challenge to mainstream approaches to psychology.

18.8 CONCLUSION

This chapter has outlined the principles and practicalities of discourse analysis, illustrating the analytic process through an engagement with brief excerpts of data and offering some critical reflections upon the approach. Although it is hoped that some indication has been provided of how discourse analysis might be undertaken, it is also hoped that readers have gained a clear sense of how discourse analysis cannot be treated merely as an analytic technique. Researchers who choose to use discourse analysis also choose to employ a range of assumptions about the social world (although the precise nature of these assumptions will vary according to the type of discourse analysis used) and must ensure that their contextualization of their study (e.g. in a literature review), research questions, analyses and discussion of the implications of the research accord with these assumptions. It is fair to say that, while discourse analysis is perhaps not a research approach for the faint-hearted, nonetheless, for those who can work with text in a sustained, detailed way and who relish the prospect of critically interrogating the 'taken for granted' of social life, it can prove most rewarding.

18.9 FURTHER READING

Potter and Wetherell's (1987) classic text remains the obvious starting point for anyone interested in discourse analysis; it is very readable and broad-ranging. Potter (1996) offers a clear and comprehensive account of the history, epistemology and practicalities of discursive approaches, with many clarifying examples. For an outline of the principles of the other major discourse analytic tradition in the UK, see Parker (1992). Wetherell, Taylor and Yates (2001a, 2001b) books are invaluable to novice analysts as they focus on the process of analysis within different traditions and present a wide range of examples. Willig (1999) provides examples of how different versions of discourse analysis can inform interventions on a range of practical issues, thereby demonstrating how questions about the utility of discourse analytic work can be answered.

19

Principles of Statistical Inference Tests

Chris Fife-Schaw

19.1   Introduction
19.2   Some basic definitions
19.3   What are bivariate statistical analyses?
19.4   Classical bivariate designs
  19.4.1   Experimental designs
  19.4.2   Quasi-experimental designs
  19.4.3   Correlational and observational designs
19.5   Theories and hypotheses
  19.5.1   Theories
  19.5.2   Hypotheses
19.6   Type I and Type II errors
  19.6.1   Type I error
  19.6.2   Type II error
19.7   Probability
  19.7.1   Basic definitions
  19.7.2   One-tailed versus two-tailed tests
  19.7.3   Statistical power
19.8   Parametric versus non-parametric tests
19.9   Choosing a statistical test
19.10 Conclusion
19.11 Further reading

AIMS

This chapter attempts to explain the ideas underlying some commonly used tests with reference to as few formulae as is possible. It aims to explain the logic of common bivariate statistical tests in the hope that when you do look at a statistics text it will make more sense to you.

Key terms

alpha criterion	probability
alternative hypothesis	random sampling
between-subjects design	raw score
bivariate statistical tests	repeated measures
conditions	sample
confounding variables	sampling distribution
critical regions	sampling error
data	statistic
dependent variable	statistical inference
descriptive statistics	statistical power
effect size	statistical significance
hypotheses	substantive significance
independent groups	test statistic
independent variable	theories
inferential statistics	treatments
measurement error	two-tailed test
non-parametric tests	Type I error
null hypothesis	Type II error
one-tailed test	unit of analysis
parameter	variable
parametric tests	within-subjects design
population	

19.1 INTRODUCTION

In a book on research methodology it is not possible to avoid a discussion of statistical techniques or approaches to data analysis. Teachers of statistics around the world know how the topic strikes fear and loathing into the hearts of many a psychology student, yet most of the ideas underlying these analyses are very straightforward. Many people see statistical formulae and assume that they will not be able to understand them, yet the vast majority involve little more than being able to add, subtract, multiply or divide numbers.

In this chapter I will attempt to explain the ideas underlying some commonly used tests with reference to as few formulae as is possible. There is not enough space in this book to provide proper explanations of all statistical tests so you will need to look at a statistics book at some point. However, the aim is to explain the logic of common statistical tests in the hope that when you do look at the statistics text it will make more sense to you. You should make sure you have read Chapter 3 on levels of measurement first, as I will assume you are familiar with these issues. Before looking at any statistical analyses you should be aware of some key concepts that many texts take for granted that you understand.

19.2 SOME BASIC DEFINITIONS

population

The **population** is the collection of all individuals of interest in a particular study. More abstractly it is the set of all 'units' of analysis defined by your problem area: for example, all people resident in the UK, all people with a particular disease, all females, etc.

Unfortunately, the term 'population' is also used in a more specific way to refer to a population of scores. The sample of people you draw upon will provide you with a sample of scores from the population of scores. This can be confusing since the population of scores probably does not exist in any real sense: for example, you get test scores from your sample but as the rest of the population has not taken the test their scores exist only at a kind of abstract, 'as if' level.

sample

A **sample** is a set of individuals selected from a population and intended to represent the population under study. Usually it is impractical to study everybody in your target population so you have to draw a sample. See Chapter 6 for a discussion of sampling issues.

unit of analysis

As psychologists we are interested in people, and this means that for many applications the **unit of analysis** (or case) is the individual respondent or participant. We assign individuals to conditions, say, and measure their responses. You should be aware that statistical tests do not require that the case be a person. The case could be a household or a rat or a stick or anything that could reasonably have data associated with it.

Our measurements or observations are called **data**. A data set is a collection of measurements. 'Data' is the plural of 'datum' and when writing about your data you should talk about 'these data' rather than 'this data' – a pedantic point, but one that journal editors will pick up on.

A **raw score** is an original measurement or observed value (a datum). A value before some form of manipulation has been done. Summaries of raw scores (averages, variance, and the like) are referred to as **descriptive statistics** (see below).

A **variable** is a characteristic or condition that changes or has different values for different individuals (e.g. height, hair colour, score on a test).

A value that describes a population is called a **parameter**. It could be a single measurement (e.g. mean score on a mathematics ability test) or derived from a set of observations *drawn from the population* (e.g. the mean maths score of all females who are above average on an English test). There is a convention in textbooks that population parameters are indicated by using Greek characters (e.g. μ, σ).

A value that describes a sample, on the other hand, is called a **statistic**. This can be a single measurement (e.g. mean maths score of the people in your sample) or derived from a set of observations (e.g. mean score of the females in your sample). Often a statistic is the best estimate you have of a population parameter since you may not be able to 'test' everybody in your target population. All sorts of numerical values that summarize your sample data are statistics. These could be means, medians, percentages, correlations, *t*-values, *F*-ratios, etc.

Inferential statistics are techniques for using sample data to make statements about the population that the sample came from. Most of the time you are interested in using inferential statistical techniques to tell you how justified you are in concluding something about the population based on the data provided by your sample.

Most psychologists collect data from samples of people. We rarely have access to the total population of people who we might have been interested in studying. Suppose, you were conducting an experiment to assess the impact of two teaching methods on mathematical ability in children. You could set up the two teaching schemes in local schools and test the children's ability before and after the schemes were put in place. Naturally, in the long term you would like to be able to recommend one scheme as being more generally useful than the other, as you would like your research to have an impact on children's education generally. However, you cannot test all children in the country on one or other of the methods; you have to draw a sample of children and then extrapolate the findings from your sample to what you think you would have found if you had tested all children.

This process of extrapolating from findings based on sample data is referred to as **statistical inference**. You try to infer something about the population from your sample. Analytical procedures that allow this sort of extrapolation are called inferential statistics.

data

raw score

descriptive statistics

variable

parameter

statistic

inferential statistics

statistical inference

test statistic

statistical significance

Most inferential statistical tests produce a number, called a **test statistic**, which has to be compared with some criterion value to determine its **statistical significance**. A *t*-test produces a *t* statistic, a Kendall's tau correlation produces a τ statistic, etc. These summarize something about the *relationship* between your variables. Statistical significance is the probability of having observed a test statistic as large as you have if there was in fact no relationship between the variables in question. Statistical significance, probability and hypotheses are considered later in more detail.

substantive significance

Substantive significance is not to be confused with statistical significance. Psychology journals are packed with statistically significant findings but this does not necessarily mean that the findings are psychologically or theoretically important. As we will see later, it is possible to get a statistically significant result associated with a relationship between variables that is so small it is of no substantive significance at all. It is also possible for a substantively significant effect to be present that is not statistically significant.

bivariate statistical tests

multivariate statistical tests

Tests involving a relationship between two variables, are referred to as. **bivariate statistical tests** When the relationship is between three or more variables (see Chapter 20), we talk about **multivariate statistical tests**.

We use test statistics when considering, say, whether two groups' scores are statistically significantly different. The probability value (*p*-value) we get will tell us how likely it was that we would have observed a difference between the groups' scores as big as we did if there really were no differences between the groups in the population. This depends to a large degree on the size of the sample but tells us nothing about *how different* the two groups' scores are. We could just say what the difference was expressed in the units of our scores (e.g. IQ points, number of 'correct' responses) but it is often helpful to express the dif-

effect size

ferences in terms of an established **effect size** metric. Common effect size metrics include Cohen's *d*, eta-squared (η^2) and R^2. There are more, but they all share in common the ability to say how big a difference or relationship has been found and there are conventions for saying whether an effect is 'small', 'medium' or 'large'. It is becoming common for journals to require authors to report effect sizes since traditional statistical significance tests do not tell us how big an effect has been revealed by a study (see also Chapter 22).

As discussed in Chapter 10, all measures of psychological constructs contain errors that are attributable to the measurement process itself. With the exception of a small class of sophisticated multivariate analyses (see Chapter 21), common inferential statistical procedures do not allow for this kind of error. Even if a statistical test is highly appropriate for the data you have, poor-quality measures

measurement error

with unknown amounts of **measurement error** could invalidate any conclusions you might wish to draw from your test. You must always seek to minimize measurement errors.

When you calculate a statistic based on data from a sample, it is likely that your sample is not absolutely representative of the population. In fact, it is highly unlikely that any sample statistic will exactly match the population parameter. So, there is something called **sampling error** which we need to know about whenever we want to make general statements about the population. Most of the time, the bigger your sample in relation to the size of population, the smaller the size of the sampling error.

sampling error

The way you draw your sample from the population of interest should be by true random selection **random sampling** if at all possible. Non-random selection processes are likely to introduce biases into your parameter estimates. Most inferential statistical techniques (see Section 19.7) assume that you have obtained your sample via random sampling procedures.

random sampling

In practice, psychologists often use non-random samples for convenience (e.g. students, attenders at the local clinic) or implicit quota designs (see Chapter 6). Much has been written on the relationship between inferential statistical procedures and sampling procedures, and those interested in the techniques of estimating the impact of sample designs, known as design effects, should consult Moser and Kalton (1971).

19.3 WHAT ARE BIVARIATE STATISTICAL ANALYSES?

In the remainder of this chapter the focus is on the use of inferential statistical procedures since, as researchers attempting to explain human behaviour generally, we are rarely interested in merely describing our sample. We would like to make theoretical claims that apply to all people in a given population.

This chapter deals with analyses that involve two variables. These analyses can be broken down into two broad categories: tests that look for *differences between groups*, as defined by one variable, on scores on another variable; and tests that detect an *association* or correlation or relationship between scores on two variables. Chapter 20 will discuss analyses that deal with more than two variables at a time, which are called *multivariate* analyses.

19.4 CLASSICAL BIVARIATE DESIGNS

Much of this book has been concerned with explaining common research designs and, at the risk of repeating material you may already have read, the following prototypical approaches commonly require bivariate analyses. It is important to understand the relationship between research design and the types of statistical procedures which are appropriate for use with them.

19.4.1 Experimental designs

dependent variable

conditions
treatments

independent variable

In experiments an independent variable is changed or altered while changes in a **dependent variable** are observed. To be sure of a cause and effect relationship between the two variables, the experimenter tries to exclude the effects of all other variables by randomly assigning people to **conditions** or **treatments** (values of the independent variable) and by controlling or holding constant other things that might affect the results. It is possible to have more than one independent variable, but we will deal with that in Chapter 20.

The **independent variable** is a variable that is controlled or manipulated by the experimenter. Usually it is a categorical/nominal level variable, and normally you have an expectation that the independent variable causes changes in the dependent variable. Levels of the independent variable are often referred to as conditions or treatments: for example, no drug treatment v low-dose treatment v high-dose treatment or teaching method A v teaching method B.

The dependent variable is the variable that is affected by changes in the independent variable. It is *never* thought of as influencing the independent variable. Chapter 4 discusses experimental designs in more detail.

independent groups
between-subjects
design

In its most basic form an experiment will randomly allocate people to one of two conditions of the independent variable, say, people taught statistics by method X and a control condition of people who are exposed to no statistics teaching. We let a period of time elapse so that method X can have some impact and then we give both groups a statistics test; this is our dependent variable. This is referred to as an **independent groups** or **between-subjects design** since none of the participants appear in both groups and we are interested in differences between groups.

repeated measures
within-subjects
design

This design is acceptable but there may be problems if, by chance, when randomly allocating people to the two groups, we allocate people who are already better at statistics to the method X group. This would make it more likely that we would get higher scores for the method X group. To get over this we could simply measure everyone's statistics ability first, then expose them to method X, and then retest their ability. This is called a **repeated measures** or **within-subjects design**. This latter design does not get over the problem that statistics ability might improve over time without help from method X (though data from a control group would help), but it does get over the problem of randomly allocated participants being different before the experiment took place.

It is important to know whether you have an independent (between-groups) design or a repeated measures (within-subjects) design to select an appropriate statistical test. You should also be aware that it is now regarded as more appropriate to call experimental subjects 'participants', even though the terminology to describe designs has yet to change: we do not yet have 'within-participants designs'.

19.4.2 Quasi-experimental designs

These are similar to true experiments except that the levels of the independent variable are not under the control of the experimenter. For example, if you want to see whether school-based anti-smoking campaigns had an effect on smoking behaviour you could not randomly allocate children to the schools that either would, or would not, have the anti-smoking intervention.

Quasi-experiments are often the best you can hope for as you do not always have any real ability to control the independent variable. There is always a possibility that any effects you show are due to unforeseen **confounding variables**. For example, smoking rates might already be different in the schools you studied; your campaign might have no effect but schools will show a difference in smoking rates after the intervention. Your 'control' school may choose to run its own anti-smoking campaign, which would be another kind of confounding variable (see Chapter 5 for more on quasi-experimentation).

confounding variables

Relationships between supposed independent and dependent variables in most questionnaire surveys are tested only within this quasi-experimental framework. If you conduct a survey and want to see what effect various background factors (social class, amount of education, etc.) have on test scores, again you cannot randomly allocate people to different levels of social class or educational experience. This is important because some survey analyses are written up to read as if they were true experiments.

19.4.3 Correlational and observational designs

These look to see if there is any systematic relationship between two variables. The aim is only to show that levels of one variable are associated with levels of another. There are no independent and dependent variables as such, as no causal relationship can usually be inferred from correlational analyses even if you have a good hunch that there is one.

For example, if you found that the size of car engines seemed to increase with the aggressiveness of their owners, as measured on a personality test, you could draw at least the following three conclusions: (i) it could be that aggressive people buy fast cars to express themselves; (ii) it could also be that owning a fast car gradually makes you more aggressive; or (iii) something else that you have not measured causes both the buying of fast cars and the development of aggressive personalities. You cannot sort this out with a correlational or observational study, but you can at least show that there is a relationship and that it is not zero.

A notable exception to this is when the temporal ordering of events is not in question. For instance, the number of cigarettes smoked when someone was 20 might be highly correlated with levels of tar found in the lungs at age 50. It seems *unlikely* that levels of tar at age 50 *caused* levels of cigarette smoking at an earlier age. The philosopher John Stuart Mill reminds us that, strictly speaking, for something to cause an effect it must temporally precede the effect so if the temporal ordering is unambiguous you can be pretty sure that the later event did not cause the earlier event. You cannot be entirely sure that the later effect was caused by the earlier event, however, because there is the possibility of a third, unmeasured variable influencing both variables which still cannot be ruled out.

Note that all three of these general approaches concern the relationship between two variables. These designs can be made multivariate by incorporating additional variables, but for our present purposes we will deal with these proto-typical cases. The experimental, and to a lesser extent, quasi-experimental designs tend to require analyses that look at differences between groups or conditions (defined by the independent variable) in scores on some outcome (the dependent variable). Correlational or observational approaches require analyses that detect associations between variables where neither variable is necessarily the dependent or independent variable (they could be, but it is not necessary that they are).

19.5 THEORIES AND HYPOTHESES

This section spells out some aspects of classical hypothesis testing. This perspective on the conducting of good research is only one of a number of views, but it is still the dominant view in psychology. It owes a lot to the theorizing of Karl Popper (1959) and is sometimes called the hypothetico-deductive model. It is also a form of positivism and assumes that there is a reality and some form of truth out there waiting for us to find it. Chapter 1 discusses this and alternative perspectives and if you are in any doubt about what is said here, refer back to that chapter.

19.5.1 Theories

theories **Theories** are statements about the underlying mechanisms of behaviour: the 'how' and 'why' of behaviour. To satisfy Popper it is essential that these are stated in such a way as to allow the potential of their being shown to be wrong. Theories that could never, in principle, be shown to be wrong are not part of good science. They **hypotheses** become acts of faith. Theories should generate specific **hypotheses** that can be tested. If these prove false then the theory can be questioned, modified or rejected.

19.5.2 Hypotheses

Hypotheses are predictions about the outcomes of experiments or studies. Usually one formally expresses a theoretically generated prediction, or an educated guess, about how an independent variable will affect a dependent variable. Conventionally we deal with two sorts of hypothesis when we do any inferential statistical tests. These are as follows.

The **null hypothesis** is what we actually test and it appears slightly odd at first sight. The null hypothesis in an experiment is the statement that the independent variable has *no effect* on the dependent variable at all *in the population*. In a correlational study the null hypothesis would normally be that two variables are not associated, or correlated, with one another *in the population*. Note that what happens in the *sample* is not what we are really interested in. The null hypothesis is often referred to as H_0.

null hypotheses

The **alternative hypothesis** is usually our 'hunch' hypothesis: that the independent variable does indeed affect the dependent variable *in the population* or that two variables are correlated with one another *in the population*. However, this is only one hypothesis in a range of possible alternative explanations about what really affects the dependent variable and we cannot treat our preferred alternative hypothesis as absolutely true. This is in part because we normally draw on data from a sample rather than from the whole population.

alternative hypothesis

For example, suppose you wanted to prove the hypothesis that 'all people have two hands' and you draw a sample of one person. If that person had two hands that would not prove that all people had two hands. Some people that you have not sampled might have more hands or, more likely, fewer. If the sample person had one or none, however, then you would have to throw out your hypothesis; it would definitely be wrong.

It is easier to show that a hypothesis is false than it is to show that a hypothesis is true. Indeed, there is a philosophical argument that we can only ever prove that something is not true: we can never show that something is always absolutely true. The alternative hypothesis is referred to as H_1.

19.6 TYPE I AND TYPE II ERRORS

19.6.1 Type I error

Type I error is the error that occurs when you reject a true null hypothesis. This is where you conclude that the independent variable did affect the dependent variable when, in fact, it did not. This can happen when, for instance, by chance you allocate people who were already high scorers to one condition and low scorers to another. When you measure the dependent variable, the difference between the conditions is due to the fact that the people were different before you started, *not* because the independent variable had any effect. In terms of correlational analyses, Type I error occurs when you say that the two variables were related to one another when, in fact, they were not.

Type I error

Publishing findings with Type I errors in them could mislead people into doing more research on a dead-end topic or making serious life-threatening decisions based on the inaccurate conclusions from your work.

19.6.2 Type II error

Type II error

Type II error occurs when you fail to reject a false null hypothesis. You conclude that the independent variable has no influence on the dependent variable when it actually does. This happens sometimes because the size of the treatment effect is very small and hard to notice in your sample. It can also happen when you get the opposite of the example given for Type I errors. Here, by chance, you allocate people who were already high scorers on the dependent variable to the treatment condition that actually lowers scores and vice versa. The effect of the experiment is to level up the two groups so that there is now no difference between treatment groups on the scores and you accept the null hypothesis of 'no differences' between groups. In fact, the independent variable had a big effect but your sampling obscured this. One solution for this example is to adopt repeated measures designs so that you know how people scored before and after the experiment.

With correlational designs Type II error occurs when you conclude that there is no relationship between your two variables when, in fact, there is. If you can publish such 'non-findings' at all, then it may discourage people from investigating a potentially important effect.

The aim is always to minimize the probability of these two types of error occurring.

19.7 PROBABILITY

19.7.1 Basic definitions

probability

The **probability** p is a measure of the chance that something will happen. Where a number of possible outcomes A, B, C, D, etc. could occur, the probability of any particular outcome is a proportion based on the following:

$$\text{Probability of outcome } A = p(A) = \frac{\text{Number of possible } A \text{ outcomes}}{\text{Total number of outcomes}}$$

Probabilities always vary between 0 and 1. The sum of the probabilities of all possible events (A, B, C, D, etc. above) must always add up to 1. Some simple probability examples are as follows:

> $p = 1$ if something always happens: for example, the probability of picking a joker out of a pack of 52 jokers
> $p = 0$ if something never happens: for example, the probability of picking a joker out of a pack of cards with no jokers in it
> $p = 0.5$ is the probability of an unbiased coin coming up heads: another way of saying this is a '1 in 2 chance'

$p = 0.25$ is the probability of picking a diamond card from a pack of 52 playing cards: another way of saying this is a '1 in 4 chance'.

The commonest application of probability notions in psychology is to decide how likely it is that your *sample-based* test statistic is found to be as big as it is by chance, assuming that your null hypothesis was, in fact, true. For example, if there really was no real difference between people who had received a medical treatment and those who had not, then could it be, or rather, how likely is it, that the observed improvement in the treatment group was as big as it was just by chance?

Suppose we have a new treatment under test, and our null hypothesis is that the mean score on our cognitive test (the dependent variable) will be no different from that found in untreated people. In other words, our null hypothesis is that the population mean for treated people is the same as that for untreated people. Figure 19.1 is a frequency distribution of all the possible differences between treatment and control group means that would be obtained if you repeatedly drew new samples and calculated the means for each new sample. This is called a **sampling distribution**. You do not have to create this distribution your- | **sampling distribution**
self: this is simply shown here to explain the logic of hypothesis testing.

The shaded areas, known as **critical regions**, contain 'extreme' or very unlikely | **critical regions**
outcomes. They are still possible differences in means even if our null hypothesis is true. The proportion of mean differences falling into the critical regions gives you the probability of observing a difference that extreme if H_0 is true.

By convention, if the probability of observing means as different from that predicted by the null hypothesis (under the assumption that the H_0 is true) is less than $p = 0.05$ (alternatively, 1 in 20 or 5%), then you reject the null hypothesis. If the probability is not less than 0.05 then you do not reject the null hypothesis. This $p = 0.05$ figure, called an **alpha criterion**, is the maximum prob- | **alpha criterion**
ability of making a Type I error.

In the above example we have looked at the difference between group/treatment means observed in your sample and what would have been predicted under H_0. The same logic applies to designs concerned with associations between variables, too. When you are interested in correlations your null hypothesis is usually (though not always) that there is no (zero) correlation between the variables. As with the means, you look to see how likely it is that, via sampling, you would have observed a correlation that big between the two variables if H_0 were actually true. Again you could create a sampling distribution of correlations and look to see if your observed correlation fell into the critical region where you would reject the null hypothesis.

Most inferential statistical techniques, whether concerned with means or correlations or some other test statistic, use sampling distributions to determine

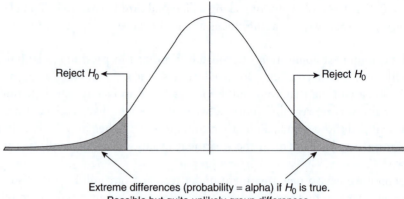

Reject H_0 ←   → Reject H_0

Extreme differences (probability = alpha) if H_0 is true.
Possible but quite unlikely group differences.

Figure 19.1   A sampling distribution of differences between group means under the assumption that the null hypothesis is true

whether the observed value falls into a critical region. Sometimes these sampling distributions make reference to population parameters and assume you have drawn random samples from the population, and sometimes the sampling distributions are constructed out of the range of possible outcomes given the particular experiment or study you are doing (see Section 19.8).

The 0.05 probability figure is not a magical figure. It is only a convention and there are times when you would not be happy to reject the null hypothesis at this level. When people are conducting particularly controversial research, such as trying to establish the existence of clairvoyance (which, if true, would undermine some well-established laws of physics), it is usual to adopt a stricter alpha criterion. This has the effect of making all your analyses more conservative.

You are free to set the alpha criterion at any value you like but you must declare it and be prepared to have to convince others that you are justified in doing this. This is an example of how some of the relativist and socially conventional processes discussed in Chapter 1 creep into a part of the research process which, from the outside, might appear concrete, highly rigorous and uncontroversial. Many would argue (e.g. Kirk, 1996) that the undue focus on p-values has actually hampered science rather than promoted it.

19.7.2 One-tailed versus two-tailed tests

one-tailed test

When carrying out hypothesis testing you must decide whether you are going to do a one- or two-tailed test of the null hypothesis. In a **one-tailed test**, you reject the null hypothesis if the difference between the observed mean, say, and that predicted under H_0 is relatively small but is in a *previously specified direction*.

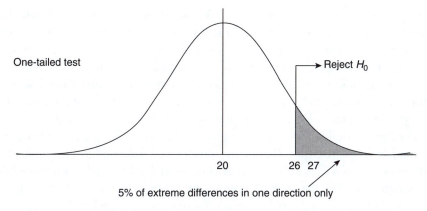

One-tailed test

Reject H_0

20   26 27

5% of extreme differences in one direction only

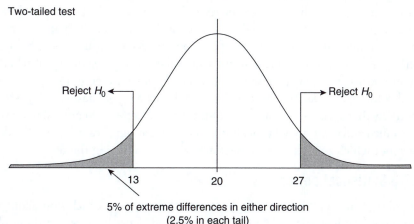

Two-tailed test

Reject H_0 Reject H_0

13   20   27

5% of extreme differences in either direction
(2.5% in each tail)

Figure 19.2 Sampling distributions of differences between group means: critical regions for one-tailed and two-tailed hypothesis tests

A **two-tailed test** requires a somewhat larger difference but is independent of the direction of difference.

two-tailed test

This distinction is best illustrated by an example. Suppose you had a wonder drug that was supposed to influence cognitive performance. If you had a strong theory about the action of this wonder drug which said that it would increase scores on the cognitive test, then if you observed no difference between treatment and control groups *or* you found that the drug group scored less, you would have disconfirmatory evidence for your theory. In this case your *null hypothesis* would be that drug treatment scores would be the same or less than those of the controls. This would be a one-tailed test.

In most psychological research, our theories are generally less well specified and we would be interested in differences in either direction. Big drops in score would be just as interesting as big gains. We would not wish to ignore a big drop in scores by doing a one-tailed test. This time our null hypothesis would be that treatment and control group means would be the same. Figure 19.2 illustrates the point. In this figure we can see that the shaded areas in the tails of both distributions occupy 5% of the total areas under the curves and thus 5% of all sampling means. In this hypothetical example, the one-tailed critical value is 26 so any observed mean for the drug group greater than 26 would lead us to reject H_0. For the two-tailed test any value greater than 27 *or* less than 13 would lead us to reject H_0. Notice that when doing a two-tailed test you have to get a bigger difference between the two group means to reject H_0. This makes the two-tailed test inherently more conservative (less prone to Type I error) and this is partly why psychology journal articles contain more two-tailed probability values.

The same logic applies to tests of hypotheses of association. If you have a strong hypothesis that two variables will be positively (or, alternatively, negatively) correlated then you can specify a one-tailed test. In most psychological applications you will be interested in strong relationships regardless of whether they are positive or negative and so two-tailed tests may be more appropriate. Use the less conservative one-tailed test only when you have a very strong hypothesis that specifies the direction of the expected effect. Do not swap between a two-tailed and a one-tailed probability just to get a 'significant' result: the decision about which to look at must be made before conducting the test.

19.7.3 Statistical power

The point of all hypothesis testing is to reach the correct conclusion about the hypotheses. We have already looked at Type I and Type II errors and the probability of making a Type I error. **Statistical power** is associated with the tests you use and is the probability that the test will correctly reject a false null hypothesis. This is the test's power to detect an effect when there really is one there to detect.

statistical power

Most textbooks refer to the probability of making a Type II error (the probability of accepting a false null hypothesis) as β (the Greek letter beta). Since the sum of the probabilities of all possible events must add up to 1, the probability of rejecting a false null hypothesis, the power of your test, is:

$$\text{Power} = p \text{ (rejecting a false } H_0) = 1 - p \text{ (accepting a false } H_0) = 1 - \beta$$

While this formula is very simple, settling on a single value for β is not straightforward. Although people often talk of this or that test as being more powerful than another, power depends on a number of factors that vary for each application. There is no single figure that always applies to each particular type of test.

One factor is the size of the treatment effect – the effect size (see Section 19.2). Put simply, if your independent variable has an effect on the dependent variable (i.e. H_0 is false) but the size of this effect, the treatment effect, is small, it is going to be harder to detect this effect. Thus you will need a more powerful test to detect the effect (with a given size of sample) than would be the case if the treatment effect was strong. If the treatment effect is large, detecting it will not be difficult. A second factor is the level you set for the alpha criterion. Setting a smaller level will make it less likely that you will reject a true null hypothesis but it will also now be harder to reject a false hypothesis, all other things being equal.

A third factor is sample size. As the sample size gets larger and approaches the size of the population, so you will increase the statistical power of your test. If there really is a treatment effect (H_0 is false) in the population, you are more likely to find it with a larger sample than with a small one. Note, however, that power is about the ability to reject a false H_0 and is not about the size of the treatment effect. You might add more and more participants to your study to increase statistical power, but this will not change the absolute magnitude of the treatment effect or its substantive significance.

For example, you might have invented an expensive intervention programme to improve scores on IQ tests. Let us assume that it does work, though you do not know it yet, but it improves IQ by only 1 point (IQ scores often have a mean of 100 and a standard deviation of around 15). You set up a controlled experiment with ten participants getting your programme and ten control participants. You find that the treatment programme group has an IQ score 1 point higher than the control. You carry out the appropriate test, you fail to reject the null hypothesis and you make a Type II error.

Disappointed but not deterred, you realize that you did not have enough statistical power, so you rerun the study with samples of 1000 in the treatment and control conditions. Again you find the treatment programme group has an IQ score 1 point higher than the control. You now have a lot of power and your test correctly leads you to reject the null hypothesis. The intervention programme has a statistically significant effect on IQ scores. However, in practical terms, this effect is too small to justify the expense of the programme and people may well question the importance of being able to improve IQ by a single point. Beware confusing statistical significance with substantive, 'real-world' significance (and see Box 19.1 for a brief discussion on the merits or otherwise of significance testing).

It is possible to use power tables to estimate the size of sample you would need to achieve a test with a given power as long as you can make some reasonable estimate of the likely size of the treatment effect (effect size). When designing a study it is highly desirable to use power tables to work out how many participants you need in advance, rather than to run the study only to find out that you had little chance of detecting the effect because you did not have enough power as you had not approached enough people. Ethical committees and grant awarding bodies are highly likely to ask you to do a power analysis before agreeing to let you conduct a study, as studies that lack sufficient power are seen in some quarters as essentially unethical (see Box 19.2). Non-significant findings will be inherently ambiguous, as you will not know whether the failure to get a significant result is a result of the null hypothesis being true or it being false and you having insufficient power to detect the effect you are looking at.

Computer programs are now available to do power calculations (e.g. G*POWER, nQuery, PASS) and as some are free there is little excuse for not using them.

Box 19.1 Significance testing v confidence limits and effect sizes

From time to time people have had serious doubts about whether the statistical null hypothesis testing I have presented here is the right way to proceed (e.g. Harlow, Mulaik & Steiger, 1997). One of the key criticisms is that the null hypothesis is usually neither scientifically interesting nor very likely to be true on a priori grounds. As an example, when comparing two groups on some measure the null hypothesis is that the difference between the means of the two groups' scores, is exactly zero down to the last decimal place – there is absolutely no difference between them. Given that we usually sample people and their scores, it is very unlikely that the group means will be exactly the same. In other words, the likelihood of the null hypothesis being true is very low indeed yet we use this as the basis for making all our statistical inferences, including whether to reject the null hypothesis as being false. We actually get no information about the probability of the null hypothesis being true from the traditional testing procedure itself.

An alternative approach has been to emphasize the reporting of confidence intervals (CIs) so that not only can decisions be made about the likelihood of any estimated value having that value in the population but we can also get an idea of the precision with which the estimate is being made (see Chapter 6). Taking the above two-group example, we could report the 95% confidence interval for the differences between the means. If the confidence interval includes zero it is not possible to predict the direction of the difference between the group means with any great degree of certainty. If it does not contain zero then we are 95% certain that we know the direction of the difference.

We can also report the effect size, which gives us an idea of the magnitude of the effect of interest as this can often be overlooked when focusing on p-values in hypothesis tests. In fact p-values conceal information about both effect size and CI and the argument runs that more useful information is conveyed by reporting a combination of effect size and CIs than by reporting the p-value associated with the null hypothesis test.

The reasons why our statistical practices retain a focus on traditional null hypothesis testing are the subject of continued debate. While some arguments are sophisticated philosophical ones, it is probably the practical ones that dominate. These include the observation that a lot of people seem to be doing it, the widespread belief that it is difficult to publish in high-prestige journals if you do not

(*Continued*)

Box 19.1   (Continued)

report conventional hypothesis tests and that many popular statistical software programs do not readily calculate confidence limits and effect sizes for you. As time marches on this latter reason fades away and many journals, particularly those published by the American Psychological Association, are encouraging the reporting of effect sizes, CIs as well as conventional hypothesis tests.

Box 19.2   How many subjects do I need? A word on effect sizes

A priori power analysis is all about making sure you set up a 'fair test' of your hypotheses. It is about planning to avoid getting an ambiguous result out of your study. Studies that lack sufficient statistical power and which yield non-significant results are inherently ambiguous – you do not know whether your null hypothesis is in fact true or that your design did not have enough power to reliably detect an effect of the size that is really there. You must plan to avoid this as conducting studies that have little a priori chance of detecting significant effects is essentially unethical – they are probably a waste of your participants' and your time.

You ought to be able to state the size of the smallest effect you wish to detect. Hard-nosed scientist folk might well ask why you are conducting a study if you have no idea what size of effect you are interested in being able to detect. If you cannot say in advance what the *smallest substantively meaningful difference* is, one might ask why you are doing the study at all.

An example might help. Suppose you wanted to measure the relative levels of depression among Republican and Democrat supporters in the wake of the re-election of George Bush – you have a hunch that Democrats might be a little depressed by the election result. You want to draw samples of Republicans and Democrats and to administer the well-known Beck Depression Inventory (BDI) and you are going to conduct a power analysis to work out how many people to get in each sample. How much of a difference in depression scores will you consider to be a psychologically meaningful difference that is worth knowing about (also known as the *critical effect size*)? If you had a vast sample of 10,000 people you would have more than enough power to detect a real difference of half a point on the BDI. However, while such a difference might be real it would probably be substantively meaningless.

Settling on a critical effect size can often seem difficult, and there is a temptation to settle on a 'big' effect size since that will usually mean you do not have to collect data from so many people as would be the case if you were planning to detect a smaller effect. The amount of effort required to collect data from a sample of a certain size should not drive the decision about the critical effect size. You must use the test manuals, past literature and your psychological knowledge to

(Continued)

gauge what size of difference would be substantively meaningful. In the case of the BDI example, the manuals for the BDI give norms for various groups including clinically depressed groups as well as non-depressed samples. The mean scores from these groups (and their standard deviations) can be used to gauge what kinds of differences in depression scores are psychologically meaningful.

19.8 PARAMETRIC VERSUS NON-PARAMETRIC TESTS

The final major distinction you need to be aware of before selecting a statistical test is whether you can do parametric or non-parametric statistical tests. A good number of the well-known statistical tests such as the *t*-test, the Pearson product moment correlation and analysis of variance (ANOVA) make assumptions about the distribution of scores in the populations. The commonest assumptions are that the scores are normally distributed (have the classic 'bell-shaped' curve) in the population or that the distribution of (hypothetical) sample means is normally distributed. They also assume that you have drawn a random sample from this population of scores. Some parametric tests assume that the variances of population scores are the same in your treatment and control **parametric tests** groups. Tests that involve these assumptions are called **parametric tests**: they make use of assumptions about the distribution of scores in the population (i.e. information about population parameters).

If, as is often the case, your data do not satisfy these assumptions then you **non-parametric** should use the **non-parametric** alternatives to the parametric tests. These do not make the same assumptions about the distributions of scores in the population and so violating these assumptions is not a problem. Sometimes you will see these tests called 'distribution-free tests'. These sorts of test are also especially appropriate for use with ordinal and categorical measures where the mean is not an appropriate measure of central tendency. To truly establish the normality of a distribution you would need to be able to estimate its mean and variance and thus it is difficult to establish this assumption with ordinal and categorical data. This is not to say that there are no parametric procedures appropriate for such measures, but these require additional special assumptions to be met and will not be considered here.

Hypothesis testing with non-parametric tests proceeds by creating sampling distributions that apply specifically to your study. In essence, most work by calculating all possible values of the relevant test statistic given your study's data, design and null hypothesis. Then they look to see whether your observed value of the test statistic is relatively extreme and therefore unlikely to have occurred by chance if your null hypothesis were true. Whilst the procedures are not identical to those used with parametric tests, I hope you will appreciate that the basic logic of hypothesis testing remains the same as described earlier in this chapter. Statements about differences in the population can be made only if you have used random sampling procedures.

Parametric tests, if appropriate for your data, should be chosen in preference to their non-parametric equivalents since they tend to be more powerful and are thus better able to detect treatment effects if they really exist. See Chapter 3 for a discussion of violations to the levels of measurement assumptions of parametric tests.

19.9 CHOOSING A STATISTICAL TEST

Most statistics textbooks provide tree diagrams (like Figures 19.4 and 19.5) that help you decide which statistical test you should use. You need to know the following before you can use such trees.

Firstly, you must decide whether you are interested in looking for relationships (e.g. correlations, associations) or differences (e.g. between groups).

Secondly, if you are interested in differences then you should identify which variable is the dependent (outcome) measure and which is the independent variable.

Thirdly, if you are interested in tests of association and you have normally distributed interval or ratio scale measures, produce a scatterplot (a graph) of scores on one variable against scores on the other. Figure 19.3 shows some hypothetical scatterplots. You should decide whether the relationship between the two variables looks linear or monotonic. Figures 19.3(a) and 19.3(b) show linear or 'straight line' relationships between the X and Y variables. Figure 19.3 (a) shows a positive linear relationship: increases in X seem to be associated with increases in Y. Figure 19.3 (b) shows a negative linear relationship; increases in X are associated with decreases in Y.

A relationship is considered to be linear if you could reasonably draw a straight line through the points. Straight lines have been added to Figure 19.3(a) and 19.3(b). If there was a perfect relationship between X and Y then all the points would lie on a straight line. As the relationships are not perfect you observe an elliptical distribution of observations around the 'best fit' straight lines.

I hope you can see that it would not be possible to do this with Figure 19.3(c) since changes at higher scores on variable X do not seem to be associated with big changes in Y. Lower down the scale, changes in X are associated with bigger changes in Y. This is a monotonic relationship. Monotonic relationships are ones where increases in one variable are always associated with increases (or, if a negative relationship, decreases) in the other variable but the rate of change is not constant or linear. Figure 19.3(c) shows a positive monotonic relationship.

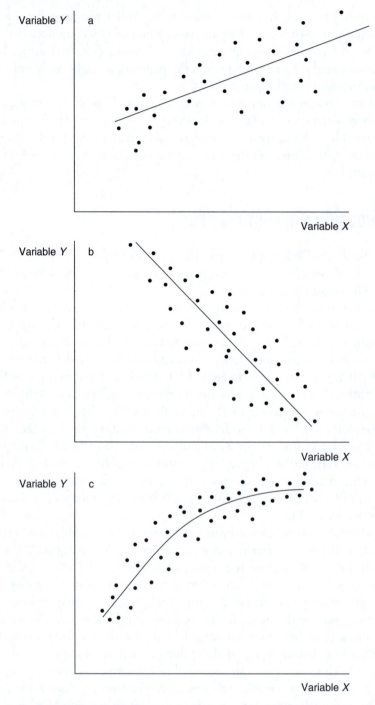

Figure 19.3 Scatterplots showing linear and monotonic relationships between two variables

If the scatterplot looks *u*-shaped or *n*-shaped or has several peaks, you will not have a simple relationship between the two variables. You will have to consult a statistics text and look at the possibility of carrying out a mathematical transformation of one or both of your variables.

Fourthly, what is the level of measurement of each variable? When testing for an association the choice of test will depend on the levels of measurement of both variables. When testing for differences between groups or conditions, the level of measurement of the *dependent* variable is crucial for test selection.

Fifthly, if you have interval level or ratio scale measures and you think you may be able to do a parametric test, you must ask whether the variables are likely to be normally distributed in the population and whether you have been able to sample at random from the population.

As noted earlier, many psychological studies rely on convenience samples so, in such cases, you will not have met the random sampling assumption. In practice, the use of parametric tests such as the *t*-test is acceptable as long as participants are *randomly assigned* to treatment conditions (see Minium, King & Bear, 1993). The justification of this is technically complex but boils down to the fact that, in most cases, the conclusion drawn from the *t*-test is the same as would have been achieved if the most appropriate statistical model had been used. However, the results from your convenience sample are not sufficient for making generalizations about the population; you will need further evidence to support those conclusions.

In practice you are also unlikely to have access to information about the distribution of scores in the population, so you will be able to look only at the distributions of scores in your sample data. There is much written about how *robust* parametric tests are to violations of the normality assumption (see Blalock, 1988). Although there are dissenting voices, there is now some consensus that minor deviations from normality will not unduly undermine the value of many common parametric tests.

If you have access to a statistics computer package you can look at diagnostic statistics that tell you how much your sample's data deviate from what would have been expected if they were normally distributed. Skewness is a figure which indicates the degree to which the distribution of scores is skewed to the left or the right. Kurtosis indicates the degree to which the distribution is more peaked or flatter than would be expected. Both figures should be 0 and have known standard errors (see Chapter 6) so confidence limits can be calculated. As a rule of thumb only, skew and kurtosis figures within the range +1 to −1 with medium to large samples are probably sufficiently close to normality to allow the use of parametric tests. You should note that some textbooks report the normal distribution as having a kurtosis of 3 rather than 0. Whilst this is correct most statistical packages now report something called 'excess kurtosis' (though still calling it kurtosis on printouts) which is simply the sample kurtosis minus 3. This has the effect of making the desirable values of skew and (excess) kurtosis both 0.

So, if your sample data appear normally distributed then it is probably safe to assume you have satisfied the normality assumption. If, however, you have multiple modes ('peaks') in your sample data or the distributions look severely non-normal, then use the equivalent non-parametric test. When in doubt, do both types of test and rely on the non-parametric test if the two tests do not lead to the same conclusion.

Finally, when testing group differences you must know if independent (separate) samples provide scores or whether the samples are matched so that either (i) each respondent (case) is paired off with another respondent assumed to be alike on some basis, or (ii) each respondent provides more than one score on a measure. This simply refers back to your research design. If you have two or more separate groups or conditions and each respondent (case) provides a single score you have what is often referred to as 'independent groups'. If your respondents provide two or more scores on a measure, say before and after an intervention, the design is a repeated measures one. In this example, each respondent's before and after scores are matched together for the purposes of the test. Studies involving matched samples are possible but relatively less common.

Unfortunately, statistical texts have yet to reach a consensus on the terminology to be used to deal with this dichotomy. This is partly because authors want to provide decision trees that are appropriate for all possible applications of tests and thus they need to use abstract terms. Here, since this chapter has discussed only the two most common types of bivariate test (tests of difference and tests of association), we can hopefully adopt simpler terminology.

Figure 19.4 should be used when you wish to look for differences between groups or differences between conditions/treatments. Figure 19.5 should be used when you are looking at the relationship between two variables.

Suppose you had two groups of people, those with maths GCSE and those without, and you wanted to see if their scores on a statistics test were different. This is a quasi-experimental research design. Let us assume the scores are on a ratio scale (number of items correct), and in your sample data the scores appear to be normally distributed in both groups (i.e. their distributions look like the one in Figure 19.1). This requires a test of differences, so you would look at Figure 19.4.

The first question you are asked is how many groups or conditions/treatments you have. You have two, so you move up the tree to the next question which asks what type of design you have. Here, your two groups are independent of one another (you cannot both have and not have maths GCSE) so you move along and up again. This leads you to the independent groups *t*-test which is a

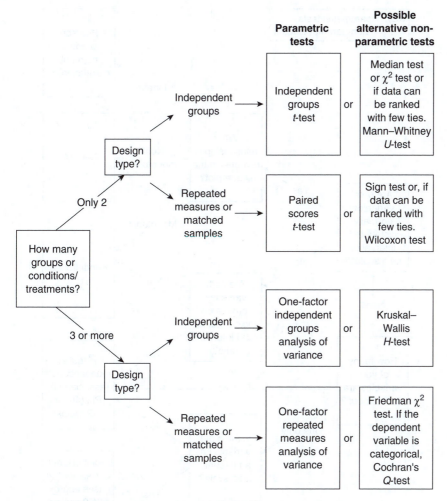

Figure 19.4 Simplified decision tree for tests of differences between groups or treatments/conditions

parametric test. As you have normally distributed interval level data you can use the *t*-test. Were you unable to satisfy these parametric assumptions you could use the Mann–Whitney *U*-test providing there were not too many people who had the same score on the test.

Now suppose you had measured attitudes towards death metal music on a seven-point, 'strongly in favour' to 'hate it' scale, and you had asked people to tell you how many times they had been to church in the last month. You want to know if church-going is associated with a dislike of death metal. Using Figure 19.5, you are first asked how many variables are dichotomous (have two

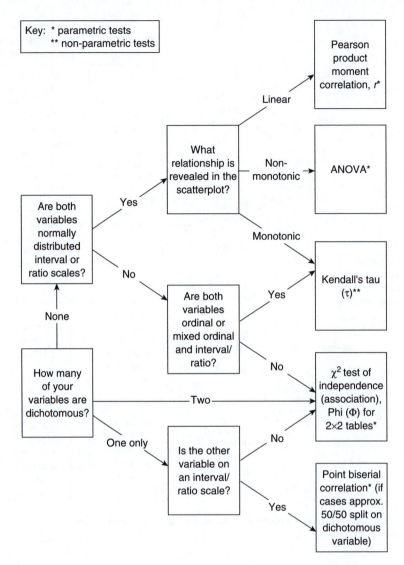

Figure 19.5 Simplified decision tree for tests of association or relationship between two variables

categories only). Neither of your measures is dichotomous so you move up to the question which asks if both variables are on interval or ratio scales. Your church attendance measure is, but strictly speaking the attitude measure is an ordinal one so you move down the 'no' branch. The next question asks if both variables are ordinal or you have a mix of ordinal and interval/ratio. Here the answer is 'yes', which leads you to the box containing Kendall's tau, a non-parametric correlation coefficient.

Both decision trees have been much simplified for the sake of clarity and there is a range of tests that could also have been included. However, for most basic bivariate tests of either difference or association, these decision trees will lead you to an appropriate analysis.

19.10 CONCLUSION

The aim of this chapter has been to describe the logic underlying hypothesis testing with simple bivariate statistical tests and give some guidelines on how to select appropriate tests. In the space of one chapter it is not possible to describe individual tests, but I hope you now have a better understanding of what they can do for you. To keep matters simple I have dealt with the two most popular classes of bivariate tests: those that test hypotheses about differences between samples and those that test for associations between variables. There are other kinds of bivariate test such as tests for trends or tests of differences in dispersion, for example. These are less common applications within psychology, but most standard texts deal with these issues. It is always important to remember that the statistical tests are a research tool and not an end in themselves. They are not uncontroversial and, as explained in Chapter 1, need to be understood for what they are if psychological research is to progress productively.

19.11 FURTHER READING

Minium *et al.*'s (1993) text is very good for explaining the reasons behind various statistical procedures and is clear and accessible. Kirk's (1996) gives a useful discussion of how statistical tests ought to be used and how, if abused, they can prove a hindrance to the advancement of psychology. Kraemer and Thiemann's (1987) is an easy-to-understand text on how to calculate statistical power and thereby estimate the numbers of participants that will be needed for a study. Of the books available on this topic this is by far the easiest to use.

G*POWER is a power calculation program freely available on the Internet from the following address: http://www.psycho.uni-duesseldorf.de/aap/projects/gpower (please cite the G*POWER authors if you use it).

20

Introduction to Multivariate Data Analysis

Sean Hammond

20.1   Introduction
20.2   Examining differences between groups
   20.2.1   Analysis of variance
   20.2.2   Discriminant analysis
20.3   Making predictions
   20.3.1   Simple regression
   20.3.2   Multiple regression
   20.3.3   Further issues in regression
20.4   Exploring underlying structure
   20.4.1   Factor analysis
   20.4.2   Cluster analysis
   20.4.3   Multidimensional scaling
   20.4.4   The myth of confirmatory methods
20.5   The special case of categorical data
20.6   Conclusion
20.7   Further reading

AIMS

This chapter is intended as an introduction to multivariate data analysis. Psychology researchers will typically work with a multitude of variables and the task of making sense of the resulting data may sometimes appear daunting. In fact, the challenge of examining multivariate data is hugely rewarding and many psychologists develop lasting and deep interest in specific multivariate data analysis techniques. Indeed, psychologists have been at the fore in the development and application of multivariate statistical methods. It is not possible to give a full coverage of the area in one short chapter, but we do hope to highlight some of the basic methods and issues that will help a researcher along the fascinating path of discovery.

Key terms

alienation coefficient
analysis of variance
bivariate
Bonferroni adjustment
canonical variate analysis
centroids
cluster analysis
configural frequency analysis
confirmatory analysis
correspondence analysis
dimensionality
discriminant function analysis
dual scaling
eigenvalue
factor analysis
factorially complex
hierarchical methods
interaction structure analysis
interpretability
latent class analysis
logistic regression
logit analysis

loglinear methods
multicollinearity
multidimensional scaling
multivariate
multivariate analysis of variance
non-hierarchical methods
oblique rotation
optimal scaling
orthogonal rotation
partial correlation
partitioning
principal components analysis
probit analysis
rank order
regionality
regression
restricted analyses
ridge estimation
Stein-type estimation
stepwise regression
stress coefficient
univariate
varimax

20.1 INTRODUCTION

multivariate
univariate, bivariate

When we collect information based upon a large number of variables, such data are termed **multivariate**. This is in contrast to data from one variable, termed **univariate**, or two variables, termed **bivariate** (see Chapter 19). By convention, data from more than two variables are known as multivariate data.

Obviously, multivariate data can convey more information about a sample of people than univariate or bivariate data. As undergraduates most of us learn the standard univariate and bivariate statistical approaches to data analysis, but we are rarely taught the more sophisticated methods of multivariate data analysis in any great detail. This is a shame because most of the more interesting research questions we might ask in the social sciences are multivariate by nature. There are simply not enough hours in the typical undergraduate psychology curriculum to do justice to all the exciting possibilities for exploring multivariate data. Obviously, therefore, this chapter can do little more than scratch the surface, but we hope that it will help the student and researcher to understand some of the more basic issues of multivariate data analysis and inspire further exploration of this fascinating area.

Psychologists collect data in order to answer one or more research questions. It should be apparent from the preceding chapters that the nature of the research question will dictate the data analytic strategies used. Multivariate data analysis techniques can be grouped according to the research question being posed. Although our research questions almost always overlap, it may be helpful to broadly categorize them into four classes:

1 questions examining the differences between groups;
2 questions concerning the prediction of particular outcomes;
3 questions exploring underlying structure;
4 questions concerning the fit of our measurements to theoretical models.

In this chapter we will look at some of the methods appropriate for the first three types of question and then we will look briefly at the special case of categorical data. The fourth type of question will be addressed fully in the next chapter on structural equation modelling (Chapter 21). Clearly, in the space of one chapter it will not be possible to give a comprehensive review of multivariate methods; a number of books that attempt to do this are reviewed at the end of the chapter. What this chapter aims to do is to act as an initial pointer to the new researcher who is looking for a data analytic method to fit his or her research questions.

20.2 EXAMINING DIFFERENCES BETWEEN GROUPS

A common problem that faces research psychologists is the one where we are interested in looking at the differences between two or more groups of people and we have a number of measures (dependent variables) on which to compare them. The temptation is to carry out a separate statistical test of group difference for each dependent variable involving the multiple use of the *t*-test or one-way **analysis of variance** (ANOVA). There are two major problems with this approach.

Firstly, we have the problem of 'weighing the odds' in favour of a significant result. As discussed in Chapter 19, statistical tests are commonly interpreted by probability estimates. What this means is that if we carried out 100 *t*-tests using random data, we would expect to obtain 5 *t*-values with an estimated probability less than or equal to 0.05 even if there were no real differences there to be found. In other words, the more tests we carry out the greater the chance we have of obtaining a statistic that will be interpreted as significant. This may lead us to a Type I error. One way around this problem is to apply an adjustment to the probability level that we use to signify a significant statistic. A commonly used method is known as **Bonferroni adjustment** (see Box 20.1), but this is not a panacea and has a number of limitations. Other methods of adjusting the probabilities for multiple statistical tests exist (Šidák, 1967; Holm, 1979) but the Bonferroni method is the simplest to apply.

analysis of variance

Bonferroni adjustment

Box 20.1   The Bonferroni adjustment for multiple tests

Here we describe the use of the Bonferroni adjustment in cases where the researcher has carried out multiple statistical tests on a single data set. We will also point out some of the limitations of this approach.

The reasoning behind the Bonferroni adjustment is that, in testing the null hypothesis of no difference between groups with multiple tests, we are inflating the probability of obtaining a statistically significant ($p < 0.05$) result. If we use 15 tests, for example, the probability that one will prove significant is not 0.05 but 0.537. The formula for identifying this probability is:

$$p = 1-(1-\alpha)^n$$

where n is the number of tests and α is the probability that we ascribe as statistically significant (usually $\alpha = 0.05$). The Bonferroni adjustment is intended to deflate the α applied to each test, so the overall error rate remains at 0.05. The formula for carrying out this adjustment is:

$$p = 1-(1-\alpha)^{\frac{1}{\sqrt{n}}}$$

This turns out to be 0.0034 for 15 tests. A shorter and more commonly used estimate is simply to divide α by the number of tests, which in our case turns out to be 0.0033. Now we only accept as significant a test that produces a significance level less than 0.003.

(Continued)

Box 20.1   (Continued)

For example, suppose that we wish to see how males and females differ in terms of personality. We obtain a large sample using a Big-5 personality test and obtain the following results by carrying out five *t*-tests with the following associated *p*-values:

Extroversion	0.021
Anxiety	0.011
Conscientiousness	0.007
Openness	0.032
Agreeableness	0.046

As we can see, all of our tests reach significance at the $p < 0.05$ level and we might be tempted to assert that the sexes manifest very different personalities. However, the probability of obtaining at least one significant result is 0.226, so the likelihood of a Type I error is quite high. The Bonferonni adjustment tells us that we need to look for a probability of 0.01 before we can assume significance. Thus we can only have confidence in the finding that the sexes differ in terms of conscientiousness.

This all seems very simple and straightforward, but unfortunately such adjustments are not without limitations. It is important to note that, while the adjustment reduces the chances of a Type I error, it increases the chance of a Type II error so that interesting results may be lost to posterity. In addition, there is an implicit assumption that all the tests being used in the analysis have similar power to discriminate the groups and the interpretation of a single finding is dependent upon the number of other tests performed, not their quality. Another limitation is that the Bonferroni adjustment tests the hypothesis that all null hypotheses are true simultaneously, and this is not normally the point of the exercise.

Finally, as discussed in the main text, the Bonferroni adjustment does not take the interrelationships between the variables into account, and this, in my view, is the strongest case for the application of a properly multivariate analysis rather than relying upon multiple bivariate tests.

Adjustments of this sort might get around one of the problems of multiple statistical tests (elevated Type I error), but another, more difficult problem is the one caused by relationships between the dependent variables. Let us consider a simple example in which an educational psychologist is comparing persistent truants with non-truant children on three variables: IQ, scholastic achievement and reading ability. Suppose that the psychologist decides to calculate three *t*-tests to examine the difference between truant and non-truant children on the three dependent variables. She or he finds that each test produces a statistically significant result at the 0.01 level. This may lead to the conclusion that the two groups of children differ on three distinct variables. However, another interpretation may be that the two groups differ significantly on only one of the variables (say, reading ability) and the other two dependent variables reflect this because reading is fundamental to both scholastic achievement and the successful completion of an IQ test. Thus, the IQ measure and the achievement ratings may be highly correlated with the reading test and the fact that they also show significant *t*-tests is an artefact of this relationship. What is needed in this situation is a method of data analysis that takes the relationships between the variables into account. We will return to this example later when we describe the technique known as discriminant function analysis.

Now let us turn to some of the strategies that are typically employed in examining the question of group differences with multivariate data. Typically, this requires that we specify a particular parameter to represent each group and we then make a comparison of that parameter. More often than not this parameter is the mean, although tests exist to compare medians and variances as well. Traditionally, when we are faced with the question of group difference we will look to the set of techniques known as ANOVA in which means are compared (see Chapter 19). In this case we have at least one variable that is measured on the nominal level. The nominal variable represents the group membership. Let us stay with the school truancy example for now; thus one of our variables may be coded 1 if the child in question is a regular truant and 2 if not. The number we give to each group is arbitrary, since all we are conveying by this level of measurement is the group membership for each individual and the number simply serves as a name (hence nominal).

We will begin by describing how group differences may be viewed in the simple bivariate situation and show how this can be generalized to the multivariate case. We will then turn to the situation where we have one independent variable and a number of dependent variables.

20.2.1 Analysis of variance

Let us assume that we have one dependent variable and one independent variable and that the independent variable is categorical. For the purpose of demonstration we will look at the case where the dependent variable is IQ score and the independent variable is truancy. We are interested in group differences, and group membership is represented by the categories of the independent variable (1 = truant, 2 = not truant).

In order to see whether the two groups are different in IQ we would normally perform a *t*-test in which the two means are compared. The *t*-test is actually a special case of the one-way ANOVA when there are just two groups to compare. If we carry out an ANOVA on this data the resulting F statistic will equal the square of the t statistic obtained by a *t*-test. This approach to testing group differences appears quite straightforward.

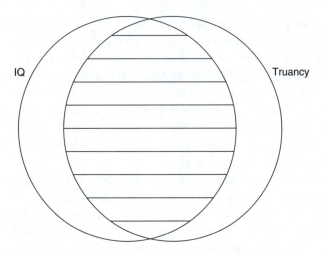

Figure 20.1 Schematic representation of the effect of IQ on truancy

Table 20.1 Summary table for a one-way ANOVA

Source of variation	SS	Degrees of freedom	MS	F
Truancy	40.00	1	40.00	16.00
Residual	120.00	48	2.50	
Total	160.00	49		

In Figure 20.1 we see a schematic diagram of the problem. Note that it looks almost identical to Figure 20.4 in our discussion of correlation in Section 20.3.1. In fact, the principles are essentially the same. We are interested in finding out how much of the dependent variable's variance can be accounted for by variation in the independent variable. This partitioning of the variance is where analysis of variance gets its name. Table 20.1 shows the ANOVA summary.

This tells us a few things about Figure 20.1. The mean square (MS) column informs us that a large amount of the variance of IQ has been accounted for by truancy. This accounted-for variance is greater than the residual or error variance. The statistic F, which tells us whether there are differences between the mean scores of the two groups, is a ratio of accounted-for variance and the residual variance represented by the truancy MS and residual MS, respectively. Because this example involves just two groups, the resulting F statistic of 16.00 is exactly equivalent to a t-test statistic of 4.00.

Let us now move on to consider the multivariate situation where we have more than one independent or 'group' variable. To illustrate this, let us assume that we have simply added the independent variable of sex into the study. We are now interested in seeing whether IQ differs between truants and non-truants as

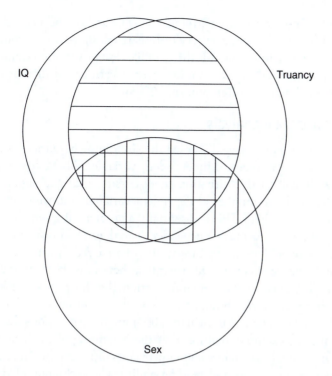

Figure 20.2 Schematic representation of the effect of IQ and sex on truancy

Table 20.2 Summary of a two-way ANOVA

Source of variation	SS	Degrees of freedon	MS	F
Truancy	33.60	1	33.60	13.58
Sex	6.20	1	6.20	2.51
Truancy by sex	6.40	1	6.40	2.59
Residual	113.80	46	2.47	
Total	160.00	49		

well as females and males. We may also be interested in the additional information of the interaction between sex and truancy with respect to IQ.

Figure 20.2 represents this situation schematically. Here, we have two independent variables accounting for a substantial amount of the IQ variance. The part at which they both intersect represents the interaction between truancy and sex. The results may look something like Table 20.2. The largest effect is that of truancy, and this is statistically significant at the 0.05 level (we know this by looking up the value of F with 1 and 46 degrees of freedom in statistical tables). Neither the sex effect nor the interaction between sex and truancy accounts for a statistically significant amount of IQ variance.

The ANOVA procedures are extremely flexible and can be adapted to analyse data derived from a very wide variety of research designs. It is beyond the scope of this brief chapter to go into all the possible design variations, and the interested reader is referred to the comprehensive treatment of this area by Winer (1978) or Hinkelmann and Kempthorne (2005).

20.2.2 Discriminant analysis

So far in this section we have discussed the situation where there is one dependent variable and a number of independent variables. At the beginning of this chapter we alluded to this situation in discussing multiple significance tests where we have a large number of dependent variables and we wish to see how our groups differ on them. This is essentially a problem of group discrimination. In other words, we are using our dependent variables to allow us to discriminate between the groups. The method most often employed in this case is multiple discriminant function analysis. Our treatment here must be very brief; should it whet the reader's appetite for more information, the short book by Klecka (1980) is a more comprehensive though very readable account. For more statistical detail, Huberty (1994) and McLachlan (2004) might also be consulted.

Let us take the example mentioned at the beginning of this chapter. We are interested in seeing how truants and non-truants differ on the three variables of IQ, scholastic achievement and reading ability. The technique of **discriminant function analysis** begins by forming a composite of the dependent variables such that this composite variable will maximally discriminate between the groups. This composite variable (or function), as in the case of multiple regression, is made up by weighting the dependent variables. A simple analysis of the group differences on this composite variable is then carried out. If there are just two groups this analysis is equivalent to a simple t-test and, as it was developed by Harold Hotelling, is known as Hotelling's T^2-test. Where there are more than two groups a large number of alternative tests are possible but they mostly use the chi-squared statistic to test for significance.

The result of our example may look like Table 20.3. Here we see that the multiple t-tests suggest that all of the variables differentiate the two groups significantly. The multivariate test tells us that the two groups can indeed be discriminated, but when we look at the weights on the discriminant function it is apparent that reading ability is the important variable and that the other two have little or no relevance. This tells us that the discriminant function (composite) is essentially one of reading ability. When we look at the group means on this function, we see that the truant group has a low score while the non-truant group has a high score (we have already observed that this difference is statistically significant).

However, IQ and scholastic achievement also have significant bivariate t-test statistics, and we are now saying that they have no relevance. This is because we

margin note: discriminant function analysis

Table 20.3 Discriminant analysis on data from the school example

	Control group mean	Truant group mean	
t-tests			
IQ	101.23	94.20	$t = 3.56$
Reading	100.83	82.63	$t = 5.62$
Achievement	104.10	88.55	$t = 5.44$
Discriminant function weights			
	Raw	**Standard**	
Reading	1.342	0.723	
Achievement	0.344	0.251	
IQ	−0.333	−0.116	
Group means			
Phobic	−1.562		
Control	1.621		

can now see that they are largely made up of reading ability. In other words, reading is necessary to perform well on the IQ test and it is also an essential part of scholastic achievement. The discriminant analysis has shown us that it is reading problems that discriminate the truant group from the non-truant group. This gives us the potential for remedial intervention, which may not have been the case had we assumed that truancy was largely a function of IQ.

This is a very simple example of discriminant function analysis and it is often the case that we are trying to discriminate between more than two groups. In this case, the analysis will generate more than one function. The maximum number of functions will be one less than the number of groups or one less than the number of dependent variables, whichever is the smaller. Each function can be assessed for statistical significance, usually by a chi-squared statistic, and they are always presented in descending significance. When multiple functions exist they must be interpreted by examining which variables have been weighted the most in forming them. The group means (sometimes called **centroids**) on the function are then examined to see how they discriminate the groups.

centroids

One of the uses that discriminant analysis is sometimes put to is to classify new cases where the group is unknown. Suppose we have a new child at our school; we have his IQ, reading ability score and scholastic achievement record and we wish to predict whether he will become a truant or not. We can use the weights generated in our discriminant function analysis to estimate his score on the function. This allows us to estimate the probable group that he belongs to. In this way we can see that discriminant function analysis serves the function of a multiple regression analysis when the criterion variable is a nominal group membership variable.

Discriminant function analysis is a very useful method but it does entail a number of strict assumptions. Most importantly, an assumption of normal distributions among the discriminating variables is made. This is also true for the traditional ANOVA procedures, but it is rather more critical with discriminant function analysis.

The larger the sample size the more reliable the results, but there are no easy 'rules of thumb' in discriminant analysis to let us know how large a sample is adequate. Certainly, each group should be large enough to enable us to argue that they are representative of the population of such people. As a general rule it would be inadvisable to carry out a discriminant function analysis with fewer than 30 subjects in each group, and much larger samples should be aimed for.

The discussion so far has assumed that the discriminating variables are measured at the interval level. Procedures for carrying out discriminant analysis on categorical data do exist, but they are not readily available in existing computer packages. The interested reader might consult Anderson (1972) for a mathematical description. Alternatively, a technique mentioned later in this chapter – called correspondence analysis – might prove useful.

One situation that we have not mentioned is the one in which we have a number of independent variables as well as multiple dependent variables. The typical **multivariate** method of data analysis in this case is **multivariate analysis of variance** **analysis of** (MANOVA). MANOVA is simply a generalization of ANOVA and discriminant **variance** function analysis, combining the generation of composites with variance partitioning. The procedure is extremely complex and general, and it can be shown that multiple regression and canonical variate analysis are also special cases of the MANOVA model. Most psychological researchers come across MANOVA when they are trying to carry out a simple ANOVA analysis with repeated measures using a computer package such as SPSS. This simply shows that nearly all ANOVA designs are a special case of MANOVA, which in this case is just the name of the program subroutine and not the specific analysis method.

For any reader who has an interest in the statistical models underlying these methods the MANOVA is a fascinating model, and an excellent introductory account is provided in Marascuilo and Levin (1983).

20.3 MAKING PREDICTIONS

Let us now turn to the second common question: how can we use our data to make predictions? For example, having carried out a piece of research showing that self-efficacy is related to recovery time after a hospital operation, how can we predict recovery time if we know a patient's self-efficacy level? Typically, this **regression** kind of question is addressed by a class of multivariate methods known as **regression** procedures. We will describe the commonest form of regression analysis,

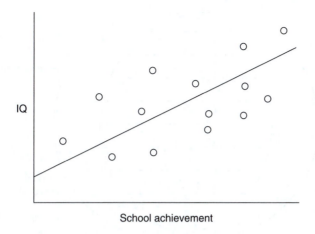

IQ

School achievement

Figure 20.3 Scatterplot of IQ against school achievement

starting with the special bivariate case where we have one predictor and one dependent variable. We will then develop our arguments to include the multivariate situation.

20.3.1 Simple regression

As an example of simple regression, we will consider the problem of predicting scholastic achievement from IQ. In Figure 20.3 we see the relationship between IQ score and reading ability represented in a scatterplot. We can see that the relationship is a positive one such that an individual with a high IQ will tend to have a high scholastic achievement. Thus if we know an individual's IQ score we can make a guess at their likely scholastic achievement score. In fact, we can do better than that: we can estimate the scholastic achievement score statistically.

To do this we first calculate the position of the regression line. This is the straight line that passes through the scattered points such that the distance from the points to the line is minimized. The slope of the line is calculated as the parameter beta (β) and the intercept (i.e. the point at which the line cuts across the X-axis) is estimated as parameter alpha (α). Given a new individual with a known IQ X, we can then estimate the achievement score Y by using the formula:

$$Y = \beta X + \alpha \qquad (20.1)$$

Thus, β is a weight which is applied to our predictor variable to optimally predict our dependent or criterion variable. The parameter α is simply a scaling parameter to transform the scale of the predictor variable to that of the criterion variable (IQ score to scholastic achievement score). This estimate is accurate only if

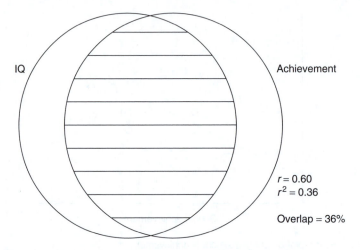

Figure 20.4   Schematic representation of a correlation between two variables

the points in the scatterplot are close to the regression line since we are using this line as our 'model' of how the two variables are related. If all the points in the plot lie on the regression line we will have an absolute correlation coefficient of 1.00 and we will have a perfectly accurate estimate. The product moment correlation coefficient refers to a relationship represented by the product of the moments around the regression line. Thus, whenever the correlation is less than 1.00 and greater than −1.00 we have some inaccuracy in our prediction.

Let us think of this correlation between IQ and scholastic achievement in another way. Figure 20.4 shows a schematic representation of the relationship in which each variable is conceptualized as a ball of variance. Where a correlation exists two variables are said to co-vary; this is represented by an overlap between the two variables. In Figure 20.4 we see that the correlation between IQ and scholastic achievement is 0.60; the squared correlation (0.36) represents the proportion of covariance or overlapping variance between the two variables. This tells us that 36% of the variance of scholastic achievement is shared with IQ and the remaining 64% is unique or residual.

Note that where correlations are concerned we assume that each variable has been standardized to have a mean of zero and a variance of 1.00. This is done automatically when we calculate the product moment correlation. Thus, if two variables have a perfect correlation of 1.00 or −1.00, they will be represented as two perfectly overlapping spheres in which 100% of the variance is shared.

20.3.2 Multiple regression

From this analysis we might be tempted to say that scholastic achievement is a function of IQ. However, we have to be very careful about making causal judgements. Causality can be shown only if three features are true:

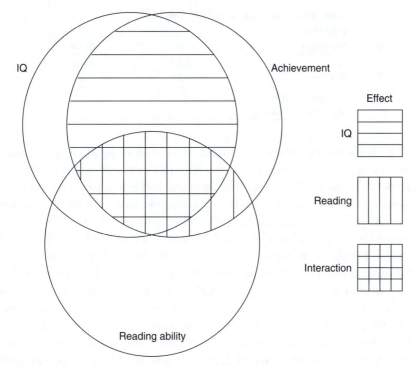

Figure 20.5 Schematic representation of a correlation between three variables

1 *A* is related to *B*;
2 *A* precedes *B*;
3 the relationship between *A* and *B* is not due to their joint relationship with *C*.

We have demonstrated point 1 and we may use theoretical argument to assert that point 2 holds, but point 3 remains a problem. It tells us to beware of confounding variables. Let us consider one such variable, reading ability. Figure 20.5 shows a schematic representation of the relationships between the three variables of scholastic achievement, IQ and reading ability. The first thing is that when we look at IQ and reading ability together we notice that we have accounted for a greater proportion of scholastic achievement than with IQ alone. We also note that some of the covariance between IQ and achievement is also shared by reading ability. If we were to take only the covariation unique to IQ and achievement and exclude that (crosshatched) part we would be partialling out the effect of reading ability. This would result in what is known as the **partial correlation**. Note that since we are talking about proportions of variance, of course, we are describing the squared partial correlation. Thus, while the correlation of IQ with achievement is 0.60 when we partial out the effect of reading ability, we may find that the resulting partial correlation becomes 0.50.

partial correlation

Table 20.4 Multiple regression with two predictors

Predictor	r	Beta
IQ	0.60	0.45
Reading	0.60	1.34

Multiple $r = 0.80$
Multiple $r^2 = 0.64$

The multiple regression method utilizes this notion of partitioning of variance to find the optimal prediction of one variable (achievement) given a number of predictors (IQ, reading ability). The fundamental idea is to account for as much of the variance of the criterion variable as possible. We have seen that the variance of the criterion variable, achievement, can be partitioned into that which is accounted for by IQ, reading ability and the interaction or overlap of the two, and that which remains, which is commonly termed the residual or unique variance.

Of course, these schematic representations of the process are rather simple. In practice we do not use such graphical methods for analysing our data but rather resort to sophisticated mathematical estimation methods. These essentially involve the generation of a composite variable consisting of the relevant parts of the predictor variables plus a rescaling coefficient. This composite is constructed in order to produce a maximal correlation between it and the criterion variable. This composite variable represents the estimate of the criterion variable given the predictor variables. Beta weights for the predictor variables are calculated as in the bivariate case. The predicted value is then calculated by:

$$Y = \alpha + \beta_1 X_1 + \beta_2 X_2 + \dots + \beta_n X_n \tag{20.2}$$

The size of the beta weight indicates the relative weight of the standardized predictor variable in question. Variables with greater weights are more relevant to the prediction equation. For our example, the results of the regression analysis are given in Table 20.4. Here we see that reading ability is the most important variable in predicting achievement.

stepwise regression It is possible to carry out a **stepwise regression** in which the computer program (no one does multiple regression by hand any more) will select the best combination of predictors for accounting for the criterion variance. One procedure is to use all the possible predictors and take them out one at a time until a more parsimonious but almost equally accurate solution results (step-down method). Alternatively, the program could select the predictors one at a time to build up the solution (step-up method). Most programs now include a method that combines both strategies (stepwise method). Personally, I have always found the step-down method to be most useful, although it is really a matter of individual preference.

The multiple regression analysis also provides a multiple correlation coefficient which represents the correlation between the composite of predictor variables and the criterion variable. The composite is simply an estimate of the criterion variable estimated by formula (20.2). Thus, if we manage a perfect prediction, Y (from (20.2)) will be identical to the criterion score for every individual. The multiple correlation between Y and the criterion variable will be perfect and will produce a coefficient of 1. The statistical significance of the multiple r is estimated by carrying out an analysis of the ratio of accounted variance over residual variance. This is exactly equivalent to the ANOVA test which provides an F statistic.

20.3.3 Further issues in regression

The procedures we have been talking about here entail a number of strict assumptions. Firstly, they are parametric methods. The use of the product moment correlation always assumes that the variables in question have a relatively normal distribution and that the relationships between the variables are assumed to be linear. If the variables cannot be assumed to be normally distributed it may be appropriate to use a non-parametric correlation coefficient as a starting point. The non-parametric product moment correlation is Spearman's rho, which is essentially a Pearsonian correlation on the data after they have been transformed into ranks. However, if this is done it is important that the researcher realizes that they are simply predicting the **rank order** of the criterion variable and not the actual value.

rank order

In addition, it is important that a relatively large sample size is used so that the sampling error, which inflates the correlation coefficient, is minimized, thus increasing the precision of the correlation estimate. This would normally mean that a multiple regression should be attempted only with a sample size in excess of 100 (Kerlinger & Pedhazur, 1973). If the sample size is smaller the reliability of the result may be open to question. However, in the research process there may be times where it is interesting to carry out the analysis on smaller samples. When reporting a regression analysis, it is important to indicate the sample size.

Another problem with the multiple regression method is that it loses accuracy when the predictor variables are highly correlated with each other. This situation is known as **multicollinearity** and causes difficulty when estimating the beta weights. In order to mitigate this problem, techniques exist such as **ridge estimation** or **Stein-type estimation**. These are not commonly available on the most widely used computer packages, so it is good policy to take care that your predictors are reasonably independent of each other by examining the simple correlations between your variables before proceeding.

multicollinearity

ridge estimation

Stein-type estimation

Other methods of regression analysis exist for cases where non-linear relationships are assumed, although these non-linear methods are theoretically and mathematically complex. Methods also exist for categorical data: these methods include **logistic regression, logit analysis** and **probit analysis.** Detailed discussion of these methods is beyond the scope of this chapter, but the interested reader is referred to Clogg and Stockley (1988) and Haberman (1978; 1979). Tabachnick and Fidell (2001) give an excellent introduction to logistic regression which is used when the criterion variable is categorical, and a more detailed coverage may be found in Hosmer and Lemeshow (1989).

One situation that we have not touched upon is the case where the researcher has more than one criterion variable as well as a number of predictor variables. In this case, one set of variables is being used to predict responses on another set of variables. The method used in this case is known as **canonical variate analysis**. Again this brief chapter cannot do justice to this method, and the interested reader is referred to the excellent introductory treatment in Hair, Anderson, Tatham and Black (1992: Chapter 5) or Tabachnick and Fidell (2001). For more detail, try Tacq (1997: Chapter 10).

20.4 EXPLORING UNDERLYING STRUCTURE

A very common research question concerns the underlying structure of our data. Often in multivariate research we are interested in finding out whether our variables imply the existence of some superordinate structure. For example, 50 questions in a personality questionnaire designed to measure the Big-5 personality factors are assumed to manifest an underlying structure comprising five traits – extroversion, anxiety, conscientiousness, openness and agreeableness. Alternatively, it might be hypothesized that a group of 30 symptoms from a checklist are clustered into two groups relating to psychological and physical symptomatology. In each of these cases we are interested in examining the underlying structure of our observed variables.

One of the main reasons for examining the underlying structure of our data is so that we can describe what is being observed in a more parsimonious way. Thus, we can describe the 30 symptoms mentioned above in terms of only 2 superordinate variables, psychological and physical symptomatology.

The underlying structure of a group of variables is implied by the interrelationships that exist between them. This means that for nearly all of the methods described below the first step is the calculation of inter-variable associations. These are usually, but not always, correlation coefficients. The table of all inter-variable correlation coefficients is known as the correlation matrix, and it is the structure implied by this matrix that is to be explored.

Although we are addressing the exploration of underlying structure, it is important to realize that no good research is entirely exploratory. The selection of the variables will have been informed by some theoretical position. The fact that we are looking at the structure implies that we have reasoned grounds for such a tactic. In other words, we will usually have some a priori expectation, at least in broad terms, of what we will discover. This expectation need not be formally stated but it will be useful to use as a yardstick when we have to interpret our analyses.

In this section, I will briefly describe three methods for analysing multivariate structure: these are factor analyses, cluster analyses and multidimensional scaling analyses. We will then turn to the issue of **confirmatory** or **restricted analyses**.

confirmatory
restricted
analyses

20.4.1 Factor analysis

One of the most widely used approaches for exploring the underlying structure of a set of variables is **factor analysis**. This is a global term describing a wide variety of different techniques developed primarily as a means of examining the existence of underlying latent traits. This means that the use of factor analysis cannot ever be said to be purely exploratory, since the most basic assumption of this method is that the structure may be described in terms of one or more bipolar constructs.

factor analysis

As with nearly all methods for examining structure, factor analysis begins with the calculation of the inter-variable correlation matrix. It is most important to note that almost all factor analysis methods require that these correlations are product moment estimates or direct estimates of covariation.

The analysis proceeds to identify the set of underlying linear traits that are best implied by the inter-variable relationships. In fact, the analysis generates underlying composite variables in much the same way that regression and discriminant analysis do. These composites are then identified and interpreted by observing their correlations or regression weights with each variable included in the analysis.

The factor analysis treats the correlation matrix as a ball of inter-variable variance and extracts chunks of variance to represent each underlying factor sequentially. These 'chunks' get smaller as each factor is extracted. The mathematical terminology for these chunks is the **eigenvalue**. Thus, the first factor extracted has a relatively large eigenvalue and each successive factor is built around a smaller chunk of variance or eigenvalue than the preceding one.

eigenvalue

As an example, let us look at a questionnaire study on environmental concern. A short 20-item checklist taken from Ashford (1994) was administered to 311 university students. Each item concerned an environmental issue such as 'global warming' and 'threat to sea mammals', and the respondents were asked to indicate the degree of concern they felt for that issue on a five-point rating scale. It was expected that the resulting 20 variables would be described by 3 underlying factors relating to global, local and wildlife concerns. A 20×20 correlation matrix was generated and a factor analysis was performed. The 3 eigenvalues extracted were 8.76, 2.93 and 1.71. The resulting structure is reported in Table 20.5. Here we

Table 20.5 The factor structure of 20 pro-environment behaviours

Variable	Factors I	II	III
Global warming	0.88	0.01	−0.26
Ozone layer	0.91	0.03	−0.28
Water pollution	0.61	0.17	0.12
Air pollution	0.69	0.12	0.14
Factory farming	0.29	0.49	0.09
Endangered wildlife	0.17	0.81	0.12
Threat to forests	0.11	0.45	−0.15
Overpopulation	0.45	0.17	0.15
Acid rain	0.60	0.17	0.21
Threat of nuclear power	0.53	−0.02	0.28
Fossil fuels	0.48	−0.13	0.37
Cruelty to animals	−0.12	0.81	0.09
Trade in rare animal products	−0.06	0.89	0.01
Litter	−0.20	0.26	0.71
Transport congestion	0.51	0.02	0.36
Waste disposal	0.47	0.03	0.43
Bulding on green belt land	0.12	0.41	0.40
Food contamination	0.22	0.01	0.69
Noise nuisance	0.01	0.03	0.81
Threat to sea mammals	0.05	0.78	0.02
Factor correlation matrix			
Factor 1	1.00		
Factor 2	0.40	1.00	
Factor 3	0.30	0.31	1.00

see that each factor is represented as a column of numbers. Each number is known as a loading, and describes the weight that each item has on the factor in question. We use the term 'loading' here to be compatible with much of the existing literature on factor analysis, but the reader should be aware that the term 'structural coefficient' is increasingly being advocated. What we can immediately see is that the large (or salient) loadings on factor 1 belong to items associated with global issues. Factor 2 has high loadings from items relating to wildlife, while factor 3 appears to be associated with local issues.

Note that some items have quite large loadings (here we take 0.35 or above as salient) on more than one factor. Thus, 'transport congestion' is seen as relevant **factorially** to both local and global issues. These items are known as **factorially complex**. **complex**

Factor analysis is essentially a descriptive method. This means that the usefulness of the technique is a function of how interpretable the solution is. However, there are a number of pitfalls in factor analysis that this simple example has not highlighted.

The first problem is deciding how many factors to extract. In this example we extracted three factors because we had good reason (from Ashford's work) to expect this solution. Often, we do not have an a priori expectation of the appropriate number of factors. Indeed, the technique allows the researcher to extract as many factors as there are variables, which would be unhelpful. The researcher has to have some broad expectation of the number of potential factors before embarking on a factor analysis. A number of strategies for deciding on the number of factors have been proposed, but none is without limitations.

One of the most commonly used criteria is also one of the worst, and this is to extract only as many factors as have eigenvalues greater than or equal to 1. This method will usually extract more factors than appropriate and so it has some value as a means of identifying an upper bound. Despite its use in common practice and its occasional recommendation in the literature, the researcher is strongly advised to avoid the use of this criterion for deciding the number of factors. The advice we present here is to use **interpretability** as the criterion for selecting the number of factors. This means that the researcher identifies the minimum and maximum number of factors and carries out an analysis for each potential solution. The solution which makes the most theoretical sense is the most appropriate. Clearly, this method involves an element of subjective interpretation, but it assumes that the researcher is in tune with the theoretical underpinnings of the data and that the interpretation is properly detailed in the dissemination of results. To find out more about alternative methods to aid in deciding the number of factors, the researcher is referred to the classic works by Cattell (1978), McDonald (1985) and Harman (1976).

interpretability

Another bone of contention in factor analysis is the issue of rotation. This is where the initial factor-loading matrix is transformed to aid in interpretation. Essentially, this involves moving the variance around to overcome the artefact where successive factors contain less variance than those preceding them. There are two types of rotation (although there are many techniques) termed orthogonal and oblique. **Orthogonal rotation** involves a transformation that forces the underlying factors to be uncorrelated with each other. **Oblique rotation**, on the other hand, allows the factors to be correlated. Some authors advise the researcher to use orthogonal rotation (Child, 1990) because it is supposed to be 'simpler'. Indeed, orthogonal rotation, using the **Varimax** technique, is the default option on many computer programs. However, psychologists rarely deal with constructs that are unrelated to each other. In our example, it would be odd if concern for global issues was not correlated with concern over other environmental issues. If we were to use orthogonal rotation in this case we would be imposing an unnecessary artefactual restriction on our data. In Table 20.5 we also see the correlations between the factors which indicate a high degree of relationship.

orthogonal rotation

oblique rotation

varimax

Factor analysis is a huge topic, but anyone wishing to use the method should take the time to find out about the various controversies and pitfalls that attend it. A good text in this vein can be found in Thompson (2004) The method is widely used, but it is also very widely misused and many poor factor-analytic studies succeed in being published, which makes it difficult for the young researcher to identify best practice from the literature. However, one rule of thumb is that if a study reports a factor solution in which the number of factors is decided by eigenvalues greater than 1 and it is then rotated by the varimax criterion without justification of the orthogonal structure, the chances are that it is an ill-considered and opportunistic analysis simply availing itself of canned computer program default options. When writing up a factor analysis the author should justify the use of the method, the choice of the number of factors extracted and the rotational strategy employed.

A final point worth highlighting is the need for a good sample size. Since the factor analysis is a variance partitioning method we need a sample size that minimizes sampling error. To produce a reliable factor solution it is advisable that a sample size of at least 200 is used where possible. As a general rule it is also recommended that there are at least four times as many subjects as variables. Smaller samples can of course be used, although the reliability of the solution may be questionable.

20.4.2 Cluster analysis

cluster analysis

Factor analysis is widely used but, as we have seen, it is not without limitations. An alternative method of exploring underlying structure which may be more supportable with the data psychologists often handle is termed **cluster analysis** (Blashfield & Aldenderfer, 1988; Everitt, Landau & Leese, 2001).

The basic premise of cluster analysis is that the variables can be grouped into discrete clusters. Thus in our environmental concerns example we might expect the variables to group into three discrete groups representing global concerns, local concerns and wildlife concerns. Unlike factor analysis, we do not expect these clusters to represent an underlying bipolar trait ranging from high to low concern but simply understand them as a descriptive set of categories. These clusters can be represented as simple nominal categories or as hierarchical arrangements in which all variables belong in one superordinate (general concern) cluster which may be broken down into more and more clusters.

partitioning non-hierarchical methods

Cluster analysis is often used to cluster people rather than variables (although the example we use here clusters variables). Commonly, this involves a variety of clustering methods termed **partitioning** or **non-hierarchical methods**. These methods usually require the user to tell the program how many clusters are expected. The program then places objects (people or variables) into the relevant clusters according to the similarity they have with each other. The idea is that objects within a particular cluster will be more similar to each other than to objects in other clusters.

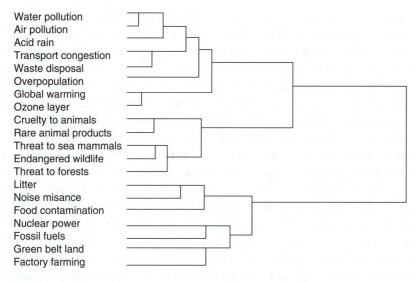

Figure 20.6 Hierarchical cluster analysis dendrogram of 20 pro-environmental behaviours

The **hierarchical methods** generally start by placing each object into its own unique cluster and then, by examining the similarity of the objects, merging the two most similar into a new cluster. The resulting N–1 clusters are then examined and another merger occurs. This continues until only one cluster remains.

Unlike factor analysis, cluster analysis does not place a great many demands upon the researcher and is accessible to a wider range of data types. Like factor analysis, it relies upon the relationships between the objects to describe the underlying structure. Factor analysis is a variance partitioning method; this means that the measure of the inter-variable relationship must be a measure of covariance or correlation. Cluster analysis, in contrast, can start from any symmetric measure of association. This means that it may be carried out using data that do not allow the use of product moment correlations. For example, Kendall's tau (τ) or the Goodman–Kruskal gamma (γ) for ordinal variables may be used and, if skewed dichotomies exist, non-parametric association coefficients such as Jaccard's index or Yule's Q. More commonly, cluster analysis uses the simple Euclidean distance coefficient.

As an example of a hierarchical cluster analysis we will use the data already used in the factor analysis above. A summary of the results is presented in Figure 20.6. This figure presents a dendrogram showing the hierarchical structure of the 20

hierarchical methods

environmental concerns. It is clear immediately that there are three distinct clusters that appear to overlap well with the factor solution of Table 20.5.

As with factor analysis, cluster analysis presents the user with the problem of specifying the number of clusters to use in describing the data structure. Again, the best way to address this problem is to develop a sound theoretical justification for the solution chosen. A number of less subjective methods have been developed but, as with factor analysis, these operate outside the substantive context of the research. One strategy that I have employed with some success is to generate a series of cluster solutions using different methods of clustering. The solution showing the most agreement across methods is the solution that may have greatest reliability. However, this procedure still requires that the researcher has some idea of the upper and lower bound for numbers of clusters.

Another challenge in the use of cluster analysis is the interpretation of the clusters. This is particularly a problem when people rather than variables have been clustered because we do not necessarily have a simple label we can apply to each person in our sample as we do for the variables, so a generalized cluster label is hard to identify.

A common strategy in identifying clusters of people is to carry out a non-hierarchical partitioning cluster analysis and then to treat the cluster membership as a criterion variable in a subsequent discriminant function analysis. In this way each cluster may be defined by the composite functions that discriminate them. When clustering people in this way the usual focus of the study is to identify some kind of typology and this is perhaps the simplest way of distinguishing between factor analysis and cluster analysis. Factor analysis assumes an underlying trait model, while cluster analysis assumes a simple type model.

20.4.3 Multidimensional scaling

multidimensional scaling

We now move on to briefly describe another method that offers yet another way of examining data structures. Parametric methods for **multidimensional scaling** (MDS) grew originally out of early work on factor analysis. However, in the 1960s and 1970s a series of non-parametric methods became available and it is these so-called non-metric methods that we commonly refer to when using the term MDS.

The basic idea of MDS is to represent data spatially by plotting variables as points in n-dimensional space. The distance between the points represents the similarity of the variables. Thus, if variable X is highly correlated with variable Y then these two variables will be situated close together on the plot. The advantage of MDS is that the structure of the data can be examined in a number of

regionality

ways. For example, we can examine the **regionality** of the space by identifying regions occupied by a particular group of variables. Alternatively, we can examine the shape of the plot; for example, whether the variables arrange themselves in a straight line or a circle.

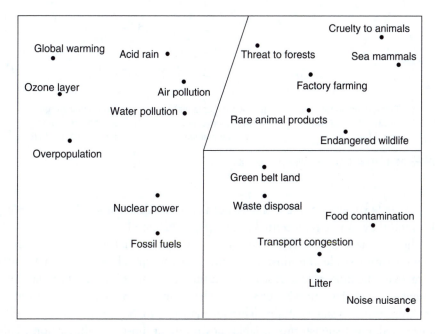

Figure 20.7   Multidimensional scaling analysis of 20 environmental concerns

Non-metric MDS has very few assumptions and is appropriate for most forms of data. Because MDS solutions may be interpreted very broadly, they are an ideal choice when carrying out entirely exploratory work. They are particularly effective for theory building since the method does not tend to impose a model on the data that may influence the interpretation as the linear factor model does. However, this may also be seen as a problem because it means that interpreting MDS solutions is often a somewhat arbitrary and subjective affair. As we have stated above, there is no replacement for some kind of a priori expectation in interpreting structure, but when these expectations do not include underlying linear traits or discrete groupings, MDS is a useful method. The combination of facet theory and MDS is a very potent research strategy since it merges the strict conceptualization of the research topic with a flexible and open-ended data analytic technique.

In order to demonstrate an MDS analysis the same environmental concern data were used. A two-dimensional plot is reported in Figure 20.7. In this plot we can see the three regions of global, local and wildlife concern emerging. It is also worth noting the almost circular structure that emerges.

Apart from the necessary subjectivity in interpretation, MDS has a problem in common with factor analysis and cluster analysis: that of choosing the number of dimensions to represent the data. It should be apparent that the maximum **dimensionality** we can expect will be one less than the number of variables. Thus,   **dimensionality**
two variables need only one dimension (a straight line) to represent them

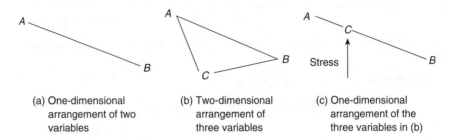

(a) One-dimensional arrangement of two variables

(b) Two-dimensional arrangement of three variables

(c) One-dimensional arrangement of the three variables in (b)

Figure 20.8 The dimensionality of three variables

(Figure 20.8(a)), while three variables need only two dimensions (Figure 20.8(b)) although they can be represented in one (Figure 20.8(c)).

When we have 20 variables the maximum dimensionality is 19: however, it would be impossible for most researchers to conceptualize a 19-dimensional space. Even the most able of researchers cannot think in terms of more than four dimensions, and even that is not simple. Three dimensions is about all any of us can hold in our heads spatially. This means that MDS, in order to be readily interpreted, must squash the variables down into at most four dimensions. This 'squashing' results in pressure as our recalcitrant variables want to express their true dimensionality and push against the constraints imposed by the MDS. This pressure is measured by an index known variously as the **stress coefficient** or **alienation coefficient** and it ranges between 0 and 1. The smaller this coefficient is, the less the pressure, and the better the data fit the MDS solution. Unfortunately, there is no hard and fast rule that says what is a 'good' stress measure. In our example the stress was 0.15, and this would normally be considered reasonable for 20 items. Advice on the size of the stress ranges widely from the very strict (Kruskal, 1964) to the more *laissez-faire* (Shye, 1988).

The only advice I can give here is to suggest that interpretability is the first and most important criterion. Clearly, if you find you can interpret a solution but the stress is very high, say 0.60, then you will need to question the tenets of your interpretation since the data do not appear to fit very well.

One drawback with MDS is the dearth of readily accessible texts describing the methods for the beginner, exceptions being Kruskal and Wish (1978) and Schiffman, Reynolds and Young (1981). Indeed, the techniques are still relatively new and are being developed and improved all the time for both general and specific research contexts. Two excellent accounts of MDS developments to date can be found in Borg and Groenen (1997) and Cox and Cox (2001).

20.4.4 The myth of confirmatory methods

So far we have been concerned to describe three methods for exploring the underlying structure of your data. It should be clear that, despite the use of the term 'explore', the effective use of these methods requires that the researcher has some theoretical expectations of what they might find. Indeed, carrying out a factor analysis without understanding that the result will suggest underlying linear structure would be a waste of time and may result in the researcher thinking that they have discovered something that they themselves imposed on the solution. Nevertheless, these methods may still be used in an exploratory way since the researcher may not have a formalized set of hypotheses but, rather, a number of broad expectations.

There is now an increasing interest in approaches claiming to be confirmatory as opposed to exploratory (see Box 20.2). Essentially, what this means is that the researcher is asked to generate a formal model of the relationships between the variables. This model is then tested for fit to the empirical data, resulting in a statistic evaluating the degree of misfit to the model. This statistic is usually based on chi-squared. The most useful of these approaches grew out of factor analysis and came to be called variously linear structural relations analysis or covariance structure analysis. In Chapter 21 we will examine the natural extension of this work under the heading of structured equation modelling.

Box 20.2   Confirmatory methods

There is now an increasing interest in methods of data analysis that are termed 'confirmatory' as opposed to 'exploratory'. A number of computer programs now exist for carrying out these analyses and they are becoming generally available. While most of these have grown out of factor analysis methods, it should be mentioned that a number of 'confirmatory' methods have also grown out of MDS (see Borg & Groenen, 1997). The basic idea is excellent: the researcher is expected to set up a model (essentially a system of hypotheses concerning the relationships between variables) and then demonstrate that his or her data conform to, or fit, the model by means of a statistical test.

At its simplest, confirmatory analyses work by restricting the data to the model in question. Thus, a confirmatory factor analysis might posit a model in which the number of factors is known and each variable is identified with one of these factors. In this way a target matrix is constructed that forms the template for the factor structure. The data, in the form of an inter-variable covariance matrix, are then made to 'fit' the target as best they can under a number of constraints. The best-fitting solution is retained and the degree of fit, often based upon the amount of variance accounted for by the model, is calculated.

Confirmatory analyses range from very simple Procrustean methods for rotation and multiple group factor analysis, to much more sophisticated methods in which extremely sophisticated models can be tested.

However, despite the attractiveness of the concept, the idea of confirmatory analysis is not without difficulties and we describe a few of them here. First,

(Continued)

Box 20.2 (Continued)

confirmatory methods are generally built on strict linear systems. This is a challenge rather than a limitation, since it means that the researcher, firstly, must find a way of couching their model in linear terms and this may sometimes be awkward. Thus, if we wanted to test the hypothesis of a circumplex relationship between our variables (meaning that the variables form a circle in Euclidean space) we would have to formally represent it in linear form. It is certainly possible to do this, but it adds an extra layer of sophistication to the analysis.

Secondly, the statistics that tell us whether the data fit the model can be severely problematic and many tend to be dependent on sample size. This suggests that a large sample size will almost inevitably produce an inflated chi-squared statistic, signifying that the data do not fit the model. A number of coefficients for fit without this drawback have been proposed but they generally do not allow statistical inference to be made, so they take on the purely descriptive status of the stress coefficient in MDS.

Thirdly, a difficulty with confirmatory methods is that, although they are termed 'confirmatory', they actually confirm nothing. Simply finding that the data do not contradict a model does not confirm that model. Note that these methods work by constraining the freedom of the solution parameters to emerge in a way that contradicts the model. Remember, too, that for each model there are a large number of competing models that may fit the data as well or better. Typically, these models are not tested. This, coupled with the weakness of the 'confirmatory' statistics, does not support the extravagant claims that are sometimes made about the use of these methods.

I do not wish to appear to be advising against the use of these methods since they can be extremely useful in the appropriate context (see, for example, the special case of item response theory mentioned in Chapter 10). However, a better term to describe such methods is as *restricted* rather than *confirmatory*. This is because the data are constrained to fit, as best as possible, the model in question. Once this terminological problem is resolved, we can get back to the basic issue in the multivariate analysis of inter-variable relationships. This is to apply a method which is appropriate to the nature of the research question and is justifiable for the data being analysed. Certainly, in many cases a restricted analysis is appropriate. Confirmation, on the other hand, comes with replication and the accumulation of research findings.

20.5 THE SPECIAL CASE OF CATEGORICAL DATA

So far we have been concentrating our description on variables derived from continuous measures. However, psychological researchers commonly have to deal with categorical data. Increasingly, with the growth of the content analysis of qualitative data there is a demand for multivariate procedures for handling categorical measures.

Traditionally, group differences with categorical variables have been analysed by chi-squared methods. In fact, these methods can be readily generalized to the multivariate situation as long as there are not too many variables. The result is a nominal equivalent of the ANOVA termed **interaction structure analysis** which derives from the partitioned chi-squared model of Lancaster (1969). However, there is very little about the technique in the literature and very few computer programs exist to help the researcher. Interested readers are referred to von Eye (1990).

interaction structure analysis

A commoner strategy is to apply the more general **loglinear methods**. These methods allow the researcher to test differences between groups analogously to ANOVA and also to test predictive models analogous to regression models. A treatment of log-linear methods is beyond the scope of this chapter, and the interested reader is referred to Everitt (1977).

loglinear methods

When the research question involves the examination of underlying structure, special methods exist for categorical variables. However, these techniques are not widely available on computer packages as yet, although SPSS now contains a package of routines specifically designed for such data. The interested reader is referred to Gifi (1990) for full and excellent coverage of these routines.

One useful technique is known variously as **correspondence analysis, dual scaling** or **optimal scaling**. This is essentially a **principal components analysis** (similar to factor analysis) of categorical data but it produces a graphical output much like MDS. In addition to exploring structure, it may also be used as a form of discriminant analysis for categorical data. Interested readers should consult Greenacre (1984), Greenacre and Blasius (1994), Nishisato (1980) or Weller and Romney (1990) or, for a more comprehensive mathematical account, Gifi (1990).

correspondence analysis

dual scaling

optimal scaling

principal components analysis

A number of methods also exist for examining typologies of respondents measured on categorical variables. The interested reader should look up references to **latent class analysis** (Clogg & Stockley, 1988; McCutcheon 1987; Hagenaars & McCutcheon, 2002) and **configural frequency analysis** (von Eye, 2002).

latent class analysis

configural frequency analysis

20.6 CONCLUSION

None of the methods reported here are typically carried out by hand, with the exception of the ANOVAs, although even these are rarely carried out without the use of a computer these days. The use of computer programs for data analysis has liberated researchers from the toil of data analysis and so, presumably, generated more time for thought and consideration of the research process. Unfortunately, the other side of this situation is that researchers have been provided with a host of very sophisticated methods for analysis of their data and there is a temptation to throw the data into the computer in the vague hope that the analysis will tell us something. There is certainly emerging a class of research in which the researchers have taken very little time to understand the basic principles and logic of the methods they use. Such work still manages to emerge in the research literature despite the best efforts of journal reviewers, and its presence at best fails to add much to the body of psychological knowledge, and at worst sets a precedent for the rest of us to misuse the powerful and often mathematically complex techniques that are increasingly available.

This chapter is certainly neither sufficiently comprehensive nor sufficiently detailed to convey the full range and limitation of multivariate data analytic methods. The purpose here has been to give the new researcher some feel for the basic classes of methods that exist. It is fervently hoped that the student researcher will seek out more detailed and critical sources before embarking on their analysis. I finish with a plea that if you are considering a multivariate analysis you will make the acquaintance of the method, its logic, its assumptions, its controversies and its theoretical underpinnings. The unquestioning use of user-friendly computer programs with their hosts of default options is becoming a significant source of suboptimality in psychological research.

20.7 FURTHER READING

An excellent treatment of multivariate data analysis and, in my opinion, the one book that all student researchers should have at their fingertips is Tabachnick and Fidell's (2001). This is written in an easy and accessible style and contains many examples in which the various computer packages are compared. Another useful text that makes effective use of examples is Hair, Tatham, Anderson and Black (1998). This provides detailed examples of a number of the most commonly used techniques. Another very useful reference book is by Nesselroade and Cattell (1988). Although quite old, this text provides a series of review chapters by different authors on a variety of data analytic methods that are particularly well targeted at postgraduate research students.

A real gem of a text that is absolutely free is the online encyclopedia by StatSoft, the publishers of STATISTICA; this can be found at http://www.statsoft.com/textbook/stathome.html Other excellent online texts are those of David Stockburger (http://www.psychstat.missouristate.edu/MultiBook/mlt00.htm) and David Lane (http://davidmlane.com/hyperstat).

If the reader is looking for a reasonably accessible introduction to the statistical background to the methods discussed here, a book that is quite old but still stands out as an excellent pedagogic text is Marascuilo and Levin's (1983) text. Tacq's (1997) is also a good starting point. However, at the more technical end of the continuum it is hard to beat Gifi's (1990). More recently Tinsley and Brown (2000) have provided a useful intermediate level text.

21

Introduction to Structural Equation Modelling

Chris Fife-Schaw

21.1   Introduction

21.2   The idea of model fitting and model comparison

21.3   Measurement models and confirmatory factor analysis

    21.3.1 Identification

    21.3.2 Estimating parameter values

    21.3.3 Modification indices and specification searches

21.4   Structural models

21.5   Analysis strategy

21.6   Other things that can be done with SEM

21.7   Cautionary notes

21.8   Conclusion

21.9   Further reading

AIMS

This chapter introduces a relatively new approach to statistical hypothesis testing that takes a model 'confirmation' approach. By following this approach researchers are encouraged to be quite systematic about what they are doing, and this is to be seen as a 'good thing'. It is included here as this approach to statistics is increasing in popularity and differs in some key respects to the approaches discussed in Chapters 19 and 20.

Key terms	
augmented model	modification indices
bootstrapping	multi-group modelling
compact model	non-recursive models
endogenous variables	observed variables
exogenous variables	parameter
fit indices	proportional reduction in error
fitting function	recursive models
identification	residual variance
Lagrange multiplier tests	specification search
latent variables	structural models
local minimum	uniqueness
measurement models	

21.1 INTRODUCTION

Structural equation modelling (SEM) is a widely used approach that is growing in popularity and one that encourages the organization of systematic research programmes. This chapter has two broad aims. One is to give an overview of the ideas underlying SEM so that articles using it, of which there is an ever-increasing number, can be better understood. The second is to encourage researchers to adopt some of these ideas in the hope of promoting greater rigour in quantitative psychological research. I will try to keep the use of jargon to a minimum but some is inevitable, I am afraid.

observed variables
latent variables
measurement models
structural models

SEM is a set of statistical procedures that can be applied to quantitative data that allow the researcher to: (i) test theoretically specified 'models' of the relationships between **observed variables** (e.g. test scores) and unobserved **latent variables**, which are sometimes called **measurement models**; and (ii) test theoretical models of the relationships between sets of latent variables, which are called **structural models**.

SEM offers immense potential for psychologists since, by and large, most of the things psychologists are interested in are unobserved latent variables, even though we may not normally think of them as such. Personality traits, for instance, cannot be observed directly and we have to infer a person's level of extroversion, say, from their answers to personality test items (observed variables). We do not know what units extroversion should be measured in and we have no direct way of measuring extroversion other than by inferring it from indirect measures such as test responses, peer reports or behaviours, etc. The same applies to attitudes, beliefs, stress, intelligence, depression, anxiety, job satisfaction and a whole host of other popular psychological constructs. Indeed, it is an interesting exercise to list those variables that we are routinely interested in that are not latent in this sense.

Although it is becoming ever more common to see SEM, it remains a mystery for many people. It has its origins in the 1960s (Jöreskog, 1970) and some of the ideas date back much further and are shared with other procedures such as regression, path analysis, factor analysis and loglinear analysis (see Chapter 20). Much of the problem has been that the literature on SEM, and early SEM computer programs, were very mathematical and tended to assume that the reader/user possessed a university-level knowledge of matrix algebra. This had the effect of restricting SEM to a highly numerate and motivated elite, and it is only in the last decade that these techniques and principles have been made readily accessible to the rest of us via more user-friendly computer packages. That said, this user-friendliness has also had the unfortunate side-effect of increasing the number of uncritical uses of SEM where the technique has been used simply because it can be used easily and looks impressive rather than because it was the appropriate analysis to do.

SEM differs from many forms of statistical analysis in that to do it you have to make explicit your theories or models of the relationships between your observed measures and latent variables and the relationships you expect between the latent variables. Doing what is pejoratively called data mining (or 'fishing') in the hope of finding something 'significant' in your data is possible within SEM but is massively time-consuming and usually unrewarding. SEM pushes you to be more rigorous in your approach to data analysis and therefore has to be a good thing, as I hope you will see.

Popular computer packages to conduct SEM include LISREL/SIMPLIS (Jöreskog & Sörbom, 1993), EQS (Bentler, 1995) and AMOS (Arbuckle, 2003) and the list is growing all the time. As this chapter is not intended to be an introduction to any particular software package I will not refer to command syntaxes directly. A good general guide to the range of packages available and the differences between them is given by Ullman (2001).

You should be aware that SEM is known by a number of alternative names, such as analysis of covariance structures, covariance structure modelling, simultaneous equation modelling and (inappropriately as we will see) causal modelling, but these all refer to the same family of procedures.

21.2 THE IDEA OF MODEL FITTING AND MODEL COMPARISON

Underlying SEM is a set of ideas about what constitutes good scientific practice. These lean heavily on the hypothetico-deductive principles discussed in Chapter 1 and assume that you already have a theoretical model about how your measurements or observations are related to latent constructs and how the latent constructs themselves are related to each other. The name of the game is to confront your theoretical model with some hard data and see to what degree your model is consistent with these data. We will see how this is done later, but if your model is not consistent with the data then (assuming the data are good) the model must be wrong and therefore either rejected or modified by respecifying the relationships in the model. If the model is consistent with the data then you can tentatively proceed with it: *you have failed to disconfirm it*. Regrettably, finding a model consistent with the data does not mean you have found 'the true model'; there may be alternative models out there that you have not tested which are as good as or better than your model.

SEM assumes that the goal of research is to generate and test a theoretical model that will allow the accurate prediction of existing and, hopefully, future data points. A theory that cannot make such predictions is not really a theory in the SEM framework. As you might expect, there are some competing pressures in this enterprise. On the one hand you want a theoretical model that provides accurate predictions, but on the other you also want to settle on a simple and parsimonious model. In general, there is little point in making a model so complex that it becomes as complex as the data it is trying to explain. The SEM analyst's task is to decide how best to strike this balance.

An example might help. Suppose you want a theory that will account for why some children get more GCSE exam passes at grade A than others. In SEM terms you want a simple but accurate model that will predict each individual child's exam performances. Assuming we knew nothing about these children as individuals, our best guess at the performance of any given child would probably be the average performance of all children in the population. This would be a very **parameter** simple model with one bit of information and a relationship, or **parameter**, in it (strictly, a parameter is a numerical quantity that describes some aspect of your model in the population). This would not be a very helpful model, though, since it would make the same prediction for each child.

We could make the model more predictive of exam performance by adding extra information about each child to the model. We could add information on their IQ scores and we might reasonably expect that adding this parameter (the relationship between IQ and exam performance) would improve the accuracy of our predictions. If we know a child's IQ we can make a guess at their exam performance because these variables tend to be correlated with each other. Put another way, we would predict that children who score above average on IQ tests would also tend to do better than average in formal exams.

It is possible to go on adding variables and relationships to the model. We could add information about each child's socio-economic status (SES), for example, since research suggests that greater socio-economic advantage tends to be associated with greater success at school and that this effect is probably independent of the effect of IQ on performance. Clearly we could go on adding information about each child to the model until it contained as many parameters as there were children whose performances we wanted to predict. At this point it would be more efficient to simply say Joe Bloggs's score was X, John Brown's score was Y, etc.

Each time we add a new parameter, accuracy will go up (or stay the same) at the expense of making the model more complicated. Ultimately, however, needing to ask for thousands of bits of information from each child to predict performance does not make much sense. We need to find a way to decide whether adding a parameter will produce a worthwhile increase in predictive power. Here we apply the principle (sometimes referred to as Occam's razor) that if two models predict something equally well then we will conclude that the more simple and parsimonious model is more likely to be the correct one.

Conceptually it helps to think about this in the following way:

$$\text{Data} = \text{Model} + \text{Error}$$

The data are the basic observations, the model is your theoretically derived neat and compact explanation or representation of the data, and the error is the amount by which the model fails to represent the data. The error is best thought of as the degree to which the predictions made by the model are inaccurate rather than some kind of mistake. In our example above the (very simple) model says that exam performance is 'caused' by IQ and SES and we can make a prediction about each child's performance based on knowledge of these two variables. However, it is unlikely that our model's predictions for each child will be 100% accurate and the degree to which we get each child's scores wrong is the error. The error is often referred to as **residual variance** in SEM since it may not truly be error but variability in the outcome that is caused by something you have not accounted for (e.g. school teaching quality). It follows from this that:

residual variance

$$\text{Error} = \text{Data} - \text{Model}$$

We need to reduce the error when we build theoretical models, and we can do this by collecting better-quality data, data with less measurement error, using better research designs and adopting better data collection strategies. The error can also be reduced by making the model's predictions conditional on additional information about each case (here a case is a child): this means changing the model by adding parameters such as teaching quality and its relationship to exam performance in the example.

How do you know if a more complicated model with more parameters is 'better' than a simple one? If we start off with a simple model, model C (called a **compact model** in the jargon), and then create a model with more parameters in it, model A (referred to as an **augmented model**), then model A should have the same or less error than model C:

compact model
augmented model

$$\text{Error(A)} < \text{Error(C)}$$

We can work out the **proportional reduction in error** (PRE) we have achieved:

proportional reduction in error

$$\text{PRE} = 1 - \frac{\text{Error (A)}}{\text{Error (C)}}$$

PRE is an index that ranges between 0 and 1. Deciding whether a PRE of, say, 0.40 is worthwhile will depend on inferential statistics (more on this later). However, we would be more impressed by a PRE of 0.40 when it involved adding only 1 more parameter to the model than we would if we had had to add 10 new parameters to achieve the same level of improvement. Also, as the number of data points/observations is usually the upper limit on the number of parameters that can be added to a model, a PRE of 0.40, say, will be more persuasive and impressive when the difference between the number of parameters added and the number that could have been added is big. SEM researchers have developed a whole range of more sophisticated alternative indices to PRE that take this into account.

The endpoint of this kind of approach is to make two decisions. The first is whether the model, even in its augmented form, makes good enough predictions (i.e. it is consistent with the data). The second is to decide whether the improved accuracy (predictive power) of an augmented model has warranted making the original compact model more complicated. Both decisions have to be based on statistical criteria, but they must also meet theoretical criteria. It is possible, for instance, to improve predictive power by adding a parameter that makes no theoretical sense. For example, we could try to predict GCSE exam performances (which are usually taken at age 16 in the UK) by using information about A-level exam performance at age 18, and the chances are that both these bits of information will be highly correlated with each other and the predictive power will be high. A theory for understanding academic performance at age 16 that uses information collected after the age of 16 is hardly of much use theoretically or practically, however.

This is the broad logic of what is going on in SEM. In practice, rather than trying to predict raw scores for cases, SEM tries to predict the variances of, and covariances (or correlations) between, observed variables. Though this sounds (and is) different from predicting a raw score, it is ultimately the same idea. When trying to account for a variance we are essentially trying to explain why a particular case's score deviates from the mean score: why does child F score X more exam passes than the average child?

21.3 MEASUREMENT MODELS AND CONFIRMATORY FACTOR ANALYSIS

SEM approaches are primarily used to test two sorts of models: (i) models of the relationships between observed and unobserved (latent) variables; and (ii) models of the relationships between latent unobserved variables. In this section I will deal with the former, often called measurement models, and a particularly popular

confirmatory factor analysis

form of measurement model testing called **confirmatory factor analysis** (CFA – but see also Chapter 20). The principles involved in model fitting that are discussed below apply equally to structural models: however, before you start to worry about testing an impressive structural model you must establish that you can measure the main latent variables of interest well.

In CFA, scores on observed variables (e.g. responses to questions) are thought

uniqueness

to be 'caused' by unobservable common factors and some **uniqueness** (a factor or an error unique to the variable). SEM deals with a matrix of the relationships between variables rather than the raw scores themselves, so this becomes a question of asking whether the patterns of covariation in the observed variables are 'caused' by variation in the unobservable factors. These unobservable factors are referred to as latent variables since they cannot be observed directly but are nonetheless thought to exist and to cause the manifestations of variables you can observe. The researcher must come up with a substantively motivated model that imposes clear constraints. These are to decide:

1 how many common factors or latent variables there are;
2 which pairs of common factors or latent variables are correlated with each other;
3 which observed variables are affected by which common factor or latent variable;
4 which observed variables are affected by a unique factor (usually error);
5 which pairs of unique factors or errors are correlated.

Notice that you are not asking the SEM package to tell you the answers to these questions: you think you know the answers already but are testing these out against the data.

Figure 21.1 gives a much abbreviated example based on a study of 235 young people in Swindon conducted as part of the Economic and Social Research Council's 16–19 Initiative. This study was concerned with the attitudes and lifestyles of young people and how these were related to occupational and political aspirations. In this simple measurement model there are six questions from the questionnaire. Three of these (Q8, Q9 and Q10) are questions from the Hammond (1988) Estrangement Scale and are thought to tap feelings of psychological estrangement. The remaining three (Q12, Q13 and Q14) are thought to tap a negative attitude towards new technology. In this example I have used the convention that latent variables (factors) are denoted by ellipses and observed variables by squares. Do not worry about the Greek letters and subscripts for now; these are included only because they are the conventional symbols used in what is known as LISREL notation.

Each observed variable has an arrow entering it from a latent variable or factor and an arrow indicating that some of the variability is 'caused' by some other source (uniqueness) of error. It is possible to specify that these sources of error are correlated with one another if this makes some substantive sense (e.g. the errors are 'caused' by the same thing) but it does not in the present example.

The important idea here is that some relationships (parameters) are constrained to have particular values (usually, but not always, zero). It is not the case, for instance, that every observed variable is related to both latent variables. Some observed variables are constrained to have no (zero) relationship with particular latent variables (e.g. Q10 and the factor Newtech). Conventionally these

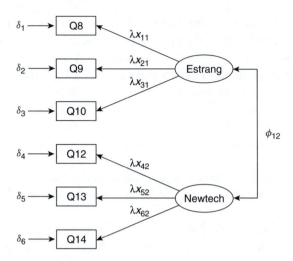

Figure 21.1   A simple two-factor model

zero relationships are not drawn in: the absence of an arrow indicates no proposed relationship.

The input into the analysis is either a correlation or covariance matrix that shows how scores on each observed variable are related to every other observed variable in your sample. This sample correlation or covariance matrix is known as **S**. Remember that the point of your model is to explain why the data are the way they are (i.e. to be able to predict them) and you want your model to be relatively simple and parsimonious. Here you want to explain why variables are correlated with each other in the way they are, and the model proposes that the reason is that the observed scores are 'caused' by certain specific latent variables or factors (two in this case).

In essence, and at the risk of oversimplifying matters greatly, the analysis package takes **S** as a starting point and asks what the correlation (or covariance) matrix would be like in the population if the constraints in the model were imposed (i.e. the model is 'right'). The covariance (or correlation) matrix generated by the model is known as **Σ**. The procedure makes estimates of the parameters in the model (the λ loadings, δ errors and ϕ factor correlations, etc.) to do this and gradually refines these until it cannot do any better. At each stage in estimating the parameters the program compares **S** and **Σ** and tries alternative parameter values in order to increase the similarity between these two matrices. Eventually it stops doing this when it cannot increase the similarity any further.

If there were no constraints imposed by the model, **S** and **Σ** would be exactly the same. Almost any set of parameter estimates would work and you would have achieved nothing. It is like having a theoretical model that says everything is related to everything else – not a very helpful model. The constraints in your model mean that **Σ** will not be exactly the same as **S**, and you can then ask how

Table 21.1   Commonly seen fit indices

Name		Desired value for good fit
χ^2	Chi-squared	Small and non-significant or, if $n > 500$, $\chi^2 < 2df$
CFI	Comparative fit index	>0.95
NNFI	Non-normed fit index	>0.95
GFI	Goodness of fit index	>0.95
AGFI	Adjusted goodness of fit index	>0.90
RMSEA	Root mean square error of approximation	<0.06
SRMR	Standardized root mean square residual	<0.08

different Σ and S are and whether this difference is so big that your model must be wrong or badly misspecified. If the difference between S and Σ is acceptably small then the parameter estimates (λs, δs, ϕs, etc.) are probably good and tell you something meaningful about the relationships between the latent and observed variables.

A number of what are known as **fit indices** can be calculated to indicate how badly Σ fits S. The best-known of these is χ^2. Importantly, and contrary to what people normally expect when doing inferential statistical analyses, you want a *non-significant and small* χ^2 value which indicates that what you observe in your data (the matrix S) is not significantly different from what you would expect to be the case in the population if the model were true (Σ).

There are a number of shortcomings to the fit index χ^2 (see Ullman, 2001, for an overview) so it is common to see researchers report a range of additional fit indices in the hope that, as a whole, they suggest the model fits the data well. Each has its own technical limitations, but if you have a good model then the majority of indices should be telling you that it is good; if not, you need to investigate the indices further. Table 21.1 gives some of the better-known indices and what is regarded as indicative of a 'good' fit: there are others, but these are probably the best known. Box 21.1 gives a brief discussion on exact and close fit indices.

fit indices

Box 21.1   The exact v close fit debate

A debate has raged for some time now concerning the criteria that the fit indices are based on (see the SEMNET archives at the address given in Section 21.9). Some, such as the χ^2 index, are what are called 'exact fit' indices since they indicate the degree to which the data and the model-implied data are exactly the same. Other indices, such as RMSEA, ask whether the fit is close enough for us to be satisfied that the main thrust of our model is true. If the fit is 'close enough' we tend to be happy to accept that our model is a good one.

(Continued)

Box 21.1 (Continued)

Putting aside any principled arguments for a moment, it is usually the case that passing the 'exact fit' tests is more difficult than passing the 'close fit' ones, and this has led to the journals filling up with articles where the authors argue that because of the well-known difficulties of passing the exact fit tests (which usually their model has just failed) they will conclude that their chosen model is still good because it has passed the close fit tests. It is argued that it is close enough to fitting for us to warrant keeping the model. Cynics have noted that when models also pass the exact fit test people tend not to have any problems reporting and relying on them.

This has led some to argue (e.g. Cameron McIntosh, SEMNET archives) that we, the academic community, are treating as 'true' models that fail an exact test but, because they have passed the close fit tests, the source of their lack of fit is no longer a topic of much interest. The model 'fits' in some sense so we do not need to expend more effort finding out why it does not fit. This, it is argued, is a recipe for the proliferation of misspecified models. On the other side of the debate the argument is that the exact tests are unrealistically strict and that otherwise good and useful models would be rejected on the basis of relatively trivial misspecifications. Advances can be made without our models having to be 100% correct in all details.

The debate has developed into a quite sophisticated one about the philosophy of SEM-based science, and it would be too difficult to do justice to all the positions here. Ultimately all the fit indices in current use, exact and close fit, require some judgement to be made about whether the values achieved should lead you to accept or reject your model. The issue is about how we agree where to place the cut-offs – something which is as much a social process as a statistical one. However this debate develops in the medium term, the best advice is to always report the χ^2 statistic, so that at least those favouring exact fit indices will know if your model has passed that test. Not reporting inconvenient results is not a very principled way to proceed.

In our present example the fit indices are as follows: $\chi^2(8) = 12.37$ ($p = 0.14$), GFI = 0.98, AGFI = 0.95, SRMR = 0.046, RMSEA = 0.048, NNFI = 0.96. All of these indices suggest that our proposed two-factor model is consistent with the data and that we have distinct measures of the two latent constructs. The correlation between the Estrang (estrangement) and Newtech (negative attitudes to new technology) latent variables or factors is 0.22. This is the estimated correlation after measurement errors in the observed variables have been removed and suggests a moderate tendency for estranged young people to have negative attitudes towards new technology (Figure 21.2).

21.3.1 Identification

identification

Before you can start to estimate the parameters in a model you need to address the question of **identification**: you must ask whether the parameters are uniquely determined or identified. If a model (or part of it) is not identified it would be possible to find an infinite number of values for the parameters that

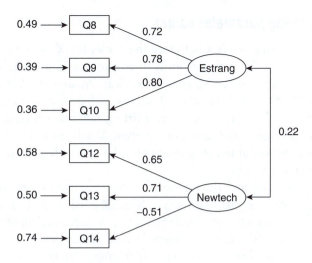

Figure 21.2 The simple two-factor model after LISREL has estimated the standardized unconstrained parameter values

would produce a population correlation/covariance matrix **Σ** that fitted the sample correlation/covariance matrix **S** and your model's constraints. This is obviously not a desirable state of affairs and arises because your model requires the estimation of more parameters than you have data points (correlations or covariances) on which to base the estimates. The problem is analogous to trying to solve the equation:

$$x + y = 10$$

An infinite number of combinations of values for x and y will satisfy this equation and it cannot be uniquely solved until you have additional information. If you also know that:

$$2x + y = 14$$

it is a simple matter to work out that x must be 4 and y must be 6.

Establishing that a model is identified is potentially quite complicated (see Long, 1983); however, this is a problem that is gradually declining in importance as computer packages become better able to detect underidentified models and warn the user that there are difficulties. Nonetheless if you get a warning that your model or parts of it are not identified this usually means that the model is misspecified and/or that you do not have enough observed variables to estimate all the specified parameters.

21.3.2 Estimating parameter values

fitting function

The values of the parameters and thence the values for Σ can be calculated in a number of ways. The most commonly used are maximum likelihood (ML), unweighted least squares (ULS), generalized least squares (GLS) and weighted least squares (WLS). There are others, but these will do for the time being. Each of these methods (algorithms) produces a **fitting function** which is an equation that generates a value to indicate how different Σ is from **S**. The program iterates (keeps doing) its estimation procedure until it cannot reduce the value of the fitting function any more.

The way these work and the reasons for choosing one method over another are beyond the scope of this chapter (see Ullman, 2001, and/or program manuals) but there are a number of pitfalls that are common to all algorithms.

local minimum

The first of these is known as finding a **local minimum**. Here the program finds a value for the fitting function that it cannot make smaller by making minor adjustments to the parameter estimates. However, were it to have started its search for the smallest value of the fitting function from somewhere else (different starting values) it might actually have found a better-fitting set of parameters. It is not easy to tell whether this has happened, though Long (1983) claims this may not be a common problem in practice.

A second kind of problem in estimating parameters concerns 'silly' parameter estimates. Sometimes a good fit can be achieved but the values of the parameters make no sense. For instance, it is possible to get negative variances or correlations with an absolute value greater than 1, even though such figures are meaningless. If this happens, your specified model may simply be wrong or some of your variables may not meet distributional assumptions (important when using certain estimation algorithms). This can also happen when your sample size is very small and the asymptotic (large sample) assumptions that drive the estimation algorithms may not be justified.

Another potential cause of silly estimates is missing data. Researchers tend to prefer to use correlation (or covariance) matrices that are generated by 'pairwise' deletion of missing values since this maximizes the number of cases contributing to each correlation. However, this means that different parts of the matrix **S** are generated by samples of different sizes, leading to a matrix that may not be internally consistent with itself. Sometimes the program will detect this, sometimes it will not. The newer versions of software packages are better at detecting this and warning the user.

21.3.3 Modification indices and specification searches

specification
search

If you find that the model does not fit, how should you change it? Trying to change a model to get a better fit is called a **specification search**. One way to do

this is to look at the **modification indices** (MIs), sometimes called **Lagrange** modification indices
multiplier tests. These indices tell you what might be expected to happen to the Lagrange multiplier
value of the χ^2 goodness-of-fit index if you freed a previously constrained path tests
to be estimated. Freeing one constrained (not estimated) path to be estimated
loses one degree of freedom and the MI then becomes a test of the hypothesis
that the parameter to be freed is equal to its former fixed value. If this is significant, then the model would fit better than it did before and the freed parameter
was probably not equal to its former fixed value.

The freeing of parameters should not be done at random but should be theoretically acceptable. Often high MIs suggest that the model is substantially misspecified. Freeing up any old parameter just because it has a large MI can result
in a much better-fitting but substantively meaningless model. Your original
model may not fit the data but, generally, you should not let the data dictate the
form of your model.

In some senses the opposite kind of problem occurs when you have specified
that a parameter should be estimated in your model but, in fact, the parameter
is so close to zero that the model might have been better specified with the parameter fixed at zero. This would make the model simpler and is generally desirable *unless* fixing the parameter at zero would be theoretically inappropriate.

One of the most straightforward approaches to finding parameters that are
probably best constrained to be zero is to compare the values of estimated parameters with their standard errors (provided by the software). This amounts to
doing a t-test to examine the hypothesis that the parameter estimate is actually
zero. If a t-value suggests that a parameter is not different from zero it might
make sense to respecify your model constraining that parameter to be zero, thus
reducing the number of parameters to be estimated and simplifying the model at
the same time. If you remember, simple is generally better in SEM.

In our two-factor CFA model all the parameter estimates are theoretically reasonable (remember that the Newtech factor is *negative* attitudes towards new
technology) and have values significantly greater than zero. The MIs suggest
that the χ^2 fit would be improved by 4.61 ($p<0.05$) if we allowed the errors of
Q8 and Q10 to be correlated. However, since there is no theoretical justification
for doing this (there is nothing about the questions which might suggest why
the errors might be correlated) and the model fits adequately anyway, this modification is not made.

If you respecify a model using your sample data then, strictly speaking, you
should not test the model on the same data set: obtain a new data set and test the
revised model on that. This is the orthodox view, but you will see revised models retested on the same sample data. The issue is whether the revision remains
theoretically coherent and consistent or is just a fishing exercise that capitalizes
on chance relationships in your sample. Replication is always desirable.

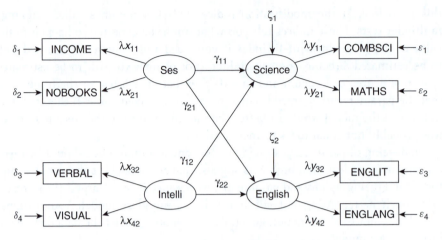

Figure 21.3 A tentative structural model of factors influencing exam performance

21.4 STRUCTURAL MODELS

In psychology we are often interested in predicting the outcome of some sort of process. In the traditional jargon of experimental psychology, we want to know which independent variables 'cause' or predict scores on our dependent variable. In SEM terms (it would have been too simple to stick with the same termino- logy) the independent variables are called **exogenous variables** and the depen- dent variables are called **endogenous variables**. The real advance of SEM is that we can deal with many or endogenous variables at the same time. The other great advance, and one which we have already dealt with, is that we can ask about the relationship between the unobserved latent factors that we are normally really interested in.

Looking at the relationship between exogenous and endogenous variables is conceptually similar to doing multiple regression (when there is a single endoge- nous variable) and path analysis (when there are many endogenous variables). When we do traditional regression or path analysis we are implicitly assuming that the observed variables are perfectly reliable and contain no error. If we were measuring height or age these measures would still contain error, but probably not enough for psychologists to worry about. We could carry on treating the observed variables as 'perfect' indicators of height and age and proceed as before. With most psychological variables the measures we have are imperfect indices of latent constructs that in *principle* we could never measure perfectly accurately. SEM offers us the chance to try to take this error in measurement into account when estimating our model parameters.

exogenous variables

endogenous variables

This is important for a number of reasons. Measurement errors usually serve to bias parameter estimates, and this tends to be in the direction of underestimating the effects of one variable on another (though not always). If we want to know how strong a relationship is between two constructs it would be desirable to estimate the size of this relationship after errors have been 'controlled' for. A second reason for wanting to eliminate errors is that the fit of our model to the data is usually bad in part because of measurement errors. Again, controlling for errors should allow a less biased assessment of our model's fit.

To illustrate this, I have expanded on the example used earlier about predicting academic ability. In Figure 21.3 I have two latent exogenous variables, Intelli (intelligence) and Ses (socio-economic status). These are both thought to cause two observed variables each. I am assessing Ses by counting the number of books in the household (NOBOOKS) and asking about household income (INCOME). Intelli is measured by getting scores on verbal (VERBAL) and visuo-spatial (VISUAL) primary ability tests.

The endogenous latent factors are slightly more refined in this example. Here I am trying to predict academic ability rather than raw examination scores and I am interested in trying to predict general ability in science (Science) and English (English) which are conceived of as latent variables here. The interesting feature here is that I am recognizing that ability in science, for example, might be measured with error if I just looked at a single exam score (e.g. people might feel unwell on the day of one of the science exams). By having two indicators of ability in science (COMBSCI and MATHS) I hope to get a more accurate assessment of ability in science than I might otherwise have got. In spite of these enhancements this model remains a fairly simple 'causal' model; Box 21.2 looks at a special case of a more complex kind of causation than SEM can deal with.

Box 21.2   Breaking the laws of causality?

A possibility offered by SEM is the testing of models containing reciprocal (or sometimes simultaneous) causal links. These are models where one endogenous latent variable is thought to 'cause' another and this endogenous variable is, in turn, thought to 'cause' the first latent variable. This is perfectly acceptable statistically, though many people have objections to models containing such relationships. This is a philosophical matter really and depends on what you regard to be necessary for something to be caused by something else.

Most formulations of causation require that the cause is temporally prior to the effect, and saying that two factors simultaneously cause each other looks like it violates this requirement. An example might suggest classes of problem where being able to test models with reciprocal causation might nevertheless be very useful.

(Continued)

Box 21.2 (Continued)

Suppose you had measured people's levels of depression and social activity. It is probably the case that when people become depressed they go out and socialize less often. The absence of social activity also adds to the level of depression, and increased depression and lowered activity reinforce each other in a spiral. Because you were not in a position to assess depression and social activity at the point at which the cycle started, and you cannot monitor levels of these variables constantly throughout the day, it is not possible to say unambiguously which cause came first. Here, essentially, the time gap between the 'cause' and the 'effect', and the subsequent influence of the 'effect' on the 'cause', is shorter than the gap between possible measurements. We still believe a temporal gap existed but we are not in a position to collect data within that time gap to work out which 'cause' came first.

non-recursive models
recursive models

Models which contain elements of mutual causation and/or feedback loops are called **non-recursive models**; those that do not are called **recursive models**.

All the principles of model comparison we have discussed so far apply to this more complex situation. We will specify a model with parameter constraints and see how well the population covariance matrix generated by the model fits the sample covariance matrix. I can ask whether the two types of academic ability are independent of one another (uncorrelated) as specified here. As the model already states that both abilities are caused by Ses and Intelli, I am asking whether they are independent after these sources of shared variation are accounted for. If the model fits well enough then I can continue with the model. If it does not fit, and the MIs suggest that I should add a path from Science to English (or vice versa), then my hypothesis that the two types of ability are independent will have to be abandoned.

21.5 ANALYSIS STRATEGY

It is unlikely that, in an introduction such as this, I will be able to set out an uncontroversial SEM strategy that will be applicable to every problem. What is presented here is more of a set of guidelines based on some fairly clear principles.

Firstly, you must be able to state what latent variables you are interested in. Secondly, you must be able to measure these well; if you cannot, then there is little point in continuing. Thirdly, you must have a theory which clearly states how you expect your latent variables to be related to each other. Any modifications made to the model must be theoretically justifiable and any resulting model must have legitimate parameter values. Finally, you must retest your model on fresh data.

What follows is a suggested analysis strategy and, if you look on SEMNET (see Section 21.9), you will see that there has been a lot of debate about this, primarily between Les Hayduk and Stan Mulaik. Some of this debate is very contentious so what I have done here is set out what might be regarded as a version of the traditional view, which you should not treat as the gospel truth but something to reflect upon. Les Hayduk (1996) argues that this is definitely the wrong approach, and the more interested among you should check out Chapter 2 of his book on this.

1   Start with a theoretically generated initial compact model (your model C). The model should be the simplest one possible, with few parameters in need of estimation. Start with a simple model that you may have to make more complex rather than a complex model that you hope to simplify. You should have some ideas about what modifications of the model would not make sense for your theory.
2   Pilot your key measures on samples drawn from your target population. Check that the measurements you are making are based on good measurement models by conducting CFAs. If these models are weak or misspecified then there is little chance that your structural model will fit well.
3   Collect your main sample data using the best possible data collection strategies available to you.
4   Test conceptually distinct subparts of your initial model. If these are not OK, then go to step 5, otherwise go to step 6.
5   Respecify the submodel(s) by relaxing constraints to make an augmented submodel(s). Only relax constraints that are conceptually OK to relax. Relax them singly or in small numbers: don't radically respecify the original model unless you have good grounds for doing this.
6   Combine the submodels into one overall global test. Again modify this only if it makes some theoretical sense.
7   Confirm the specification of the final model on a new sample of data.

In practice you probably will not have the resources to do what is essentially (at least) three data collections. This is a fact of life, but you should beware of testing your measurement models and the structural models on the same data set. Using only one sample necessarily makes any of your conclusions sample-specific.

21.6 OTHER THINGS THAT CAN BE DONE WITH SEM

Firstly, SEM packages will deal with models that contain only observed variables, which can be a useful alternative to conventional regression-based path modelling packages. You do not have to have any latent variables to go model testing, and this is useful if you believe your measures contain no error (i.e. are perfect indices of the key constructs).

bootstrapping

Secondly, it is possible to do what is called **bootstrapping** when you have doubts about variable distributions. This involves taking lots of random samples of a given size k ($k < N$) from your sample data and estimating the parameters and fit indices many times over. Doing this allows you to make estimates of the standard errors associated with each parameter and fit index which, in turn, lets you draw up confidence intervals for each estimate. This is a relatively specialized statistical technique, but one which is gradually becoming commoner in the psychological literature.

Thirdly, one of the most promising areas that developments in SEM allow is the testing of measurement and structural models in more than one group at a time. This is called **multi-group modelling**. A common application is in the development of psychometric tests for use in other cultures. For example, a test developed in one country, say the UK, might be translated into another language and the researcher wants to know whether the underlying measurement model has remained the same as it was in the UK. You can collect sample data from both countries and ask the SEM package to test whether the measurement model (a CFA model) is exactly the same in both places. 'Exactly the same' would mean that the item loadings, inter-factor correlations and errors were constrained to be identical in both countries. The analysis will give a single set of fit indices that tell you whether the model fits well simultaneously in both countries. If it does not you can relax constraints (e.g. perhaps allow item loadings to be different between countries) and see whether the revised, less strictly equivalent, model fits.

multi-group modelling

This can be extended to substantive structural models too. You might develop a theory of factors influencing political identification among males and then see whether the model holds for females too and is therefore equally applicable to both sexes.

Fourthly, so far the discussion has been about measurement and structural models which are conceptually extensions of factor analysis and multiple regression/path models. SEM can be used to conduct analyses that we might previously have thought of doing using group difference tests such as the t-test and analysis of variance. As we have already seen, one of the virtues of SEM procedures has been the ability to estimate relationships between variables with measurement errors removed. This can be transferred to group difference testing so that you end up testing whether there is a difference in scores on the latent variable even though, necessarily, you have data only on the observed variables. This is an important possibility, since when you find a group difference using a traditional t-test, say, you are unsure whether this difference is a difference attributable to differences in measurement errors or in the 'true' latent variable you are interested in.

Regrettably, conducting the equivalent of a humble *t*-test even with the friendlier computer packages is still quite difficult to do and, indeed, understand! Hopefully, more user-friendly implementations will come along soon.

21.7 CAUTIONARY NOTES

The commonest objection raised by critics is that SEM analysts often claim to be testing causal models even though the input data are correlations/covariances. Since correlation does not imply causation, claims made that causal relationships have been established cannot be supported. At best SEM can show only that a suggested causal model is consistent with observed correlations.

When doing SEM it is very encouraging to believe that when your pet theoretical model seems to fit the data you have somehow proved your model to be correct. Regrettably, since you will not have tested all possible alternative models, some of which might fit the data even better, all you can really conclude is that until other models have been tested, yours will have to be regarded as the currently 'least bad' model rather than the 'best' or 'true' model. A related criticism is levelled at the use of the term 'confirmatory', particularly when SEM is used for confirmatory factor analysis. It is often pointed out that nothing is actually 'confirmed' in CFA, but, rather, that models are not disconfirmed. Sean Hammond's suggestion in Chapter 20, section 20.4.4, that the term 'restricted' is used seems like a good compromise.

SEM and related model-fitting approaches have often been criticized for their emphasis on prediction at the expense of real explanation. It is quite possible to produce a model to predict something well without really having been able to explain the phenomena of interest. For example, we might find that socio-economic status is a good predictor of academic attainment without really knowing what it is about having a high SES that causes children to perform better. I am sure the reader can probably make some good guesses as to what these aspects of SES might be, but a well-fitting model might nevertheless be achieved by simply stating that SES predicts academic performance.

While prediction is clearly not the same thing as explanation, theories that claim to explain phenomena but cannot predict them are of limited utility in SEM terms. If no predictions can be made it becomes difficult to see in traditional hypothetico-deductive terms how such theories are to be tested.

SEM currently deals primarily with linear relationships between variables. Because SEM analyses are based on correlations and/or covariances which assess only the degree of linear relationships between variables, they cannot easily deal with data that contain true non-linear relationships. Some transformations of data are possible (see Ullman, 2001) and specialist packages for non-linear problems are gradually appearing on the market, but in the meantime it is incumbent on researchers to be clear about whether they expect linear relationships between variables before embarking on an SEM analysis.

Finally, this is still a developing field and many problems remain to be addressed. Frustratingly, advice in the specialist texts naturally reflects current wisdom and this changes all the time as this is an area of considerable research activity. Fit indices, initially hailed as the best thing since sliced bread, were soon shown to be flawed or applicable only in special cases which your own data never seem to be examples of. Estimation algorithms that were claimed to be capable of dealing with strangely distributed variables are suddenly found to require sample sizes of several thousand before they will produce good parameter estimates; and so on. All this means that a certain willingness to learn about the field is necessary if you are to become an effective user of SEM.

21.8 CONCLUSION

In this chapter I hope to have given you some idea of what is going on when people apply SEM approaches to data analysis. It may seem a bit dry, but SEM really does have a lot to offer to psychology. The ability to estimate relationships between unobservable latent variables after measurement errors have been excluded is a major advance for psychologists whose research interests are primarily about constructs that cannot be measured directly. Coupled with this, SEM brings with it a more overtly rigorous approach to hypothesis testing and model building, which must be viewed as a good thing in a political climate where psychology is struggling to be recognized, and to maintain its status, as a 'real' science.

21.9 FURTHER READING

An introduction to the whole SEM area that includes references to software packages is Ullman's (2001) large chapter in a very well-written and generally useful multivariate statistics book by Tabachnick and Fidell and there are not many better explanations around. Other good introductions include Hoyle's (1995) and Maruyama's (1997) texts.

If you have access to the Internet you can look up the Web page of the SEMNET interest group at http://www2.gsu.edu/~mkteer/semnet.html which includes details of how to join its e-mail discussion group. If you join you can send queries to this group and contribute to the very lively debates that seem to be conducted at a frenetic pace.

22

Meta-analysis

David O'Sullivan

22.1   Introduction
22.2   Quantifying the review process
22.3   Steps in conducting a meta-analysis
   22.3.1   Formulating the problem
   22.3.2   Identification of studies
   22.3.3   Coding and data extraction
   22.3.4   Data analysis
   22.3.5   Interpreting the effect size statistic
22.4   Conclusion
22.5   Further reading

The aim of this chapter is to introduce the method of quantitative literature review or meta-analysis. This involves a set of statistical hypothesis-testing techniques that take a model 'confirmation' approach. The chapter will briefly highlight some of the primary challenges in effective literature reviews and then introduce the basic concepts of meta-analysis. It aims to show how to make effective use of this strategy by providing a worked example of the simplest case. While, for most applications, greater detail may be required, it is intended that this chapter should encourage students and researchers to explore further the rich array of meta-analytic methods and to seriously consider using this approach as a major part in the literature review process of their research.

Key terms

apples and oranges problem	narrative review
associations	population effect
clinical significance	power
ecological validity	treatment effects
effect size	Type I errors
file drawer problem	Type II errors
generalizability	weighted effect size

22.1 INTRODUCTION

In psychology it is rare that a single piece of research answers a question once and for all. There are various reasons why this should be so, particularly in the behavioural sciences. The prime reasons have to do with the nature of the subject area and research methods used. There is always a tension between tight laboratory-based settings where everything is controlled, such that **ecological validity** becomes questionable, and loose field-based settings, where the control of variables becomes difficult. In the broad view this is not necessarily problematic as the complexity of psychological issues needs to be studied from multiple viewpoints. Indeed, sticking rigidly to particular methodological vantage points can lead to blind spots, with a resultant lack of progress.

ecological validity

Another factor is the probabilistic logic we use to determine whether a research contribution shows an effect. It goes something like this: we can never be sure whether there really is an effect, but with the application of the appropriate statistical analysis we can determine the probability of the result being due to chance. Although we try to guard against it as far as we can, there is always the chance of a false positive or a false negative finding. Thus, over-reliance on single findings can ultimately prove to be misleading.

Finally, we have to accept that most of our findings are grounded in the particular sample and setting of the study. While the hope is that our results are generalizable, this cannot be guaranteed. So, for example, results of studies on highly intelligent university students relating to cognitive functioning may have little relevance to more general samples.

For all these reasons, and more, we need to use multiple research findings to explore a given area. This is very evident in any presentation of research findings. The introduction, or literature review, fulfils the purpose of identifying the important research in the area, placing it in an evaluative order and providing an appraisal frame on which the worth of the current research contribution can be based. This means that our literature reviews require us to identify and accumulate evidence for or against a particular position. Meta-analysis is a term used to describe the situation where our qualitative appraisal of the literature is supported by a quantification of evidence.

Like all sciences, development in psychology is a continual process of knowledge accumulation and refinement. Even a cursory glance at the literature would demonstrate that the demand for knowledge accumulation is being satisfied. The number of journals being published is growing year by year, and still there seem to be more articles than there are journal slots available. The refinement of knowledge can be challenging in psychology because of the non-linear way in which it is produced. As much as anything else it is a function of the complexity of studying the human mind and behaviour. Add to this different methodologies, samples and lack of agreement at the level of definitions and the complexity of the task becomes apparent.

The task in knowledge refinement is not so much to adjudicate on the value or significance of a particular work as to spot the underlying trends and principles within a body of work. Literature reviews seek to achieve this aim. However, the device of a literature review as a method of meta-analysis is not without its difficulties. The achievement of a comprehensive literature review is hampered by the sheer volume of research that is being published. Mastering this is a continuing challenge to professional researchers and becomes an increasingly difficult task for practitioners who strive for evidence-based practice. With such a large knowledge base the narrative literature review becomes unwieldy and unequal to the task. Moreover, in these circumstances the ability of the human mind to reliably and validly achieve this task is questionable (Glass, McGraw & Smith, 1981).

In order to make the review work as a piece or argumentation and manage the material that needs to be assimilated, analysed and interpreted, the researcher has to be selective in the material that is used to reach conclusions. Thus coverage changes from being comprehensive to selective, evaluating the most important sources. Of necessity the researcher must make a series of subjective decisions which can introduce bias. We are predisposed to organize chaos into patterns: we often perceive shapes and objects when no such things exist. This tendency to seek out patterns or positive results is magnified in the face of increasing levels of knowledge. Disconfirming evidence can easily be overlooked. Given the in-built biases in our cognitive system, we know that this might not be the best method on which base a scientific scrutiny. Moreover, the method of study selection is not apparent and has led to the charge that reviewers may choose studies for reasons other than a thorough evaluation of scientific worth (Wolf, 1986: 10).

How can we be sure that authors have not dismissed studies because they do not suit their purposes (Knipschild, 1994)? Indeed, one of the failings of traditional narrative reviews is that they are silent on how the methodology of the studies was assessed (Knipschild, 1994). This lack of comprehensive coverage and the possibility of bias render narrative literature reviews an unsafe way of refining knowledge, particularly in climates where society needs answers to questions of a psychological nature which have been arrived at in a reliable way.

22.2 QUANTIFYING THE REVIEW PROCESS

Although the literature review can be regarded as a form of meta-analysis in the loosest sense of the term, it is probably more appropriate to move to a tighter definition at this stage. From now on we will take it to mean the statistical procedures or methods whereby data are combined from different studies (Moncrieff, 1998) and the subsequent interpretation of these results. At this stage it is also important to delineate the type of research studies that are amenable to meta-analysis, as our tightening of the definition has implications here. We are examining empirical data rather than theoretical contributions, the data need to be quantitative rather than qualitative, the findings need to be configured (or be capable of being configured) in a statistical form that is comparable, and the constructs under examination must be the same or similar. How this latter point is operationalized is important. It can vary from comparing studies where there is a pure replication to those where there is conceptual replication. The difficulty with conceptual replication is that you may be comparing studies that are actually different from each other – the **apples and oranges problem**, not comparing like with like. Conclusions that you draw may not be relevant. The way to overcome this is only to compare studies where there is pure replication. However, you may end up with too few studies to compare, and therefore effect the **generalizability** of your conclusions. Achieving this balance is a delicate task.

apples and oranges problem

generalizability

Although meta-analysis answers some of the problems posed by narrative reviews, it also brings some important benefits to the process of research synthesis. Knipschild (1994) points out two such advantages which can also act as preparation for the carrying out of a trial. One advantage is that a systematic review will allow the field to be comprehensively studied, and in this way a researcher will know how much a new trial will add to knowledge. This is an effective way of putting a value on proposed research initiatives. By its very nature meta-analysis will require the researcher to contact the key authors in the area. It is important to locate, as we will see later, trials that have failed to produce a significant result. These tend not to be published, but stored away in filing cabinets, leading to the well-known **file drawer problem** (Rosenthal, 1979). Negative trials can provide good information on what does not work, and in this way the researcher, rather than remaking all the classic mistakes over again, learns from the experience of others in the field.

file drawer problem

Historically the first step in combining the results of studies was to use each study as a vote in a referendum on the research question being asked. All the studies that addressed this question were identified and their votes, whether they found an effect or not, were counted. The result was based on this ballot. This is an intuitively attractive idea, but flawed. It runs counter to the probabilistic nature of hypothesis testing. A negative result does not mean there was no effect. It means that an effect, if there was one, could not be detected within acceptable limits. Therefore, a negative result may not be a vote against the question as we have no way of distinguishing between true negative results and false negative results. Of course the opposite can occur as well, we have some false positive results in our yes votes. This is the eternal problem of **Type I** and **Type II errors**. A pragmatist might argue that these would balance themselves out and that if a question hangs on one or two votes it should not be called. However, there is a practical issue here in the applied setting. Treatment studies can often fail to reach significance levels, not because there is no treatment effect, but because, due to necessarily small numbers, it is not possible to detect the effect statistically, although the effect does have a clinical impact (Moncrieff, 1998). An example will be sufficient to illustrate the problems that this can cause.

Suppose I am trying to evaluate the effectiveness of a new type of reading intervention for dyslexic readers. There has been anecdotal evidence that this approach is more effective than the traditional methods of teaching reading and there have been a few trials. I would like to see what the research says before I commit to an expensive retraining program for teachers in the area. First of all, I establish inclusion criteria.

1 The studies included must have involved an intervention using this particular teaching technique.
2 The studies must have had a comparison group that received conventional remedial teaching.
3 The treatment group must have been composed of individuals who had been diagnosed as having a reading difficulty explained by dyslexia.
4 The participants must have been randomly assigned to either the control or treatment group.

Next, I develop a strategy for finding relevant trials. I start with a search of the relevant databases, bibliographies, conference proceedings, etc. From those that I identify I contact authors and follow citations so as to identify more trials. My search yields four trials. I place these in a contingency table (see Table 22.1) and, having counted the 'votes', resolve the question of whether this new form of teaching is more effective than conventional methods.

On the face of it this solves the problem: only one of the four studies found that this type of intervention was effective. So clearly the use of this type of intervention is unwarranted. However, the data are troubling. First of all, we know that the lack of a significant result may be the result of a trial not having sufficient **power**, and this is most often due to the trial having low numbers. This pattern certainly seems to be evident with studies A–C, and these were early studies. We also know from reading these studies that although the effects were not statistically significant the authors argued that there were results present that showed **clinical significance**. That, you suspect, is why a trial (study D) with a larger sample and sufficient power to detect the supposed effect was commissioned.

Type I
Type II errors

power

clinical
significance

Table 22.1 Statistical significance for dyslexic intervention

Trial	N	Significant result	Non-significant result
A	20		1
B	24		1
C	20		1
D	60	1*	

*$p<.05$

Although at first sight an easy task, the interpretation of the data in Table 22.1 is far from unproblematic.

To follow our hunch and interpret the results on the basis of trial D, which we feel gives the best representation of what is happening, is to fall into the trap of **narrative review**: choosing representative trials on non-objective grounds. On the face of it the only way forward is that we must run at least three more trials which have positive results and overturn what we suspect is a wrong result. Apart from anything else this would result in a large expenditure of effort and, not least, has the smack of scientific gerrymandering of the constituency of trials to get the result we want. There must be a way to use the data that we have to answer our original question.

This was the next step in the development of the meta-analytic technique. Instead of looking at the significance level alone, we examine the treatment effect of the trials and combine these effects across all the trials. By combining data from different studies, power can be increased. In addition, by combining studies across a variety of settings the range of effectiveness of the treatment can be measured (Moncrieff, 1998).

It was a problem similar to this, the debate over the effectiveness of psychotherapy as a treatment, that introduced the techniques of meta-analysis into psychology. Eysenck (1952), in a seminal piece of work concluded that, after 20 years of evaluation and hundreds of trials, research effort had failed to demonstrate that psychotherapy had any effect. Effectively Eysenck had held a type of ballot. The resulting controversial statement was hotly and sometimes nastily debated, then as now. It took over 25 years for a definitive counter-response to emerge. Smith and Glass (1977) moved away from pure significance testing and instead examined the direction and magnitude of **treatment effects** across studies. Using this approach they concluded that psychotherapy did indeed work. The method they used for analysis they called meta-analysis. The introduction of meta-analysis in psychology illustrates the cross-fertilization that goes on among fields of scientific enquiry. It drew on the ideas of Tippett (1931) who, in interpreting the results of agricultural field trials, concluded that taking the probabilities of a series of studies together could determine whether a result was due to a new agricultural technique or chance. It was Cochran (1937) who devised a method for combining the sizes of effects across independent studies that laid the statistical foundation for the meta-analytic approach taken by Smith and Glass.

One interesting conclusion from Smith and Glass's (1977) work is that they found no great difference in the average impact of various types of therapy. Therapies differientiate themselves from each other principally on the basis of theories of human nature and development, techniques and intervention strategies. And yet, as they were found to work equally they must presumably work for reasons other than method or theoretical orientation.

Box 22.1   A historical note

Although the first quantitative meta-analysis was published by Pearson (1904), it was not until the period of the late 1970s and early 1980s that the technique was introduced to the field of psychology (Glass, McGraw & Smith, 1981). It took several years for its impact to be absorbed. In the late 1980s there were under 100 articles on meta-analysis in social science journals. This rocketed in the following years, so that by the early years of the twenty-first century there were over 1000 (Field, 2003). There has been a levelling off in recent years: Hunt (1997) argues that this represents the approach finding its niche in the discipline.

22.3 STEPS IN CONDUCTING A META-ANALYSIS

We now turn to what is intended to be a more practical account of the process of meta-analysis. The reader should appreciate that this is merely a taster; should your appetite be whetted, greater detail and many wider applications are discussed in the meta-analytic literature.

22.3.1 Formulating the problem

From the theory and the research in a specific area is it possible to locate unanswered questions? Although the raw material for meta-analysis is previous knowledge, the synthesis of existing studies should lead to new knowledge. To a large extent the technique has been associated with the examination of group differences, particularly in the area of treatment effects. This was the classic approach taken by Glass, McGraw and Smith (1981). However, as well as differences between groups that have been created experimentally, differences between naturally occurring groups can be examined. In addition to differences between groups, associations between variables can be explored; this approach can be used in individual difference research or validity generalization. Within this mix of approaches meta-analysis can be used to address three broad questions. Firstly, what, if any, research has been conducted in the area? Secondly, how best can the available research best be summarized. If the researchers are concerned with conceptual replication rather than pure replication, they will notice that there is often a great deal of variability between studies in terms of, for example, sample characteristics, outcome measures, etc. In this situation the researchers may be in a position to answer a third broad question and identify the variability between studies and explain why this has led to different results. There is no reason why certainly the first two and often all three questions cannot be answered in a meta-analysis. Indeed, meta-analysis is well placed to answer these questions.

22.3.2 Identification of studies

This is the most important stage of the meta-analytic method. Meta-analysis synthesizes the results of large numbers of studies, and it is by summarizing all the available data rather than selected sections of it that its conclusions are strengthened. This is also the most difficult stage. Although the advent of searchable electronic databases makes locating suitable studies easier, they do introduce their own problems, as we shall see later. In addition, the databases are by their nature specialized and there is no guarantee that all the relevant studies have been indexed. An illustrative example will be useful here. Torgerson, Porthouse and Brooks (2003) were interested in locating and synthesizing the results of interventions within the area of adult literacy and numeracy. Their search terms included adult literacy; adult numeracy; adult basic education; worksite education; and workplace education. They electronically searched the following databases: PsycInfo, Educational Resources Information Centre (ERIC), Social Science Citation Index (SSCI), the Campbell Collaboration's Social, Psychological, Educational and Criminological Trials Register (C2-SPECTR), System for Information on Grey Literature in Europe (SIGLE) and Criminal Justice Absracts (CJA). Using the bibliographies of the included reviews, they conducted a manual search for potential trials that had not been identified in the electronic searches.

They identified 4555 papers that were of possible interest. Their next step was to identify the relevant papers from amongst these. By its very nature this is a process of selection where the judgement of the researcher(s) is brought into play. It is important that this stage is conducted as objectively as possible. Failure here invites the criticism of subjectivity that has been levelled against narrative reviews. Indeed, it is important when evaluating meta-analyses to be aware of how subjectivity, by introducing a selection bias, influences the conclusions drawn. This problem can be guarded against by the use of explicit inclusion and exclusion criteria and then applying them in a way that is reliable and repeatable.

Torgerson *et al.* (2003) then examined this base of 4555 papers against their inclusion criteria of 'evaluations of interventions aimed at increasing the literacy or numeracy in study populations of adults'. Studies had to be randomized controlled trials, controlled trials or a review of these. In addition, they had to have been carried out in an English-speaking country and written in English. The final criterion was that they had to be either published or unpublished between the years 1980 and 2002. There was also a number of exclusion criteria. They could not be studies where the first language of the participants was not English or if some or all of the participants were under 18. In addition, they could not be studies that were interventions of a pre- and post-test design or non-interventions. In the initial screening, titles and abstracts were used. For the four main databases (PsycInfo, ERIC, CJA and SIGLE) two of the researchers, working independently, applied the inclusion/exclusion criteria. The papers in the two smaller databases (SSCI and C2-SPECTR) were screened by one researcher. This resulted in a pool of 168 papers. This second double screening was based on the full papers. All disagreements about exclusion or inclusion were discussed and resolved, such that 100% agreement was reached.

22.3.3 Coding and data extraction

Torgerson *et al.* (2003) coded their studies as either RCT (randomized controlled trial), CT (controlled trial) or review. The purpose of this coding was to provide a description of the findings in general and also, if there was variability within the pool of studies, a description of how the studies differed from each other in terms of critical aspects of the studies. In order to summarize or compare studies with each other, data need to be extracted from the studies in a focused and standardized manner.

The data need to capture the study in a relevant way and need to be extracted consistently across studies. Of relevance would be the name of the study or, if blinding is used, the study number, source of the data and the type of design. In addition, there should be a description of the study groups: how many used, how many in them, the age and sex distribution of the groups, and how the groups were derived. If there was an intervention, what it was and how long it lasted. Also, what the dependent variables were and how they were measured. The results also need to be summarized, which would include the descriptive statistics of dependent measures for the groups as well as test statistics, degrees of freedom and *p*-values. The protocol may need to be piloted on a few studies before the final format is fixed (Berman & Parker, 2002).

22.3.4 Data analysis

It is the use of effect size that makes meta-analysis possible. In synthesizing the research data we are no longer interested in whether there was a significant result or not, rather we are interested in the effect of, say, an intervention, its strength and direction. Using the effect size we are able to code the research findings on a scale that is independent of the number of participants that took part in the study. There are many different effect size measures, some of which are particularly suited to particular types of research situations. Indeed, some effect size measures can be computed in different ways. This is mentioned not to increase confusion, but, rather, to lessen it as one encounters different effect size statistics and methods of computation in the literature. Nevertheless it can be said that there are two main types of statistics that are encountered – **effect size** measures for differences between groups, and measures for **associations** between variables.

effect size

associations

Some studies will provide estimates of the effect size. For those that omit them, they will have to be calculated. Wolf (1986: 25) provides the basic formula for group differences, known as a standardized difference and denoted d:

$$d = \frac{\bar{x}_1 - \bar{x}_2}{SD}$$

This standardized difference is the effect size and is equal to the difference between the treatment group mean and the control group mean, divided by a measure of standard deviation. Typically it is the standard deviation of either the control group or the pre-test group that is used. This is because these groups are not affected by the treatment or intervention (Glass *et al.*, 1981), although either standard deviation could be used since homogeneity of variances is assumed (Wolf, 1986: 25). For correlational studies the basic computation is to average the correlation of the two variables across the studies. Typically Pearson's correlation coefficient is used (Wolf, 1986: 28–29).

Let us return to the fictitious example we used previously when illustrating the votes in the ballot method. Although the effect sizes are not reported in these studies, it is relatively easy to calculate them from the descriptive statistics given in the papers. Then it is easy to work out the average effect size; the sum of the effect sizes divided by the number of studies (Wolf, 1986: 26). For the data from Table 22.2 the average effect size is:

$$\frac{0.53 + 0.23 - 0.16 + 0.47}{4} = 0.27$$

As we know, one of the advantages of using a measure of effect size over inferential statistics is that the measure is relatively unaffected by the sample size, and so results with different sample sizes can be compared with each other. What we are interested in is not the sample *per se*, but what they tell us about the population from which they are drawn. However, each effect size represents the true **population effect** size plus error and, like all statistics, the larger the sample the more likely the effect size is a true estimate of the effect size in the population

population effect

Table 22.2 Effect sizes for dyslexic intervention

Trial	N	df	Treatment group	Control group	SD	d
A	20	9	20.8	15.1	10.7	0.53
B	24	11	29.1	23.5	24.1	0.23
C	20	9	24.2	25.7	9.6	-0.16
D	60	29	24.4	17.4	14.6	0.47

(Clark-Carter, 2003). With this in mind, and on examining the data in Table 22.2, it would not be unreasonable to argue that as study D had most participants this study may provide the best estimate of the true effect size. Extending this argument, the calculation of effect size should take this into account so as to minimize the amount of error, rather than according each effect size an equal weighting. Various methods have been used to form a **weighted effect size** (WES) of individual studies in such a way. An intuitively appealing way is to use the number of participants as the weight. One formula that would take account of this would be to multiply each effect size by the degrees of freedom and then divide these by the sum of the degrees of freedom:

$$WES = \frac{\sum(\bar{x}_1 - \bar{x}_2)df}{\sum df}$$

For the data in Table 22.2 this would result in:

$$WES = \frac{0.53 \times 9 + 0.23 \times 11 - 0.16 \times 9 + 0.47 \times 29}{9 + 11 + 9 + 29} = 0.34$$

This represents a spread of 17% between the scores of the treatment and control groups in favour of the treatment group.

22.3.5 Interpreting the effect size statistic

Once we have calculated the effect size we need to be in a position to say what it means. One of the more popular effect sizes is Cohen's d (1988), which is used to quantify the degree of difference between groups' means. Pearson's r can be used to represent the size of a relationship or also the degree of difference between group means. Indeed, most measures of effect size can be converted between each other (Rosenthal, 1991). Cohen provided a handy metric for interpreting effect sizes that can be seen in Table 22.3.

For our example above we would interpret the effect size we found as being a small to medium effect. Although the use of conventional guidelines can be useful, they need to be applied with caution, as different areas will have different

Table 22.3 Interpretation of effect sizes

Large	$d=0.80$	Large	$r=0.50$
Moderate	$d=0.50$	Moderate	$r=0.30$
Small	$d=0.20$	Small	$r=0.10$

effect sizes that are regarded as practically or clinically significant. As Welkowitz, Ewen and Cohen (1982) point out, they should not be used if the relevant effect size for a particular area is known. In general, this can be determined from the literature in the field. Of course, if the area is new this can be problematic. One way out of this, as Glass *et al.* (1981) suggest, is to examine the literature in a related area. Nevertheless, in the face of no established effect size estimates being available, the conventional guide may be the only option available. In this situation the interpretation of a small effect size can be difficult, particularly when evaluating treatments and especially when these treatments have life-and-death consequences. Although psychological treatments would not generally be regarded as having this type of impact, the counter-argument could be made for behavioural interventions within medical settings.

The issue is how a treatment effect expressed as a decimal of a standard deviation – such as 0.01 or 0.06 – relates to its practical or clinical significance. The debate over this issue has led to the recognition that a small effect size does not mean that the treatment effect is similarly small (Lipsey & Wilson, 1993). For instance, Rosenthal (1991) reports that the effect of aspirin on heart attacks was judged as conclusive when the effect size reached 0.07. This would be a small effect size using Cohen's (1988) guidelines, and would have represented a 3.5% difference between those groups getting the aspirin treatment and those that were not. However, because of its life-and-death impact, this difference was regarded as clinically significant.

Box 22.2

In the early twentieth century there was uncertainty over how effective inoculation was against typhoid fever. Results varied and samples were small. Pearson (1904) calculated the correlation between mortality and inoculation in each sample and then averaged this across all the samples. In this way chance factors were balanced out and the effectiveness of inoculation was demonstrated. This very first use of meta-analysis was used to answer a life-and-death question. Although statistical and methodological sophistication has increased, the basic idea is encapsulated here.

Related to the issues of interpreting the effect size is the question of whether the effect size is an overestimate of the population effect size and, if so, to what extent. This is a problematic issue for two main reasons. Studies with positive results are more like to be submitted for publication. Greenwald (1975) has estimated that those with significant results are eight times more likely to be submitted. In addition, once submitted, such studies are more likely to be published. This is because editors frequently use statistical significance as a quality control measure for selecting studies for publication (Gillett, 2001), and, as we have previously indicated, a lack of a significant result does not imply a lack of a treatment effect. This publication bias means that those studies that have the strongest effects are more likely to be published, and consequently any meta-analysis of these studies is likely to overestimate the population treatment effect. This is not an insignificant problem as the rigorous methodology of meta-analysis can give scientific credence to erroneous conclusions (Begg, 1994), and this is a serious misuse of meta-analyses. On top of this, those conducting meta-analyses also make judgements on the studies to be included. This selection process is designed to avoid the apples and oranges problem. However, it can also introduce an element of bias.

There are several ways in which this tendency can be minimized. It is important to explicitly define the inclusion and exclusion criteria that were used to select the studies. Also, the strategy used to retrieve the studies needs to be made explicit. This strategy should include both the obvious and not so obvious databases in addition to other sources of studies such as conference proceedings and bibliographies, as well as contacting authors for unpublished studies. To the extent that these steps are made overt, the reader is able to make judgements on the likely presence of bias. Locating unpublished studies is a non-trivial task, and it is not possible ever to know if all of them have been located. Rosenthal (1979) has approached this problem from a different angle using the fail-safe method. He developed a formula for estimating how many non-significant studies you would need to find, which presumably would be in the unpublished literature, to show that there was no effect. Clearly, if you only needed a few studies, then these could be hidden in somebody's filing cabinet drawer. Under these circumstances, it would be wise not to pay too much regard to the reported effect. Reviewing the participants in the studies used can also help us come to a judgement. Studies with larger numbers of participants are more likely to have effect sizes that are closer to the effect size of the population. If the meta-analysis were comprised of studies with small sample sizes, then this would alert our suspicions. More likely there would be a mixture, and the presence of small studies with small sample sizes may be distorting the effect size. Here we would seek to see if the individual effect sizes of the studies have been weighted on the basis of their sample size. Avoiding false positives (Type I error) as well as ensuring that the discovery of novel relationships is not suppressed (false negatives, Type II error) is a perennial problem not just for meta-analysis, but also for all of scientific psychology.

Not all meta-analyses are based on large study sets. Shoham-Salomon, Avner and Neeman (1989) conducted one on paradoxical interventions using only ten studies. Here the therapist encourages the behaviour that the client is trying to change – the anxious are told to worry, as it were. For some reason this often has the opposite effect. They found that the effect was robust and it worked as effectively as a range of other therapies. That said, with such a small base it was not possible to determine how and why it worked. However, the value of meta-analyses using small study numbers is more to focus future research than to reach firm conclusions.

22.4 CONCLUSION

This chapter has introduced the concept of meta-analysis. In the space provided it is not possible to explore the many more sophisticated developments in the field. The interested reader is referred to the literature discussed below. Our hope here is that the reader of this chapter is in a position to critique published meta-analyses and may be inspired to apply these principles to their own work.

Box 22.3   The principal strengths of meta-analysis

Meta-analysis can synthesize the results of large numbers of studies. Traditional narrative analyses would be overwhelmed by tasks of this size.

By focusing on the direction and strength of effects, it can uncover relationships that are hidden when the levels of significance are analysed.

As well as summarizing previous research data, it can highlight what is lacking in a field and thereby point to future research directions.

By emphasizing methodology it standardizes how research is summarized. Although the aim is to be objective, there are series of subjective judgements at crucial stages. However, by following explicit methodological steps, researchers are reminded of the difficulties of these judgements and when they are overt readers can judge to what extent bias may have entered into the process.

By exposing the process of review, in a way that narrative reviews can never approach, readers are presented with a more differentiated summary of findings in an area.

22.5 FURTHER READING

Hunt (1997) provides a clear and comprehensive presentation of meta-analysis in terms of its history and contribution to scientific progress in a number of fields. Wolf's (1986) text is a good source for many of the statistical formulae and their uses, as well as their rationale. An alternative source is Lipsey and Wilson's (2001) text, which is good for practical worked examples. It would be wrong not to present the counter-arguments to meta-analysis: Eysenck is a fervent critic, and discussion of his 'Meta-analysis and its problems' (1994) is worth reading.

Ralf Schwarzer has written a freely available computer program for carrying out meta-analyses, and this program comes with an excellent manual. It may be obtained at: http://www.fu-berlin.de/gesund/gesu_engl/meta_e.htm

References

Abraham, C. & Hampson, S. E. (1996). A social cognition approach to health psychology: Philosophical and methodological issues. *Psychology and Health*, *11*, 223–241.

Adams, E. W. (1966). On the nature and purpose of measurement. *Synthese*, *16*, 125–129.

Ainsworth, M. D. S., Blehar, R. M. C., Waters, E. & Wall, S. (1978). *Patterns of attachment: A psychological study of the Strange Situation.* Hillsdale, NJ: Erlbaum.

Albrecht, T. L., Johnson, G. M. & Walther, J. B. (1993). Understanding communication processes in focus groups. In D. L. Morgan (Ed.), *Successful focus groups: Advancing the state of the art.* London: Sage.

Alcalá-Quintana, R. & García-Pérez, M. A. (2004). The role of parametric assumptions in adaptive Bayesian estimation. *Psychological Methods*, *9*, 250–271.

Allen, M. J. & Yen, W. M. (1979). *Introduction to measurement theory.* Belmont, CA: Wadsworth.

American Psychological Association (1992). *APA Ethics Code.* Washington, DC: American Psychological Association.

Anderson, J. A. (1972). Separate sample logistic discrimination. *Biometrika*, *59*, 19–36.

Andreassi, J. L. (2000). *Psychophysiology: Human behavior and physiological response* (4th ed.). Mahwah, NJ: Lawrence Erlbaum Associates.

Andrich, D. (1988). *Rasch models for measurement.* Beverly Hills, CA: Sage.

Arbuckle, J. L. (2003). *Amos 5.0 update to the Amos user's guide.* Chicago: Smallwaters Corporation.

Archer, J. (2004). The trouble with 'doing boy'. *The Psychologist*, *17*, 132–136.

Argyle, M. (1972). *The psychology of interpersonal behaviour.* Harmondsworth: Penguin.

Ashford, P. (1994). *Proenvironmentalism: Identity and the media.* PhD thesis, University of Surrey.

Ashworth, P. (2003a). The origins of qualitative psychology. In J. A. Smith (Ed.), *Qualitative psychology: A practical guide to research methods* (pp. 4–24). London: Sage.

Ashworth, P. (2003b). An approach to phenomenological psychology: The contingencies of the lifeworld. *Journal of Phenomenological Psychology*, *34*, 145–156.

Atkinson, J. & Heritage, J. (Eds) (1984). *Structures of social action: Studies in conversation analysis*. Cambridge: Cambridge University Press.

Atkinson, J. W. (1958). *Motives in fantasy, action and society*. New York: Van Nostrand.

Atkinson, P., Coffey, A., Delamont, S., Lofland, J. & Lofland, L. (2001). *Handbook of ethnography*. London: Sage.

Auerbach, C. & Silverstein, L. (2003). *Qualitative data: An introduction to coding and analysis*. New York: New York University Press.

Axelrod, R. (Ed.) (1976). *Structure of decision*. Princeton, NJ: Princeton University Press.

Back, L. (1993). Gendered participation: Masculinity and fieldwork in a south London adolescent community. In D. Bell, P. Caplan & W. J. Karim (Eds), *Gendered fields: Women, men and ethnography* (pp. 215–232). London: Routledge.

Backs, R. W. (1998). A comparison of factor analytic methods of obtaining cardiovascular autonomic components for the assessment of mental workload. *Ergonomics*, 41, 733–745.

Baker, F. (2001). *The basics of item response theory*. ERIC Clearinghouse on Assessment and Evaluation, University of Maryland, College Park, MD. (http://edres.org/irt).

Bales, R. F. (1950). *Interaction process analysis: A method for the study of small groups*. Cambridge, MA: Addison-Wesley.

Bandura, A. (1997). *Self-efficacy: The exercise of control*. New York: Freeman.

Bandura, A., Ross, D. & Ross, S. A. (1961). Transmission of aggression through imitation of aggressive models. *Journal of Abnormal and Social Psychology*, 63, 575–582.

Bandura, A., Ross, D. & Ross, S. A. (1963). Imitation of film-mediated aggressive models. *Journal of Abnormal and Social Psychology*, 66, 3–11.

Bandura, A. & Walters, R. H. (1963). *Social learning and personality development*. New York: Holt.

Banks, M., Bates, I., Breakwell, G., Bynner, J., Emler, N., Jamieson, L. & Roberts, K. (1992). *Careers and identities*. Milton Keynes: Open University Press.

Banks, S. P. (2004). Identity narratives by American and Canadian retirees in Mexico. *Journal of Cross-Cultural Gerontology*, 19, 361–381.

Barbour, R. S. & Kitzinger, J. (Eds) (1998). *Developing focus group research: Politics, theory and practice*. London: Sage.

Barker, C., Pistrang, N. & Elliott, R. (2002). *Research methods in clinical psychology* (2nd ed.). New York: Wiley.

Barker, G. N. & Rich, S. (1992). Influences on adolescent sexuality in Nigeria and Kenya: Studies from recent focus group discussions. *Studies in Family Planning*, 23, 199–210.

Barnes, R., Auburn, T. & Lea, S. (2004). Citizenship as practice. *British Journal of Social Psychology*, 43, 187–206.

Bateson, G. (1972). *Steps to an ecology of mind*. New York: Ballantine.

Basch, C. E. (1987). Focus group interview: An underutilized research technique for improving theory and practice in health education. *Health Education Quarterly*, 14, 411–448.

Baumann, U., Laireiter, A. R. & Krebs, A. (1996). Computer-assisted interaction diary on social networks, social support, and interpersonal strain. In J. Fahrenberg & M. Myrtek (Eds) *Ambulatory assessment: Computer assisted psychological and psychophysiological methods in monitoring and field studies*. Göttingen: Hogrefe and Huber.

Beattie, A. (1991). The evaluation of community development initiatives in health promotion: A review of current strategies. In *'Roots and Branches': Papers from the OU/HEA 1990 Winter School on Community Development and Health* (pp. 212–235). Milton Keynes: HEU/Open University.

Beattie, G. (2003). *The new psychology of body language*. London: Routledge.

Bechtel, W. & Richardson, R. C. (1993). *Discovering complexity: Decomposition and localization as strategies in scientific research*. Princeton, NJ: Princeton University Press.

Begg, C. B. (1994). Publication bias. In H. Cooper & L. V. Hedges (Eds), *Handbook of research synthesis* (pp. 521–529). New York: Russell Sage Foundation.

Beike, D. R., Lampinen, J. M. & Behrend, D. A. (Eds) (2004). *The self and memory*. New York: Psychology Press.

Bell, M. M. & Gardiner, M. (Eds) (1998). *Bakhtin and the human sciences: No last words*. London: Sage.

Bellisle, F., Dalix, A. M. & De Castro, J. M. (1999). Eating patterns in French subjects studied by the 'weekly food diary' method. *Appetite, 32*(1), 46–52.

Bentler, P. M. (1995). EQS: *Structural equations program manual*. Encino, CA: Multivariate Sotware Inc.

Berg, B. (1995). *Qualitative research methods for the social sciences* (2nd ed.). Boston: Allyn & Bacon.

Berman, N. G. & Parker, R. A. (2002). Meta-analysis: Neither quick nor easy. *BMC Medical Methodology, 2*:10 (http://www.biomedcentral.com/1471-2288/2/10).

Billig, M. (1988). Methodology and scholarship in understanding ideological explanation. In C. Antaki (Ed.), *Analysing everyday explanation: A casebook of methods*. London: Sage.

Birnbaum, A. (1968). Some latent trait models and their use in inferring an examinee's ability. In L. F. Lord & M. Novick (Eds), *Statistical theories of mental test scores*. Reading, MA: Addison-Wesley.

Birnbaumer, N. & Ohman, A. (Eds) (1993). *The structure of emotion*. Berlin: Hogrefe and Huber.

Blair, R. J. R., Jones, L., Clark, F. & Smith, M. (1997). The psychopathic individual: A lack of responsiveness to distress cues? *Psychophysiology, 34*(2), 192–198.

Blake, R. & Hiris, E. (1993). Another means for measuring the motion aftereffect. *Vision Research, 33*, 1589–1592.

Blake, R. & Sekuler, R. (2005). Perception (5th ed.). New York: McGraw-Hill.

Blalock, H. M. Jr (1988) *Social statistics* (rev. 2nd ed.). Singapore: McGraw-Hill.

Blascovich, J. & Kelsey, M. (1990). Using electrodermal and cardiovascular measures of arousal in social psychological research. In C. Hendrick & M. S. Clark (Eds), *Research methods in personality and social psychology*. Newbury Park, CA: Sage.

Blashfield, R. K. & Aldenderfer, M. S. (1988). The methods and problems of cluster analysis. In J. R. Nesselroade & R. B. Cattell (Eds), *Handbook of multivariate experimental psychology*. London: Plenum.

Blinkhorn, S. F. & Johnson, C. (1990). The insignificance of personality testing. *Nature, 348*, 671–672.

Bloor, M., Frankland, J., Thomas, M., & Robson, K. (2001). *Focus groups in social research*. London: Sage.

Blum, G. S. (1949). A study of psychoanalytic theory of psychosexual development. *Genetic Psychology Monographs, 39*, 3–99.

Blumer, H. (1969). *Symbolic interactionism*. Englewood Cliffs, NJ: Prentice Hall.

Bogardus, E. (1926). The group interview. *Journal of Applied Sociology, 10*, 372–382.

Bond, T. G. & Fox, C. M. (2001). *Applying the Rasch model: Fundamental measurement in the human sciences*. Mahwah, NJ: Erlbaum.

Borg, I. & Groenen, P. (1997). *Modern multidimensional scaling*. New York: Springer.

Bormann, H. (1972). Fantasy and rhetorical vision: The rhetorical criticism of social reality. *Quarterly Journal of Speech, 58*, 396–407.

Boulton, M. (Ed.) (1994). *Challenge and innovation: Advances in social research on HIV/AIDS*. Brighton: Falmer.

Bramley, N. & Eatough, V. (2005). An idiographic case study of the experience of living with Parkinson's disease using interpretative phenomenological analysis. *Psychology & Health, 20*, 223–235.

Brazelton, T. B. & Cramer, B. G. (1991). *The earliest relationship: Parents, infants and the drama of early attachment*. London: Karnac Books.

Breakwell, G. M. (1994). The echo of power: An integrative framework for social psychological theorizing. *The Psychologist, 7*(2): 65–72.

Breakwell, G. M. (Ed.) (2004). *Doing social psychology research*. Oxford: Blackwell/BPS.

Breakwell, G. M. & Canter, D. V. (1993). *Empirical approaches to social representations*. Oxford: Oxford University Press.

Bringer, J., Johnston, L. & Brackenridge, C. (2004). Maximising transparency in a doctoral thesis: The complexities of writing about the use of QSR*NVIVO within a grounded theory study. *Qualitative Research, 4*, 247–265.

British Psychological Society (2004). *The BPS Code of Conduct, Ethical Principles and Guidelines*. Leicester: BPS (http://www.bps.org.uk/the-society/ethics-rules-charter-code-of-conduct/ethics-rules-charter-code-of-conduct_home.cfm).

Brocki, J. & Wearden, A. (2006). A critical evaluation of interpretative phenomenological analysis in health psychology. *Psychology & Health, 21*, 87–108.

Brockmeier, J. & Carbaugh, D. (Eds) (2001). *Narrative and identity: Studies in autobiography, self and culture*. Amsterdam: John Benjamins.

Bruner, J. (1990). *Acts of meaning*. Cambridge, MA: Harvard University Press.

Bryant, P. & Bradley, L. (1985). *Children's reading problems*. Oxford: Blackwell.

Bryant, P. E. (1990). Empirical evidence for causes in development. In G. Butterworth & P. E. Bryant (Eds), *Causes of development*. New York: Harvester Wheatsheaf.

Bull, P. (2004). The analysis of equivocation in political interviews. In G. M. Breakwell (Ed.), *Doing social psychology research*. Oxford: Blackwell.

Burawoy, M., Burton, A., Ferguson, A. A. & Fox, K. J., with Gamson, J., Hurst, L., Julius, N. G., Kurzman, C., Salzinger, L., Schiffman, J. & Ui, S. (1991). *Ethnography unbound: Power and resistance in the modern metropolis*. Berkeley: University of California Press.

Burman, E. (1992). Feminism and discourse in developmental psychology: Power, subjectivity and interpretation. *Feminism & Psychology, 2*, 45–59.

Burman, E. (1995). 'What is it?' Masculinity and femininity in cultural representations of childhood. In S. Wilkinson & C. Kitzinger (Eds), *Feminism and discourse: Psychological perspectives*. London: Sage.

Burman, E. & Parker, I. (1993a). Introduction – discourse analysis: the turn to the text. In E. Burman & I. Parker (Eds), *Discourse analytic research: Repertoires and readings of texts in action*. London: Routledge.

Burman, E. & Parker, I. (Eds) (1993b). *Discourse analytic research: Repertoires and readings of texts in action*. London: Routledge.

Burr, V. (2003). *Social constructionism* (2nd edn.). London: Routledge.

Cabinet Office (1999). *Modernising government*. Cm 4310. London: Stationery Office (http://www.cabinet-office.gov.uk/moderngov/whtpaper/index.htm).

Cacioppo, J. T., Tassinary, L. G. & Berntson, G. G. (2000). *Handbook of psychophysiology*. Cambridge: Cambridge University Press.

Caldirola, D., Bellodi, L., Caumo, A., Migliarese, G. & Perna, G. (2004). Approximate entropy of respiratory patterns in panic disorder. *American Journal of Psychiatry*, *161*, 79–87.

Campbell, A. (2004). Words, words, words. *British Journal of Developmental Psychology*, *22*, 509–513.

Campbell, D. T. & Stanley, J. (1966). *Experimental and quasi-experimental designs for research*. Chicago: Rand McNally.

Campbell, J. M. (1992). Treating depression in well older adults: use of diaries in cognitive therapy. *Issues in Mental Health Nursing*, *13*(1), 19–29.

Campos, J. J., Anderson, D. I., Barbu-Roth, M. A., Hubbard, E. M., Hertenstein, M. J., & Witherington, D. (2000). Travel broadens the mind. *Infancy*, *1*, 149–219.

Campos, J. J., Hiatt, S., Ramsay, D., Henderson, C. & Svejda, M. J. (1978). The emergence of fear of the visual cliff, In M. Lewis & L. Rosenblum (Eds) *The development of fear*. (pp. 149–182), New York: Plenum.

Campos, J. J., Svejda, M. J., Bertenthal, B., Benson, N. & Schmid, D. (1981). Self-produced locomotion and wariness of heights: new evidence from training studies, paper presented at the meeting of the Society for Research in Child Development, Boston.

Campos, J. J., Svejda, M. J., Campos, R. G. & Bertenthal, B. (1982). The emergence of self-produced locomotion: its importance for psychological development in infancy. In D. Bricker (Ed.) *Intervention with at-risk and handicapped infants*, (pp 195–216), Baltimore, MD: University Park Press.

Cappello, M. (2005). Photo interviews: Eliciting data through conversations with children. *Field Methods*, *17*, 170–182.

Carlson, J. G., Seifert, A. R. & Birnbaumer, N. (1994). *Clinical applied psychology*. New York: Plenum.

Carlson, N. R. (2004). *Physiology of behaviour* (8th edn). Boston: Pearson.

Carr, W. & Kemmis, S. (1986). *Becoming critical: Education, knowledge and action research*. London: Falmer.

Cattell, R. B. (1978). *The scientific use of factor analysis*. London: Plenum.

Cattell, R. B. (1981). *Personality and learning theory*, Vols I and II. Berlin: Springer.

Catterall, M. & Maclaran, P. (1997). Focus group data and qualitative analysis. *Sociological Research Online*, *2*(1): (http://www.socresonline.org.uk/2/1/6.html).

Chalmers, H. & Colvin, J. (2005). Addressing environmental inequalities in UK policy: An action research perspective. *Local Environment*, *10*(4), 1–28.

Chamberlain, P., Camic, P. & Yardley, L. (2004). Qualitative analysis of experience: Grounded theory and case studies. In D. Marks & L. Yardley (Eds), *Research Methods for Clinical and Health Psychology*. London: Sage.

Chambers, R. (1998) Beyond 'Whose reality counts?' New methods we now need. In O. Fals Borda (Ed.), *People's participation: Challenges ahead*. Bogotá: Tercier Mundo.

Chapman, E. (2002). The social and ethical implications of changing medical technologies: The views of people living with genetic conditions. *Journal of Health Psychology*, 7, 195–206.

Charmaz, C. (1990). Discovering chronic illness: Using grounded theory. *Social Science and Medicine*, 30, 1161–1172.

Charmaz, K. (2000). Grounded theory: Objectivist and subjectivist methods. In N. Denzin & Y. Lincoln (Eds), *Handbook of qualitative research* (2nd edn). Thousand Oaks, CA: Sage.

Child, D. (1990). *The essentials of factor analysis*. London: Cassell.

Christensen, L. B. (1988). *Experimental methodology* (4th edn). Boston: Allyn & Bacon.

Clark-Carter, D. (2003). Effect size: The missing piece in the jigsaw. *The Psychologist*, 16, 636–638.

Clogg, C. C. & Stockley, J. W. (1988). Multivariate analysis of discrete data. In J. R. Nesselroade & R. B. Cattell (Eds), *Handbook of multivariate experimental psychology*. London: Plenum.

Cochran, W. G. (1937). Problems arising in the analysis of a series of similar experiments. *Journal of the Royal Statistics Society*, 4, 102–118.

Cohen, J. (1960). A coefficient of agreement for nominal scales. *Educational and Psychological Measurement*, 20, 37–46.

Cohen, J. (1988). *Statistical power analyses for the behavioural sciences* (2nd edn). Hillsdale, NJ: Erlbaum.

Conner, M., Fitter, M. & Fletcher, W. (1999). Stress and snacking: A diary of daily hassles and between-meal snacking. *Psychology and Health*, 14(1), 51–63.

Conrad, P. (1987). The experience of illness: Recent and new directions. *Research in the Sociology of Health Care*, 6, 1–31.

Converse, P. E. (1964). The nature of belief systems in mass publics. In D.E. Apter (Ed.), *Ideology and discontent*. New York: Free Press.

Cook, T. D. & Campbell, D. T. (1979). *Quasi-experimentation: Design and analysis issues for field settings*. Chicago: Rand McNally.

Cooke, B. & Wolfram Cox, J. (2005). *Fundamentals of action research*, Vols I–IV. London: Sage.

Cooper, C. (2002). *Individual differences*. London: Hodder Arnold.

Corkrey, R. & Parkinson, L. (2002). A comparison of 4 computer-based telephone interviewing methods: Getting answers to sensitive questions. *Behavioural Research Methods, Instruments and Computers*, 34, 354–363.

Cornsweet, T. N. (1962). The staircase-method in psychophysics. *American Journal of Psychology*, 75, 485–491.

Cornsweet, T. N. & Teller, D. Y. (1965). Relation of increment thresholds to brightness and luminance. *Journal of the Optical Society of America*, 55, 1303–1308.

Cox T. F. & Cox M. A. (2001). *Multidimensional scaling* (2nd edn). Boca Raton, FL: Chapman & Hall.

Coxon, A. P. M. (1994). Diaries and sexual behaviour: The use of sexual diaries as method and substance in researching gay men's response to HIV/AIDS. In M. Boulton (Ed.), *Challenge and innovation: Methodological advances in social research on HIV/AIDS. Social aspects of AIDS*. London: Taylor & Francis.

Coxon, A. P. M. (1999). Parallel accounts? Discrepancies between self-report (diary) and recall (questionnaire) measures of the same sexual behaviour. *AIDS Care, 11*, 221–234.

Crittenden, P. (1998). Truth, error, omission, distortion, and deception: An application of attachment theory to the assessment and treatment of psychological disorder. In S. M. Clany Dollinger & L. F. DiLalla (Eds), *Assessment and intervention issues across the life span*. London: Lawrence Erlbaum.

Croft, C. A. & Sorrentino, M. C. (1991). Physician interaction with families on issues of AIDS: What parents and youth indicate they desire. *Journal of Health Behavior, Education and Promotion, 15*(6), 13–22.

Cronbach, L. J. (1951). Coefficient alpha and the internal structure of tests. *Psychometrika, 16*, 297–334.

Cronbach, L. J. (1971). Test validation. In R. L. Thorndike (Ed.), *Educational measurement*. Washington, DC: ACE.

Cronbach, L. J., Gleser, G. C., Nanda, H. & Rajaratnam, N. (1972). *The dependability of behavioral measurements: Theory of generalizability for scores and profiles*. New York: Wiley.

Crowne, D. P. & Marlowe, D. (1964). *The approval motive: Studies in evaluative dependence*. New York: Wiley.

Dale, A., Gilbert, G. N. & Arber, S. (1985). Integrating women into class theory. *Sociology, 19*, 384–409.

Dallos, R. & Draper, R. (2005). *An introduction to family therapy* (2nd edn). Maidenhead: Open University Press.

Dallos, R. & Vetere, A. (2005). *Researching psychotherapy and counselling*. Maidenhead: Open University Press.

Davies, B. & Harré, R. (1990). Positioning: The discursive production of selves. *Journal for the Theory of Social Behaviour, 20*, 43–63.

Davies, B. & Harré, R. (1999). Positioning and personhood. In R. Harré & L. van Langenhove (Eds), *Positioning theory*. Oxford: Blackwell.

Davies, J. B. (2004). Time for a paradigm shift: Bring on the physics revolution. *The Psychologst, 17*, 692–693.

Davison, M. L. & Sharma, A. R. (1990). Parametric statistics and levels of measurement: factorial designs and multiple regression. *Psychological Bulletin, 107*, 394–400.

de Gruijter, D. N. M. & van der Kamp, L. J. T. (2005). Statistical test theory for education and psychology (http://icloniis.iclon.leidenuniv.nl/gruijter).

De Leuw, E., & Hox, J. (2001). Trends in household survey nonresponse: A longitudinal and international comparison. In R. Groves, D. Dillman, J. Eltinge & R. Little (Eds), *Survey nonresponse*. New York: Wiley.

Delli-Carpini, M. & Williams, B. A. (1994). Methods, metaphors and media research: The uses of TV in political conversation. *Communication Research, 21*(6), 782–812.

Dempster, J. (2001). *The laboratory computer: A practical guide for physiologists and neuroscientists*. San Diego, CA: Academic Press.

Denzin, N. & Lincoln, Y. (2005). *The Sage handbook of qualitative research* (3rd edn). Thousand Oaks, CA: Sage.

Derrida, J. (1976). *Of grammatology* (trans. G. Chakravorty Spivak). Baltimore, MD: Johns Hopkins University Press.

Diamond, L. M. (2001). Contributions of psychophysiology to research on adult attachment: Review and recommendations. *Personality and Social Psychology Review, 5,* 276–295.

Dickinson, J. J., & Poole, D. A. (2000). Efficient coding of eyewitness narratives: A comparison of syntactic unit and word count procedures. *Behavior Research Methods, Instruments and Computers, 32,* 537–545.

Dobson, V. G. & Rose, D. (1985). Models and metaphysics: The nature of explanation revisited. In D. Rose & V.G. Dobson (Eds), *Models of the visual cortex.* Chichester: Wiley.

Drew, P. (2003). Conversation analysis. In J. A. Smith (Ed.), *Qualitative psychology. A practical guide to research methods.* London: Sage.

Dunn, N. J., Seilhamer, R. A., Jacob, T. & Whalen, M. (1993). Comparison of retrospective and current reports of alcoholics and their spouses on drinking behavior. *Addictive Behaviors, 17,* 543–555.

Dworkin, S. F. & Wilson, L. (1993). Measurement of illness behavior: Review of concepts and common measures. In P. M. Conn (Ed.), *Paradigms for the Study of Behavior.* New York: Academic Press.

Eatough, V. & Smith, J. A. (in press). I feel like a scrambled egg in my head: An idiographic case study of meaning making and anger using interpretative phenomenological analysis. *Psychology & Psychotherapy.*

Edley, N. & Wetherell, M. (1999). Imagined futures: Young men's talk about fatherhood and domestic life. *British Journal of Social Psychology, 38,* 181–194.

Edmunds, H. (1999). *The focus group research handbook.* Lincolnwood, IL: NTC Business Books.

Edwards, D. & Potter, J. (1992). *Discursive psychology.* London: Sage.

Elliott, R. (1986). Interpersonal process recall (IPR) as a process research method. In L. Greenberg & W. Pinsof (Eds), *The psychotherapeutic process.* New York: Guilford Press.

Elliott, R., Fischer, C. T. & Rennie, D. L. (1999). Evolving guidelines for publication of qualitative research studies in psychology and related fields. *British Journal of Clinical Psychology, 38,* 215–229.

Ellis, C. (1998). Exploring loss through autoethnographic inquiry: Autoethnographic stories, co-constructed narratives, and interactive interviews. In J. Harvey (Ed.), *Perspectives on loss: A sourcebook* (pp. 49–61). Philadelphia: Brunner/Mazel.

Ellis, D. G (1993). *Small group decision making.* New York: McGraw-Hill.

Ellis, J. & Kiely, J. (2005) Action inquiry strategies: Taking stock and moving forward. In B. Cooke & J. Wolfram Cox, *Fundamentals of action research.* London: Sage.

Ely, R., Melzi, G., Hadge, L., McCabe, A. (1998). Being brave, being nice: Themes of agency and communion in children's narratives. *Journal of Personality, 66,* 257–284.

Embretson, S. E. & Reise, S. (2000). *Item response theory for psychologists.* Mahwah, NJ: Erlbaum.

Erdberg, P. & Exner, J. E. (1984). Rorschach assessment. In G. Goldstein & M. Hersen (Eds). *Psychological assessment.* New York: Pergamon.

Evans, M. (1993). Reading lives: How the personal might be social. *Sociology, 27,* 5–13.

Evans, R. I., Rozelle, R. M., Mittelmark, M. B., Hansen, W. B., Bane, A. L. & Havis, J. (1978). Deterring the onset of smoking in children: knowledge of immediate physiological effects and coping with peer pressure, media pressure and parent modeling. *Journal of Applied Social Psychology, 8*(2), 126–135.

Everitt, B. S. (1977). *The analysis of contingency tables*. London: Chapman & Hall.

Everitt B. S., Landau, S. & Leese, M. (2001). *Cluster analysis*. London: Arnold.

Ewing, K. P. (2000). Dream as symptom, dream as myth: A cross-cultural perspective on dream narratives. *Sleep and Hypnosis, 2*(4), 152–159.

Exner, J. (1986). *The Rorschach: A comprehensive system* (2nd edn). Chichester: Wiley.

Eysenck, H. J. (1952). The effects of psychotherapy: An evaluation. *Journal of Consulting Psychology, 16*, 319–324.

Eysenck, H. J. (1994). Meta-analysis and its problems. *British Medical Journal, 309*, 789–792.

Eysenck, H. J. & Eysenck, S. B. G. (1975). *Manual for the Eysenck Personality Questionnaire*. London: Hodder & Stoughton.

Eysenck, H. J. & Eysenck, S. B. G. (1976). *Psychoticism as a dimension of personality*. London: Hodder & Stoughton.

Ezzy, D. (1998). Theorizing narrative identity: Symbolic interactionism and hermeneutics. *Sociological Quarterly, 39*, 239–252.

Fals Borda, O. (2001). Participatory action research in social theory: Origins and challenges. In P. Reason & H. Bradbury (Eds), *Handbook of action research: Participative inquiry and practice* (pp. 27–37). London: Sage.

Farell, B. & Pelli, D. G. (1998). Psychophysical methods. In R. H. S. Carpenter & J. G. Robson (Eds), *Vision research: A practical guide to laboratory methods* (pp. 129–136). Oxford: Oxford University Press.

Farsides, T. (2004). Cognitive mapping: Generating theories of psychological phenomena from verbal accounts and presenting them diagrammatically. In G. M. Breakwell (Ed.), *Doing social psychology research*. Oxford: Blackwell.

Feldman, C. F. (2001). Narratives of national identity as group narratives: Patterns of interpretive cognition. In J. Brockmeier & D. Carbaugh (Eds), *Narrative and identity: Studies in autobiography, self and culture* (pp. 129–144). Amsterdam: John Benjamins.

Field, A. P. (2003). Can meta-analysis be trusted? *The Psychologist, 16*, 642–645.

Field, A. & Hole, G. (2003). *How to design and report experiments*. London: Sage.

Fielding, N. (Ed.) (2003). *Interviewing*. London: Sage.

Fisch, B. J. (1999). *Fisch and Spehlmann's EEG primer: Basic principles of digital and analog EEG* (3rd edn). Amsterdam: Elsevier.

Fischer, G. & Molenaar, I. (1995). *Rasch models: Foundations, recent developments and applications*. London: Springer.

Fisher, R. A. (1935). *The design of experiments*. Edinburgh: Oliver & Boyd.

Fleiss, J. L. (1971). Measuring nominal scale agreement among many raters. *Psychological Bulletin, 76*, 378–382.

Flick, U. (1998). *An introduction to qualitative research*. London: Sage.

Fontana, A. & Fry, J. H. (2000). The interview: From structured questions to negotiated text. In N. K. Denzin & Y. S. Lincoln (Eds.), *Handbook of qualitative research* (2nd edn). Thousand Oaks, CA: Sage.

Forbat, L. (2005). *Talking about care: Two sides to the story*. Bristol: Policy Press.

Freeman, P. R. (1973). *Table of d' and β*. Cambridge: Cambridge University Press.

Fried, R. & Grimaldi, J. (1993). *The psychology and physiology of breathing*. London: Plenum.

Frith, H. (2000). Focusing on sex: Using focus groups in sex research. *Sexualities, 3,* 275–297.

Frith, H. & Kitzinger, C. (1998). Emotion work as a participant resource: A feminist analysis of young women's talk-in-interaction. *Sociology: Journal of the British Sociological Association, 32*(2), 305–321.

Frosh, S., Phoenix, A. & Pattman, R. (2003). Taking a stand: Using psychoanalysis to explore the positioning of subjects in discourse. *British Journal of Social Psychology, 42,* 39–53.

Fuller, T. D., Edwards, J. N., Vorakitphokatom, S. & Sermsri, S. (1993). Using focus groups to adapt survey instruments to new populations: Experience from a developing country. In D. L. Morgan (Ed.), *Successful focus groups: Advancing the state of the art.* London: Sage.

Gage, N. L. (1963) *Handbook of research on teaching.* Chicago: Rand McNally.

Gale, A. & Eysenck, H. O. (Eds) (1993). *Handbook of individual differences: Biological perspectives.* Chichester: Wiley.

Gaskell, G., Wright, D. & O'Muircheartaigh, P. (1993). Reliability of surveys. *The Psychologist, 6,* 500–503.

Gaventa J. & Cornwall, A. (2001). Power and knowledge. In P. Reason & H. Bradbury, *Handbook of action research: Participative inquiry and practice.* London: Sage.

Gergen, K. J. (1989). Warranting voice and the elaboration of the self. In J. Shotter & K. J. Gergen (Eds), *Texts of identity.* London: Sage.

Gergen, K. J. (1994). *Realities and relationships: Soundings in social construction.* Cambridge, MA: Harvard University Press.

Gergen, K. J. (1998). From control to co-construction: New narratives for the social sciences. *Psychological Inquiry, 9*(2), 101–103.

Gervais, M.-C. (1993). *How communities cope with environmental crises: The case of the Shetland oil spill.* Paper presented at the BPS Social Psychology Section Annual Conference, Jesus College, Oxford, September.

Gescheider, G. A. (1997). *Psychophysics* (3rd edn). Hillsdale, NJ: Lawrence Erlbaum.

Gibbs, G. R. (2002). Qualitative data analysis: Explorations with NVivo. Buckingham: Open University Press.

Gibson, E. J., & Walk, R. D. (1960). The 'visual cliff'. *Scientific American, 202,* 64–71.

Gifi, A. (1990). *Nonlinear multivariate analysis.* Chichester: Wiley.

Gilgun, J. F., Daly, K. & Handel, G. (1992). *Qualitative methods in family research.* London: Sage.

Gillett, R. (2001). Meta-analysis and bias in research reviews. *Journal of Reproductive and Infant Psychology, 19*(4), 287–294.

Giorgi, A. & Giorgi, B. (2003). Phenomenology. In J. A. Smith (Ed.), *Qualitative psychology: A practical guide to research methods* (pp. 25–50). London: Sage.

Glaser, B. G. & Strauss, A. L. (1967). *The discovery of grounded theory.* Chicago: Aldine.

Glaser, R. (1963). Instructional technology and the measurement of learning outcomes. *American Psychologist, 18,* 519–522.

Glass, G., McGraw, B. & Smith, M. L. (1981). *Meta-analysis in social research.* Beverly Hills, CA: Sage.

Glitz, B. (1998). *Focus groups for libraries and librarians.* New York: Forbes Custom Publishing.

Goetz, J. P. & LeCompte, M. D. (1984). *Ethnography and qualitative design in educational research.* London: Academic.

Goffman, E. (1961). *Asylums.* Chicago: Aldine.

Goldberg, D. (1972). *The detection of psychiatric illness by questionnaire.* London: Oxford University Press.

Golsworthy, R. & Coyle, A. (1999). Spiritual beliefs and the search for meaning among older adults following partner loss. *Mortality,* 4, 21–40.

Gomm, R., Hammersley, M. & Foster, P. (2000). *Case study and generalization.* In R. Gomm, M. Hammersley & P. Foster (Eds), *Case study method.* London: Sage.

Gottman, J. M. (1982). Emotional responsiveness in marital communications. *Journal of Communications,* Summer, 108–120.

Green, D. M. & Swets, J. A. (1966). *Signal detection theory and psychophysics.* New York: Wiley.

Greenacre, M. (1984). *Theory and application of correspondence analysis.* New York: Academic.

Greenacre, M. & Blasius, J. (1994). *Correspondence analysis in the social sciences.* New York: Academic Press.

Greenbaum, T. L. (1998). *The handbook for focus group research.* London: Sage.

Greenbaum, T. L. (2000). *Moderating focus groups: A practical guide for group facilitation.* Thousand Oaks, CA: Sage.

Greenwald, P. C. (1975). Consequences of prejudice against the null hypothesis. *Psychological Bulletin, 82,* 1–20.

Greenwood, D. J. & Levin, M. (1998). *Introduction to action research.* London: Sage.

Groves, R., Fowler, F., Couper, M., Lepkowski, J., Singer, E. & Tourangeau, R. (2004). *Survey methodology.* Hoboken, NJ: Wiley.

Gulliksen, H. (1950). *Theory of mental tests.* New York: Wiley.

Guttman, L. (1941). The quantification of a class of attributes: A theory and method of scale construction. In P. Horst *et al.* (Eds), *The prediction of personal adjustment.* New York: Social Science Research Council.

Haberman, S. J. (1978). *The analysis of qualitative data,* Vol. 1. New York: Academic.

Haberman, S. J. (1979). *The analysis of qualitative data,* Vol. 2. New York: Academic.

Hair, J. F., Anderson, R. E., Tatham, R. L. & Black, W. C. (1992). *Multivariate data analysis.* New York: Macmillan.

Hair J. F., Tatham R. L., Anderson R. E. & Black W. (1998). *Multivariate data analysis.* New York: Prentice Hall.

Hagenaars J. A. & McCutcheon A. L. (2002). *Applied latent class analysis.* Cambridge: Cambridge University Press.

Hall, J. L. (1981). Hybrid adaptive procedure for estimation of psychometric functions. *Journal of the Acoustical Society of America, 69,* 1763–1769.

Halliday, A. M., Butler, S. R. & Paul, R. (1987). *A textbook of clinical neurophysiology.* Chichester: Wiley.

Hambleton, R. K., Swaminathan, H. & Rogers, H. J. (1991). *Fundamentals of item response theory.* London: Sage.

Hammersley, M. (1992). *What's wrong with ethnography? Methodological explorations.* London: Routledge.

Hammersley, M. & Atkinson, P. (1995). *Ethnography: Principles in practice* (2nd edn). London: Routledge.

Hammond, S. (1988). *The meaning and measurement of adolescent estrangement.* PhD thesis, University of Surrey.

Harlow, L. L., Mulaik, S. & Steiger, J. H. (Eds) (1997). *What if there were no significance tests?* Hillsdale: Lawrence Erlbaum.

Harman, H. (1976). *Modern factor analysis.* Chicago: University of Chicago Press.

Harper, D. J. (1994). The professional construction of 'paranoia' and the discursive use of diagnostic criteria. *British Journal of Medical Psychology, 67,* 131–143.

Harré, R. (1979). *Social being.* Oxford: Basil Blackwell.

Hart, E. & Bond, M. (1995). *Action research for health and social care: A guide to practice.* Buckingham: Open University Press.

Harvey, L. O., Jr (1986). Efficient estimation of sensory thresholds. *Behavior Research Methods, Instruments and Computers, 18,* 623–632.

Hayduk, L. A. (1996). *LISREL: Issues, debates and strategies.* Baltimore, MD: Johns Hopkins University Press.

Helmholtz, H. von (1962). *Treatise on physiological optics.* New York: Dover. (Originally published in 1866.)

Henkel, R. E. (1975). Part–whole correlations and the treatment of ordinal and quasi-interval data as interval data, *Pacific Sociological Review, 18,* 3–26.

Henwood, K. L. (1993). Women and later life: The discursive construction of identities within family relationships. *Journal of Ageing Studies, 7,* 303–319.

Henwood, K. L. & Pidgeon, N. (1992). Qualitative research and psychological theorizing. *British Journal of Psychology, 83,* 97–111.

Henwood, K. L. & Pidgeon, N. F. (2001). Talk about woods and trees: Threat of urbanisation, stability and biodiversity. *Journal of Environmental Psychology, 21,* 125–147.

Henwood, K. L. & Pidgeon, N. F. (2003). Grounded theory in psychological research. In P. Camic, L. Yardley & J. Rhodes (Eds), *Qualitative research in psychology* (pp. 131–155). Washington, DC: American Psychological Association Press.

Hepburn, A. & Wiggins, S. (2005). Size matters: Constructing accountable bodies in NSPCC helpline interaction. *Discourse & Society, 16,* 625–645.

Hilder, J. (1997). *Notes on the use of focus groups in organizational settings.* Unpublished manuscript, Social Psychology European Research Institute, University of Surrey.

Hinkelmann, K. & Kempthorne, O. (2005). *Design and analysis of experiments: Advanced experimental design.* Chichester: Wiley.

Hobbs, D. & May, T. (Eds) (1993). *Interpreting the field: Accounts of ethnography,* Oxford: Clarendon Press.

Hoepfl, M. (1997). Choosing qualitative research: A primer for technology education researchers. *Journal of Technology Education, 9* (http://www.borg.lib.vt.edu/JTE/jte-v9n1/hoeofl.html).

Hollander, J. A. (2004). The social context of focus groups. *Journal of Contemporary Ethnography, 33,* 602–637.

Hollway, W. (1989). *Subjectivity and method in psychology: Gender, meaning and science.* London: Sage.

Holm, S. (1979). A simple sequentially rejective multiple test procedure. *Scandinavian Journal of Statistics, 6,* 65–70.

Holstein, J. & Gubrium, J. F. (Eds) (2003). *Inside interviewing: New lenses, new concerns*. London: Sage.

Holsti, O. R. (1969). *Content analysis for the social sciences*. Reading, MA: Addison-Wesley.

Holter, I. M. & Schwartz-Barcott, D. (1993). Action research: What is it, how has it been used and how can it be used in nursing? *Journal of Advanced Nursing, 18*, 298–304.

Hosmer, D. W. & Lemeshow, S. (1989). *Applied logistic regression*. Chichester: Wiley.

Hoyle, R. H. (1995). *Structural equation modelling: Concepts, issues and applications*. London: Sage.

Huber, R., Ghilardi, M. F., Massimini, M. & Tononi, G. (2004). Local sleep and learning. *Nature, 430*, 78–81.

Huberty, C. J. (1994). *Applied discriminant analysis*. Chichester: Wiley.

Hui, C. H. & Triandis, H. C. (1989). Effects of culture and response format on extreme response style. *Journal of Cross-Cultural Psychology, 20*, 296–309.

Hulin, C. L., Drasgow, F. & Parsons, C. K. (1983). *Item response theory*. Homewood, IL: Dow Jones-Irwin.

Hull, D. L. (1988). *Science as a process*. Chicago: University of Chicago Press.

Hunt, M. (1997). *How science takes stock: The story of meta-analysis*. New York: Russell Sage Foundation.

Hutchinson, K. & Wegge, D. (1991). The effects of interviewer gender upon response in telephone survey research. *Journal of Social Behavior and Personality, 6*, 575–584.

Hyden, L.-C. & Bulow, P. H. (2003). Who's talking: Drawing conclusions from focus groups: Some methodological considerations. *International Journal of Social Research Methodology, 6*(4), 305–321.

Israel, J. (1972). Stipulations and construction in the social sciences. In J. Israel & H. Tajfel (Eds), *The context of social psychology*. London: Academic.

Jacobson, N. S., Fokllette, W. C. & Ravenstorf, D. (1984). Toward a standard definition of clinically significant change. *Behaviour Therapy, 17*, 308–311.

Jarrett, R. L. (1993). Focus group interviewing with low-income minority populations. In D. L. Morgan (Ed.), *Successful focus groups: Advancing the state of the art*. Newbury Park, CA: Sage.

Jennings, J. & Coles, M. G. (Eds) (1991). *Handbook of cognitive psychophysiology: Central and autonomic nervous system approaches*. Chichester: Wiley.

Jezzard, P., Matthews, P. M. & Smith, S. (2001). *Functional MRI: An introduction to methods*. Oxford University Press: Oxford.

Jordan, S. & Roberts, C. (2000). *Learning and residence abroad: Introduction to ethnography for language learners*. Oxford Brookes University, Thames Valley University and King's College London.

Jöreskog, K. G. (1970). A general method for analysis of covariance structures, *Biometrika, 57*, 239–51.

Jöreskog, K. G. & Sörbom, D. (1993). *LISREL 8: Structural equation modeling with the SIMPLIS command language*. Hillsdale, NJ: Scientific Software International/Erlbaum.

Jovchelovitch, S. (2000). Corruption flows in our blood: Mixture and impurity in representations of public life in Brazil. In M. Chaib & B. Orfali (Eds), *Social representations and communicative processes*. Jönköping: Jönköping University Press.

Junker, B. H. (1972). *Fieldwork: An introduction to the social sciences.* Chicago: University of Chicago Press.

Kalfs, N. & Willem, S. (1998). Large differences in time use for three data collection systems. *Social Indicators Research, 44,* 267–290.

Kelly, G. A. (1955). *The psychology of personal constructs,* Vols 1 and 2. New York: Norton.

Kemmis, S. & McTaggart, R. (1988). *The action research planner.* Geelong: Deakin University Press.

Kenny, A. J. (2005). Interaction in cyberspace: An on-line focus group. *Journal of Advanced Nursing, 49,* 414–422.

Keppel, G. & Saufley, J. R. (1980). *Introduction to design and analysis: A student's handbook.* San Francisco: Freeman.

Kerlinger, F. N. & Lee, H. B. (2000). *Foundations of behavioral research* (4th edn). Belmont, CA: Wadsworth/Thomson Learning.

Kerlinger, F. N. & Pedhazur, E. J. (1973). *Multiple regression in behavioral research.* New York: Holt, Rinehart and Winston.

Kidder, L. H. & Fine, M. (1987). Qualitative and quantitative methods: When stories converge. In M. M. Mark & L. Shotland (Eds), *New directions in program evaluation.* San Francisco: Jossey-Bass.

Kiernan, B. D., Cox, D. J., Kovatchev, B. P., Kiernan, B. S. & Giuliano, A. J. (1999). Improving driving performance of senior drivers through self-monitoring with a driving diary. *Physical and Occupational Therapy in Geriatrics, 16*(1–2), 55–64.

King, G., Keohane, R. O. & Verba, S. (1994). *Designing social enquiry: Scientific inference in qualitative research.* Princeton, NJ: Princeton University Press.

King, R. M. & Wilson, G. V. (1992). Use of a diary technique to investigate psychosomatic relations in atopic dermatitis. *Journal of Psychosomatic Research, 35,* 697–706.

King-Smith, P. E., Grigsby, S. S., Vingrys, A. J., Benes, S. C. & Supowit, A. (1994). Efficient and unbiased modifications of the QUEST method: Theory, simulations, experimental evaluation and practical implementation. *Vision Research, 34,* 885–912.

King-Smith, P. E. & Rose, D. (1997). Principles of an adaptive method for measuring the slope of the psychometric function. *Vision Research, 37,* 1595–1604.

Kirk, R. E. (1996). Practical significance: A concept whose time has come. *Educational and Psychological Measurement, 56,* 746–759.

Kitcher, P. (1993). *The advancement of science.* New York: Oxford University Press.

Kitzinger, J. (1994). The method of focus group interviews: The importance of interaction between research participants. *Sociology of Health and Illness, 16*(1), 103–121.

Klecka, W. R. (1980). *Discriminant analysis.* London: Sage.

Klee, R. (1997). *Introduction to the philosophy of science.* New York: Oxford University Press.

Klein, S. A. (2001). Measuring, estimating, and understanding the psychometric function: A commentary. *Perception & Psychophysics, 63,* 1421–1455.

Klein, S. A. & Macmillan, N. A. (Eds) (2001). Psychometric functions and adaptive methods. *Perception & Psychophysics, 63,* 1277–1455.

Kline, P. (1993). *Handbook of psychological testing.* London: Routledge.

Klopfer, W. G. & Taulbee, E. S. (1976). Projective tests. *Annual Review of Psychology, 27,* 543–568.

Knipschild, P. (1994). Systematic reviews: Some examples. *British Medical Journal, 309*, 719–721.

Knodel, J. (1993). The design and analysis of focus group studies: A practical approach. In D. L. Morgan (Ed.), *Successful focus groups: Advancing the state of the art*. London: Sage.

Kontsevich, L. L. & Tyler, C. W. (1999). Bayesian adaptive estimation of psychometric slope and threshold. *Vision Research, 39*, 2729–2737.

Kraemer, H. C. & Thiemann, S. (1987). *How many subjects? Statistical power analysis in research*. Newbury Park, CA: Sage.

Krippendorf, K. (1980). *Content analysis: An introduction to its methodology*. Beverly Hills, CA: Sage.

Krosnick, J. A., Holbrook, A. L., Berent, M. K., Carson, R. T., Haneman, W. M. *et al.* (2002). The impact of 'no opinion' response options on data quality. *Public Opinion Quarterly, 66*, 371–403.

Krosnick, J. A. & Schuman, H. (1988). Attitude intensity, importance and certainty and susceptibility to response effects. *Journal of Personality and Social Psychology, 54*, 940–952.

Krueger, R. A. (1993). Quality control in focus group research. In D. L. Morgan (Ed.), *Successful focus groups: Advancing the state of the art*. London: Sage.

Krueger, R. A. (1994). *Focus groups: A practical guide for applied research* (2nd edn). London: Sage.

Krueger, R. A. & Casey, M. (2000). *Focus groups: A practical guide for applied research* (3rd ed.). Newbury Park, CA: Sage.

Kruskal, J. B. (1964). Nonmetric multidimensional scaling: A numerical method. *Psychometrika, 29*, 1–27.

Kruskal J. B. & Wish, M. (1978). *Multidimensional scaling*. Beverly Hills, CA: Sage.

Kuder, G. & Richardson, M. (1937). The theory of the estimation of test reliability. *Psychometrika, 2*, 151–160.

Kuhn, T. S. (1962). *The structure of scientific revolutions*. Chicago: University of Chicago Press.

Kutas, M. & Dale, A. (1997). Electrical and magnetic readings of mental functions. In M. D. Rugg (Ed.), *Cognitive neuroscience*. Hove: Psychology Press.

Kvale, S. (1996). *Interviews: An introduction to qualitative research interviewing*. London: Sage.

Labovitz, S. (1975). Comment on Henkel's paper: The interplay between measurement and statistics. *Pacific Sociological Review, 18*, 27–35.

Lakoff, G. (1990). *Women, fire and dangerous things*. Chicago: University of Chicago Press.

Lakatos, I. (1970). Falsification and the methodology of scientific research programmes. In I. Lakatos & A. Musgrave (Eds), *Criticism and the growth of knowledge*. Cambridge: Cambridge University Press.

Lamiell, J. T. (1995). Rethinking the role of quantitative methods in psychology. In J. A. Smith, R. Harré & L. Van Langenhove (Eds), *Rethinking methods in psychology*. London: Sage.

Lancaster, H.O. (1969). *The chi-squared distribution*. New York: Wiley.

Lasen, A. (no date). *A comparative study of mobile phone use in public places in London, Madrid and Paris.* Digital World Research Centre, University of Surrey.

Lee, R. M. & Fielding, G. (2004). Tools for qualitative data analysis. In M. Hardy & A. Bryman (Eds), *Handbook of data analysis* (pp. 529–546). London, Sage.

Legg, C., Puri, A. & Thomas, N. (2000). Dietary restraint and self-reported meal sizes: Diary studies with differentially informed consent. *Appetite, 34,* 235–243.

Levine, M. W. (2000). *Fundamentals of sensation and perception* (3rd edn). Oxford: Oxford University Press.

Lewin, K. (1943). Forces behind food habits and methods of change, *Bulletin of the National Research Council, 108,* 35–65.

Lewin, K. (1948). Action research and minority problems. In G. W. Lewin (Ed.), *Resolving social conflicts: Selected papers on group dynamics by Kurt Lewin.* New York: Harper.

Lewis, A. & Porter, J. (2004). Interviewing children and young people with learning difficulties. *British Journal of Learning Disability, 32,* 191–197.

Libman, E., Fichten, C. S., Bailes, S., & Amsel, R. (2000). Sleep questionnaire versus sleep diary: Which measure is better? *International Journal of Rehabilitation and Health, 5,* 205–209.

Light, R. J. (1971). Measures of response agreement for qualitative data: Some generalisations and alternatives. *Psychological Bulletin, 76,* 175–181.

Lincoln, Y. S. & Guba, E. G. (1985). *Naturalistic inquiry.* Beverly Hills, CA: Sage.

Linell, P. (2001). A dialogical conception of focus groups and social representations. In U. Sötterlund Larson (Ed.), *Sociocultural theory and methods: An anthology.* Department of Nursing, University of Trollhöttan/Uddevalla.

Linn, R. L. & Slinde, J. A. (1977). The determination of the significance of change between pre and post testing periods. *Review of Educational Research, 47,* 121–150.

Lipsey, M. W. & Wilson, D. B. (1993). The efficacy of psychological, educational, and behavioural treatment: Confirmation from meta-analysis. *American Psychologist, 48,* 1181–1209.

Lipsey, M. W. & Wilson, D. B. (2001). *Practical meta-analysis.* Thousand Oaks, CA: Sage.

Lipton, P. (1991). *Inference to the best explanation.* London: Routledge.

Llewellyn, G. (1991). Adults with an intellectual disability: Australian practitioners' perspectives. *Occupational Therapy Journal of Research, 11,* 323–335.

Long, J. S. (1983). *Confirmatory factor analysis.* Newbury Park, CA: Sage.

Lorber, M. F. (2004). Psychophysiology of aggression, psychopathy, and conduct problems: A meta-analysis. *Psychological Bulletin, 130,* 531–552.

Lord, F. M. (1980). *Applications of item response theory to practical testing problems.* Reading, MA: Addison-Wesley.

Lord, F. M. & Novick, M. (1968). *Statistical theories of mental test scores.* Reading, MA: Addison-Wesley.

Lowenthal, D. (1985). *The past is a foreign country.* Cambridge: Cambridge University Press.

Luce, R. D. & Tukey, J. W. (1964). Simultaneous conjoint measurement: A new type of fundamental measurement. *Journal of Mathematical Psychology, 1,* 1–27.

Luce, R. D., Krantz, D. H., Suppes, P. & Tversky, A. (1990). *Foundations of measurement, volume 3: Representation, axiomatisation and invariance.* New York: Academic Press.

Lundh, L. G. & Sperling, M. (2002). Social anxiety and the post-event processing of socially distressing events. *Cognitive Behaviour Therapy, 31*, 129–134.

Lunt, P. (1996). Discourse of savings. *Journal of Economic Psychology, 17*, 677–690.

Lunt, P., & Livingstone, S. (1996). Focus groups in common and media research. *Journal of Communication, 42*, 78–87.

Lynn, P., Beerten, R., Laiho, J. & Martin, J. (2001). *Recommended standard final outcome categories and standard definitions of response rate for social surveys.* Working Papers of the Institute for Social and Economic Research 2001–23. University of Essex, Colchester.

McAdams, D. P. (1999). Personal narratives and the life story. In O. P. John & L. A. Pervin (Eds), *Handbook of personality: Theory and research* (2nd edn). New York: Guilford Press.

McAdams, D. P. (2004). The redemptive self: Narrative identity in America today. In D. R. Beike, J. M. Lampinen & D. A. Behrend (Eds), *The self and memory* (pp. 95–115). New York: Psychology Press.

McCutcheon, A. L. (1987). *Latent class analysis.* Newbury Park, CA:Sage.

McDonald, R. P. (1985). *Factor analysis and related methods.* Hillsdale, NJ: Erlbaum.

McLachlan G. J. (2004). *Discriminant analysis and statistical pattern recognition.* Chichester: Wiley.

Macmillan, N. A. & Creelman, C. D. (2005). *Detection theory: A user's guide* (2nd edn). Mahwah, NJ: Lawrence Erlbaum.

McTaggart R. (2005). Is validity really an issue for participatory action research. In B. Cooke & J. Wolfram Cox, *Fundamentals of action research.* London: Sage.

Mcllenberg, G. J. (1999). A note on simple gain score precision. *Applied Psychological Measurement, 23*, 87–89.

Madill, A. & Doherty, K. (1994). 'So you did what you wanted then': Discourse analysis, personal agency, and psychotherapy. *Journal of Community & Applied Social Psychology, 4*, 261–273.

Magina, C. A. (1997). Some recent applications of clinical psychophysiology. *International Journal of Psychophysiology, 25*(1), 1–6.

Manis, J. G. & Metzer, B. N. (1967). *Symbolic interactionism: A reader in social psychology.* Boston: Allyn & Bacon.

Marascuilo, L. A. & Levin, J. R. (1983). *Multivariate statistics in the social sciences.* Monterey, CA: Brooks/Cole.

Markham, A. N. (2004). Internet communication as a tool for research. In D. Silverman (Ed.), *Qualitative research: Theory, method and practice* (pp. 95–124). London: Sage.

Marsh, P., Rosser, E. & Harré, R. (1978). *The rules of disorder.* London: Routledge & Kegan Paul.

Marshall, C. & Rossman, G. B. (1999). *Designing qualitative research* (3rd edn). London: Sage.

Maruyama, G. M. (1997). *Basics of structural equation modeling.* London: Sage.

Mather, G., Verstraten, F. & Anstis, S. (Eds) (1998). *The motion aftereffect. A modern perspective.* Cambridge, MA: MIT Press.

May, V. (2004). Narrative identity and the re-conceptualization of lone motherhood. *Narrative Inquiry, 14*(1), 169–189.

Merton, R. K. & Kendall, P. L. (1946). The focused interview. *American Journal of Sociology*, *51*, 541–557.

Michell, J. (1997). Quantitative science and the definition of measurement in psychology. *British Journal of Psychology*, *88*, 355–383.

Michell, J. (1999). *Measurement in psychology: A critical history of a methodological concept*. Cambridge: Cambridge University Press.

Michell, J. (2000). Normal science, pathological science and psychometrics. *Theory and Psychology*, *10*, 639–667.

Michell, L. (1998). Combining focus groups and interviews: telling how it is: Telling how it feels. In R. Barbour & J. Kitzinger (Eds), *Developing focus group research* (pp. 36–46). London: Sage.

Michell, L. & West, P. (1996). Peer pressure to smoke: The meaning depends on the method. *Health Education Research*, *11*(1), 39–49.

Miles, M. B. & Huberman, A. M. (1994). *Qualitative data analysis*. London: Sage.

Miles, S. & Rowe, G. (2004). The laddering technique. In G. M. Breakwell (Ed.), *Doing social psychology research*. Oxford: Blackwell.

Milgram, S. (1974). *Obedience to authority*. New York: Harper & Row.

Milgram, S. (1983). *Obedience to authority: An experimental view*. New York: HarperCollins.

Mill, J. S. (1950). *A system of logic*. New York: Harper. (Originally published in 1874.)

Minami, M. (2000). The relationship between narrative identity and culture. *Narrative Inquiry*, *10*(1), 75–80.

Minium, E. W., King, B. M. & Bear, G. (1993). *Statistical reasoning in psychology and education*. New York: Wiley.

Mislevy, R. J. (1993). Foundations of a new test theory. In N. Frederiksen, R. J. Mislevy & I. Bejar (Eds), *Test theory for a new generation of tests*. London: Erlbaum.

Moncrieff, J. (1998). Research synthesis: Systematic reviews and meta-analysis. *International Review of Psychiatry*, *10*, 304–311.

Moore, J., Canter, D., Stockley, D. & Drake, M. (1995). *The faces of homelessness in London*. Aldershot: Dartmouth.

Moran, D. (2000). *Introduction to phenomenology*. London: Routledge.

Morgan, D .L. (1988) *Focus groups as qualitative research*. Newbury Park, CA: Sage.

Morgan, D. L. (1997). *Focus groups as qualitative research* (2nd edn). Thousand Oaks, CA: Sage.

Morgan, D. L. & Krueger, R. A. (1997). *Focus group kit*. London: Sage.

Morris, D. (2002). *Peoplewatching*. London: Vintage.

Moscovici, S. (1976). *Social influence and social change*. London: Academic.

Moser, C. A. & Kalton, G. (1971). *Survey methods in social investigation*. London: Heinemann.

Myers, G. (2000) Becoming a group: Face and sociability in moderated discussions. In S. Sarangi and M. Coulthard (Eds), *Discourse and Social Life* (pp. 121–137). Harlow: Pearson.

Myrick, H., Anton, R. F., Li, X., Henderson, S., Drobes, D., Voronin, K. & George, M. S. (2004). Differential brain activity in alcoholics and social drinkers to alcohol cues: Relationship to craving. *Neuropsychopharmacology*, *29*, 393–402.

Nesselroade, J. R. & Cattell, R. B. (Eds) (1988). *Handbook of multivariate experimental psychology* (2nd edn). London: Plenum.

Neugebauer, H. (1929). Das Gefühls und Willensleben meines Sohnes in seiner frühen Kindheit. *Zeitschrift für Angewandte Psychologie, 34*, 275–310.

Nezlek, J. B. (1991). Self-report diaries in the study of social interaction. *Contemporary Social Psychology, 14*(4), 205–210.

Nigro, G. & Wolpow, S. (2004). Interviewing young children with props. *Applied Cognitive Psychology, 18*, 549–565.

Nishisato, S. (1980). *Analysis of categorical data: Dual scaling and its applications.* Toronto: University of Toronto Press.

Nitko, A. J. (1988). Designing tests that are integrated with instruction. In R. L. Linn (Ed.), *Educational measurement.* New York: Macmillan.

Nunnally, J. C. (1978). *Psychometric theory.* New York: McGraw-Hill.

Nunnally, J. C. & Bernstein, I. (1994). *Psychometric theory.* New York: McGraw-Hill.

O'Brien, K. (1993). Improving survey questionnaires through focus groups. In D. L. Morgan (Ed.), *Successful focus groups: Advancing the state of the art.* London: Sage.

Oldroyd, D. (1986). *The arch of knowledge: An introductory study of the history of the philosophy and methodology of science.* New York: Methuen.

Oostenveld, R. & Praamstra, P. (2001). The five percent electrode system for high-resolution EEG and ERP measurements. *Clinical Neurophysiology, 112*, 713–719.

Oppenheim, A. N. (1992). *Questionnaire design, interviewing and attitude measurement.* London: Pinter.

O'Reilly, K. (2004). *Ethnographic methods.* London: Routledge.

Palmer, R. (1969). *Hermeneutics.* Evanston, IL: Northwestern University Press.

Park, R. E. (1967). *On social control and collective behaviour: Selected papers.* Chicago: University of Chicago Press.

Parker, I. (1992). *Discourse dynamics: Critical analysis for social and individual psychology.* London: Routledge.

Parker, I. (1997). Discourse analysis and psychoanalysis. *British Journal of Social Psychology, 36*, 479–495.

Parker, I. & Burman, E. (1993). Against discursive imperialism, empiricism and constructionism: Thirty-two problems with discourse analysis. In E. Burman & I. Parker (Eds), *Discourse analytic research: Repertoires and readings of texts in action.* London: Routledge.

Parker, I., Georgaca, E., Harper, D., McLaughlin, T. & Stowell-Smith, M. (1995). *Deconstructing psychopathology.* London: Sage.

Parkes, C. M. (1971). Psycho-social transitions: A field for study. *Social Science and Medicine, 5*, 101–115.

Pashler, H. & Wixted, J. (Eds) (2002). *Methodology in experimental psychology.* Chichester: Wiley.

Pearson, K. (1904). Report on certain enteric fever inoculation statistics. *British Medical Journal, 3*, 1243–1246.

Pelli, D. G. & Farell, B. (1995). Psychophysical methods. In M. Bass (Ed.), *Handbook of optics*, Vol. I (2nd edn). New York: McGraw-Hill.

Pentland, A. (1980). Maximum likelihood estimation: The best PEST. *Perception & Psychophysics, 28*, 377–379.

Performance and Innovation Unit (2001). *Better policy delivery and design: A discussion paper* (http://www.strategy.gov.uk).

Peters, M. L., Sorbi, M. J., Kruise, D. A., Kerssens, J. J., Verhaak, P. F. M., & Bensing, J. M. (2000). Electronic diary assessment of pain, disability and psychological adaptation in patients differing in duration of pain. *Pain, 84*, 181–192.

Piaget, J. (1952a). *The origins of intelligence in the child*. New York: Basic Books.

Piaget, J. (1952b). *The child's conception of number*. London: Routledge & Kegan Paul.

Pidgeon, N. & Henwood, K. (2004). Grounded theory. In M. Hardy & A. Bryman (Eds), *Handbook of data analysis*. London: Sage.

Plummer, K. (Ed.) (1981). *The making of the modern homosexual*. London: Hutchinson.

Pomerantz, A. M. (1986). Extreme case formulations: A new way of legitimating claims. *Human Studies, 9*, 219–229.

Popper, K. R. (1959). *The logic of scientific discovery*. London: Hutchinson.

Potter, J. (1996). *Representing reality: Discourse, rhetoric and social construction*. London: Sage.

Potter, J. (2003). Discourse analysis. In M. Hardy & A. Bryman (Eds), *Handbook of Data Analysis*. London: Sage.

Potter, J. & Collie, F. (1989). 'Community care' as persuasive rhetoric: A study of discourse. *Disability, Handicap & Society, 4*, 57–64.

Potter, J. & Wetherell, M. (1987). *Discourse and social psychology: Beyond attitudes and behaviour*. London: Sage.

Powell, G. E. & Adams, M. (1993). *Introduction to research on placement*. Paper presented at the Clinical Psychology Forum, 12–16 March, British Psychological Society.

Pullman, P. (1998). *The subtle knife*. London: Scholastic Point.

Radley, A. & Chamberlain, K. (2001). Health psychology and the study of the case: From method to analytic concern. *Social Science and Medicine, 3*, 321–332.

Rapoport, R. N. (1972). Three dilemmas in action research. In P. A. Clark (Ed.), *Action research in organisational change*. London: Harper & Row.

Rasch, G. (1960). *Probabilistic models for some intelligence and attainment tests*. Copenhagen: Danish Institute for Educational Research.

Ray, P. & Page, A. C. (2002). A single session of hypnosis and eye movement desensitisation and reprocessing (EMDR) in the treatment of chronic pain. *Australian Journal of Clinical and Experimental Hypnosis, 30*, 170–178.

Reason, P. (1988). *Human inquiry in action: Developments in new paradigm research*. London: Sage.

Reason, P. & Bradbury, H. (Eds) (2001a). *Handbook of action research: Participative inquiry and practice*. London: Sage.

Reason, P. & Bradbury, H. (2001b). Introduction: Inquiry and participation in search of a world worthy of human aspiration. In P. Reason & H. Bradbury (Eds), *Handbook of action research: Participative inquiry and practice* (pp. 1–14). London: Sage.

Reason, P. & Torbert, W. (2001). The action turn: Toward a transformational social science. *Concepts and Transformations, 6*(1), 1–37.

Reicher, S. (2000). Against methodolatry: Some comments on Elliott, Fischer, and Rennie. *British Journal of Clinical Psychology, 39*, 1–6.

Reid, K., Flowers, P. & Larkin, M. (2005). Exploring lived experience: An introduction to interpretative phenomenological analysis. *The Psychologist, 18*, 20–23.

Reuband, K. & Blasius, J. (1996). Face-to-face, telephone and mail questionnaires: Response rates and pattern in a large city study. *Kölner Zeitschrift für Soziologie und Sozialpsychologie, 48*(2), 296–318.

Reuben, D. B., Wong, R. C., Walsh, K. E. & Hays, R. D. (1995). Feasibility and accuracy of a postcard diary system for tracking healthcare utilization of community-dwelling older persons. *Journal of the American Geriatrics Society, 43*, 550–552.

Rich, M. & Patashnick, J. (2002). Narrative research with audio-visual data: VIA and NVivo. *International Journal of Social Research Method, Theory and Practice, 5*, 245–261.

Richards, L. (2000). *Using NVivo in qualitative research* (2nd edn). Melbourne: QSR International.

Ricoeur, P. (1970). *Freud and philosophy*. New Haven, CT: Yale University Press.

Ridderinkhof, K. R. & van der Stelt, O. (2000). Attention and selection in the growing child: views derived from developmental psychophysiology. *Biological Psychology, 54*, 55–106.

Robson, C. (2002). *Real world research*. Oxford: Blackwell.

Roethlisberger, F. J. & Dickson, W. J. (1939). *Management and the worker*. Cambridge, MA: Harvard University Press.

Rorschach, H. (1921). *Psychodiagnostics*. Berne: Huber.

Rose, D. (1988). ZSCORE: A program for the accurate calculation of d' and β. *Behavior Research Methods, Instruments and Computers, 20*, 63–64.

Rose, D. & Dobson, V. G. (1985). Methodological solutions for neuroscience. In D. Rose & V. G. Dobson (Eds), *Models of the visual cortex*. Chichester: Wiley.

Rose, R. M., Teller, D. Y. & Rendleman, P. (1970). Statistical properties of staircase estimates. *Perception & Psychophysics, 8*, 199–204.

Rosenhan, D. L. (1973). On being sane in insane places. *Science, 179*, 250–268.

Rosenthal, R. (1979). The 'file drawer' problem and tolerance for null results. *Psychological Bulletin, 86*, 638–641.

Rosenthal, R. (1991). *Meta-analytic procedures for social research*. Beverly Hills, CA: Sage.

Rothschild, Lord (1971). *The organisation and management of government research and development* (Cmnd. 4814). London: HMSO.

Rust, J. & Golombok, S. (1999). *Modern psychometrics: Science of psychological assessment*. London: Routledge.

Rustin, M. (2002). Research, evidence and psychotherapy. In C. Mace, S. Morley & B. Roberts (Eds), *Evidence in the psychological therapies*. Hove: Brunner/Routledge.

Salmon, P. (2003). How do we recognise good research? *The Psychologist, 16*(1), 24–27.

Samar, V. J., Swartz, K. P. & Raghuveer, M. R. (1995). Multiresolution analysis of event-related potentials by wavelet decomposition. *Brain and Cognition, 27*, 398–438.

Sammer, G. (1998). Heart period variability and respiratory changes associated with physical and mental load: Non-linear analysis. *Ergonomics, 41*, 746–755.

Sapsford, R. & Jupp, V. (Eds) (1996). *Data collection and analysis*. London: Sage.

Schaie, K. W. (1965). A general model for the study of developmental problems. *Psychological Bulletin, 64*, 92–107.

Schiffman, S. S., Reynolds, M. L. & Young, F. W. (1981). *Introduction to multidimensional scaling*. New York: Academic.

Schuetz, A. (1998). Autobiographical narratives of good and bad deeds: Defensive and favorable self-description moderated by trait self-esteem. *Journal of Social and Clinical Psychology, 17*, 466–475.

Schuman, H. & Presser, S. (1996). *Questions and answers in attitude surveys: Experiments on question form, writing and context.* London: Sage.

Schwartz, M. S. & Andrasik, F. (2003). *Biofeedback: A practitioner's guide.* New York: Guilford Press.

Schwartz, A., Campos, J. & Baisel, E. (1973). The visual cliff: cardiac and behavioral correlates on the deep and shallow sides at five and six months of age. *Journal of Experimental Child Psychology, 15*, 86–99.

Scott, J. (2006). *Documentary research.* London: Sage.

Scott, J. & Xie, Y. (2006). *Quantitative social science.* London: Sage.

Sedgwick, E. (1990). *The epistemology of the closet.* London: Penguin.

Seidel, J. V., Kjolseth, A. & Seymour, J. A. (1988). *The Ethnograph: A user's guide.* Littleton, CO: Qualitative Research Associates.

Shadish, W. R., Cook, T. D. & Campbell, D. T. (2001). *Experimental and quasi-experimental designs for generalized causal inference.* Boston: Houghton Mifflin.

Shaughnessy, J. J., Zechmeister, E. B. & Zechmeister, J. S. (2006). *Research methods in psychology* (7th edn). Boston: McGraw-Hill.

Shavelson, R. J. & Webb, N. M. (1991). *Generalizability theory.* London: Sage.

Sherliker, L. & Steptoe, A. (2000). Coping with new treatment of cancer: A feasibility study of daily diary measures. *Patient Education and Counseling, 40*(1), 11–19.

Shoham-Salomon, V., Avner, R. & Neeman, R. (1989). You're changed if you do and changed if you don't: Mechanisms underlying paradoxical interventions. *Journal of Consulting and Clinical Psychology, 57*, 590–598.

Shye, S. (1988). *Multiple scaling.* Amsterdam: North-Holland.

Šidák, Z. (1967). Rectangular confidence regions for the means of multivariate normal distributions. *Journal of the American Statistical Association, 62*, 625–633.

Silverman, D. (Ed.) (2004). *Qualitative research: Theory, method and practice.* London: Sage.

Simpson, M. (Ed.) (1996). *Anti-gay.* London: Freedom Editions.

Singer, J. A. (1997). How recovered memory debates reduce the richness of human identity. *Psychological Inquiry, 8*, 325–329.

Singer, J. A. (2004). Narrative identity and meaning making across the adult lifespan: An introduction. *Journal of Personality, 72*, 437–460.

Skidelsky, R. (1992). *John Maynard Keynes: A biography. Vol. 2: The economist as saviour, 1920–1937.* London: Macmillan.

Skinner, B. F. (1953). *Science and human behaviour.* New York: Macmillan.

Skinner, C., Holt, D. & Smith, T. (1989). *Analysis of complex surveys.* New York: Wiley.

Slater, L. (2004). *Opening Skinner's box: Great psychological experiments of the twentieth century.* New York: W. W. Norton.

Smith, J. A. (1993). The case study. In R. Bayne & P. Nicolson (Eds), *Counselling and psychology for health professionals* (pp. 249–265). London: Chapman & Hall.

Smith, J. A. (1996). Beyond the divide between cognition and discourse: Using interpretative phenomenological analysis in health psychology. *Psychology and Health, 11*, 261–271.

Smith, J. A. (1999). Towards a relational self: Social engagement during pregnancy and psychological preparation for motherhood. *British Journal of Social Psychology, 38*, 409–426.

Smith, J. A. (2003). *Qualitative psychology: A practical guide to methods.* London: Sage.

Smith, J. A. (2004). Reflecting on the development of interpretative phenomenological analysis and its contribution to qualitative research in psychology. *Qualitative Research in Psychology, 1*, 39–54.

Smith, J. A., Harré. R. & Van Langenhove, L. (1995a). *Rethinking methods in psychology.* London: Sage.

Smith, J. A., Harré. R. & Van Langenhove, L. (1995b). Idiography and the case study. In J. A. Smith, R. Harré & L. Van Langenhove (Eds), *Rethinking psychology* (pp. 59–69). London: Sage.

Smith, J. A. & Osborn, M. (2003). Interpretative phenomenological analysis. In J. A. Smith (Ed.), *Qualitative psychology. A practical guide to research methods* (pp. 51–80). London: Sage.

Smith, M. J. (2005). *Philosophy and methodology in the social sciences.* London: Sage.

Smith, M. L. & Glass, G. V. (1977). Meta-analysis of psychotherapy outcome studies. *American Psychologist, 32*, 752–760.

Solesbury, W. (2001). *Evidence based policy: Whence it came and where it's going.* Working Paper 1, ESRC UK Centre for Evidence Based Policy and Practice.

Spearman, C. (1907). Demonstration of formulae for true measures of correlation. *American Journal of Psychology, 18*, 161–169.

Spencer, L., Faulkner, A. & Keegan, J. (1988). *Talking about sex.* London: Social and Community Planning Research.

Spencer, L., Ritchie, J., Lewis, J. & Dillon, L. (2003). *Quality in qualitative evaluation: A framework for assessing research evidence.* London: Cabinet Office.

Spradley, J. P. (1979). *The ethnographic interview.* New York: Holt, Rinehart & Winston.

Spradley, J. P. & Mann, B. J. (1975). *The cocktail waitress: Women's work in a man's world.* New York: Wiley.

Stanton, B., Black, M., Laljee, L. & Ricardo, I. (1993). Perceptions of sexual behaviour among urban early adolescents: translating theory through focus groups. *Journal of Early Adolescence, 13*(1), 44–66.

Steinschneider, M., Kurtzberg, D. & Vaughan, H. G. (1992). Event-related potentials in developmental neuropsychology. In I. Rapin & S. J. Segalowitz (Eds), *Handbook of Neuropsychology*, Vol. 6. Amsterdam: Elsevier Science.

Steptoe, A., & Wardle, J. (1999). Mood and drinking: A naturalistic diary study of alcohol, coffee and tea. *Psychopharmacology, 141*, 315–321.

Stevens, S. S. (1946). On the theory of scales of measurement, *Science, 103*, 677–680.

Stewart, D. W. & Shamdasani, P. N. (1990). *Focus groups: Theory and practice.* Newbury Park, CA: Sage.

Steyaert, C. & Bouwen, R. (2004). Group methods of organizational analysis. In C. Cassell & G. Simon (Eds), *Essential Guide to Qualitative Methods in Organizational Research.* London: Sage. pp. 140–153.

Stine, W. W. (1989). Meaningful inference: The role of measurement in statistics. *Psychological Bulletin, 105*, 147–155.

Stockley, D. (1998). *Report of rough sleepers' views and experiences for the Salvation Army in evidence to the Social Exclusion Unit.* London: Salvation Army.

Strauss, A. & Corbin, J. (1990). *Basics of qualitative research: Grounded theory procedures and techniques.* Newbury Park, CA: Sage.

Strauss, A. & Corbin, J. (Eds) (1997). *Grounded theory in practice.* London: Sage.

Strauss, A. & Corbin, J. (1998). *Basics of qualitative research: Techniques and procedures for developing grounded theory* (2nd edn). Newbury Park, CA: Sage.

Stringer, E. T. (1996). *Action research: A handbook for practitioners.* London: Sage.

Stringer, E. T. (1999). *Action research* (2nd edn). London: Sage.

Strong, J. & Large, R. G. (1995). Coping with chronic low back pain: An idiographic exploration through focus groups. *International Journal of Psychiatry in Medicine, 25,* 371–387.

Sudman, S. & Bradburn, N. M. (1982). *Asking questions: A practical guide to questionnaire design.* San Francisco: Jossey-Bass.

Suen, H. K. (1990). *Principles of test theories.* Hildsdale, NJ: Erlbaum.

Surakka, V. & Hietanen, J. K. (1998). Facial and emotional reactions to Duchenne and non-Duchenne smiles. *International Journal of Psychophysiology, 29*(1), 23–33.

Svejda, M. & Schmid, D. (1979). The role of self-produced locomotion in the onset of fear of heights on the visual cliff. Paper presented at the meeting of the Society of Research in Child Development, San Francisco.

Swantz, M.-L., Ndedya, E. & Masaiganah, M. S. (2001). Participatory action research in Southern Tanzania, with special reference to women. In P. Reason & H. Bradbury (Eds), *Handbook of action research: Participative inquiry and practice* (pp. 386–395). London: Sage.

Tabachnick, B. G. & Fidell, L. S. (2001). *Using multivariate statistics.* Boston: Allyn & Bacon.

Tacq, J. (1997). *Multivariate analysis techniques in social science research: From problem to analysis.* London: Sage.

Taylor, C. (1985). Self-interpreting animals. In *Philosophical papers: Vol. 1. Human agency and language* (pp. 45–76). Cambridge: Cambridge University Press.

Taylor, M. M. & Creelman, C. D. (1967). PEST: efficient estimates on probability functions. *Journal of the Acoustical Society of America, 41,* 782–787.

Taylor, S. M., Elliot, S., Eyles, J., Frank, J. *et al.* (1991). Psychosocial impacts in populations exposed to solid waste facilities. *Social Science and Medicine, 33,* 441–447.

Teichert, D. (2004). Narrative, identity and the self. *Journal of Consciousness Studies, 11*(10–11), 175–191.

Thomas, J. (1993). *Doing critical ethnography.* London: Sage.

Thompson, B. (2004). *Exploratory and confirmatory factor analysis: Understanding concepts and applications.* Washington, DC: American Psychological Association.

Tinsley H. E. A. & Brown S. D. (2000). *Handbook of applied multivariate statistics and mathematical modeling.* New York: Academic Press.

Tippett, L. H. (1931). The method of statistics. London: Williams & Norgate.

Tizard, B., Blatchford, P., Burke, J., Farquar, C. & Plewis, I. (1988). *Young children at school in the inner city.* Hove: Erlbaum.

Todman, J. B. & Dugard, P. (2001). *Single-case and small-n experimental designs: A practical guide to randomization tests.* Mahwah, NJ: Lawrence Erlbaum Associates.

Torgerson, C. J., Porthouse, J. & Brooks, G. (2003). A systematic review and meta-analysis of randomised controlled trials evaluating interventions in adult literacy and numeracy. *Journal of Research in Reading, 26*, 234–255.

Townsend, J. T. & Ashby, F. G. (1984). Measurement scales and statistics: The misconception misconceived. *Psychological Bulletin, 96*, 394–401.

Treisman, M. & Watts, T. R. (1966). Relation between signal detectability theory and the traditional procedures for measuring sensory thresholds: Estimating d' from results given by the method of constant stimuli. *Psychological Bulletin, 66*, 438–454.

Treutwein, B. (1995). Adaptive psychophysical procedures, *Vision Research, 35*, 2503–2522.

Treutwein, B. & Strasburger, H. (1999). Fitting the psychometric function. *Perception and Psychophysics, 61,* 87–106.

Turner, B. A. & Pidgeon, N. F. (1997). *Man made disasters* (2nd edn), Oxford: Butterworth-Heineman.

Turpin, G., Barley, V., Beail, N., Scaife, J., Slade, P., Smith, J. A. & Walsh, S. (1997). Standards for research projects and theses involving qualitative methods: Suggested guidelines for trainees and courses. *Clinical Psychology Forum, 108*, 3–7.

Tyrrell, R. A. & Owens, D. A. (1988). A rapid technique to assess the resting states of the eyes and other threshold phenomena: The modified binary search (MOBS). *Behavior Research Methods, Instruments and Computers, 20*, 137–141.

Ullman, J. B. (2001). Structural equation modeling. In B. G. Tabachnick & L. S. Fidell (Eds), *Using multivariate statistics* (4th edn). Boston: Allyn & Bacon.

Ulrich, R. & Miller, J. (2004). Threshold estimation in two-alternative forced-choice (2AFC) tasks: The Spearman–Kärber method. *Perception & Psychophysics, 66*, 517–533.

Ussher, J. M. & Mooney-Somers, J. (2000). Negotiating desire and sexual subjectivity: Narratives of young lesbian avengers. *Sexualities, 3*, 183–200.

Uzzell, D. L. (1979). Four roles for the community researcher. *Journal of Voluntary Action Research, 8*(1–2), 66–76.

Van der Linden W. & Hambleton R. (1997). *The handbook of modern item response theory.* London: Springer.

Van der Molen, B. (2000). Relating information needs to the cancer experience. 2. Themes from six cancer narratives. *European Journal of Cancer Care, 9*(1), 48–54.

Van der Molen, M. W. & Molenaar, P. C. M. (1994). Cognitive psychophysiology: A window to cognitive development and brain maturation. In G. Dawson & K. W. Fischer (Eds), *Human behavior and the developing brain.* New York: Guilford.

Vetere, A. & Gale, T. (1987). *Ecological studies of family life.* Chichester: Wiley.

von Eye, A. (1990). *Introduction to configural frequency analysis.* Cambridge: Cambridge University Press.

von Eye, A. (2002). *Configural frequency analysis: Methods, models, and applications.* Earlbaum: New York.

Wagner, H. & Manstead, A. (Eds) (1989). *Handbook of social psychophysiology.* Chichester: Wiley.

Waite, B. M., Claffey, R. & Hillbrand, M. (1998). Differences between volunteers and non-volunteers in a high demand self-recording study. *Psychological Reports, 83*(1), 199–210.

Walker, P., Lewis, J., Lingayah, S. & Sommer, F. (2000). *Prove it: Measuring the effect of neighbourhood renewal on local people.* London: New Economics Foundation (http://www.neweconomics.org/gen/z_sys_PublicationDetail.aspx?PID=2).

Wallwork, J. & Dixon, J. A. (2004). Foxes, green fields and Britishness: On the rhetorical construction of place and national identity, *British Journal of Social Psychology, 43*, 21–39.

Warnock, M. (1987). *Memory*. London: Faber and Faber.

Watson, A. B. & Pelli, D. G. (1983). QUEST: A Bayesian adaptive psychometric method. *Perception & Psychophysics, 33*, 113–120.

Watzlawick, P. (1964). *An anthology of human communication*. Palo Alto, CA: Science and Behavior Books.

Watzlawick, P., Beavin, J. & Jackson, D. (1967). *Pragmatics of human communication*. New York: Norton.

Weille, K. L. (2002). The psychodynamics of consensual sadomasochistic and dominant-submissive sexual games. *Studies on Gender and Sexuality, 3*, 131–160.

Welkowitz, J., Ewen, R. B., & Cohen, J. (1982). *Introductory statistics for the behavioral sciences*. San Diego, CA: Harcourt Brace Jovanovich.

Weller, S. C. & Romney, A. K. (1990). *Metric scaling: Correspondence analysis*. London: Sage.

Wellings, K., Branigan, P. & Mitchell, K. (2000). Discomfort, discord and discontinuity as data: Using focus groups to research sensitive topics. *Culture, Health and Sexuality, 2*, 255–267.

Wengraf, T. (2001). *Qualitative research interviewing: biographic narrative and semi-structured methods*. Thousand Oaks, CA: Sage.

Werner, O. & Schoepfle, G. M. (1987). *Systematic fieldwork. Volume 1: Foundations of ethnography and interviewing*. London: Sage.

Wetherell, M. (1998). Positioning and interpretative repertoires: Conversation analysis and post-structuralism in dialogue. *Discourse & Society, 9*, 387–412.

Wetherell, M. (2001). Debates in discourse research. In M. Wetherell, S. Taylor & S. J. Yates (Eds), *Discourse theory and practice: A reader*. London: Sage.

Wetherell, M. & Potter, J. (1992). *Mapping the language of racism: Discourse and the legitimation of exploitation*. Hemel Hempstead: Harvester Wheatsheaf.

Wetherell, M., Taylor, S. & Yates, S. J. (Eds) (2001a). *Discourse theory and practice: A reader*. London: Sage.

Wetherell, M., Taylor, S. & Yates, S. J. (Eds) (2001b). *Discourse as data: A guide for analysis*. London: Sage.

Wetherill, G. B. & Levitt, H. (1965). Sequential estimation of points on a psychometric function. *British Journal of Mathematical and Statistical Psychology, 18*, 1–10.

Whyte, W. F. (1991). *Participatory action research*. London: Sage.

Whyte, W. F. (1943). *Street corner society: The social structure of an Italian slum*. Chicago: University of Chicago Press.

Widdicombe, S. (1993). Autobiography and change: rhetoric and authenticity of 'Gothic' style. In E. Burman & I. Parker (Eds), *Discourse analytic research: Repertoires and readings of texts in action*. London: Routledge.

Wiggins, S. (2004). Good for 'you': Generic and individual healthy eating advice in family mealtimes. *Journal of Health Psychology, 9*, 535–548.

Wilkinson, S. (1998). Focus group methodology: A review. *International Journal of Social Research Methodology, 1*, 181–203.

Wilkinson, S. (2003). Focus groups. In J. A. Smith (Ed.), *Qualitative psychology: A practical guide to research methods* (pp. 184–204). London: Sage.

Wilkinson, S. (2004a). Focus groups. In G. M. Breakwell (Ed.), *Doing social psychology research*. Oxford: Blackwell.

Wilkinson, S. (2004b). Focus group research. In D. Silverman (Ed.), *Qualitative research: Theory, method and practice* (pp. 177–199). London: Sage.

Willig, C. (Ed.) (1999). *Applied discourse analysis: Social and psychological interventions*. Buckingham: Open University Press.

Willig, C. (2001). *Introducing qualitative research in psychology: Adventures in theory and method*. Buckingham: Open University Press.

Wilson, C. & Powell, M. (2003). A guide to interviewing children. *Applied Cognitive Psychology, 17*(2), 249.

Wilson, G. D. & Patterson, J. R. (1968). A new measure of conservatism. *British Journal of Social and Clinical Psychology, 7*, 264–290.

Winborne, D. G. & Dardaine, R. P. (1993). Affective education for 'at risk' students – the new urban principles. *Urban Review, 15*(2), 139–150.

Winer, B. J. (1978). *Statistical principles in experimental design*. New York: McGraw-Hill.

Winkielman, P. & Cacioppo, J. T. (2001). Mind at ease puts a smile on the face: Psychophysiological evidence that processing facilitation elicits positive affect. *Journal of Personality and Social Psychology, 81*, 989–1000.

Wirth, L. (1928). *The ghetto*. Chicago: University of Chicago Press.

Wolf, F. M. (1986). *Meta-analysis: Quantitative methods for research synthesis*. Beverly Hills, CA: Sage.

Wolke, D., Meyer, R. & Gray, P. (1994). Validity of the Crying Pattern Questionnaire in a sample of excessively crying babies. *Journal of Reproductive and Infant Psychology, 12*(2), 105–114.

Woodworth, R. S. & Schlosberg, H. (1954). *Experimental psychology* (rev. edn). London: Methuen.

Wooffitt, R. (2001). Analysing factual accounts. In N. Gilbert (Ed.), *Researching social life* (2nd edn). London: Sage.

Yardley, L. (2000). Dilemmas in qualitative research. *Psychology and Health, 15*, 215–228.

Yin, R. K. (2003). *Case study research: Design and methods* (3rd edn). Thousand Oaks, CA: Sage.

Young, K. & Kramer, J. (1978). Local exclusionary policies in Britain: The case of suburban defence in a metropolitan system. In K. Cox (Ed.), *Urbanization and conflict in market societies*. London: Methuen.

Zani, A. & Proverbio, A. M. (2002). *The cognitive electrophysiology of mind and brain*. San Diego, CA: Academic Press.

Ziller, R. C. (1973). *The social self*. Oxford: Pergamon Press.

Ziller, R. C. (2000). Self-counselling through re-authored photo self narratives. *Counselling Psychology Quarterly, 13*, 265–278.

Zorbaugh, H. W. (1929). *The Gold Coast and the slum: A sociological study of Chicago's Near North Side*. Chicago: University of Chicago Press.

Index

This index is in word by word order. Diagrams are indicated by **italics**. Only first authors of articles are included. Illustrations of concepts and methods are listed under the main heading of 'examples'; studies and experiments are listed under 'studies'.

ABA design 100–2, *101*
ABAB design 102
ability tests 187
Abraham, C. 373
absolute thresholds
    162–7, 168–74
absolute zero 56
abstracts 32
acquiescence bias 222, 245
action orientation 370, 375–6
action research 302, 311–19
    challenges 319
    criteria 315–18
    description 311–13
    features 315–16
    types 313–14
active process facilitation 286
Adams, E.W. 53
adaptive techniques, stimulus
        detection 169
advanced theory structures
        10–15
AEP/AER 154
age cohorts 19
age data 223
ageing process 148
Ainsworth, M. D. S. 128, 134
Albrecht, T. L. 280, 285
Alcalá-Quintana, R. 173
alienation coefficient 438
Allen, M. J. 193
alpha coefficient 195, 198
alpha criterion 399, 400, 403
alternative hypothesis 397
American Psychological
    Association 39

analysis *see also* data analysis
analysis of variance (ANOVA)
        417, 419–22
analytic induction 140
ancillary data 247
Anderson, J. A. 424
Andrich, D. 207
anomalies 14
anonymity 42, 229
ANOVA 417, 419–22
anthropology 302, 303, 329
APA 39
apples and oranges problem 470
applied psychophysiology 149
approximate value 58
Arbuckle, J. L. 447
Archer, J. 385
archetypal narratives 270–1
Argyle, M. 126, 131
Ashford, P. 431
Ashworth, P. 325
aspirations, data from
        questionnaires 227
assistants, for research 36
association, tests of 407, 409,
        411–12, *412*, 476
assumptions
    in interview questions 238
    in questionnaires 221
assumptive world 305–6
Atkinson, J. 371
Atkinson, J. W. 185
attention, in data collection 142
attitudes, data from
        questionnaires 226–7
Auburn, T. 373

audio recording 142, 215, 242,
        249–50, 291, 332, 352
audit trails 144
auditing, external 363
Auerbach, C. 242
augmented models
        449, 450, 461
authentication of data,
        interviews 252
average evoked potential
        (AEP) 154
average evoked response
        (AER) 154
Axelrod, R. 294
axial coding 360–1

Back, L. 307
back-translation 222
background data 223–5
Backs, R. W. 153
balanced repeated
        replication 117
Bales, R. F. 129
Bandura, A. 12, 28–9, 43
Banks, S. P. 224, 270
Barbour, R. S. 276
Barker, G. N. 278
Barnes, R. 373
Basch, C. E. 281
Bateson, G. 133
Baumann, U. 265
Bear, G. 62, 409
Beattie, A. 126, 316
Bechtel, W. 17
Begg, C. B. 479
behaviour, and physiology 148

behaviour sequences,
coding 136–9
behavioural data 225–6
behavioural research
diaries as intervention 257
and linguistic observations 132
behavioural significance 310
behavioural theory, and
observation 133
Beike, D. R. 266
Bell, M. M. 266
Bellisle, F. 258
Bentler, P. M. 447
Berg, B. 276, 277
Berman, N. G. 475
Bernstein, I. 191, 208
Bertenthal, B. 80, 81
between-subject designs
74–81, 394, 410
bias
acquiescence 222, 245
cultural 139
and focus groups 284
forced-choice staircases 172
in historical accounts 307
from interviewer effects 248–50
and nonresponse 112
over/underreporting 226, 260
parameter estimates
in SEM 459
participant 33–4, 35, 41,
72, 262
in questionnaire responses
215, 221
researcher 139, 362
response 186–7, 245
sample/sampling/selection
34, 35, 41, 94, 118, 248
Billig, M. 375
Binet, Alfred, objective tests 187
biofeedback 149
biological sex data, in
questionnaires 223, 226
biosignal data,
quantification 156–8
Birnbaum, A. 203, 205
bisection, stimuli 177
bivariate statistical analysis
389–413
choice of test 407–13
classical designs 393–6
definitions 390–3
parametric/non-parametric
tests 406–7
probability 398–406
theories and hypotheses 396–7
Type I/II errors 397–8
see also multivariate data
analysis; statistical
analyses; structural
equation modelling

bivariate statistical tests
392, 407–13
Black, W. 430
Blackie Test 185
Blair, R. J. R. 151
Blake, R. 178
Blalock, H. M. Jr. 62, 409
blank trials 163–4
Blascovich, J. 148
Blashfield, R. K. 434
Blasius, J. 243, 441
blind experiments 13
Blinkhorn, S. F. 201
blood oxygen level dependent
(BPLD) data 156
blood pressure
measurement 152–3
blood volume measurement
152, 153
Bloor, M. 278, 280
Blum, G. S. 185
Blumer, H. 344
Bogardus, E. 276
bogus pipeline tactic 226
BOLD, fMRI data 156
Bond, M. 302, 311, 312,
314, 315, 316, 317
Bond, T. G. 207
Bonferroni adjustment 417–18
bootstrapping 462
Borg, I. 438, 439
Bormann, H. 295
Boulton, M. 226
BPS 39, 40–2
Bradburn, N. M. 212, 218,
223, 226
Bradbury, H. 314, 315, 318
Bradley, L. 79, 86
Bradley, T. B. 133
Bramley, N. 328
Brazelton, T. B. 133
break characteristics 284
Breakwell, G. M. 8, 231, 276
Bringer, J. 251
British Psychological Society
39, 40–2
Brocki, J. 328
Brockmeier, J. 268
Bruner, J. 325
Bryant, P. 79
Bryant, P. E. 86
budgets see costing; funding
Bull, P. 242
Burawoy, M. 302
Burman, E. 369, 371, 376, 384
Burr, V. 369, 370, 371

Cabinet Office 312
Caldirola, D. 153
Campbell, A. 385
Campbell, D. T. 93, 95

Campbell, J. M. 258
Campos, J. J. 80, 81
canonical variate analysis 430
CAPI 118, 244
capnometry measures 153
Cappello, M. 245
CAQDAS 353
cardiac response 152
Carlson, J. G. 152
Carlson, N. R. 148
Carr, W. 313
carry-over effects 82
case identifiers 229
Casey, M. 279
CASI 244
catchall questions 238
categorical data, multivariate
procedures 440–1
categorical measurement 53–4
categorical responses, in
questionnaires 215, 216
categorical structuring 251
categorical variables 70
categorization
in coding schemes 136, 250–1
in grounded theory
353–6, 358–9
of phenomena 7
see also classification
category integration 358
category renaming/labelling 358
category splitting 358
CATI 118, 244
Catterall, M. 277, 279
causality 69, 79–81, 459–60
mechanisms 17
and validity 73
ceiling effects 72–3, 188
census 107
central limit theorem 109
centroids 423
CFA (confirmatory factor
analysis) 439–40, 450–7
Chalmers, H. 317
Chamberlain, P. 356
Chambers, R. 313
change, measurement 196–7
change interventions 315
Charmaz, C. 360
Charmaz, K. 360
Child, D. 433
children, interviewing 244–7
Christensen, L. B. 86
Clark-Carter, D. 476–7
classical bivariate designs 393–6
classical test theory 189–99
classification
of measurement 53–8
see also categorical;
categorization
clean measure 83

clinical psychophysiology 148–9
clinical significance 471–2, 478
Clogg, C. C. 430, 441
close fit 453–4
closed-ended response
    formats 214, 215
cluster analysis 434–6
clustering
    in sampling 115
    of themes in IPA 335, 337–8
co-construction, of narratives
    269, 302
Cochran, W. G. 472
Code of Conduct, Ethical
    Principles and Guidelines 308
codes of conduct
    BPA/APA 39, 308
    see also guidelines
coding errors 214–15
coding schemes 134–8
    axial coding 360–1
    categories 136, 250–1
    in content analysis 292–34
    in discourse analysis 375
    in meta-analysis 475
    in observational research
        129, 131
    open coding 353–6
cognition, hot/cool 327
cognitive psychology,
    and IPA 325
cognitive psychophysiology 148
Cohen, J. 144, 198, 477, 478
Cohen's d 477
Cohen's kappa 198
cold calling 243
communication processes,
    in groups 281
community development
    projects 314
compact models 449, 450
compensatory rivalry 100
complete observer role 131
complete participant 130, 140
complex sample designs 115–17
composite variable 428
computer-assisted personal
    interviews (CAPI) 118, 244
computer-assisted qualitative data
    analysis software
    (CAQDAS) 353
computer-assisted
    self-interviews (CASI) 244
computer-assisted telephone
    interviews (CATI) 118, 244
computers, in categorical
    measurement 54
concepts, operational
    definitions 30–1
concurrent validation 202

confidence intervals (CIs)
    110–11, 404
confidence levels 110
confidentiality 34, 42, 229, 296
configural frequency analysis 441
confirmability 317
confirmatory factor analysis
    (CFA) 439–40, 450–7
confounding, of variables 74, 395
conjoint measurement theory 57
Conner, M. 258
Conrad, P. 324
consent, informed 39–40, 236,
    291, 307–8
consistency, in psychometric
    tests 192–8
consistency across time 195–7
constant comparison method 356
constants, in age-related
    studies 19–20
construct validation 202–3
constructionist approach 16
content analysis 250–1,
    269–71, 292–4, 356
content validity/validation
    186, 200
content-oriented focus group 286
context effects
    in focus groups 297
    in questionnaires 219–20
contexts
    in discourse analysis 376
    importance in ethnography
        303–4, 305
    for research 28
continuous recording of data 143
continuous variables 58
control variables 101
controlled experiments 13
Converse, P.E. 217
Cook, T. D. 93, 95
Cooke, B. 34
cool cognition 327
Cooper, C. 149
Corbin, J. 128, 138, 360
core analysis, in grounded
    theory 358–61
Corkrey, R. 244
Cornwell, A. 312
correlation
    between true and observed
        scores 191
    and causality 69
    intraclass 116
    multiple correlation
        coefficient 429
    and regression 426, 427
correlation matrix 430
correlational designs/studies
    86, 395–6

correspondence analysis 441
costing 36
    see also funding
counterbalancing 84
Cox, M. A. 438
Cox, T. F. 438
Coxon, A. P. M. 258, 259
credibility, in action research 317
criteria
    for action research 315–18
    for experiments 67
    for qualitative research 383–4
criterion, in stimulus
    detection 165
criterion referenced tests 188–9
criterion validation 201–2
criterion variable 425, 428
critical discursive psychology 372
critical effect size 405
critical regions 399, 401
Crittenden, P. 135
Cronbach, L.J. 189, 194,
    200, 203
Cronbach's alpha 195, 198
cross case analysis 338
cross-cultural research 222
    see also cultural research;
        ethnographic research
cross-individual analysis 270
cross-modal matching 176
cross-sectional design 19
Crowne, D. P. 222
Crowne-Marlowe Social
    Desirability Scale 222
cultural differences 129
cultural issues
    and analysis of data 270
    observational research
        42, 129, 139
cultural research 303, 304
    and action research 314
    development of psychometric
        tests 462
    see also cross-cultural
        research; ethnographic
        research

Dale, A. 148, 224
Dallos, R. 126, 132, 133
Dark Materials 308
data, definition 21
data analysis
    collapsing measurements 61
    discourse analysis 377–82
    focus groups 291–5
    in grounded theory 346, 353–61
    interviews 237–8, 250–2
    IPA studies 332–8
    in meta-analysis 475–80
    narratives 269–71

data analysis *cont.*
  qualitative/quantitative
      treatment 21, 302
  and theoretical background 13
  see also bivariate statistical
      analysis; multivariate data
      analysis; statistical
      analyses; structural
      equation modelling
data collection
  ancillary 247
  in diary technique 258–9
  ethnography 306
  psychophysiology 149–55
  from questionnaires 223–7
  IPA studies 329–32
  medium of interview 243–4
  narrative techniques 267–9
  participant observer
      research 141–2
  through focus groups 277
data dredging 158
data elicitation 18
  see also data collection
data extraction, in
      meta-analysis 475
Data Protection Act 1998 42, 229
data recording 142–3, 242,
      247, 249–50, 263–4, 291
data storage, in grounded
      theory 352–3
Davies, B. 372
Davies, J. B. 138
Davison, M. L. 61
De Leuw, E. 112
debriefing, of participants 41, 239
deception 40–1, 142, 226
decision trees 61, 407, *411, 412*
deduction 9, 21
Delli-Carpini, M. 281
demarcation indicators 167
demographic data 223–5
dependability, in action
      research 317
dependent variables
      70–3, 394, 395
  see also endogenous
      variables
Derrida, J. 370
descriptive statistics 391
design effect 116
design factor 117
designs *see* research designs
detection thresholds
      162–7, 168–74
developmental psychology,
      and observation 133
developmental
      psychophysiology 148
Diamond, L. M. 148

diary techniques 255–65
  data collected 258–9
  format 263–4
  pilot studies 264
  sample maintenance 265
  strengths and weaknesses
      259–63
  types of records 256–7
diastolic blood pressure 152, 153
Dickinson, J. J. 266
Dickson, W. J. 102
difference tests
  in bivariate analysis 407,
      409, 410–11, *411,* 462
  in multivariate analysis 416–24
difference thresholds 174–5
differential dropout 248
differential treatment 67
dimensionality, MDS 437–8, *438*
direct elicitation of data 18
disciplinary knowledge 349
discourse analysis 367–86
  data analysis 377–82
  description 368–73
  evaluation 382–4
  practical applications 373
  problems 384–6
  sampling 374
  technique 375–7
Discourse and Social Psychology:
      Beyond Attitudes and
      Behaviour 368
discrete variables 58
discriminant function
      analysis 422–4, 436
discursive analysis 295
discursive psychology 371
discursive research 326
dissemination of research 47
distributions 107–10
  noise/signal-plus-noise 164
Dobson, V. G. 5, 8
Doherty, K. 384, 385
'don't know' response
      217–18, 245
double hermeneutic 324
double negatives, in
      questions 238
double-barrelled questions 221, 238
downweighting 116
Draper, R. 126, 133
Drew, P. 332
dropout 33–4, 98, 262
dual scaling 441
Duhem-Quine thesis 11
Dunn, N. J. 259
Dworkin, S. F. 258

e-focus groups 296
e-mail interviewing 244

Eatough, V. 328, 330
eclecticism 22
ecological validity 86, 468
Edley, N. 372
education, action research 314
Edwards, D. 371
EEG 153–5, 158
effect size 392, 402, 404,
      405, 476–80
effective sample size 117
egocentricity of childhood 246
eigenvalues 431
electoral registers 113
electrocardiography 152
electrodermal activity 150–1
electroencephalography
      (EEG) 153–5, 158
electromyography 149
electro-oculography 151
Elliott, R. 142, 326
Ellis, C. 129, 269
Ellis, D. G. 129
Ellis, J. 314
Ely, R. 266
email interviewing 244
Embretson, S. E. 203
emergent designs 347, 348–9
  see also experimental designs
empowerment, through action
      research 314, 315
encoding, in data collection 142
endogenous variables 458–60
  see also dependent variables
environment
  for interviews 245
  see also location
Environment Agency 317–18
epsem designs 114
  see also random sampling
equipment for research 35, 38
Erdberg, P. 185
error variance 190
errors
  in classical test theory 190
  in measurement
      59, 392, 459
  in parameter estimation 456
  on psychophysical tasks 178–9
  in psychophysiological
      measurement 157–8
  in SEM 449
  in stimulus detection
      techniques 173
essentialism 278–9, 287
estimates
  population parameter 213
  precision 111
ethical codes
  BPS/APA 39, 308
  guidelines on deception 40

ethical issues
  participant observer
    research 130
  research feasibility 38–43, 46–7
  and specific research
    questions 28–9
ethical principles 39–42
ethnicity questions 224
ethnographic research 302–11
  description 302–5
  problems in 305–9
  quality measurement 309–11
  see also cross-cultural
    research; cultural research
ethogenics 305
evaluation
  and action research 316
  in discourse analysis 382–4
  in experimental method 85–6
  qualitative research 310–11
Evans, M. 328
Evans, R. I. 226
Everitt, B. S. 434, 441
evidence based policy
  312–13, 317–18
evoked potential
electroencephalography 154
Ewing, K. P. 266
exact fit vs. close fit 453–4
examples
  anti-social behaviour, and
    causality 70
  behaviour sequences,
    coding schemes 136
  criminal behaviour, theoretical
    background 12
  defence mechanisms 10
  dream interpretation
    diaries 258, 263
  drug treatment, one-tailed
    test 401
  extroversion, ordinal
    measurement 55
  hypotheses 68–71
  inkblot test, theoretical
    background 13
  knowledge tests, item
    characteristic
    curve 205–6
  learning environment,
    carry-over effects 82
  learning theory 10
  nonsense syllable pairs,
    theoretical background 13
  peer teaching,
    pre-experiments 91–2
  reading, experimental
    design 74, 76, 77, 78
  self-efficacy, theoretical
    background 12

examples *cont.*
  sexuality, social
    construction 369
  speed checks, treatment
    withdrawal 103
  truancy, and causality 69
exhaustiveness 53
Exner, J. E. 185
exogenous variables 458–60
  see also independent variables
expectations, data from
  questionnaires 227
experience-altered measure 83
experiential research 326
experimental action
  research 313–14
experimental designs 74–85, 347
  psychophysical
    parameters 178–80
  psychophysiological
    parameters 158–9
  see also emergent designs;
    pre-experiments;
    quasi-experimental
    designs; research designs
experimental method 66–86
  and causality 69
  designs 74–85
  difficulties in 86
  evaluation 85–6
  historical development 66–7
  implications for
    psychology 66–7
  reliability and validity 73–4
  variables 69–73
experimental observation 128
experimental treatment 67
experimenter effects 248–50, 362
experiments
  criteria 67, 70
  definition 67–8
explanations
  for interviews 236–7, 240
  for participants of focus
    groups 282–3
  of phenomena 7–8
exploratory observation 127–8
external auditing 363
external validity 86, 91, 93
extraneous variables 12
eye movements 151–2
Eysenck, H. J. 55, 200
Eysenck Personality
  Questionnaire 55
Eysenck, S. B. G. 55, 200
Ezzy, D. 266

face validity 200
face-to-face interview
  surveys 118

factor analysis 431
factorially complex items 432
factual knowledge tests 187, 227
fair tests 120
faking good 187
Fals Borda, O. 314
false memories 271
falsifiability, of themes 9–11, 12
fantasy theme analysis 295
Farsides, T. 251
feedback
  focus groups 296
  of results in psychophysical
    experiments 179
feedback loops, in
  institutional interviewing 246
Feldman, C. F. 271
file-drawer problem 470, 479
filter questions 230
Fisher, R. A. 66
fit indices 453–4
fit and work accounts 362
Fitter, M. 258
fitting function 456
fixed variables 70
Fleiss, J.L. 198
Flick, U. 302
floor effects 72–3, 188
flow of work, grounded
  theory 346, *348*
fMRI 155–6, 158
focal stimuli 281–3
focus groups 275–97
  data analysis 291–5
  data recording 291
  design and planning 283–6
  development of
    technique 276–7
  feedback of results 296
  focal stimuli 281–3
  future development 296–7
  implementation 286–91
  uses 277–81
focused coding 354
Fontana, A. 330
Forbat, L. 374
forced-choice staircases 172
forced-choice techniques 167–8
forgetting *see* memory and
  forgetting
formulae
  alpha coefficient 195
  classical test theory 192–3
  Cohen's kappa 198
  KR20 194
  power 402
  probability 398
  proportional reduction in
    error (PRE) 449
  split half reliability coefficient 194

formulae cont.
standardized difference 476
weighted effect size 477
Foucaldian discourse
analysis 371
Fourier analysis 154
fractionation 177
Freeman, P. R. 166
Fried, R. 153, 158
Frith, H. 279, 285
Frosh, S. 372
Fuller, T. D. 281
fully structured interviews 237
functional explanations 7, 8
functional magnetic resonance
imaging (fMRI) 155–6, 158
funding 43–6
see also costing

gain score 196
Gale, A. 149
Gale, T. 128, 130, 131
galvanic skin response 150–1
Gaskell, G. 226
gatekeepers, for
participants 34–5
Gaventa, J. 312
gender
effect on interviews 243
and focus groups 284–5
and questionnaires 223
generalizability theory 189
generalization of studies
91, 106–7, 329
and manipulation 20
see also transferability
Gergen, K. J. 269, 381
Gervais, M.-C. 280, 285
Gibbs, G. R. 375
Gibson, E. J. 79
Gifi, A. 441
Gilgun, J. F. 131
Gillett, R. 479
Giorgi, A. 325
Glaser, B. G. 344, 350
Glaser, R. 188
Glass, G. V. 469, 472, 473, 476, 478
Glitz, B. 279
global focus groups 296–7
Goetz, J. P. 302
Goffman, E. 128
going native 128
Goldberg, D. 213
Gomm, R. 129
Gottman, J. M. 136
Green, D. M. 164, 165, 166
Greenacre, M. 441
Greenbaum, T. L. 276, 286,
296, 297
Greenwood, D. J. 312, 316, 317

Greewald, P. C. 479
Grimaldi, J. 153, 158
Groenen, P. 438, 439
grounded theory 295, 345–63
data analysis 346, 353–61
data storage 352–3
design 348–50
method 346–8
reports 357–8, 361–3
sampling 350–2
use 344–6
group difference see difference
group discrimination 422
group dynamics 128
group interviews see focus
groups; interviews
group process 276, 280–1
group size, focus groups 285–6
groups, participant observer
research 130–1, 140
Groves, R. 117
Guba, E. G. 310, 317
guessing parameters 204
guidelines
for coding schemes 135
see also codes of conduct
Gulliksen, H. 194
Guttman, L. 203, 204

Haberman, S. J. 430
Hagenaars, J. A. 441
Hair, J. F. 430
Hall, J. L. 171, 179
Halliday, A. M. 148
Hambleton, R. 190
Hambleton, R. K. 190
Hammersley, M. 129, 329
Hammond, S. 451
Harlow, L. L. 404
Harman, H. 433
Harper, D. J. 374
Harré, R. 128, 305, 326, 329, 372
Hart, E. 302, 311, 313, 314,
315, 316
Harvey, L. O. Jr. 173
Hawthorne effect 102
Hayduk, L. A. 461
heart, cardiac response 152
heart rate variability 153,
156, 157, 158
Helmholtz, H. von 66
Henkel, R. E. 61, 62
Henwood, K. L. 344, 348,
350, 355, 358
Hepburn, A. 370
hermeneutic inquiry 324
hidden assumptions, in
questionnaires 221
hierarchical methods,
cluster analysis 435

Hilder, J. 282, 283, 296
Hinkelmann, K. 422
historical accounts, bias 307
historical diaries 257, 261
history effects 92, 96
Hobbs, D. 302
Hoepfl, M. 277
holistic structuring, of
interview data 251
Hollander, J. A. 276, 277,
279, 282, 284, 285, 286, 297
Hollway, W. 371
Holm, S. 417
Holsti, O. R. 292
Holter, I. M. 311, 314
homogenous samples 329
Hosmer, D. W. 430
hot cognition 327
Huber, R. 155
Huberty, C. J. 422
Hui, C. H. 222
Hull, D. L. 16
Hunt, M. 473
Hutchinson, K. 243
Hyden, L. C. 280
hypotheses 7, 68, 396–7
analytic induction 140
and causality 69
in discourse analysis 375, 376
use of interviews 236
null 397, 398, 399, 404
post-hoc 11
use of questionnaires
212–13, 213–14
in scientific method 6
testing 120, 402, 406–7
and theory testing 12, 22–3
hypothetical questions 219
hypothetico-deductive model 396

ICC 205, 205
identification, parameters
in SEM 454–5
identity
and IPA 327
and self-narrative 266
idiographic studies 189, 326
implicit theories 4–5
income questions, in
questionnaires 225
incomplete counterbalancing 84
independent (between subject)
designs 74–81, 394, 410
independent ethics
committees 39
independent variables
70, 394, 395
see also exogenous variables
indexing systems, grounded
theory data 354–6, 358–9

indirect elicitation of data 18
individual differences 149
individual psychometric tests 189
induction 9, 21
inductive approach to data 326–7
inferential statistics 391, 399–400
inflated scores 95
information processing ability,
    and physiology 148
informed consent 39–40,
    236, 291, 307–8
inkblot test 185
instructions, diary technique 264
instrumentalism 16
instrumentation effects 97–8
integration of
    methodologies 22–3
intelligence
    measurement 52, 188
    see also psychometric tests
intentions, data from
    questionnaires 227
inter-observer analysis 144
inter-rater consistency 197–8
inter-rater reliability
    144, 251–2, 294
inter-variable variance 431
interaction structure analysis 441
interactive voice response
    (IVR) 244
interia *see* criteria
intermittent recording of data 143
internal consistency 194–5
internal validity 91
internet
    and discourse analysis 384
    interviews using 244
    on-line focus groups 296–7
    tools for psychophysical
        research 180
    virtual discussion groups 297
    virtual interviews 119
internet surveys 119
interpretability, in factor analysis 433
interpretation
    in IPA report writing 338–9
    of texts in discourse
        analysis 375–7
interpretative component 134
interpretative orientation
    138–9, 144
interpretative phenomenological
    analysis (IPA) 295, 324–40
    data analysis 332–8
    data collection 329–32
    description 324–5
    place in psychology 325–6
    report writing 338–40
    research questions 326–7
    sampling 327–9

interpretative repertoires 370
    see also discourse analysis
interpretative research 302
interpretative thematic
    analysis 345
interval measurement 55–6, 61–2
interview protocol 241
interview schedules 237, 331–2
interviewer bias/effects 248–50
interviews 234–53
    analysis of data 250–2
    with children 244–7
    concluding 239
    conduct of 241–2
    introductions and
        explanations 236–7, 240
    in IPA studies 330–1
    medium for 243–4
    pilot studies 240–1
    relationship with
        observational research 132
    reliability and validity of
        data 247–50
    reporting in research 252–3
    semi-structured 242, 329–30
    structural format 235–9
    structured 237
    surveys 118
    unstructured 237–8, 241, 242
    use 234–5
intraclass correlation 116
intragroup process 280
intra-modal matching 176
intrapersonal group process 280
invasion of privacy 26, 41–2
investigative journalism 130, 141
IPA *see* interpretative
    phenomenological analysis
IQ tests 52, 56
IRT 302–7
iso-intensity contours 176
Israel, J. 8
item characteristic curves
    (ICC) 205, *205*
item parameters 204
item response theory (IRT) 203–7
IVR 244

Jacobson, N. S. 197
jargon *see* terminology
Jarrett, R. L. 280, 288
Jennings, J. 148
Jordan, S. 302
Jöreskog, K. G. 446, 447
Jovchelovitch, S. 277
Junker, B. H. 129
just noticeable difference 174

Kalfs, N. 265
kappa, Cohen's 198

Kelly, G. A. 4–5, 138
Kemmis, S. 311, 313
Kendall, P. L. 276, 289
Kenny, A. J. 297
Kerlinger, F. N. 429
Kidder, L. H. 326
Kiernan, B. D. 258
King, B. M. 62, 409
King, G. 106
King, R. M. 258
King-Smith, P. W. 173, 174
Kirk, R. E. 400
Kitcher, P. 16
Kitzinger, C. 279
Kitzinger, J. 276, 277
Klecka, W. R. 422
Klee, R. 16
Klopfer, W. G. 185
Knipschild, P. 469, 470
Knodel, J. 284
knowledge tests 187, 227
Kontsevich, L. L. 174
KR20 formula 194
Krippendorf, K. 292
Krosnick J. A. 218, 221
Krueger, R. A. 276, 277, 279
Kruskal, J. B. 438
Kuder, G. 194
Kuhn, T. S. 14
kurtosis 409–10
Kutas, M. 148
Kvale, S. 330

laboratory-based experiments 92
Labovitz, S. 61
Lagrange multiplier tests 457
Lakatos, I. 11, 14
Lakoff, G. 290
Lamiell, J. T. 13
Lancaster, H. O. 441
language
    and behavioural research 132
    constructing reality 368–70
    Foucaldian discourse
        analysis 372
    and observational research 139
    post-structuralist view 383
large samples 119
    see also sample size
Lasen, A. 307
latent class analysis 441
latent variables 446, 447, 460
Latin square design 84
leading questions 219, 238, 289
Legg, C. 258
level of measurement 53–63
levels of observation 132–3
Levin, M. 312, 316
Lewin, K. 313, 314
Lewis, A. 245

Lewis, J. 302, 364
Libman, E. 259
lifeworld 325
Light, R. J. 198
Likert scale (alternative rating
scale) 217, 227
Lincoln, Y. S. 310, 317
Linell, P. 277, 278, 297
Linn, R. L. 196
Lipsey, M. W. 478
Lipton, P. 69
listening skills, focus group
moderators 290–1
literature reviews 15
in grounded theory 348–50
in research planning 31–3
see also meta-analysis
literature searches, in
meta-analysis 474–5
Llewellyn, G. 285
loading, in factor analysis 432
local minimum 456
location
for focus groups 286
see also environment
logistic regression 430
logit analysis 430
loglinear methods 441
Long, J. S. 456
longitudinal cohort sequential
design 20
longitudinal studies
design 19
participant attrition 33
Lorber, M. F. 151
Lord, F. M. 190, 197, 204, 205
Lowenthal, D. 307
Luce, R. D. 53, 57
Lundh, L. G. 258
Lunt, P. 278, 281
Lynn, P. 111–12

Maclaran, P. 277, 279
Madill, A. 384, 385
Magina, C. A. 148
magnetoencephalography
153, 154, 158
magnitude estimation 175–6
manipulation
of experimentees 18, 20–1
of variables 74
manipulation checks 21
MANOVA 424
Marascuilo, L. A. 424
market research 276
Markham, A. N. 296
Marsh, P. 128, 305
matching 77–81
stimulus detection 176
materials for research 35–6

Mather, G. 177
maturation effects 91, 96, 97
maximum variation, in
sampling 352
May, V. 271
McAdams, D. P. 266, 270
McDonald, R. P. 433
McGraw, B. 469, 473
McLachlan, G. J. 422
MDS 436–8, 437
mean 55, 109, 188
meaning-making 325
measurement
of intelligence 52, 188
of outcomes 71
psychophysiological 147–59
published scales and
measures 228
of quality in ethnographic
research 309
in research 52–63
and theoretical
backgrounds 13
validation with
questionnaires 213, 214
see also psychometric tests
measurement errors 59, 392, 459
measurement models
see latent variables
median 55
Mellenberg, G. J. 196
member categories 355
member validation 362
memo writing 357–8
memory and forgetting
in data collection 142
in stimulus detection 179
mentalist discourse 385
Merton, R. K. 276, 289
meta-analysis 120, 467–80
description 468–9
development of technique 471–3
stages 473–80
strengths 480
type of studies 470
see also literature reviews
method of adjustment 169
method of constant stimuli 168
method of difference 69
method of limits 169–70
method of single stimuli 175
method of a thousand
staircases 172–3
methodologies see research
methods
Michell, J. 57, 207
Michell, L. 278, 285, 290
Miles, S. 251
Milgram, S. 73, 127
Mill, J. S. 69

Minami, M. 268
Minium, E. W. 62, 409
MIs 457
Mislevy, R. J. 190
model comparison, SEM 447–50
models
in grounded theory
building 359–60
parameter 204–7, 204,
205, 206
testing with
questionnaires 213–14
true score 190
see also structural equation
modelling
moderator styles, focus
groups 287–8
modification indices (MIs) 457
modifications, to research
designs 38
Moncrieff, J. 471, 472
monotonic relationships 407, 408
Moore, J. 307
Moran, D. 324
Morgan, D. L. 276, 279
Morris, D. 126
Moser, C. A. 393
MRI 155–6, 158
multicollinearity 429
multidimensional scaling
methods (MDS) 436–8, 437
multi-group modelling 462
multiple correlation
coefficient 429
multiple regression 426–9, 458
multiple-response items
215, 216, 227
multiple time series designs
98–102, 99, 102–3
multivariate analysis of
variance (MANOVA) 424
multivariate data analysis 415–42
categorical data 440–1
difference between
groups 416–24
predictions 424–30
underlying structure of
data 430–40
see also bivariate statistical
analysis; statistical
analyses; structural
equation modelling
multivariate statistical tests 392
muscle activity, measurement 149–50
mutual exclusivity 53
Myers, G. 278
Myrick, H. 156

narrative account, in IPA 338
narrative reviews 472

narrative techniques 266–71
  data analysis 269–71
  eliciting data 267–9
  structure 266–7
  types 268
national identity 270–1
nationality questions 224
naturalistic observations
      41–2, 128–9, 130,
      303, 309–10
naturalistic settings 303
NECG designs 93–6, 94
network structuring 251
Neugebauer, H. 256
Nezlek, J. B. 258
Nigro, G. 245
Nishisato, S. 441
Nitko, A. J. 188
'noise', affecting stimulus
      detection 162–3, 164, 173
nomothetic 326
non-attitude response
      (don't know) 217–18, 245
non-compliance, participant
      33, 34
non-contact 112
non-equivalent control group
      (NECG) designs 93–6, 94
non-hierarchical methods,
      in cluster analysis 434
non-parametric tests 61, 62, 406
non-participant observation 129
non-recursive models 460
nonresponse rate 112–13
non-verbal data
  and discourse analysis 385
  in interviews 242
norm referenced tests 188
normal distribution 108–10,
      109, 188, 406
normal science 14
normative tests 188
norms 188
note-taking
  in interviews 242
  in participant research 142–3
novel syntheses, of data 14–15
Novick, M. 190, 197, 204
null hypothesis 397, 398,
      399, 404
nulling 177–8
Nunnally, J. C. 191, 198, 208
nursing, action research 314

objective tests 187–8
oblique rotation 433
O'Brien, K. 281
observation, as human
      activity 126
observational designs 395–6

observational research 125–45
  of behaviour and speech 132–3
  coding schemes 134–8
  description and types 126–31
  ethnographic 304, 307–8
  invasion of privacy 41–2
  orientations 138–9
  participant 139–43
  theoretical perspectives 133–4
  validity 144–5
observed scores 191
observed variables
      446, 447, 460
observer drift 144
observer as participant 131
Occams' razor 15, 448–50
occupation questions 224–5
Ockham's razor 15, 448–50
Oldroyd, D. 9, 16
O'Muircheartaigh, P. 226
one-parameter models
      204, 205–7
one-tailed tests 400, 401–2, 401
ongoing focus groups 296–7
on-line see also internet
on-line focus groups 296–7
Oostenveld, R. 155
open coding 353–6
open questions 289, 290
open-ended questions/
      answers 237
open-ended response
      formats 214, 215
openness of inquiry 363
operational definitions
      30–1, 37, 71
operationalism 16
Oppenheim, A. N. 212, 218
optimal scaling 441
order effects 82
ordinal measurement
      54–5, 56–7, 59–60, 61–2
organizational action
      research 314
orthogonal rotation 433
Osborn, M. 324, 330, 333, 338
outcome measures 71
outcomes of research,
      anticipating 43
overdetermination 10
overreporting
  diaries 260
  questionnaires 226
oximetry measures 153

PAFs 113
Palmer, R. 324
panic disorder 153
paradigm shifts 14
paralinguistic features 132

parameter estimation
  bias 459
  statistical values 456
  using questionnaires 213
parameter models 204–5,
      204–7, 204, 205, 206
parameters 204, 391, 448, 454–5
parametric tests 61–2, 406
parental consent 40
Park, R. E. 309
Parker, I. 369, 370, 371,
      372, 376, 384
Parkes, C. M. 305
partial correlation 427
participant attrition/mortality
      (dropout) 33–4, 98, 262
participant bias 33–4, 35, 41,
      72, 262
  see also sampling/sample
      bias; sampling error
participant non-compliance
      33, 34
participant observational
      research 129–31, 139–43
participant as observer 130–1
participants
  availability 38
  debriefing 41, 239
  ethical rights 39–42
  in ethnographic research 306
  manipulation 18, 20–1
  in observational
      research 129–31, 139–43
  refusal 112, 236
  selection methods
      35, 235–6, 315
  suitability 33–5
  talking with for data
      recording 143
  see also respondents
participatory action research 314
partitioning methods 434
path analysis 458
payment of participants, ethics 40
Pearson, K. 473, 478
Pearson's r 477
Pentland, A. 172
perceptual effects, stimulus
      detection 177–8
Performance and Innovation
      Unit 313
performance tests 187
person parameters 204
personality measurement 55, 185
Peters, M. L. 256
phenomena, explanations 7–8
phenomenological data 303
phenomenological
      psychology 325
phenomenology 324, 345

photoplethysmographs 152
Piaget, J. 71, 83
Pidgeon, N. F. 344, *348*, 350, 360
pilot studies 36–7, 73
    for diary technique 264
    for interviews 240–1
    for questionnaires 229
    and small sample research 120
    for structural equation
        modelling 461
planning process 26–38
    checklist 46–7
    ethical considerations 38–43
    funding 43–6
    see also pilot studies;
        research designs
plethysmography 152, 153
Plummer, K. 369
point scales 59–60, 216,
    217, 226–7
point of subjective equality
    (PSE) 175
Pomerantz, A. M. 376
Popper, K. R. 9
population census 107
population effect 476, 478–9
population parameter
    estimation 213
populations 106–7, 113, 390
positioning 372
positivism 16, 13
post hoc content analysis 237–8
post hoc hypotheses 11
post-interview data
    interpretation 251
postcard diaries 256
postcode address files (PAF) 113
postdictive validation 201–2
Potter, J. 368, 371, 374, 375,
    376, 383
Powell, G. E. 120
power
    and action research
        313, 314, 315
    and significance of results 471
power tests 187
PQRST complex 152
practical issues, in research
    design 46–7
pragmatism 16
pre-experiments 90–2
precision
    estimates 111
    in experimental design 71–3
predictions 424–30
predictive validity 201
Presser, S. 220, 221
principal components
    analysis 441
privacy, invasion 26, 41–2

private diaries 261
probability 398–406
probability distributions 107
probability surveys 115
probes/probing questions
    241, 289
probit analysis 430
problem-focused research 315
problems in research 45
process explanations 7, 8
process facilitation
        moderator style 287
process-orientated focus
        group 286
progressive hypothesizing 140
projective tests 185–6
prompts
    for diary maintenance 265
    in interviews 241, 331
proof of theories 9–11, 12
proportional reduction in error
        (PRE) 449–50
protection of participants 39
PSE 175
psychodynamic theory,
    and observation 133
psychological disorders
        148–9, 185
psychometric *see also*
        measurement
psychometric function
        163, *164*, 168
    allowing for errors 179
psychometric tests 183–208
    classical test theory 189–99
    development and use 184
    IQ tests 52, 56
    item response theory 203–7
    for other cultures 462
    types 185–9
    validity and reliability 190–203
psychophysical methods 161–80
    absolute thresholds
        162–7, 168–74
    difference thresholds 174–8
    forced-choice techniques 167–8
    tips for experiments 178–9
psychophysiological
        methods 147–59
psychophysiology 148–9
PsycINFO database 32
publication
    of diaries 257
    of research 43
published measures/scales 228
Pullman, P. 308
pupillary response 151, 152

qualitative content analysis 293–4
qualitative data 21, 302

qualitative research 120, 134
    evaluation 309–11, 383–4
    see also action research;
        discourse analysis; ethno-
        graphic research; grounded
        theory; interpretative
        phenomenological analysis;
        interviewing; self-recording
        methods
quantification
    of attributes for measurement 57
    of projective tests 186
    of psychophysiological data 156
quantitative content
        analysis 292–3
quantitative data 21
quantitative research *see* meta-
        analysis; statistical analyses
quantitative variables 70
quasi-experimental designs
        89, 92–103, 395
    see also experimental designs;
        pre-experiments; research
        designs
questioning skills 289
questionnaires 211–31
    advantages and
        disadvantages 212
    aims 212–14
    combined with diary
        techniques 259
    layout 228–31
    length 229
    mode of completion 118–19
    nonresponse 112
    relationship between
        variables 395
    response formats 214–18
    self-report 186–7
    terminology and wording
        218–23, 228
    type of information
        gathered 223–7
questions
    in focus groups 290–1
    in grounded theory
        designs 349–50
    for internal consistency 247
    for IPA interviews 330–1
    for IPA project 327
    literal interpretation 246
    order 229–30, 239
    order effects 219–20
    structure 289
    wording 218–23, 238–9, 290
    see also research questions
quota sampling 117–18

Radley, A. 328
random sampling 108, 114–15, 393

randomization 76–7
rank ordering 54–5, 62
ranking scales 216, 217
Rapoport, R. N. 312
Rasch, G. 203, 204
Rasch models 204, 205–7
rating scales 59–60, 216,
    217, 226–7
ratio scale measurement
    56–7, 60
rationalism, in theory testing 15
raw scores 391
Ray, P. 258
reactance effects 263
reaction time, stimulus
    detection 177
reactivity effects 144
real life studies 41–2, 128–9,
    130, 303, 309–10
real limits 59
real-time focus groups 296, 297
realism 16
Reason, P. 314, 315, 318, 320
receiver operating characteristic
    (ROC) curves 166, *167*
recording, data 142–3, 242,
    247, 249–50, 263–4, 291
recovered memories 271
recruitment of participants
    34, 283, 285
    see also sample selection
recursive models 460
redemptive self narrative 270
reduced scores 95
reference lists, in textbooks 32
reflexivity 363
    see also self-reflexiveness
refusals 112, 236
regionality 43
regression line 425
regression procedures 424–30
regression towards mean 95
Reicher, S. 326
Reid, K. 328
relabelling, of grounded theory
    categories 358
related groups (within-subjects)
    designs 74–6, 81–5, 394, 410
relational rules 7, 9, 294
relativism 16
relativity 138
reliability 73
    as construct validation 202
    interview data 247–50
    participant observer
        research 144
    of psychometric tests 190–9
reliability coefficient
    191, 193, 194, 198–9
reliability index 191

reliability theory 189–99
reliable change index 197
REM sleep 152
Rendleman, P. 172
repeated groups/measures
    designs 74–6, 81–5,
    394, 410
repertory grid 189
replication, to establish reliability 73
reports
    action research 319
    ethnographic 307
    grounded theory 357–8, 361–3
    of interviews 252–3
    IPA 338–40
    of study for participants 34
research
    anticipating outcomes 43
    dissemination 47
    goals 66
    materials and equipment
        35–6, 38
    planning *see* planning
        process; research designs
    topic selection 26–7
research designs 18–22
    choice 31
    focus groups 283–6
    grounded theory 348–50
    modifications 38
    observational 395–6
    practical issues 33–8, 46–7
    specific research
        questions 27–31
    see also emergent designs;
        experimental designs;
        planning process;
        pre-experiments;
        quasi-experimental
        designs; single-case designs
research methods
    choice 31
    integrating methodologies 22–3
    and theory testing 17–22
    see also pilot studies
research proposals 44–6
research questions 27–31
    in meta-analysis 470–1, 473–4
    in multivariate data
        analysis 416
    use of discourse
        analysis 373–4
researcher bias/effects
    248–50, 362
researcher categories, in
    grounded theory 355
residual variance 449
resources for research 35–6, 38
respiration, measurement
    153, 159

respondents
    emotional response in
        interviews 239, 241
    in ethnographic
        research 306
    in questionnaires 229
    see also participants
response bias 186–7, 245
response formats
    interviews 237–8
    questionnaires 214–18, 222
response rate 111–12
response set 187
response variables *see*
    dependent variables
responses 7
restricted analyses 440–1
Reuband, K 243
Reuben, D. B. 256
revolution, in theories 14
Rich, M. 242
Richards, L. 375
Ricoeur, P. 266, 324
Ridderinkhof, K. R. 148
ridge estimation 429
right to withdraw 41
Robson, C. 128, 133, 135,
    140, 144
ROC curves 166, *167*
Roethlisberger, F. J. 102
role retraction moderator
    style 287
Rorschach, H. 185
Rose, D. 5, 8, 166
Rose, R. M. 172, 174
Rosenhan, D. L. 130
Rosenthal, R. 470,
    477, 478, 479
Rosser, E. 128, 305
Rothschild, Lord 312
rounding numbers, in
    measurement 58
Rowe, G. 251
Rustin, M. 126

Salmon, P. 126
Samar, V. J. 155
Sammer, G. 153
sample bias *see* sampling/
    sample bias
sample maintenance 262, 265
    see also participant attrition/
        mortality; participant non-
        compliance
sample selection 91, 235–6
    in action research 315
    for pilot studies 241
    population samples 113–18
    see also recruitment of
        participants

sample size 34, 37, 77, 108, 119
  allowing for nonresponse 112
  discriminant function
    analysis 424
  effective 117
  in factor analysis 434
  for interviews 235
  IPA studies 327–8
  in meta-analysis 479, 480
  and multiple regression 429
  pilot studies 120
  and standard error 111
  and statistical power 403
samples 329, 390, 391
sampling/sample bias 34, 35,
    41, 94, 118, 248
  see also participant bias;
    sampling error
sampling distributions 107–10,
    399–400, 400, 401
  sampling error 393
  see also participant bias;
    sampling/sample bias
sampling frames 113, 119
sampling techniques 105–20
  confidence intervals/levels
    110–11, 404
  discourse analysis 374
  distributions 107–10
  generalization of studies 106–7
  IPA studies 327–9
  effect of nonresponse 111–13
  random sampling 108,
    114–15, 393
  survey mode 118–19
  theoretical 350–2
  types of selection 113–18
sampling without
  replacement 114
satisficing responses 218
saturated categories 358–9
scales
  interval 55–6, 61–2
  ordinal 54–5, 56–7, 59–60, 61–2
  published 228
  ranking 54–5, 216, 217
  rating 59–60, 216, 217, 226–7
  ratio 56–7, 60
  unidimensional 202
scaling, stimulus detection 177
scaling methods 436–8, 437
scatterplot graphs 407, 408, 409
Schaie, K. W. 19
schematic diagrams 420, 421
Schiffman, S. S. 438
Schmid, D. 80, 81
Schuetz, A. 267
Schuman, H. 220, 221
Schwartz, A. 80
Schwartz, M. S. 149

Schwartz-Barcott, D. 311, 314
science, sociological view 15–16
scientific approach 5
scientific method 6
  see also experimental method
screening, for focus
    groups 283–4
Sedgwick, E. 369
seed numbers 114
Seidel, J. V. 294
selection
  of participants 35, 235–6,
    283, 315
  of population samples 113–18
selection bias see sampling/
    sample bias
selection-maturation
    interaction 94–5
selective attention 142
selective encoding 142
selective memory 142
self-completion
    questionnaires 118
self-narrative, and identity 266
self-paced trials 167
self-recording methods 256–72
  diary techniques 256–65
  narrative techniques 266–71
  self-report questionnaires 186–7
self-reflexiveness
  in data recording 143
  required of diaryists 262–3
  of researcher 5, 307
self-report questionnaires 186–7
self-selection of material,
    diarists 262
semi-structured interviews
    242, 329–30
semi-structured questions 289
sensational measurements 175–8
sense-making, focus groups
    279, 281
sensitive issues
  in interviews 241–2
  in questionnaires 223, 230
sensitivity, of experiments 77
separate group designs
    74–81, 394, 410
sequence analysis, of
    behaviour 136–8
sequential design 19
Shamdasani, P. N. 280, 285,
    287, 297
shared histories, in focus
    groups 285
Shavelson, R. J. 190
Sherliker, L. 258
Shoham-Salomom, V. 480
Shye, S. 438
Šidák, Z. 417

signal-plus-noise distribution 164
significance
  clinical 471–2, 478
  in research 310
  statistical 392
  substantive 392
silence, use in focus groups 290
Silverman, D. 276
simple random sampling
    108, 114–15, 393
simple regression 425–6
Simpson, M. 369
Singer, J. A. 266, 271
single-case designs 100–2,
    101, 120, 270, 326,
    328, 334–8
skewness 409
Skidelsky, R. 312
skin conductance 151
skin potentials 150
skin resistance 150, 151
Skinner, B. F. 66
Skinner, C. 117
Slater, L. 130
small samples 119–20
  see also sample size
Smith, J. A. 138, 276, 293, 295,
    324, 325, 326, 328, 329,
    330, 333, 335, 338–9
Smith, M. 151
Smith, M. L. 469, 472, 473
social class, in questionnaires
    224–5
social constructionism
    134, 279–80, 368–9
social contexts 305, 345
social desirability, and
    questionnaire answers 221–2
social psychophysiology 148
social stratification 224–5
socio-economic status, in
    questionnaires 224–5
Sod's Law 47
Solesbury, W. 312
spatial forced-choice
    experiments 168
Spearman, C. 194
specific research
    questions 27–31
specification searches 456–7
speed tests 187
Spencer, L. 218, 302, 310
sphygmomanometers 152
split-half reliability coefficient 194
spontaneous
    electroencephalography 154
spontaneously generated diaries/
    narratives 261, 268
Spradley, J. P. 302
SQUIDs 154

stability, in reliability 195
staircase methods 170–3
standard deviation from
mean 109, 188
standard error of measurement
(SEM) 110, 111, 115,
116, 117
in classical test theory 191, 196
in item response theory 207
standard stimulus 174
standardized alpha 195
standardized difference
formula 476
Stanton, B. 278, 282
statistical analyses 37, 61
BOLD fMRI data 156
see also bivariate statistical
analysis; data analysis;
multivariate data analysis;
structural equation modelling
statistical inference 391, 399–400
statistical power 119, 120, 402–4
statistical regression towards
mean 95
statistical significance 392
statistical tests 392, 400–13,
417–23, 450–62, 476
statistics 13
and levels of measurement 61–3
see also statistical analyses
Stein-type estimation 429
Steinschneider, M. 148
steps, in stimulus detection
169–70
stepwise regression 428
Stevens, S. S. 53
Stewart, D. W. 280, 285,
287, 297
Steyaert, C. 281
stimuli 7
for focus group research 281–2
human response to 162–3
stimulus detection 162–80,
164, 165, 166, 167
stimulus intensity 169–74,
170, 175–8
Stine, W. W. 62
stipulative statements 8
Stockley, J. W. 430, 441
storytelling, in projective tests 185
Strasburger, H. 174
stratification 115–16
Strauss, A. 128, 138, 360
Strauss, A. L. 344, 350
stress coefficient 438
Stringer, E. T. 311, 317
Strong, J. 278
strong programme view of
science 16
structural content analysis 294

structural equation modelling
(SEM) 445–64
analysis strategy 460–1
criticisms 463–4
description 446–7
measurement models
446, 450–7
structural models 458–60
theoretical model testing
447–50
uses 461–2
see also bivariate statistical
analysis; multivariate
data analysis; statistical
analyses
structural models 446, 458–60
structured interviews 237
structured observation 129
structured questions 189, 289
studies
abortion questions 220–1
African-American women's
focus group 280, 288
altruism 8, 151
anti-social behaviour,
Duhem-Quine thesis 11
attitudes to illness, focus
groups 277
Bobo doll experiment,
ethics 28–9
cancer patients,
cross-individual
analysis 270
chronic illness, grounded
theory model 360
church going/death metal,
statistical analysis 411–12
Crying Pattern
Questionnaire 259
depression and social activity,
SEM studies 459–60
dyslexia
matching technique 79
meta-analysis 471–2,
477–8, 477
facial expressions, muscle
activity measurement 150
faked mental illness study 130
football hooliganism, ethogenic
research 305
homelessness, ethnographic
research 307
homosexuality and religion,
discourse analysis
377–82
IQ, statistical analysis
418–23, 425–8,
448–50, 458, 459
Maths GCSE, statistical
analysis 410–11

studies cont.
medical treatment diaries 258
mobile phone use, ethnographic
research 308
obedience to authority
experiments 73–4, 127
Piaget's conservation of
number experiment 83–4
reading speed,
pre-experiments 90–1
retired Americans,
narratives 270
Shetland community focus
groups 280
social anxiety and distress,
diaries 258–9
Strange Situation study
128, 134–5
television, influence 281
unemployment
narratives 269–70
visual cliff avoidance 79–81
Welsh environment,
grounded theory
350–1, 357
women's experiences
of aggression 333–8
young people's lifestyles, SEM
study 451, 452, 455
substantive coding 353–6
substantive significance 392
substantively meaningful
difference 406
Sudman, S. 212, 218, 223, 226
Suen, H. K. 190, 208
superconducting quantum
interfering devices
(SQUIDs) 154
supervision, in participant
research 141
Surakka, V. 150
survey mode 118–19
surveys, sampling
techniques 105–20
Svejda, M. 80, 81
Swantz, M.-L. 314
sweat gland activity 150–1
Swets, J. A. 164, 165, 166
symbolic interactionism 344
systematic error 190
systematic random sampling 114
systemic theory, and
observation 133
systolic blood pressure 152

t-tests 409–10, 410–11, 411,
417–19, 419, 420, 422,
457, 462
Tabachnick, B. G. 430
talking with participants 143

Taylor, C. 324
Taylor, M. M. 172
Taylor series approximation 117
Teichert, D. 266
telephone interviews/
    research 118, 243
Teller, D. Y. 172, 173
temporal forced-choice
    experiments 168
temporal ordering of events 395
terminology
    in discourse analysis 376
    statistics 390–3
    use of jargon in interviews 238
    use in questionnaires
        218–23, 228
test stimulus 174
test validation 213
test-retest reliability 195–6
testing effects 91, 96–7
tests *see* psychometric tests;
    statistical tests; theory testing
texts, and discourse analysis
        370, 375–6
thematic analysis
        270, 333, 336–7
Thematic Apperception Tests 185
thematic content analysis 293
thematic structuring, of
    interview data 251
theoretical agnosticism 350
theoretical memos 357–8
theoretical sampling 350–2
theoretical saturation 359, 362
theoretical sensitivity 349
theory/theories 4, 15–17,
        133–4, 282, 347, 396
theory building 4, 6–9
    from qualitative data 344
    grounded theory 359–61
theory testing 9–15
    and hypotheses 12, 22–3,
        119, 120
    observational research
        dimension 127–8
    research methods 17–22
    see also structural equation
        modelling
thick descriptions 305
thin descriptions 305
Thomas, J. 309
Thompson, B. 433
thousand staircases
    method 172–3
three-parameter models
        205, 205, 206, 206
thresholds, in stimulus
    response 163
time event analysis 138
time sampling 143

time series designs 96–102,
        97, 103
time series with non-equivalent
    control group (TSNECG)
    designs 98–102, 99, 102–3
timetables
    for diaries 257
    for research 35, 37–8, 41
Tippett, L. H. 472
Tizard, B. 74
topic guides, focus groups 288–9
topographical EEG maps
        154, 155, 157
Torgerson, C. J. 474, 475
Townsend, J. T. 62
transcription
    analysis of data during
        333, 334–5
    of recordings 242, 291,
        332, 352–3, 374
transducers 149
transferability, in action
    research 317
treatment effects 472, 478
treatment withdrawal designs 103
treatments, independent
    variable 394
Treisman, M. 163
Treutwein, B. 173, 174
trial intervals 167
trials, stimulus 163, 165, 167, 168
Triandis, H. C. 222
triangulation 145, 258, 363
true score model 190–1
true score theory 189–99
TSNECG designs 98–102,
        99, 102–3
Turner, B. A. 360
Turpin, G. 328
two-alternative forced-choice
    experiments 168
two-factor models 452, 455, 457
two-parameter models
        204–5, 205, 206, 206
two-tailed tests 401–2, 401
Type I/II errors 397–8, 399,
        402, 418, 471, 479–80
Tyrrell, R. A. 172

Ullman, J. B. 447
Ulrich, R. 168
unbiased estimator 110
'uncategorizable' measurement
    category 54
uncertainty, in stimulus
    detection 179
unconscious 185
underreporting
    diaries 260
    questionnaires 226

undetermination, in theory
    testing 15
unidimensional scale 202
uninterrupted time series
    designs 96–102, 97, 103
uniqueness 450–1
unit of analysis 390
univariate 416
universal laws 17
unstructured interviews
        237–8, 242
unstructured observation 129
unstructured questions 289
unsystematic error 190
upweighting 116
Ussher, J. M. 266
Uzzell, D. L. 302

validity 73
    content 186, 200
    of diary techniques 263
    ecological 86, 468
    external 86, 91, 93
    internal 91
    interview data 247–50
    participant observer
        research 144–5
    psychometric tests 199–203
    and questionnaires
        213, 214, 231
value judgements
    in interview questions 238
    in questionnaires 219
Van der Molen, B. 270
Van der Molen, M. W. 148
Van Langenhove, L. 326, 329
variability, of discourse 376–7
variables 69–73, 391
    confounding of 74, 395
    continuous 58
    control 101
    criterion 425, 428
    dependent 70–3, 394, 395
    discrete 58
    endogenous 458–60
    in ethnography 310
    exogenous 458–60
    extraneous 12
    independent 395
    latent and observed
        446, 447, 460
    natural control 128–9
    see also bivariate statistical
        analysis; multivariate
        data analysis
variance, analysis of
        417, 419–22, 424
variance error 190
variance estimation 116–17
Vetere, A. 128, 130, 131, 132

video recording
  analysis 144, 242
  observation 129, 134–5,
    142, 291
  self-recording 268
  to remove bias 249–50
virtual discussion groups 297
virtual interviews 119
von Eye, A. 270, 441

Wagner, H. 148
Waite, B. M. 260
Walker, P. 316
Wallwork, J. 373
Warnock, M. 328
Watson, A. B. 173
Watzlawick, P. 133
web *see* internet
Weber fraction 174
Weber's law 174
weighted effect size 477
weighting 113, 116
Weille, K. L. 330
welfare of participants 39
Welkowitz, J. 478
Weller, S. C. 441
Wellings, K. 279, 284

Werner, O. 306
Wetherell, M. 368, 370, 372,
  374, 375, 376–7
Wetherill, G. B. 171
Whyte, W. F. 131, 309, 314
Widdicombe, S. 375
Wilkinson, S. 251, 276, 277,
  279, 285, 286, 290, 295
Williams, B. A. 281
Willig, C. 371, 373
Wilson, C. 245
Wilson, G. D. 228
Wilson, L. 258
Winborne, D. G. 278
Winer, B. J. 422
Winkielman, P. 150
Wirth, L. 309
within-subject designs
  74–6, 81–5, 394, 410
Wolf, F. M. 469, 476
Wolke, D. 259
women
  socio-economic status 224
  telephone interviewing 243
Woodworth, R. S. 175
Woodworth Personal Profile 186
Wooffitt, R. 374

wording
  in interviews 238
  in questionnaires 218–23, 228
  in questions 290
work flow 346, *348*
workability of solutions 317
workshops, discourse
  analysis 377–82
writing memos 357–8
writing reports
  action research 319
  in ethnography 307
  grounded theory
    studies 357–8, 361–3
  IPA studies 338–40

Yardley, L. 356, 383
Yin, R. K. 328
Young, K. 306
young people,
  socio-economic status 224

Zani, A. 148
Ziller, R. C. 185, 268
Zorbaugh, H. W. 309